THE EMPLOYMEN

The Employment Relationship

Examining Psychological and Contextual Perspectives

Edited by

JACQUELINE A-M. COYLE-SHAPIRO
LYNN M. SHORE
M. SUSAN TAYLOR
LOIS E. TETRICK

OXFORD
UNIVERSITY PRESS

*This book has been printed digitally and produced in a standard specification
in order to ensure its continuing availability*

OXFORD
UNIVERSITY PRESS

Great Clarendon Street, Oxford OX2 6DP

Oxford University Press is a department of the University of Oxford.
It furthers the University's objective of excellence in research, scholarship,
and education by publishing worldwide in

Oxford New York

Auckland Cape Town Dar es Salaam Hong Kong Karachi
Kuala Lumpur Madrid Melbourne Mexico City Nairobi
New Delhi Shanghai Taipei Toronto
With offices in
Argentina Austria Brazil Chile Czech Republic France Greece
Guatemala Hungary Italy Japan South Korea Poland Portugal
Singapore Switzerland Thailand Turkey Ukraine Vietnam

Oxford is a registered trade mark of Oxford University Press
in the UK and in certain other countries

Published in the United States
by Oxford University Press Inc., New York

© Oxford University Press 2004

ISBN 978-0-19-928683-6

In memory of my Mother
To Mark for his rock solid support
—J. C-S.
To Ted, Jason, and Benjamin for their constancy and support
In memory of my parents who inspired me to write
—L. S.
To past and present researchers of the employment relationship
My first employer, the Wilby Theater in Selma, Alabama
—S. T.
To Bill for his continuing support through the years
—L. T.
To all the participants at the Houston Workshop and especially Dana,
Eric, and Lynda, who helped "the trains run on time," as well as
all the scholars who have paved the way in advancing our
understanding of the employment relationship.

Preface

The Employment Relationship: Examining Psychological and Contextual Perspectives had its beginning in a conversation among presenters, discussants, and the audience at a well-attended symposium on the psychological contract research at the 2001 National Academy of Management Meetings in Washington, DC. The papers presented during the symposium generated many comments from all parties regarding the increasingly large body of work on the psychological contract and the employment relationship. In particular, there were frequently appearing and reappearing "troublesome issues" within that large and growing body of work. These troublesome issues included: (*a*) potentially overlapping conceptual domains among a number of social exchange frameworks, including the psychological contract, perceived organizational support (POS), and the leader member exchange (LMX); (*b*) all too frequent references to the norm of reciprocity as the "be all and end all" explanation for an infinite list of outcomes linked to the employment relationship; (*c*) increasing questions about the importance and conceptualization of the organization's role in the psychological contract; (*d*) questions about the reliability and validity of measures used to assess the psychological contract; and (*e*) the need for more complex, as opposed to simpler, conceptualizations of the development of violations in the psychological contract. The general consensus around these issues at the end of the symposium was that it would be difficult for research to progress on the psychological contract in particular and the employment relationship in general until some of these troublesome issues were addressed.

In subsequent cocktail hour and dinner meetings after the originating symposium, the editors of this book somewhat naively decided to secure funding for a Research Network Workshop with a view to inviting fifteen scholars working in areas related to the troublesome issues to begin to address them. The process involved participants completing preparatory reading prior to the Workshop, which was held over two-and-a-half days and involved small group discussions with plenary sessions. After much cajoling, planning, and organizing, this conference was held in the Psychology building at the University of Houston, May 10–12, 2002. Its unique and successful (we hope) structure resulted in three jointly authored research papers that were presented at a symposium titled Research Workshop Networks: A methodology for developing the employee organization relationship, August 9–14, 2002 at the National Academy of Management Meetings in Denver. Toward the end of the Workshop, participants were asked to consider developing the ideas discussed in Houston by contributing a chapter to this book. The rest, as they say, is history. In gazing at the now complete typescript, which adopts a unique and also multidisciplinary approach to address and extend the original troublesome issues, while also establishing policy implications and a future research agenda for the employment relationship, we admit to a bit of pride in the final product.

We also feel an enormous obligation to those who worked with us throughout this long journey and thus acknowledge those who helped along the way.

Acknowledgements

The four editors are very grateful to our respective institutions for their support: The London School of Economics and Political Science; The Beebe Institute of Personnel and Employment Relations at Georgia State University; The Graduate School of Management at the University of California, Irvine; The Robert H. Smith School of Business and the Center for Human Capital, Innovation and Technology, at the University of Maryland, College Park; The Department of Psychology and the C. T. Bauer School of Business at the University of Houston; and The Department of Psychology at George Mason University.

We also would like to thank Eric Dunleavy, Dana Glenn, and Lynda Villanueva for all their help throughout the Workshop in Houston and who quite simply made our job so much easier.

We could not have done this without the Workshop participants, who gave up their time during the Mother's Day weekend and who made the workshop an exciting and stimulating experience.

Finally, we would like to thank Carolina Villaverde for her word processing skills in helping get this book into a final format with continued enthusiasm.

Contents

List of Contributors   xi

List of Figures   xviii

List of Tables   xix

Introduction   xxi

Part I. The Nature of the Employment Relationship from Social Exchange, Justice, Industrial Relations, Legal, and Economic Literatures

1. The Employment Relationship through the Lens of Social Exchange   5
   Jacqueline A-M. Coyle-Shapiro and Neil Conway

2. Justice and Employment: Moral Retribution as a Contra-subjugation Tendency   29
   Robert Folger

3. Industrial Relations Approaches to the Employment Relationship   48
   John Kelly

4. Legal Theory: Contemporary Contract Law Perspectives and Insights for Employment Relationship Theory   65
   Mark V. Roehling

5. The Economic Dimension of the Employment Relationship   94
   Richard N. Block, Peter Berg, and Dale Belman

6. Commonalities and Conflicts Between Different Perspectives of the Employment Relationship: Towards a Unified Perspective   119
   Jacqueline A-M. Coyle-Shapiro, M. Susan Taylor, Lynn M. Shore, and Lois E. Tetrick

Part II. Examining Constructs to Capture the Exchange Nature of the Employment Relationship

7. Employer-oriented Strategic Approaches to the Employee–Organization Relationship   135
   Lynn M. Shore, Lyman W. Porter, and Shaker A. Zahra

8. The Employment Relationship from Two Sides: Incongruence in Employees' and Employers' Perceptions of Obligations   161
   Elizabeth Wolfe Morrison and Sandra L. Robinson

9. Job Creep: A Reactance Theory Perspective on Organizational Citizenship Behavior as Overfulfillment of Obligations   181
   Linn Van Dyne and Jennifer Butler Ellis

10. Perceived Organizational Support   206
    Robert Eisenberger, Jason R. Jones, Justin Aselage, and Ivan L. Sucharski

11. The Role of Leader–Member Exchange in the Dynamic Relationship
    Between Employer and Employee: Implications for Employee
    Socialization, Leaders, and Organizations   226
    Robert C. Liden, Talya N. Bauer, and Berrin Erdogan

**Part III. Developing an Integrative Perspective of the Employment
Exchange; Creating a Whole that is More than the Sum of Individual
Parts; Looking Toward the Future; Developing a Research Agenda**

12. Taking Stock of Psychological Contract Research: Assessing Progress,
    Addressing Troublesome Issues, and Setting Research Priorities   253
    M. Susan Taylor and Amanuel G. Tekleab

13. Changes in the Employment Relationship Across Time   284
    René Schalk

14. Understanding the Employment Relationship: Implications for
    Measurement and Research Design   312
    Lois E. Tetrick

15. Employment Relationships in Context: Implications for Policy
    and Practice   332
    David R. Hannah and Roderick D. Iverson

16. Directions for Future Research   351
    *Lynn M. Shore, Lois E. Tetrick, Jacqueline A-M. Coyle-Shapiro,
    and M. Susan Taylor*

Index   365

List of Contributors

Justin Aselage is a graduate student in Social Psychology at the University of Delaware. His research interests include applications of social exchange theory to the employee–employer relationship, employee creativity, and intrinsic motivation in the workplace. He recently published an article in the *Journal of Organizational Behavior* proposing an integration of two social exchange approaches to the employee–employer relationship, organizational support theory, and psychological contract theory.

Talya N. Bauer (Ph.D., Purdue University) is Associate Professor of Organizational Behavior and Human Resource Management at Portland State University. Her research interests include the socialization of new employees, applicant reactions to selection, employee recruitment, and job choice, as well as leader–member exchange. Her research on these topics has appeared in the *Academy of Management Journal, Personnel Psychology, Journal of Applied Psychology,* and *Research in Personnel & Human Resource Management.* She is on the editorial board of the *Journal of Applied Psychology and Personnel Psychology* and serves as an ad hoc reviewer for the *Academy of Management Journal* and *Academy of Management Review.* She was Program Planning Chair for the 2001 SIOP Conference and is on the Program Planning Committee for the 2003 SIOP Conference.

Dale Belman is an associate professor in the School of Labor and Industrial Relations at Michigan State University, with a Doctorate in economics from the University of Wisconsin–Madison. His research is in the areas of collective bargaining, government regulation of labor markets, and public sector employment, as well as studies of the employment relationship in trucking and construction. He has published articles in the *Industrial and Labor Relations Review, Industrial Relations,* the *Review of Economics and Statistics,* and the *Journal of Business and Economic Statistics,* and has co-authored *How New is the New Employment Contract* and *Sailors of the Concrete Sea: The Work and Work Life of Truck Drivers.*

Peter Berg is an associate professor at the School of Labor and Industrial Relations at Michigan State University. He received his Ph.D. in economics from the University of Notre Dame. His research interests include organizational change in the United States and Germany, high performance work systems, work life policies and practices in the United States and Europe, comparative employment relations, and work restructuring in U.S. hospitals. Dr. Berg has authored or co-authored numerous publications in leading academic journals, and is co-author of the book *Manufacturing Advantage: Why High Performance Work Systems Pay Off* (Cornell/ILR University Press).

Richard N. Block is Professor in the School of Labor and Industrial Relations at Michigan State University. He received a Ph.D. in Industrial and Labor Relations from Cornell University in 1977. Professor Block has done research on and is the author of numerous articles and books on issues in labor and employment law, the relationship between law and practice and industrial relations, industrial relations and competitiveness, industrial relations and structural economic change, employee privacy, and international labor standards. His work has appeared in all major journals in the industrial relations field. His most recent books are *Labor Standards in the United States and Canada* and *Bargaining for Competitiveness: Law, Research, and Case Studies*, both published by the W. E. Upjohn Institute for Employment Research.

Jennifer Butler Ellis is a Professor of Practice and the Director of the Ernst and Young Accounting Business Communication Center in the Eli Broad College of Business at Michigan State University. She received her Ph.D. from Michigan State University. Professor Ellis's research interests are in organizational and interpersonal communication. Her current research focuses on memorable messages, employee psychological contracts, and employee perception of quality communication and work-life promises and violations. Her work has been published in *Communication Monographs* and *Communication Research*.

Neil Conway is a Lecturer in Organizational Psychology at Birkbeck College, University of London. He was awarded his Ph.D. at the Department of Organizational Psychology, Birkbeck. He has recently published articles on the psychological contract in the *Journal of Organizational Behavior,* the *Journal of Vocational Behavior*, and the *Human Resource Management Journal*. His current research interests include the psychological contract, part-time work, and researching everyday affect and behavior.

Jacqueline A-M. Coyle-Shapiro is a Reader in Organizational Behavior in the Department of Industrial Relations at the London School of Economics, where she received her Ph.D. Her current research interests include the employment relationship, psychological contracts, organizational citizenship behavior, and organizational change. She has published in such journals as the *European Journal of Work and Organizational Psychology, Journal of Applied Behavioral Science* and the *Journal of Vocational Behavior*. She is a Consulting Editor and has served as Guest Editor for the *Journal of Organizational Behavior*.

Robert Eisenberger is a Professor of Psychology and Director of the Social Psychology graduate program at the University of Delaware. His research interests include employee motivation, intrinsic motivation and creativity, and learned industriousness. He is author of more than sixty publications in such journals as *Psychological Review, Psychological Bulletin, American Psychologist, Journal of Applied Psychology*, and *Journal of Personality and Social Psychology*. Two special reports of his research have been carried on National Public Radio, and reports have also appeared in the *American Psychological Association Monitor, Encyclopedia Britannica Science and the Future Yearbook, Science News*, and *Report on Educational Research*. Dr. Eisenberger's research has been funded by grants from the National Institute of Mental Health. He was co-recipient of the award for the Best Paper on Organizational Behavior at the 2001 Academy of Management Conference.

Berrin Erdogan (Ph.D., University of Illinois at Chicago) is Assistant Professor of Organizational Behavior/HRM at Portland State University. Her research focuses on leader–subordinate relationships, organizational justice perceptions, person–organization fit, and organizational culture. She has published in journals such as *Human Relations* and *Human Resource Management Review*. She is on the editorial board of the *Journal of Management*, and serves as an ad hoc reviewer for the *Journal of Applied Psychology* and *Journal of Business Research*.

Robert Folger is a Professor in the Management Department at the College of Business at the University of Central Florida. He received his Ph.D. from the University of North Carolina, Chapel Hill. Professor Folger has published more than ninety publications on organizational justice, work motivation, trust, and decision-making. Currently, he is working on moral emotions. He has served on the editorial boards of the *Academy of Management Review, Journal of Organizational Behavior, Organizational Behavior and Human Decision Processes*, and *Social Justice Research*. Professor Folger has received a number of awards for his research, including the Best Book Award of the International Conflict Management Association in 1999 for *Organizational Justice and Human Resource Management* (co-authored with Russell Cropanzano) and the New Concept Award from the Academy of Management's OB Division in 1986.

David R. Hannah is an Assistant Professor of Management and Organization Studies at Simon Fraser University. He received his Ph.D. from the University of Texas at Austin. His research interests include the protection and management of trade secrets in organizations, employee socialization, psychological contracts, and cultural relationships between sport and business. His work has been published in *Organization Science* and the *Journal of Sport Management*.

Roderick D. Iverson is a Professor of Human Resource Management at the Faculty of Business Administration, Simon Fraser University. He received his Ph.D. in Industrial Sociology from the University of Iowa. Roderick's main research interests include the areas of employee withdrawal (absenteeism, voluntary turnover, and downsizing), psychological contracts, organizational, union, and dual commitment, occupational injury, and high-performance work systems. He was awarded the Best Paper prize by the HR Division at the Annual Academy of Management meetings in 1999 and 2000. Roderick currently serves on the editorial boards of *Asia Pacific Journal of Human Resources, Human Resource Management Review, Journal of Occupational Health Psychology*, and the *International Journal of Selection and Assessment*.

Jason R. Jones is a graduate student in Social Psychology at the University of Delaware. His research interests focus on attributional processes contributing to perceived organizational support, and characteristics of the person and work environment that contribute to the experience of flow on the job.

John Kelly is a Professor of Industrial Relations at Birkbeck College, University of London, with a Ph.D. from London University (1979). His main research interests are trade unions and industrial conflict. He is the co-editor of *Union Organization and*

Activity (2004) and *Labour Movement Revitalization in Comparative Perspective* (2004), and author of *Rethinking Industrial Relations: Mobilization, Collectivism and Long Waves* (1998), *Working for the Union* (1994, with Ed Heery), and *Trade Unions and Socialist Politics* (1988). He was formerly editor of the *British Journal of Industrial Relations* and has published in a wide range of journals including the *British Journal of Industrial Relations, European Journal of Industrial Relations, Human Relations,* and *Work, Employment, and Society.*

Robert C. Liden (Ph.D., University of Cincinnati) is Professor of Management at the University of Illinois in Chicago. His research focuses on interpersonal processes as they relate to such topics as leadership, groups, career progression, and employment interviews. He has more than fifty publications in journals such as the *Academy of Management Journal, Academy of Management Review, Journal of Applied Psychology, Journal of Management,* and *Personnel Psychology*. In 2000, he was inducted into the Academy of Management Journals' Hall of Fame as a charter bronze member. He won awards (with co-authors) for the best article published in the *Academy of Management Journal* during 2001, as well as the best article published in Human Resource Management during 2001. He has served on the editorial boards of the *Journal of Management* since 1994 and the *Academy of Management Journal* from 1994 to 1999. He was the 1999 Program Chair for the Academy of Management's Organizational Behavior Division, and was Division Chair in 2000–1.

Lyman W. Porter is Professor of Management in the Graduate School of Management at the University of California, Irvine, and was formerly Dean of that School. Prior to joining UCI in 1967, he served on the faculty of the University of California, Berkeley. Currently, he serves as a member of the Academic Advisory Board of the Czechoslovak Management Center, and a member of the Board of Trustees of the American University of Armenia, and was formerly an External Examiner for the National University of Singapore. Professor Porter is a past president of the Academy of Management. In 1983, he received that organization's "Scholarly Contributions to Management" Award, and in 1994 its "Distinguished Management Educator" Award. He has also served as President of the Society of Industrial-Organizational Psychology (SIOP), and in 1989 was the recipient of SIOP's "Distinguished Scientific Contributions" Award. Professor Porter's major fields of interest are organizational psychology, management, and management education. He is the author, or co-author, of eleven books and more than eighty articles in these fields. His 1988 book (with Lawrence McKibbin), *Management Education and Development* (McGraw-Hill), reported the findings of a nationwide study of business school education and post-degree management development.

Sandra L. Robinson (Ph.D., Northwestern University) is an Associate Professor of Organizational Behavior and Human Resource Management in the Sauder School of Business, University of British Columbia. She currently holds a Distinguished University Scholar Chair. Professor Robinson's research focuses on trust, employment relationships, psychological contracts, workplace deviance, and territoriality in organizations. Her work has appeared in a variety of journals, such as *Administrative Science Quarterly, Academy of Management Journal, Academy of Management Review, Journal of Applied Psychology*, and *Harvard Business Review*. She has received various awards for her research including the Faculty Research Excellence award from the University of British Columbia, the Ascendant Scholar Award from the Western Academy of Management, and the Cummings Scholar Award from the OB Division of the Academy of Management. Professor Robinson is an editor of the *Journal of Management Inquiry* and she currently serves on the editorial boards of the *Academy of Management Journal*, the *Journal of Engineering and Technology Management*, the *Journal of Applied Psychology*, and the *Journal of Organizational Behavior*.

Mark Roehling is an Assistant Professor in the School of Labor and Industrial Relations, Michigan State University. He received his Ph.D. in Human Resource Management from the Eli Broad School of Management, Michigan State University, and his law degree from the University of Michigan. His primary research interests include rights and responsibilities in the employment relationship (psychological, legal, and ethical perspectives), and interdisciplinary studies in human resources and the law (e.g. employer and employee perceptions of legal constraints and the impact of their perceptions on organizational behavior, and critical reviews integrating behavioral science and legal perspectives). Professor Roehling has published in such journals as *Personnel Psychology, Journal of Applied Psychology, Employee Responsibilities and Rights Journal, Human Resource Management, Journal of Business Ethics, Journal of Business and Psychology, Journal of Managerial Studies*, and *Journal of Management History*, and serves on the editorial review boards of *Human Resource Planning* and the *Employee Rights and Responsibilities Journal*. He is a member of the Academy of Management, the Society for Industrial and Organizational Psychology, the Industrial Relations Researchers Association, and the Academy of Legal Studies in Business.

René Schalk holds a special chair in Policy and Aging at Tilburg University in the Netherlands and is a faculty member of the department of Organization Studies at Tilburg University. He earned his Ph.D. in Social and Organizational Psychology from Nijmegen University, the Netherlands. His research focuses on complexity and dynamics in organizations, with a special focus on the psychological contract, contingent work, international differences, and policy and aging. He is a consulting editor of the *Journal of Organizational Behavior*, and editorial board member of the *Journal of Managerial Psychology*. He is co-editor of the book *Psychological Contracts in Employment: Cross-national Perspectives*, and is author of books on absenteeism and older employees (in Dutch).

Dr. Lynn M. Shore is a Professor of Management at San Diego State University. She received her Ph.D. in Industrial/Organizational Psychology from Colorado State University in 1985. Her research on the employee–organization relationship focuses on the influence of social and organizational processes, and her work on diversity has examined the impact that composition of the work group and employee/supervisor dyads has on the attitudes and performance of work groups and individual employees.

She has published numerous articles in such journals as *Academy of Management Journal, Academy of Management Review, Journal of Applied Psychology, Personnel Psychology, Journal of Organizational Behavior, Human Relations,* and *Journal of Management*. Dr. Shore is a Fellow of the American Psychological Association and the Society for Industrial and Organizational Psychology. She served as the Chair of the Human Resources Division of the Academy of Management. Dr. Shore is an Associate Editor for the *Journal of Applied Psychology*.

Ivan L. Sucharski is a graduate student in the Social Psychology graduate program at the University of Delaware. His research interests include employees' perceptions of support from multiple sources within organizations, and employees' identification with the organization. His most recent publication appeared in the *Journal of Applied Psychology* and explored how perceptions of supervisor support influence perceived organizational support.

M. Susan Taylor is Dean's Professor of Human Resources and Director of the Center for Human Capital, Innovation, and Technology (HCIT) at the Robert H. Smith School of Business, University of Maryland at College Park. She received her Ph.D. from Purdue University and is current working in the areas of organizational justice, strategic human resource management, the employee–organization relationship, and managerial career transitions. Taylor has published in such journals as the *Academy of Management Journal, Administrative Science Quarterly, Journal of Applied Psychology, Organizational Science, Personnel Psychology,* and *Organizational Behavior and Human Decision Processes*.

Amanuel G. Tekleab is an Assistant Professor at Clarkson University. He received his Ph.D. from the Robert H. Smith School of Business, University of Maryland. His current research interests include psychological contracts, organizational socialization, team processes, justice, compensations, and strategic human resource management. Tekleab has recently published in the *Journal of Organizational Behavior*.

Lois Tetrick received her doctorate in Industrial and Organizational Psychology from Georgia Institute of Technology in 1983. Prior to joining the faculty at George Mason University as Director of the Industrial and Organizational Psychology Program, she was on faculty at Wayne State University and at the University of Houston. At Wayne State University, she was Program Director of the Industrial and Organizational Psychology Doctoral Program and served as the interim director of the Masters of Arts in Industrial Relations. At the University of Houston, she was Director of the Industrial and Organizational Psychology Program and co-director of the Occupational Health Psychology minor within the Department of Psychology. Professor Tetrick has served as Associate Editor of the *Journal of Applied Psychology* and is currently an Associate Editor of the *Journal of Occupational Health Psychology*. She also serves on the editorial board of the *Journal of Organizational Behavior*. Dr. Tetrick's research has focused primarily on individuals' perceptions of the employment relationship and their reactions to these perceptions, including issues of occupational health and safety, occupational stress, and organizational/union commitment. She is active in the

Society for Industrial and Organizational Psychology (SIOP) and was recently elected to represent SIOP on the American Psychological Association Council of Representatives. She also is active in the Academy of Management and is Past-Chair of the Human Resources Division. Dr. Tetrick is a fellow of the Society for Industrial and Organizational Psychology, the American Psychological Association, and the American Psychological Society.

Linn Van Dyne is Associate Professor of Management in the Eli Broad Graduate School of Management at Michigan State University. She received her Ph.D. from the University of Minnesota in Strategic Management and Organizations. Her research focuses on proactive behaviors (e.g. helping, voice, and minority influence) and the effects of work context, roles, and groups on employee behavior. She has published in a range of journals including the *Academy of Management Journal, Academy of Management Review, Journal of Applied Psychology,* and the *Journal of Organizational Behavior.*

Elizabeth Wolfe Morrison (Ph.D., Northwestern University) is a Professor of Management and Organizational Behavior at the Stern School of Business, New York University, and Chair of the Management Department. She has won several research awards, including the Cummings Scholar Award from the OB Division of the Academy of Management. Professor Morrison's research focuses on proactive behaviors by employees, newcomer adjustment, psychological contracts, and employee voice and silence. Professor Morrison has published articles in a range of journals, including *Academy of Management Journal, Academy of Management Review, Journal of Applied Psychology, Journal of Organizational Behavior,* and *Organizational Behavior and Human Decision Processes.* She is on the editorial board of the *Journal of Organizational Behavior* and the *Journal of Management.*

Shaker Zahra is Paul T. Babson Distinguished Professor of Entrepreneurship at Babson College. Shaker has also been a visiting professor at Georgia Tech and in several universities in Sweden, Finland, France, Poland, and Hong Kong. He received his Ph.D. in business administration from the University of Mississippi. His research focuses on technology strategy, innovation, and technology-based competition. His research has appeared in the *Academy of Management Journal, Academy of Management Review, Academy of Management Executive, Strategic Management Journal, Journal of Management, Journal of Business Venturing, Journal of Management Studies, Entrepreneurship: Theory & Practice, Decision Sciences, Information Systems Research,* and *Production Operations Management,* among others. He has also published/edited five books and edited special issues of *Academy of Management Review, Academy of Management Executive,* and *Entrepreneurship: Theory & Practice.* Shaker's research has received several research awards, including best papers from *Academy of Management Journal, Journal of Management,* and *Entrepreneurship: Theory & Practice.*

List of Figures

7.1 Agent development of the EOR · 143

9.1 Job creep—a reactance theory perspective on OCB as over-fulfillment of employee obligations · 182

11.1 The role of LMX in the development of the employer–employee relationship · 231

11.2 The moderating influence of socialization tactics on the relation between LMX and the employer–employee relationship · 238

12.1 An integrative psychological contract model · 275

13.1 Framework: Society, organization, and employee · 285

14.1 Conceptual framework for assessing the employment relationship · 313

14.2 Multilevel conceptualization of the employment relationship · 314

14.3 Reflective and formative measurement models of the employment relationship · 324

15.1 The effect of national-level factors on employers' HRM toolkits · 336

15.2 Model of how HRM policies influence employees' attitudes and behaviors · 338

15.3 Contextualized model of employment relationships · 344

16.1 Agents in the employment relationship · 359

16.2 The employment relationship · 362

List of Tables

1.1 Key themes in social exchange research and future directions 6

3.1 Trade union density (% of workers in unions) and collective bargaining coverage (%), six countries, 1980–97/8 52

3.2 Collective bargaining coverage, hourly wage rates, and wage premia (Great Britain and the United States) 53

4.1 Summary of key legal provisions pertaining to individual employment contracts for selected countries 69

4.2 Summary comparison of relational, neoclassical, and classical theories of contract 85

5.1 Mean days of paid annual leave, by size of establishment and years of service, United States, 1990–7 111

5.2 Percentage of employees in various benefit plans, by full/part-time status, United States, 1999–2000 112

6.1 Conflicts and commonalities between the different perspectives to the employment relationship 125

7.1 Views of organization strategy 138

7.2 Agent and employee influence on the EOR 145

13.1 Means of employee obligations 288

13.2 Means of employer obligations 289

13.3 Means of fulfillment of employer obligations 289

13.4 Satisfaction with type of contract of Dutch employees 294

13.5 Correlations of employee, employer, and fulfillment of employer obligations with age 303

16.1 Comparison of conceptual frameworks 352

Introduction

There has been a long-standing interest in understanding the relationship between employees and employers. This interest has been pursued across disciplines that have not necessarily converged in their understanding of the employment relationship. The purpose of this volume is to explore a number of the dominant disciplinary perspectives, discuss potential ways of integrating the different perspectives and highlight how researchers could incorporate different elements of perspectives into research, and offer suggestions for future theoretical and conceptual development, as well as highlighting future research avenues.

This volume is organized into three parts. The first part presents five theoretical perspectives on the employment relationship. First, Coyle-Shapiro and Conway examine the employment relationship from the perspective of social exchange theory. This is followed by Folger's chapter, which provides a synthesis of justice theory as it relates to the employer–employee relationship. Kelly presents an overview of industrial relations approaches to understanding the relationships between employers and employees. In the next chapter, Roehling presents a review and integration of legal theory and modern contract law and thus presents the employment relationship as being a contract either in the sense of a formal contract or a relational contract from the purview of modern contract law. Moving more to a macro-level, the last discipline's perspective to be presented is economics. Block, Berg, and Belman draw on neoclassical economic theory as it relates to the employment relationship. To conclude this section, Coyle-Shapiro, Taylor, Shore, and Tetrick provide a comparison of these disciplines' approaches to considering the employment relationship.

The second part of this volume focuses on more recent considerations of the employment relationship, primarily those based on exchange theory. Shore, Porter, and Zahra lead off this section by comparing four strategy theories and assessing their implications for the employment relationship from an organizational perspective. Morrison and Robinson focus on the antecedents and consequences of incongruence between employees and their employer. This is followed by Van Dyne and Butler Ellis, who introduce the concept of "job creep" in the employment relationship and use reactance theory to examine this phenomenon. Liden, Bauer, and Erdogan examine the role of leader–member exchange in the socialization of newcomers as well as the consequences of LMX for the employment relationship. This chapter is followed by Eisenberger, Jones, Aselage, and Sucharski, who examine how organizational support theory (OST) can be extended to advance our understanding of the employment relationship.

Part III turns the focus to the future. First, Tekleab and Taylor review the psychological contract literature, identifying some troubling issues and suggesting future theorizing and research to address these issues. Schalk, in the following chapter, discusses the dynamic nature of the employment relationship resulting from societal and organizational changes, as well as individual growth and development. Tetrick then discusses past measurement approaches to assessing the employment relationship and suggests necessary measurement and methodological refinements that need to be made to advance the quality of the research on the employment relationship and thus our understanding of this phenomenon. This section concludes with two chapters discussing implications for policy and future research. Iverson and Hannah discuss national contexts and human resource management considerations in managing employment relations from a policy and practice perspective. The editors then conclude with a chapter suggesting directions for future research beyond those suggested by the authors of the individual chapters.

It is hoped that readers of this volume will come away with new, at least to them, perspectives of the employment relationship, having viewed the employment relationship from the perspectives of multiple disciplines and from both the organizational and individual employee perspectives. In addition, it is hoped that readers will consider the extent to which the exchange construct might be useful in integrating this multidisciplinary perspective into a more interdisciplinary, integrative model of the employment relationship. Lastly, such integrations are expected to advance our understanding of how the employment relationship develops and the outcomes associated with various facets of the employment relationship for individual employees, organizational units, organizations, and larger economy and societal units.

PART I

THE NATURE OF THE EMPLOYMENT RELATIONSHIP FROM SOCIAL EXCHANGE, JUSTICE, INDUSTRIAL RELATIONS, LEGAL, AND ECONOMIC LITERATURES

The nature of the employment relationship has been an important but amorphous topic probably since the very first time one individual struck a bargain with another, trading labor for otherwise inaccessible valued outcomes. While that first employment relationship was likely fairly simple in nature, this is certainly not true today. Today, employment exchanges vary widely from short-term, primarily but not exclusively monetary exchanges, for example, a cab ride to the airport, to incredibly complex, all-encompassing, and "virtually never ending" relationships between some employees and their employer.

What then is the true essence of the employment relationship? Is it simply an economic exchange or a relationship that begins with economic origins but soon broadens in scope to an enduring social relationship? Is it a legally enforceable contract between two parties, albeit one involving parties who participate as "whole persons" rather than as group of knowledge and skills working for a group of pay and benefits? Is it a relationship which by its very nature is fraught with inherent conflicts of interest where employees need protection from the powerful employer? In fact, as the first five chapters of the book will show, the employment relationship is in some sense each of these, none of these, and yet all of these.

For this reason, we begin *The Employment Relationship: Examining Psychological and Contextual Perspectives* with a section devoted to five distinctly different perspectives—social exchange, justice, industrial relations, legal, and economic. In the final chapter of this part, we examine these perspectives for both conflicts and commonalities, and strive for a synthesis that is richer, more continuous, and more parsimonious than the five separate perspectives. We also seek to encourage readers to view the employment relationship with new eyes, and hopefully to research it with a higher level of understanding than would have been the case without the reading of Part I.

Chapter 1 by Coyle-Shapiro and Conway examines the employment relationship through the eyes of the social exchange literature. The authors remind us that theorists such as Homans, March, Simon, Gouldner, and Blau provided a foundation for the development of several social exchange concepts uniquely applicable to the employment relationship, for example, the leader member exchange (LMX), organizational citizenship behaviors (OCBs), perceived organizational support (POS), and psychological contract. Coyle-Shapiro and Conway organize their chapter around three critical components of social exchange theories: content of the exchange, process of the exchange, and the parties to the exchange. The authors urge researchers to seek greater insight into the processes through which the exchange develops over time as well as its embeddedness in larger exchange networks, and in doing so portray the uniqueness of this important perspective for the employment relationship.

Chapter 2 by Folger opens with Simon's metaphor of the employment relationship as an exchange whereby the employee receives economic inducements provided by the employer in exchange for allowing the employer to have a "blank check" of organizational prerogative, in terms of the virtually unlimited duties that may be required of an individual once on the job. However, Folger also identifies important constraints to management's discretion in exceeding the "zone of acceptability" in exercising their authority—there is considerable support for both procedural and interactional justice as important determinants of individual attitudes and behaviors. Folger's writing informs us that the employment relationship is shaped not only by the inducements and contributions of the two parties but also by a tendency of individual employees to blanch against the constraints of a higher organizational authority, as well as strong societal sanctions that are likely to be levied against employers who ignore the "human covenant" and respond to a favorable imbalance of power in the employment relationship by treating employees unfairly.

Kelly in Chapter 3 provides an industrial relations (IR) perspective on the employment exchange. Kelly structures his chapter around several common themes in the IR literature, including the unavoidable structural conflict of interest between employee and employer, the hierarchical and unequal character of the relationship between the two parties, the relative power differential favoring the employer, the indeterminacy of the relationship that gives rise to different forms of regulation on the relationship—unilateral by employer, bilateral through collective bargaining, and trilateral through the involvement of governments—and the many levels (national, industry, enterprise) at which this regulation plays out. The chapter vividly portrays the implications of these themes for the employment relationship and emphasizes both the uniqueness and the continuing relevance of the IR perspective for the employment relationship.

In Chapter 4, Roehling argues that the heavy emphasis on promise-based obligations in the context of the employment relationship because of their legally enforceable, contractual nature is passé; since even neoclassical contract theory accepts the binding nature of obligations reflecting a broader societal acceptance, for example, customs, past practices, etc., even in the absence of mutually agreed promises. The author's primary emphasis, however, is on the more recent relational contracting legal theory that originated in the work of Macneil. He informs the reader of a legal theory that characterizes contractual relationships, including the employment one, in a manner falling far to the right of the most balanced social exchanges. Terming relational theory "the most useful" of the legal contract theories for understanding the employment relationship, the author highlights its implications for the role of fairness in the employment relationship, the importance of context, and the limitations of promises. In doing so, Roehling establishes the continuing importance of a legal lens to our understanding of the employment relationship, particularly in an era of increasing employment legislation that is markedly relational in nature.

Block, Berg, and Belman present the final perspective from an economics perspective in Chapter 5. The authors base their writing on neoclassical economic theory and depict an employment exchange whereby both parties strive to maximize their respective utilities, profits for the organization, and the overall utility of employment for the individual, in the face of market factors that neither can control. The authors demonstrate that employees' decisions about their level of participation in the labor force depend heavily on the amount of salary and benefits that an employer offers them. Similarly, employers are willing to engage in a number of different employment relationships as long as they permit the organization to compete effectively in the marketplace. Overall, neoclassical economic theory argues that the market delivers higher outcomes to both individuals and society when unconstrained, assuming a fairly competitive market. Yet, national values for individual rights, including property rights and beliefs about the competitiveness of markets, produce employment legislation that differs considerably in the protection and benevolence awarded to individual employees. The result of these national differences are varying "default employment relationships" for different countries: For example, the organization and individual employees in America and the organization with a collective union representative of employees in Europe. Overall, the economic perspective portrays organizational and employee (union) parties striving for their own respective economic "best deal" and being relatively ambivalent toward the needs or desires of the other party—adding yet a final distinctive view of the employment relationship.

Chapter 6 by Coyle-Shapiro, Taylor, Shore, and Tetrick concludes Part I. The chapter evokes the imagery of a pentagonal prism formed by the five perspectives through which one may view the employment relationship, causing different images and different contextual factors to dominate and recede as one peers through the various prism sides. Chapter 6 identifies both conflicts and commonalities across the perspectives and lays the foundation for a unified view of the employment relationship that is the focus of Chapter 16.

1

The Employment Relationship through the Lens of Social Exchange

JACQUELINE A-M. COYLE-SHAPIRO AND NEIL CONWAY

1.1 Social exchange approach to the employment relationship

Almost half a century ago, Homans (1958: 597–8) wrote "[exchange]...is one of the oldest theories of social behavior, and one that we still use every day to interpret our own behavior...[but] this view has been much neglected by social scientists." Presently, social exchange is a dominant theoretical framework used to examine the employment relationship as exemplified by research on psychological contracts (Rousseau 1995) and perceived organizational support (Eisenberger et al. 1986) and its consequences on employee attitudes and behavior. However, while there is a great deal of belief in the existence of social exchange-based transactions underpinning the employment relationship, we would argue that social exchange still remains theoretically underdeveloped, that some of its key assumptions remain untested, and that the empirical base for social exchange is large in terms of the number of studies, but very narrow in terms of methods employed, most often focusing on the simple contribution–inducement exchanges assessed through correlations. Social exchange theory has been used to examine a variety of organizationally desired outcomes and to examine how employees view their relationship with their employer in different cultures and under different contractual arrangements. Overall, the empirical evidence seems to support the universality of social exchange as a framework for understanding the employment relationship (Shore and Coyle-Shapiro 2003).

Against this backdrop, the aims of this chapter are to review the origins of social exchange theory, examine the main developments and applications since the early seminal works, assess the limitations of the theory, and outline issues for future consideration. Throughout this chapter, we focus on the content, process, and parties to social exchange as these headings constitute useful themes for organizing much of the research in the area and capture the defining building blocks of social exchange, namely, the parties involved, what is exchanged (i.e. content), and how the exchange occurs (i.e. process). From the early work on social exchange, we trace the development of the main ideas and highlight areas of convergence and divergence amongst different contributors. Table 1.1 provides an overview of the contents of this chapter.

Table 1.1. *Key themes in social exchange research and future directions*

	Content/type of exchange	Process of exchange	Parties to the exchange
Early work	Exchange of material and non-material goods (Homans) Inducements–contributions (March and Simon) Social and economic exchange (Blau)	Balance in relationship (Homans) Profit maximization (Homans) Individual satisfaction (March and Simon) Exchange has implication for organizational stability/survival (March and Simon) Reciprocity norms (Gouldner) Heteromorphic and homomorphic reciprocity (Gouldner)	Employee–organization (March and Simon) Employee–organization, where groups provide equity standards (Homans) Workgroup sets standards of employee behavior (Blau) Importance of indirect parties to the exchange (Blau) Power imbalance across parties (Blau)
Advancements	Detailed classification of resources to be exchanged (Foa and Foa) Transaction/productive exchanges (Emerson) Potent inducements (e.g. POS)	Reciprocity typologies: Generalized, balanced, and negative (Sahlins) Factors that propel (e.g. indebtedness) or disrupt (e.g. violation) the ongoing exchange	Networks of individuals and groups (Emerson) Conceptualizing/operationalizing the employer's perspective (Tsui et al.)
Trends	Convergence developing on specification of resources to be exchanged However, Emerson highlights that the resources to be exchanged may be dependent upon actions of the exchange partners—resources may not be independently exchanged	Promoting of concepts to understanding types and duration of reciprocity	Divergence in terms of level of the exchange and parties to the exchange
Limitations	Distinction between direct and indirect exchanges not captured Multiple meanings of exchanged resources overlooked Necessary and boundary conditions of exchange need stating	Process of exchange not explored through "process" theories (cf. Langley), but rather through "variance" theories	Exchanges tend not to be nested in broader social/group context
Prospects	Develop process (cf. Langley) approaches that acknowledge the interplay of exchange content, party, and process: Nested in context More flexible in terms of dealing with time issues, the precision of the exchange, sense-making of exchange partners Incorporates multiple parties and levels of analysis		

1.2 Origins of social exchange theory

In reviewing the origins of exchange theory and its development, we concentrate on the work of Homans (1958), March and Simon (1958), Gouldner (1960), and Blau (1964) as these works, collectively, are heavily drawn upon by researchers examining the employment relationship through the lens of exchange. These early writings were also very rich in ideas, a number of which have been highly influential to later research on social exchange (e.g. social/economic exchanges), while a number of other ideas presented in these early works have not received the same attention and have not been adopted or developed subsequently by researchers (e.g. direct and indirect exchanges; the effects of groups on individual exchanges). Furthermore, it is probably fair to say that these writings constitute the only seminal works in the area of social exchange with regard to work settings. However, these contributions do not represent the beginning of social exchange theory as these authors note their debt to earlier researchers such as Mauss (1925) and Malinowski (1922). The texts by Homans (1958), March and Simon (1958), Gouldner (1960), and Blau (1964) are, however, the starting point and authority for more recent research, where certain ideas proposed in these texts are often accepted uncritically and assumed to provide social exchange "laws."

1.2.1 Content of the exchange

Homans (1958) lays out a skeleton theory of exchange in the context of how individuals interact within groups. Specifically, Homans (1958: 606) views social behavior as "an exchange of goods, material goods but also non-material ones, such as the symbols of approval or prestige." In a similar vein, March and Simon (1958), drawing heavily on the work of Barnard (1938), outline an inducements–contributions model to capture the exchange relationship between an employee and the organization. They viewed the exchange as one where the organization offered inducements in return for employee contributions.

Homans (1958) and March and Simon (1958) did not categorize inducements nor did they specify the type of relationship that would emerge between exchange partners, which was subsequently addressed by Blau (1964). Blau (1964) was influenced by the work of Homans (1958) and while retaining the basic principles of exchange, he distinguished between economic and social exchange. Blau (1964) defines economic exchange as one where the nature of the exchange is specified and the method used to assure that each party fulfills its specific obligations is the formal contract upon which the exchange is based. In contrast, social exchange involves unspecified obligations—"favors that create diffuse future obligations, not precisely specified ones, and the nature of the return cannot be bargained about but must be left to the discretion of the one who makes it" (Blau 1964: 93). Thus, one party needs to trust the other to discharge future obligations (i.e. to reciprocate) in the initial stages of the exchange and it is the regular discharge of obligations that promotes trust in the relationship.

This early work, primarily adopting a sociological perspective (the exception is March and Simon 1958), views the content of exchange relationships as encompassing tangible benefits as well as intangible benefits such as affection, approval, and respect. As such, there is a high degree of convergence between these early contributors regarding the content of the exchange relationships. Blau's distinction between economic and social exchange has been particularly influential and carried forward to current research exploring exchange relationships in organizational settings (cf. Eisenberger et al. 1986; Rousseau 1995; Tsui et al. 1997; Shore 1999). Subsequent work by social psychologists added greater precision to the mapping of the content of the exchange (see Section 1.3.1).

1.2.2 Process of the exchange

Early studies began with a focus on the outcomes driving the exchange process (e.g. balance, profit maximization) prior to a more detailed explication of the underlying process through examining the norm of reciprocity.

In Homans' (1958) view, individuals strive for balance in their exchanges with their exchange partner and also seek to maximize profit from the exchange—the difference between the value of what is received and the cost of what is given in return. March and Simon (1958) view the process of the exchange between an employee and the organization in a similar manner. Individual employees are more satisfied when there is a greater difference between the inducements offered by the organization and the contributions given in return. From the organization's perspective, its survival and continued existence is contingent upon the contributions of employees being sufficient to generate the inducements that subsequently are perceived as adequate by employees in terms of eliciting the necessary contributions. In other words, March and Simon (1958) recognize the contingent interplay between the inducements offered and the contributions needed in return, where these contributions need to be sufficient to warrant the organization continuing to provide the same level of inducements.

Although Homans (1958) and March and Simon (1958) conceptualized the process of the exchange in terms of the outcomes received, some degree of reciprocation is needed for the exchange partners to attain their desired outcomes (e.g. March and Simon posit that an individual employee will be more satisfied with his or her outcomes when the organization engages in greater reciprocation than the individual). The underlying process was made more explicit by Gouldner (1960) in his seminal work on the norm of reciprocity. The norm of reciprocity is very much visible in current research that examines the employment relationship. Almost all social exchange research refers to this work as evidence of the existence of the "norm of reciprocity," although the assumption is largely unelaborated and untested. Gouldner suggests that the norm of reciprocity makes two demands: "(1) people should help those who have helped them and, (2) people should not injure those who have helped them" (1960: 171). Recognizing that prior work on reciprocity implied that the amount to be reciprocated is roughly similar to that given (i.e. equivalent), Gouldner (1960) expanded the meaning of equivalence by distinguishing between heteromorphic and homeomorphic reciprocity. The former means that what is exchanged between two parties is different but equal in perceived value. The latter involves exchanges where the content or the circumstances under which things are exchanged are identical. For example, a colleague helps out another when he or she is under pressure to meet a work deadline. This act is subsequently reciprocated when the former colleague finds himself or herself in a similar position attempting to meet a deadline. The recipient of past help now helps the colleague and the circumstance in which it was given (in time of need) is identical. However, Gouldner (1960) notes that the adequacy of this conceptual distinction is an empirical issue. Regarding how the norm of reciprocity operates, Gouldner (1960) argues that the strength of an obligation to repay is contingent upon the value of the benefit received. Benefits are more valued when (a) the recipient is in greater need; (b) the donor cannot afford to (but does) give the benefit; (c) the donor provides the benefit in the absence of a motive of self-interest; and (d) the donor was not required to give the benefit. Therefore, highly valued benefits create a stronger obligation to reciprocate.

The norm of reciprocity plays an important role in the development of social exchange relationships by perpetuating the ongoing fulfillment of obligations and strengthening indebtedness. However, an important consideration is when repayment will take place and what factors influence the timeliness of repayment. Blau (1964: 99) argues that the timing of reciprocation is important—"posthaste reciprocation of favors, which implies a refusal to stay indebted for a while and hence an insistence on a more businesslike relationship is condemned as improper." The underlying rationale is that remaining obligated for a period of time to another party and the trust that the obligations will be discharged serves to strengthen the social exchange. Furthermore, the social exchange process takes time to develop, beginning with minor transactions in which little trust is required. If the recipient reciprocates the small benefits received, this acts as a demonstration of their trustworthiness facilitating the ongoing conferring of benefits and discharging of obligations.

In summary, this work, primarily grounded in sociology, developed from a common base and highlighted two key issues in how exchange relationships operate—the felt obligation to reciprocate and the timing of reciprocation. Furthermore, this work highlighted the interdependency between the content of the exchange and the process of the exchange. Gouldner (1960) views the starting mechanism (i.e. felt obligation) of the exchange process as contingent upon the value of prior benefits, while Blau (1964) sees an individual's unwillingness to remain indebted to another for an adequate period as being influential in the type of exchange that subsequently develops. For Gouldner, the content of what is exchanged influences the process while Blau views the process (i.e. the timing of reciprocation) as influencing the content of the subsequent exchange.

1.2.3 Parties to the exchange

A key point of divergence amongst early contributors concerns the parties to the exchange. In particular, the work of March and Simon (1958) is clearly demarcated in their focus on the employee–organization relationship. In doing so, the organization is treated as a single unified entity where management takes the responsibility for managing any change in the inducements–contributions balance. In contrast, the work of Homans (1958) and Blau (1958) emphasized the dyadic exchange between individuals located in a group context.

Homans (1958) argued that in addition to establishing balance and maximizing "profit" individuals would also attempt to ensure that no one else in the group earned greater profit, thus incorporating equity between group members into the exchange. Blau (1964) developed the idea of exchange between individuals nested in a group context further by considering the effects of groups on the exchange process between individuals and also how the group as a collective react to the exchange relationship. For Blau, treating exchange dyads in isolation was far too simplistic, "Crusoe and Friday were a dyad that existed in isolation, but most associations are part of a broad matrix of social relations" (Blau 1964: 32). The social context exerts a number of important influences on the exchange process. First, Blau (1964) argues that a dyadic exchange is influenced by the "role set" that each partner belongs to as this defines the alternatives forgone and, hence, the costs incurred to obtain the rewards from the present dyadic exchange. Second, the group may exert influence on exchange partners not to deviate from the group standard governing exchange transactions. Third, Blau (1964) distinguishes between direct and indirect exchanges. Transactions in a given exchange are located in other exchanges that may occur in the background but which may be of greater saliency. For example, an employee who helps a colleague with no expectation of reciprocation or who refuses the offer of gaining a future benefit may gain social approval from his or her immediate boss. In this situation, the direct exchange (i.e. helping out a colleague) cannot be fully understood without taking into account the indirect exchange (i.e. the benefit of social approval). Thus, the act of reciprocation did not come from the recipient who received help but rather from a witness to the act.

A final aspect of Blau's (1964) work that is of relevance here is how groups react to the exchange relationship. Of central importance is the role of power and, in particular, how the collective judge the exercise of power in the exchange relationship; "the significance of power imbalances for social change depends, therefore, on the reactions of the governed to the exercise of power" (Blau 1964: 29). Employees received benefits from the organization in return for complying with the directives of the superior and making additional contributions to the organization. If the group of employees judges that the demands are fair considering the benefits received, Blau (1964) argues that this will generate collective approval and bestow legitimacy on the superior's authority. In turn, this collective approval will manifest itself in group pressures that promote compliance with the superior's directives and simultaneously reinforce the power imbalance in the relationship. However, if the group evaluates the exchange as unfair, this is likely to lead to hostility among members and the communication of anger to each other. Mutual support amongst group members may facilitate opposition to the employer through union organization. Thus, Blau (1964) recognizes that individuals may respond individually or collectively in their exchange relationship with their superior.

What emerged from this early work are different views of the parties to the exchange and the degrees to which the context in which exchanges occur is considered. Blau (1964) probably presents the most comprehensive portrayal of the context of exchanges by not only taking into account how groups influence a particular dyadic exchange but also considering responses to the exchange at the individual and collective levels. The effect of groups on individuals was a fundamental contribution of the Human Relations School (Roethlisberger and Dickson 1939), which is currently recognized as having an important influence on individual behavior (George 1990; Robinson and O'Leary-Kelly 1998). Ang et al. (2003) demonstrate how workgroups (in particular, task interdependence) heightens social comparison processes that in turn give rise to differing perceptions of an individual's view of the employment relationship and their contribution to the relationship. However, the role of groups is seldom considered in employment relationship research, which tends to focus on individual level responses to the exchange relationship and examines this without considering the group context.

Summary

Early work on social exchange examined the exchange process at a fundamental level. Most notably, considerable efforts were directed towards debating and justifying whether it was reasonable to suppose that any type of exchange takes place at all. This early work provided a considerable degree of convergence in outlining the content of the exchange relationships and the norm of reciprocity as the process underlying the exchange. Yet, at the same time, and at this early stage of development, different views are apparent with regard to the parties to the exchange and the context in which the exchange is located.

1.3 Main developments on early work

This section provides a review of some of the main extensions to social exchange theory since the early seminal works, and also presents research on related concepts examining the employment relationship that draws heavily from the early theoretical work on social exchange. The latter work includes the psychological contract, perceived organizational support (POS), leader–member exchange (LMX), and the employment relationship as defined from the employer's perspective. These concepts are reliant on social exchange for providing their underlying operating mechanism. As such, they can be considered as extensions of the social exchange idea. They have in a number of instances provided concepts, such as psychological contract violation, which have further increased our understanding of social exchange.

1.3.1 Content of the exchange

The first main advancement here has been attempts to add greater precision to the contributions–inducements exchange (e.g. Foa and Foa 1975, 1980; Emerson 1972, 1981). Coming from a social psychological perspective and considering interpersonal relationships, the work of Foa and Foa (1975, 1980) specified in greater detail the content of exchange relationships; that is, the resources exchanged. Following in the sociological tradition, Emerson (1981) elaborated on the types of the exchange relationships thereby moving the conceptualization beyond a reciprocal exchange. The second main advancement has been the identification of inducements (e.g. organizational support) that seem particularly important in ensuring employee contributions in organizations.

Adding precision to the contributions–inducements exchange
In an attempt to overcome the lack of specificity of what is exchanged, Foa and Foa (1980: 79) suggest that most resources can be categorized as falling into one of six classes: (a) money—"any coin, currency, or token which has some standard unit of exchange"; (b) goods—"tangible products, objects or materials"; (c) services— "activities on the body or belongings of a person which often constitute labor for another"; (d) information—"advice, opinions, instruction or enlightenment"; (e) status—"expression of evaluative judgment which conveys high or low prestige, regard or esteem"; (f) love—"expression of affectionate regard, warmth or comfort."

Foa and Foa (1980) order these resources in terms of their degree of concreteness/ symbolism and particularism/universalism. Particularism refers to the significance of the individual who provides the resource. According to Foa and Foa (1980), love is more particularistic because it matters from whom we receive affection and socio-emotional support, while money is the most universalistic of the resources. Goods and information are more particularistic than money but less particularistic than status and services. Concreteness refers to the observability of the resources exchanged. Services and goods are concrete while status and information are more symbolic. Love and money fall in between as they can be exchanged in concrete and symbolic form. Empirically, the authors find support for an individual's preference for exchanges between proximal rather than distal resources, where proximal refers to the exchange of a resource with another resource from the same or a neighboring category, as organized according to the concreteness/symbolism and particularism/ universalism dimensions, thus supporting Gouldner's (1960) idea of homeomorphic reciprocity.

Berg and Wiebe (1993) argue that a simple distinction between economic and social resources may obscure subtle but important aspects of the exchange and hence the contribution of Foa and Foa's (1980) resource theory is that it "reflects similarities and differences in the behaviors that motivate exchange and in the effects produced through the exchange of different resources" (Berg and Wiebe 1993: 98). The majority of work on resource theory has empirically tested the exchange of resources under experimental conditions or in particular types of relationships (friendship and romantic relationships). Berg and Wiebe (1993), based on two empirical studies in organizations, conclude that resource theory is useful for examining resources exchanged in work settings. Specifically, the authors find that there are differences between quality circle members and non-members in terms of the resources given and received—in particular, particularistic and symbolic resources.

In line with Foa and Foa's (1980) prediction, employees prefer the exchange of similar resources (Berg and Wiebe 1993).

Furthermore, Foa and Foa (1980) offer time as a third dimension and argue that some resources take more time than others to exchange (money can be exchanged quickly, but love takes time). The implication is that the opportunity to exchange resources that require time may be limited in relationships that have a short-term focus. Foa and Foa's (1980) argument that the timing is contingent upon the nature of the resource to be exchanged is also consistent with Blau's (1964) view that a willingness to feel indebted to another party is an important element in the development of a social exchange relationship. The value of specifying resources along the dimensions of particularism/universalism and concreteness/symbolism has been recognized in more recent work on psychological contracts (e.g. McLean Parks and smith 1998).

While the focus of prior work was on independent contributions to the exchange, Emerson (1981) highlighted the potential for interdependence between each party's contributions to the exchange relationship. First, Emerson (1981) distinguished social relationships into transaction and productive exchanges. Transaction exchanges are either negotiated or reciprocal. Negotiated transactions involve mutually contingent contributions to the exchange in which the two contributions evolve into a social process (terms of employment that is the culmination of the bargaining process). Reciprocal transactions involve separately performed contributions in which the initiating process (i.e. the initial contribution) is given in a non-contingent manner—if reciprocated, then a reciprocal transaction has occurred. Productive exchanges are similar to Barth's (1966) notion of incorporation. The key distinguishing feature of this type of exchange is that separately obtained benefits by either party are not possible. Emerson (1981) uses the analogy of "it takes two to tango" and under this type of exchange, if both parties perform well, both will benefit—if one party performs poorly, neither will benefit. The benefit or value from the exchange results from behavioral contributions that have little value if accomplished solely. The offer of training and development might be closer to this type of exchange—there is little benefit to either party unless the employer offers it and the employee is a willing participant.

These advancements on earlier work provided a detailed specification of resources exchanged and extended the conceptualization of exchange relationships beyond reciprocal exchanges. They do not, however, provide insight into whether certain inducements are more important than others in terms of eliciting contributions, which is the issue we turn to next.

Importance of certain organizational inducements

Research on POS and LMX represent important extensions to capturing the content of exchange relationships in a work context. POS captures an individual's perception concerning the extent to which the organization values his or her contributions and cares about his or her well-being (Eisenberger et al. 1986). Thus, researchers adopting a POS framework argue that from the array of possible inducements offered by organizations, organizational support is likely to be particularly important.

Informed by Foa and Foa's resource theory, LMX relationships involve the exchange of information, material resources, and support. The greater the exchange of these resources, the higher the quality of the LMX relationship (Wayne et al. 1997). Wayne et al. (1997) find that there is a reciprocal relationship between LMX and POS, although the direction of the relationship seems to be stronger in the direction of LMX to POS.

Empirical evidence is strongly supportive of the relationship between POS and LMX and organizational commitment, organizational citizenship behavior, performance, the desire to remain with the organization, and a lower likelihood of performing withdrawal behaviors such as absenteeism and tardiness. POS and LMX extend social exchange theory by highlighting which inducements are important in prompting employee reciprocation and thus present clear prescriptive guidelines for organizations to fully realize employee contributions. The idea that supportive actions toward employees will be reciprocated in kind by employees is essentially similar to Foa and Foa's prediction of proximal exchanges (i.e. similar resources will be exchanged with one another). Hence, the validity of POS and LMX rely on the validity of the theory of proximity.

1.3.2 Process of the exchange

We concentrate on the following advancements: The extension made to the norm of reciprocity and the conceptualization of the "ongoingness" of the exchange. The former stems from Sahlins' (1965) work in anthropology and the latter draws heavily on social and organizational psychology. Together, these advancements broaden our understanding of the process of reciprocation and the psychological triggers that serve to maintain (e.g. indebtedness) or disrupt and potentially end (e.g. violation) exchange relationships.

Reciprocity
Gouldner's (1960) conceptualization of the norm of reciprocity, although widely cited, is limited in focus compared to the subsequent work of Sahlins (1965, 1972). Sahlins (1965) derived his work partly from Mauss's (1925) theory of gift giving that suggests individuals have a moral obligation (a) to give gifts, (b) to accept gifts, and (c) to repay for gifts received, and also the work of Malinowski (1922) who viewed exchanges as either "pure gifts," partial or conditional repayment, or an equivalent repayment which he termed "barter."

Sahlins (1972) broadened the conceptualization of reciprocity by developing a typology based on three dimensions: (a) immediacy of returns—the timing by which the recipient needs to reciprocate in order to discharge the obligation which could range from simultaneous reciprocation to indefinite; (b) equivalence of returns— the extent to which exchange partners return the same resource; (c) interest—the degree to which exchange partners are interested in the exchange process. From these three dimensions, Sahlins (1972) outlines three forms of reciprocity: Generalized, balanced, and negative.

Generalized reciprocity is altruistic in orientation where there is a lack of concern over the timing and the content of the exchange. According to Sahlins (1972), repayment may be conditional upon what the recipient can afford and when they can reciprocate but this does not preclude the situation where reciprocation never occurs. Hence, this form of reciprocity is viewed as "sustained one-way flow" (Sahlins 1972: 194). Balanced reciprocity is characterized by quid pro quo and a perfectly balanced exchange is one where there is a simultaneous exchange of an equivalent resource. However, Sahlins (1972: 194–5) states that "balanced reciprocity may be more loosely applied to transactions which stipulate returns of commensurate worth or utility within a finite period of time." Finally, negative reciprocity is characterized by a taking orientation in which exchange partners have opposite interests and attempt to maximize their own utility at the expense of the other. In the main, employment relationship researchers tend to assume that balanced reciprocity governs the employment relationship. Rarely do researchers empirically examine the form of reciprocity governing the exchange. However, recent attempts to measure Sahlins' (1972) forms of reciprocity may provide the stimulus for closer examination of the norm of reciprocity in organizational settings (Tetrick et al. 2004).

Ongoingness of the exchange
We review indebtedness as playing a role in the maintenance of the exchange relationship and the contribution of psychological contract breach as a disruption to the ongoing nature of the exchange. Building on Homans, Greenberg (1980: 5) argues that the strength of obligation to reciprocate—indebtedness—is likely to be influenced by (a) the donor's motives, (b) the magnitude of the rewards and costs incurred by the recipient and donor as a result of the exchange, (c) the locus of causality of the donor's action, and (d) cues emitted by comparing others. Therefore, an individual is likely to experience greater indebtedness when they perceive that the donor is more concerned with the recipient's welfare than their own at the time the help was given; when the donor's net costs for the help and the recipient's net rewards of the help are great; when the recipient perceives that they requested the help rather than it being offered by the donor; and when the donor gives cues that the debt still exists despite the recipient believing that it was repaid.

Following from this, Greenberg (1980) argues that the greater the magnitude of the indebtedness, the greater the discomfort experienced and the stronger the attempts to deal with or reduce the felt indebtedness. To reduce the indebtedness, an individual may cognitively restructure the situation or engage in reciprocation. The former is more likely when the cognitions associated with the act of help are ambiguous, there are few witnesses to the helping act, future interaction with the donor is unlikely, and the recipient perceives that the opportunity to reciprocate is minimal. An individual is more likely to reduce indebtedness by reciprocating when he or she has been reinforced in the past for reciprocating help and there is the opportunity to reciprocate the donor directly or indirectly via a third party.

Work on the role of dispositions suggest that exchange-related dispositions may be important in explaining how individuals vary in their response to the exchange relationship. In particular, an individual's acceptance of the norm of reciprocity (Coyle-Shapiro 2002), exchange ideology (Eisenberger et al. 1986, 2001; Coyle-Shapiro and Neuman 2004), and creditors' ideology (Eisenberger et al. 1987; Coyle-Shapiro and Neuman 2004) have been found to moderate how individuals respond to the resources received in an exchange relationship. As Eisenberger et al. (1987: 744) note, "partners may differ in their readiness to reciprocate benefits on the basis of ideologies concerning the most effective ways to strengthen exchange relationships." Creditors prefer to have others in their debt and this is accomplished by repaying a partner with a greater amount than that received (Greenberg and Westcott 1983). Therefore, the role of indebtedness and individual dispositions may play an important role in the strengthening of social exchange relationships.

Indebtedness is indirectly captured in the POS and psychological contract research through felt obligation and employee obligations to the employer. Eisenberger et al. (2001) found a positive relationship between employee perceptions of organizational support and their felt obligation to care about the organization and help it achieve its goals. In psychological contract research, employees may reduce their indebtedness as a consequence of the employers fulfilling their obligations to them by cognitively increasing what they feel they are obligated to give the employer (Coyle-Shapiro and Kessler 2002). In this research, indebtedness manifests itself in the strength of obligation toward the exchange partner.

Probably the most important construct in psychological contract theory, in terms of understanding how psychological contracts affect employee attitudes and behaviors, is that of "breach." Breach is defined as occasions where an employee believes that their organization has failed to fulfill any of its promises (Robinson and Rousseau 1994) and is essentially a disruption to the ongoing exchange process that is the psychological contract.

Psychological contract breach has been an important conceptual addition to research on social exchange as it identifies one of the most important ways that ongoing exchange relationships are disrupted. Furthermore, with the established links between psychological contract violation and the intention to quit and other forms of employee withdrawal, it also provides social exchange with a concept that helps us understand how exchange relationships might end. Finally, breach provides a way of viewing social exchange in terms of "events" rather than variables, which is typical of most empirical research in organizations on social exchange. Conway and Briner (2002) argue that the operation of the psychological contract consists of sequences of events embedded in an ongoing relationship. They note that the psychological contract is by definition an exchange process consisting of a series of related events experienced and interpreted by the employee and agents of the organization. Using a daily diary study that facilitated the capturing of broken promises (i.e. breach) and exceeded promises close to when they actually happened, they found support for the relationship between the psychological contract and everyday fluctuations in emotion and affect and the importance of attributions in the interpretation of psychological contract events. Qualitative data from the diary study revealed a number of discrete and highly salient psychological contract "episodes" over the two-week diary duration period (Conway and Briner 2000). "Episodes" here refers to an ongoing sequence of broken and exceeded promises that take the form of narratives, where events in the sequence are perceived by the participant as being causally related to one another. To the extent that social exchange relationships are characterized by sequences of exchange events over time, which we argue below, then psychological contract breach represents an important type of event in the unfolding of social exchange.

1.3.3 Parties to the exchange

Subsequent work shifted attention away from dyadic exchanges by examining exchanges between groups and in exchange networks. The second main development focused attention on the employer's perspective to the exchange in contrast to the emphasis of prior work on the employee perspective.

Emerson (1981) extended the idea of exchanges beyond the dyad by directing attention to: (a) groups involving two or more actors and (b) networks involving three or more actors. A corporate group has two defining characteristics: It confronts its environment (which could be another group) as a single social unit and it is dealt with as a single unit. For example, collective bargaining over the terms and conditions of the employment relationship can be thought of as an exchange between two groups—organizational representatives representing the organization and trade union representatives representing employees as a collective.

Networks, in contrast, are relatively autonomous decision-making actors occupying positions in a structure. Emerson (1981) defines network connections as a set of two or more connected exchange relations where the connection may be positive (an exchange in which one relation is contingent upon an exchange in another) or negative (an exchange in one relation is contingent upon non-exchange in the other). To illustrate, an exchange between a focal employee X and supervisor Y may (or may not) be independent of the exchange between the supervisor and other employees. An independent exchange would involve the supervisor–employee dyad being non-contingent upon the supervisor–other employees' exchanges. In contrast, the employee and supervisor may exchange and the supervisor obtains a resource that is valued and may be passed on to other employees and used to obtain benefits from these employees. In this case, the exchange between the supervisor and other employees is dependent upon the exchange between the supervisor and focal employee. Therefore, the timing of the reciprocation and the benefits to be passed to other employees from the supervisor is dependent upon the exchange with the focal employee. Thus, Emerson's (1981) idea of interdependency adds an additional layer of complexity to understanding relationships whereby the resource to be exchanged in a particular exchange is dependent upon that resource being received from another exchange relationship. That said, we would argue that this may be a more accurate reflection of exchanges in organizations as a system of interdependent exchanges. For example, a supervisor's exchange relationship with his or her subordinate may be dependent on the supervisor's exchange relationship with those higher up in the hierarchy. This idea would be consistent with an individual having multiple psychological contracts in organizations in which the fulfillment of some obligations by his or her immediate supervisor may be contingent upon the supervisor's relationship with senior-level managers.

The complexity inherent in viewing exchanges within organizations through networks and groups presents organizational researchers with operationalization challenges in terms of the parties involved. The majority of research on social exchange is still anchored in adopting a single party's perspective, namely, the individual employee. Tsui et al. (1997) provided one of the first empirical examinations of the employer's perspective to the exchange relationship with employees. The authors develop a typology of employment relationships based on two dimensions: Balance (between the inducements offered by the employer and the expected contributions from employees) and content of the exchange (economic and social exchange). Briefly, a balanced economic exchange (quasi-spot contract) occurs when the employer offers short-term purely economic inducements in return for highly specified outcomes. A balanced social exchange (mutual investment) occurs when both parties offer an open-ended and long-term investment to each other. The underinvestment approach occurs when the employer expects open-ended commitment and long-term investment from employees in return for short-term economic inducements. The overinvestment approach is categorized by the employer offering long-term investment in return for highly specified employee outcomes. The key finding of their empirical study is that a mutual investment employment relationship is positively associated with employee attitudes and performance. This work took an important step in defining the employment relationship from the employer perspective, yet at the same time, Emerson's (1981) ideas on networks have not received sufficient attention in the arena of the employment relationship.

Summary
In terms of the content of the exchange, an advancement that is consistent with the seminal works is greater precision in the specification of the exchange and the importance of similarity in the resources exchanged. Subsequent work on the process of the exchange propose additional reciprocity typologies and also examine factors that influence the ongoing exchange, in terms of compelling parties to fulfill or to end their exchange with the other party. Advancements on the parties to the exchange have highlighted the embeddedness of exchange relationships in social structures and reaffirm prior work in distinguishing between direct and indirect exchanges as well as the interdependency amongst exchanges. Although convergence and the development of ideas are clearly apparent in the work addressing the content and process of the exchange, there is less convergence in terms of the parties of the exchange—who is party to the exchange and whether the exchange is conceptualized as a dyad, group, or network.

1.4 Limitations of social exchange and directions for future research

In this final section, we discuss what we consider to be some of the main limitations of social exchange research and propose ways of possible development. As with previous sections, we have organized the discussion under the themes of content, process, and parties.

We begin with considering the content of the social exchange and argue that our existing understanding is too simplistic and reductionist, in that the demarcation between inducements and contributions is often viewed as unproblematic; the wider symbolic meanings of items exchanged is overlooked; the logic of proximal exchanges is not very compelling; empirical work assumes but never explicitly measures exchange, thus potentially masking any number of other explanations for the relationship between inducements and contributions; and finally that the necessary conditions for adopting a social exchange framework are often overlooked.

1.4.1 *Content of the exchange*

Social exchange research to a very large extent assumes that there is a clear demarcation between the inducements offered and the contributions expected, where the exchange in commodities is separated by an unspecified period of time. This assumption ignores the possibility that what is exchanged between the two parties may provide simultaneous benefit to each. Taking training and development as an example, this is often viewed as an organizational inducement to employees. However, employees may rightfully interpret that training may result in the expansion of their role and raise performance expectations and could well see the receipt of training as a "cost" rather than as a "reward" as intended by the organization. Furthermore, for the benefits of training to be fully realized the two parties need to "jointly contribute." This type of exchange, labelled as a productive exchange by Emerson (1981), is largely overlooked in employment relationship research that to a greater extent assumes that the exchange is reciprocal whereby the contributions of each exchange are separate and clearly demarcated. Emerson (1981) argues that some exchanges may involve a joint exchange activity where the two parties' contributions are interdependent to achieving an outcome for both. In the context of the employment relationship, some aspects of the overall exchange relationship may depend on the employee and employer engaging in a joint activity where the outcome for both is contingent upon their joint actions rather than their independent actions. In reality, the employment relationship may involve exchanges that are negotiated and reciprocal and, furthermore, some aspects may be akin to a productive exchange.

Second, the range of symbolic meanings of items exchanged is overlooked in social exchange research. As Blau (1964: 96) noted, "since the utility of a given benefit cannot be clearly separated from that of other rewards derived from a social association, it seems difficult to apply the economic principles of maximizing utilities to social exchange." As acknowledged in research on interpersonal relationships (Kelley 1979), interactions yield symbolic outcomes, which may occur as a direct result or as an act of inference by one of the parties from more concrete commodities that are exchanged. Take the example of an employee who helps out his colleague by showing him how to perform a task more quickly. The colleague may appreciate the assistance and see it as a "loan" of others' time, which he or she is expected to return later. The act may also be read by the colleague as the receipt of skill acquisition and more generally an indication of technical and social support. Alternatively, the colleague may have ambivalent feelings about the offered help, feeling that the help undermines their self-esteem and publicizes difficulties he or she is having completing the work, consistent with research that has found that visible support (as opposed to "invisible" support where the recipient of the support is not consciously aware of the other party's support) transactions can have a negative effect on well-being (see Bolger et al. 2000 for a review). Clearly, understanding the full range of meanings attached to a transaction is crucial to understanding how an employee is likely to respond to the receipt of an inducement.

Third, the logic of a commodity being exchanged with another commodity to which it is broadly proximal and similar in content, as argued by Foa and Foa (1980) and underpinning POS and LMX research, is not very compelling and somewhat at odds with other concepts included under social exchange theory. For instance, a major motivation for entering an exchange is that the parties can provide goods to one another that they could not acquire on their own, which runs directly counter to the exchange of similar commodities. Further, certain concepts that are underpinned by an implicit theory of proximal exchange are often conceptualized in broad terms encapsulating such a wide range of exchangeable resources that the idea of proximal exchange is not very informative. If we take the example of perceived organizational support, this concept includes employee judgments of how their performance is appraised, whether their pay is fair, whether the organization cares about their well-being, and promotional opportunities covering most if not all of the six separate resources as outlined by Foa and Foa. If the idea of proximity is to have value, the boundaries of the resources to be exchanged need to be defined more narrowly. Otherwise, it amounts to little more than stating that "a wide variety of things will be exchanged for a wide variety of things."

Fourth, many social exchange studies—such as those conducted in the fields of the psychological contract, POS, and LMX—conduct correlational questionnaire survey studies between inducements and contributions and assume that these are linked in an underlying social exchange. Whether the employee sees their behavior as performed in exchange for the inducement is not assessed in these studies. Hence, there are any number of possible explanations that may account for the association between, say, POS and organizational citizenship behavior, of which social exchange may be but one. To the extent that alternative explanations are accounting for the observed correlation, these associations will need to be discounted to arrive at a more conservative estimate of the "true" relationship accounted for by social exchange processes.

Finally, an exchange-based framework may be limited in the extent to which relationship behavior can be understood and one reason for this is that exchange frameworks are often applied without consideration of necessary conditions. In certain contexts, there are operating policies and practices where behaviors are performed in the knowledge that there will be no reciprocity. From an anthropological perspective, Fiske (1991) outlines a number of relational models that individuals use in relating to others. These include communal sharing, authority ranking, equality matching, and market pricing. According to Fiske (1991: 21), "people use these relational models to initiate social action, to understand what other people are up to, and to respond appropriately." The underlying exchange process differs between the four models. The equality matching and market pricing models parallel Gouldner's (1960) homeomorphic and heteromorphic reciprocity. Market pricing involves the exchange of unlike commodities in proportion to work done or contributions made, whereas under equality matching the exchange partners give each other the same thing.

In contrast, communal sharing (similar to what Clark and Mills 1979; Mills and Clark 1994 term "communal exchange") is a non-contingent form of exchange, where what an individual gets from another does not depend on what was previously given and does not create an obligation to return anything. Mills and Clark (1994) distinguish exchange and communal relationships based on the norms governing the relationship. The former is characterized by the giving and receiving based on the norm of reciprocity. The latter is characterized by the giving of benefits to meet the needs of the other party based on the norm of concern for the welfare of the other party. The authority-ranking model, in contrast, would emphasize an obedience norm in which the giver bestows benefits to the recipient based on their authority to command those benefits. In this respect, individuals engage in certain acts because they have a sense of moral obligation predicated on the authority of their superiors. There is some emerging empirical evidence that employees engage in acts that benefit the organization out of a concern for the welfare of the organization (Blader and Tyler 2000). Thus, it would seem that an exclusive reliance on exchange-based frameworks may not do justice to the range of norms that may govern how individuals act in their relationship with their employer and would require expanding the basis of behavior beyond straightforward reciprocity.

A number of these criticisms can be addressed by expanding how we view process approaches to the exchange, which can potentially provide a means for examining the psychology behind both parties to the exchange while capturing the context and content of that exchange.

1.4.2 Process of the exchange

While most real-life social exchanges are likely to reflect ongoing exchange processes—and this is clear from examples and illustrations of exchanges in the writings of Blau, Homans, and Gouldner—much of the latter theorizing and empirical research do not reflect processes but are more akin to what Mohr (1982) and more recently Langley (1999) refer to as variance theories. In support of this, Fromkin and Snyder (1980) argue that exchange theories almost exclusively focus on profit maximization in the immediate situation and thus ignore the potential consequence of a single exchange on subsequent exchange behavior. Mohr (1982) and Langley (1999) draw the distinction between variance theories that are characterized by relationships between independent and dependent variables that tend to reflect rather static models where causation is oversimplified, in contrast to process theories that attempt to capture sequences of events involving multiple parties, where the timing between events varies and data is diverse and can include, for example, such things as changing relationships, expectations, intentions, emotions, and sensemaking (Langley 1999). We believe that social exchange encounters are by their nature more closely allied and correctly modeled by a process theory approach.

While making sense of such processes is a demanding challenge involving conceptualizing events and patterns between them in an area where there is very little conceptual development and the data collected are likely to be difficult to analyze (Langley 1999), we believe the potential rewards through using such an approach would greatly enrich social exchange theory and the existing empirical base, which is dominated by survey research and experiments of dubious external validity.

Research of this nature would lend itself to the integration of content, process, and parties into a single model. Existing research on social exchange and related concepts (such as POS) tends to overemphasize the commodity being exchanged rather than the exchange *interaction* itself. Further, research on social exchange is very rarely "social" in the sense that it seeks to incorporate both parties' perspectives to the exchange, or considers how parties view the social situation and interpret exchange events.

Research would thus benefit from focusing on the intentions and expectations of the parties as well as the commodity being exchanged. Research on interdependence theory (Holmes 2002; Kelly et al. 2002; Rusbult and Lange 2003) may provide a useful approach for theorizing social exchange processes in employment relationships. Interdependence theory is fairly complex and aims to examine each party's needs, expectations, cognitions, and motives in relation to one another relevant to a particular situation. Interdependence theory advances the main dimensions of situations, where each situation determines the interdependence of the two parties and also identifies the interpersonal dispositions (e.g. avoidance/comfort with dependence) of persons A and B that are likely to influence decisions in each situation. Movement from one state to another is formulated through matrices and transition lists. Rusbult and Van Lange (2003) argue that such a theory provides the concepts and logic for analyzing, explaining, and predicting relationship interactions. The concepts proposed under interdependence theory could also be incorporated into process approaches indicated by Langley (1999).

While we are suggesting that there is potential merit in adopting a process theory approach to further our understanding of the employment relationship, at the same time it could be argued that the idea of exchange is often stretched too far, with research on social exchange processes too often assuming employees to be overly willing to and capable of strategizing and monitoring complex exchanges. What is possibly more plausible is that the ongoing exchange of contributions for inducements is under the control of more automated than conscious processes resulting in the formation of habituated work behavior. This argument is based on two interrelated ideas. First, how social exchanges may evolve into the development of habits. In long-term social exchange relationships, the exchange of contributions for inducements becomes so diffuse that it is no longer possible to make direct linkages between a discrete contribution and a discrete inducement. Hence, the causality implied in exchange relationships (i.e. inducement X → contribution Y → inducement X, and so on) becomes so distant in the mind of the employee—and interrelated with other ongoing exchanges between the two parties—that effectively the inducement– contribution linkage becomes decoupled. The employee adopts a more automated policy of assuming that as long as they carry out their range of contributions, inducements will remain forthcoming without having to monitor the specific linkages of the exchange. Second, while this is occurring, research on habits proposes that the frequent performance of a behavior leads to the formation of a habit, and that when a behavior is performed many times the intentions behind the behavior become largely irrelevant and the behavior is performed with little or no conscious thought (Rusbult and Van Lange 1996; Ajzen 2001). In other words, much of the behavior at present considered part of a social exchange between employee and employer can be interpreted at least in part as being habits and under the control of automatic processes.

Interpreting exchange in this way leads to a number of ways of reconsidering "exchange," by drawing on habit research. For example, an exploitative relationship where an employee continues to offer contributions to the organization even though the equity of the exchange is deteriorating can be construed as a habit disorder, renegotiation and violation of exchanges can be seen from the perspective of breaking habits, and exchanges that end over time can be paralleled with habit extinction.

1.4.3 Parties to the exchange

The predominant emphasis of some of the early work (Homans, March, and Simon) focused on the exchange as a dyadic one, although Homans (1958) recognized the influence of the group. March and Simon (1958), while retaining the dyadic focus, view the exchange as one between an individual employee and the organization relying on Levinson's (1965) thesis of anthropomorphization. The emphasis on the dyadic exchange dominates current employment relationship research. Most recent research on the organization's perspective to the exchange has treated the organization as a single entity, relying on anthropomorphic assumptions. However, if we look at the increasing trend into researching organizational commitment, the idea of treating the organization as a single entity is becoming increasingly problematic. Almost twenty years ago, Reichers (1985) argued that rather than considering the organization as a single monolithic entity, it is more useful to view an organization in terms of its various constituencies, each with its own goals, which may not necessarily overlap. Empirical research into different foci of commitment is relatively recent, yet there is compelling initial evidence that the distinctions are worth making (see Reichers 1985; Becker 1992; Becker et al. 1996; Chen et al. 2002; Stinglhamber and Vandenberghe 2003). At present, the four main distinctions between foci within the organization are based around organizational hierarchy, namely co-workers, supervisors, top management, and the organization. We would recommend that future research into social exchange adopt a more fine-grained analysis toward the treatment of the organization's perspective and recognize that employees collectively may influence the content and process of the exchange.

Organizations are complex exchange systems and, as such, a number of exchanges may be occurring simultaneously, which may have consequences for other exchanges. An exchange does not occur in isolation nor can an exchange be conceptualized as an isolated event. If we take an example of organizations where employees, as a collective group, have some form of representation in the exchange relationship, then we may see the following exchanges occurring: Between two groups (employees and managers being represented in the collective exchange process) that would be reflected in some form of negotiation over the terms of the exchange relationship; against this collective exchange, there are exchanges among employees, managers, and between employees and managers. Furthermore, the extent to which any single exchange relationship operates may be contingent upon the prior successful interchange of resources in another exchange. For example, an employee may help out a colleague (a direct exchange) if he or she has fulfilled his or her exchange with his or her supervisor. Thus, the potential employee–employee exchange is dependent upon the "state" of the employee–supervisor exchange. If the employee–employee exchange occurs, the employee who donates the help may or may not be the recipient of future benefits from his or her colleague. However, he or she may receive benefits from another party (i.e. the supervisor who was not party to the employee–employee exchange but who was an observer to the exchange). Therefore, reciprocal actions by one party may be dependent upon other exchange relationships and the conferring of benefits may come from an individual not party to the "direct" exchange. Although simplistic, this example illustrates two dimensions of exchanges overlooked in most research: Direct and indirect exchanges and interdependency amongst exchanges.

While it would pose difficult challenges for researchers to examine the entirety of exchanges in organizations, we see several possible avenues for empirical investigation. First, examining direct and indirect exchanges between employees and their supervisor and, in particular, how indirect exchanges contribute to the "ongoingness" of direct exchanges or act as a stimulus to the breakdown of direct exchange relationships. Second, the role of interdependency in networks of exchanges may be important for understanding the potential consequences of psychological contract breach, in terms of a breach triggering off a chain of further breaches to other members in the network. Third, exploring how collective exchanges influence or are influenced by dyadic exchanges. For example, does a collective exchange set the parameters within which individuals exchange, and how do individual exchanges impact on collective exchanges?

Summary
A number of theoretical and methodological limitations of social exchange theory were highlighted. We suggest that a means of addressing most of these limitations is to treat social exchange as an ongoing *process*. One possibility is to draw on the various available strategies for analyzing processes, as outlined by Langley (1999). Furthermore, in order to track exchanges with sufficient precision over time, considerable innovation is required in the type of methods used to study exchanges, and certainly beyond typical questionnaire surveys whether they be cross-sectional or longitudinal.

1.5 Conclusion

Social exchange has proved to be an incredibly enduring area of investigation and the basic idea of give-and-take in the employment relationship is intuitively appealing. Social exchange has also been used as an assumed mechanism for a wide range of related concepts, such as the psychological contract, organizational fairness and justice, perceived organizational support, and LMX. However, social exchange theory has often been applied uncritically, operationalized incompletely, and used implicitly—for example, in research on the psychological contract—rather than the components of social exchange theory being examined directly. There is a good understanding of what is exchanged in the employment relationship between employee and employer in terms of the wide range of possible inducements and contributions and how these various elements correlate with each other. However, there is less understanding as to the dynamics of social exchange, both in terms of how social exchange unfolds over time and how exchanges imbedded in larger exchange networks operate. In other words, theoretical approaches that seek to link together content, process, and parties to the exchange are required, involving further conceptualization and innovation in methodologies. We have suggested a number of possible avenues that require revisiting ideas contained in earlier works and drawing on advances in the study of relationships outside of work psychology.

Acknowledgments

We would like to thank Lynn Shore, Lois Tetrick, Amanuel Tekleab, and Linn Van Dyne for their constructive comments on an earlier version. Neil Conway is a Leverhulme Trust Research Fellow and would like to thank the Trust for their support.

References

Ajzen, I. (2001). "Nature and operation of attitudes". *Annual Review of Psychology*, 52: 27–58.
Ang, S., Van Dyne, L., and Begley, T. M. (2003). "The employment relationships of foreign workers versus local employees: A field study of organizational justice, job satisfaction, performance and OCB". *Journal of Organizational Behavior*, 24: 561–83.

Barnard, C. I. (1938). *The Functions of the Executive.* Cambridge, MA: Harvard.

Barth, F. (1966). *Models of Social Organization.* London: Royal Anthropological Institute.

Becker, T. E. (1992). "Foci and bases of commitment: Are they distinctions worth making?" *Academy of Management Journal,* 35: 232–44.

—— Billings, D. M., Eveleth, D. M., and Gilbert, N. L. (1996). "Foci and bases of employee commitment: Implications for job performance". *Academy of Management Journal,* 39: 464–82.

Berg, J. H., and Wiebe, F. A. (1993). "Resource exchange in the workplace: Exchange of economic and interpersonal resources", in U. G. Foa, J. Converse, Jr., K. Y. Toernblom, and E. B. Foa (eds.), *Resource Theory: Explorations and Applications* (San Diego: Academic Press), 97–122.

Blader, S. L., and Tyler, T. R. (2000). "Beyond reciprocity: The role of relationship orientation in explaining cooperative organizational behavior". Paper presented at the Annual Meeting of the Society for Industrial and Organizational Psychology, New Orleans.

Blau, P. (1964). *Exchange and Power in Social Life.* New York: Wiley.

Bolger, N., Zuckerman, A., and Kessler, R. C. (2000). "Invisible support and adjustment to stress". *Journal of Personality and Social Psychology,* 79(6): 953–61.

Chen, Z. X., Tsui, A. S., and Farh, J-L. (2002). "Loyalty to supervisor vs. organizational commitment: Relationships to employee performance in China". *Journal of Occupational and Organizational Psychology,* 75(3): 339–56.

Clark, M. S., and Mills, J (1979). "Interpersonal attraction in exchange and communal relationships". *Journal of Personality and Social Psychology,* 37: 12–24.

Conway, N., and Briner, R. (2000). "Employee reactions to transgressed psychological contracts: A daily diary study". Paper presented at the Society of Industrial and Organizational Psychology Conference, New Orleans.

—— and Briner, R. B. (2002). "A daily diary study of affective responses to psychological contract breach and exceeded promises". *Journal of Organizational Behavior,* 23: 287–302.

Coyle-Shapiro, J. A-M. (2002). "A psychological contract perspective on organizational citizenship behavior". *Journal of Organizational Behavior,* 23: 927–46.

—— and Kessler, I. (2002). "Reciprocity through the lens of the psychological contract: Employee and employer perspectives". *European Journal of Work and Organizational Psychology,* 11: 1–18.

—— and Neuman, J. (2004). "Individual dispositions and the psychological contract: The moderating effects of exchange and creditor ideologies". *Journal of Vocational Behavior,* 64: 150–164.

Eisenberger, R., Huntington, R., Hutchison, S., and Sowa, D. (1986). "Perceived organizational support". *Journal of Applied Psychology,* 71: 500–7.

—— Cotterell, N., and Marvel, J. (1987). "Reciprocation ideology". *Journal of Personality and Social Psychology,* 53: 743–50.

—— Armeli, S., Rexwinkel, B., Lynch, P. D., and Rhoades, L. (2001). "Reciprocation of perceived organizational support". *Journal of Applied Psychology,* 86: 42–51.

Emerson, R. M. (1972). "Exchange theory Part I: A psychological basis for social exchange", in J. Berger, J. Zelditch, and B. Anderson (eds.), *Sociological Theories in Progress,* Vol. 2 (Boston: Houghton Mifflin).

—— (1981). "Social exchange theory," in M. Rosenberg, and R. Turner, (eds.) *Social Psychology: Sociological Perspectives* (New York: Basic Books).

Foa, U. G., and Foa, E. B. (1975). *Resource Theory of Social Exchange.* Morristown, NJ: General Learning Press.

—— and —— (1980). "Resource theory: Interpersonal behavior as exchange," in K. J. Gergen, M. S. Greenberg, and R. H. Willis (eds.), *Social Exchange: Advances in Theory and Research* (New York: Plenum Press), 77–94.

Fiske, A. P. (1991). *Structures of Social Life.* New York: Free Press.

Fromkin, H. L., and Snyder, C. R. (1980). "The search for uniqueness and valuation of scarcity: Neglected dimensions of value in exchange theory," in K. J. Gergen, M. S. Greenberg, and R. H. Willis (eds.), *Social Exchange: Advances in Theory and Research* (New York: Plenum Press).

George, J. M. (1990). "Personality, affect and behavior in groups." *Journal of Applied Psychology,* 75: 107–16.

Gouldner, A. W. (1960). "The norm of reciprocity". *American Sociological Review,* 25: 161–78.

Greenberg, M. S (1980). "A theory of indebtedness," in K. J. Gergen, M. S. Greenberg, and R. H. Willis (eds.), *Social Exchange: Advances in Theory and Research* (New York: Plenum Press).

—— and Westcott, D. R. (1983). "Indebtedness as a mediator of reactions to aid," in J. D. Fisher, A. Nadler, and B. M. DePaulo (eds.), *New Directions in Helping* (New York: Academic Press), 85–112.

Holmes, J. G. (2002). "Interpersonal expectations as the building blocks of social cognition: an interdependence theory perspective". *Personal Relations,* 9: 1–26.

Homans, G. C. (1958). "Social behavior as exchange". *American Journal of Sociology,* 63: 597–606.

Kelley, H. H. (1979). *Personal Relationships.* Hillsdale, NJ: Erlbaum.

—— Holmes, J. G., Kerr, N. L., Reis, H. T., Rusbult, C. E., and Van Lange, P. A. M. (2002). *An Atlas of Interpersonal Situations.* New York: Cambridge University Press.

Langley, A. (1999). "Strategies for theorizing from process data". *Academy of Management Review,* 24(4): 691–710.

Levinson, H. (1965). "Reciprocation: The relationship between man and organization". *Administrative Science Quarterly,* 9: 370–90.

Malinowski, B. (1922). *Argonauts of the Western Pacific: An Account of Native Enterprise and Adventure in the Archipelagoes of Melanesian New Guinea.* London: Routledge (Republished, New York: Dutton, 1962).

March, J. G., and Simon, H. A. (1958). *Organizations.* New York.

Mauss, M. (1925). *The Gift.* Glencoe, IL: Free Press, 1954. (Republished, New York: Norton, 1967.)

McLean Parks, J., and smith, f. (1998). "Organizational contracting: A 'rational' exchange?" in J. J. Halpern and R. N. Stern (eds.), *Debating Rationality: Non Rational Aspects of Organizational Decision Making* (Ithaca, NY: Cornell University Press), 125–54.

Mills, J., and Clark, M. S. (1994). "Communal and exchange relationships: Controversies and research," in R. Erber and R. Gilmour (eds.), *Theoretical Frameworks for Personal Relationships* (Hillsdale, NJ: Lawrence Erlbaum Associates).

Mohr, L. B. (1982). *Explaining Organizational Behavior.* San Francisco: Jossey-Bass.

Reichers, A. E. (1985). "A review and reconceptualization of organizational commitment". *Academy of Management Review,* 10: 465–76.

Robinson, S. L., and Rousseau, D. M. (1994). "Violating the psychological contract: Not the exception but the norm". *Journal of Organizational Behavior,* 15: 245–59.

—— and O'Leary-Kelly, A. M. (1998). "Monkey see, monkey do: The influence of work groups on the antisocial behavior of employees". *Academy of Management Journal,* 41: 658–72.

Roethlisberger, F. J., and Dickson, W. J. (1939). *Management and the Worker.* Cambridge, MA: Harvard University Press.

Rousseau, D. M. (1995). *Psychological Contracts in Organizations: Understanding Written and Unwritten Agreements.* Thousand Oaks, CA: Sage.

Rusbult, C. E., and Van Lange, P. A. M. (1996). "Interdependence processes," in E. T. Higgins and A. W. Kruglanski (eds.), *Social Psychology: Handbook of Basic Principles.* New York: Guildford.

—— and —— (2003). "Interdependence, interaction and relationships". *Annual Review of Psychology,* 54: 351–75.

Sahlins, M. (1965). "On the sociology of primitive exchange," in M. Banton (ed.), *The Relevance of Models for Social Anthropology.* London: Tavistock.

—— (1972). *Stone Age Economics.* New York: Aldine de Gruyter.

Shore, L., and Coyle-Shapiro, J. A-M (2003). "New developments in the employee–organization relationship". *Journal of Organizational Behavior,* 24: 443–50.

—— Tetrick, L. E., and Barksdale, K. (1999). "Transactional and relational exchange relationships". Paper presented at the Society for Industrial and Organizational Psychology, Atlanta.

Stinglhamber, F., and Vandenberghe, C. (2003). "Organizations and supervisors as sources of support and targets of commitment: A longitudinal study". *Journal of Organizational Behavior,* 24(3): 251–70.

Tetrick, L. E., Shore, L. M., Tsui, A. S., Wand, D. X., Glenn, D., Chen, N., Liu, H., Wang, X., and Yan, H. (2004). "Development of a measure of generalized, balanced, and negative reciprocity in employment relationships". Paper to be presented at the Inaugural Conference of the International Association for Chinese Management Research, Beijing, June.

Tsui, A. S., Pearce, J. L., Porter, L. W., and Tripoli, A. M. (1997). "Alternative approaches to the employee–organization relationship: Does investment pay off?" *Academy of Management Journal,* 40: 1089–121.

Wayne, S. J., Shore, L. M., and Liden, R. C. (1997). "Perceived organizational support and leader–member exchange: A social exchange perspective". *Academy of Management Journal,* 40: 82–111.

2

Justice and Employment: Moral Retribution as a Contra-subjugation Tendency

ROBERT FOLGER

2.1 Introduction

"[I]n a...species given to strong status rivalry there is a natural propensity for adults to behave dominantly. This results in a dislike of being dominated oneself, and it makes for subordinate rebellion against superiors" (Boehm 2000: 84).

"The disposition in question is...one that makes us resentful of being *unduly* subordinated, however that happens to be defined individually—or culturally" (Boehm 1999: 170).

The employment relationship has aspects amenable to notions about contracts (e.g. the mutual obligations of contracting parties), and this chapter on organizational justice and the employment relation reflects a contract-based perspective. In particular, fairness in honoring contracts extends beyond terms formally stipulated, touching upon implicit and assumed understandings as well. Parties to a contract need not have identical interests, and concerns about fairness often arise with regard to those areas in which interests conflict. Certainly, no one believes that the interests of employers and employees always coincide isomorphically. The employment relationship thus constitutes a way of providing both employers and employees with opportunities for some mutual interest despite some conflict of interest. Presumably, each side's perceptions about matters of fairness in the relationship can influence the relationship itself—and what flows from it—in various ways.

Indeed, subsequent material in this chapter will summarize the results of empirical studies concerning fairness-related effects on aspects of organizational functioning. Prior to addressing selected topics in that vein, however, let me provide a brief overview or roadmap of the topics covered. An initial section sketches a big-picture perspective on the role of authority in the employment relationship, based on Simon's (1951) classic treatment. A second introductory section then relates Simon's views with fairness issues broadly conceived as moral precepts placing limits of legitimacy on how employees view the exercise of managerial authority. That section extends Simon's treatment of the employment relationship by pointing to a moral component seemingly missing from his analysis (or at least not explicitly addressed).

Simon's (1951) views represent a way to conceptualize the employment relationship as grounded in the economic viability of contractual terms on which the two central parties, employer (i.e. management) and employee, could agree in advance about the former's right to make subsequent demands on the latter, given mutually established expectations regarding compliance. In contrast, moral considerations such as fairness provide an additional yardstick beyond economic viability for judgments about legitimate limits to authority—those that proscribe certain instances of its exercise as abusive. The research findings concerning fairness-based reactions of employees thus bears witness to ways in which a relationship initiated by mutually agreed-upon terms of economic viability nonetheless may have to contend with social dynamics other than purely economic motivations.

My treatment of such dynamics also adopts a big-picture perspective by referring to two concepts discussed elsewhere (Folger 1998), bounded autonomy and the human covenant. Here, as in that prior discussion, I juxtapose them with Simon's (1951) analysis as a way to frame the relevance of the research findings—but this time additionally drawing from a sweeping assessment of human nature by a prominent anthropologist and primatologist Christopher Boehm (e.g. 1999, 2000), the gist of whose fundamental thesis I previewed in terms of the two opening quotations. After a summary of selected findings from the organizational justice literature, I return to themes that overlay the bounded autonomy and human covenant notions with ideas inspired by Boehm's work. In particular, I consider implications for a contemporary workplace climate now so widely noted as calling into question the psychological understandings of the employment relationship heretofore not so nearly destabilized as it appears at present.

2.2 Authority and the employment contract

Simon's (1951) article provides a way of thinking about the employment relationship by conceptualizing some of its central features in abstract terms and by deriving implications based entirely on standard economic theorizing. In particular, he focused on both *authority* and *contract* by relating them to one another: "The authority relationship that exists between an employer and an employee, a relationship created by the employment contract, will play a central role in our theory" (Simon 1951: 293). Simon used symbolic notation to express his ideas algebraically. Here, I follow his convention to "call our employer B (for 'boss'), and our employee W (for 'worker')" (p. 294) for the sake of ease in quoting some of his formulaic expressions. For example, he used x in referring to an element of the set of behaviors that W might need to perform on the job. Simon thereby described authority as a central feature of the employment relation in the simplest possible terms: "We will say that B exercises *authority* over W if W permits B to select x" (p. 294). In other words, an employee's boss tells the former what to do.

Of course, telling people what to do cannot count as an exercise of authority if they refuse. Authority does not consist of exercising brute force but instead encompasses a form of autonomy or discretion by both parties. On the one hand, bosses use their discretion regarding which x to "select" on a given occasion—that is, in deciding what directives to give employees. On the other hand, employees retain some auto-nomy in using their discretion about which x to "permit" (e.g. perhaps not following directives they consider illegal). Simon thus summarizes as follows: "In general, W will accept authority only if x_0, the X chosen by B, is restricted to some given subset (W's 'area of acceptance') of all the possible values" (p. 294).

Simon shed further light on this role of authority by distinguishing between employment contracts and sales contracts. In the first of those two contractual forms, an employee agrees to accept management authority and management agrees to pay the employee a stated wage. That contrasts with sales contracts (e.g. ordinary purchases) in which a "buyer...promises to pay a stated sum of money; but the seller [unlike management as employer]...promises in return a specified quantity of a completely specified commodity" (p. 294). In addition, "the seller is not interested in the way in which his commodity is used once it is sold" (p. 294), whereas clearly employees have a stake in what management might want them to do.

Simon noted that this distinction draws attention to some questions about the rationale underlying employment contracts and conditions favoring their adoption: "Why is W willing to sign a blank check, so to speak, by giving B authority over his behavior? If both parties are behaving rationally—in some sense—under what cir-cumstances will they enter into a sales contract and under what circumstances an employment contract?" (p. 295). In turn, he then offered the following conjectures as grounds for a formal model elaborated mathematically in further sections of his article (Simon 1951: 295):

1. The worker, W, accepts an employment contract with management (boss, B) "only if it does not matter to him 'very much' which x (within the agreed-upon area of acceptance) B will choose or if W is compensated in some way for the possibility that B will choose an x that is not desired by W (i.e., that B will ask W to perform an unpleasant task)."

2. "It will be advantageous to B to offer W added compensation for entering into an employment contract if B is unable to predict with certainty, at the time the contract is made, which x will be the optimum one, from his standpoint. That is, B will pay for the privilege of postponing, until some time after the contract is made, the selection of x."

These conjectures thus address Simon's questions about the employment contract by suggesting: (a) when and why employees agree to accept an employment offer; and (b) when and why an employer would make such an offer.

Specifically, Simon modeled his conjectures by adopting the standard rationality assumption that each side wants to maximize its own interest-satisfaction, so they enter into those agreements perceived as mutually advantageous (an economic validity constraint). Sales and employment agreements, however, differ fundamen-tally in terms of what the parties can know about the satisfaction of those interests at the time when they reach an agreement. According to Simon's modeling of conditions that yield sales contracts for labor, "the rational procedure for B and W

would be first to determine a preferred x" (i.e. settle on details about the specified commodity), "and then to proceed to bargain about w" (p. 297) in relation to their respective satisfaction functions for interest maximization. Thus, a sales-contracted laborer "agrees to perform a specific, determinate act... in return for an agreed-upon price" (pp. 297–8)—such as when you agree to pay someone a specified amount for installing a particular type of security system in your home before the end of the month.

In contrast, an employment contract involves further uncertainties about interest-satisfaction, such as when an employer does not know in advance exactly which performances of particular work might prove most advantageous (e.g. employees sometimes have assignments shifted), and employees do not know in advance exactly which functions they might perform and whether the offered compensation will satisfactorily offset disadvantages incurred by performing such functions (e.g. vis-à-vis opportunity costs). Actually, Simon considered situations involving such uncertainties in terms of their prospects for sales contracts based on *estimates* of how to maximize satisfaction. His mathematical proofs showed a rational preference for employment contracts over sales contracts as a function of either of two parameters: (a) the more uncertainty for management associated with payoffs from different types of labor functions performed (i.e. not knowing exactly what workers might need to do); and (b) the greater employees' indifference across various labor functions (i.e. the wider and more all-inclusive the area of acceptance, or tolerance for unpleasantness—given, of course, the level of offsetting compensation upon which the parties had agreed in advance).

Under an employment contract, which inevitably introduces more error than sales contracts from estimates associated with uncertainty, management and a prospective employee "could agree upon a specified wage,... to be paid by the former to the latter, and upon a specified procedure that will be followed, *at a later time when the actual values for all x... [i.e., respective satisfaction to each party] are known*, for selecting a specific x [assignment, directive, etc.]" (p. 298). Although Simon acknowledged that various methods might be used to determine job directives when the time for such decisions arose, he went on to note the simplicity of having the employee (W) "permit B to select x from some specified set, X (i.e. for W to accept B's authority)"—and that, of course, "this is precisely what we have defined as an employment contract" (p. 298).

Note here some clarifications about Simon's language, which may seem dated. Obviously, the typical case today can involve a boss who selects which employee to hire but does not draw from personal investments to pay wages in the manner of an owner-entrepreneur (i.e. Simon's "B" is the manager acting as a representative of the organization). Reference to "bosses" and "workers" also might not sound very contemporary. Here, I have retained Simon's language not only for ease of quoting his algebraic expressions but also as the foreshadowing for an element of potential conflict in this relationship—"bossiness." Indeed, as both my review of fairness-related research findings and my subsequent discussion of bounded autonomy and human covenant ideas conjoined with Boehm's (1999, 2000) work will try to show, such connotations point to the crux of potentially problematic implications introduced by the very open-ended uncertainties associated with future management directives that Simon made the defining element of the employment relationship—namely, as involving an inherently *incomplete* agreement, with eventual resolution of uncertainties initiated *unilaterally* by one party (i.e. management) rather than the other. Indeed, the same element probably underlies the acknowledgment—as reflected in now-common use of phrases like *psychological contract*—that some degree of subjectivity remains nascent as background to the objective terms of explicit contracts.

It might seem doubtful that individuals today see their acceptance of the organization's paycheck as an exchange whereby they must willingly accede to whatever directives management might care to issue. That is, at first blush Simon's blank-check metaphor has an anachronistic tone seemingly at odds with contemporary practice, or at least it might seem not as applicable today as when Simon wrote. For example, many positions in today's workplace are often posted according to a set of duties that provide applicants with descriptions of at least a reasonable range of assignments to which they might be asked to respond.

Three kinds of replies, however, counter that suggestion. First, it does not undercut Simon's key insight about the fundamental qualitative difference between spot-market purchases of highly specific commodities or discretely specified labor (i.e. sales contracts) and the establishment of an ongoing, dynamic (and hence, inherently more open-ended, uncertain, and ambiguous) relationship when agreeing on an employment contract. Second, although the two types of contracts can certainly be reconceptualized as lying along a continuum of specificity rather than necessarily occupying two sharply contrasting loci in that conceptual space, the employment contract does clearly introduce a formal hierarchy of authority absent from sales contracts. Galbraith (1973), in fact, drew from Simon in pointing to hierarchy as a mechanism for dealing with unexpected exceptions and unforeseeable complexities otherwise hard to accommodate by means of the mutual-adjustment process more characteristic of equal-status bargainers in a negotiation (e.g. home buyers and sellers).

Third, certain features of employment-contract jobs—as much today as ever, if not more—should make us question that a detailed job posting would eliminate or vitiate the relevance of the blank-check metaphor. For example, accepting a job with even the most detailed descriptions of possible assignments posted in advance leaves open occasions for management whim, as movies like *9 to 5* remind us in their portrayal of personal tasks a boss might ask a secretary to perform (e.g. selecting a present for the boss's spouse). Less anecdotally, the evidence of constant reorganization and restructuring in response to contemporary market competitiveness highlights the extent to which no job remains fixed anymore.

On a related note, some readers might wonder how to locate Simon's sales-versus-employment distinction in relation to current terminology illustrating the reciprocal obligations of the employment relationship—such as references to transactional versus relational, social versus economic exchange, and so on (e.g. Blau 1964; Foa and

Foa 1980; Rousseau 1995; Tsui et al. 1997). Simon (1951) achieved elegant simplicity by framing his sales-versus-employment distinction at the highly abstract level of equations that no doubt helped yield its publication within an *Econometrica* article, but this abstractness might make readers feel in need of additional details to clarify the exact nature of the difference. That feeling should subside, however, once recognition of Simon's fundamental point hits home fully: The employment contract formally establishes an asymmetrical role relationship of authority and subordination by which both sides agree in advance that only one (i.e. management) is ultimately "in charge."

Moreover, the authoritative position granted management cross-cuts distinctions such as social–economic or transactional–transformational, etc., in ways perhaps ill-construed if too much emphasis centers on granting authority in return for economic compensations such as the offered wage (e.g. obviously some idea about safe working conditions and the like also constitutes part of the total package). At the risk of misconstruing someone not alive for a rejoinder, I want to suggest the adaptability of Simon's analysis as an alternative to dichotomies such as economic versus social exchange or transactional versus transformational leadership when taken as either–or categorizations. I argue that: (a) with respect to such terms as implying dichotomous classifications, Simon's conception of the employment relationship is mute or neutral— that is, even some mix or blend of them would remain amenable to his analysis (the fact of an authoritative position in a ranked hierarchy does not change, although its "flavor" might); and (b) because economic and other forms of compensation in return for labor represent a *constant* across the sales–employment divide whether as a categorical distinction or as end-points on a continuum, that economic-transaction component cannot signal a decisive feature for *distinguishing* between the two.

Differences such as transformation versus transactional and economic versus social exchange do, however, point to a missing ingredient in Simon's analysis—one that I refer to as a moral component in loose terms initially and will then further elaborate in various ways throughout, beginning with the following section on fairness research. Nonetheless, I assert that we should think in terms of layered, embedded, and simultaneous views about norms of conduct within the employment relationship rather than by referring to contemporary dichotomies in an either–or fashion. Consider a homely example that applies even to the purest forms of economic transactions like sales contracts or spot-market purchases, such as when buying toothpaste at the drugstore. If the clerk selling you some toothpaste were to sneeze and you were to utter something like "Bless you," this sequence of events would demonstrate your having layered norms about politeness rituals on top of the more narrowly bounded contours that ordinarily circumscribe the basis for this particular type of encounter in the first place (namely exchanges between buyers and sellers). Thus, you would also have acknowledged norms equally applicable within an employment relationship (surely there is no reason to forego showing your boss the same courtesy), which thereby illustrates how norms of social conduct, moral or otherwise, can apply rather universally in ways that transcend conceptually distinguishable categories regarding the specific basis for an interaction.

More generally, people show adherence to certain types of socio-moral norms in ways illustrating a generic applicability that can cut across particular contexts—such as the generic concept of fairness, rather than any given conception of it (e.g. as equity, equality, or need, and so forth). A moral precept proscribing wrongful harm, for example, can apply at least abstractly across a variety of social contexts that otherwise differ greatly in their specific characteristics. The clerk who seems to show undue regard for others' health by sneezing directly in peoples' faces (not covering his or her mouth when coughing, etc.) can become targeted for disapproval—not only from customers despite any lack of prior thoughts about sneeze-regulation as even a tacit consideration governing this particular type of exchange, but also from mere observers as otherwise disinterested third parties. Such reasoning implies that some types of fairness concerns might apply despite the exact character of a given exchange or interaction. Bringing fairness concerns to bear on the employment relationship as an issue otherwise underplayed by Simon's analysis thus provides a context for the following section.

2.3 Fairness, authority, and the employment relation

In simple terms, then, Simon's (1951) analysis described a central feature of the employment relationship with language worth repeating because of its implications for fairness: The employee "sign(s) a blank check, so to speak, by giving (to management)...authority over his behavior" (p. 295). Employees ordinarily know a number of things in advance, when they first agree to work for a given employer, about the beneficial consequences thereby made available (e.g. annual salary, length of paid vacations). On Simon's analysis, however, the very nature of that relationship—the reason why a firm would hire labor by means of an employment contract rather than a labor contract—establishes a fundamental asymmetry in it. Employees not only remain in the dark about the full scope of their possible duties (because some will be determined on an as-needed basis), but also lock themselves into predetermined levels of beneficial consequences (e.g. a first-year's annual salary set upon hiring) without knowing nearly as much about possible differences in aversiveness associated with tasks across the range of those that might be assigned.

Moreover, the employee has little or no say over assignments because that condition—granting authority to management—constitutes precisely the agreement made in advance when entering into an employment-contract arrangement. The only proviso, in Simon's words, consists of W's assumption about the nature of the original agreement: To repeat, that "W will accept authority only if x_0, the x chosen by B, is restricted to some given subset (W's 'area of acceptant') of all the possible values" (Simon 1951: 294). This proviso thereby relates to implicit psychological contracts in that employees presumably have some ideas about the range of forthcoming tasks at the time of hiring. Simply put, exceeding that range can initiate speculations about perceived unfairness—and the open-ended uncertainties of that range suggest room for generic and abstract notions of fairness to play a part alongside more delimited conceptions pertaining only to considerations deemed normative or rational in economic terms. Later sections will review the organizational justice literature on this topic. First, however, a theoretical review follows as grounds for making some conceptual distinctions.

2.3.1 Forms of justice

The organizational justice literature often traces its roots to work on equity theory by Adams (1965). Subsequent treatments also classify that theory under the heading of *distributive justice*, which refers to fairness of outcomes (e.g. pay). Adams (1965), for example, described perceptions of inequity algebraically along the following lines: $O_A/I_A \neq O_B/I_B$ (where O stands for outcomes, I for inputs, A for the perceiver's existing rate of return, and B for some referent rate considered for purposes of comparison).

Thibaut and Walker (1975) initiated work on *procedural justice* that subsequently became influential in the organizational justice literature as well. They addressed formal decision-making in dispute-resolution hearings structured with different roles for the disputants and the third-party decision-maker (whose authority allowed imposing an outcome distribution). Among other results, a general finding showed that the perceived fairness of those procedures influence the perceived fairness of the outcome distribution (for a review, see Lind and Tyler 1988). In turn, procedural fairness stemmed from the extent to which disputants perceived that they had opportunities for making their views known during the hearing—a process ingredient that became known as *voice* (e.g. Folger 1977). Leventhal (1980) and Leventhal et al. (1980) subsequently argued that procedures seem most fair when they: (a) take into account the opinions of the various affected parties (i.e. voice for all stakeholders); (b) are applied consistently across people and over time; (c) are free from bias such as vested interest; (d) rely on accurate information; (e) allow for corrective measures (e.g. appeal mechanisms) for subsequent adjustments deemed necessary; and (f) reflect ethical standards of propriety.

Bies (1987) and Bies and Moag (1986) introduced the term *interactional justice* as referring to yet another set of fairness considerations (most recently elaborated in Bies 2001), and the distinctiveness of distributive, procedural, and interactional justice has since been verified empirically (e.g. Cohen-Charash and Spector 2001). The core of this concept essentially relates to considerations of human dignity and respect for persons. In part, such respect manifests itself in the manner, style, and demeanor (e.g. politeness) of communications—for example, when authorities explain the reasons behind the actions they take. Issues involving further aspects of interactional justice include those such as the following: Derogatory judgments, deception, invasion of privacy, and disrespect—in turn exemplified by inconsiderate actions, abusive words or actions, and various forms of coercive treatment (for an elaboration, see Bies 2001).

The work on interactional justice in particular suggests the variety of ways in which employees might come to perceive that bosses have exceeded legitimate authority. Essentially, the interactional justice concept implies that the employee's area of acceptance not only includes a boss's decisions about task assignments and other kinds of directives (potentially influencing perceptions of distributive justice, procedural justice, or both) but also a boss's interpersonal conduct toward subordinates—in short and even more generally, all treatment of employees, whether by individual representatives of management regarding their own subordinate(s) or by virtue of company policy, collective directives (e.g. from "headquarters"), and the like, applying to subgroups or to everyone a firm employs. Interactional justice—sometimes described by an "interpersonal" subcomponent pertaining to more general treatment with dignity and respect as well as by an "informational" subcomponent pertaining to communication qualities such as adequate and honest explanations (see e.g. Colquitt and Greenberg 2001)—clearly shares conceptual overlap with the showing-consideration component of leadership, not to mention similar characteristics called "transformational" or seen as comprising "social" rather than merely economic exchange. Such overlap should hardly seem surprising if fairness norms reflect even more transcendent ideas about morality and human conduct as widely shared views guiding how we treat other people in the course of our everyday lives.

Another conceptual similarity exists between interactional justice and perceived organizational support (POS) (Eisenberger et al. 1986). Many of the items loading highest on POS as a factor have at least a superficial similarity to those used in measuring interactional justice (e.g. Moorman 1991). Typically, interactional justice items address supervisory conduct by someone to whom subordinates report directly, whereas POS addresses considerate support from the organization as a whole. An even closer parallel, however, exists now that researchers have also measured perceived supervisory support (PSS) as a separate construct (e.g. Kottke and Sharafinski 1988).

Moreover, Simon's (1951) analysis provides grounds for extending consideration about interactional justice beyond mere support per se. Supportive consideration enables employees to work effectively. The employment relation refers to roles contracted for the purpose of having work done but interactions in the workplace also constitute interpersonal relations among people as human beings. Norms for interpersonal conduct, therefore, can acquire moral content imported to the workplace from the larger context of social relations in general. When hired, employees presumably assume that ceding authority to management for making task assignments and workplace directives, etc., will not entail management acting in ways contrary to such norms. In other words, employees have an area of acceptance circumscribed not only by an implicitly agreed-upon sense about the range of potential work assignments but also by moral norms (e.g. fair treatment) pertaining to human conduct in general. I return to this theme after reviewing more specific categories of justice studies.

2.4 Justice in the workplace

Two recent meta-analyses (Cohen-Charash and Spector 2001; Colquitt et al. 2001) as well as various literature reviews (e.g. Folger and Cropanzano 1998; Konovsky 2000) provide the basis for the following summary. This summary does not aim at comprehensiveness, so readers should consult the sources cited for further material.

2.4.1 Pay and benefits

A large number of studies in the early equity literature concerned reactions to pay based on distributive justice (see Adams and Friedman 1976), whereas the more recent literature has included the role of procedural and interactional justice. Because confirmation of the latter's distinctiveness has gained widespread acceptance only relatively recently, however, many effects noted in relation to procedural justice have come from studies whose scales for that measure probably conflated it with at least some elements of interactional justice.

Obviously, pay itself can also act as an antecedent to justice perceptions, so it should come as no surprise that the meta-analysis by Cohen-Charash and Spector (2001) yielded a weighted mean r of 0.32 for the correlation of distributive justice with amount of pay raise. The same antecedent also showed a non-significantly different r of 0.20 for procedural justice, reflecting that justice perceptions themselves tend to correlate with one another and hence with both their antecedent and consequences. On the other hand, the same meta-analysis failed to find significant effects on either distributive or procedural justice from the level of salary. Taken together, these results suggest changes in salary at the time of annual raises can alter the fairness perceptions established at the time of hiring.

Changes from the nature of the original contract can also occur when companies institute pay practices that differ from traditional salary arrangements. Some suggestive evidence bearing on that point comes from Lee et al. (1999), who found in a longitudinal study that employee fairness perceptions about the introduction of a skill-based pay plan varied as a function of associated communications. Other studies indicate the importance of perceived fairness in conjunction with the use of group-level pay plans such as gainsharing (e.g. Cooper et al. 1992; Welbourne et al. 1995; Dulebohn and Martocchio 1998).

Perhaps the studies most directly related to the preceding analysis based on Simon's (1951) conception of the employment contract, which suggests that its open-ended or "blank check" nature will cause scrutiny of changes according to fairness criteria, have involved settings in which B finds that circumstances call for altering w in ways that neither party to the relationship might have anticipated at its outset. Schaubroeck et al. (1994), for example, found that fairness perceptions based on management explanations influence turnover (i.e. perceived fairness kept it in check) when unexpected economic conditions led to a pay freeze. Even more dramatic results of that nature come from a study that tracked indications of employee-theft rates in two plants subject to temporary wages as well as in a matched plant where wages remained constant for periods of time that began prior to the salary cuts and extended beyond it (Greenberg 1990). Here, the interactional justice of respectful, informative communications mitigated amounts of company property stolen during the pay-cut period.

Other employee reactions to pay changes after the initial salary level at hiring can have a potentially detrimental impact on work organizations in ways less directly ascertainable than those just noted with respect to turnover and theft. Indeed, every time a performance review leads to salary adjustments, such changes to w in effect mark the equivalent of a renegotiated contract—except that the typical employee already stands in a fixed relationship with a given *B* by then, and the latter would normally not view the scope of his or her authority as needing any alteration at that point. Employees not inclined to seek other jobs (or unable to do so, at least with sufficient convenience) might, therefore, feel at least occasionally trapped in an employment relationship that no longer always corresponds to the one they perceived as agreed-upon at the outset of the relationship. Refusing specifically assigned *x*s (job duties identified on an as-needed basis) rarely, if ever, constitutes a live option—for at least two reasons. First, allowing *B* the prerogative to make such assignments was part of the original agreement itself; and second, refusing to perform assigned work can easily lead to consequences more negative than the employee wants to endure (e.g. dismissal).

Skarlicki and Folger (1997) argued that under such circumstances employees often resort to various forms of subtle and largely covert actions as means by which to retaliate for perceived unfairness in management's exercise of its authority. Organ (1990) had already noted how workplace effectiveness is enhanced when employees engage in organizational citizenship behaviors (OCBs) that go above and beyond the call of duty based on explicit assignments, and the association of fairness perception with OCBs is well-established (e.g., see the review by Konovsky 2000). Skarlicki and Folger (1997) called its dark-side complement organizational retaliatory behavior (ORB). They showed that in conjunction with performance reviews determining pay raises, employees manifested a range of anti-organization and anti-supervisor actions as a function of perceived unfair treatment regarding distributive, procedural, and interactional combinations (with the last producing the single largest independent affect).

2.4.2 Reaction to authority itself

The "blank check" role of authority in work organizations, as highlighted by Simon's (1951) analysis of the employment relationship, implies that employees respond based on conceptions of presumed acceptability regarding management prerogatives. As suggested in Section 2.4.1, changes to pay arrangements can thus reflect varying degrees of acceptability, with concomitant effects on other employee reactions. Procedures, policies, and everyday management conduct have impact beyond simply assigned duties for wages, however, and the concept of procedural justice in particular—along with the respect-and-dignity core of interactional justice—has always spoken directly to the perceived legitimacy of authority.

Indeed, a central thrust in pushing fairness conceptions beyond equity and distributive justice has parallel Simon's (1951) analysis in highlighting how people react to the institutionally embedded nature of relations with authorities as encompassing concerns broader than the *quid pro quo* of direct exchange in its simplest form. A survey of citizen reactions to encounters with police (Tyler and Folger 1980) helps illustrate this point. Tyler and Folger classified these encounters as initiated either by the citizens (e.g. contacting police after being robbed) or by the police (e.g. stopping motorists) and as leading to results deemed either favorable (e.g. recovery of goods stolen, no fine for traffic violation) or unfavorable (e.g. goods not recovered, fine issued). Independently of such factors, the results showed citizens' views of police as influenced positively to the extent that these respondents felt they had been treated with dignity and respect.

This study predated the work by Bies (1987) and Bies and Moag (1986) on interactional justice, but although framed in procedural justice terms at the time, the interpretation of its effects indicates how much of the organizational justice literature has applied either one or the other of those constructs in ways that diverge not only from simple exchange notions but also from the original (Thibault and Walker 1975) basis for distinguishing between distributive and procedural justice. As noted by Lind and Tyler (1988), the original distinction proposed an instrumental, or means–ends, connection. As the means for conducting deliberations that determine outcome distributions, procedures should seem fair to the extent that they embody the types of arrangements most conducive to rendering fair outcome distributions (e.g. the use of accurate measurement, consistently applied). Lind and Tyler (1988) identified a second, alternative conception of procedures, however, as associated with an alternative—non-instrumental or expressive—function whereby social conditions accord with fundamental values. Such values, also reflected in the interactional justice themes of dignity and respect, coincide with norms of conduct that employees believe apply to all human relationships (not only in the workplace), but the occasion for their potential applicability looms much larger in the extended and institutionalized context of the employment contract as opposed to simple exchange per se (*qua* sales contract). Essentially, such reasoning formed the basis for the continuing emphasis by Tyler on the role of procedural justice in shaping such authority-related matters as endorsement of leaders and compliance with the law (e.g. Tyler 1994).

2.5 Morality beyond fairness

I argue that adherence to moral mandates about social conduct in general, even more than those about fairness in particular, points to an incompleteness in Simon's (1951) analysis. Essentially, this incompleteness stems from underplaying the role of two types of moral norms that imply the possibility of dueling priorities—one specific to the contracted employment relationship, and the other related to human sociality in more general terms. Simon's analysis can be read as at least implicitly incorporating the fairness of keeping promises as agreed-upon commitments: If you (as employee) promise to do what I (as employer) might require, I promise in return to give you certain kinds of benefits (wages, etc.) along lines stipulated in advance. Here, the fairness of reciprocity also reinforces the fairness of promise keeping.

A second type of moral norm, however, has roots distinct from promise-keeping and reciprocity: "First, do no harm," as expressed historically in codes of conduct for physicians. The relevance of moral norms for physicians bears directly on the hierarchical ranking of management and employees in work organizations. Similarities and analogies between the two abound. Both involve an authority-ranked relationship based on voluntary consent rendered in advance of specific interactions. To gain care-giving benefits from a physician, for example, requires following the directives of medical regimens (e.g. taking certain dosages of prescribed drugs) issued by that authority only after he or she has determined what seems necessary for you to do. The contractual basis for compensation, of course, reverses the $B-W$ structure—you pay the authority! Nonetheless, the logic of reciprocity-in-exchange remains parallel. The incentive for agreeing to abide by instructions consists of anticipated benefits, but as enhanced health (in return for compliance with regimen directives) rather than as financial remuneration.

Complaints about physician arrogance and incivility, however, show that patients as well as third-party observers also have fairness-based expectations about their rights as grounded more fundamentally in valuing human dignity than in the reciprocity of exchange. Similarly, Kantian ethical philosophy distinguishes between the *categorical* (non-contingent) imperative of proscribed indignity and so-called *hypothetical* norms with an if–then, contingent structure whereby "then" deliverances gain entailment only by first having "if" conditions met. In short, both the doctor's office and the workplace represent situations in which two different moral groundings for fair treatment can vie for priority. On the one hand, such norms as promise-keeping, reciprocity-in-exchange, and the deference to which legitimately granted authority has an entitlement ("rank hath its privileges") call for tolerant compliance from those occupying relatively more subordinate positions in formally ranked hierarchies entered voluntarily (e.g. military command-and-control structures). On the other hand, moral obligations of respect for human dignity draw lines between civility and incivility (albeit sometimes "fuzzy") with some "do not cross" proscriptions at least implicitly independent of rank-ordered status.

This characterization sheds new light on differentiations among distributive, procedural, and interactional justice. In line with Simon's (1951) analysis, the rationale underlying the employment relationship has the distributive justice of equitably reciprocated exchanges as its core, although the structural aspects of procedures directly instrumental to determining resource distribution clearly stem from that same rationale. The non-instrumental or so-called relational aspects of procedural treatment, however, coincide with the sense of interactional justice as comprised of categorically imperative prohibitions against degrading, demeaning, abusively uncivil misconduct toward others—no matter their rank.

2.5.1 The human covenant and bounded autonomy

Elsewhere (Folger 1998) I introduced two concepts—*bounded autonomy* and the *human covenant*—as candidate ideas for ways to think about addressing the moral lacunae in Simon's (1951) analysis. Much in the spirit of his work on *bounded rationality* (e.g. Simon 1957), I described bounded autonomy as a notion about limits. Bounded rationality refers to the limits on human mental functioning that nature imposes; put simply, none of us is omniscient. Similarly, none of us is omnipotent. The latter truism not only captures one way of thinking about bounded autonomy—namely, in terms of naturally imposed limits on the ability to bring about whatever we want (e.g. humans cannot fly merely by flapping their arms)—but also indicates that bounded rationality is a subset of bounded autonomy.

Unlike bounded rationality as a product of limitations to human mental life that nature imposes, however, the full extent of our bounded autonomy also stems from a social and socially constructed source—that is, from limits we impose on one another. Moreover, as my earlier drugstore-clerk example suggested, the ways in which we seek to constrain one another's behavior extend beyond the bounds imposed merely by the requirements of economic viability (the core of Simon's analysis) or of reciprocity in exchange (chiefly distributive justice or the purely instrumental function of procedural justice). What I call the human covenant refers to socially shared understandings about the moral considerations seen as applicable for governing interpersonal interactions and social conduct in general, which thereby establish boundaries of acceptable behavior among human beings. In particular, general moral proscriptions (e.g. do not murder) serve to mark wrongful conduct as out-of-bounds.

Fairness norms constitute a significant part of the human covenant and hence place restrictions on economic agents in addition to the requirements for economic viability in Simon's analysis. Again, even the sales contract as a purely economic exchange provides examples to illustrate this point. The economic viability of price adjustments according to supply-and-demand dynamics implies something like "whatever the market will bear" as the sole constraining factor, for example, but "it's unfair" reactions to snow-shovel prices hiked upwards immediately after a blizzard (cf. Kahneman et al. 1986) indicate that the public governs its own purchasing behavior in ways not bounded exclusively either by the laws of economics or the legislative statutes of a given jurisdiction.

2.5.2 An evolutionary aside: Human ambivalence about authority

Customs vary worldwide, as does the content of locally observed moral mandates. Anthropologist/primatologist Christopher Boehm, however, brings substantial evidence to bear on a case he makes for a thesis about one particular evolutionary path backwards both toward "a likely candidate for the first behaviour to be labeled as morally deviant... bullying behaviour" (Boehm 2000: 79) and toward its origins in a proclivity for status rivalries coupled nonetheless with an aversion for conflict: "Morality is the human invention that addresses such problems, and it is based very heavily upon ancestral dispositions. These were the raw materials, out of which moral communities were forged." (Boehm, 2000: 97). I tried to capture some of Boehm's notions about human ambivalence regarding domination with the quotations that opened this chapter. Here I say more about bullying or bossiness (the abuse of power).

People attend to "*behavior* [that] *threatens the autonomy of others and thereby becomes deviant*" (Boehm 1999: 67, emphasis in original). Hence, "A particularly disvalued form of deviancy arises when... [someone in a position of authority] belittles, bullies, or otherwise tries to control another" (p. 67; cf. Boehm 1993). Because subordinates want "a kind of mutual respect that leaves individual autonomy intact" (Boehm 1999: 68), "a leader is likely to be watched quite vigilantly by... [those] whose personal autonomies will be at stake if he tries to become bossy or otherwise aggrandize his prerogatives" (p. 69). Moreover, "Preferred qualities in leaders often are expressed negatively: an *absence* of arrogance, overbearingness, boastfulness, and personal aloofness" (p. 69, emphasis in original), which behooves leaders in general to "avoid any sign of assertive self-aggrandizement" (p. 72). Those "otherwise capable individuals [who] are irascible, arrogant, stingy, or meanspirited, and do not manage to control these tendencies" often encounter difficulties "gaining or maintaining the leadership role" (p. 72). Boehm (2000) also makes the case that subordinates judge such conduct against a "standard proscription-list of aggressive, self-interested behaviours... that cause conflict within the group" (p. 87). Such acts of "moral malfeasance" (p. 87), which are "likely to cause conflict within the group, and degrade the overall quality of social life—for everyone" (p. 86), come from "individuals who are abusing power or who are acting in some other predatory or otherwise antisocial capacity" (p. 87).

In compiling this description, however, I have taken a considerable liberty: Although I think the tone should hardly strike anyone as incongruent with employee attitudes likely to surface with regularity in today's workplace, all of the quotations in the preceding paragraph come from Boehm's characterizations of what he called the *egalitarian ethos* found among extant foraging nomads and similarly ascribed to hunter-gatherers during ancestral times. Boehm hypothesizes that small bands evolved egalitarian behavior (e.g. applying negative social sanctions as leveling mechanisms in a counter-dominant or anti-despot fashion) about 100,000 years ago, but that strand of our evolutionary history built on top of proclivities for dominance and submission inherited from our primate cousins—suppressed by egalitarianism but still nascent. This egalitarianism broke down upon the advent of agriculture, larger societies, the rise of governments, and other social institutions (e.g. religious establishments) that created hierarchies as well as formal rules, codified regulations, and power/status rankings or rigid social stratification. All these tended to displace the leveling ethos otherwise still found in hunter-gatherer groups today.

If Boehm is correct, then "moral systems are driven very heavily by considerations of power" (2000: 80)—and here, notably, Boehm cites Weber (1947). Independent of the evidential strength for Boehm's arguments, surely it cannot seem far-fetched to suspect that systems with a unilateral flow of authority will tend to invite resentment and activities generated for the sake of exercising a countervailing thrust. Ancient Romans framed the issue as a rhetorical question by asking *Quis custodiet ipsos custodies*, or who will keep the keepers themselves. The theme of power's potential as a corrupting influence—that is, when people abuse the prerogatives granted to them—gains credence both from empirical reviews (e.g. Keltner et al. 2003) and from "the higher the monkey climbs, the more you see his behind" as an aphorism attributed to Saint Bonaventura (de Waal 1996). In light of the possibility that the management prerogatives of authority might invite abuse and correspondingly encourage resentment of unfairness such as that identified in the organizational justice literature, therefore, let us consider the picture developing in today's workplace.

2.6 Implications of current workplace trends

Other authors in this volume provide ample evidence for the so-called "new psychological contract" as a modern development. For the sake of brevity, therefore, I rely here on Stone (2001) as a comprehensive source to which readers can refer for more extensive description as well as voluminous documentation and reference sources. In brief, elements of the "old" contract include "long-term promise of long-term job security, orderly promotional opportunities, longevity-linked pay and benefits, and long-term pension vesting," all of which "encouraged worker attachment to the firm" (p. 524), whereas the new model includes such elements as "general skills training, upskilling of jobs, networking opportunities, [and] contact with firm constituents for employees at all levels of the firm" (pp. 524–5) as substitutes consistent with making employees more employable elsewhere rather than assuming the employment relationship as one of sustained attachment. I single out only what Stone refers to as human capital and social capital implications of these trends.

On general skills training and the upskilling of jobs as related to the former, Stone puts it this way:

It becomes clear from an examination of the writings of prominent management theorists that corporations are searching to find a way to make the shift away from long-term career employment not only acceptable, but desirable. By promising employees the opportunity to develop their human capital, the new psychological contract tries to do this. Employers promise employability and training so that, in return, employees will see themselves as entrepreneurs marketing their own human capital in a market place (p. 570).

Similarly with respect to the latter, "Not only can employees raise their human capital, they can raise their social capital by meeting and interacting with others in different departments within the firm, with customers and suppliers of the firm, and with competitors" (p. 571).

Collapsing across human–social capital, conflicts of interest can arise between employer and employee over the ownership of this capital (obtained by skills development and networking among constituencies):

The issue typically arises when an employee leaves one employer and goes to work for a competitor. Increasingly, the original employer, fearing that valuable knowledge possessed by the employee will fall into the hands of a competitor, will seek to prevent the employee from taking the job or utilizing the valuable knowledge. Disputes about employees' use of intellectual property in the posttermination setting have increased because firms recognize that their employees' human capital is one of their most valuable assets (p. 575).

Stone's (2001) law-review article addressed matters of jurisprudence attendant to such issues, so she couched implications in terms of a judicial recommendation—namely, that "courts should take the tacit understandings of the new psychological contract into account" (p. 577). Her further commentary fleshes out this point:

The terms of this contract bear directly on issues of employee human capital. As we have seen, one of the most important terms of the new psychological contract is that employers will provide employees with training, skill development, networking opportunities, and general human capital. In situations in which such assurances have been given by an employer, subsequent efforts of the employer to place restrictions on the portability of the employee's general human capital should be regarded as suspect (p. 577).

The remainder of this "Disputes over Ownership of Human Capital" section of Stone's (2001: 576) article not only described ways in which these conflicting interests between employer and employee have begun to play out during the modern era, but also noted how the courts have wrestled with such developments (e.g. regarding not-to-compete or not-to-disclose provisions of contracts).

My point is a simple one: If the courts have not yet come to a wholly unified conclusion, if law-review articles find the need to give courts advice about what they should do, and if such advice includes admonitions about attending to the new psychological contract's tacit understandings, then what further evidence do we need that open-ended uncertainties exist in the employment relationship now more than ever? Moreover, does a business climate populated with Enron-like scandals encourage employees to think management's exercise of authority will not try to take advantage of looseness in the "area of acceptance?"

2.7 Conclusion

In short, bosses garner via employment contracts the right to tell workers what to do as well as how and when—but although such rights have the blank-check quality described by Simon, they should remain circumscribed by responsibilities and morally obligatory proscriptions of interpersonal mistreatment that pertain to the conduct and demeanor exhibited when issuing such directives. Employees who react negatively to perceived mistreatment and injustice in the workplace might well exhibit an egoistic bias by too readily externalizing blame toward management, but perhaps this tendency also reflects a certain inherent distrust of authority that Boehm (1999, 2000) sees as a pandemic quality of human nature. Moreover, Simon's (1951) analysis suggests that although a give-and-take reciprocity by which deals get struck underlies the fundamental logic of the employment relationship, that same logic entails a unilateral flow of control in the aftermath as governing how initially unresolved issues will get settled. Even though that transfer of power takes place by voluntary consent, we should not become surprised if it is sometimes abused or if employees sometimes incline toward subversive rebelliousness over perceived grievances. After all, perhaps that is only fair.

References

Adams, J. S. (1965). "Inequity in social exchange," in L. Berkowitz (ed.), *Advances in Experimental Social Psychology*, Vol. 2 (New York: Academic Press), 267–99.

Adams, J. S., and Friedman, S. (1976). "Equity theory revisited: Comments and annotated bibliography," in L. Berkowitz (ed.), *Advances in Experimental Social Psychology*, Vol. 9 (New York: Academic Press), 43–90.

Bies, R. J. (1987). "The predicament of injustice: The management of moral outrage," in L. L. Cummings and B. M. Staw (eds.), *Research in Organizational Behavior*, Vol. 9 (Greenwich, CT: JAI Press), 289–319.

—— (2001). "Interactional (in)justice: The sacred and the profane," in J. Greenberg and R. Cropanzano (eds.), *Advances in Organizational Justice* (Stanford, CA: Stanford University Press), 89–118.

—— and Moag, J. S. (1986). "Interactional justice: Communication criteria for fairness," in B. Sheppard (ed.), *Research on Negotiation in Organizations*, Vol. 1 (Greenwich, CT: JAI Press), 43–55.

Blau, P. M. (1964). *Exchange and Power in Social Life*. New York: Wiley.

Boehm, C. (1993). "Equalitarian Behavior and reverse dominance hierarchy". *Current Anthropology*, 34: 227–54.

—— (1999). *Hierarchy in the Forest: The Evolution of Egalitarian Behavior*. Cambridge, MA: Harvard University Press.

—— (2000). "Conflict and the evolution of social control". *Journal of Consciousness Studies*, 7: 79–101.

Cohen-Charash, Y., and Spector, P. E. (2001). "The role of justice in organizations: A meta-analysis". *Organizational Behavior and Human Decision Processes*, 86: 278–321.

Colquitt, J. A., Conlon, D. E., Wesson, M. J., Porter, C. O. L. H., and Ng, K. Y. (2001). "Justice at the millennium: A meta-analysis of 25 years of organizational justice research". *Journal of Applied Psychology*, 86: 425–45.

—— and Greenberg, J. (2001). "Doing justice to organizational justice: Forming and applying fairness judgments," in S. W. Gilliland, D. D. Steiner, and D. P. Skarlicki (eds.), *Theoretical and Cultural Perspectives on Organizational Justice* (Greenwich, CT: Information Age), 217–42.

Cooper, C. L., Dyck, B., and Frohlich, N. (1992). "Improving the effectiveness of gainsharing: The role of fairness and participation". *Administrative Science Quarterly*, 37: 471–90.

De Waal, F. (1996). *Good Natured: The Origins of Right and Wrong in Humans and Other Animals*. Cambridge, MA: Harvard University Press.

Dulebohn, J. H., and Martocchio, J. J. (1998). "Employee perceptions of the fairness of work group incentive pay plans". *Journal of Management*, 24: 469–88.

Eisenberger, R., Hunington, R., Hutchison, S., and Sowa, D. (1986). "Perceived organizational support". *Journal of Applied Psychology*, 71: 500–7.

Foa, U. G., and Foa, E. B. (1980). "Resource theory: Interpersonal behavior as exchange," in K. J. Gergen, M. S. Greenberg, and R. H. Willis (eds.), *Social Exchange: Advances in Theory and Research* (New York: Plenum Press), 77–94.

Folger, R. (1977). "Distributive and procedural justice: Combined impact of 'voice' and improvement on experienced inequity". *Journal of Personality and Social Psychology*, 35: 108–19.

—— (1998). "Fairness as a moral virtue," in M. Schminke (ed.), *Managerial Ethics: Morally Managing People and Processes* (Mahwah, NJ: Lawrence Erlbaum), 13–34.

—— and Cropanzano, R. (1998). *Organizational Justice and Human Resource Management*. Thousand Oaks, CA: Sage.

Galbraith, J. (1973). *Designing Complex Organizations*. Reading, MA: Addison-Wesley.

Greenberg, J. (1990). "Employee theft as a reaction to underpayment inequity: The hidden cost of pay cuts". *Journal of Applied Psychology*, 75: 561–8.

Kahneman, D., Knetsch, J. L., and Thaler, R. H. (1986). "Fairness and the assumptions of economics". *Journal of Business*, 59: S285–300.

Keltner, D., Gruenfeld, D. H., and Anderson, C. (2003). "Power, approach, and inhibition". *Psychological Review*, 110: 265–84.

Konovsky, M. A. (2000). "Understanding procedural justice and its impact on business organizations". *Journal of Management*, 26: 489–511.

Kottke, J. L., and Sharafinski, C. E. (1988). "Measuring perceived supervisory and organizational support". *Educational and Psychological Measurement*, 48: 1075–9.

Lee, C., Law, K. S., and Bobko, P. (1999). "The importance of justice perceptions on pay effectiveness". *Journal of Management*, 25: 851–73.

Leventhal, G. S. (1980). "What should be done with equity theory? New approaches to the study of fairness in social relationships", in K. Gergen, M. Greenberg, and R. Willis (eds.), *Social Exchange: Advances in Theory and Research* (New York: Plenum Press), 27–55.

—— , Karuza, J., and Fry, W. R. (1980). "Beyond fairness: A theory of allocation preferences," in G. Mikula (ed.), *Justice and Social Interaction* (New York: Springer-Verlag).

Lind, E. A., and Tyler, T. R. (1988). *The Social Psychology of Procedural Justice*. New York: Plenum Press.

Moorman, R. H. (1991). "Relationship between organizational justice and organizational citizenship behaviors: Do fairness perceptions influence employee citizenship?" *Journal of Applied Psychology*, 76: 845–55.

Organ, D. W. (1990). "The motivational basis of organizational citizenship behavior," in B. M. Staw and L. L. Cummings (eds.), *Research in Organizational Behavior*, Vol. 12 (Greenwich, CT: JAI Press), 43–72.

Rousseau, D. M. (1995). *Psychological Contracts in Organizations: Understanding Written and Unwritten Agreements*. Thousand Oaks, CA: Sage.

Schaubroeck, J., May, D. R., and Brown, F. W. (1994). "Procedural justice explanations and employee reactions to economic hardship: A field experiment". *Journal of Applied Psychology*, 79: 455–60.

Simon, H. A. (1951). "A formal theory of the employment relation". *Econometrica*, 19: 293–305.

—— (1957). *Administrative Behavior: A study of Decision-Making Processes in Administrative Organization*. New York: Macmillan.

Skarlicki, D. P., and Folger, R. (1997). "Retaliation in the workplace: The roles of distributive, procedural, and interactional justice". *Journal of Applied Psychology*, 82: 434–43.

Stone, K. V. W. (2001). "The new psychological contract: Implications of the changing workplace for labor and employment law". *UCLA Law Review*, 48: 519–661.

Thibault, J. W., and Walker, L. (1975). *Procedural Justice: A Psychological Perspective*. Hillsdale, NJ: Erlbaum.

Tsui, A., Pearce, J. L., Porter, L. W., and Tripoli, M. (1997). "Alternative approaches to the employee-organization relationship: Does investment in employees pay off?" *Academy of Management Journal*, 40: 1089–121.

Tyler, T. R. (1994). "Psychological models of the justice motive: Antecedents of distributive and procedural justice". *Journal of Personality and Social Psychology*, 67: 850–63.

—— and Folger, R. (1980). "Distributional and procedural aspects of satisfaction with citizen-police encounters". *Basic and Applied Social Psychology*, 1: 281–92.

Weber, M. (1947). *The theory of social and economic organization*: translated by A. M. Henderson and T. Parsons. New York: Free Press.

Welbourn, T. M., Balkin, D. B., and Gomez-Mejia, L. R. (1995). "Gainsharing and mutual monitoring: A combined agency-organizational justice interpretation". *Academy Management Journal*, 23: 513–30.

3

Industrial Relations Approaches to the Employment Relationship

JOHN KELLY

3.1 Themes underlying the employment relationship

Industrial relations (IR), increasingly known as employment relations (ER), has been defined as follows:

Employment relations is the study of the regulation of the employment relationship between employer and employee, both collectively and individually, and the determination of substantive and procedural issues at industrial, organizational and workplace levels (Rose 2001: 6).

The employment relationship can be defined, at a basic level, as an exchange in which the employer hires labor to produce goods and services in order to make a profit whilst the employee sells his or her capacity to work in order to earn income. IR is not a discipline but a field of study, comprising contributions from across the social sciences, including economics, sociology, psychology, law, and politics. Consequently, it is not a straightforward matter to isolate and discuss "an IR approach" to the employment relationship because there are variations both within and between disciplines and between countries. Nevertheless, it is possible to discern a number of major themes which are common to most approaches to the subject and which constitute the distinctive attributes of the field, particularly when compared to human resource management (HRM) and organizational behavior (OB). The chapter begins by discussing each of these themes. It then moves on to look at the ways in which they have shaped our understanding of the regulation of IR through collective bargaining. We look in turn at the effects of collective bargaining on employees and on employers before discussing several ways in which the parties have tried to construct more cooperative industrial relations, both at the level of the enterprise—through partnership agreements—and at the level of the national economy—through social pacts between unions, employers, and the state.

3.1.1 Cooperation and conflict

First, and common to many IR approaches, is the proposition that the employment relationship is partly cooperative—the parties have a shared interest in the success of the employing business—but also entails an unavoidable, structural conflict of interest between worker and employer, which cannot be designed out of the system by better management. Different analyses of conflict have been provided by different writers and they vary in their implications for theory and practice. One theme stresses the exploitative character of employment as owners of capital seek to extract surplus value from labor. Wages are therefore necessary to hire labor and create profit but are simultaneously a deduction from profits. Or in the language of HRM, whilst it is true that workers are a productive asset for a company and should therefore be protected, they are at the same time a cost that may periodically need to be reduced (Storey 2001). Within the British banking and financial services sector, for example, at least fifteen major companies have signed partnership agreements with unions since the mid-1990s, but in the three years 1998–2000 almost 75,000 jobs were shed by these and other companies in the sector (Gall 2001: 364, 371).

3.1.2 Inequality

A second theme is the necessarily hierarchical and unequal character of the employment relationship. It is the employer who has the legal right to hire and fire, to direct workers' activity, and to fix terms and conditions of employment, albeit within legal and other regulations that may constrain these rights and/or lay down rights for employees. One manifestation of this inequality is revealed in the 1996 figures on the ratio of chief executive pay to average manual worker pay in manufacturing industry. In Germany the ratio was 10:1, in the United Kingdom 18:1, and in the United States 27:1 (Rubery and Grimshaw 2003: 13).

3.1.3 Power

A third feature of employment is that it is a relationship of power. As already mentioned, the employer enjoys a series of wide-ranging legal rights, including the right to exercise authority over employees. In addition, the average level of unemployment in European capitalist economies since 1980 has been around 10 percent (Rubery and Grimshaw 2003: 143). This means that the individual employee is typically more dependent on their employer for work than vice versa, a fact that often becomes clear when employers fire and replace striking workers. The balance of power between the parties is complex and is influenced by a number of variables, in particular by intense product market competition, by employee skills, and by organizational resources such as trade unions.

3.1.4 Indeterminacy

Fourth, the contract of employment itself is necessarily indeterminate: The employer rarely hires a fixed quantity of effort but hires the employee's capacity to work for a fixed period of time. In the absence of any meaningful consensus about fair levels of effort, the amount of work to be performed within that period will be the subject of debate and conflict. Under conditions of high unemployment and weak trade unions, employers will typically try to raise effort levels despite employee complaints about work intensity and stress (see below).

The indeterminacy of the employment relationship leads to different forms of regulation by the parties involved, employers, unions, and the state, as they seek to pursue their interests. Issues in employment may be regulated unilaterally by the employer, as in 58 percent of British workplaces in 1998 (Millward et al. 2000: 96); bilaterally, by unions and employers, typically through collective bargaining; and trilaterally, through the involvement of the state. The emphasis in much of the HRM literature is on the employer as the key agent of regulation and restructuring, as is clear from the following definition of the field:

Human resource management is a distinctive approach to employment management which seeks to achieve competitive advantage through the strategic deployment of a highly committed and capable workforce using an array of cultural, structural and personnel techniques (Storey 2001: 6).

Within the field of IR, there is more emphasis on the other parties and on the interrelations and conflicts between them.

3.1.5 Levels of regulation

Fifth, regulation of the employment relationship is normally conducted at several different levels within most national industrial relations systems: At the national level itself, at industry or sector level, and at the level of the enterprise (or company). Within both Europe and the United States there has been a process of decentralization of collective bargaining and a growing range of issues, such as working practices, that are now subject to regulation within the firm (Katz 1993). In some countries, such as Spain, for example, bargaining at enterprise level continues to be closely linked to, or articulated with, bargaining at higher levels. In countries such as Britain, by contrast with weak employers' associations, the decentralization of collective bargaining has taken a "disorganized" rather than "organized" form as industry-wide bargaining has simply been abandoned by employers (Traxler 1995).

The thrust of these two previous points is that "institutions matter": Enduring sets of rules or values make a difference to many of the outcomes valued by workers and employers, and a growing body of research in industrial relations is addressing the question of "which institutions matter and how they matter" (Pontusson 2000: 325; see also Peters 1999). The "varieties of capitalism" approach provides one of the more fruitful ways of thinking about these issues. According to Hall and Soskice (2001), we can distinguish three different national varieties of capitalist system based around clusters of the following variables: IR institutions, especially bargaining and consultative structures; employee motivation practices; systems of training and education; patterns of corporate governance; and types of interfirm relations. Liberal market economies (LMEs) such as the United Kingdom and the United States typically have decentralized bargaining, low bargaining coverage, high levels of workforce insecurity and flexibility, limited systems of work-related training, corporate governance systems geared to short-term profit maximization, and interfirm relations regulated primarily by contracts and markets. These stand in contrast to the more coordinated market economies (CMEs), such as Germany, which operate with more centralized or coordinated bargaining, greater employment protection, extensive systems of work-related training, and trust-based networks of corporate governance. The Mediterranean economies (MEs), such as Spain, can be thought of as a hybrid form, characterized by coordinated bargaining but weak systems of workforce training. Within the LMEs, conflicts of interest are more likely to be settled by the exercise of power and therefore levels of strike activity are typically higher in these economies, such as the United Kingdom, United States, and Canada, for example, than in the CMEs (Monger 2003). In the latter cases, such as Germany and the Netherlands, conflicts of interest are more likely to be settled through negotiation within a dense network of institutions (Rubery and Grimshaw 2003: 157–70).

3.1.6 Good industrial relations

Finally, there is a strong normative thrust in much IR literature towards the pluralist view that a "good" IR system, at whatever level, is one that optimizes both productive efficiency and fair treatment for employees, where the latter category is often taken to include effective voice in enterprise or workplace decision-making (cf. Osterman et al. 2001). Given the conflicts of interest in the employment relationship and the imbalance of power between workers and employers, there is a strong presumption in favor of power resources and institutions that can protect workers against unfettered market regulation and employer power, whether these be unions, collective bargaining arrangements, or some form of state regulation. Contrast this position with the view enshrined in the definition of HRM, quoted earlier, in which the employer's concern for "competitive advantage" is paramount.

This set of themes has led IR researchers over the years to pose a number of distinctive questions about the employment relationship and to generate a set of findings about the conditions under which workers and employers can pursue their respective interests. In the remainder of this chapter, I discuss each of these in turn. First, there is a substantial literature that compares the impact of different modes of employment regulation on both employer and employee outcomes. The main comparison normally made is between collective bargaining and unilateral employer regulation. Second, and in light of arguments about the rigidities and costs of collective bargaining, there is an equally extensive literature on recent forms of labor–management cooperation. The latter part of the chapter therefore examines "partnership" agreements in a number of different countries.

3.2 The effects of collective bargaining on employees

The first point to make here is that researchers in the two major liberal market economies, the United States and the United Kingdom, are often prone to exaggerate the declining influence of collective bargaining because they generalize from a handful of what turn out to be atypical cases. As Table 3.1 shows, the proportion of workers whose pay is regulated by collective bargaining between unions and employers (bargaining coverage) did indeed fall significantly in both these countries during the past twenty years. But what is equally clear is that bargaining coverage is both very high and stable throughout most of the coordinated and Mediterranean economies of western and northern Europe, even where the proportion of workers belonging to unions is very low. In Spain, for example, less than 20 percent of workers are members of a trade union but over 80 percent have their pay rises fixed by sector level negotiations between union confederations and employers' associations.

The analysis of conflicting interests in the employment relationship has led IR researchers to focus attention on wages and conditions of work. Typically, pay rates determined by collective bargaining in the unionized sector of the economy are compared with rates in the non-union sector decided unilaterally by the employer, and the differences are striking (Table 3.2).

Not only are pay rates higher, on average, under collective bargaining, but the wage premium is particularly high for the less advantaged workers in the labor market, such as ethnic minorities, women, and the less skilled, although more so in Britain than the United States. The absolute figures should be interpreted with care since they are unadjusted for other wage determinants such as age, education level, or workplace size, but even when these and other control variables are taken into account there remain significant differences. In recent years, the issue of workforce

Table 3.1. *Trade union density (% of workers in unions) and collective bargaining coverage (%), six countries, 1980–97/8*

	Trade union density			Bargaining coverage		
	1980	1990	1997	1980	1990	1998
France	22.2	13.9	9.9	85	95	95
Germany	34.9	32.1	27.1	76	76	80
Italy	49.6	39.1	36.8	85	83	90
Spain	8.3	12.1	17.4	60	60	86
United Kingdom	56.3	42.8	34.4	83	65	30
United States	20.2	14.8	14.2	26	18	16

Sources: Union density: France, Germany, Italy, Spain, and the United Kingdom: Ebbinghaus and Visser (2000: Table WE.13/14a); United States: Golden et al. (1999: Table 7.1) and US Bureau of Labor Statistics, www.bls.gov. Bargaining coverage: Waddington and Hoffman (2000: Table 1.5); Blau and Kahn (2002: Table 3.1); European Commission (2000: Chart 8).

Table 3.2. *Collective bargaining coverage, hourly wage rates, and wage premia*
(Great Britain and the United States)

Type of worker	Collective bargaining (£)	Not covered by collective bargaining (£)	Wage premium (union: non-union pay)	
			GB 1998 (%)	US 1997 (%)
Male	9.31	9.15	1.7	15.7
Female	7.97	6.26	27.3	12.8
White	8.65	7.87	9.9	14.9
Non-white	8.95	6.77	32.2	15.1
Non-manual	9.79	9.54	2.6	n/a
Manual	6.78	5.18	30.9	49.7

Sources: Great Britain: Metcalf et al. (2000: Table A.1); United States: Mishel et al. (2001: Tables 2.35, 2.36).

diversity has become more prominent in HRM research, with particular attention paid to the needs and interests of women workers (Liff 2003). It appears from the evidence on pay rates that collective bargaining makes a substantial difference to the earnings of women in general and to low skilled, ethnic minority women in particular. In other words, not only do unions raise wages they also reduce inequality between different segments of the workforce.

If we look at trends over time there is an equally powerful union effect. A recent study of the U.S. telecommunications industry showed that between 1983 and 1998 non-union clerical, sales, and technical workers experienced a dramatic reduction in median real weekly wages of approximately 20 percent (real wage changes are calculated by taking money wage changes and adjusting by the consumer price index). Unionized workers, by contrast, saw their wages increase by between 2 percent (clerical and sales staff) and almost 6 percent (technical staff) over the same period (Keefe and Batt 2002: Table 5). In the American construction industry, the hourly wage gap between union and non-union workers has widened significantly in recent years. In 1984, the gap for craft workers was 55 percent but by 1999 this had grown to 68 percent. Translated into actual pay rates, a unionized building craft worker in 1999 earned on average $32.33 per hour; his or her non-union counterpart made just $19.21 per hour (Thieblot 2002: Table 8.3).

In addition to their bargaining impact on pay levels, unions also have a significant egalitarian effect on the distribution of earnings. One of the most commonly used measures of earnings inequality is the 90:10 wage ratio. This is calculated as the ratio of the ninetieth percentile (the gross earnings figure below which 90 percent of workers fall) to the tenth percentile (the comparable figure below which 10 percent fall). In 1994, the 90:10 ratio for Sweden, with powerful unions, 85 percent union density, and a similar level of bargaining coverage, was 2.20; the figure for the United States, with union density and bargaining coverage both below 20 percent, was almost twice as high, at 4.35 (Machin 1999: Table 11.3). Broadly speaking, the more the power wielded by unions through high levels of collective bargaining coverage, the lower the degree of wage inequality.

In principle, union power could achieve these results in a number of ways: By compressing earnings at the top of the wage distribution; by raising the earnings of those at the bottom; or by a combination of the two. The evidence suggests the union effect is far more powerful at the bottom as compared to the top end of the wage distribution. Data from thirteen OECD countries for the mid-1980s to the mid-1990s show that high paid workers (the ninetieth percentile) experienced significant real wage growth of around 20 percent, both in countries with high bargaining coverage such as Germany and Italy and in those with low coverage such as the United Kingdom and Japan. The big comparative differences show up in the experiences of low wage workers, defined as those on the tenth percentile. They experienced rates of real wage growth comparable to their high earning peers where unions were powerful and bargaining coverage was high, as in Belgium, Finland, or Germany. But where union power and bargaining coverage fell steeply, as in New Zealand and the United States, for example, low paid workers saw their earnings decline in real terms over this ten-year period (OECD 1996: Chart 3). In other words, unions deliver a wage premium for workers in general, but are especially powerful and effective in protecting the earnings of the lowest paid groups in the labor market. Serious erosion of union power, whatever its other effects, has a significant and damaging impact on these workers.

Unions, of course, aim to do more than simply protect or increase workers' interests in wage rises. Typically, they will try to negotiate policies that restrain the exercise of managerial power around issues of job protection and the management of redundancy. Job protection policies might include redeployment or work sharing, whilst agreed redundancy procedures would normally cover notice periods for affected workers, methods for avoiding redundancy, selection criteria for individual workers, compensation levels, and corporate assistance with job seeking by those made redundant. Across Europe, many of these measures are now legal requirements on employers but unions will often seek to negotiate improvements to the statutory minima (OECD 1999). As one might expect, employment protection laws are most stringent in those countries with powerful union movements, as indicated by bargaining coverage or union density: Italy and Spain by contrast with the United States and Australia, for example. Contrary to the widespread neoliberal view that employment protection laws (EPL) will reduce employment levels (or growth rates) and raise the unemployment level, the OECD analysis found no such effects (1999: 88; see also Esping-Andersen and Regini 2000). Bivariate associations between EPL and unemployment levels became insignificant when additional variables were introduced into the analysis and multivariate statistics calculated.

An earlier OCED study examined the association between union presence and employee feelings of job insecurity. Across twenty OECD countries the proportion of workers who said they were worried about the future of their company rose from 28 percent in 1992 to 35 percent in 1996 (OECD 1997: Table 5.3). Between 1991 and 1995, the proportion of German and British workers who reported they were "worried about job security" rose even more dramatically, from 29 to 42 percent

(OECD 1997: Table 5.4). Demographic and economic factors both played a part in accounting for the rise in feelings of insecurity. Workers with low levels of skill or education report higher levels of insecurity and so do workers in economies with slow or negative growth. But unions also make a difference: Feelings of insecurity are lower where there is high bargaining coverage; and where there is a relatively high ratio of welfare benefits to average earnings, the latter being most commonly found in the Scandinavian countries with powerful union movements (OECD 1997).

Unions also play a role in regulating the amount of effort employees are required to expend within the working day, as well as regulating the length of the working day itself. Effort levels are an important issue for unions and their members for two reasons: First, as noted earlier, the indeterminacy in the employment relationship means that the rate at which employees are required to work is always potentially problematic. Second, there is a lot of evidence suggesting that the past twenty years has witnessed a signifi-cant intensification of work as employers have successfully sought to squeeze more effort out of employees. In a 1992 survey of almost 3500 British employees, 62 percent reported they had to expend more effort in their jobs than five years previously and 53 percent said that stress levels had increased. Another British survey, carried out in 1998 but using management respondents, found as much as 39 percent stating that employee effort levels had risen during the previous five years, discounting the idea that reports of intensification reflect employee biases (Green 2001: 66, 68). Comparative data from twelve European countries shows a similar trend. In 1991, 24 percent of employees in these countries said they had to work at "very high speed" but by 1996 the figure had risen to 31 percent (Green and McIntosh 2001: Table 1). Interview quota-tions from qualitative research convey the flavor of the phenomenon:

Jobs built up that I had no control over completing and I wasn't being able to—as hard as I worked, and I worked all the hours under the sun—but every day things would be added to my list that would never get done. So I ended up, well, I got stressed... (Utilities manager quoted in Wichert 2002: 101).

The big thing is going home at night time and not being able to relax because you've got work spinning round in your head and you're thinking "God, I'll never get it all ready." (College lecturer quoted in Nolan 2002: 121).

The strongest predictor of the international rise in effort levels is change in trade union density, an approximate measure of union power (Green and McIntosh 2001: Table 6). Countries with the steepest declines in union density—Britain and Ireland, for example, compared to Belgium, Denmark, and Spain—have recorded the sharpest increases in effort levels, an association that suggests it is the changing balance of power at the workplace that has permitted employers to drive up effort levels.

3.2.1 Unions, collective bargaining, and employee "voice"

The decline in unionism and collective bargaining in some countries has had one final consequence for employees. In liberal market economies, such as the United States and the United Kingdom, the trade union has been the most widespread form of worker representation generally available to employees for the exercise of "voice" as a counterweight to the hierarchy of managerial power. In 1980, 64 percent of British workplaces recognized trade unions for bargaining, and just over half of these had also created separate consultative committees. By 1998, the incidence of union recognition for bargaining had dropped substantially to 42 percent and there had been a slight fall in the numbers of consultative committees (Millward et al. 2000: Tables 4.6 and 4.10). Meanwhile, over the same period, a growing number of British employers created management-dominated communication bodies such as briefing groups: The incidence of these rose from 36 percent of workplaces in 1984 to 65 percent in 1998 (Millward et al. 2000: Table 4.12).

In most European countries the IR system is regulated at several different levels and is structured around two channels of influence, the trade union and the works council (European Commission 2000). The latter is a legally mandated information and consultative body, operating at workplace level and comprising representatives elected by the whole workforce (union and non-union alike). The works council provides some form of worker influence even where union density is low and as a result works council elections normally have a level of voter turnout far in excess of union density. For example, the 1994 works council elections in Germany recorded a turnout of 78 percent although union density that year was just below 30 percent (Calmfors et al. 2001: Table 4.5). Most European workers have some form of workplace voice even where union density is low or falling.

In contrast, the decline in union density in countries such as Britain and the United States tends to have a more dramatic effect on worker influence, an outcome corroborated by data on employee perceptions of the amount of say they have in workplace decisions. Data from a nationally representative British employee sample showed that 63 percent of employees were satisfied with their influence over decisions affecting their work back in 1985. After the rise of briefing groups and direct communications in the ensuing years, but following the decline in union representation, that figure actually fell to 46 percent in 1989 and has hardly changed since (Jowell et al. 1997, 2001; Kelly 1998: 46). Curiously, a U.S. employee survey carried out in 1994 arrived at much the same estimate of what the authors described as "the representation gap," the difference between the amount of influence employees said they wanted and the amount they actually exercised. According to Freeman and Rogers (1999: 48–9), 53 percent of U.S. employees had less involvement in workplace decisions than they would have liked. We should not make too much of the similarity in numbers because of differences in question wording and in levels of union influence between Britain and the United States. Nevertheless, it is interesting that a small majority of both British and U.S. employees appears dissatisfied with management's organization of decision-making and involvement.

The decline in employee perceptions of voice has one further consequence which links into the literature on procedural and substantive justice and employee perceptions of fairness. In a 1998 British employee survey ($N = 18,641$), non-managerial respondents were asked to rate their managers on a number of dimensions, including how fairly they treated employees. One of the best predictors of employees' perceptions of fair treatment was union recognition for collective bargaining and the presence of a consultative committee. By contrast, non-union forms of employee involvement and communication made no difference to employee perceptions of fair treatment (Millward et al. 2000: Table 4.17).

3.3 Unions, collective bargaining, and employers

Given that unions exercise power in pursuit of worker interests, pushing up wage rates above those in the non-union sector, protecting jobs, and providing employees with a voice in enterprise decision-making, what is their impact on the employer? One school of thought, influenced by neoclassical economics, argues that unions pursue worker interests at the expense of the employer. On this view, a rise in labor costs can only be absorbed by firms through higher prices, lower profits, or both. Competitive product markets and tight monetary policy have arguably suppressed the high price route in many sectors and contributed to the recent low inflation across the OECD (Franzese Jr. and Hall 2000: Table 6.1). Consequently, the predicted effect of unions would show through in lower profits, and therefore in less investment and reduced employment in unionized firms. The corollary is that non-union employers would have a powerful incentive to avoid unions, whilst those already unionized would have an equally strong incentive to eliminate them or escape their influence (Kleiner 2002).

An alternative approach, known as the "Harvard school," argues there is far more potential for cooperation between labor and capital because of shared interests and that good IR does not require the elimination of unions (Freeman and Medoff 1984). First, it is suggested unions do not always seek to maximize wages, because of the negative consequences of doing so, and may therefore pursue a policy of wage moderation. Second, in a climate of good IR, unions and management may cooperate to raise labor productivity, thereby offsetting any negative wage impact on profits. Third, the higher wages paid to union workers should attract more, and better, job applicants and reduce labor turnover. With a more stable and longer-tenure workforce, employers have more incentive to invest in training and that effect should further raise labor productivity. Finally, insofar as unions provide workers with an independent voice, employers will be better informed about worker preferences and concerns as compared to their non-union counterparts.

Central to the research paradigm in this area is the construction of two sets of firms, matched on as many variables as possible, such as size, product range, degree of product market competition, technology, and labor force composition, but differing in respect of union status. In theory, a comparison of this type should control for the key determinants of company performance so that any residual differences between the groups can be attributed to union presence. In practice, it is difficult to control for more than a small number of variables.

The empirical evidence has shown partial support for both perspectives. Consistent with the neoclassical approach, there appears to be a fairly robust negative association in the United States and the United Kingdom between measures of union presence and several measures of financial performance including rate of profit and value added (Freeman and Medoff 1984: Tables 12.1 and 12.2; Kleiner 2002: 298–9; Metcalf 2003: Table 3). However, and in support of the Harvard approach, there are other studies that have shown a positive union–profitability connection (Metcalf 2003). Evidence from Germany shows that there is no simple connection between the presence of a works council and workplace performance (Frege 2002). In line with the Harvard approach, Frege's explanation is that works councils vary significantly in their strength and in the policies they pursue within firms, so *a priori* there is no reason to expect a uniform link between council activity and company performance. Evidence on unions and productivity is even more mixed: In both the United States and the United Kingdom studies over the past twenty years have found every possible association from negative to positive. Finally, it does appear to be true that unionized firms have lower labor turnover than their non-union counterparts.

There is one final piece of aggregate evidence that bears on the question of union power and its effects and that concerns the shares of national income accruing to labor and capital, respectively. A powerful and militant labor movement might be expected to increase the percentage share of national income taken by wages and salaries at the expense of profits. By dividing national income into these two categories and plotting trends over time (and across countries), we can construct a rather crude measure of changes in the power of organized labor as compared with employers. The measure is crude, though still useful, because national income shares are also affected by other factors such as levels of capital investment. However, what the available data show is that the profit share in national income fell steeply across Europe from approximately 36 percent in the late 1960s to 30 percent in the mid-1970s, a shift that was closely correlated with the great strike wave of that period (the U.S. figures were 37 and 33 percent, respectively) (Armstrong et al. 1991; Kelly 1998: Table 6.2). By 1999, however, it had recovered a full ten percentage points (but just four points in the United States), a remarkable shift in income redistribution from labor to capital in a relatively short period of time (European Commission 2000: Chart 43).

The most reasonable interpretation of this evidence is that from the standpoint of the unionized employer, IR have improved significantly in recent years: Profit rates and profit shares are higher and union power, measured by rates of strike activity for example, is less of a problem than in the past. However, in those national economies with a substantial non-union sector, such as the United Kingdom and the United States, but not most of western Europe, a different comparison can be drawn, between the performance of the union and the non-union firm. On that comparison, the unionized firm may still be less attractive to the profit-maximizing employer than its non-union rival, especially in the United States where the union wage premium is still very high (see above). As a result, a number of academic commentators and policy-makers have begun to explore different ways of regulating the employment relationship.

3.4 The search for "cooperative" industrial relations

One of the major arguments in industrial relations during the past twenty years has revolved around the capacity of economies regulated by unionized collective bargaining to adapt to intensified product market competition. For critics of unions and collective bargaining, this "old system" established high and standard rates of pay and employment that were often only loosely connected to fluctuations in corporate performance. Increasingly, employers said they wanted "flexibility"—in staffing levels, in job descriptions, and in pay levels—and many sought union cooperation in trying to achieve these goals. In the United States and the United Kingdom, these firm level initiatives have appeared in various guises over the past twenty years: Quality of Work Life Programs, Labor–Management Cooperation Committees, Quality Circles, and most recently Labor–Management partnerships (Kochan and Osterman 1994). Throughout the coordinated economies of western Europe, by contrast, the term partnership has a rather different meaning and has often taken the form of a tripartite agreement, or "social pact," between union confederations, employers' associations, and the state (Pochet and Fajertag 2000). We will first examine the enterprise level arrangements and then turn to the social pacts.

3.4.1 Enterprise partnership agreements

The literature on partnership in the United Kingdom and the United States is growing rapidly and has become increasingly diverse. In particular, there is a large and growing body of case studies, usually, though not always, of a single organization with a partnership agreement. Whilst some studies are rigorous, such as Marks et al. (1998) in the United Kingdom or Rubinstein and Kochan (2001) in the United States, there is also a substantial body of journalistic and uncritical cases, heavily based on the views of a handful of partisan informants and seriously under-theorized (see Kelly 2004 for details). A recent study by the author attempted a more systematic assessment by comparing a set of outcomes from twelve United Kingdom partnership firms with the same outcomes from a control group of twenty-six non-partnership firms, matched for employment size, product range, and union status. The partnership firms included some well-known examples such as Barclays Bank, Blue Circle Cement, and the food retailer Tesco. This type of comparison allows us to control for the impact of variables such as firm size or technology and arrive at a more accurate estimate of the effects of partnership agreements. These agreements normally include three major sets of provisions, reflecting the main interests of each of the parties: For workers, a commitment to some form of employment security; for the employer, union acceptance of various forms of flexibility; and for the union, an undertaking from the employer that it will be able to exert significantly more influence over corporate business decisions. The outcomes examined in the research comprised standard IR variables, namely wages, hours of work, employment levels, profit rates, and union density, and they were measured over a 2–3 year period prior to the signing of a partnership agreement and for a number of years after the agreement.

Overall, the evidence showed there were no significant differences between partnership and non-partnership firms in employee wage rises, hours of work, paid holidays, union density changes, or rates of profit. For example, hourly wage rates in three partnership banks (Barclays, Cooperative, and NatWest) increased by an average of 16.1 percent over the period 1998–2002; wage rates in four similar non-partnership banks rose by 17.6 percent over the same period. Gross profit margins rose by 3.7 percent per annum in the two partnership retail stores, Asda and Tesco, during 1999–2001; they increased by a very similar figure—3.2 percent—in two non-partnership retail chains. On the other hand, and from the employer's perspective, jobs were shed at a faster rate in partnership firms operating in highly competitive sectors, although they were also created at a faster rate in buoyant sectors such as retail. For example, the partnership water and sewage company Hyder cut its workforce by 40.1 percent in the ten years 1991–2001 but the average workforce reduction in the nine non-partnership water and sewage companies over the same period was 26.1 percent. Whilst it appears from this evidence that employers gain more than workers from these agreements, the overall outcomes for both parties are rather disappointing when set beside the rhetoric about partnership as a new era of industrial relations (Kelly 2004).

There is one additional reason for being skeptical of claims about a new period of labor–management "cooperation" and that concerns the role of employer coercion, either prior to, or in conjunction with, "partnership" agreements. Several employers, faced with economic and IR problems, seriously considered de-unionization as an option before selecting the "partnership" route, namely, Legal and General, National Power, and Tesco, whilst others threatened de-unionization or plant closure in order to secure union compliance with a "partnership" agreement, namely, Allied Domecq, Blue Circle, Bulmers, Hyder, Rover, and United Distillers (Marks et al. 1998: 213, 217; Bacon and Storey 2000: 413–14; Haynes and Allen 2001: 172). Similar evidence of the articulation of employer coercion and "cooperation" has also been reported in the United States. In nine of the thirteen case studies of labor–management "cooperation" examined by Walton et al. (1994), unions and workers were faced with major sanctions designed to secure their compliance with management demands, including lockouts and dismissals (Table 11.1). In the U.S. context, this is perhaps not so surprising because employers have shown a considerable propensity to use coercive and illegal tactics in their desire to avoid or eliminate unions. During the 1950s, illegal dismissals of union activists affected one in every twenty union organizing campaigns; by 1990, and despite a sharp decline in the volume of union organizing, activists were then being illegally fired at the much higher rate of one in four campaigns (Kleiner 2002: 296).

3.4.2 Coordinated bargaining and social pacts

A rather different approach to labor–management cooperation has been adopted in some of the coordinated economies of western Europe where tripartite national agreements have been signed between union confederations, employers' associations, and governments. Social pacts, as they are now known, have appeared in Belgium (from 1998), Finland 1995, Ireland 1987, Italy 1995, the Netherlands 1993, and Spain 1996 (European Commission 2000: 80–5). Taken as a whole, they have covered three broad sets of issues: Wages and working time, items traditionally regulated by sectoral collective bargaining; labor market reforms, such as the regulation of dismissals; and welfare reform, in particular the regulation of pensions and unemployment benefits. There are variations between countries: Wage moderation has comprised a central component of social pacts in Belgium, Ireland, and Italy, for example, but less so in Spain. Under the rules governing the European Monetary Union, governments are obliged to hold public debt below 3 percent of Gross Domestic Product and many have therefore been eager to reduce the costs of large welfare Programs, including state pensions and unemployment benefits. Many have also taken the view that contentious reforms will be easier to implement if they enjoy the support of their national trade union movements, many of which are still very powerful. This calcu-lation was reinforced by the defeat of the French Right in 1997, two years after its attempted pension reforms were aborted in the face of a general strike. Labor market reform has been a highly salient issue in countries such as Italy and Spain whose workers enjoy a comparatively high degree of protection against dismissal (Blau and Kahn 2002: Tables 3.4 and 3.5). Employers have lobbied hard for reforms under the rubrics of flexibility and competitiveness. Union leaders in these countries have generally taken the view that it is preferable to negotiate unpalatable reforms than oppose from the outside. Spanish unions, however, managed to do both; when negotiations over reforms to unemployment benefit broke down in spring 2002, the two major union confederations mobilized several million workers for a general strike in June. With more strikes threatened in the autumn, the government backed down and abandoned virtually all of its proposals (Hamann and Kelly 2003). In contrast, centralized wage negotiations in the Netherlands, involving a union movement with a much weaker mobilizing capacity than its Spanish counterparts, have produced some of the lowest real wage increases in Europe throughout the 1990s (European Commission 2000: Chart 44). Taken as a whole, the evidence suggests that there is considerable variation in the content and outcomes of social pacts, particularly when compared to the outcomes of enterprise-level partnerships in the United Kingdom.

3.5 Conclusions

The decline in union power in many countries has led some commentators to the view that IR as a field of study is increasingly anachronistic and therefore has little future unless it can reinvent itself and appropriate some of the language and the concerns of the fashionable HRM agenda (cf. Kaufman 1993). In fact, as this chapter has tried to show, there is a strong case for believing that the core themes of IR approaches to the employment relationship are of continuing relevance. First, the analytical focus on conflicts of interest and on power continues to be relevant in a world where many features of the employment relationship are both salient for many people and at the same time highly contentious. In spring 2003, for example, the annual shareholder meetings of several major U.K. corporations were lobbied by unions and pressure groups protesting at CEO pay rises; the three union confederations in France called a general strike to protest at planned reforms to the pensions system; and American Airlines avoided filing for bankruptcy only because it negotiated a series of major work and pay reforms with its unions. Second, and contrary to the spirit of labor–management cooperation at the heart of the HRM agenda, employer disempowerment and coercion of employees continues to be a widespread feature of contemporary employment relations. IR researchers are highly attuned to the presence of coercion because of the operating assumption that the employment relationship is a site of conflicting interests and a relationship of power. Third, whilst the "demise of unions and collective bargaining" view might seem plausible in the United States, it makes little sense in Europe because of the high levels of bargaining coverage and the political role of unions in social pacts and in membership mobilization.

References

Armstrong, P., Glyn, A., and Harrison, J. (1991). *Capitalism Since 1945*. Oxford: Blackwell.

Bacon, N., and Storey, J. (2000). "New employee relations strategies in Britain: Towards individualism or partnership?" *British Journal of Industrial Relations*, 38(3): 407–27.

Blau, F. D., and Kahn, L. M. (2002). *At Home And Abroad: U.S. Labor Market Performance in International Perspective*. New York: Russell Sage Foundation.

Calmfors, L., Booth, A., Burda, M., Checchi, D., Naylor, R., and Visser, J. (2001). "The future of collective bargaining in Europe," in T. Boeri, A. Brugiavini, and L. Calmfors (eds.), *The Role of Unions in the Twenty-First Century* (Oxford: Oxford University Press), 3–134.

Ebbinghaus, B., and Visser, J. (2000). "A comparative profile," in B. Ebbinghaus and J. Visser (eds.), *Trade Unions in Western Europe Since 1945* (London: Macmillan Reference), 33–74.

Esping-Andersen, G., and Regini, M. (eds.) (2000). *Why Deregulate Labour Markets?* (Oxford: Oxford University Press).

European Commission (2000). *Industrial Relations in Europe 2000*. Luxembourg: Office for Official Publications of the European Communities.

Franzese Jr., R. F., and Hall, P. A. (2000). "Institutional dimensions of coordinating wage bargaining and monetary policy," in T. Iversen, J. Pontusson, and D. Soskice (eds.), *Unions, Employers and Central Banks: Macroeconomic Coordination and Institutional Change in Social Market Economies* (New York: Cambridge University Press).

Freeman, R. B., and Medoff, J. L. (1984). *What Do Unions Do?* New York: Basic Books.

—— and Rogers, J. (1999). *What Workers Want*. Ithaca, NY: ILR Press.

Frege, C. M. (2002). "A critical assessment of the theoretical and empirical research on German works councils". *British Journal of Industrial Relations*, 40(2): 221–48.

Gall, G. (2001). "From adversarialism to partnership? Trade unionism and industrial relations in the banking sector in the UK". *Employee Relations*, 23(4): 353–75.

Golden, M., Wallerstein, M., and Lange, P. (1999). "Postwar trade union organization and industrial relations in twelve countries," in H. Kitschelt, P. Lange, G. Marks, and

John D. Stephens (eds.), *Continuity and Change in Contemporary Capitalism* (New York: Cambridge University Press), 194–230.

Green, F. (2001). "It's been a hard day's night: The concentration and intensification of work in late twentieth century Britain". *British Journal of Industrial Relations*, 39(1): 53–80.

——and McIntosh, S. (2001). "The intensification of work in Europe". *Labour Economics*, 8(2): 291–308.

Hall, P. A., and Soskice, D. (2001). "An introduction to the varieties of capitalism," in P.A. Hall and D. Soskice (eds.), *Varieties of Capitalism: The Institutional Foundations of Comparative Advantage* (New York: Oxford University Press), 1–70.

Hamann, K., and Kelly, J. (2003). "The domestic sources of differences in labour market policies". *British Journal of Industrial Relations*, 41(4).

Haynes, P., and Allen, M. (2001). "Partnership as union strategy: A preliminary evaluation". *Employee Relations*, 23(2): 164–87.

Jowell, R. et al. (eds.), *British Social Attitudes*, various years, from 1984.

Katz, H. C. (1993). "The decentralization of collective bargaining: A literature review and comparative analysis". *Industrial and Labor Relations Review*, 47(1): 3–22.

Kaufman, B. E. (1993). *The Origins and Evolution of the Field of Industrial Relations in the United States.* Ithaca, NY: ILR Press.

Keefe, J., and Batt, R. (2002). "Telecommunications: Collective bargaining in an era of industry reconsolidation," in P. F. Clark, J. T. Delaney, and A. C. Frost (eds.), *Collective Bargaining in the Private Sector* (Champaign, IL: Industrial Relations Research Association), 263–310.

Kelly, J. (1998). *Rethinking Industrial Relations: Mobilization, Collectivism, and Long Waves.* London: Routledge.

——(2004). "Social partnership agreements in Britain: Labor cooperation and compliance". *Industrial Relations* (in press).

Kleiner, M. M. (2002). "Intensity of management resistance: Understanding the decline of unionization in the private sector," in J. T. Bennett and B. E. Kaufman (eds.), *The Future of Private Sector Unionism in the United States* (Armonk, NY: M.E. Sharpe), 292–316.

Kochan, T. A., and Osterman, P. (1994). *The Mutual Gains Enterprise.* Boston, MA: Harvard Business School Press.

Liff, S. (2003). "The industrial relations of a diverse workforce," in P. Edwards (ed.), *Industrial Relations: Theory and Practice*, 2nd edn. (Oxford: Blackwell), 420–46.

Machin, S. (1999). "Wage inequality in the 1970s, 1980s and 1990s," in P. Gregg and J. Wadsworth (eds.), *The State of Working Britain* (Manchester: Manchester University Press), 185–205.

Marks, A., Findlay, P., Hine, J., McKinlay, A., and Thompson, P. (1998). "The politics of partnership? Innovation in employment relations in the Scottish spirits industry". *British Journal of Industrial Relations*, 36(2): 209–26.

Metcalf, D. (2003). "Union effects on productivity, profitability and investment," in J. Addison and C. Schnabel (eds.), *International Handbook of Trade Unions* (Cheltenham: Edward Elgar).

——, Hansen, K., and Charlwood, A. (2000). *Unions and the Sword of Justice: Unions and Pay Systems, Pay Inequality, Pay Discrimination and Low Pay.* London: London School of Economics, Centre for Economic Performance, Discussion Paper 452.

Millward, N., Bryson, A., and Forth, J. (2000). *All Change at Work? British Employment Relations 1980–1998, as Portrayed by the Workplace Industrial Relations Survey Series.* London: Routledge.

Mishel, L., Bernstein, J., and Schmitt, J. (eds.) (2001). *The State of Working America 2000–01* (Ithaca, NY: Cornell University Press).

Monger, J. (2003). "International comparisons of labour disputes in 2000". *Labour Market Trends*, 111(1): 19–27.

Nolan, J. (2002). "The intensification of everyday life," in B. Burchell, D. Ladipo, and F. Wilkinson (eds.), *Job Insecurity and Work Intensification* (London: Routledge), 112–36.

OECD (1996). "Earnings inequality, low-paid employment and earnings mobility". *OECD Employment Outlook*, 59–108.

—— (1997). "Is job insecurity on the increase in OECD countries?" *OECD Employment Outlook*, 129–60.

—— (1999). "Employment protection and labour market performance". *OECD Employment Outlook*, 49–89.

Osterman, P., Kochan, T. A., Locke, R. M., and Piore, M. J. (2001). *Working in America: A Blueprint for the New Labor Market*. Cambridge, MA: MIT Press.

Peters, B. G. (1999). *Institutional Theory in Political Science: The New Institutionalism*. London: Pinter.

Pochet, P., and Fajertag, G. (2000). "A new era for social pacts in Europe," in G. Fajertag and P. Pochet (eds.), *Social Pacts in Europe: New Dynamics*, 2nd edn. (Brussels: European Trade Union Institute), 9–40.

Pontusson, J. (2000). "Labor market institutions and wage distribution," in T. Iversen, J. Pontusson, and D. Soskice (eds.), *Unions, Employers and Central Banks: Macroeconomic Coordination and Institutional Change in Social Market Economies* (New York: Cambridge University Press).

Rose, E. (2001). *Employment Relations. Continuity and Change: Policies and Practices*. Harlow: Pearson.

Rubery, J., and Grimshaw, D. (2003). *The Organization of Employment: An International Perspective*. London: Palgrave.

Rubinstein, S. A., and Kochan, T. A. (2001). *Learning from Saturn: Possibilities for Corporate Governance and Employee Relations*. Ithaca, NY: ILR Press.

Storey, J. (2001). "Human resource management today: An assessment," in J. Storey (ed.), *Human Resource Management: A Critical Text*, 2nd edn. (London: Thomson Learning), 3–20.

Thieblot, A. J. (2002). "The fall and future of unionism in construction," in J. T. Bennett and B. E. Kaufman (eds.), *The Future of Private Sector Unionism in the United States* (Armonk, NY: M. E. Sharpe), 149–71.

Traxler, F. (1995). "Farewell to labour market associations? Organized versus disorganized decentralization as a map for industrial relations," in C. Crouch and F. Traxler (eds.), *Organized Industrial Relations in Europe: What Future?* (London: Ashgate), 3–19.

Waddington, J., and Hoffman, R. (2000). "Trade unions in Europe: Reform, organisation and restructuring," in J. Waddington and R. Hoffman (eds.), *Trade Unions in Europe: Facing Challenges and Searching for Solutions* (Brussels: European Trade Union Institute), 27–79.

Walton, R. E., Cutcher-Gershenfeld, J. E., and McKersie, R. B. (1994). *Strategic Negotiations: A Theory of Change in Labor–Management Relations*. Boston: Harvard Business School Press.

Wichert, I. (2002). "Stress intervention: What can managers do?" In B. Burchell, D. Ladipo, and F. Wilkinson (eds.), *Job Insecurity and Work Intensification* (London: Routledge), 154–71.

4

Legal Theory: Contemporary Contract Law Perspectives and Insights for Employment Relationship Theory

MARK V. ROEHLING

4.1 Introduction

Across disciplines, researchers have found it useful to view the employment relationship through a contract lens (e.g. implicit contracts, Williamson 1993; psychological contracts, Rousseau 1989). Despite the fact that all uses of the contract perspective to study the employment relationship can be traced to the field of law and the legal conceptualization of contracts, the richness of legal theories of contract is not adequately reflected in the employment relationship literature. Discussions of legal contract principles typically emphasize classical, and some would argue outdated, principles of contract law (e.g. the necessity of "a meeting of the minds," an emphasis on "bargained for promises"). Diverging legal theories of contract and their evolution over time receive only slight acknowledgment, if any, from employment relationship researchers. As a result, the potential contribution of contract scholarship to employment relationship theory has been underrealized. This chapter is intended to help address that limitation by increasing researchers' awareness of contemporary Anglo-American contract law perspectives, and by identifying insights for employment relationship theory that are provided by those contract perspectives.

This chapter is organized in four sections. It begins by placing the application of contract principles to the employment relationship in a broader context. This is accomplished by: (a) tracing the evolution of employment rights from master–servant law to rights based on contract; (b) briefly discussing the juridification of the employment relationship that has occurred in Europe, the United States, and other industrialized countries; and (c) identifying selected aspects of current legal schemes regulating employment relationship (in industrialized nations) that have implications for employment contracting. The second section provides an overview of classical contract law and neoclassical or modern contract law, briefly describing and contrasting the two distinct but related models of legal contract. The third section focuses on Ian Macneil's relational contract theory (1980), a "post-modern" theory of contracting behavior (Knapp 2002). Relational contract theory has already had a significant impact in the employment relationship literature (e.g. Rousseau 1989). This section seeks to enhance further the theory's contribution to the understanding of employer–employee relationships by providing a discussion of relational contract theory that expands significantly upon the existing treatment that it has received in the employment relationship literature. Therefore, the discussion of relational contract theory goes into much greater depth than the overview provided of classical and neoclassical contract law. The chapter concludes by identifying and discussing specific observations from the legal contract literature that are deemed to have potential relevance to theorizing about the nature of the employment relationship.

4.2 The broader context: The evolution of employment contracts and the juridification of employer–employee relationships

4.2.1 Master–servant relationship: Status versus contract

According to Honeyball (1989), it is inevitable that contract plays a major part in any analysis of employment. However, this has not always been the case. The generally recognized preindustrial precursor of the law regulating the "employer–employee" relationship, the law of the "master–servant relationship," was not a matter of contract, but one of status (Carlson 2001). That is, the obligations of master and servant were determined not by their agreement, but were imposed by the English common law based on their status as either "master" (a principal who employs another to perform services and who has the right to control the service provider's conduct) or "servant" (the person providing services whose conduct is subject to the control of the principal; Bakaly and Grossman 1995; Freedman 1989). Once the existence of the master–servant relationship was established (not all workers were considered "servants"), the law frequently dictated the rate and method of pay, the term of the employment, and the grounds for terminating the relationship (Blackstone 1765; Carlson 2001).

4.2.2 The rise of the employment contract law following the industrial revolution

The shift from employment law based on status to a system based on contract occurred over several centuries. Employment law scholars Bakaly and Grossman (1991) identify the fourteenth century enactment of the Statute of Laborers as marking the beginning of that shift. The Statute made it a criminal offense to demand (or to pay) wages higher than a reasonable rate, providing evidence that employees were beginning to bargain directly with employers over conditions of employment (Bakaly and Grossman 1995).

The Industrial Revolution in England is credited with bringing about the decline of the master–servant relationship, and completing the shift from employment as a factor of status to employment as a factor of contract (Bakaly and Grossman 1995; Freedman 1989). The old master–servant relationship, which was predicated on simple and direct relationships without much variation in work related duties and legal rights, failed to address the complexity resulting from an explosion of new occupations, new ways of organizing work, and a growing risk to the public associated with the new forms of work (Carlson 2001). Consistent with classical contract law theories (discussed later), the hallmark of the contractual approach to the employer–employee relationship was the voluntary consent of both parties to the relationship and its terms. Briefly, the relationship between an employer and employee was said to exist when, pursuant to an expressed or implied *agreement of the parties*, one person (the employee) undertakes to perform services or do work under the direction and control of another (the employer) (Friedman 1989).

4.2.3 *The juridification of the employment relationship*

Juridification, in the employment-labor field, refers to the extent to which the employment relationship is subjected to regulation through legal means, which includes legislation, administrative regulation, treaties, and to some extent judicial decisions (Gladstone 1997). The juridification of the employment relationship arguably goes back at least as far as the enactment of the Statute of Laborers in the fourteenth century. However, the onset of the juridification process is more commonly associated with the nineteenth-century passage of protective workplace legislation in Great Britain (e.g. the Factory Acts) and continental Europe (e.g. German "Bismarckian" labor regulations of the 1880s).

In most industrialized countries (e.g. Belgium, Canada, France, Germany, Japan, Mexico, United Kingdom, United States), the juridification of the employment relationship involves the increased regulation of both individual employee rights (e.g. protection from discrimination) and collective employment rights (i.e. the right to organize unions and other aspects of industrial relations law). Clear evidence of juridification can be found in most areas of employment: Individual employee contracts, safety, health, pensions, benefits, wages, hours, leaves, and dismissals (Keller 1997).

4.2.4 *Summary of key aspects of current regulatory schemes*

It is neither possible nor desirable to review each of the regulatory schemes that have resulted from the juridification process in the various countries of the world. This section makes several general observations regarding employment regulatory schemes that have particular relevance to employment contracts in industrialized nations, providing a number of country-specific examples in order to illustrate the different approaches to employment regulation.

Nearly all countries have multiple layers or levels of employment regulation. For example, in the United States, private sector employment relationships are regulated by Federal, State, and in some communities, local laws (e.g. the San Francisco city ordinance prohibiting discrimination in employment based on body weight). For companies with international operations, there may also be U.S. treaty obligations relating to employment (e.g. NAFTA). In addition, all employers are, at least to some extent, regulated by common law (or judge-made law) principles relating to the employment relationship. Similarly, employment in the countries of the European Union is governed by the regulations and directives from the Council of Ministers, decisions of the European Court of Justice, the national laws of members states, relevant treaties, and in the case of the United Kingdom, common law principles (to a more limited extent than in the United States). Within some member countries, regional legislative bodies (e.g. the parliament for the Flemish region of Belgium) may enact law regulating employment in their region. Also, since members of the European Union are members of the International Labor Organization (ILO), they are also subject to the extensive labor standards of the ILO.

The regulatory schemes in all industrialized countries provide at least some "minimum standards" that all employment contracts, individual or collective, must comply with. These minimum standards are typically established through a collection of statutes, regulations, and in some countries, judicial decisions, that address topics such as wages, hours of work, leaves, workplace injuries, and discrimination in employment based on personal characteristics (e.g. race, nationality, sex). Thus, in all industrialized countries the freedom of employers and workers to agree upon whatever terms of employment they might negotiate (i.e. the freedom to contract) is significantly constrained. There are, however, meaningful differences across countries in the extent to which the parties have freedom to negotiate. This is particularly true with regard to the contract of employment between the *individual* and the employer, or the "individual contract of employment."

Table 4.1 summarizes selected legal provisions pertaining to individual employment contracts in a non-random sample of industrialized countries. It does not purport to reflect all of the differences in legal requirements for employment contracts across countries, or even across different types of employees (e.g. full- versus part-time) within each country. Rather, Table 4.1 is intended to *illustrate* the types of differences found across countries in their regulation of individual employment contracts of private sector, non-civil servant, full-time employees. The first column focuses on legal requirements pertaining to the formation of individual employment contracts of indefinite (i.e. ongoing) duration, and the second column focuses on employment contracts that are expected to last only for a specified or fixed period of time (e.g. seasonal employment, employment to complete a specific project that will end in the foreseeable future). All reviewed countries provide that employment contracts of indefinite duration may be entered into either orally or in writing. However, as a result of a directive of the Council of Ministers, employers in European Union member countries (Belgium, France, Germany, and the United Kingdom in Table 4.1) are required to give employees written notice of certain basic terms and conditions of employment within a specified period after the employment relationship begins. Similarly, while Japanese employers may enter into employment contracts orally or in writing, by statute, employers with ten or more employees must set forth specific work rules that must be filed with a government agency and communicated to employees. Some countries further require that a specific language be used

Table 4.1. *Summary of key legal provisions pertaining to individual employment contracts for selected countries*

Country	Formation of individual employment contract for an indefinite period	Formation of individual employment contract for a fixed period	Relationship of individual and collective contracts	Termination of individual contracts—private sector
Belgium	May be written or oral; written contracts must be in the language specified for the relevant regions (e.g. in the Flemish region, Dutch). Every company with employees must have written work regulations which are drafted by the Works Council or in the absence of a Works Council, the employer. Deviations from the work regulations are possible; individual employment contracts but must be in writing	Must be in writing	The terms of the individual contract must comply with all relevant collective bargaining agreements (conducted at national, industry, or company level) *unless* they provide more protection to the employee	Required notice to all employees (length of notice varies for type of employees) Required compensation for employees discharged without good reason (amount of compensation varies for type of employee and length of service)
Brazil	May be written or oral. Statute specifically recognizes "tacit agreement" created through behavior of the parties	May be written or oral. The law permits a fixed term only for certain types of work-related services (e.g. temporary business activities, professional athletes, seasonal workers)	If a collective agreement takes affect, its provisions substitute for any individual contracts within its scope	Employees who have worked less than ten years for the same employer may be discharged without "just cause." However, if discharge is not for just cause, the employee is entitled to indemnification that varies by length of service and salary level

Table 4.1. (Continued)

Country	Formation of individual employment contract for an indefinite period	Formation of individual employment contract for a fixed period	Relationship of individual and collective contracts	Termination of individual contracts—private sector
				Employees with more than ten years service may be dismissed only for "serious fault." Failure of employer to prove serious fault generally results in reinstatement and back pay
Canada	May be oral or in writing, expressed, or implied	May be written or oral. Unless specified otherwise, individual contract assumed to be for an indefinite term	Collective bargaining agreements preclude individual employment contracts for all employees in the relevant collective bargaining unit, *unless* the collective agreement expressly allows individual contracts	The parties may specify the notice period so long as the minimum statutory notice requirements are met. If notice period is not specified in the contract, courts require reasonable notice under the circumstances (e.g. in light of length of service, availability of suitable employment). No notice is required if termination is for a just cause. If termination is found not to be for a just cause, the employee will be ordered reinstated, normally with back pay
France	May be oral or written However, after the employment relationship begins, the employer is required to give the employee	Must be in writing and pertain to the performance of a precise task set forth in the Labor Code (e.g. replacement	If a collective agreement takes affect, its provisions substitute for any individual contracts	Terminations after agreed upon trial period must be with notice and for cause Required notice period varies by

	written notice of the terms and conditions of employment All written employment contracts must be in French	of absent employee, temporary employment to meet a seasonal need)	within its scope, *except* where the terms of the individual contract are more favorable to the employee	type of employee and length of service Required compensation for employees discharged without good reason varies by length of service and the prejudice (damages) suffered by the employee
Germany	May be oral or written However, after the employment relationship begins, the employer is required to give the employee written notice of the terms and conditions of employment	Must be in writing and are permissible in few, relatively narrow circumstances set forth in specific legislation	The terms of the individual contract must comply with all relevant collective bargaining agreements (concluded at national, industry, or company level) *unless* they provide more protection to the employee	Required notice with period varying depending on length of employee service Every termination must be reviewed by the Works Council if there is one in the facility
Japan	May be written or oral Employers with ten or more employees must set forth terms of employment in work rules that must be filed with a government agency and communicated to employees New work rules that negatively affect workers rights or employment conditions may not be implemented unilaterally	May be written or oral The maximum term of employment that can be fixed in a contract is one year, except for contractors intended to continue until the completion of a specific project	If a union represents three-fourths of the workers in a similar job classification in a given workplace, the remaining (non-union) workers of similar kind employed in the same place will be bound by the same collective agreement	As a minimum procedural requirement, employers must give thirty days notice of dismissal or thirty days wages in lieu thereof If an employer obtains prior recognition from the relevant government agency that the dismissal is for cause, neither advance notice nor payment is required

Table 4.1. (Continued)

Country	Formation of individual employment contract for an indefinite period	Formation of individual employment contract for a fixed period	Relationship of individual and collective contracts	Termination of individual contracts—private sector
				There no statutory provision requiring just cause for the dismissal of employees. However, a doctrine prohibiting abusive discharge has evolved, and dismissal is generally considered permissible only on the grounds of a serious cause Employees disputing the dismissal may file a lawsuit seeking injunctive relief (e.g. suspend the dismissal) and payment for lost wages
Mexico	May be oral or written, expressed, or implied The key is a finding that one person rendered personal service to another under the latter's direction or control, in consideration for payment, *regardless how that relationship came about*	May be oral or written	Collective agreement cannot provide conditions which are less favorable to workers than those by existing agreements at the time the collective agreement is executed Generally, collective agreement precludes individual worker contracts in the enterprise, even if they	Dismissal without cause is possible, but is the basis for required compensation (which varies based on length of service and salary level) Employers must notify employees in writing of the cause for the dismissal or it will be deemed unjustified Even when dismissal is for just cause, certain workers (e.g. those with fifteen years of service, or

			are not members of the union	who were incapacitated as a result of a work-related condition) many be entitled to mandatory "severance premiums"
United Kingdom	May be oral or written, expressed or implied However, after the employment relationship begins, the employer is required to give the employee written notice of certain basic terms and conditions of employment Notification of changes in the specified terms and condition employment contract must of given to the employee in writing	Must be in writing	Most collective agreements are not "gentlemen's agreements" that are not legally binding Collective agreement can become legally enforceable through incorporation (express or implied) into individual employment contracts	The parties may agree upon the grounds for dismissal and procedural requirements (e.g. notice period) that can be enforced through a breach of contract claim brought in the courts In addition to any contract rights, employees who meet certain eligibility requirements (e.g. two years length of service) also have statutory protection from "unfair dismissal"; the employer must show that the dismissible of an eligible employee was fair and reasonable
United States	May be oral or written, express or implied (lack of an effective disclaimer to the contrary)	May be oral or written, express, or implied (absent an effective disclaimer to the contrary)	Collective bargaining agreements preclude individual employment contracts for all employees in the relevant collective bargaining unit	Employment at-will is the prevailing doctrine (i.e. unless agreed otherwise, employees may be discharged without notice or without just cause) Significant erosion of the at-will doctrine as a result of judicial decisions

by employers in any written employment contract (e.g. Belgium, France). In contrast to the foregoing, there are other countries which have essentially no formal requirements regarding the form of indefinite contracts. For example, Mexico's law focuses on whether an employer–employee relationship existed *in fact*, regardless of whether there was a formal, or even explicit, agreement. Also, legislation in Brazil provides that tacit employment agreements created through the behavior of the parties may be legally enforceable.

With some notable exceptions (e.g. the United States), in most industrialized countries there is a presumption that the term of employment is indefinite unless specified otherwise. Some of the countries recognizing this presumption (e.g. those that are members of the European Union) require that in order to effectively rebut the presumption, employment contracts for a fixed period must be in writing. Other countries, such as Brazil, only allow fixed period contracts for certain types of work (e.g. temporary business activities, professional athletes, seasonal workers).

Table 4.1 also indicates differences between countries in the relationship of individual employment contracts to collective employment contracts. The primary difference is between regulatory schemes which provide that if a collective employment agreement exists, employers are precluded from entering individual employment contracts with employees covered by the collective agreement (e.g. Japan, United States), and those regulatory schemes that allow individual employment contracts among employees also covered by a collective employment agreements to the extent that the terms of the individual contract meet or exceed the protection provided the employee by the collective employment agreement. That is, individual contracts may supplement the terms of an applicable collective employment agreement if it benefits the employee.

The final column in Table 4.1 reports key provisions relating to the termination of individual employment contracts of private sector/non-civil servant employees, focusing on notice requirements and the extent to which the law generally requires good or just cause for the dismissal of an employee. Provisions regarding providing employees advance notice of dismissal vary from required notice to essentially all employees (e.g. Belgium, Germany, Japan) to no generally required notice (e.g. the United States). The notice requirements of a number of countries fall between the two identified extremes. For example, Canada has a minimum statutory notice requirement, but no notice is required if termination is for just cause. Also, the mandatory notice requirements of some countries only apply after some minimum length of service has been met (e.g. an agreed upon trial period, France; a period specified by statute, United Kingdom). In summary, the vast majority of countries require some kind of notice before dismissing an employee, with the required notice period often varying by the length of service of the employee or the specific grounds for dismissal. Even in the United States, where there is no generally required notice for the dismissal of private sector employees, the parties may agree upon notice requirements that may be enforced by the courts, for example, through a breach of contract claim.

The extent to which different countries' regulatory schemes generally require good or just cause for the dismissal of an employee (i.e. provide substantive legal protection against arbitrary dismissals) may also be placed on a continuum. At one end are countries that require that employers establish good cause in order to effectively terminate employment. If the employer cannot meet that burden, the employee is typically reinstated and compensated (e.g. Canada). At the other end of the continuum is the United States where, without a contrary agreement, private sector employment is generally presumed to be "at-will" (i.e. there is no need for the employer to establish good cause for the dismissal).

A number of countries fall between these continuum anchors, rejecting the presumption that employment is at-will, but allowing employee dismissals that are not for good cause so long as the dismissed employee is compensated. For example, dismissal without cause is possible in Mexico, but is the basis for required compensation which varies based on length of service and salary level. Further, a number of regulatory schemes provide employees greater protection after a specified length of service has been met. For example, employees in Brazil with less than ten years of service with the same employer generally may be dismissed without good cause, but if the dismissal is without good cause, the employee will be entitled to compensation that varies by length of service and the employee salary level. Employees with less than ten years of service are not entitled to reinstatement even if the dismissal was not for good cause. However, employees who have worked ten years or more for the same employer cannot be terminated except for "serious fault" (a standard higher than good cause), and if that standard is not meet, the employee will be entitled to reinstatement and back pay. In summary, the regulatory schemes of almost all industrialized countries reflect the general belief that employees have some legitimate interest in the continuation of their employment relationships and, therefore, employees should receive some protection from arbitrary dismissals (i.e. compensation and/or reinstatement).

The foregoing discussion of selected legal provisions pertaining to individual employment contracts supports the observation, previously made by others (e.g. Keller 1997), that the individual contract of employment has much greater importance in some countries. That is, the regulation of employment in some countries (e.g. Canada, United Kingdom, United States) gives less preeminence to collective employees rights, and allows greater opportunities for individual employees' negotiation of the terms and conditions of employment than the regulation of employment in other countries (e.g. Germany).

4.2.5 Juridification and the appropriateness of the contract lens

The suitability of the contractual framework for the employment relationship has been questioned based on the argument that as a result of the juridification of the employment relationship that has occurred in recent decades, freedom of contract no longer operates between the parties. That is, it is argued, the legal regulation of employment is now so extensive that the parties, employers and employees, are no longer free to engage in contracting in any meaningful sense (Browne 1997; Haines 1989).[1] This argument highlights the importance of recognizing the richness of contract theories. The claim that a contractual framework is no longer appropriate because freedom of contract has been constrained by the increasing regulation of the employment relationship reflects a particular, classical view of what constitutes a contract. There are, however, other theories of contract that place much less emphasis on "freedom of contract," and which incorporate government regulation of exchange relationships into their explanation of contracting behavior (e.g. relational contract theory, discussed at length below). Thus, one's assessment of the suitability of the contractual framework for the employment relationship may depend on the theory of contract that is adopted (e.g. classical, neoclassical, or relational).

4.3 Classical and neoclassical models of contract law

Classical contract law had its heyday in the English and American legal systems during the late nineteenth and early twentieth centuries. In the classical contract model, a contract is a bilateral agreement that consists of a bargained-for exchange of promises. The exchange is deliberately carried through by the process of offer and acceptance with the mutual intention of creating a binding deal. It was presumed that the parties deal at arm's length, and that the parties have nearly unlimited freedom to chose the content of a contract. Under the classical contract model, courts needed to see objective evidence of a meeting of the minds regarding the promises that were exchanged in order for the promises to be binding. Highly formal rules of offer, acceptance, and consideration (providing something of value for promise received) had to be complied with in order for the court to find the kind of objective evidence that would create a legally binding contract. The contractual rights and obligations of the parties were determined based on what happened at the moment in time when the contract was formed (i.e. prior relationships or the subsequent course of dealing between the parties were not taken into account).

The rigid formalism of the classic contract model was not well suited for the complexity of ongoing exchange relationships, and the inevitable fairness issues that arise in such relationships. As one contract scholar recently observed, the rules of classical contract "were often responsive to neither the actual objectives of the parties, the actual facts and circumstances of the parties' transaction, nor the dynamic nature of contracts. Instead, the rules of classical contract law were centered on a single abstraction, the reasonable person; on a single kind of promise, the bargain promise; and on a single moment in time, the moment of contract formation" (Eisenberg 2000: 1749). Classical contract law was further criticized based on the finding that its formal rules did not explain the results in actual cases (Feinman 2000).

Neoclassical contract law evolved in response to the criticisms of classical contract law, emerging in roughly the middle half of the twentieth century. It is referred to as "neoclassical" because it addresses certain shortcomings of classical contract law rather than offering a wholly different conceptualization of contract law

(Hillman 1997). The primary differences between classical and neoclassical contract law may be summarized as follows. First, although freedom of contract is still a central concern, and contracting is still viewed as being fundamentally about the parties achieving their own ends, in contrast to classical contract law, neoclassical contract law assumes that the ends sought by the parties must be balanced by, or even subordinated to, social values and policies in some circumstances. As a result, the obligations that are legally enforceable under neoclassical contract law obligations are not limited to those based on bargained-for promises objectively consented to by the parties. In addition to promise-based obligations, neoclassical contract obligations may also include specific obligations imposed by the law to avoid unfairness or injustice to a party under the particular circumstances (e.g. to avoid the unconscionable taking advantage of a contracting party in an inherently weaker position, or to recognize a party's justified reliance on the representations of the other—even though the representation did not constitute a bargained-for promise), as well as a general obligation to act in good faith when dealing with one's contracting partner.

Second, also in contrast to classical contract law, neoclassical contract law assumes that the ends sought by the parties must be understood in terms of the context out of which they arise. Accordingly, albeit to a limited extent, neoclassical contract law gives some recognition to the dynamic nature of exchange relationships. For example, in limited circumstances, neoclassical law may take into account events occurring before the moment the contract was formed (e.g. prior course of dealings between the parties) and events occurring after the moment the contract was formed in order to construct the terms of the contract.

Third, although neoclassical law still employs a body of rules to determine whether an enforceable contract exists, and if so its terms, in contrast to classical contract rules based on axioms thought to be self-evident, the rules applied under neoclassical contract law are sometimes subjective (e.g. they may involve inquiries into the actual mental state of both parties) and not always applied in the same way (e.g. the rules of contract construction may vary by type of contract). There would seem to be little dispute that neoclassical contract law represents a significant theoretical advancement of the classical contract law model. However, there are contract scholars who argue that neoclassical contract law is still woefully inadequate to deal with the true nature of most exchange relations, including employment. One of the most notable critics is Ian Macneil, the putative father of relational contracting theory (Macneil 1980). His theory and its application to the employment relationship are the focus of the section that follows.

4.4 A post-modern perspective: Relational contracting theory

Relational contract theory and its continuum of transactional–relational exchange behavior (referred to as the discrete–relational continuum in the legal literature) were introduced by Ian Macneil in the field of contract law.[2] Since being imported into the organizational behavior-management (OB-management) literature, the continuum has been widely adopted in writings and research relating to the employment relationship. It has been used to characterize the nature of employee *psychological contracts* (e.g. Nelson et al. 1991; Herriot and Pemberton 1996), specific employee–employer *obligations* (e.g. Robinson and Rousseau 1994), and *employment relationships in general* (e.g. Sparrow 1996; Hendry and Jenkins 1997) as either "transactional" or "relational." The transactional–relational continuum has also been applied prescriptively. For example, Rousseau and Wade-Benzoni (1994) suggest that depending on an employer's business strategy, employers should seek to develop psychological contracts that fall at a particular location on the continuum, and Hall and Moss (1998) recommend that in order to compete in today's business environment, employers should promote employment contracts that are "relational." As noted in Section 4.1, this section seeks to enhance the theory's contribution to the understanding of employer–employee relations by providing a discussion of Macneil's relational contract theory that expands significantly upon the existing treatment that the work has received in the employment relationship literature, and by identifying and discussing specific insights from relational contract theory that are deemed to have potential relevance to theorizing about the nature of the employment relationship.

4.4.1 Overview of Macneil's contract scholarship

Ian Macneil is a lawyer who introduced the concept of a "relational contract" in the legal literature (Macneil 1974, 1978), and has since published numerous detailed works addressing the continuum and relational contract theory (Macneil 1980, 1983, 1985, 1986, 1987, 2000). Macneil distinguishes between *contracting behavior* and *contract law*. His theory of relational contract focuses on behavior, and it has implications for contract law scholarship. Macneil's work may be viewed as an attempt to: (a) describe contracting behaviors, and (b) influence thinking about contract law in a way that would, ultimately, make the law more reflective of actual contracting behavior.

Macneil's theory adopts a view of contract that contrasts sharply with traditional definitions, classical or neoclassical: "By contract I mean no more or no less than the relations among parties to the process of projecting exchange into the future" (Macneil 1980: 4). Noticeably absent is any reference to "promise," or terms with special legal meaning, such as "offer," "acceptance," or "consideration." According to Macneil, contracts-in-law (i.e. those enforceable by the legal system) are just a small fraction of the contracts that exist in the modern world (Macneil 1980: 5). A core proposition of relational contract theory is that every transaction (i.e. exchange) is embedded in complex relations (i.e. a social context), and the understanding and effective analysis of transactions requires the recognition and consideration of the relations in which the transactions occur (Macneil 1985, 2000).

4.4.2 The transactional (discrete)–relational continuum:
Discrete contracts

According to Macneil, exchange occurs in various patterns along a continuum ranging from highly *discrete* to highly *relational.* Discrete contracts are characterized by short duration, limited personal interactions, and easily measured objects of exchange (i.e. those things that the parties do or provide each other in the relationship). Everything is clearly defined. The parties are bound precisely and tightly. As a result of these characteristics, discrete contracts require only a minimum of future cooperation between the parties. Discrete exchange is said to involve the separation of the transaction from all else between the participants. Its ideal occurs when there is nothing else between the parties, never has been, and never will be. The parties view themselves as free of entangling strings (e.g. friendships, altruistic desires). Discrete exchange is epitomized by the one-time, market exchange between a buyer and seller in which the parties had no previous relations and no expectations of possible future relations (Macneil 1980, 1985, 1987)

Purely discrete exchange is not possible (Macneil 1974, 1980). This point warrants emphasis and, therefore, I will return to it. For now, it should be understood that when Macneil refers to discrete contract, he means *relatively* discrete.[3] An example of a relatively discrete exchange would be an out-of-town traveler's one-time, cash purchase of gasoline from a gas station located along an interstate highway, in an area in which she has never been and does not expect to be again. The traveler and attendant make an exchange of money for a monetizable commodity, gas, without expectation of future interactions (Macneil 1985).

4.4.3 The transactional (discrete)–relational continuum:
Relational contracts

While discrete exchange may be described relatively succinctly, the nature of relational exchange requires a more involved description. My goal in the following discussion is to provide a parsimonious description of relational contract, focusing on what I believe are its essential, defining characteristics. This description is based on a review of Macneil's works (Macneil 1974, 1978, 1980, 1983, 1985, 1986, 1987, 1989, 2000), and interpretations, criticisms, and applications of his work by other contract scholars (e.g. Goetz and Scott 1981; Whitford 1985; Feinman 2000; Armour 1994; Spiedel 2000) and behavioral science researchers (e.g. Dwyer et al. 1987; Kaufman and Stern 1988; Barnett 1992; Provan and Gassenheimer 1994). Relational contracts can be described as having several characteristic traits that are conceptually distinguishable, but interrelated. Before discussing them, I would note that one could reasonably divide the "relational pie" into more or fewer pieces. Macneil's work regarding relational contract has been criticized as complex and somewhat difficult to read (Whitford 1985). The level at which I have identified the characteristics of relational contracts reflects a judgment regarding the appropriate balance between preserving the distinctiveness of important characteristics of relational contracts and the goal of providing a description that is more parsimonious than that provided in Macneil's original works.

Extended duration
Relational exchange involves repeated performances that are of a "significant duration" (Macneil 1987: 275; Feinman 2000). The term *significant duration* is never explicitly defined, and must be understood in the context of the broader theory of relational contract which looks at the extent to which an exchange relationship must be projected into the future as a dimension of the relationship that significantly impacts its structure (Armour 1994). Significant duration can be understood to mean of such duration that the precise terms of exchange cannot be fully specified at the present, making cooperation and other aspects of relational contracting, discussed below, necessary in order for the exchange to be carried out successfully. Although there is a tendency to treat "relational contacts" as synonymous with "long-term contracts," as others have pointed out, "temporal extension per se is not *the* defining characteristic of relational contracts" (emphasis added; Eisenberg 2000: 814). Some long-term contracts may lack other key aspects of relational exchange. For example, a long, fixed-term lease with fixed-rent in which the tenant is responsible for maintenance, insurances, and taxes may involve little relationship between the landlord and tenant. In contrast, depending on other aspects of the exchange relation, a two-week contract to remodel a room may be highly relational (Eisenberg 2000).

As the foregoing discussion suggests, the development of highly relational employment contracts does not necessarily require a permanent, lifetime, or even long-term exchange relationship. What is more central to the development of highly relational employment, I would argue, is the existence of a shared belief that the employment relationship will continue into *a future that is of unspecified duration*. More than, for example, a legally binding guarantee of lifetime employment, such a belief promotes cooperation, the sharing of benefits and burden in the relationship (discussed below), and other characteristics of relational contracts.

Objects of exchange
The objects of relational exchange include both quantities that are difficult or impossible to measure or specify and easily measured quantities *that are not in fact measured*. The difficulty of measuring or specifying what is being exchanged may be due to the nature of what is being exchanged (its intricacies, complexity, or intangible nature), uncertain future conditions, and/or the interaction of the two. The relevant inquiry is not simply "to what extent does the exchange involve objects of exchange that can or can not be measured?" It must also be asked, "if the exchange involves objects of exchange that can be measured, are they *in fact* measured?" A finding that exchange partners do not bother to measure objects of exchange that can be easily measured is indicative of relational exchange (Macneil 1978).

In the employment context, the objects of exchange include those tangible and intangible things that an employee receives from employment that are of some value to the employee, and those things that the employee contributes to the employer which are of some value to the employer. Objects of exchange that employees receive are more specific and more tangible to the extent that their value to the employee is readily reducible to a monetary value that can be presently calculated. Examples of non-specific, intangible objects of exchange include the following *if they are of value to the employee*: Meaningful, challenging, or interesting work; personal recognition; opportunities for social interaction; and status or prestige associated with a position. Examples of objects of exchange that are relatively specific and tangible include: An agreed upon hourly wage or salary; a specific benefit package, particularly where the employer provides a statement of the monetary cost or value of the benefits; and paid holidays. Turning to what employees contribute to the relationship, objects of exchange are intangible and characteristic of relational employment to the extent that the details of the contribution cannot be fully specified in advance. Examples of relatively non-specific or intangible subjects of exchange that may be contributed by employees include: Loyalty; the exercise of employee judgment, discretion, creativity, or initiative in the performance of work; and engaging in general, non-job-specific behaviors for the benefit of the employer. The objects of exchange that the employer receives are lacking in relational character if all that the employee is contributing is strict performance of well-specified tasks.

Involvement of parties

Relational exchange involves more extensive, whole-person relations between the parties. The parties respond to the "whole person" in the sense that they respond to many aspects of another's character and background, permitting feelings to enter into the relationship. For example, in a highly relational employment relationship the employee is not narrowly viewed as a service-or skill-providing unit. Rather, the employee is seen as a whole person, with a work life, a personal or non-work life, feelings, emotions, etc. Similarly, the employee has a broader, more holistic view of the employer, its component parts, obligations to other employees, and the demands it faces in its environments. The employee's more holistic view might be described as "an understanding of the business." The interaction of whole persons in relational exchange is both a potential source of additional rewarding social exchange, and a potential source of conflict that may be disruptive to the exchange relationship if not successfully managed.

Cooperation

Future cooperation between or among the parties to relational exchange is antici-pated. In discrete transactions, almost no future cooperation will be required because each party produces either the money or the bargained-for commodity at the time and place agreed upon (Macneil 1980). However, because relational exchange involves ongoing exchange, the nature of which cannot be fully specified at present, the parties must cooperate with each other as circumstances relevant to the exchange relationship unfold over time in order for the exchange relationship to be successfully continued. Cooperation almost inevitably requires flexibility.

Benefits and burdens

Relational exchange involves a sharing of the benefits and burdens of the parties' exchange relationship. In discrete transactions, benefits and burdens are sharply divided. Each party is allocated certain benefits and certain burdens (with associated risks), and the parties are rigidly held to the allocation that was made. The sharing of benefits and burdens that is characteristic of relational exchange can be viewed as arising from the interaction of fairness concerns (e.g. the norm of reciprocity; Gouldner 1960), which requires that parties to a relationship maintain some kind of equivalence in their exchange.

Obligations associated with relational exchange

According to Macneil, the different exchange behavior patterns "give rise" to normative obligations (shared beliefs about the parties' mutual responsibilities) which parallel the categories of behavior that are necessary for the exchange pattern to be successful (Macneil 1989). While there are obligations that are associated with all successful exchange in modern contracts, obligations that are characteristic of relational exchange can be distinguished from discrete obligations on several dimensions: Specificity, source, and substance.

In extreme discrete contracting, obligations are specific and founded on promise (Macneil 1980). In extreme relational contracting, obligations are non-specific, leaning toward the diffuse, and ill-defined, and the relation itself develops obligations, "with only modest input from individual promise" (Macneil 1980: 17). A fundamental tenet of relational contract theory is that in contracting behavior, obligations between the parties are not limited to those based on promise; promise can never cover more than a fragment of the total situation (Macneil 1980). Accordingly, Macneil has argued that promise-centered theories of contract are inadequate to deal with complex contractual relations without distortion and omission (Macneil 1985). Obligations arising out of the parties' relationship(s) include obligations based on customs, status, habits, expectations created by the status quo, and social norms (Macneil 1980). Also, for certain relationships in society, some relational obligations may come from external sources (e.g. government regulation of the employment relationship; Macneil 2000).

An example of a normative relational obligation identified from Macneil's work is the obligation to act in good faith when dealing with an exchange partner. Other relational norms that are related to fairness, and have been identified by Macneil (1980) as necessary for successful relational exchange, include the duty to provide restitution for losses caused, and the duty to meet the reasonable expectations of one's exchange partner. In a highly discrete exchange, lack of good faith and fairness is not only tolerated, it is largely expected (hence the maxim "caveat emptor" or "buyer beware").

Relational obligations do not involve specific monetary obligations *that may be presently calculated* (e.g. payment of specific hourly wage or salary). Contrary to suggestions in the OB-management literature, this does not mean that any obligation that relates to money is non-relational or "transactional." For example, an employer's feeling of obligation to share company profits with his or her employee, where there is uncertainty about the amount, involves a sharing of benefits of relationship and is relational in nature. Similarly, an employee feeling an obligation to accept a reduction in pay if necessary to keep the employer financially afloat involves the sharing of burdens, and would also be relational in nature if it arose from norms associated with the relationship, and not as a result of a bargained-and-paid-for promise.

4.4.4 *The transactional and relational ideals versus modern contracts*

In contrast to the ideals that may or may not exist in the real world, but which have been the focus of attention in the OB-management literature, Macneil describes "modern contracts" as involving both relational and discrete aspects. Like the relational ideal, modern contractual relations generally involve primary personal relations, tend toward long life, and tacit assumptions abound. But there are important differences between the relational ideal and modern contractual relations. First, modern relational contracts "are ridden with measurement and specificity" (Macneil 1980: 22). But the complexity of modern society calls for processes and structures that tend to organize even the most specific and measured exchange into relational patterns, and all modern relational contracts also involve a great deal of exchange that cannot be or is not measured (e.g. social exchange; Macneil 1980: 22–3). Second, modern relations tend to include both sharp divisions of benefits and burdens and a sharing of them (Macneil 1980). For example, employees may receive a precise wage for performing specific job tasks (dividing benefits and burden), but they may also share prosperity with management through bonus schemes or more comfortable working conditions. They may also share hard times through such employer actions as layoffs, reduced bonuses, and pay cuts. Third, modern contractual relations tend to combine both discrete and relational obligations. The source of obligations may include promises, the relation itself (i.e. based on customs, habits, expectations, status, and social norms), and externally provided norms (e.g. constraints imposed by employment legislation).

4.4.5 *The inherently relational nature of employment*

It is important to recognize that relational contract theory is a general theory of exchange behavior (Macneil 1985, 2000), and the transactional–relational continuum was introduced by Macneil in a much broader context than the one in which it is being applied in the employment relations literature. The continuum describes the full range of exchanges that occur within society, from one-time, arm's length transactions conducted under market conditions to marital relations. When the full range of exchange is considered, virtually all, if not all, employment relationships fall closer to the relational end of Macneil's continuum than to the discrete end. Stated another way, employment is, relatively speaking, inherently relational. Support for this claim can be found in the many specific references Macneil makes to employment. Macneil frequently uses the employment relationship as an example of a relational contract (cf. Macneil 1980), and he identified employment relationships as among those structures that are "obviously relational in nature" (Macneil 1978: 858). Also, Macneil observed that employment is an "extremely relational contract, no matter how strenuously a party attempts to make it discrete" (Macneil 1985: 492), and in describing the nature of the most discretely organized economy possible, he states that "of course, no employment is possible" (Macneil 1985: 489).

By focusing on important elements of relational contracting, discussed above, the relational nature of employment relationships can be more particularly demonstrated. Employment relationships necessarily involve some uncertainty that precludes a specification of all of the terms and conditions of exchange. It has been observed that no job can be completely specified in advance, eliminating all employee discretion (Fox 1974; cf. Levinson et al. 1962). Unlike the single performances involved in the discrete exchange ideal, employment, even part-time employment, involves multiple performances. Commons (1924) has argued that the employment contract "is not a contract, it is a continuing implied *renewal* of contracts at every minute and hour, based on the continuance of what is deemed, on the employer's side, to be satisfactory service, and, on the laborers' side, what is deemed to be satisfactory conditions and compensation" (Commons 1924: 285).

The relational nature of employment in the United States, and in many other societies, is further promoted by the set of obligations imposed on the employment relationship by the government. Employment legislation creates obligations that arise as a result of the employment relationship (Macneil 1980). Even in the absence of promises or agreements between the parties, based upon the existence of a specific relationship between the parties (i.e. that of employer and employee), employers are obligated to employees in a variety of ways relating to non-discriminatory treatment, safety and health, minimum wages, pension contributions, hours of work, etc. (Macneil 2000).

It has been suggested that employment agencies such as Manpower and Kelly create purely transactional agreements with workers. Even though this kind of temporary employment may contain relatively more discrete aspects than the traditional employment relationship, depending on the extent to which the formal contractual arrangement influence the parties' actual contractual relations, it still does not come close to reaching the pure discrete ideal. In contrast to the discrete ideal, even contract employees' work involves multiple performances that cannot be fully specified, in every detail, in advance. Moreover, expectations relating to future exchange are likely to creep in (e.g. the possibility of the contract being renewed or the employee being brought on as a "regular" employee), and many of the relational obligations imposed by society apply to contract employees (e.g. health and safety laws). In sum, when the full exchange continuum is considered, all working relationships that may be fairly characterized as involving "employment" are relatively more relational than discrete.

4.4.6 Summary comparison of contract theories

Numerous comparisons between classical, neoclassical, and relational contract theories have been made or suggested. Table 4.2 summarizes those comparisons. The three general categories of contract theories that have been discussed in this chapter

Table 4.2. *Summary comparison of relational, neoclassical, and classical theories of contract*

Dimension	Relational	Neoclassical	Classical
Scope	Broadest: All exchange involving at least some economic activity	Narrower: No longer attempts to encompass all transactions (e.g. excludes labor law from the scope of contract law)	Broad: All consensual transactions
Formality	Informal: Substantive reasoning reflecting social values	Formal rules tempered by consideration of context and fairness in some circumstances	High: Formal rules based on self-evident axioms
Objectivity	Highly subjective: Contract assessment depends on the subjective mental state of the parties	Rules are sometimes subjective (e.g. inquire into the mental state of one or both parties)	Highly objective: Focuses on the directly observable state of the world (e.g. the "plain meaning" rule); actual intent not relevant
Degree of standardization	Highly individualized: Application of law depends on situation-specific variables; "contextualized with a vengeance"	Still a unitary body of rules, however, they are fragmented in that they are not always applied the same way (e.g. may vary by type of contract)	Highly standardized: Clear rules framed at a high level of generality
Basis/source of contractual obligations	Obligations are non-specific, based on customs, status, habits, expectations created by the status quo, social norms, and external sources, "with only modest input from individual promise"	Promises, but only enforced only under appropriate conditions. Also, obligations based on equitable and fairness considerations imposed by law in limited circumstances	Bargained-for promises
Static–dynamic	Highly dynamic: Determination of rights and obligations takes in stream of events before and after the relationship of the party	Dynamic: In limited circumstances, may take into account events occurring before or after the moment the contract was formed	Static: Rights and obligations determined based on what occurred at the moment in time when a contract was formed
Assumptions regarding rationality of actors	Recognizes various limits on cognitions (e.g. bounded rationality, defective capability)	Recognizes various limits on cognitions (e.g. bounded rationality, defective capability)	Assumes highly rational actors

are compared on seven dimensions. Many of the comparisons have already been elaborated upon in earlier sections, and others are relatively straightforward. Therefore, in this section I will focus on several key observations regarding the comparison of relational contract theory to the other theories. It should be apparent that classical contract law is the antithesis, in virtually all regards, of relational contract theory (e.g. the exclusive focus on promise as "the" source of obligations, the total separation of contract formation from the relationships in which most exchange occurs, the presumption that the parties are dealing at arm's length). The assumptions on which classical contract law are based suggest that it is most appropriately applied to discrete or transactional exchange, the end of the exchange continuum that relational contract theory is least interested in explaining.

While neoclassical contract law shares more similarities with relational contract theory, there are important differences suggesting that relational contracting is not merely a new, "tweaked" version of neoclassical contract law, but represents a fundamentally different theory of contract. For example, compared to neoclassical contract law, relational contract dramatically broadens the scope of contract law. Macneil describes contracts as encompassing "all human activities in which economic exchange is a significant factor" (Macneil 2000). This definition includes in the scope of contract, for example, exchange activities that are not primarily economic, but which have some economic aspects, such as family relations. Also, although neoclassical contract law takes into account the context of the parties' exchange (e.g. customary practice, prior course of dealing), it does so only to a very limited extent. In contrast, relational contract theory emphasizes that virtually all exchange is embedded in relations and a broader context that must be taken into account in order to understand the nature of the contract, and where disputes have arisen, to arrive at workable solutions. In the words of one contract scholar, relational contract theory "is contextual with a vengeance" (Feinman 2000: 703).

Finally, another important difference between neoclassical and relational contract theory is the role that fairness and justice considerations play. Good faith when dealing with an exchange partner, a sharing of the benefits and burdens of the contract, and other obligations related to fairness (described earlier) are core obligations that are central to the theory's explanation of relational contracting behavior. In contrast, neoclassical contract law largely adopts the classical law proposition that parties are free to pursue their self-interest. It is only in very limited circumstances that neoclassical law requires that the ends the party seeks be subordinated to social values relating to fairness. In short, fairness is a core consideration in relational contract theory, but is largely a peripheral consideration in neoclassical contract law.

4.5 Concluding observations and implications for employment relationship research

This chapter was intended to promote insights for employment relationship theory by increasing researchers' awareness of contemporary Anglo-American contract law perspectives. The evolution of employment legal rights from master–servant to rights based on contract was briefly traced, and two contemporary contract perspectives, neoclassical contract law and relational contract theory, were described and compared to classical contract law (and each other). The foregoing discussion and analysis is the basis for several observations that have implications for employment relationship research, and in particular, the psychological contract literature.

4.5.1 The usefulness of a contract framework for studying the employment relationship

It has been argued that freedom of contract no longer operates between employers and employees due to the increasing legal regulation of the employment relationship, and that as a result, the usefulness of the contract framework for understanding the employment relationship has been significantly undermined (e.g. Browne 1997). The increasing regulation of employment and the resulting lack of freedom to contract are relevant *if* one adopts a classical contract law perspective, or to a lesser extent, *if* one adopts a neoclassical contract law perspective. However, it is not a relevant concern from a relational contract perspective. From a relational contract perspective, governmental regulation of the employment relationship is a factor that may shape the nature of the exchange relationship, but does not, no matter how extensive, eliminate contracting behavior. For example, governmental regulations that embody relational norms (e.g. prohibiting unfair discrimination or the arbitrary treatment of employees) promote more highly relational employment by creating relational obligations (referred to earlier as relational obligations coming from "external sources"; discussed earlier).[4] Other governmental regulations, depending on their character, might impede the development of highly relational employment (e.g. laws requiring highly specified, written employment contracts). In sum, relational contract theory takes into account, and helps explain, the affect of governmental regulation on the employment relationship; no assumption of relational contract theory is challenged by the increased regulation of the employment relationship.

Given the variety of contractual perspectives that exist, and the significant differences in their postulates and underlying assumptions, rather than asking the question, "Is a contract framework still useful for studying employment relationship?" it would seem that a more appropriate question is, "Which contract framework is likely to be most useful in the study of employment relationships?" Of the three perspectives discussed in this chapter, the answer suggested by the foregoing discussion is clear: Relational contract theory. This is not to suggest that other theories (not discussed in this chapter) or new theories of contract might not be found to be equally useful. The important point for employment relationship researchers is that there is not "a" legal theory of contract, and when attempting to import, borrow, or adapt from the legal literature, available contract theories should be identified and evaluated for their usefulness.

4.5.2 The importance of context

A fundamental proposition of relational contracting theory is that the consider-ation of context (past dealings, industry customs, societal or organizational norms) is essential when attempting to understand a contracting relationship (e.g. when determining the parties' intent, or when assessing the fairness of the parties' actions in the contract relationship). Of course, the importance of contextual analysis when studying employment relationships has already been recognized by employment relationship scholars. In a sense, relational contracting theory provides additional, converging evidence reinforcing the importance of context in that it is based on a different perspective (i.e. a legal scholar's perspective) and the assessment of a wider range of exchange relationships than addressed in the employment relationship literature (e.g. employment, commercial, familial). Relational contracting theory might be viewed as elevating the importance of considering context in exchange relations ("contextualizing with a vengeance"), and Macneil's analysis of the role of context in exchange relations in general (Macneil 1980) may provide employment relationship researchers strategies for conducting contextual analysis of employ-ment relationships.

4.5.3 The central role of fairness in employment

Given the inherently relational nature of most employment relationships (discussed earlier), relational contract theory provides further theoretical support for the importance of fairness and justice concerns in the employment relationship. While fairness was essentially a non-concern in classical contract law, relational contract theory posits that good faith, reciprocity, and other fairness concerns are core obligations in relational contracting (such as employment), and that it is essential for those core obligations to be met if relational contracting is to be successfully main-tained. The reading of Macneil's original works by justice researchers may lead to new insights regarding the roles of justice and fairness in employment relationships.

4.5.4 The potential limits of "promise" in conceptualizing the psychological contract construct

This chapter's discussion of the transactional–relational continuum and the broader theory of relational contract (Macneil 1980) in which it is embedded draws attention to, and has implications for, an ongoing issue in the psychological contract literature. While there is broad agreement that at a general level the employee psychological contract construct refers to beliefs about the terms of exchange between employees and employers (e.g. Argyris 1960; Schein 1980; Rousseau 1995), in defining, opera-tionalizing, and discussing the construct, different researchers focus on theoretically distinguishable beliefs. Most notably, with varying degrees of clarity, some researchers appear to focus on expectations (e.g. Kotter 1973; Farmer and Fedor 1999), others on obligations (e.g. Coyle-Shapiro and Kessler 2000; King 2000), and other researchers on promises or promise-based obligations (e.g. Rousseau and Tijoriwala 1999; Guest and Conway 2002). As indicated earlier, relational contract theory explicitly addresses the role of promises in contracting. In this section, the usefulness of focusing on promises in understanding contracting behavior is further expounded upon and linked to the psychological contract literature.

Macneil introduced the relational contract concept to address limitations in traditional contract scholarship, including its over-reliance on promise as the basis of contracts (Macneil 1978, 1980). He sought to draw attention to actual contracting behavior, which, he argued, did not limit obligations to those based on promises. Macneil has repeatedly expressed his strongly held view that a promise framework, or an analysis based on promise, inhibits our ability to understand contracting behavior. For example, after describing how the focus on contract law instead of contract behavior inhibits our ability to understand contract, Macneil goes on to state: "But an even more serious hindrance to understanding is the limitation of contract to 'promise or a set of promises'" (Macneil 1980: 5). He has also stated that promise-centered theories of contract "virtually guarantees that we will not understand highly relational contract behavior" (Macneil 1985: 508), and that our knowledge of relational contracting "is hindered in part by immense intellectual barriers we put in the way of its acquisition, *particularly those created by our addiction to promise*" (Macneil 1985: 525, emphasis added). Bluntly stated, relational contract theory involves a clear rejection of a promise framework for understanding contracting behavior.

The lack of attention to the broader theory of relational contract has resulted in a situation that might be described as ironic. Macneil, a lawyer writing in the legal literature, was trying to influence contract law to overcome its "addiction to promise" and give greater recognition to the obligations created by contracting relations. However, when his work was imported into the OB-management literature (a behavioral science literature), classical contract law's emphasis on the promissory nature of contracts was reintroduced. Arguably, the application of Macneil's relational contract concept to a promise-centered conceptualization of psychological contracts involves the use of a concept (relational contract) to describe its antithesis (a promise-centered conceptualization of contract).

There is no question that promises are a basis for exchange obligations, and have a role to play in explaining contracting behavior—legal or psychological.[5] The question is, "Should there be an exclusive focus on promises or promise-based obligations in defining the psychological contract construct?" Based on the reasoning provided by Macneil, a focus on promise would seem to be too limited, and prove to be deficient in terms of adequately capturing the psychological phenomenon most researchers seem to be interested in when they discuss "psychological contracts."

Perhaps it is possible to rebut Macneil's argument regarding the limitations of a promise focus, and support the use of promise as the focal belief in the psychological contract construct. However, based on my review, to date, no such rebuttal arguments have been offered in the literature. Rather, it appears that the focus on promises in conceptualizing the psychological contract construct is primarily supported by reference to classical contract law notions of what constitutes a legal contract (i.e. the argument that "legal contracts involve promises, therefore psychological contracts should focus on promises"). There is a need for researchers to give much greater attention to defining the psychological contract, and providing support for the definition that they adopt. If competing definitions persist, as appears likely, there will be a need for empirical research assessing which approach to defining and operationalizing the psychological contract construct is most consistent with widely agreed upon links in the construct's nomological network.

4.5.5 The opportunity for employment relationship researchers to contribute to legal scholarship

Relational contract theory and other postmodern theories incorporate principles from the behavioral sciences, but their writing remains very propositional. For example, the theory identifies a number of characteristics said to be associated with relational exchange (discussed earlier) but little attempt has been made to investigate the extent to which those characteristics cluster and are found together in actual exchange relations. Also, it is argued that reducing exchange obligations to writing has the effect of reducing the relational nature of an exchange relationship (Macneil 1980). To what extent, if any, does the use of written employment contracts inhibit the development or maintenance of relational exchange? Research investigating these and other relational contract theory propositions in employment settings may contribute to both the legal-contract literature and the employment relationship literature.

Notes

1. I would note that there are those who would also dispute this claim by arguing that we are currently in a period of dejuridification, consistent with growing pressure to deregulate and free up business in order to meet the competitive demands associated with globalization, and as a result, conditions for employment contracting are likely to become more favorable (Gladstone 1997).
2. Macneil's early writing about relational contract used the term "transactional contract" (Macneil 1974). In subsequent works, however, the transactional term was abandoned in favor of "discrete exchange" (Macneil 1980). At present, although Macneil and other relational contract theorists generally use the latter term, the OB-management literature typically uses the former. For the purposes of this chapter, the term "transactional" can be equated with "discrete" and used interchangeably. In an attempt to distinguish his theory from theories incorporating relational language and/or principles (e.g. Williamson 1993), Macneil (2000) suggested a new title, "essential contract theory." This title has not, as of yet, caught on in the literature. Therefore, to avoid potential confusion, this chapter will continue to refer to the theory reflected in Macneil's work (e.g. Macneil 1980, 1985, 2000) as "relational contract theory."
3. In recognition of the non-existence of purely discrete exchange, Macneil renamed the discrete pole of his exchange continuum "as if discrete" (Macneil 2000).

4. Macneil has described the body of American workplace regulations (e.g. anti-discrimination law, workmen's compensation, safety regulations) as exemplifying "relational contract law" (Macneil 2000: 897).
5. While Macneil rejects the promise framework, he still recognizes the obvious role that promises play in contracting behavior. But Macneil argues that promise is the essence of *discrete* contracting behavior, and that the more that a relationship relies on promise, the more discrete it is (Macneil 1983: 360). Thus, a conceptualization of psychological contracts that is framed in promise focuses on the discrete aspects of contracting behavior.

References

Argyris, C. (1960). *Understanding Organizational Behavior.* Homewood, IL: Dorsey Press.

Armour, M. N. (1994). "A nursing home's faith duty to care: Redefining a fragile relationship using the law of contract". *Saint Louis University Law Review*, 39: 217–83.

Bakaly, C. G., and Grossman, J. M. (1995). *The Modern Law of Employment Relationships.* New York: Aspen.

Barnett, R. E. (1992). "Conflicting visions: A critique of Ian Macneil's relational theory of contract". *Virginia Law Review*, 78: 1175–206.

Blackstone, W. (1765). *Commentaries on the Laws of England,* London: Thomas Tegg.

Browne, J. (1997). "The juridification of the employment relationship: Implications and issues," in F. Meenan (ed.), *Legal Perspectives—The Juridification of the Employment Relationship* (Dublin: Oak Tree Press), pp. 23–36.

Carlson, R. R. (2001). "Why the law still can't tell an employee when it sees one and how it ought stop trying". *Berkeley Journal of Employment and Labor Law*, 22: 295–368.

Commons, J. R. (1924). *Legal Foundations of Capitalism.* New York: Macmillan.

Corbett, W. R. (2001). "Waiting for the labor law of the twenty-first century: Everything old is new again". *Berkeley Journal of Employment and Labor Law*, 23: 259–306.

Coyle-Shapiro, J., and Kessler, I. (2000). "Consequences of the psychological contract for the employment relationship: A large scale survey". *Journal of Management Studies*, 37(7): 903–30.

Dwyer, F. R., Schurr, P. H., and Oh, S. (1987). "Developing buyer-seller relationships". *Journal of Marketing*, 52: 11–27.

Eisenberg, M. A. (2000). "Why there is not law of relational contracts". *Northwestern University Law Review*, vol. 94: 805–21.

Farmer, S. M., and Fedor, D. B. (1999). "Volunteer participation and withdrawal: A psychological contract perspective on the role of expectations and support". *Nonprofit Management and Leadership*, 9(4): 349–67.

Feinman, J. M. (2000). "Relational contract theory in context". *Northwestern Law Review*, 94: 737–48.

Fox, A. (1974). *Beyond Contract: Work, Power, and Trust Relations.* London: Faber.

Freedman, W. (1989). *The employment contract.* Westport, CT: Quorum Books.

Gladstone, A. (1997). "Legal perspectives—the juridification of the employment relationship," in F. Meenan (ed.), *Legal Perspectives—The Juridification of the Employment Relationship* (Dublin: Oak Tree Press).

Goetz, C. J., and Scott, R. E. (1981). "Principles of relational contracts". *Virginia Law Review*, 67: 1089–150.

Gouldner, A. W. (1960). "The norm of reciprocity: A preliminary statement". *American Sociological Review*, 25: 161–78.

Guest, D. E., and Conway, N. (2002). "Communicating the psychological contract: An employer perspective". *Human Resource Management Journal*, 12(2): 22–38.

Haines, B. W. (1989). "English labour law and separation from contract". *Journal of Legal History,* 1: 262–96.

Hall, T. H., and Moss, J. E. (1998). "The new protean career contract: Helping organizations and employees adapt". *Organizational Dynamics,* 26(3): 22–38.

Hendry, C., and Jenkins, R. (1997). "Psychological contracts and new deals". *Human Resource Management Journal,* 7(1): 38–45.

Herriot, P., and Pemberton, C. (1996). "Contracting careers". *Human Relations,* 49(6): 757–91.

Hillman, R. A. (1997). *The Richness of Contract: An Analysis and Critique of Contemporary Theories of Contract Law,* Dordrecht: Kluwer Academic Publishers.

Honeyball, S. (1989). "Employment law and the primacy of contract". *Modern Law Review,* 228: 97–108.

Kaufman, P. J., and Stern, L. W. (1988). "Relational exchange norms, perceptions of unfairness, and retained hostility in commercial litigation". *Journal of Conflict Resolution,* 32: 534–52.

Keller, W. L. (1997). *International Labor and Employment Laws,* Vol. 1. Washington, DC: BNA Books.

King, J. E. (2000). "White-collar reactions to job insecurity and the role of the psychological contract: Implications for human resource management". *Human Resource Management,* 39(1): 79–92.

Knapp, C. L. (2002). "Taking contracts private: The quiet revolution of contract law". *Fordham Law Review,* 71: 761–98.

Kotter, J. P. (1973). "The psychological contract: Managing the joining up process". *California Management Review,* 15: 91–9.

Levinson, H., Price, C., Munden, K., Mandl, H., and Solley, C. (1962). *Men, Management, and Mental Health.* Cambridge, MA: Harvard University Press.

Macneil, I. R. (1974). "The many futures of contracts". *Southern California Law Review,* 47: 691–816.

——(1978). "Contracts: Adjustment of long-term economic relations under classical, neo-classical, and relational contract law". *Northwestern Law Review,* 72: 854–905.

——(1980). *The New Social Contract: An Inquiry into Modern Contractual Relations.* New Haven: Yale University Press.

——(1983). "Values in contract: Internal and external". *Northwestern Law Review,* 78: 340–418.

——(1985). "Relational contract: What we do and do not know". *Wisconsin Law Review,* 483–525.

——(1986). "Contract in China: Law, practice, and dispute resolution". *Stanford Law Review,* 38: 303–97.

——(1987). "Relational contract theory as sociology: A reply to professors Lindenberg and de Vos". *Journal of Institutional and Theoretical Economics,* 143: 272–90.

——(2000). "Relational contract theory: Challenges and queries". *Northwestern Law Review,* 94: 877–907.

Nelson, D. L., Quick, J. C., and Joplin, J. R. W. (1991). "Psychological contracting and newcomer socialization: An attachment theory foundation". *Journal of Social Behavior and Personality,* 6: 55–72.

Provan, K. G., and Gassenheimer, J. B. (1994). "Supplier commitment in relational contract exchanges: A study of interorganizational dependence and exercised power". *Journal of Management Studies,* 31: 55–68.

Rousseau, D. M. (1989). "Psychological and implied contracts in organizations". *Employee Responsibilities and Rights Journal,* 2: 121–39.

——(1990). "New hire perceptions of their own and employer's obligations: A study of psychological contracts". *Journal of Organizational Behavior,* 11: 389–400.

—— (1995). *Psychological Contracts in Organizations: Understanding Written and Unwritten Agreements*. Thousand Oaks, CA: Sage.

—— (1998). "The 'problem' of the psychological contract considered". *Journal of Organizational Behavior*, 19: 665–71.

Rousseau, D. M., and Tijoriwala, S. A. (1999). "What"s a good reason to change? Motivated reasoning and social accounts in promoting organizational change". *Journal of Applied Psychology*, 84(4): 514–28.

—— and Wade-Benzoni, K. A. (1994). "Linking strategy and human resource practices: How employee and customer contracts are created". *Human Resource Management*, 33: 463–89.

Schein, E. H. (1980). *Organizational Psychology*. Engelwood Cliffs, NJ: Prentice Hall.

Sparrow, P. R. (1996). "Transitions in the psychological contract: Some evidence from the banking sector". *Human Resource Management Journal*, 6(4): 75–93.

Spiedel, R. E. (2000). "The characteristics and challenges of relational contracts". *Northwestern University Law Review*, 94: 823–46.

Whitford, W. C. (1985). "Ian Macneil's contribution to contracts scholarship". *Wisconsin Law Review*, 545–60.

Williamson, O. E. (1993). "Opportunism and its critics". *Managerial and Decision Economics*, 14(2): 97–108.

5

The Economic Dimension of the Employment Relationship

RICHARD N. BLOCK, PETER BERG, AND DALE BELMAN

5.1 Introduction

At its most basic level, the employment relationship is a matter of economics. Individuals offer their skills and abilities to an employer for a price. Economic considerations, such as wages, salaries, and levels of benefits, are major factors in individual and firm decisions to establish the employment relationship. Economic forces and markets also exert a strong influence on the employment relationship, once established. The vast majority of private employers operate in market environments and many are subject to competition that is global in scale. Even public employers are indirectly subject to market forces to the extent that these determine levels of government funding.

Neoclassical economics provides the dominant theoretical approach to understanding the employment relationship as an economic transaction. This theory stresses that individuals and firms make, respectively, utility-maximizing and profit-maximizing choices based on market-determined prices that they cannot influence. In a perfectly competitive environment, the choices they make lead to optimal outcomes for individuals, firms, and society as a whole.

Whereas economic theory provides a tool to understand the employment relationship, the extent to which societies allow market forces to determine or dominate the nature of the employment relationship is a public policy decision reflected in the laws that govern employment and labor relations. Some countries, such as the United States, have strongly based their public policy toward labor and employment on neoclassical economic theory and assumptions of competitive labor markets. Other countries, most notably those in the European Union, have regulated the employment relationship with greater recognition of imperfect competition in the labor market; the European Union has been much more willing than the United States to provide employees with specific legal rights in the employment relationship (Block et al. 2003).

This chapter examines the economic dimension of the employment relationship on three levels. First, we discuss how economic theory describes the employment relationship. Second, we examine how economic theory is used to create social and legal structures that define the employment relationship, using the United States and

the European Union as case examples. Third, we consider how these differing social
and legal structures based on assumptions of economic theory manifest themselves
in structuring employment at the firm level.

5.2 The economic foundations of the employment relationship

The neoclassical economic theory of the firm and consumer behavior provides an integrated explanation of the employment relationship as a set of transactions that opti-
mize individual and social welfare.[1] First fully synthesized by Marshall (1891), it
premises that economic actors rationally seek their own best ends: Firms maximize
profits and employees/consumers select their best possible bundle of commodities
(including leisure) given their endowments (employee's skills and abilities) and tastes.
Given a competitive market in which: (a) consumers choose "rationally" and freely;
(b) consumer satisfaction increases with consumption; (c) firms' production technologies are not everywhere characterized by economies of scale and are well known;
and (d) consumers and firms are mobile and informed about their markets, price competition is efficient, and provides the goods, services, and leisure most valued by society.
This model is general enough to incorporate diverse dimensions of the employment
relationship including safety and health, life cycle decisions, and non-standard work,
and the evaluation of alternative labor market policies. Within economic theory, the
employment relationship may be viewed from the perspective of employee decisions
about work and employment (labor supply), the firm's hiring decisions (labor demand),
and finally the integration of the supply and demand sides of a market, as well as
conditions that cause competitive markets to produce undesirable outcomes.

5.2.1 The labor supply decision

Individuals' decisions about work are a consequence of decisions about consumption. Individuals are seen as optimizing their well-being (utility) through consuming
goods and leisure subject to constraints on their income and time and market prices
inclusive of their wage rate. Utility increases with the consumption of goods and
leisure. In the economic model, work does not of itself create utility; rather, it is a
means of earning income that permits individuals (employees) to purchase utility-
creating goods and leisure. This view that consumption, rather than work, creates
well-being shapes public policy in countries such as the United States, where the
desires of consumers for low prices are favored over the desires of workers for high
wages and legal rights.

The relationship between work and utility is formalized in theory through
constraints on individuals' expenditures and time. Consumption purchases cannot
exceed individuals' earnings from working at their going wage and non-labor
income. As time is finite over the model's decision period, leisure time is limited by
individuals' decisions about consumption and, in turn, about working time. While
leisure does not have a price in the market (e.g. it cannot be formally purchased),

its implicit price is the wage rate—the income foregone by taking leisure. Based on their tastes and preferences, employees then chose their optimal (utility maximizing) combination of leisure and consumption, given the wage available to them in the market and their non-labor income.[2]

Wages play a central role in employee decisions about labor market participation and working time. Higher wages increase labor market participation, but their effect on working time is ambiguous. Increased wages motivate individuals both to reduce leisure time (as its implicit cost is higher) and increase leisure (as higher incomes induce increased consumption of most goods). Although the effect of wages on individual work time is ambiguous, higher wages draw additional workers into a market and result in a positive relationship between the wage and labor supply at the level of the market. Decisions about labor supply are influenced not only by wages in the individual's current labor market, but wages in related labor markets in which individuals might reasonably obtain employment, as well as the prices of goods and services individuals wish to purchase.

5.2.2 *The labor demand side*

Although firms may, for a time, pursue ends such as maximizing market share, economic theory stylizes firms as maximizing profits, the difference between revenue and costs, in the long term. Inputs, including labor, are available to the firm at the market price and the firm, facing these prices and the technical relationship between inputs and outputs (the production function), selects the set of inputs that provide the greatest return. While the firm's problem differs somewhat in the short and long terms, the fundamental rule for profit maximization is that use of an input is increased to the point at which the increment to revenue (the product of the increment to output and the price of output) from an additional unit of that input is equal to its unit cost. Most production processes are characterized by diminishing returns, the increment to output is positive but declines as additional units of a particular input are applied. This produces a negative relationship between the price of an output and the amount demanded by a firm, the downward-sloping labor demand curve of the firm. As the rule on unit costs is applied to all inputs, marginal output per dollar spent is equalized across inputs and the use of inputs is affected by (a) its incremental productivity and price, (b) the incremental productivity and price of other inputs, and (c) the price of output.

One's employability depends on the wage one is willing to work at and whether one possesses the skills and abilities to be considered an acceptable productive input. However, the firm's demand for a particular type of labor is affected not only by its own price (the wage) or quality, but also by the price of other types of labor as well as the prices of other inputs. Market driven shifts in these prices will cause the firm to adjust its use of inputs, including labor. As suggested by Marshall, labor demand is more sensitive to changes in its own wage when (a) consumer demand is sensitive to changes in the price of output, (b) when other inputs can readily be substituted for labor in the production process, and (c) when the prices of other factors are not sensitive to increased demand for those factors.[3]

5.2.3 *The interaction of supply and demand in the labor market*

The market wage for a particular type of labor is determined in the labor market through the interaction of the labor supply and demand. The interaction of firms and workers through the market moves supply and demand toward equality and establishes a market clearing—equilibrium—wage. Suppose that the market wage is above the level that equates supply and demand. At this wage, more labor is offered than firms are willing to hire. Some of those who are not employed may offer their work for less than the market wage. The lower wage increases the demand for labor by firms (since demand rises with declines in the wage), and reduces supply as individuals withdraw from the market. As the wage falls, unemployment is reduced by continued absorption and withdrawal of workers until there are no additional workers who are willing but unable to find work at the going wage. Supply and demand are restored to equality and the downward adjustment of the wage ends. This process explains why increased competition from low wage labor can cause downward pressure on wages and force people out of the labor market. Achieving equilibrium in the labor market is a dynamic process that can alter the employment relationship and often change the conditions of employment.

From a theory perspective, there is no unmet demand for labor and no involuntary unemployment at the point of market equilibrium. All the labor that is willing to work at the going wage is employed; firms' demand for labor is exactly met. The market may be moved off this equilibrium, which in a world of change is no more than a tendency, by shifts in output prices or the prices of non-labor inputs, by changes in technology, by changes in consumer tastes, or by government policy. Such changes will initially result in an imbalance between supply and demand but adjustments in the market wage moves the market to a new equilibrium. Prices, in this case the wage, play the central role in conveying information about market conditions and initiating actions by firms and individuals that restore equilibrium. They are the medium through which society signals economic actors how to reallocate resources to adjust to changes in technology, in tastes, or to conditions in other markets.

5.2.4 *Market transactions and social welfare*

Neoclassical economic theory does not just claim that this is a *good* way to organize the workplace. Rather, it maintains that under perfect competition the optimizing decisions of market participants produce the *best* possible outcomes for both individuals and society. As such, government or other intervention in properly functioning markets is unlikely to improve individual or social welfare. Suppose that government desires to increase employees' earnings and intervenes by establishing a "minimum wage" above the competitive wage. Although some employees realize an improvement in their incomes and labor income on aggregate may rise, for society as a whole the gain is illusory. Most of the gain to labor comes from redistribution of income from other productive inputs, but the higher wage also reduces employment as employers substitute other inputs for the more expensive labor and consumers respond to higher production prices by reducing consumption. And while producers affected by the minimum wage use too much capital, energy, and other inputs relative to society's endowment, the labor released from that production is underutilized, being either unemployed or employed in an unregulated sector at a lower wage. In sum, a minimum wage raises costs, reduces output, and results in a smaller and less desirable set of consumption goods than was previously available. Society would be better off with an unregulated regime, in this case a regime without a minimum wage.

Regulation may also be objectionable because it prevents employees from arranging their leisure, consumption, and conditions of work to best fit their desires. Presumably, employees in a competitive market can choose suitable work and hours to fit their needs and wants. Those who desire shorter hours, safer conditions, or greater security from dismissal are at liberty to find employers who offer such employment packages. Others, less desirous of these conditions, can seek employment contracts that address their particular wants. By limiting freedom of contract, laws that regulate the conditions of labor preclude at least some employees from establishing their desired balance of consumption but do not improve the consumption of other employees (who have previously attained the now regulated conditions through individual bargaining).

5.2.5 Market failures

The conclusion, that markets produce socially desirable outcomes, is only assured where markets are reasonably competitive: Firms and individuals are price takers and prices are determined by the interaction of market supply and demand. Such outcomes may not be obtained where there are market imperfections: Where there is monopoly or monopsony (one buyer) in the labor market, when information about markets is incomplete, where participants are immobile, or where participants decisions do not allow for the effect of those decisions on others.

In the presence of market imperfections, prices no longer provide the appropriate signals to individuals or firms or these parties are unable to respond to those signals. For example, when there are monopsonies or oligopsonies, few buyers in the labor market, those buyers will maximize their profits by setting a wage below the competitive wage and employing too little labor. Labor will be misallocated across markets relative to the socially optimal allocation—away from its best use.

Competitive markets will also not produce individually or socially optimal outcomes if the information available to firms and individuals is incomplete or if labor is immobile. The efficient functioning of the market system requires that relevant information about markets be conveyed by price signals and that individuals and firms are able to respond. The wages paid by firms and industries reflect both worker productivity and working conditions. If workers value better working conditions and are aware of the conditions which are offered by firms, firms which offer substandard conditions will have to pay a premium, a compensating differential, to recruit sufficient numbers of employees. This compensates workers for the poor conditions, protects the profitability of firms that offer better conditions, and provides an incentive for improving conditions. When information is lacking on working conditions, workers cannot signal their preferences for better conditions and there is no incentive for employers to provide the conditions which workers desire (and are willing to pay for in a reduced wage). This problem is most acute where dangers are not readily apparent, as is often the case with occupational illness.

Market processes will also fail to produce socially optimal outcomes where individual decisions affect the utility of others, such as when a large employer moves a manufacturing facility from a small- or medium-sized city. In such instances, individuals' decisions will be based on their individual gains and losses and will not account for the wider consequences of their decisions, such as the loss of jobs in firms that depend on the existence of the facility. Wages and prices will not reflect the social dimension of decisions and, as a consequence, market adjustments will then reflect individual rather than social gains or costs.

5.2.6 Implications of the neoclassical model for labor market policy

The neoclassical economic theory carries clear prescriptions for labor market policy. If one believes that that markets are fundamentally competitive, social welfare is best served by policies that lessen market imperfections and remove barriers to competition. Efforts to improve the functioning of markets through regulatory policies which affect the price mechanism may be intended to achieve desired social ends, but they inevitably carry the cost of reducing economic efficiency. These strong conclusions are modified if one believes that market imperfections are pervasive and not readily overcome, or that markets do not appropriately value social and non-economic outcomes. Under such conditions, there is additional latitude for improving social welfare and economic conditions through restructuring and regulation without negative effects on efficiency.

Economic theory's most powerful insights into the employment relationship may, however, come not from attending to the implications for optimality and social welfare, but rather from its focus on the operation of markets and their consequences. Firms and individuals operate across a multiplicity of markets. The logic of markets compels actors to be, to a great degree, economically rational if they are to survive and prosper. There are many different approaches to the employment relationship within firms, but those approaches must permit firms to compete effectively in their markets. Nations are in a somewhat different position as they have been better able to structure national markets and impose barriers to international markets in the interests of national goals. Even national systems may, however, provide less shelter from market pressures in the future as changes in transportation, communication, and the international trading system expose ever larger segments of each nation's economy to world markets.

5.3 Norms, societal beliefs, laws, and legal doctrine

In Section 5.2, we discussed the economic principles underlying employment. The extent to which these economic principles form the basis for organizing and defining the terms of the employment relationship vary across countries.

We use the United States and the European Union as benchmarks for comparison. Although the United States and the European Union are both western capitalist economies, we contend that the United States and Europe represent fundamentally different concepts of the employment relationship and these different concepts account for the observed differences between the United States and the European Union with respect to the legislated labor standards (Block et al. 2003).[4] The employment relationship in the United States is much more influenced and shaped by neoclassical economic thought than the employment relationship in Europe. These different concepts can be illustrated in differing societal beliefs in four areas: (a) the importance of individual rights; (b) the principle of the corporation as a legal individual; (c) the importance of property and property rights; and (d) views regarding the appropriateness of government regulation of markets, including the labor market. This part of the chapter will explore these beliefs in the United States and Europe.[5]

5.3.1 Societal beliefs and assumptions

Individual rights and employment

The United States. Attempting to understand the social order in the United States, five sociologists noted that "individualism lies at the very core of American culture" (Bellah et al. 1985: 142). Lipset has observed that the "the American creed can be subsumed in four words: Antistatism, individualism, populism, and egalitarianism" and that its "institutions reflect the effort to apply universalisitc principles emphasizing competitive individualism and egalitarianism" (Lipset 1989: 26).

There are two employment-related implications that flow from the belief in individualism. The first is the assumption that the "normal" default employment relationship is individual rather than collective (Block 1990). Consistent with the neoclassical model, the employment relationship is presumed to be a relationship between two individuals in a competitive labor market, with the employee maximizing utility and the employer maximizing profit. Neither can be forced into establishing or continuing a relationship as to do so will require an individual employee or employer to agree to enter into a relationship or to accept terms and conditions of employment that will not maximize utility or profit, resulting in an outcome that is both inconsistent with individual rights and is associated with a misallocation of resources.

The second major implication revolves around views of individuals acting collectively and the freedom of association. There is a tension between the political principle of freedom of association and the economic principle of efficient labor markets as seen through the lens of neoclassical economic theory. While freedom of association is valued, the neoclassical theory of the employment relationship, postulating a competitive labor market with individual employers and workers, each of whom has no influence on the price of labor, suggests that permitting workers to associate for purposes of collective bargaining has the potential to create inefficient suboptimal outcomes by giving workers monopoly power to influence wages, the price of labor.

In the United States, this tension is resolved by incorporating within the freedom to associate the freedom not to associate if one so desires, thereby addressing the neoclassical economic problem of suboptimal markets. By permitting employees to refuse to engage in collective activity and to act individually in the labor market, individuals/employees whose utility is maximized by accepting the (assumed market optimal) wage offered by the employer may do so, contrary to the wishes of those in the collectivity who chose to associate. Employees have the fundamental right to act as utility-maximizing individuals, and the collectivity may not impair that right.[6]

Europe: Unlike the United States, the European Union does not place a high value on individualism in the labor market. In Europe, unionism and collectivization of the employment relationship is considered a legitimate way and is often the dominant way of determining terms and conditions of employment. In many European countries, union density is greater than 50 percent of the labor force and workers covered under labor union contracts exceed 80 percent. Unions in Europe are afforded status such that individual employees are required to subsume their individual interests to the interests of collectivities to a much greater extent than in the United States. Indeed, unions are recognized as legitimate representatives of employees in the Treaty of Amsterdam and are given explicit roles in European Union policy-making (Treaty of Amsterdam 1997; Szyszczak 1999). In addition, labor unions in some European countries serve quasi-public roles. For example, in Sweden and Belgium labor unions manage the unemployment insurance system (Visser 1996: 191).

The European system of labor relations assumes a basic economic model of the labor market that is at variance with the U.S. model. The European model assumes that the normal labor market situation is not competitive. Rather, employers have substantial market power to maintain wages below competitive market rates. By establishing labor unions as the normal representative of the employees, countervailing power is established in the labor market. If union power offsets employer power, the assumption is that wages and terms and conditions of employment close to those that would emerge from a competitive market will be agreed upon.

The individuality of the corporation

The United States: As law in the United States has evolved, corporations are legal individuals. With the exception of the right to vote, corporations have the same rights as persons. Corporations may make contracts, buy and sell assets, hire and terminate employees, and engage in some political activity, such as contributions to candidates and speaking out on issues. This individuality makes corporations equivalent to employees in the eyes of the law. Although corporations are, technically, nothing more than collectivities of shareholders who combine their assets, their individuality supports the assumption that their size does not distort the labor market when they participate as employers. Thus, the neoclassical presumption of competitive markets can be applied, as the corporation's individuality supports a presumption that both employer and employee have no influence on the price of labor.

Europe: In Europe, there is a much greater willingness than in the United States to recognize corporations for what they are, businesses that are large collectivities of shareholders with substantial market power, the existence of which may be inconsistent with the price-taker assumptions of the neoclassical model. While their size gives corporations the opportunity to realize economies of scale and efficiencies in production, this size can also provide corporations with monopsony or oligopsony power in the labor market, leading to suboptimal outcomes. With less willingness to accept the notion of the corporation as a person, there is more willingness on the part of the European Union to recognize differences between employees, on the one hand, and corporations as employers on the other. Thus, at least with respect to the labor market, European law requires corporations to deal with unions as a countervailing force. In other words, the European Union does not assume that legal individuality necessarily implies economic individuality. European law does not assume equality between the corporation and the individual employee; it assumes inequality. Equality is obtained through forcing employers to deal with unions.

The importance of private property

United States: A third important value in the United States is the high status given to private property (Kaufman 1997). The importance of private property was noted by Perlman (1966) (orig. pub. 1928). Comparing the labor movement in the United States with the labor movements in other countries, Perlman observed that the distinctive characteristic of the U.S. labor movement was an inability to stay organized for "want of inner cohesiveness." A major reason for this lack of solidarity, according to Perlman, was the strength of the institution of private property. Perlman observed that the labor movement was, fundamentally, an infringement on the right of the employer to use its property as the employer saw fit. Whether this infringement was by economic or legislative means, it was viewed as an infringement and would be resisted (Perlman 1966, orig. ed. 1928).

In the United States, more recent writing on this issue noted that legal doctrine has established beyond question the principle of deference to employers and their property. Atleson cites as examples cases in which the public nature of privately owned shopping malls were at issue (Atleson 1983: 91–6, Lloyd Corp).

The high status given to property rights permits employers to resist expansions of employee rights by claiming that granting employees such rights would not only be economically inefficient (as employers are presumed to maximize profits and efficiency in competitive markets), but also a violation of the employer's property rights. Thus, as will be discussed below, property rights is the basis for giving U.S. employers wide latitude to resist union organizing at the place of employment, and is likely the reason why there is no mandated employee participation in firms.

Finally, a key corollary of the right of private property is full freedom of contract. This, in essence, is the right of an individual to dispose of or do with his or her property as he or she sees fit.[7] By minimizing the constraints on private property, employers are assured of the authority to allocate productive inputs, capital, and labor in manner that they see fit, and that, presumably, maximizes their profits. In the neoclassical model, such profit maximization contributes to the efficient and optimal allocation of resources.

Europe: In contrast to the United States, there is a willingness in the European Union to place constraints on the business use of private property. Because corporations are not seen as economic individuals, and because there is no presumption that the exercise of private property rights by a corporation will necessarily lead to the most efficient allocation of resources, the private property rights of corporations in Europe are more circumscribed than they are in the United States. Thus, statutes have recognized the role of employees as legitimate stakeholders in the firm and given them rights of participation in a variety of decisions. Works council legislation in Germany, France, the Netherlands, and Sweden among other countries provides employees with rights to information, consultation, and co-decision. In Germany, works councils possess rights of co-determination over social policy issues such as payment methods, work schedules, recruitment, promotions, and dismissals. Information and consultation rights apply to issues of personnel planning, work organization, new technology, and job content. In addition, works councils have the right to information on company financial and economic matters and must be informed in good time about planned changes that may disadvantage workers (Visser and Van Ruysseveldt 1996). The European Union now requires large firms that wish to incorporate in more than one EU country to create employee consultation systems (European Union, Council Directive 2001/86/EC).

In addition, the European Union provides substantial protection to employees in the event of an ownership change in a firm. The European Union requires that the successor employer honor the employment "contract," the basic terms and conditions of employment provided to the employees by the predecessor. EU employees are protected from dismissal due solely to the change in ownership, and are entitled to information and consultation with their representatives. If there is a collective agreement in place, it must be honored (Blainpain 1999). Works council legislation and EU directives on transfer of ownership significantly challenge managerial prerogative and the supremacy of property owners in the employment relationship.

Skepticism regarding government intervention

United States: The three beliefs discussed above feed quite logically into a fourth belief that is found in the United States: A skepticism regarding government intervention in markets in general, and therefore, in the labor market (Block 1992). Given the U.S. assumption that markets are generally competitive and function best if parties are left to maximize utility and profits on their own, government intervention would simply impair the otherwise efficient functioning of the market. This skepticism does not mean that there is no government regulation of markets in the United States. It does mean, however, that the burden of proof is always on those advocating government intervention to demonstrate that markets, left to their own devices, have failed or have produced undesirable outcomes. Additionally, the existence of government intervention in markets is constantly being re-evaluated, with the costs and benefits of regulation under persistent scrutiny (Schwab 1997). Merely because government intervention exists does not mean it must always exist, as indicated by the movements to deregulate the airlines, trucking, and telecommunications industries in the 1970s and 1980s (Block and McLennan 1985; Keefe and Boroff 1994).

Europe: Because the European Union is less concerned about individualism than in the United States, it is less willing to see the corporation as an individual, has less concern about the rights of corporations to exercise property rights, and is less willing to see markets as competitive, the European Union is far more willing than the United States to place governmental constraints on the employment relationship. Thus, as noted, the European Union regulates the employment relationship to a much greater extent than does the United States (Block et al. 2003).

5.3.2 Employment laws and legal doctrine

Legal doctrine regulating employment is a useful barometer of a society's norms and values vis-à-vis the employment relationship. It is reasonable to believe that, in a democracy, laws and legal doctrine reflect, albeit in a rough way, the values of the populace that elects the lawmakers.

Europe and the United States have different approaches to protecting workers. In Europe, worker protection is a component of human rights (Harris and Darcy 2001; Samuel 2002). Thus, the European Union directives prohibiting discrimination in employment on the basis of sex, race, religion, age, disability, or sexual orientation[9] are grounded on constitution-like documents, including the Treaty on European Union[10] and the Treaty Establishing the European Community.[11] They are also part of the broader principle of social inclusion that is central to the European Union.[12]

Freedom of association is also so established. The Charter of Fundamental Social Rights makes freedom of worker association and the right to join unions a fundamental EU right.[13] The Treaty of Amsterdam formally incorporates unions, along with management, into the policy-making process of the European Commission by requiring the Commission to consult with representatives of labor and management on matters of social policy (Treaty of Amsterdam 1997; Szyszczak 1999). Moreover, a large number of European countries have established corporate systems in which a high-level labor organization represents workers in national-level negotiations with employers and the state (Turner 2002). This demonstrates that collective worker representation is not only constitutionally protected in the European Union, but may be seen as the preferred method of establishing terms and conditions of employment. Employees are believed to be best off if they subordinate their individual interests to the worker collectivity.

In the United States, on the other hand, legal employment protection has no constitutional basis, nor is it anchored in concepts of human rights (Adams 2002; Gross 2002); it is created through statute. This characteristic makes employee rights in the United States subject not only to legislative changes, but also to judicial interpretations influenced by the attitudes, values, and views of judges. This section of the chapter will explore the relationship between U.S. social norms discussed above and employment legislation in two important areas: Anti-discrimination laws and laws governing collective bargaining.

Anti-discrimination laws

Since 1964, the United States, at both the federal and state levels, has enacted numerous laws that prohibit employment discrimination based on the personal characteristics of individuals. These characteristics include race, national origin, religion, gender, age, and disability. The rationale for these laws was that individuals were being prevented from obtaining employment or advancing in their current employment based on factors that were unrelated to their qualifications or expected productivity. In essence, then, these statutes may be viewed as enhancing the operation of the competitive labor market. In addition, because these laws protected individuals from discrimination, they were consistent with the value of individualism.

While they were consistent with the principle of the functioning of the market and individualism, these laws were inconsistent with the principles of private property and government non-intervention in the labor market. To say that a business could not make a hiring decision based on certain criteria was, in a sense, requiring an employer, a property owner, to permit on the owner's premises an individual whom it may not otherwise permit on the premises. Thus, anti-discrimination laws created tension between values in the United States: The importance of the market and individualism, on the one hand, and the importance of private property and governmental non-intervention in the market, on the other. These tensions would appear in the interpretations of the statutes.

U.S. law prohibiting discrimination on the basis of race and gender has evolved to give racial and religious minorities and women substantial protection (Wolkinson and Block 1996: 24–8).[14] On the other hand, the judiciary has been much less willing to impose restrictions on employers in age and disability discrimination cases. Some insight into why this has been the case can be obtained from the U.S. Supreme Court's 2000 decision in Kimel et al. v. Board of Regents et al. In that case, Kimel and others had brought suit against their respective employers, state universities in Florida, alleging violation of the Age Discrimination in Employment Act, which Congress had applied to the states. The Court ruled, however, that the provision of the law which applied to the states violated the U.S. constitution, which prevents the federal government from requiring states to subject themselves to suits from their citizens in the absence of a willingness to submit themselves to suits. The court pointed out that unlike race and gender, age was not a "suspect classification." Put differently, the Supreme Court simply did not believe that discrimination on the basis of age was of sufficient seriousness that discriminating on that basis, by a state as an employer, could not be constitutional. This was because there could, conceivably, be a link between productivity and age. The Court, therefore, found a transaction-based rationale for age-based discrimination.[15]

This case illustrates the constitution–legislative distinction between Europe and the United States. In Europe, the right to be free from discrimination in employment is incorporated in constitution-like documents. In the United States on the other hand, because the right to be free from discrimination in employment is legislative rather than constitutional, it may be limited by constitutional principles that are superior to legislation; in the case of Kimel, the dominant constitutional principle was the sovereign rights granted to individual states within the governing principles of the United States.

Discrimination on the basis of disability was addressed in Sutton v. United Airlines. There, the Supreme Court determined that job applicants with 20/200 uncorrected vision but 20/20 corrected vision who had applied for positions as airline pilots were not disabled for purposes of the ADA because their disability was corrected. In other words, a person with a corrected or mitigated disability would not be considered disabled for the purposes of the ADA, and, therefore, not entitled to protection. This was because a disability, if corrected or mitigated, did not "substantially limit" a life activity. As such, the Court had no need to determine whether the employer's requirement, a minimum of 20/100 uncorrected vision, was necessary for its business.

The dissent, on the other hand, pointed out that the legislative history of the ADA demonstrated that Congress had meant to define disability in its unmitigated or uncorrected form. More generally, the dissent stated that "I believe that, in order to be faithful to the remedial purpose of the Act, we should give it a generous, rather than a miserly, construction" (Sutton v. United Airlines).

Thus, the Supreme Court has substantially narrowed the coverage of both the age and disability discrimination statutes, consistent with the long-standing principles of property rights and minimization of government intervention in the labor market. This is most starkly revealed in *Sutton.* In that case, offered a clear choice between two fairly conflicting views, an expansive reading of "disability" and a narrow one, the Supreme Court consciously chose the narrow reading, thus favoring property rights and minimal government intervention in the labor market.

Collective bargaining and the law

Collective bargaining in the United States is governed primarily by one statute, amended on several occasions. The National Labor Relations Act (NLRA), first enacted in 1935 as the Wagner Act, provided most private sector employees,[16] except those in railroads and airlines,[17] with the right to self-organize into unions and to bargain collectively with a bargaining representative of their own choosing. Among other things, the purpose of the Wagner Act was to equalize bargaining power between employers and employees.[18]

A law encouraging collective bargaining runs generally counter to the mainstream culture of individualism in the United States. For a period of 130 years in U.S. history, from 1806 through 1935, judicial decisions had generally repressed and made illegal union activity (Lieberman 1960). The NLRA was enacted in 1935, in the midst of the Great Depression, the most serious economic crisis in the history of the United States. It is reasonable to believe that its passage was an aberration caused by unusual circumstances. That this is the case is indicated by subsequent legislative activity surrounding the NLRA. The 1947 Taft–Hartley amendments created rights of employees not to participate in organizing activity and put numerous constraints on unions. The 1958 Landrum–Griffin Act placed additional constraints on unions in collective bargaining and regulated the internal affairs of unions. Attempts to amend the NLRA to expand union rights were defeated in 1977, 1990, and 1993 (Block 1997). Only the 1974 Health Care Amendments to the NLRA, which brought non-profit private health care institutions under the coverage of the NLRA, can be seen as an exception to the post-1935 trend of narrowing the rights of unions (Block 1997).

This statutory evolution indicates the skepticism with which collective activity is viewed in the United States. While recognizing, in 1935, that there was a power imbalance between employers and individual employees and that collective action was necessary to balance that power,[19] the Congress of the United States was willing to permit individual employees to weaken the bargaining power of the collectivity through individual action and to permit employers to exercise property rights that were the source of their superiority at bargaining power. The importance of property rights and individual rights were be explored in two doctrines under U.S. labor law: Organizing, bargaining, and the rights of strikers.

With respect to bargaining, the law requires an employer to bargain collectively with the union representing its employees. Section 8(d) of the NLRA defines bargaining as "the performance of the mutual obligation of the employer and the representative of the employees to meet at reasonable times and confer in good faith with respect to wages, hours, and other terms and conditions of employment,…" (National Labor Relations Act as amended). In 1958, the U.S. Supreme Court decided that the parties were obligated to bargain only over "wages, hours, and other terms and conditions of employment" (NLRB v. Borg Warner, 356 U.S. at 349). By the same token, then, the parties were not obligated to bargain over matters not considered "wages, hours, and other terms and conditions of employment" (NLRB v. Borg Warner, 356 U.S. at 349). Thus, by the early 1960s, the question arose whether some subjects about which one party may wish to bargain might not be considered "wages, hours, and other terms and conditions of employment," thereby obviating the obligation to bargain over that issue and creating a class of management decisions that affected employment but that the employer could make unilaterally, without negotiating with the union. The issue was ultimately addressed in First National Maintenance Corp. v. NLRB in 1981.

The employer in *First National Maintenance* provided cleaning and janitorial services to various nursing homes. The First National Maintenance employees at one of the customers, Greenpark, had unionized. Because First National Maintenance and Greenpark had developed a dispute over the amount of the fee Greenpark would pay First National Maintenance, First National Maintenance informed its Greenpark employees that its contract with Greenpark would be terminated, and, in turn, they would be terminated. The union requested bargaining over the decision to terminate the contract and the employees. First National Maintenance refused and the Supreme Court found in favor of First National Maintenance noting:

...in establishing what issues must be submitted to the process of bargaining, Congress had no expectation that the elected union representative would become an equal partner in the running of the business enterprise in which the union's members are employed. Despite the deliberate open-endedness of the statutory language, there is an undeniable limit to the subjects about which bargaining must take place:

The Court went on to state:

Management must be free from the constraints of the bargaining process to the extent essential for the running of a profitable business (452 U.S. 666, 678–79).

No statute or other source was cited for this statement. In essence, the Court was asserting, consistent with the neoclassical model, that employers operating freely will cause optimal outcomes, and based on the dominant cultural assumption of property rights, an unwillingness to encroach upon a zone of property-based management rights it considered inviolate. Again, the basic assumption is that the optimal employment decisions in society are made by the employer free of regulatory labor market constraints.

Strikers and non-strikers

The greater status of individuals vis-à-vis the collectivity is illustrated in the U.S. Supreme Court decisions in Pattern Makers v. NLRB, issued in 1985, and Trans World Airlines (TWA) v. International Federation of Flight attendants, issued in 1989.

In the Pattern Makers case, the U.S. Supreme Court found it unlawful for a labor union to enforce upon its members an internal union rule that prevented them from resigning either during a strike or lockout or when a strike or lockout was imminent. The Court stated that "(b)y allowing employees to resign from a union at any time, (the law) protects the employee whose views come to diverge from those of his union. ... (the union rule) curtails this freedom to resign from full union membership" (473 U.S. 95, 107). The four justices in dissent viewed the union as a legitimate economic instrument, noting "(i)n a strike setting, therefore, "[t]he mutual reliance of his fellow members who abide by the strike for which they have all voted outweighs ... the admitted interests of the individual who resigns to return to work" (473 U.S. 95 at 130).

The TWA case grew out of a 1986 strike against TWA by the union representing its flight attendants. Under prior collective agreements, there existed at the airline a long-established system of job posting and bidding which was designed to permit the longest service senior flight attendants to fly out of the domiciles (home bases) and select the routes and schedules that they wished. The system was also designed to avoid laying off longer service employees by permitting the longer service employees whose positions were eliminated to displace shorter service employees. The result of this system was that the longest service employees had the most desirable positions available.

When the employees struck, TWA informed the union that it had decided to hire replacements for striking employees. The replacements would be assigned based on whatever vacancies (domiciles, routes, or schedules) were available on the hire date. If an employee chose to abandon the strike, he or she would also be assigned based on available vacancies. More senior crossovers, however, would not be permitted to bump less senior replacements. In addition, and more importantly, when the strike ended, the strikers would be assigned based on the available vacancies, as the Company would not permit the more senior strikers to displace the less senior replacements and any less senior crossovers. The result was that senior employees who struck lost their more desirable positions, although they continued to be employed by TWA.

The U.S. Supreme Court ruled that TWA had no legal obligation to permit the more senior strikers to displace less senior crossovers and replacements. The Court noted that the law protects "an employee's right to choose not to strike,... and, thereby, protects employees' rights to 'the benefit of their individual decisions not to strike'..." (489 U.S. 426, 436). The court then went on to observe that

(t)o distinguish crossovers from new hires in the manner (the union) proposes would have the effect of penalizing those who decided not to strike in order to benefit those who did (489 U.S. 426, 438).

The dissent pointed out what the Court was really doing was choosing to favor the crossovers, those who chose not to strike and not to engage in collective activity.

The dissent observed:

The Court... allows TWA to single out for penalty precisely those employees who were faithful to the strike until the end, in order to benefit those who abandoned it. What is unarticulated is the Court's basis for choosing one position over the other. If indeed one group or the other is to be "penalized,"... what basis does the Court have for determining that it should be those who remained on strike rather than those who returned to work? I see none, unless it is perhaps an unarticulated hostility toward strikes (489 U.S. 426, 447).

The dissent, in essence, challenged the majority to articulate the value judgment and assumptions underlying its decision, that it preferred that any losses associated with the strike be incurred by those who participated in collective action, rather than on those who declined to participate in the collective action. The majority, therefore, was protecting the right of the individual employee to abandon the group, and pursue his or her own utility-maximizing interest, even if it meant that the group would be worse off as a result. When faced with a choice that required deferring to the individual's right not to strike, or to the collective right to strike, the Court chose the former, consistent with U.S. values.

Ultimately, values derived to a large extent from the neoclassical economic model of the labor market and an assumption of competitive markets determined the outcome of the case, and, more importantly, the relative rights of the individual and the collectivity. Consistent with the neoclassical model, employees have the fundamental right to act as utility-maximizing individuals, and the collectivity may not impair that right.

5.4 Experiences at the firm level

The preceding discussion suggests that the legal and policy environment in the United States is more favorable to employers vis-à-vis employees and unions than the legal and policy environment in the European Union. At the firm level, this difference would be expected to manifest itself in greater legal requirements on companies in their firm-level employment practices in the European Union relative to the United States. In this section, we compare the experiences of EU and U.S. employees in two human resource policy areas: Paid annual leave and part-time work. These areas were chosen because they are areas in which the European Union has enacted directives, in which the United States has enacted no legislation, and in which the United States Bureau of Labor Statistics (BLS) has collected data in the United States. Thus, the minimum requirements in the European Union established by the directives can be compared with market-determined firm-level outcomes in the United States.

5.4.1 Paid annual leave

The European Union requires member countries to provide workers with at least four weeks of paid annual leave.[20] The United States has no legal requirement that any employee receive paid annual leave. Consistent with the U.S. practice, the existence and amount of paid annual leave available to employees is based on employer discretion, the market, and the provisions contained in collective bargaining agreements.

The market in the United States dictates that full-time employees receive annual leave. In 1999, 90 percent of all full-time employees in U.S. private industry received some paid annual leave (United States Bureau of Labor Statistics, undated). In 2000, that percentage was up to 91 percent (United States Bureau of Labor Statistics, undated).

Employees in the United States who receive paid annual leave receive far less than their counterparts in the European Union. As shown in Table 5.1, in the 1990s, the most recent time period for which the BLS has published data, only employees who had a tenure of twenty years in medium and large firms had paid leave at approximately the EU minimum.[21] Moreover, only about one-third of employees had ten or more years of tenure with the same employer (United States Bureau of Labor Statistics, "Percent of . . ."). As the median employer tenure for employees twenty-five years of age and over during the 1990s was between 4.7 and 5 years (United States Bureau of Labor Statistics, "Median Years . . ."), it is reasonable to conclude that the typical full-time employee in the United States in the 1990s received from 11–14 days of paid leave each year, with variation around this mean. This is more than one week less than the four-week/twenty-day minimum required in the EU.

5.4.2 Full-time and part-time workers

As part of the legal regulation of employment in the European Union, it is generally a violation of EU law for firms to discriminate against part-time employees by denying them benefits that are otherwise available to full-time employees (European Union,

Table 5.1. *Mean days of paid annual leave, by size of establishment and years of service, United States, 1990–7*

Year	1 Year of service		5 Years of service		10 Years of service		20 Years of service	
	Small	Med–large	Small	Med–large	Small	Med–large	Small	Med–large
1990	7.6		11.5		13.5		15	
1991		9.3		13.4		16.5		20.4
1992	7.6		11.5		13.5		15.1	
1993		9.4		13.6		16.6		20.4
1994	7.8		11.5		13.4		14.8	
1995		9.6		13.9		16.9		20.4
1996	7.1		11.5		13.9		15.4	
1997		9.6		13.8		16.9		20.3

Source: United States Bureau of Labor Statistics.

Council Directive 97/81/EC and *Council Directive 98/23/EC*). Such differential treatment between part-time and full-time employees is not prohibited in the United States. Table 5.2 presents data from the U.S. Bureau of Labor Statistics on the percentage of private sector employees with access to and participation in various employee benefit plans (incidence), by full- and part-time status, in 1999 and 2000, the last time these data were collected.

As can be seen, in 1999 and 2000, there was a substantial disparity in benefit access and participation between full- and part-time employees in the United States. The percentages for part-time workers represent a lower bound since some part-time employees may choose not to take benefits that are offered. However, this possibility is unlikely to close the significant difference in benefits between part- and full-time workers. With the exception of access to and participation in child care and survivor income insurance, the incidence of part-time employees in various benefit plans was always less than one-half of the incidence of full-time employees in comparable plans. Moreover, with respect to the two benefits in which incidence was equal, the full-time incidence was so low as to suggest that these benefits are rarely provided.

5.5 Summary and conclusion

This chapter examined the economic dimension of the employment relationship. The chapter first explored the basic neoclassical economic model of the employment relationship. It showed that neoclassical economic theory conceives of employers/firms as profit maximizers, and employees as utility maximizers, attempting to maximize utility obtained from the combination of income and leisure. Both are considered to be price-takers in the market, with no influence over the price of labor. The section then considered the possibility of market failures due to imperfections in the labor market.

Table 5.2. *Percentage of employees in various benefit plans, by full/part-time status, United States, 1999–2000*

Benefit	Employment status	1999	2000
Annual leave	Full-time	90	91
	Part-time	43	39
Accidental death, dismemberment insurance	Full-time	52	50
	Part-time	11	8
Retirement plans	Full-time	56	55
	Part-time	21	18
Child care	Full-time	6	5
	Part-time	6	3
Dental care	Full-time	39	35
	Part-time	10	6
Paid holidays	Full-time	87	87
	Part-time	36	39
Life insurance	Full-time	68	65
	Part-time	15	11
Long-term disability	Full-time	32	31
	Part-time	4	4
Medical care	Full-time	64	61
	Part-time	14	13
Sickness and accident insurance	Full-time	43	39
	Part-time	15	12
Paid sick leave	Full-time	63	N/A
	Part-time	19	N/A
Survivor insurance	Full-time	4	2
	Part-time	1	1
Vision care	Full-time	22	21
	Part-time	6	4

Source: U.S. Bureau of Labor Statistics.

Finally, the section pointed out that the key contribution of economics is its emphasis on markets, both product markets and labor markets, as the fundamental basis of the employment relationship. The employment relationship would not exist if there were not a market for the goods or services produced by the firm/employee and the employer and employee did not derive economic benefit from the relationship.

The next section of the chapter focused on the four beliefs that are linked to the economic concept of employment in the United States: The importance of individual rights; the principle of the corporation as a legal individual; the importance of property and property rights; and views regarding the appropriateness of government regulation of markets. It was shown these beliefs have a basis in the economic conception of employment as it is conceived in the United States. It was also shown that in Europe, where there is a much greater willingness than in the United States to question the economic basis of the employment relationship, these four beliefs are not held nearly as strongly.

The final section of the chapter demonstrated how these differences in the conception of employment between the United States and Europe are experienced at the firm level. Exploiting the fact that the European Union regulates the employment relationship to a much greater extent than the United States, this section analyzed the difference between EU legislation in unregulated firm-level practices in the United States in two areas: Paid annual leave and differences between full- and part-time workers. The analysis showed that the regulations applied to firms in the European Union were more favorable to employees than the unregulated, market-driven outcomes in the United States.[22]

Based on this chapter, it is clear that neoclassical economic theory underlies employment and employment policy in the United States. This is in marked contrast to the European Union, where the employment relationship is considered to have substantial social content. As the European Union continues to evolve into an integrated economy that is not dissimilar to the United States, the contribution to the economic welfare of workers/citizens of the differing emphases on the economic dimension of employment will become an increasingly important issue.

Notes

1. Recent presentations of neoclassical economics as it relates to the employment relationship may be found in Ehrenberg and Smith (2000), Kaufman and Hotchkiss (1999), and Polachek and Siebert (1993).
2. Although institutional constraints normally prevent an individual from ceasing work at the precise moment that the marginal utility of leisure exceeds the marginal utility of an additional monetary unit of income, one can conceive of real world income–leisure tradeoffs. Teachers, for example, are professionals who normally earn less than professionals with comparable levels of education. This difference in compensation can be interpreted as the price of purchasing leisure in the form of summers and long breaks during the school year.
3. More sophisticated labor demand models better mimic the observed operation of labor markets by taking into account such factors as hiring and training costs, the presence of unions, imperfect information, and legislation.
4. For a similar analysis comparing the United States and Canada, see Block and Roberts (2000) and Block et al. (2003).
5. In limiting the chapter to comparing the United States and Europe, we acknowledge that we do not address a third model of the employment relationship—the East Asian model. This model is heavily influenced by Confucianism, which is "concerned with the correct observance of human relationships within a hierarchically oriented society" (Oh and Kim, 2002: 210). For example, both Lee (1992) and Lee (1997) have emphasized the importance of Confucianism in understanding the Korean economic system. Both point out that Confucianism emphasizes the maintenance of proper relationships between those in higher authority and those in subservient positions, for example, between the ruler and ruled, or the government and people.
6. See pp. 108–9, below.

7. For a historical perspective on private property in the context of the founding of the United States, see Beard (1913, 1935).

8. This is precisely what happened in the United States in 1991 after the 1989 U.S. Supreme Court decision in Ward's Cove Packing Co. v. Antonio (490 U.S. 642). In *Ward's Cove,* the Supreme Court, reversing eighteen years of settled anti-discrimination law in the United States, ruled that an employer need only show a business *justification* for an employment practice that resulted in disparate impact on racial or ethnic or minorities. Under a 1971 U.S. Supreme Court decision, Griggs v. Duke Power Co. 401 U.S. 424, the employer was required to demonstrate the employment practice creating a disparate impact was *necessary* for the business. Congress, in 1991, legislatively enacted the *Griggs* "business necessity standard," in effect overturning the Supreme Court's decision in *Wards Cove* (Wolkinson and Block 1996: 36–8).

9. See for example, most recently for gender, Council Directive 97/81/EC of 15 December 1997 on the Burden of proof in Cases of Discrimination Based on Sex; Council Directive 2000/43/EC of 29 June 2000 Implementing The Principle of Equal Treatment Between Persons Irrespective of Racial or Ethnic origin; and Council Directive 2000/78/EC of 27 November 2000 Establishing A General Framework for Equal Treatment in Employment and Occupation, at http://europa.eu.int/eur-lex/en/search/search_lif.html, accessed June 13, 2003.

10. See Treaty on European Union, December 24, 2002, at http://europa.eu.int/eur-lex/en/treaties/dat/EU_consol.html, accessed June 13, 2003.

11. See Treaty Establishing the European Community, December 24 2002, at http://europa.eu.int/eur-lex/en/treaties/dat/EC_consol.html, accessed June 13 2003.

12. For a very recent example of a pronouncement by the European Union on the matter of the social inclusion of persons who are disabled, see *Council Resolution of 6 February 2003 on Social Inclusion—Through Social Dialogue And Partnership* (2003/C 39/01), at http://europa.eu.int/eur-lex/en/search/search_oj.html, accessed June 27, 2003.

13. See Charter of Fundamental Rights of the European Union, Articles 12, 28 at http://www.europarl.eu.int/charter/pdf/text_en.pdf, accessed June 27, 2003.

14. See, most recently, for example, Desert Palace Inc. v. Costa, U.S. Supreme Court, 2003, at www.findlaw.com/casecode/supreme.html, accessed June 11, 2003.

15. See also Albertsons v. Kirkingburg (1999) and Murphy v. United Parcel Service (1999) in which the U.S. Supreme Court found, respectively, that an uncorrectable vision deficiency that resulted in truck driver having 20/200 vision in one eye and corrected high blood pressure were not disabilities under the Americans with Disabilities Act.

16. There are both employer and employee exclusions from the act. For example, the employees of an employer are not covered by the NLRA if the employer does affect interstate (a very small number of employers), if the employer is a public employer, or if the employer is an agricultural employer. Excluded employees of covered employers include supervisors, managers, and confidential employees who work for managers involved in labor relations matters. Employers and employees in railroads and airlines are covered by the Railway Labor Act, which provides employees with basically the same rights as the National Labor Relations Act. See National Labor Relations Act, as amended.

17. The Railway Labor Act has regulated labor relations on the railroads since 1926, and on the airlines since 1934.

18. The preamble to the Wagner Act, states, in relevant part:
    (t)he inequality of bargaining power between employees who do not possess full freedom of association or actual liberty of contract, and employers who are organized in the

corporate or other forms of ownership association substantially burdens and affects the flow of commerce, and tends to aggravate recurrent business depressions, by depressing wage rates and the purchasing power of wage earners in industry and by preventing the stabilization of competitive wage rates and working conditions within and between industries. Experience has proved that protection by law of the right of employees to organize and bargain collectively... promotes the flow of commerce by removing certain recognized sources of industrial strife and unrest,...and by restoring equality of bargaining power between employers and employees.

19. See National Labor Relations Act, Sec. 151.
20. Council Directive 93/104/EC of 23 November 1993 Concerning Certain Aspects of the Organization of Working Time, at http://europa.eu.int/eur-lex/en/search/search_lif.html.
21. Table 5.1 presents data on small and medium–large firms because that it how the data are presented by the BLS. A small firm is defined as a firm with less than 100 employees (United States Bureau of Labor Statistics, "Employee Benefits...").
22. In areas in which the United States chooses to legislate, its labor standards are also lower than the labor standards promulgated at the EU level. See Block et al. (2003).

References

Adams, R. (2002). "America's 'Union-Free' movement in light of international human rights standards". Paper presented at Michigan State University-AFL-CIO Conference on Worker Rights, East Lansing, Michigan, October.

Albertsons, Inc. v. Kirkingburg (1999). U.S. Supreme Court, No. 98-591, at www.findlaw.com/casecode/supreme.html.

Americans With Disabilities Act of 1990 at www.usdoj.gov/crt/ada/pubs/ada.txt.

Atleson, J. B. (1983). *Values and Assumptions in American Labor Law*. Amherst, MA: University of Massachusetts Press.

Beard, C. A. (Orig. 1913 and 1935). *An Economic Interpretation of the Constitution of the United States*, 1965 edn. New York: Free Press.

Bellah, R. N., Madsen R., Sullivan, W. M., Swidler, A., and Tipton, S. M. (1985). *Habits of the Heart: Individualism and Commitment in American Life*. Berkeley and Los Angeles: University of California Press.

Blanpain, R. (1999). *European Labour Law*. The Hague, London, Boston: Kluwer Law International.

Block, R. N. (1990). "American industrial relations in the 1980's: Transformation or evolution," in J. Chelius and J. Dworkin (eds.), *Reflections on the Transformation of Industrial Relations* (Metuchen, NJ and London: IMLR Press/Rutgers University and Scarecrow Press), 17–48.

—— (1992). "The legal and institutional framework for employment security in the United States," in K. Koshiro (ed.), *Employment Security and Labor Market Flexibility* (Detroit: Wayne State University Press), 127–49.

—— (1997). "Rethinking the National Labor Relations Act and Zero-Sum Labor Law: An industrial relations view". *Berkeley Journal of Employment and Labor Law*, 18(1): 30–55.

—— and McLennan, K. (1985). "Structural economic change and industrial relations in the United States manufacturing and transportation sectors since 1973," in H. Juris, M. Thompson, and W. Daniels (eds.), *Industrial Relations in a Decade of Economic Change* (Madison, WI: Industrial Relations Research Association).

Block, R. N., and Wolkinson, B. W. (1986). "Delay in the union election campaign revisited: A theoretical and empirical analysis," in D. B. Lipsky and D. Lewin (eds.), *Advances in Industrial Relations: A Research Annual*, Vol. 3 (Greenwich, CT and London: JAI Press), 43–82.

—— and Roberts R. (2000). "A comparison of labour standards in the United States and Canada". *Relations Indusrielles/Industrial Relations*, 55(2): 273–307.

—— Berg, P., and Roberts, K. (2002). "Comparing and quantifying labor standards in the United States and the European Union". *International Journal of Comparative Labor Law and Industrial Relations*, 19(4): 441–69.

—— Roberts, K., and Clarke, R. O. (2003). *Labor Standards in the United States and Canada*. Kalamazoo, MI: W.E. Upjohn Institute for Employment Research.

Board of Trustees of the University of Alabama v. Garrett (2001). No. 99-1240, U.S. Supreme Court, at www.findlaw.com/casecode.

Ehrenberg, R. A., and Smith, R. S. (2000). *Modern Labor Economics: Theory and Public Policy*, 7th edn. Reading, MA: Addison-Wesley.

European Foundation for the Improvement of Living and Working Conditions (2002). "European Company Statute in Focus," *European Industrial Relations Observatory OnLine*, at www.eiro.eurofound.ie/2002/06/feature/EU0206202F.html.

European Union, *Charter of fundamental Rights of the European Union*, at www.europarl.eu.int/charter/pdf/text_en.pdf.

—— *Council Directive 93/104/EC of 23 November 1993 Concerning Certain Aspects of the Organization of Working Time*, at http://europa.eu.int/eur-lex/en/search/search_lif.html.

—— *Council Directive 97/81/EC of 15 December 1997 Concerning the Framework Agreement on Part-Time Work Concluded by UNICE, CEEP and the ETUC*, at http://europa.eu.int/eur-lex/en/search/search_lif.html.

—— *Council Directive 98/23/EC of 7 April 1998 on the Extension of Directive 97/81/EC on the Framework Agreement on Part-Time Work Concluded by UNICE, CEEP and the ETUC to the United Kingdom of Great Britain and Northern Ireland*, at http://europa.eu.int/eur-lex/en/search/search_lif.html.

—— *Council Directive 2001/23/EC of 12 March 2001 on the Approximation of the Laws of the Member States Relating to the Safeguarding of Employees' Rights in the Event of Transfers of Undertakings, Businesses or Parts of Undertakings or Businesses*, at http://europa.eu.int/eur-lex/en/search/search_lif.html, accessed June 24, 2003.

—— *Council Directive 2001/86/EC of 8 October 2001 Supplementing the Statute for a European Company With Regard to the Involvement of Employees*, at http://europa.eu.int/eur-lex/en/search/search_lif.html, accessed June 24, 2003.

—— *Council Regulation (EC) No 2157/2001 of 8 October 2001 on the Statute for a European Company (SE)*, at http://europa.eu.int/eur-lex/en/search/search_lif.html, accessed June 24, 2003.

Fibreboard Corp. v. NLRB (1964). U.S. Supreme Court, 379 U.S. 203, at www.findlaw.com/casecode.

First National Maintenance Corp. v. NLRB (1981). U.S. Supreme Court, 452 U.S. 666, at www.findlaw.com/casecode.

Goldman, A. (2001). "Cultural and economic perspectives concerning protection of workers' social dignity", in R. Blainpain (ed.), *Labour Law, Human Rights, and Social Justice* (The Hague: Kluwer), 9–28.

Griggs v. Duke Power Co. (1971). U.S. Supreme Court, 401 U.S. 424, at www.findlaw.com/casecode.

Gross, J. (2002). "A logical extreme: Proposing human rights as the foundation for workers' rights in the U.S." Paper presented at Michigan State University-AFL-CIO Conference on Worker Rights, East Lansing, Michigan, October.

Harris, D., and Darcy, J. (2001). *The European Social Charter*, 2nd ed. Ardsley, NY: Transnational Publishers.

Hazen Paper Co. v. Biggins (1993). U.S. Supreme Court, 507 U.S. 604, at www.findlaw.com/casecode.

Hudgens v. NLRB (1976). Supreme Court, 424 U.S. 507, U.S. at www.findlaw.com/casecode.

Kaufman, B. E. (1997). "Labor markets and employment regulation: The view of the 'old' institutionalists," in B. E. Kaufman (ed.), *Government Regulation of the Employment Relationship* (Madison, WI: Industrial Relations Research Association), 11–56.

—— and Hotchkiss, J. I. (1999). *The Economics of Labor Markets*, 5th edn. Fort Worth, TX: Dryden Press.

Keefe, J., and Boroff, K. (1994). "Telecommunications labor-management relations after divestiture," in P. B. Voos (ed.), *Contemporary Collective Bargaining in the Private Sector* (Madison, WI: Industrial Relations Research Association), 303–72.

Kimel et al. v. Board of Regents et al. (2000). U.S. Supreme Court, No 98-791, at www.findlaw.com/casecode.

Lechmere, Inc. v. NLRB (1992). U.S. Supreme Court, 502 U.S. 527, at www.findlaw.com/ casecode.

Lee, M. B. (1992). "Korea," in M. Rothman, D. R. Briscoe, and R. D. C. Nacamulli (eds.), *Industrial Relations Around the World* (Berlin and New York: Walter de Gruyter).

Lee, Y-h. (1997). *The State, Society, and Big Business in South Korea*. London and New York: Routledge.

Lieberman, E. (1960). *Unions Before the Bar*, Rev. Ed. New York: Oxford Book Company.

Lipset, S. M. (1989). *Continental Divide: The Values and Institutions of the United States and Canada*. Toronto and Washington, DC: The C.D. Howe Institute and the National Planning Association.

Lloyd Corporation v. Tanner (1972). U.S. Supreme Court, 407 U.S. 551, at www.findlaw.com/casecode.

Marsh v. State of Alabama (1946). U.S. Supreme Court, 326 501, U.S. at www.findlaw.com/casecode.

Marshall, A. (1891). *Principles of Economics*. London: MacMillan and Co.

Millis, H. A., and Clark Brown, E. (1950). *From the Wagner Act to Taft-Hartley: A Study of National Labor Policy and Labor Relations*. Chicago: University of Chicago Press.

Murphy v. United Parcel Service, Inc. (1999). U.S. Supreme Court, No. 97-1992.

National Labor Relations Act as amended at www4.law.cornell.edu/uscode/29/ch7schII.html.

NLRB v. Babcock and Wilcox Co. (1956). U.S. Supreme Court, 351 U.S. 105, at www.findlaw.com/casecode.

NLRB v. Borg-Warner Corp., U.S. Supreme Court, 356 U.S. 342. 1958 at www.findlaw.com/casecode.

NLRB v. Virginia Electric and Power Co. (1941). U.S. Supreme Court, 314 U.S. 469, at www.findlaw.com/casecode.

Oh, T. K., and Kim, E. (2002). "The impact of Confucianism in East Asian business enterprise," in Z. Rhee and E. Chang (eds.), *Korean Business and Management: The Reality and The Vision*. Elizabeth, NJ and Seoul: Hollym.

Perlman, S. (1966). *A Theory of the Labor Movement* (orig. pub. 1928, 1966 edn.). New York: Augustus M. Kelley.

Polachek, S. W., and Siebert, W. S. (1993). *The Economics of Earnings*. Cambridge: Cambridge University Press.

Samuel, L. (2002). *Fundamental Social Rights: Case Law of the European Social Charter*, 2nd edn. Strasbourg: Council of Europe.

Schwab, S. J. (1997). "The law and economics approach to workplace regulation," in B. E. Kaufman (ed.), *Government Regulation of the Employment Relationship* (Madison, WI: Industrial Relations Research Association), 91–123.

Szyszczak, E. (1999). "The new parameters of European labour law," in D. O'Keefe and P. Twomey (eds.), *Legal Issues of the Amsterdam Treaty* (Oxford and Portland, OR: Hart).

Sutton v. United Airlines (1999). U.S. Supreme Court, No. 97-1943, at www.findlaw.com/casecode.

Title VII of the Civil Rights Act of 1964, at www.eeoc.gov/laws/vii.html.

Trans World Airlines, Inc. v. Independent Federation of Flight Attendants (1989). U.S. Supreme Court, 489 U.S. 426, at www.findlaw.com/casecode.

Treaty of Amsterdam (1997). At http://europa.eu.int/eur-lex/en/treaties/dat/amsterdam.html, accessed June 24, 2003.

Turner, T. (2002). "Corporatism in Ireland: A comparative perspective," in D. D'Art and T. Turner (eds.), *Irish Employment Relations in the New Economy* (Dublin: Blackhall).

United States Bureau of Labor Statistics, "Employee benefits in small private industry establishments, 1996." News Release 98-240 at www.bls.gov/ncs/ebs/sp/ebnr0004.txt.

—— "Percent of employed wage and salary workers 25 years and over who had 10 years or more of tenure with their current employer by age and sex, selected years, 1983–2002". *Labor Force Statistics from the Current Population Survey*, at www.bls.gov/news.release/tenure.toc.htm.

—— "Median years of tenure with current employer for employed wage and salary workers by age and sex, selected years, 1983–2002". *Labor Force Statistics from the Current Population Survey*, at www.bls.gov/news.release/tenure.toc.htm.

—— *National Compensation Survey—Benefits*, undated at www.bls.gov/ncs/ebs/ home.htm.

Visser, J., and Van Ruysseveldt, J. (1996). "Robust corporatism, still? Industrial relations in Germany", in J. Van Ruysseveldt and J. Visser (eds.), *Industrial Relations in Europe* (London: Sage).

Wards Cove Packing Co. v. Atonio (1989). U.S. Supreme Court, 490 U.S. 642, at www. findlaw.com/casecode.

Wolkinson, B. W., and Block, R. N. (1996). *Employment Law: The Workplace Rights of Employees and Employers.* Cambridge, MA and Oxford: Blackwell

6

Commonalities and Conflicts Between Different Perspectives of the Employment Relationship: Towards a Unified Perspective

JACQUELINE A-M. COYLE-SHAPIRO, M. SUSAN TAYLOR,
LYNN M. SHORE, AND LOIS E. TETRICK

6.1 Introduction

Part I allows us to view the employment relationship through a pentagonal prism composed of social exchange, justice, industrial relations, and economic and legal perspectives. As we rotate the prism, allowing the light to refract through different sides, various features of the employment relationship move into the foreground and dominate, while others recede. When gazing through some sides of the prism, the surrounding context so dominates our view that it is difficult to see the relationship at all, while in other cases, the context itself is virtually unnoticeable. Yet, rotating the prism across these views, we observe many similarities as well as some significant conflicts. By blending the angles across the five-sided prism, we interweave color, form, and texture to produce a rich gestalt of the employment relationship that is impossible to achieve through any single perspective. These then are our objectives in Chapter 6. We begin by examining the individual sides of the prism, the five perspectives.

6.2 Five views of the employment relationship

6.2.1 Social exchange view of the employment relationship

Social exchange theorists have viewed the employment relationship as an exchange of tangible and intangible benefits (see Chapter 1). As such, it is the emphasis on the exchange of the intangible benefits that differentiates social exchange from economic exchange. Eisenberger et al. (1986) propose that fulfilling important socio-emotional needs in the workplace is similar to fulfilling individual needs for respect, caring, and support in interpersonal relationships. The authors argue that perceived organizational support (POS) fulfills the need for self-esteem by communicating recognition of employees' contributions (Armeli et al. 1998), the need for emotional support by signaling to employees that the organization can be relied upon to help when required, and the need for social approval by communicating that they are adhering to organizational norms. Therefore, a social exchange perspective on the employment relationship goes beyond the exchange of tangible benefits to include the fulfillment of socio-emotional needs.

Underpinning this type of exchange is trust and the norm of reciprocity. As a social exchange relationship involves unspecified obligations, exchange partners are required to trust the other to discharge their obligations and also accept the norm of reciprocity that obligates an individual to return favorable treatment. Exchange partners can demonstrate their trustworthiness by reciprocating benefits received. As such, social exchange relationships take time to develop as exchange partners begin to demonstrate their trustworthiness and show that they accept the norm of reciprocity governing the relationship.

6.2.2 Justice view of the employment relationship

Adopting a justice perspective to the employment relationship (see Chapter 2) starts from the position that the employment contract is an incomplete agreement stemming from uncertainties arising from how the organization's management uses its authority. Injustice comes into play when in employees' eyes management exceeds the range of acceptability in exercising their prerogatives. In its totality, a justice perspective captures how individuals perceive their exchange relationship in terms of fairness and represents an important mechanism for managing the employment relationship.

Researchers have drawn attention to different dimensions of fairness: Distributive (outcomes), procedural (formal procedures), and interactional (interpersonal and informational). The conceptual distinction is supported empirically and suggests that individuals evaluate more than the fairness of the outcomes received from their employment relationship. In particular, procedural and interactional justice seem to have a substantial effect on the legitimacy employees bestow upon management's authority and by implication, how they react to changes initiated by management.

A justice perspective is not limited to viewing the employment relationship in terms of perceived reciprocal fairness (an instrumental motive) but also identifies the moral mandates about social conduct held by society in general (the moral norm of respect for human dignity) as an important regulator of the fairness of management actions in the context of the employment relationship. Thus, the employment relationship should not be evaluated exclusively in terms of fairness of reciprocity but also moral considerations as to social conduct in organizational settings.

6.2.3 Industrial relations view of the employment relationship

A key assumption underlying an industrial relations (IR) approach (see Chapter 3) is the existence of an inherent conflict of interest between management and employees. This conflict stems from a power imbalance favoring the employer over the individual employee in the exchange relationship and resulting inequalities in the exchange. The implication, therefore, is a conflict that is based on what the two parties are willing to contribute to the relationship—the employer, by and large, will attempt to elicit the maximum contributions from employees and employees may not be willing to give the desired contributions, especially in view of the indeterminacy of the relationship. The focus of an IR approach is on the relationship between the employer and employees, as a collective, and how to regulate the relationship in view of the conflicts that exist.

In light of this, the IR literature tends to emphasize the regulation of the relationship at the national, industrial or organizational levels according to the type of national industrial relations systems that exist. Consequently, employment systems vary across countries from those characterized by greater unilateral actions by the employer to resolve conflicts of interests (e.g. the United States and the United Kingdom) to those using a high degree of cooperation and coordination to resolve conflicts of interests through negotiations in centralized forms of collective bargaining (e.g. Germany and the Netherlands). In other countries, the regulation of the employment relationship also involves governments where tripartite national agreements are signed by unions, employers, and governments covering basic terms and conditions of employment (e.g. Finland and Italy).

Currently, within IR research, there is a debate concerning whether highly sophisticated collective bargaining mechanisms serve to constrain organizations' flexibility to cope with increasing competitive pressures and hence, some IR researchers have focused their attention on more cooperative systems of industrial relations especially in countries where union power has declined (in particular, the United States and the United Kingdom). However, the jury is out in terms of whether such "partnership" agreements between unions and management do indeed provide outcomes that are mutually beneficial, especially if they have been introduced in a context of employer coercion.

6.2.4 The legal view of the employment relationship

Legal theory also offers a unique perspective on the employment relationship (see Chapter 4) existing between an individual employee and his or her employer. Prior to the industrial revolution, parties' obligations in the employment relationship were determined by English common law based on a status distinction between "master" and "servant." The coming of the industrial revolution and its accompanying complexities shifted the basis of each party's obligations in the employment relationship to an explicit or implied contractual agreement between the two and also increased the level of legal regulation of the employment relationship. This enhanced juridification resulted in many differences across the employment legislation of different countries regarding the length of employment, employers' responsibility to notify employees of the terms of agreement, employers' responsibility to give advance notice of termination, legally permissibly grounds for termination, and employers' latitude to form individual contracts with employees already covered by collective agreements.

Over time, rigidities in classic contract models led to the development of neoclassical contract law, around the second half of the twentieth century. While retaining a focus on the freedom of contracting, neoclassical contract law also: (a) allowed for the subjugation of parties' needs to those of social values and policies; (b) imposed obligations by law, rather than simply by agreement, in order to prevent unfairness or injustice to the other party; (c) considered the ends sought by parties in the context under which they arise, thereby allowing for dynamism in the relationship; and (d) enhanced the subjectivity of rules applied to determine the existence of a contract between parties.

Despite improvements, some critics still deemed neoclassical contract theory incapable of regulating most exchange relationships, including employment. Led by Ian Macneil (1980), legal scholars subsequently developed a relational form of contract law. Note that psychological contract researchers have adopted Macneil's (1980) work as the foundation for the transactional versus relational dimensionality of parties' mutual obligations (Robinson and Rousseau 1994; Herriot and Pemberton 1996). According to Macneil (1980), employment relationships cannot be "very discrete" in nature but vary along a continuum from "relatively discrete" to "highly relational." Highly relational contracts as applied to the employment relationship:

(1) are of extended duration such that the exact terms of the exchange cannot be specified at the time of its formation and thereby require cooperation between parties and other characteristics (discussed below) in order to make the relationship successful;

(2) avoid measurement or specification of the objects of exchange—that is, objects exchanged between employee and organizational parties include a mixture of those difficult and easy to measure or specify; however *even the easily measured objects are not in fact measured*, thereby reinforcing the relational nature of the exchange;

(3) involve parties' participation as "whole people" based on their full range of characteristics, not just the knowledge or skills needed on a job; the notion of whole person involvement yields the potential for additional rewards and conflicts within the relationship;

(4) emphasize future cooperation so that cooperation between parties is mandated due to the nature of an ongoing exchange where terms cannot be fully specified at its initiation;

(5) specify parties' sharing of benefits and burdens in a relational contract rather than making a sharp division between which party receives what benefit and/or burden as is the case in discrete transactions;

(6) develop normative relational obligations that are based on customs, status, habits, and expectations linked to the status quo as well as promise-based ones.

Overall, relational contact theory is helpful in explaining the employment relationship because it considers context, parties' fairness and justice concerns, and the limitations of promises as the sole basis of parties' obligations to each other.

6.2.5 The economic view of the employment relationship

An economic perspective on the employment exchange emphasizes the distinctive-ness of the two parties within this relationship, yet, views each as primarily focused on maximizing the utility of their own individual outcomes. Thus, organizations seek to maximize profit and participate in different forms of employment relation-ships if they assist in competing effectively in the market. Similarly, the employee party, which may function as an individual or a collective (representative labor unions), seeks to maximize the utility of his or her returns by engaging in different levels of labor force participation (none, part-time, full-time, overtime, etc.), depending on the size of the wage offered.

Neoclassical economic theory assumes that both individuals and society will achieve the best possible outcomes under conditions of perfect competition within the marketplace. Thus, as long as markets are reasonably competitive, attempts to regulate their activities are likely to lower the organization's competitiveness and constrain employees' efforts to maximize their utility by adjusting work hours and seeking out employers offering the best packages of wages and benefits.

Societies differ, however, in the extent to which they accept the tenets of neoclassical economic theory. For example, the American society, which sub-scribes more fully to a neoclassical interpretation, strives to minimize marketplace regulation. Because individual action and rights are considered paramount in America and the collective action of employees is seen as a potential threat to the healthy competition of the marketplace, individuals are given the right to engage in or *refrain from* bargaining collectively over wages, hours, and conditions of employment. Therefore, the default employment relationship in America is that between organizational employer and individual employee who negotiate wages and conditions of employment. The employee's power in this negotiation is based on the property rights to his or her labor, knowledge, skills, and relationships, and the size of that power will vary depending on the existing supply and demand in the labor market

Conversely, in Europe, markets are not seen as naturally competitive but as dominated by the greater economic power of several large employers; individualism is not a dominant value. Thus, the default European employment relationship is that between an organization and the unions representing its employees. The collectiviza-tion of employment relationships, through the actions of labor unions, is the dominant means of offsetting employer power and of determining wages and conditions of employment. Worker rights are one component of human rights in Europe, and thus European workers generally receive more lucrative terms of employment with respect to paid time off and benefits than do Americans. European countries also afford more power to part-time workers, generally awarding them the same employment protection and benefits as full-time workers.

In summary, the economic perspective on employment relationships showcases the tangible economic concerns of both parties within the employment relation-ship, each functioning in the midst of market forces that they cannot control. An economic analysis shows how the relative power of each party to the relationship, as well as the nature of the employee party (whether individual or collective), are affected by strong values held within the society in which the relationship is embedded. Such values affect the passage of legislation, judicial interpretations, and also common practice. This analysis identifies distinctive characteristics of the employment exchange in America and Europe based on differing beliefs about the competitiveness of the marketplace and differing preferences for individualism versus collectivism. We turn now to an examination of conflicts and then commonalities between the different perspectives (see Table 6.1).

6.3 Conflicts between perspectives

Our analysis identifies several differences in viewing the employment relationship through the lens of the five perspectives. These differences concern the nature of the relationship, the level of analysis at which it unfolds, and important contextual influences. We address the largest and most important conflict first, that concerning the nature of the relationship.

6.3.1 Nature of the relationship

From an economic perspective, parties to the employment relationship have an ambivalent, impersonal view of one another, as both organization and employee (whether individual or collective) are highly focused on maximizing the utility of their own economic outcomes, they form and maintain the employment relationship solely for this purpose, and are both at the mercy of market forces beyond their control. The employment relationship lasts as long as both parties believe the relationship can maximize their economic utilities through it and ends when either one discovers a better deal elsewhere.

Conversely, the IR and justice perspectives envision an exploitative employment relationship involving a far more powerful organization with little or no concern for employee welfare, which holds a "blank check" right to require that employees perform any work task under any kind of condition. The exploitative employer is held in check either by the bargaining power of the employee's union collective (IR), or the realization that extremely outlandish actions, such as urging employees to retain shares of stock in a company known by organizational leaders to be failing, will bump soundly against the moral code of society in general and result in serious and painful sanctions (justice).

Finally, the social exchange and legal relational contract perspectives are outliers to envision a mutually beneficial employment relationship of indeterminate length that is motivated by the need for each party to fulfill a series of needs or desires that cannot be satisfied on its own. Over time, the relationship develops into a broad-based exchange that includes tangible and intangible aspects, both those that were promised as well as those evolving from local practices or customs. From

Table 6.1 *Conflicts and commonalities between the different perspectives to the employment relationship*

	Social exchange	Justice (moral principles model)	Industrial relations	Legal (relational contracting)	Economic
Nature of the exchange	Mutually beneficial	Exploitative	Exploitative	Mutually beneficial	Ambivalence
Level of analysis	Primary emphasis on individual level within peer group context	Individual within organizational context	Group level (employee collective)	Individual within organization	Organization and individual level
Basis of the exchange	Tangible and intangible (approval, support)	Tangible and intangible (morally acceptable treatment)	Primary focus on tangibles (wages, working conditions)	Tangible and intangible (recognition, prestige)	Primary focus on tangible aspects of exchange (wages)
Regulation of exchange/implications for maintaining the relationship	Self-imposed regulation through trust	Societal moral norms of conduct	Collective bargaining	Acting in good faith	Balance/imbalance in supply and demand
Process of exchange	Norm of reciprocity	Reciprocation based on fairness	Conflicts of interest and power—negative and balanced reciprocity	Sharing of benefits and burdens (norm of reciprocity)	Transaction exchange based on individual—utility maximizing; organization—profit maximization
Aims of the exchange	Development of an enduring relationship based on trust	Morally acceptable employer behavior and satisfactory employee performance	Productive efficiency and distributive justice	Mutually satisfying and rewarding relationship	Individual and societal welfare in competitive markets
Contextual influences on the exchange	Peer groups	Broader social context through importation of prevailing norms of conduct	IR institutions (e.g. collective bargaining arrangements)	Influence of culture and external regulation on obligations	Economic forces and markets

social exchange and relational contract perspectives, the employment relationship produces a mutual sense of trust and trustworthiness between parties, the cooperative behavior needed to work through evolving exchange obligations and broad heuristics to treat the other party benevolently and with respect (such as the tendency to act in good faith), compensate the other party for damages suffered, and satisfy reasonable expectations.

Although presented at the extreme, the social exchange and relational contracting views of the nature of the employment relationship differ so significantly from the other perspectives (in particular, IR and economic perspectives). To this we add differences in the levels of analysis that are associated with different perspectives, the outcomes of the exchange and contextual effects. While synthesis may seem improbable, there are points of similarity that create opportunities for cross-disciplinary integration to create greater understanding of the employment relationship.

6.3.2 Levels of analysis

Three perspectives, social exchange, justice, and legal (relational contract theory), argue that the level of analysis for the employment relationship is most appropriately that between individual employee and organizational employer. Conversely, the IR and (frequently, but not always) the economic perspective propose that the level of analysis is often that of the organizational employer and the collective employee representative, generally the union. The exception within the economic perspective occurs when one contrasts the American employment relationship, framed largely around individual employee and organizational employer, with that of Europe and much of Asia which envision a collective, either union or employee group, on the employees' side. We expect the conflict in the level of analysis makes the development of public policy and legislated or organizationally initiated attempts to change the nature of the employment relationship very hard to achieve because of differences in the conceptualization of who is party to the exchange.

6.3.3 Aims of the exchange

The aims of the employment relationship also vary considerably across the five perspectives. Once again the social and legal (relational contract theory) perspectives are closest in nature due to a common social exchange foundation. Thus, the social exchange perspective will yield an enduring exchange relationship that is well grounded in mutual trust that develops between the parties, while the relational contract generates a similar mutually satisfying and rewarding relationship, of "indeterminate length." Conversely, the justice and the IR perspectives diverge by including an element of productive efficiency that largely develops through employee and organizational performance based on distributive justice (IR) or moral principles governing treatment (justice). Finally, somewhat similarly to the justice and IR perspectives, an economic view aims for individual and societal welfare, assuming conditions of competitive markets as an important aim.

6.3.4 *Contextual influences on the employment relationship*

Different contextual factors influence the employment relationship within each perspective. From a social exchange perspective, the dominant contextual influence is that of the peer group in which each party to the exchange is located. Thus, both employer and employee beliefs about and actions toward the employment exchange are affected by those of their peers within and outside the organization itself. Conversely, the justice perspective is impacted through the prevailing moral norms of conduct, which tend to affect local levels from the broader social context from which they are imported. IR institutions, such as collective bargaining or consultative structures tend to be the most direct contextual effects on the industrial relations perspective. Both variances in national and regional cultures as well as external legislation provide an influential context for relational contract theory by, for example, constraining or reinforcing behavioral heuristics to act in good faith, or by compensating the other party's losses. And last but not least, market forces create the most influential context for the economic perspective by constraining the parties' ability to maximize their respective utilities.

Overall, the conflicts between the five perspectives appear daunting and vast. However, there are also important commonalities that we discuss below.

6.4 Commonalities between the different perspectives

6.4.1 *Basis of the exchange*

With regard to the basis of the exchange relationship, there is a broad degree of convergence amongst a number of different approaches, in particular, social exchange, justice, and the legal perspectives (relational contracting). These three perspectives view the employment relationship as an exchange of tangible and intangible resources. Social exchange focuses on socio-emotional needs (approval, self esteem, and emotional support; see Eisenberger et al. 1986) while a justice perspective suggests that treating individuals honestly, with dignity and respect, are important elements of the exchange relationship (Bies and Moag 1986). However, the legal perspective is less clear about the exact nature of those intangible resources, identifying a number of possibilities: Challenging work, personal recognition, and prestige, for example (see Chapter 4). Thus, the intangibles emphasized within the social exchange and justice literatures speak to more universalistic basic human needs; the legal perspective suggests saliency of intangibles to the exchange partners is important.

Although an IR approach primarily focuses on the tangible outcomes of the employment relationship, "bread and butter" issues such as wages, benefits, job security, and working conditions (Filppelli 1984), it also pays attention to intangibles in the exchange to the extent that they influence the tangibles received. Specifically, an IR approach considers process issues such as how employees are treated in the exchange and hence, procedural issues are important for instrumental reasons. Collective bargaining agreements usually include an agreement on procedures to be adopted in fulfilling the substantive elements of the agreement. The economic perspective has as its primary focus, the exchange of tangible resources, with far less attention, if any, paid to the exchange of intangibles.

Most employment relationships arguably can be characterized as involving the exchange of tangible and intangible resources, although they may differ in the nature and degree of the intangible resources offered and received. Even in relationships of limited duration and with clearly specified tasks, the argument could still be made that Folger's (see Chapter 3) "human covenant" underpins the relationship. Further, violations of moral codes of conduct by employers (e.g. demeaning behavior, public ridicule, and destructive criticism) act to spark a range of negative employee organizational behaviors and the demise of the relationship itself. At the extremes, the intangible basis of the employment relationship is dominant through the lens of social exchange, while it is "virtually" absent through the economic lens. Thus, gazing through the different sides of a prism, one sees different shades of color on the emphasis placed on the intangibility of the employment relationship.

6.4.2 *Process of the exchange*

The norm of reciprocity underlies three of the five approaches to the employment relationship: Social exchange, justice, and relational contracting. The latter two approaches focus on equitably reciprocated exchanges such that what each party contributes and sacrifices in an exchange relationship is deemed fair. As outlined in relational contract, this involves the sharing of "benefits and burdens" so that there is a degree of equivalence in the exchange. In a similar vein, social exchange theory draws on the work of Gouldner (1960), who views equivalence as an important underlying mechanism in how exchange relationships operate.

These three perspectives emphasize a balanced form of reciprocity in how they view the process of the exchange but fail to capture the potential types of reciprocity that *seem* to characterize the economic and IR perspectives. Sahlins (1972) identified two additional forms of reciprocity: Generalized reciprocity and negative reciprocity. The former has an altruistic orientation with little concern about the content of the exchange, while the latter is reflected in exchanges where partners have opposite interests and are attempting to maximize their own utility. The latter type of reciprocity may underpin the employment relationship from an economic and IR perspective. In neoclassical economic theory, both parties attempt to maximize their own utility— the individual is assumed to be a utility maximizer and the organization strives to maximize profits. Both parties are driven by their own self-interest and by and large, they have opposing interests. In the IR perspective, a starting assumption is the existence of inherent conflicts of interests between labor and capital and that unions pursue employee interests at the expense of the employer (these elements of an IR perspective would be disputed by researchers who have drawn attention to more cooperative labor-management systems).

Overall, there is a significant degree of convergence amongst the approaches in terms of the role of reciprocity in the employment relationship. Beyond this, the focus and/or assumption about which form of reciprocity underpins the employment relationship is divided between balanced reciprocity and negative reciprocity.

6.4.3 Regulation of the exchange

The type of regulation that underlies the relationship reflects assumptions about the motives and intentions of the exchange partners. For example, social exchange and relational contracting hold a mutual assumption that the two parties to the exchange have honorable motives and will act in good faith. Consequently, each party's trust in the other becomes crucial to the maintenance of that relationship. At the time, if trust is broken, this may lead ultimately to the demise of the relationship. A justice perspective relies on prevailing standards of moral conduct to at least maintain civility in the exchange relationship. Together, these regulatory mechanisms rely on forces internal to the employment relationship as a way of prolonging it.

The IR and economics perspectives have external regulatory mechanisms in place (note also that classical and neoclassical legal perspectives may rely on the courts and legal system in relationship breakdowns). Although IR systems vary across countries, if a collective bargaining agreement is breached, then grievance procedures are in place to allow unions to enforce the "contract." Whether the employer enforces the agreement may be contingent upon the power of the union and its ability to muster support for collective action in the form of strikes.

From an economic perspective, the supply and demand in the labor market acts as a regulatory mechanism to the relationship, preventing either party from developing and indefinitely retaining monopolistic power in the relationship. Instead, the threat of either economic failure due to the inability to compete effectively (organization) or the availability of alternative sources of labor and employment (individual) enable each party to retain some power and influence in the context of the employment relationship.

In summary, the perspectives are split along the issue of internal versus external regulatory mechanisms that reflect different underlying assumptions about the motives of each party and the extent to which trust or mistrust forms the basis of the employment relationship. We turn now to the discussion of whether the approaches can be synthesized into a more holistic perspective on the employment relationship.

6.5 Towards a unified perspective

Conflicts existing between the five perspectives have clear implications for targeted actions likely to be undertaken by those viewing the employment relationship from an economic or industrial relations perspective versus those viewing it from a social exchange, legal or justice perspective. For example, the target of public policy attempts to regulate the employment relationship might focus on the union as a means of collectively targeting employees and similarly, pieces of legislation or public policy directives as well as the managerial actions may be directed to employees as a collective. Conversely, when individual employees are the primary party on the employees' side, as is the case in the social exchange, justice, and legal relational contract, one must ask whether they possess sufficient economic or social power to resist regulatory, public policy, and organizational attempts that give little, if any, consideration to employees' interests.

As the perspectives have some fundamental conflictual positions on aspects of the employment relationship, the issue of whether these five sides of a prism can be synthesized to produce a new unified perspective is debatable. Possibly, a more realistic aim is the continuing blending of a number of angles of a prism to arrive at a different color, a slightly different texture and form. Thus, the consideration of the different perspectives may provide a more comprehensive lens through which to view the employment relationship. That is, the individual (influenced by societal values) is part of a collective, interacting with the "organization" that in turn is subject to external competitive market pressures and labor markets and is located in a particular societal and cultural context.

In an effort to encourage synthesis across perspectives of the employment relationship, we develop an integrative model of the employment relationship (see Chapter 16) based on these theoretical perspectives and recent developments of constructs based on exchange theory (Part II). This model pays attention to multiple organizational levels that influence an employee's view of the employment relationship and at the same time considers the effect of external influences (e.g. societal values, culture, legislation, labor markets, and unions) on the organization, and how this subsequently impacts upon the employment relationship of groups and individuals.

References

Armeli, S., Eisenberger, R., Fasolo, P., and Lynch, P. (1998). "Perceived organizational support and police performance: The moderating influence of socioemotional needs". *Journal of Applied Psychology*, 83: 288–97.

Bies, R. J., and Moag, J. S. (1986). "Interactional justice: Communication criteria for fairness," in B. Sheppard (ed.), *Research on Negotiation in Organizations*, Vol. 1 (Greenwich, CT: JAI Press), 43–55.

Eisenberger, R., Huntington, R., Hutchison, S., and Sowa, D. (1986). "Perceived organizational support." *Journal of Applied Psychology*, 71: 500–7.

Filippelli, R. (1984). *Labor in the US: A History.* New York: Knopf.

Gouldner, A.W. (1960). "The norm of reciprocity". *American Sociological Review,* 25: 161–78.

Herriot, P., and Pemberton, C. (1996). "Contracting careers." *Human Relations,* 49(6): 757–91.

Macneil, I. R. (1980). *The New Social Contract: An Inquiry Into Modern Contractual Relations.* New Haven: Yale University Press.

Robinson, S. L., and Rousseau, D. M. (1994). "Violating the psychological contract: Not the expectation but the norm." *Journal of Organizational Behavior,* 15: 245–59.

Sahlins, M. (1972). *Stone Age Economics.* New York: Aldine de Gruyter.

PART II

EXAMINING CONSTRUCTS TO CAPTURE THE EXCHANGE NATURE OF THE EMPLOYMENT RELATIONSHIP

In Part I, we reviewed the employment relationship from five perspectives outlining their commonalities and conflicts. We argued that while there are fundamental conflicts amongst the different perspectives, there is some common ground. However, these conflicts may be too great to synthesize the perspectives, yet there is scope for greater integration amongst the disciplinary perspectives.

In this part, our objectives are twofold: First, to incorporate theories that have not previously been used to examine the employment relationship and investigate the extent to which they advance our understanding of the employment relationship; and second, to build and extend existing employment relationship research by exploring the perceptions of the two parties to the exchange and the processes that underlie the exchange framework.

Chapter 7 by Shore, Porter, and Zahra examines the value of strategy theories for the relationship between organizations and employees. In doing so, this chapter attempts to link macro-level theories to the micro-level of an individual's perception of the employment relationship. The authors focus on four theories: agency theory, upper echelon, resource-based view (RBV), and dynamic capability perspective and assess the implications of each theory for organizational representatives and employees. By way of conclusion, the chapter outlines several avenues for future research that will provide greater integration between macro- and micro-views of the employment relationship.

Morrison and Robinson in Chapter 8 extend psychological contract research by examining the nature of incongruent perceptions between the two parties to the exchange. The authors argue that incongruence in perceptions stems from the nature of the mutual obligations that exist and the cognitive processes that affect how employees and organizational representatives interpret each other's contributions to the relationship. Wolfe Morrison and Robinson examine potential antecedents to incongruence and the implications of incongruent perceptions on key outcomes of the exchange relationship: Misallocation of resources, conflict, and tension.

Chapter 9 by Van Dyne and Butler Ellis presents a new model of "job creep" in the context of the employment relationship. The authors argue that job creep occurs as a result of a slow and subtle process in which an individual expands their obligations by including previously defined extra role behaviors—in other words, what was once viewed as discretionary citizenship behavior becomes a perceived obligation. Van Dyne and Butler Ellis argue that this fundamentally changes the nature of the employment relationship by focusing attention on the overfulfillment of the employee side of the exchange. The authors conclude by examining the consequences of job creep on the employee and peers' reactions, drawing on reactance theory.

Chapter 10 by Eisenberger, Jones, Aselage, and Sucharski outlines how organization support theory (OST) can be extended to advance our knowledge of the employment relationship. The authors outline a number of ways by which OST can make additional contributions to our understanding of the exchange relationship. Specifically, the authors demonstrate how social accounts may influence employees' perception of the treatment they receive. Second, they examine how socialization may affect the development of perceived organizational support (POS) in the early stages of the relationship, and assess the relevance of POS in contingent employment relationships. Finally, the authors argue that POS may play an important role in the relationship between human resource management practices and organizational performance.

Liden, Bauer, and Erdogan in Chapter 11 integrate leader–member exchange theory and socialization theory in the development of the employee–employer relationship. The authors argue that multiple organizational agents influence employees' perception of the employment relationship and the influence of the immediate leader may be particularly salient to the socialization of newcomers. Furthermore, organizational and national culture may be important contextual influences on the role of leaders in the socialization process. This chapter highlights some key issues for future research in examining the views of newcomers to the employment relationship.

7

Employer-oriented Strategic Approaches to the Employee–Organization Relationship

LYNN M. SHORE, LYMAN W. PORTER, AND
SHAKER A. ZAHRA

7.1 The employee–organization relationship

The nature of the employment relationship has been the subject of considerable interest in the literature. Most prior contributions on the topic, however, have come from industrial/labor relations, human resource management, organizational behavior, and industrial/organizational psychology scholars. Many of these researchers have focused on the individual level of analysis, while making inferences about the macro-effects of the employment relationship. In contrast, strategy and macro-organizational theorists generally have not given in-depth attention to employment relationships and their implications for individuals. Only recently have scholars linked the strategy and human resource management literature and discussed implications for the employment relationship. The focus of these recent analyses has been on categories of employees (e.g. clerical employees or programmers), not on the *individual* employee (cf. Lepak and Snell 1999; Shaw and Delery 2003; Wang, Tsui, Zhang, and Ma 2003). Yet, a consideration of the basic formulations of strategy theories can be informative about the nature of the relationship between the individual employee and the organization. In particular, such a consideration of several different strategy perspectives provides the basis for analyzing how the two key components of this interaction—the organization's agents and the employee—can influence the resulting employee–organization relationship (EOR). This analysis in turn permits the construction of a set of testable propositions for linking strategy theory with the EOR.

A key feature of the EOR is that one of the two parties involved—the organization—consists of multiple agents (Shore and Tetrick 1994; Rousseau 1995; Guest and Conway 2002). While presumably organizational agents work in concert to achieve corporate strategy, there is increasing evidence of a great deal of variability in the extent to which individuals and groups within organizations work toward common goals, or have a common vision of the organization. In a recent survey of 200 senior executives, only 12 percent reported that the majority of their workforce understood the company's strategic priorities (Accenture 2003). Therefore, inconsistency and confusion can result both across agents and over time in crafting the organization's approach to the EOR (Shore and Tetrick 1994).

The complexity and ever-changing nature of the EOR, the multiple agents involved, and the lack of understanding and agreement that often exists between the parties in the EOR, has made it difficult to provide clarity in this literature. However, given the evidence that an organization's strategies and goals influence the behavior of those who are members (Hallier and James 1997), we have opted to use that lens as an organizing framework for examining the EOR. In particular, we argue that organizational strategies and goals, as understood by multiple agents, determine the employer's approach to the EOR. Likewise, but not examined in this chapter, the individual's strategies and goals pertaining to work and life contribute to that side of the relationship. The resulting EOR, therefore, is formed by the strategies and goals of the two parties to the relationship, which can result in a relationship in which their respective strategies and goals are either aligned or misaligned. The remainder of this chapter focuses on the strategy perspectives of one of these parties, the employer, and how those perspectives can help to provide insights for understanding the nature of EORs that emerge.

7.2 Views of organization strategy

Strategic management scholars have applied different theories in their analyses of the firm and the sources of its competitive advantage. Early theories of the firm emphasize problems arising from agency relationships. Contemporary strategy research highlights the importance of a firm's upper echelon for value creation. Other researchers adopt a resource-based view or a dynamic capability perspective of the firm and the sources of a competitive advantage, defined as the ability of the firm to achieve superiority over its rivals. Each of these theories highlights different sources for value creation (defined here as superior financial performance compared to the firm's major industry or leading competitors). The strategy literature has argued for the firm's human resources (HR) as one potential source of value creation (Becker and Gerhart 1996). Empirical evidence is accumulating to support the impact of investment in human capital (e.g. training and development that enhances employee knowledge) on firm performance (cf. Huselid 1995; Delery and Doty 1996).

Though the four strategy theories discussed in this chapter have been used successfully at different levels of analysis, agency theory has been applied most frequently to top management and organizational elites. The upper echelon theory highlights the role of senior managers in shaping the values and characteristics of middle managers and other employees at lower levels of the hierarchy. Empirical analyses using fit models (e.g. Miles and Snow 1978; Porter 1980) have focused directly on functional areas (units) and specialized firms, defined as companies that compete in a single industry or have a single product. The resource-based view (RBV) is a theory of the firm and, as such, applies to company-wide operations. Finally, discussion of dynamic capabilities has examined firms, units, and individual activities, exhibiting a great deal of robustness in these analyses. Benefits from these capabilities are most obvious at the firm level of analysis.

We analyze these four theories described above because they make specific reference to human capital as a source of value creation, espousing different assumptions about the role of human capital in this regard. Together, the four theories provide a rich view of how the EOR could influence organizational performance and value creation. Table 7.1 presents these theories and the following sections discuss them in turn, outlining their potential implications for understanding the EOR.

7.2.1 Agency perspective

Agency theory suggests that when ownership and control of the firm are separated, the probability of misalignment in the goals of the principals (employers) and agents (employees) increases. While the term "agent" is synonymous with "employee" within agency theory, we depart from this labeling throughout the chapter. Instead, we use the term "agent" when referring to an individual who is acting as a representative of the organization in the enactment of the EOR, and "employee" when describing situations where the individual is representing his or her own interests in relation to the EOR.

Employees have an incentive to misrepresent their skills and abilities, act opportunistically, or even shirk their responsibilities. Problems arising from adverse selection and moral hazard also contribute to poor organizational performance (Eisenhardt 1989). Adverse selection refers to an employee's misrepresentation of her or his interests, skills, and abilities to gain a better contract with the firm. Moral hazard refers to the situation where the principal (employer) cannot directly observe the employee's behavior or when monitoring the employee's performance is too costly to be worthwhile. Principals, therefore, have to devise effective systems that monitor employees' behavior. Control systems are one such mechanism. Incentive programs also motivate employees to bond with the organization.

Under agency theory, legal contracts define with a high degree of specificity what employees should (not) do. Agency theory thus emphasizes the economic exchanges that transpire between the firm and its employees, underscoring the important role of formal contracts and financial incentives in creating a strong bond between the firm and its employees. This formalized and explicit approach to the EOR is consistent with the perspective in agency theory that employees seek to avoid risk (Gerhart and Trevor 1996). As such, the theory overlooks the psychological aspects of the EOR, where a sense of identification, feelings of belonging, values, or norms may drive employees to care deeply about their jobs and firms and identify with their specific tasks. Such deviations highlight a need for fit between individual and organizational goals, a view taken by the upper echelon perspective.

7.2.2 Upper echelon theory

This theory suggests that the organization, culture, and systems manifest the values, goals, and aspirations of senior executives (Hambrick and Mason 1984). These values and goals determine the firm's competitive strategy (i.e. the approach the organization

Table 7.1. *Views of organization strategy*

Organization strategy theories	Agency	Upper echelon	Resource-based view	Dynamic capability perspective
Key scholars	Jensen and Meckling (1976)	Hambrick and Mason (1984)	Penrose (1959); Barney (1991, 2001); Grant (1996)	Teece et al. (1997)
Concept of the firm	Nexus of contracts	Institution in the image of founders and senior managers	Bundle of resource stocks and flows that create capabilities that generate competitive advantage	Evolving set of key capabilities that could be deployed quickly and effectively for strategic advantage in dynamic environments
Locus of advantage	Efficiency	Equilibrium (fit)	Capability	Dynamic capabilities and strategic change
Strategic role of HR	Input	Execution of strategy	Uniqueness that delays imitation Firm-specific skills	Fresh flows of unique capabilities Adaptation
Employment relationship	Formal, codified, and grounded in dominant legal frameworks. Employer-centered formal exchange predominates.	Formal contracts and emphasis on tight fit with company. Employer invests in keeping valuable, key employees and seeks to control employees through governance systems.	Bundles of HR practices used to create unique competencies for competitive advantage. Core employees with trust-based social exchange relationships, non-core with temporary or contractual relationships.	Psychological contracts used to develop strong ties with company. Focus on creating and exploiting unique skills. Relationship is increasingly transient. Trust-based relationship, especially among knowledge employees.

adopts in competing, where it competes, and against whom). A strategy's ultimate success hinges on the resources and capabilities of the organization. Both tangible and intangible resources are crucial in this respect (Barney 2001). Different competitive strategies require different bundles of resources. Fit between the firm's competitive strategy and resources are paramount for market and competitive success. The theory highlights the importance of matching the skills of senior executives and employees with the demands of strategy implementations; these demands reflect the nature of the competitive arena in which the firm competes and the goals it aims to accomplish.

Upper echelon theory highlights the importance of managerial characteristics in shaping the firm's strategic decisions (e.g. diversification). The importance of fit between the organization's competitive strategy and its human resources and capabilities has been popularized in Miles and Snow (1978) and Porter (1980). Both typologies suggest that there are different strategies, and the successful execution of each of these strategies requires different managerial and human resource management (HRM) skills (Delery and Doty 1996). Thus, the importance of HRM and, indeed, the nature of the EOR depend heavily on the nature of the strategy followed by the firm.

One shortcoming of the fit perspective is that managers and their organizations do not know *a priori* what appropriate fit is. Also, the firm's external environment might change in unpredictable ways that compel managers to alter their strategic course. What does the firm do with employees who no longer fit the objectives and direction of the chosen competitive strategy? Downsizing, rightsizing, layoffs, and other restructuring activities have enabled some companies to achieve a successful turnaround. Yet, these actions have also deeply injured the employment relationship that once prevailed in companies (Baruch and Hind 1999). Employees are reported to be more cynical than ever at efforts intended to restructure and reorganize companies (O'Neil and Lenn 1995). These employees are also less likely to be loyal to their companies (Brockner et al. 1992). Restructuring efforts may stifle innovation. Finally, the concept of fit itself is difficult to gauge (Venkatraman 1986). Fit is transient and misalignments might be more prevalent than fit, which raises a question about the value added of the fit arguments.

7.2.3 Resource-based view

Another influential research stream within the strategy literature builds on the RBV of the firm. Penrose (1959) formulated the original arguments of this view and Barney (1991, 2001) recast it as a way of looking into how companies derive competitive advantage. It suggests that an organization can gain a competitive advantage by accumulating and deploying valuable and rare tangible and intangible resources that are difficult to imitate (Zahra and Nielsen 2002). The stock (how much and what types) and flows (changes in) of these resources can determine the nature of these capabilities and, as a result, the firm's competitive advantage (Wright et al. 2001). Intangible resources occupy a central role in the RBV (Grant 1996) because they are often difficult for competitors to imitate since they are not visible to outsiders. When they are spotted, competitors cannot fully decipher which resources are being used and how they are used (Reed and DeFillippi 1990), which delays imitation by the competition. It is also difficult to compress the development cycle for some intangibles. These qualities make the firm's human resources a prime intangible resource for companies that seek to create an enduring competitive advantage. Intangible resources (e.g. HR) take time to develop, are hard for outsiders to fully understand, and/or are difficult to imitate. HR also allows the firm to leverage its other key assets in ways that create and sustain a competitive advantage. A highly skilled labor force can harness and exploit innovative technologies in ways that increase the firm's competitive superiority relative to its rivals. HR also enables the firm to understand the knowledge that resides outside its boundaries, import this knowledge, and then effectively use it in innovative ways (Zahra and George 2002).

Intangible resources (e.g. employee motivation and commitment to the company) can create a competitive advantage on their own. Alternatively, they could be used to leverage the firm's tangible assets. When they leverage tangible assets, intangibles can protect the firm against rapid imitation of existing and potential rivals. This leveraging process might explain the persistence of heterogeneity in firms' strategic choices and financial performance (e.g. return on equity).

A key implication of the RBV is the importance of investing in building the firm's HR assets, resources, and capabilities (Lepak and Snell 1999). Thus, the EOR should matter a great deal within the RBV. The EOR determines the motivation and dedication of employees, their attachment to the firm, and their organizational commitment. Companies have the responsibility to cultivate and harvest the expertise and knowledge of their employees and use that knowledge as a foundation for making strategic changes that enhance the firm's competitive position and financial performance.

The RBV raises an important question: Should the firm build capabilities internally or use external sources, or combine both? Following the RBV internal control of assets is preferred. While internalization of human capital enhances a firm's core capabilities, there are also associated costs such as staffing, training, compensation, and benefits that need to be considered (Rousseau and Wade-Benzoni 1994). Furthermore, possession of resources does not confer an advantage on the firm; the firm must work hard to transform that resource into a capability. This requires integration and the combination of various resources (Zahra and Nielsen 2002). Thus, the RBV suggests that employee skills that are essential to the firm's competitiveness should be developed and maintained internally, while those skills that are of limited value can be contracted or outsourced (Lepak and Snell 1999). If the firm opts to use external sources for strategic and financial considerations, integration becomes imperative for value creation.

The implications of the RBV for the EOR have not been examined systematically and few normative prescriptions emerge from past analyses. Still, the RBV does not necessarily advocate control of assets as long as the firm can ensure sufficient supply of resources for its operations and that these sources are carefully managed and integrated. The EOR, therefore, can be transient in nature, raising an interesting question about the structuring of employment contracts about the pay, rewards, and termination of employees. However, this practice can give the firm flexibility in responding to changing circumstances. It can also enable the firm to get rid of the "deadwood." It could also give the firm access to up-to-date skills that can be used quickly. Conversely, companies might lose their key sources of advantage if they rely excessively on the transient labor force. The firm might lose the important "organizational memory" that allows it to build and keep its absorptive capacity current. Transient employees may have little incentive to share their knowledge with the "employing" firm and, therefore, important experiences and knowledge are lost. Proprietary knowledge is an important source of competitive advantage in dynamic markets (Grant 1996) and it is hard to keep this knowledge from outsiders when the EOR is transient. These views are fundamental to understanding the dynamic capability perspective.

7.2.4 Dynamic capability perspective

According to this view, a firm's dynamic capabilities are a key determinant of its ability to create and sustain a competitive advantage, especially in rapidly changing markets. These capabilities evolve over time, resulting from the integration of multiple capabilities as well as defining the paths of new capabilities (Teece et al. 1997). Dynamic capabilities are grounded in the firm's knowledge base, which is formed over time based on experiences and the composition of the labor force. Accordingly, the firm should seek to attract and retain employees with unique talents and skills. Investments are made in HR in a way that keeps these resources current and integrated. The currency is necessary because skills become dated or obsolete. Without upgrades, core competencies become core rigidities that limit the organization's ability to innovate and compete. Currency of organizational skills is assured by the reskilling of the workforce and hiring talented employees, as would be expected under familiar theories of human capital. Integration, both formal and informal, is essential for creating dynamic capabilities and keeping them current.

The need for currency and integration poses a dilemma for a firm's executives. The higher a firm's focus on integration, the less flexibility it has in revamping or upgrading some of its HR. Legal constraints, business ethics, and reputational effects often combine to limit a company's discretion in letting go of or replacing people. There are also limits to what companies can do to upgrade their employees' skills. The need for currency and integration also requires a flexible organization, one in which it is easy to retain core competencies while replenishing the skill base of the firm. Understandably, networks are becoming widely recognized organizational forms. They allow the organization to retain proprietary knowledge while promoting the absorption of externally created knowledge.

A network organizational form can alter the EOR in significant ways. In these organizations, relationships are transient and are subject to change, especially in dynamic environments. Hierarchies are replaced with structures intended to enable employees to communicate and collaborate across existing boundaries. Employees (and other agents) are encouraged—indeed, expected—to find their own space within the firm.

Within this framework, employees are expected to behave entrepreneurially by seeking and bearing calculated risks that allow them to use their creativity in ways that redefine their roles and responsibilities while enriching the firm's performance. As such, the organization provides the context and framework for the employment relationship, but the nature of this relationship is subject to considerable ambiguity and change.

Social rather than hierarchical controls are important in network organizations (O'Donnell 2000). Where roles change in response to environmental dynamism, trust- and relationship-based controls become especially important for coordination. In dynamic environments where the competition centers on the creation and exploitation of new knowledge, social controls become crucial as traditional agency theory solutions fail to motivate employees or give them an incentive. Knowledgeable employees possess valuable information that the organization cannot fully comprehend or capture, making the formal monitoring of employees costly and inefficient. In knowledge-based competitive environments, it is necessary to exercise discretion in order to adapt to continuously changing environments. Hierarchical controls can stifle initiative and reduce discretion.

The need for social controls stems also from the very nature of network organizations, which are characterized by complex interdependence among their various participants (Roth and O' Donnell 1996). Units of a large corporation, for example, often enjoy considerable autonomy. Subsidiaries of multinationals have unique mandates, develop unique cultures, and pursue different competitive strategies. Yet, overall organizational goal achievement requires integration and coordination. Information asymmetry between the firm's headquarters and its division managers requires giving managers greater degrees of discretion in leading their operations, without inducing rigidity into the firm's formal structure. Social controls, as just discussed, require trust. In turn, trust is based on fulfilling mutual obligations among exchange parties, which does not always happen in the EOR (Shore and Barksdale 1998). When fulfilled, high mutual obligations can enhance employees' commitment to the firm and their identification with its values. When this commitment is recognized and appreciated, employees are apt to work harder to achieve the firm's goals and accomplish its mission (Lepak and Snell 1999).

7.3 Agent and employee influence on the EOR

In this Section, we further develop our ideas linking each of the four strategy theories we described above in relation to the EOR. A challenge is to propose mechanisms through which macro-level theories of the firm may influence the EOR, a cross-level phenomenon. A common theme in both strategy and EOR literatures is the inclusion of agents of the firm, and we thus spotlight this element of the EOR in subsequent discussions. However, it is important to note that views of the agent are quite variable across these theoretical domains. Researchers in business strategy discuss the agent of the firm from a rational perspective. That is, agents are self-interested but through proper incentives will align their interests with the firm allowing for the successful attainment of organizational goals (cf. Eisenhardt 1989). EOR literature, such as psychological contracts (Rousseau 1995) and perceived organizational support (Eisenberger et al. 1986; Shore and Shore 1995), typically refer to the organization without specifically theorizing about the agents who represent it. In both cases, the assumption is that organizational agents work on behalf of the organization. However, evidence (cf. Liden et al. 1997) suggests that agents (e.g. managers) differ in many ways, even in the same organizational environment and when carrying out similar roles as organizational agents.

We seek to address this gap in the EOR literature by theorizing about the role of the agent in developing and maintaining the employee–organization exchange relationship. Our approach is to use the four theories of strategy described above to provide a basis for understanding how agents of the firm may behave while enacting the EOR. We propose that a sense-making process occurs when agents consider how best to enact strategic initiatives, yielding greater variability than has been suggested in theories of the firm.

Figure 7.1 depicts the process through which agents develop EORs. Multiple factors may influence the agent of the firm who is expected to carry out the firm's strategies by means of the EOR (Hallier and James 1997), including the organizational culture, the personal interests and power base of the agent, the agent's understanding of the

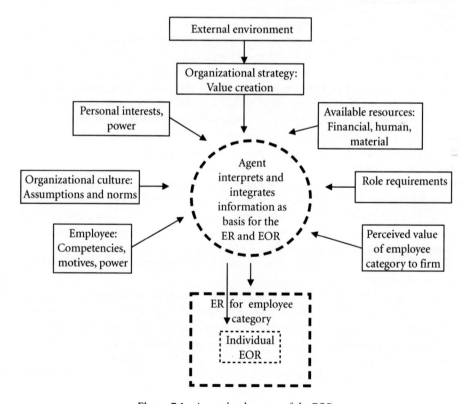

Figure 7.1. *Agent development of the EOR.*

strategy, available resources, role requirements, the perceived value of the group (human capital), and perceived employee characteristics. Through consideration of these varied factors, the agent develops ideas for carrying out the strategy through the development or revision of the employment relationship (ER) described below, and the EOR.

The ER has been studied as a group-level phenomenon, in which employees in particular roles (e.g. technically skilled employees) are viewed by agents of the firm as having a designated exchange with the organization. Tsui et al. (1997) examined the ER for different categories of employees, and showed that the ER can take several forms. Using inducements and contributions, they created four categories of employ-ment relationships, two balanced (inducements and contributions were both either high or low) and two unbalanced (when inducements was high, contributions was low, or vice versa). In another model, Lepak and Snell (1999) expanded on existing views of the ER (cf. Rousseau 1995; Tsui et al. 1995) by arguing for the critical role of human capital (i.e. the value and uniqueness of a particular group to the accomplish-ment of the organization's objectives) in determining different types of ERs.

In Figure 7.1, we specify how the EOR is embedded in the ER. While variability is expected in the EOR, the ER establishes the parameters within which such variations occur. The exchange of inducements and contributions reflected in the ER are influenced by multiple factors, such as occupation and industry (cf. Becker 1964; Freeman 1972). As an example, much evidence exists for labor markets, both internal and external, and how these influence employee opportunities, salary, and benefits (Scarpello et al. 1995). Likewise, differing expectations and employee obligations will be found in diverse settings and will vary based on whether specified by the agent or employee (Herriot et al. 1997; Porter et al. 1998). The EOR is thus influenced by the nature of the ER, though individual employees will have somewhat varied EORs depending on among other things, the relationship with his or her immediate man-ager (Graen and Scandura 1987; Graen and Uhl-Bien 1995), managerial potential (Wayne et al. 1997), and the necessity for the employee's particular skills or knowledge for the success of the firm (Lepak and Snell 1999).

A final element in the model in Figure 7.1 is the employee. As stated previously, the EOR represents the relationship between the employee and organization. Thus, we argue that perceived employee competencies, motives, and power are considerations for the agent who is developing the EOR. However, note that we have intentionally put the spotlight on the agent as the core focus in our subsequent discussion linking strategy theories to the EOR, in light of our goal of further developing the employer side of the EOR.

Now that we have described key factors that may influence the agent in develop-ing and enacting the EOR, we further refine our ideas using the lenses of the four strategy theories. Table 7.2 summarizes the ways in which agents and employees may influence the EOR, which we describe in more detail below. As shown in Table 7.2, we outline several ways in which agents influence the EOR, including specification of the EOR, and the role and the motives of the agent in establishing and maintaining the EOR within each of the four theoretical perspectives. Likewise, individual employees influence the EOR through their competencies (knowledge, skills, and

Table 7.2. *Agent and employee influence on the EOR*

Sources of influence on the EOR		Agency	Upper echelon	Resource-based view perspective	Dynamic capability
Agent (organizational representative)	Specification (variability across agents in executing the EOR)	Highly standardized EOR	Variability across agents based on different roles in carrying out the strategy and varying interpretations of strategy	EOR differences based on distinctions between core and non-core employees; low variability across agents within core/non-core segments of employees	Many distinctions among agents; highly individualized EOR
	Role of agent	Carry out formalized contracts	Align EOR with top management strategy	For core, define EORs that encourage commitment; for non-core define EORs to address present organizational needs	Adjust the EOR as needed
	Motives	Assure conformity to the contracts	Support top management directives	Attract and retain core employees	Attract, enhance, and retain currently relevant employee capabilities
Individual (recipient of the EOR)	Competencies (KSAs)	Role-based competencies influence EOR	Relevance of competencies to current strategy	Possessing capabilities that are unique and not easy to replace or acquire	Possessing and updating firm-relevant and unique KSAs including social/network competencies
	Motives	Self-serving	Emphasize the individual's fit with the strategy	Leverage not easily replaceable capabilities	Continually enhance capabilities
	Power/influence	Initial contract, or renegotiation	Degree of fit allows for influence in determining the EOR	Degree of uniqueness and difficult to replace or acquire capabilities	Highly competency based, and constantly changing

abilities), motives, and power bases, and each of the four theories suggest different implications of these individual attributes for the EOR.

7.3.1 Agency perspective

Agent influence

From an agency perspective, there should be relatively little variation in how different agents of the organization structure and implement employment relationships with employees. Each agent would be expected to establish a highly standardized (for that organization) relationship with each employee who reports to the agent. The role of the agent is to put into practice formalized contracts that lay out clear expectations for the behavior and performance of the employee. It would not be part of an agent's role to deviate from this formalized and standardized contract format. Thus, it would be a breach by the agent of the responsibilities of the role if ad hoc or informal types of employment relationships were established with one or more employees.

The motive of an agent in carrying out the employer's part of the EOR within the agency perspective is to gain adherence and compliance of the employee with the formal contract. An inability or unwillingness to obtain and maintain such adherence of the employee represents a failure to appropriately represent the employer's interests. Therefore, the agent would be motivated to guard against this possibility because of the potential negative consequences that could follow from a lack of contract conformity, including a threat to the agent's own self-interest if held responsible by upper management (Hallier and James 1997).

Individual influence

This perspective emphasizes the economic relationship between employees and the organization, suggesting that the EOR consists of formalized agreements in which there is a specification of rights and responsibilities for job holders. Through standardized selection procedures, the organization seeks role- or job-based competencies, and role-based competencies in turn define the basis for the EOR. Employees, therefore, are expected at hire to have the competencies to carry out the responsibilities of the job, and would be afforded certain rights as part of their fulfillment of job responsibilities.

Under agency theory, the interests and goals of principals and agents are not necessarily aligned. This suggests that employees will be motivated by self-interest, seeking formalized agreements that protect their rights and include specification of responsibilities. Consequently, any given individual employee should have relatively little influence on the EOR, since agreements between employees and the organization are primarily job based.

7.3.2 Upper echelon perspective

Agent influence

In the upper echelon perspective, there would be considerable variability across agents from one organization to another in establishing and implementing EORs with employees. This variability would depend on the particular "fit" of the organization's strategy to the firm's external environment. In addition, however, there would also be variability across agents within an organization depending on the particular role that each agent has in carrying out the organization's strategy as set by top management.

Using the Miles and Snow (1978) typology, agents in a "defender" type of organization would establish EORs much more like those described in agency theory, with the relationships being grounded in contracts that specified explicit expectations and standards of performance. For organizations at the other end of the Miles–Snow spectrum, "prospector" organizations, agents would be expected to set up EORs that were more jointly determined with employees and which took into consideration, within limits, their views and expectations. Agents in "analyzer" organizations would influence EORs in a manner that was not as rigid as that of those in defender organizations, but also less flexible than the relationships in prospector organizations. Similarly, using the Porter (1980) typology, agents in "low cost producer" organizations would attempt to establish considerably different EORs from those in, say, "niche player" or "innovator" organizations. Again, the point is that there would be variability in agent-established and -implemented EORs from one organization to another based on the strategy being followed by the top echelon. Within any given organization, the variability across agents in influencing the EOR would depend on the specific role obligations of the agent in relation to the organization's strategy for interacting with its environment. In addition, however, and not to be minimized, is that within-firm agent influence variability would depend on a given agent's interpretation of what constitutes the strategy of top management. It cannot be assumed that all agents within an organization would interpret the strategy in the same way, and hence EORs could vary by that factor as well as by the role of the agent.

Regardless of the variability of agent-influenced EORs across organizations, and within the same organization, based on the factors discussed above, all agents in this (upper echelon) perspective would have one common role element: To align any given EOR with top management's strategy—as interpreted by the agent. Thus, in this perspective the agent "translates" the organization's strategy into sets of EORs that are structured to be consistent with, and support, that strategy. Assuming that the top echelon has both developed and communicated a coherent strategy, the agent's role imperatives with respect to EORs are clear. Likewise, in this perspective, the motives of the agent representing the employer should be unambiguous: To support strategy directions set by top management. Any employment arrangement that would potentially deviate from that objective would be resisted by the agent, even if beneficial to the other party (i.e. the employee).

Individual influence
The upper echelon perspective is a top-down approach to governance in which the focus is on linking competitive strategy and employee capabilities. As a result, employee competencies that support strategy will greatly influence the EOR. Depending on the strategy that is enacted by senior executives, different employee

capabilities will be sought and rewarded. For example, using Miles and Snow's (1978) typology, prospector firms need employees who have the ability to effectively recruit new hires and skills that contribute to an increase in market share. Defender firms, however, need employees who have skills that allow the firm to maintain market share and control costs (Scarpello et al. 1995). Likewise, individual employees will likely be motivated to emphasize their fit with current strategy. That is, employees will attempt to show their contribution to market growth when working for executives enacting a prospector strategy, and employees in firms enacting a defender strategy will seek ways to show their contribution to internal efficiency efforts and toward minimizing costs. The upper echelon perspective further suggests that agents of the firm seek to align any particular EOR with corporate strategy, so that employees who are perceived to have the capabilities to support the strategy will have the greatest amount of power and influence in determining the EOR.

7.3.3 Resource-based view

Agent influence
The discussion in the RBV of unique and valuable resources, when applied to employees, is akin to Handy's (1989) idea of the shamrock organization in which employees can be placed in distinct categories reflecting their value to the firm. Handy defined "core" employees as those who have essential organizational knowledge and skills. Building on this idea, we propose that core employees are deemed by the organization to be critical and distinctive human resources who could not easily be replaced, whereas non-core employees are those viewed as more commodity-like resources and relatively easily substitutable. The type of influence of the agent in developing EORs with employees will depend heavily on a distinction between "core" and "non-core" employees for a given organization. Thus, agents in dealing with the former type of employees would have different levels and types of influence on EORs, compared to those agents interacting with non-core employees. Within each segment of employees, the influence of agents would be relatively similar, and across the two segments it would be different.

For core employees, the role of the agent is to try to design the EOR in such a way that it promotes the development of employee commitment to the employer. This clearly is a more challenging role than simply, say, carrying out formalized contracts as in an agency perspective or aligning the EOR with top management strategy in an upper echelon-determined fit strategy. The reason is that it is not automatically clear to the agent how this can be done, and, therefore, the role requirements for the agent are relatively ambiguous. For non-core employees, the agent's role is more straightforward: To design the EOR to meet basic organizational needs and objectives. The agent should not be concerned with how the EOR will affect the employee's organizational commitment, in contrast with the core employee situation.

The motives for the agent in the RBV are to be able to attract and retain critical core employees. To the extent that this can be accomplished, the agent will be in a position to receive greater rewards and recognition from the employer. Obviously, there will be many variables not under the direct control of the agent that will affect the core employee's response to the EOR, but the agent should be motivated to give attention to those features of the EOR that can be influenced directly by the agent. For non-core employees, the agent is motivated to make cost-efficient EORs that do not hinder meeting basic organizational objectives.

Individual influence

The RBV of the firm suggests that intangible, rare competencies create a competitive advantage for the firm. These employee competencies therefore have a strong influence on the development and revision of the EOR. The RBV suggests that firms encourage the commitment of core employees whose special competencies create opportunities for the success of the firm. Often, organizations invest in the development of such competencies and are particularly intent on retaining employees whose competencies are viewed as irreplaceable.

The RBV of the firm implies that employees will be motivated to leverage capabilities by emphasizing that their knowledge, skills, and abilities are not easy for the firm to replace, as these capabilities allow employees to influence the EOR to their advantage. Being viewed as part of the "core" enhances the employee's ability to influence the EOR, and being "non-core" suggests little power and influence on the EOR. Likewise, empirical evidence suggests that employees seek EORs that are typified by high commitment by both parties (Rhoades and Eisenberger 2002). Individuals make efforts to negotiate or revise agreements that reflect employer commitment, including developmental opportunities, promotions, and participation in decision-making (Wayne et al. 1997, 2002).

7.3.4 Dynamic capability perspective

Agent influence

Following the dynamic capability perspective, there would be expected to be many variations in the way that agents design and execute EORs to serve the purposes of the employer. Thus, the degree of agent influence, and the type or nature of that influence, on the EOR should range considerably from one agent to another within an organization, and among agents across organizations. The reason is that the EOR from the dynamic capability perspective is expected to be highly individualized, depending not only on who the employee is but also on the changing sets of circumstances faced by the employer in making rapid adaptations to the external environment. No two EORs are expected to look exactly the same if the strategy of the organization is viewed in this way.

The role of the agent representing the employer in the dynamic capabilities approach would be to fashion an EOR that meets the current and specific requirements of the organization *and* that is sufficiently flexible to meet changing needs and environmental demands faced by the employer. The agent's role is to be nimble in influencing the nature and content of EORs under the agent's purview. Again, as is the case with agents in the RBV perspective dealing with core employees, the challenges for the agent in carrying out this role are much higher than in the agency and upper echelon perspectives, discussed earlier.

An employer's representative, from a dynamic capability perspective, is to try to attract and retain employees with currently relevant capabilities but also to be prepared to alter EORs as needed. The more an agent can keep the EOR flexible while meeting the employer's current objectives, the more the agent can make subsequent changes that will meet a revised set of needs. These motives of the agent, of course, may be in direct conflict with those of the employee. The employee is likely to want as much certainty as possible in the EOR (Shore and Tetrick 1994), while the agent is motivated to do exactly the opposite: Keep the EOR as flexible and open-ended as possible.

Individual influence

The dynamic capability perspective suggests that firms seek employees who possess firm-relevant and unique competencies that meet the firm's current needs. Critical competencies will change with the demands of the external environment, and so employees who are able to not only develop and retain needed competencies, but also adapt to changing firm demands, will be highly sought after. Further, flattened organizational structures have intensified the value of social networks so that the dynamic capability perspective suggests that such social skills will be critical to firm success. Thus, the EOR from this perspective will be quite individualized, and influenced by currently needed competencies and social linkages.

The dynamic capability perspective implies that employees will be motivated to continually enhance their capabilities and retain their position in valued networks. Employees will seek to negotiate EORs that create developmental opportunities for enhanced capabilities and marketability (Herriot and Pemberton 1995). Furthermore, employees realize the criticality of "being in the know" so that they can adapt to changing competitive strategies and external environmental pressures, and provide critical knowledge to the firm. Thus, social networks have the potential to enhance employee abilities to negotiate and modify the EOR in ways that serve their own interests, while also serving the interests of the firm.

7.4 Propositions

Each of the four strategy theories analyzed in this chapter suggests somewhat different ways of viewing the impact of the firm on the EOR. It is our goal to provide mechanisms for linking organizational strategy and the EOR as a means of further developing the organizational aspect in research on the EOR. As described above, the four theories of strategy imply differential influences of agents and individual employees on the EOR. Below, we provide further development of our arguments linking strategy theory with the EOR and offer a set of testable propositions.

Proposition 1 *Strength of agent influence: The strength of agent influence on the EOR, relative to the influence of the individual, will decrease from the AT to UE to RBV to DC strategy perspectives.*

The relative strength of agent versus employee influence on the EOR obviously will determine the extent to which EORs are potentially modifiable as a result of employee needs, intents, and actions. Proposition 1 hypothesizes that an agent will have the most power to structure and enforce an EOR when the relationship is viewed from an agency theory (AT) perspective, and relatively the least power—in relation to the individual—in the dynamic capability (DC) perspective. The upper echelon (UE) and resource-based view (RBV) perspectives would be intermediate in this respect. The rationale is that in an AT perspective at one end of the continuum of amount of agent influence, the employer (organization) structures formalized contracts to be imposed and executed by the agent in a fixed manner. Consequently, from the AT perspective, the individual employee has relatively little power to modify EORs. The reverse is true when viewing organizations from the DC perspective, where individualized EORs are established based on variations in the scarcity and uniqueness of individual employee capabilities in accordance with external market changes and (to a lesser extent) internal changes in social dynamics. Thus, when viewed from a DC perspective, the individual is a "bigger player" in relation to the agent.

Proposition 2   *Variability of agent influence: The amount of variability of agent influence on EORs within organizations will increase from the AT to UE to RBV to DC* · *strategy perspectives.*

The pattern of constructed EORs within a given organization will be affected by the degree of uniformity of influence from agent to agent. When such variability is low, one EOR will look much like another EOR, but when variability is high there is much more opportunity for distinctive or unique EORs to be established for particular employees. In Proposition 2, the prediction is that variability of agent influence (among an organization's set of agents) will increase from the AT through the UE and RBV to the DC perspective. All agents in the former perspective are expected to represent the organization in ways that perform standardized and formalized EORs. When analyzing organizations (employers) from a more RBV or DC perspective, different agents will be viewed as dealing with subsets of employees differentiated by the degree to which their capabilities are core for the organization and made relatively valuable by contextual factors. Thus, the amount of within-organization agent influence in establishing and building EORs is expected to be much greater than when considered from AT or UE strategic frameworks.

Consider, for example, differences between organizations in the amount of agent influence that may be present. In highly formalized organizations such as the military, agency theory and upper echelon theory predictions may be quite applicable. Directives flow from the top to the bottom of the organization, and the agent has little influence on the EOR. In fact, the ER and EOR are likely very similar in such settings. In contrast, the growth in service-based, knowledge-intensive industries, where organizations are flatter and less hierarchical in order to respond quickly to changing environments, suggests a fit with RBV and DCP theory predictions. Agents in such industries are likely to have much more latitude in determining EORs to ensure needed capabilities (knowledge and skills) among employees in response to rapidly evolving environmental challenges.

Proposition 3 *Who speaks for the organization? The clarity of "who represents (speaks for) the organization" in the EOR will diminish from the AT to UE to RBV to DC strategy perspectives.*

The issue of "who speaks for the organization?" in constructing EORs is critical for understanding the nature and characteristics of the resulting EORs that emerge from the process. The answer to the question of who speaks for the "E," or employee—in virtually any EOR involving professional, technical, and managerial employees—is presumably clear: Only the individual speaks for himself or herself. That is not, however, the case with the "O" or organization side of the relationship. Different answers are possible (as could be demonstrated, e.g. when this question is posed to a sample of employees or of students of organizations). We propose that the degree of ambiguity is accentuated in some of the four organizational strategy perspectives discussed earlier more than others. Thus, clarity should be greatest in the AT perspective, where a designated agent for the principal would represent the employer. Almost the same degree of clarity would exist in the UE perspective, except in those instances where there have been recent changes in top management or in the specific directions of top management strategy. In both perspectives, views of either the owner (AE) or top management (UE) set the direction that agents of the firm need to follow. In the RBV and DC perspectives, particularly the latter, greater elements of uncertainty and ambiguity are introduced because of the shifting nature of employer requirements. The "O" becomes fuzzier and therefore the clarity of who represents the employer is also affected. These perspectives are aligned with "newer" organizational forms that are flatter and rely more heavily on networks. Restructuring and other organizational change efforts also mean more frequent changes in the agents who represent the firm. Issues surrounding this basic question are a prime topic for future research that attempts to link organizational strategies to the specific relationships of employees to the employer.

Proposition 4 *Stability of EORs across time: EORs will be most stable across time in the AT and UE strategy perspectives (compared to RBV and DC perspectives).*

If EORs are relatively stable over time, both agents and employees can rely on the fulfillment of the EOR with associated advantages for the firm (Morrison and Robinson 1997). Based on the basic elements of the four different strategy perspectives discussed in this chapter, it could be assumed that EORs will have more stability across time in the AT and UE frameworks than in the RBV and DCP frameworks. This is because owners and top management are viewed as more in control of EORs in these two strategy perspectives and can exert more consistent—even if wrong or incorrect—pressure for stability versus change. From RBV and DC perspectives, the context, particularly the external environment, is a more important element in the overall equation. Assuming the tendency for constant change in most external environments, it would follow that maintaining EOR stability would be less valued in these frameworks.

Proposition 5 *Alignment between EORs and firm strategy: AT and the UE perspectives should have the greatest likelihood of alignment between EORs and firm strategy, followed by the RBV, with the dynamic capabilities perspective suggesting the least likelihood of alignment between the EOR and firm strategy.*

Alignment between the firm strategy and the EOR is a critical issue for successful organizational performance. In order for a given organizational strategy to be enacted, internal systems, including the EOR, must support the strategy. The four theories of the firm presented imply different degrees of alignment between the strategy and the EOR, in part because of the proposed mechanisms for creating consistency in agent actions for enacting and revising EORs. Agency theory and upper echelon perspectives suggest mechanisms for creating uniformity in agent actions, either based on formal contracts (AE) or top management directives (UE).

In contrast, the RBV suggests two types of employees—core and non-core—which create some pressures that can lead to potential misalignment. The core are those employees who are viewed as central to the organization's goals, and are more likely to receive the "perks" of long-term employment and investment in professional development. Conversely, non-core employees are more likely to be temporary or contract workers who are viewed as less critical to the organizational strategy, giving the firm flexibility in changing times. The non-core may be seeking ways to move to a core position (e.g. by acting committed), creating pressures to modify the EOR. The presence of contingent or non-core employees may also undermine the EOR for the core by lowering organizational trust levels (Pearce 1993). Likewise, agents may have different ideas about how to create commitment through the EOR, and market pressures may cause refinements of the EOR that contribute to perceptions of employer violation, hence undermining specific corporate strategies. Considerable evidence is accumulating that the perceived violation of organizational promises can greatly undermine the EOR and lower employee support of the organization (cf. Robinson et al. 1994; Morrison and Robinson 1997; Turnley and Feldman 1999).

The DC perspective suggests the possibility of significant challenges in creating alignment between the strategy and the EOR. Pressures to create highly individualized EORs are likely to contribute to social comparisons (Ang et al. 2003) that may create perceptions of injustice—undermining efforts to retain employees with currently relevant capabilities. A fairly extensive body of literature is accumulating that suggests the important role of fairness in the establishment and maintenance of EORs (cf. Wayne et al. 1997, 2002; Masterson et al. 2000).

Proposition 6 *Sources of changes in situational dynamics and resulting EOR—Firm strategy alignment: For each theory of the firm, alignment of the firm's strategy and the EOR will be influenced by changes in specific sources of situational dynamics.*

Proposition 6a   *For AT, changes in the regulatory environment provide the greatest potential source of misalignment.*

Proposition 6b   *For UE theory, revised corporate strategy, either based on new executive leadership or changes in market conditions, provides the greatest potential source of misalignment.*

Proposition 6c   *For the RBV, market changes that influence the degree to which investments in core employees create a market advantage for the firm provide the greatest potential source of misalignment.*

Proposition 6d   *For the DC perspective, market pressures for ongoing changes in needed capabilities provide the greatest potential source of misalignment.*

Clearly, EORs are likely to be strongly influenced by contextual or situational factors. It is therefore important to try to understand which particular factors are most likely to be seen as having the greatest influence when viewed from different strategy perspectives. In AT, changes in the regulatory environment provide the greatest potential source of misalignment between the strategy and the EOR. The formalized contractual process is likely to create entrenched systems typified by rules and regulations. As organizations attempt to revise their strategy in response to these regulatory changes, AE suggests that the very systems that create stability (contracts, rules, and procedures) may also lead to inflexibility in the EOR. An AT perspective suggests that even though both agents and employees are likely to have some difficulties with modifying the EOR, this is more likely for employees because they will view the formalized agreement as representing explicit firm promises.

In the UE theory, revisions in the corporate strategy, either based on new executive leadership or changes in market conditions, provides the greatest potential source of misalignment between the strategy and the EOR. This is because agents may have varying interpretations of these changes, particularly depending on their organizational role. For example, an agent who works in an area of new growth or firm redirection is likely to create alignment between the revised strategy and the EOR given the imperatives of such a task and the benefits inherent in such alignment. In contrast, an agent whose role involves reduction in force due to redirected strategy may be more challenged to create alignment between the new strategy and the EOR, particularly if remaining employees are critical to firm success (Brockner et al. 1987).

The RBV suggests that market changes may influence the degree to which investments in previously identified core employees create an advantage for the firm. New strategies that redirect resources away from those employees who up to now have been considered core may provide the greatest potential source of misalignment. Agents given the task of revising the EOR of former core employees may find this especially challenging, provided that such relationships likely are based on social exchanges that imply broad and diffuse obligations and high levels of trust (Blau 1964).

In the DC perspective, market pressures creating ongoing changes in needed capabilities provide the greatest potential source of misalignment, particularly since individualized EORs must represent a "coherent" means of operationalizing strategy. DC perspective suggests that agents must continually create, revise, and sever EORs in an effort to support firm competitiveness. Thus, it is advantageous for firms to establish EORs that do not provide guarantees of security, in order to respond quickly to market pressures for employee capabilities that meet current and future strategic needs of the firm.

7.5 Conclusions

The goal of this chapter was to use the four theories of organizational strategy as a starting point for developing new ways of thinking about the organization side of the EOR. Though some researchers have put forth thought-provoking ideas for linking macro- and micro-perspectives of the EOR (cf. Rousseau and Wade-Benzoni 1994; Tsui et al. 1997), much more development is needed, with particular focus on the firm itself.

The four theories of organizational strategy presented offer several new ways of thinking about the EOR. These theories suggest the importance of strategy as a unifying framework for organizational members. The actual strategy as well as the interpretation of the strategy by both parties to the EOR—that is, agents as organizational representatives, and individual employees—can have a strong impact on the success of the firm. These theories, however, also vary in terms of the degree to which agents and employees would be expected to play a role in developing the EOR. Agency and upper echelon theories imply a coherency of EORs flowing from either the principal (AT) or senior management (UE) views of organizational strategy, which are then enacted by agents through the EOR. In contrast, the RBV and DC perspectives imply greater variability in EORs, given the important role of employee capabilities as a source of competitive advantage.

Different concepts of the firm underlie each theory, ranging from a nexus of contracts in AT to an evolving set of key capabilities in the DC perspective. In contrast, most of the EOR literature, whether focusing on the employment relationship (Tsui et al. 1997; Tsui and Wang 2002), psychological contracts (Rousseau 1995), or perceived organizational support (Eisenberger et al. 1986), refers to the "organization" as though there is a common understanding of the term. Yet, the theories described here suggest different theoretical framings of "the firm," each of which has distinct implications for the EOR.

This chapter focused on two sources of influence on the EOR—the agent and the individual employee—and showed how each source would be theorized to operate differently depending on the strategy theory applied. We have proposed that the strength of agent influence on the EOR, relative to the influence of the individual employee, will vary depending on which theory of the firm is applied. Clearly, elaboration of these ideas, along with empirical testing, should help to further develop the EOR literature.

Another contribution of this chapter is the discussion of alignment between organizational strategy and the EOR through the four lenses provided by the theories. The EOR through its influence on employee behavior plays a critical role in the success of the firm. For example, the DC perspective highlights the dilemma many organizations face today in seeking the effective alignment of strategy and EORs. This perspective argues for the strong influence of the quickly changing environment, creating pressures for revision of the EOR. Through revisions, potential violations are more likely, creating challenges for maintaining alignment.

We believe that several different streams of research need development to build on our ideas. First, more attention should be given to the employer side of the EOR. While a great deal of evidence establishes the importance of the organizational context in both the corporate strategy and human resource strategy literature, much of the EOR literature involves individual perceptions without consideration of the actual context. Furthermore, researchers have built links between the corporate strategy and human resource strategy literature, and more recently the ER literature (cf. Lepak and Snell 1999; Wang et al. 2003). As yet, these more macro-literatures have focused on organizational differences, and have not been systematically applied to understanding the relationship that the individual employee has *within* an organization, as depicted in the EOR. This chapter provides one approach for creating connections between more macro-influences on the EOR to more micro-views of this relationship.

Second, we have not discussed the impact of specific organizational strategies on the EOR. While an emerging area of the literature is beginning to link types of strategies, the employment relationship (ER), and firm effectiveness (Wang et al. 2003), further theoretical and empirical work is clearly needed. Of particular importance is future research that extends to the micro-level by adding the EOR to models of organizational strategy and the ER. We also believe there is a need for EOR research that links strategy with individual performance outcomes as well as firm performance.

A third area of needed research is the development of ideas about the agent. Throughout this chapter, we discuss the agent without explicating who may play that role. While prior conceptualizations have proposed that the immediate supervisor, recruiters, and top management may all be viewed by employees as agents in the EOR (Shore and Tetrick 1994; Rousseau 1995), clearly empirical research is needed, especially with regard to the interactions within and among these various sets of organizational agents.

Finally, we encourage both conceptual and empirical work that explores the degree of match between the employment relationship offered by the firm and the EOR desired by the employee. Theories of the firm imply that agents carry out corporate strategy by offering EORs supportive of organizational goals, without considering the impact of matches and mismatches. Yet, if matches in EORs desired by individuals are not considered, agents face challenges that have implications for the welfare of the firm, such as employee commitment and turnover. Furthermore, there are many potential factors that will affect the degree of matching, which need to be explored. For example, new hires may have limited understanding of the strategy that underlies an offer of employment, and may make assumptions about the EOR that are in fact unlikely, given the direction of the firm. Likewise, organizational leaders may assume that employees will see the necessity of changes in the EOR for firm success, without considering how such changes may create matches or mismatches for existing employees.

An ongoing challenge for the EOR literature will be to understand the relationships between employees and employers through the integration of macro- and micro-perspectives. This chapter provides a starting point for scholars who seek to contribute to this nascent body of literature. We believe this is an area of the literature that is ripe for further development and can improve our understanding of the EOR.

References

Accenture (2003). www.accenture.com.

Ang, S., Van Dyne, L., and Begley, T. M. (forthcoming). "The employment relationships of foreign workers versus local employees: A field study of organizational justice, job satisfaction, performance, and OCB". *Journal of Organizational Behavior*, 24: 561–83.

Barney, J. (1991). "Firm resources and sustained competitive advantage". *Journal of Management*, 17: 99–120.

—— (2001). "Resource-based theories of competitive advantage: A ten-year retrospective on the resource-based view". *Journal of Management*, 27: 643–50.

Baruch, Y., and Hind, P. (1999). "Perpetual motion in organizations: Effective management and the impact of the new psychological contracts on 'survivor syndrome' ". *European Journal of Work and Organizational Psychology*, 8: 295–306.

Becker, B., and Gerhart, B. (1996). "The impact of human resource management on organizational performance: Progress and prospects". *Academy of Management Journal*, 39: 779–801.

Becker, G. S. (1964). *Human Capital*. New York: Columbia University Press.

Blau, P. M. (1964). *Exchange and Power in Social Life*. New York: Wiley.

Brockner, J. S., Grover, S., Reed, T., DeWitt, R., and O'Malley, M. (1987). "Survivors' reactions to layoffs: We get by with a little help from our friends". *Administrative Science Quarterly*, 32: 526–41.

—— Tyler, T. R., and Cooper-Schieder, R. (1992). "The influence of prior commitment to institution on reactions to perceived unfairness: The higher they are, the harder they fall". *Administrative Science Quarterly*, 17: 241–61.

Delery, J. E., and Doty, D. H. (1996). "Modes of theorizing in strategic human resource management: Tests of universalistic, contingency, and configurational performance predictions". *Academy of Management Journal*, 39: 802–35.

Eisenberger, R., Huntington, R., Hutchinson, S., and Sowa, D. (1986). "Perceived organizational support". *Journal of Applied Psychology*, 71: 500–7.

Eisenhardt, K. (1989). "Agency theory: An assessment and review". *Academy of Management Review*, 14: 57–74.

Freeman, R. B. (1972). *Labor Economics*. Englewood Cliffs, NJ: Prentice Hall.

Gerhart, B., and Trevor, C. O. (1996). "Employment variability under different managerial compensation systems". *Academy of Management Journal*, 39: 1692–712.

Grant, R. M. (1996). *Contemporary Strategy Analysis: Concepts, Techniques, Applications*. Malden, MA: Blackwell.

Graen, G. B., and Scandura, T. A. (1987). "Toward a psychology of dyadic organizing," in L. L. Cummings and B. Staw (eds.), *Research in Organizational Behavior* (Greenwich, CT: JAI Press), 9, 175–208.

—— and Uhl-Bien, M. (1995). "Development of leader–member exchange (LMX) theory of leadership over 25 years: Applying a multi-level, multi-domain perspective". *Leadership Quarterly*, 6: 219–47.

Guest, D. E., and Conway, N. (2002). "Communicating the psychological contract: An employer perspective". *Human Resource Management Journal*, 12: 22–38.

Hallier, J., and James, P. (1997). "Middle managers and the employee psychological contract: Agency, protection, and advancement". *Journal of Management Studies*, 34: 703–28.

Hambrick, D. C., and Mason, P. A. (1984). "Upper echelons: The organization as a reflection of its top managers". *Academy of Management Review*, 9(2): 193–206.

Handy, C. (1989). *The Age of Unreason*. London: Hutchinson.

Herriot, P., and Pemberton, C. (1995). *New Deals*. Chichester: Wiley.

—— Manning, W. E. G., and Kidd, J. M. (1997). "The content of the psychological contract". *British Journal of Management*, 8: 151–62.

Huselid, M. A. (1995). "The impact of human resource management practices on turnover, productivity, and corporate financial performance". *Academy of Management Journal*, 38: 635–72.

Jensen, M. C., and Meckling, W. (1976). "Theory of the firm: Managerial behavior, agency costs, and ownership structure". *Journal of Financial Economics*, 3: 305–60.

Lepak, D. P., and Snell, S. A. (1999). "The human resource architecture: Toward a theory of human capital allocation and development". *Academy of Management Review*, 24: 31–48.

Liden, R. C., Sparrowe, R. T., and Wayne, S. J. (1997). "Leader–member exchange theory: The past and potential for the future," in G. R. Ferris (ed.), *Research in Personnel and Human Resource Management* (Greenwich, CT: JAI Press), 47–119.

Masterson, S. S., Lewis, K., Goldman, B. M., and Taylor, M. S. (2000). "Integrating justice and social exchange: The differing effects of fair procedures and treatment on work relationships". *Academy of Management Journal*, 43: 738–48.

Miles, R., and Snow, C. C. (1978). *Organizational Strategy, Structure, and Process*. New York: McGraw-Hill.

Morrison, E. W., and Robinson, S. L. (1997). "When employees feel betrayed: A model of how psychological contract violation develops". *Academy of Management Review*, 22: 226–56.

O'Donnell, S. W. (2000). "Managing foreign subsidiaries: Agents of headquarters, or an interdependent network?" *Strategic Management Journal*, 21: 525–48.

O'Neil, H. M., and Lenn, D. J. (1995). "Voices of survivors: Words that downsizing CEOs should hear". *Academy of Management Executive*, 9: 23–34.

Pearce, J. L. (1993). "Toward an organizational behavior of contract laborers: Their psychological involvement and effects on employee co-workers". *Academy of Management Journal*, 36: 1082–96.

Penrose, E. (1959). *The Theory of the Growth of the Firm*. Oxford: Oxford University Press.

Porter, L. W., Pearce, J. L., Tripoli, A. M., and Lewis, K. M. (1998). "Differential perceptions of employers' inducements: Implications for psychological contracts". *Journal of Organizational Behavior*, 19: 769–82.

Porter, M. (1980). *Competitive Strategy*. New York: Free Press.

Reed, R., and DeFellippi, R. J. (1990). "Causal ambiguity, barriers to imitation, and sustainable competitive advantage". *Academy of Management Review*, 15: 88–102.

Robinson, S. L., Kraatz, M. S., and Rousseau, D. M. (1994). "Changing obligations and the psychological contract: A longitudinal study". *Academy of Management Journal*, 37: 137–52.

Rhoades, L., and Eisenberger, R. (2002). "Perceived organizational support: A review of the literature". *Journal of Applied Psychology*, 87: 698–714.

Roth, K., and O'Donnell, S. (1996). "Foreign subsidiary compensation strategy: An agency theory perspective". *Academy of Management Journal*, 39: 678–703.

Rousseau, D. M. (1995). *Psychological Contracts in Organization: Understanding Written and Unwritten Agreements*. Thousand Oaks, CA: Sage.

—— and Wade-Benzoni, K. A. (1994). "Linking strategy and human resource practices: How employee and customer contracts are created". *Human Resources Management*, 33: 463–89.

Scarpello, V. G., Ledvinka, J., and Bergmann, T. J. (1995). *Human Resource Management: Environments and Functions*. Cincinnati, OH: South-Western.

Shaw, J. D., and Delery, J. E. (2003). "Strategic HRM and organizational health," in D. A. Hofmann and L. E. Tetrick (eds.), *Health and Safety in Organizations: A Multilevel Perspective* (San Francisco: Jossey Bass), 233–60.

Shore, L. M., and Barksdale, K. (1998). "Examining degree of balance and level of obligation in the employment relationship: A social exchange approach". *Journal of Organizational Behavior*, 19: 731–44.

—— and Shore, T. H. (1995). "Perceived organizational support and organizational justice," in R. Cropanzano and K. M. Kacmar (eds.), *Organizational Politics, Justice, and Support: Managing Social Climate at Work*, Westport: CT (Quorum Press), 149–64.

—— and Tetrick, L. E. (1994). "The psychological contract as an explanatory framework in the employment relationship," in C. Cooper and D. Rousseau (eds.), *Trends in Organizational Behavior* (New York: Wiley), 1: 91–109.

Teece, D. J., Pisano, G., and Shuen, A. (1997). "Dynamic capabilities and strategic management". *Strategic Management Journal*, 18: 509–33.

Tsui, A. S., and Wang, D. X. (2002). "Employment relationships from the employer's perspective: Current research and future directions," in C. L. Cooper and I. T. Robertson, (eds.), *International Review of Industrial and Organizational Psychology* (Chichester: John Wiley), 77–114.

—— Pearce, J. L., Porter, L. W., and Hite, J. P. (1995). "Choice of employee–organization relationship: Influence of external and internal organizational factors," in G. R. Ferris (ed.), *Research in Personnel and Human Resources Management* (Greenwich, CT: JAI Press), 117–51.

—— Pearce, J. L., Porter, L. W. and Tripoli, A. M. (1997). "Alternative approaches to the employee– organization relationship: Does investment in employees pay off?" *Academy of Management Journal*, 40: 1089–121.

Turnley, W. H., and Feldman, D. C. (1999). "The impact of psychological contract violations on exit, voice, loyalty, and neglect". *Human Relations*, 52: 895–922.

Venkatraman, N. (1986). "The concept of fit in strategy research: Toward a verbal and statistical correspondence". *Academy of Management Review*, 14: 423–44.

Wang, D., Tsui, A. S., Zhang, Y., and Ma, L. "Employment relationships and firm performance: Evidence from an emerging economy". *Journal of Organizational Behavior*, 24: 511–35.

Wayne, S. J., Shore, L. M., and Liden, R. C. (1997). "Perceived organizational support and leader–member exchange: A social exchange perspective". *Academy of Management Journal*, 40: 82–111.

Wayne, S. J., Shore, L. M., Bommer, W. H., and Tetrick, L. E. (2002). "The role of fair treatment and rewards in perceptions of organizational support and leader–member exchange". *Journal of Applied Psychology*, 87: 590–8.

Wright, P. M., Dunford, B. B., and Snell, S. A. (2001). "Human resources and the resource-based View of the Firm". *Journal of Management*, 17: 701–21.

Zahra, S. A., and George, G. (2002). "Absorptive capacity: A review, reconceptualization, and extension". *Academy of Management Review*, 27(2): 185–203.

—— and Nielsen, A. P. (2002). "Sources of capabilities, integration and technology commercialization". *Strategic Management Journal*, 23: 377–98.

8

The Employment Relationship from Two Sides: Incongruence in Employees' and Employers' Perceptions of Obligations

ELIZABETH WOLFE MORRISON AND
SANDRA L. ROBINSON

8.1 Introduction

The employment relationship involves two parties, the employee and the employer. Yet our understanding of the employment relationship has emerged largely from research that has focused on the perspective of the employee. That is, research has given little consideration to the perceptions of the employer, and has generally failed to integrate or compare the perspectives of the two parties to the relationship (Coyle-Shapiro and Kessler 2002; Tekleab and Taylor 2003). As we will explain in this chapter, the employee and employer can, and often do, have very different perceptions of their relationship with one another. Indeed, as the literature on psychological contracts suggests, employees and employers are more likely than not to perceive the core components of the employment relationship quite differently from one another. These differing perceptions have been referred to as *incongruence* (Morrison and Robinson 1997). The purpose of this chapter is to discuss why incongruence is such a common occurrence, consider the implications of incongruence for employees and organizations, and explore how incongruence can be reduced and managed.

We believe that it is important for organizational scholars and managers to recognize and understand the notion of incongruence in employment relationships. From a research standpoint, doing so can help to inform our understanding of employment relationships more broadly, and can help scholars to move away from implicitly assuming a single "objective" reality to those relationships. An understanding of incongruence is also important from a practical standpoint. As we will discuss, incongruence between employees' and employers' perceptions of their obligations and behavior toward one another can result in tension, conflict, and other negative outcomes for the individual and the organization. Awareness of the prevalence of incongruence and its underlying causes can help the parties to more effectively resolve disagreement and manage the employment relationship.

In this chapter, we examine and discuss divergent perceptions that employees and employers have regarding two specific aspects of their relationship. Specifically, we explore differing perceptions of employee and employer obligations to one another, and differing perceptions of how well those obligations are being met. We discuss the nature of these incongruent perceptions, factors that create them, some important implications of incongruence, and how the gap between employee and employer perceptions can be minimized. Before doing so, we provide some background on psychological contracts in employment relationships which is the foundational framework for our analysis.

8.2 Psychological contracts

The concept of a psychological contract was originally identified over thirty years ago to refer to mutual expectations in employment relationships (Argyris 1960; Levinson et al. 1962; Schein 1965). Rousseau (1989) reintroduced the concept in the late 1980s, although she conceptualized it as an individual-level cognition, rather than a mutual understanding. That is, Rousseau defined a psychological contract as an individual's perceptions of what he or she owes another party in an exchange relationship, and of what that other party owes in return. From this reconceptualization, a wave of empirical and theoretical research on this phenomenon emerged.

According to the current literature, the psychological contract is composed of an employee's beliefs about reciprocal, promissory obligations between himself or herself and the organization. These beliefs relate to what each party is entitled to receive and bound to provide in exchange for the other's contributions (Rousseau 1989). Although the psychological contract is an individual-level construct, it reflects beliefs about goods and services that are to be exchanged in the context of a dyadic relationship. The notion of exchange is an important part of this construct (Shore and Barksdale 1998). The employee expects to make contributions to the relationship, but these are contingent, in part, on expected contributions by the employer (Rousseau 1989). Thus, it involves not what one would *like* from the relationship, or what he or she *expects* from the relationship, but rather, what one believes *should or must be exchanged* because of promises that have been made or obligations that have been established between the two parties (Robinson 1996; Rousseau 1989).

A second central characteristic of the psychological contract is that it is inherently perceptual and subjective (Rousseau 1989). It is a set of beliefs shaped by multiple sources of input and by cognitive and perceptual biases (Shore and Tetrick 1994). As such, an employee's psychological contract may not accurately correspond to the formal written employment contract, the judgment of a neutral or observing third party, or the perceptions of the employer or agents of the employing organization (Rousseau 1989). It is important to recognize, however, that psychological contracts, although perceptual and subjective, are very real to the individuals who hold them. Indeed, attitudes and behaviors are influenced quite heavily by an individual's perception of his or her obligations, and perceptions of how well the other party's obligations have been fulfilled (Shore and Tetrick 1994; Robinson 1996; Lester et al. 2002; Tekleab and Taylor 2003).

The notion of a psychological contract provides a potentially fruitful framework for understanding some of the challenges associated with managing the employment relationship. In particular, it provides a framework for understanding how and why the two parties to an employment relationship will tend to have different perceptions of what is owed to one another and of how well those obligations are being fulfilled. Knowledge about psychological contracts, and how they form and change over time, can provide insight into these forms of divergent perceptions, as well as insight into how to manage them.

8.2.1 Incongruence in the psychological contract literature

The concept of incongruent perceptions has been a theme in the psychological contract literature. Several decades ago, Kotter (1973) noted that employee and organizational expectations of what they are to give and receive can be quite different. Kotter explained how the contract formed during recruitment generally has mismatches, but neither employee nor boss typically recognize or confront these mismatches. Over time, however, the employee may begin to experience these mismatches in the form of disappointment or frustration (Kotter 1973). More recently, Morrison and Robinson (1997), in their model of how psychological contract breach develops, argued that incongruence is one of two fundamental ways by which perceptions of psychological contract breach and contract violation occur.

A few studies have attempted to empirically examine incongruence. Herriot et al. (1997) examined and compared perceptions of employment contracts between a group of employees and a group of managers, and found that these two groups saw obligations differently. Goldman et al. (1996) studied employee–employer dyads, and found no relationship between perceptions of obligations between the two parties. Further, Lester et al. (2002) found that employees are more likely than their supervisors to perceive that the organization has failed to keep all of the obligations comprising the employee's psychological contract.

Although some important insights stem from each of the papers noted above, there are many aspects of incongruence that have not been fully explored, and limited attention has been given to how it can be managed. Hence, our goal here is to discuss more fully incongruence between the perceptions of employees and employers. We begin by proposing that there are two main types of incongruent perceptions that are especially relevant to the employment relationship. Although both employees and employers seem to accept the notion of reciprocity between themselves (Coyle-Shapiro and Kessler 2002), they may hold highly divergent views about the specific obligations that they owe one another, as several scholars have noted (Kotter 1973; Rousseau 1989; Morrison and Robinson 1997). As well, they can have divergent views about how well those obligations have been fulfilled

(Lester et al. 2002), an issue that has not been discussed as much in the literature. We refer to the former as *obligation incongruence* and the latter as *fulfillment incongruence*.

We believe that it is very important to distinguish between these two types of incongruence and to treat them separately. First, they are qualitatively distinct phenomena. Although both involve different perceptions by the two parties about the obligations between them, one examines differing perceptions about the type of obligations that exist, whereas the other focuses on how well those obligations are fulfilled. Thus, it is possible for one type of incongruence to exist and be problematic within a relationship without the other type. More importantly, these two types of incongruence have different causes, and thus different remedies.

8.3 Obligation incongruence

Obligation incongruence reflects the extent to which employee and employer (i.e. agents of the organization) have different perceptions of what they owe one another; that is, the specific contributions and inducements that should be exchanged between the two parties. The employee and employer may disagree about whether a particular obligation exists, or they may disagree about the specifics of that obligation or its meaning (Morrison and Robinson 1997). For example, an agent of the organization may perceive that an employee is obligated to work overtime when needed, whereas this obligation is not a part of how the employee views his or her psychological contract. Alternatively, both parties may agree that overtime work is "part of the deal," but they may have different beliefs about how much overtime is expected or about how the employee will be compensated for overtime. These differing perceptions can exist right from the start, or they can develop over time as the beliefs and perceptions of one or both parties change.

Morrison and Robinson (1997) noted three interrelated reasons why, at any point in time, employees and employers often hold very different perceptions about the obligations between them. One is that employees and organizational agents enter into employment relationships with different cognitive schemata, or different starting assumptions about what *should be* the mutual obligations between employees and employers. A second reason for obligation incongruence is that employment agreements are typically numerous, complex, and ambiguous (Morrison and Robinson 1997). As a result, they are subject to interpretation and sense-making processes that are inherently subjective and imperfect. A third factor contributing to obligation incongruence is poor or insufficient communication (Morrison and Robinson 1997). Employer and employee typically converse very little about their obligations to one another, even though the promises that give rise to perceived obligations are often vague, incomplete, and subject to change. Below, we expand upon Morrison and Robinson's (1997) ideas to more fully explain why perceptions of obligations often diverge. In particular, we discuss more fully the role of imperfect sense-making processes that are central to the formation of obligation incongruence.

8.3.1 *Different schemata*

Schemata are cognitive frameworks that represent organized knowledge about a given concept (Taylor and Crocker 1981). Schemata guide what people notice, what they remember, and how they interpret incoming information. One type of schema that people hold relates to employment relationships; that is, guiding beliefs about what a typical employment relationship entails (Rousseau 2001). Both employees and agents of the organization come to the employment relationship with such schemata. These mental models shape the development of the employee's psychological contract. In addition, organizational agents' schemata shape their beliefs about mutual obligations between the organization and employees in general, beliefs that they are likely to generalize to specific employees and specific employment agreements.

Both employees and agents of the organization begin to develop their cognitive schemata about employment relationships early in life. During childhood and adolescence, people develop generalized values about fairness, hard work, and reciprocity. These values, shaped by family, school, church, and peer group, affect a young adult's assumptions about work obligations and entitlements. In addition, cues from family, the media, and day-to-day interactions with people who are working provide specific ideas about what one should expect to give and receive in an employment relationship. These assumptions and expectations about employment relationships may be realistic or unrealistic, and they may be highly idiosyncratic (Rousseau 2001).

Past work experience can also contribute to the highly individualized nature of both employees' and organizational agents' schemata. Most people work for several different organizations throughout their career and it is not uncommon for employees and managers to switch occupations or industries. As they move from one work environment to another, people take their expectations and assumptions with them, which flavors their interpretation of new employment relationships. For example, an employee who worked at an organization that provided on-site child care may come to believe that employers are and *should be* responsive to child care demands. Similarly, an organizational agent may have worked primarily with employees who do not desire much growth in their careers, and thus applies a schema developed from that experience to contexts with other types of employees. In sum, employees' and organizational agents' prior work experiences will shape their cognitive schemata regarding employment relationships, which in turn will influence their unique perceptions of the obligations in a given employment relationship.

Employees' and employers' schemata are likely to differ not only as a function of their unique past experiences, but also as a function of their different roles and vantage points in the relationship. Employers, for example, may be focused on getting a good return on their labor investments. As a result, their schemata may emphasize employee, rather than employer, contributions. Employees, on the other hand, may be viewing the employment relationship through the lens of their own career goals. Hence, their schemata are more likely to focus on those things that employers should provide for employees, with less relative emphasis on employee obligations.

Additionally, general beliefs about employment obligations are affected by employees' and organizational agents' respective national cultures, and the values that stem from their cultural backgrounds. In particular, individuals from collectivistic cultures may have different expectations about employment obligations than individuals from individualistic cultures. Because collectivists place higher value on group harmony, equality, and in-group cooperation (Hofstede 1980; Triandis et al. 1988), they may be more likely than individualists to expect social support and equal treatment of employees.

Similarly, cultural values such as power distance, quantity/quality of life, and uncertainty avoidance (Hofstede 1980) may shape one's perceptions about the roles and obligations of employees and organizations. Employees who come from high power distance cultures, for example, may be less likely to include initiative-taking, assertiveness, or decision-making within their schema of employee obligations, as high power distance societies are ones in which people are very respectful of status differences and deferential to authority figures (Hofstede 1980). In addition, employees from more "feminine" cultures (Hofstede 1980) will be more likely to believe that employers are obligated to provide job security, good benefits, and considerable vacation time. Thus, different schemata, and hence incongruent perceptions about obligations are especially likely when the employee and employer have different cultural backgrounds (Morrison and Robinson 1997).

In sum, schemata are shaped through prior unique experiences and backgrounds (Fiske and Taylor 1984) and are highly idiosyncratic to the person holding them. As a result, an employee and an agent of the organization often possess very different mental models for what an employment relationship should entail. These mental models, in turn, guide how the two parties view and interpret the obligations that exist within a given employee–employer relationship. The more different the mental models, the greater the potential for incongruence between the employee's psychological contract and the perceptions about mutual obligations held by agents of the organization.

8.3.2 *Complex and ambiguous stimuli subject to sense-making*

Obligation incongruence stems not just from differing cognitive schemata, but also from the nature of the obligations that typically exist between an employee and organization. The psychological contract literature highlights that the full set of promises and obligations in a given employment relationship is large and complex (Morrison and Robinson 1997; Rousseau 1995). As the number of different obligations increases, so does the likelihood of a gap between different individuals' perceptions of those obligations. When people must attend to and remember a large number of items, they are more likely to overlook, forget, or misconstrue some of them (Griffin and Ross 1991). This implies that, particularly when there are numerous elements to the relationship, employee and organizational agent are likely to store, and later recall, different representations of the promises that they made to one another at earlier points in time.

The psychological contract literature also highlights that employment promises and obligations are often vague, ambiguous, and incomplete (Rousseau and Greller 1994; Morrison and Robinson 1997). These features imply that employment obligations will be subject to interpretation and cognitive sense-making processes. When individuals are faced with unclear or ambiguous information, they engage in a process of "filling in the gaps" by relying on contextual cues and prior information (Griffin and Ross 1991). This process is subjective and imperfect, and two parties are likely to reach different conclusions from the same information.

During the job interview and selection process, for example, employee and employer typically discuss what the job candidate should expect to contribute and receive. Although both sides participate in these discussions, what they take away from the conversation may be very different, because each party is interpreting and making inferences in the absence of complete information. Some of these interpretations are based on explicit and unambiguous statements or promises. In these cases, there is less potential for divergence in interpretation. Other inferences, however, are drawn from subtle cues such as body language, how various questions are answered, and vague or indirect statements that scholars have referred to as *implicit promises* (Shore and Tetrick 1994; Rousseau 1995). In these cases, the potential for differing perceptions of what the two parties agreed to is more likely (Morrison and Robinson 1997). As one example, imagine that the employer conveys an obligation (e.g. "we would expect you to spend some time out in the field before you could be promoted") and the employee responds with silence. The employer might interpret this silence as agreement, when in fact, the employee may not be accepting the idea at all (Morrison and Milliken 2000).

Research in the area of perception has shown that motives, needs, and goals affect what people notice in an ambiguous situation and how they interpret information and fill in the gaps when information is missing (Griffin and Ross 1991). As noted, employees and agents of the organization typically have different motives and goals. Whereas employers are generally concerned with ensuring sufficient contributions from employees, flexibility to meet the needs of the organization, and consistency across employees doing similar work, employees may have career goals and aspirations that include such things as rapid advancement, increasing responsibility, ability to balance work and family demands, and earning a good living. These differing goals may cause the two parties to attend to different information. Employees may pay particular attention to information relevant to their career objectives, and to try to glean cues about advancement from subtle statements made during the recruitment process. Employers, on the other hand, may be focusing attention on very different issues, picking up on certain cues and missing others.

Temporal changes also affect the sense-making process and can contribute to divergent perceptions. Over time, the expectations and perceptions of both parties (employee and employer) evolve and change. Rousseau and McLean Parks (1993) used the term *contract drift* to refer to situations where the passage of time alters a party's understanding of the terms of a particular contract. Morrison and Robinson (1997) similarly noted how perceptions of promises decay or become distorted in memory. These changes in perceptions are not random, but rather, involve positive illusions and self-serving biases (Taylor and Brown 1988). For example, an employee may be unlikely to see how his or her own poor performance has contributed to changes in perceived obligations and may come to expect greater contributions from the employer. Likewise, employers may, over time, inflate their perceptions of what employees are obligated to do, but not adjust their perceptions of the organization's obligations. Consistent with this notion of contract drift, Robinson et al. (1994) demonstrated in a longitudinal study that employees came to see their own obliga- tions as decreasing over time whereas they came to perceive that their employer owed them more during that same period.

There may also be actual changes in the employment relationship. When this occurs, it may not be realistic to retain prior beliefs about each party's obligations, yet beliefs may not change in accordance with the changing reality. For example, an organization that is experiencing difficult financial conditions may no longer be able to promise yearly bonuses that were customary in the past (Morrison and Robinson 1997). Employees, however, may still feel entitled to receive such bonuses, resulting in a gap between employee and employer views about obligations.

8.3.3 Insufficient communication

By sharing their assumptions and perceptions, parties to a relationship can work toward common understanding of what they owe one another and adjust that under- standing as circumstances change over time (Kotter 1973; Morrison and Robinson 1997). In the context of the employment relationship, however, there are many reasons why the parties may fail to communicate sufficiently about their obligations to one another. One reason for this failure to communicate is what psychologists have called *the false consensus effect* (Ross et al. 1977; Marks and Miller 1987). This term refers to the tendency to see one's own judgments as relatively common and appropriate while viewing alternative responses as uncommon or inappropriate. For instance, if an employer views it as appropriate for employees to be accessible via cellular phone or beeper when on vacation, he or she will be likely to assume that others would agree with this view. Making this assumption, the employer will then see little need to discuss or clarify this issue with employees.

Status differences may also impair communication. Research shows that status differences inhibit communication in general and that people are often inhibited from communicating with people in positions above them (Athanassiades 1973; Roberts and O'Reilly 1974). More specifically, the power asymmetry that typically exists between employee and employer can significantly impact on the nature of the communication between them. In many cases, employers hold greater power than employees, meaning that the latter may feel that they are unable to negotiate or question the terms of the relationship (Rousseau 2001). This is particularly likely when the employee is from a high power distance culture (Hofstede 1980). As a result of these communication barriers, gaps in perceptions or assumptions are likely to persist or even magnify between employees and organizational agents.

At the same time that employees are failing to sufficiently communicate with agents of the organization, they may be communicating quite a bit among themselves (Rousseau 1995). Through their discussions with one another, employees may develop shared understandings and conclusions about employment obligations among themselves but these shared understandings may have little bearing on what agents of the employing organization perceive to be true. In other words, social information processing (Salancik and Pfeffer 1978) and social contagion (Erickson 1988) are likely to occur. These processes of information sharing and collective sense-making are motivated by the need to reduce uncertainty. Under conditions of uncertainty, people communicate with one another, and through this communication, they develop socially derived interpretations of their environment (Festinger 1954; Salancik and Pfeffer 1978).

Research on social contagion suggests that individuals are more likely to adopt the attitudes and perceptions of their friends, people whom they see as similar to themselves, and people with whom they are interdependent and frequently interact (Krackhardt and Porter 1986; Erickson 1988; Rice and Aydin 1991; Meyer 1994). These dynamics suggest that employees' views of their psychological contracts will tend to mirror the views of their peers and those with whom they work on a regular basis. However, whereas employees' beliefs and perceptions will tend to converge among themselves, they will not necessarily converge with the beliefs and perceptions of organizational agents. Moreover, employees will be more likely to assume that their beliefs are "correct" or "accurate" since they are shared with peers, a dynamic likely to intensify the false consensus effect (Festinger 1954; Morrison and Milliken 2000).

8.4 Fulfillment incongruence

Our discussion so far has focused on the many reasons why employee and employer will tend to hold divergent views of their obligations to one another. In other words, we have focused on how employees' psychological contract will often fail to correspond with how organizational agents view the employment agreement. In this section, we discuss why employee and employer are also likely to hold divergent views of how well they have fulfilled their obligations to one another (i.e. *fulfillment incongruence*), a topic that has been less often discussed in the literature.

We argue that, for a variety of reasons, employees will be more likely than organizational agents to perceive that they have fulfilled their obligations to the organization, and more likely to perceive that the organization has fallen short in fulfilling its obligations to the employee. At the same time, employers will be more likely to perceive that the organization is adequately meeting its obligations to employees, and less likely to perceive that the employee is adequately meeting his or her obligations. Consistent with this view, Kotter (1973) argued that employees tend to underappreciate the inducements offered by the organization, while simultaneously overestimating their own contributions. In addition, Tsui et al. (1997) found that employees and organizational agents hold different perceptions of the inducements that organizations are offering their employees. In another study, Coyle-Shapiro and Kessler (2002) found that managers are more positive than employees in their assessment of the organization's fulfillment of obligations.

In the sections below, we discuss some of the factors that give rise to differing perceptions of how well obligations are being fulfilled. We argue that fulfillment incongruence stems in part from the fact that the employee and organizational agent generally hold different beliefs about the obligations that exist between them in the first place. Second, fulfillment incongruence stems from perceptual biases and distortions. Finally, we discuss how social comparison processes can lead to incongruent perceptions regarding fulfillment.

8.4.1 *Different perceptions of obligations*

As discussed in the prior section, there are many obligations that are part of a given employment relationship, and the employee and employer have different beliefs about the nature and existence of those obligations. This fact alone can create disagreement about how well obligations are being fulfilled (Lester et al. 2002). If party A perceives a particular obligation to have been established, and party B does not, party B may fail to satisfactorily meet that obligation simply because he or she is unaware of party A's expectation. Moreover, in such a situation, only party A will perceive that obligations have been unmet. For instance, imagine that an employee believes the organization promised to promote him or her after one year in an entry-level position, yet the employer does not share this view. In this case, failure to be promoted after a year will be viewed by the employee as an unfulfilled promise, yet the employer may believe that all employment promises are being met. As another example, the employer and employee may both agree that "long hours" are expected, but if they have different ideas of what this means, the employee may believe that he or she is meeting this obligation whereas the employer will have a different evaluation.

What we are suggesting, then, is that divergence between the employee's psychological contract and employer perceptions about obligations are often at the root of incongruent perceptions about fulfillment. Hence, all of the factors that create obligation incongruence—different cognitive schemata, complex and ambiguous input subject to imperfect sense-making, and failure to communicate sufficiently— also ultimately increase the occurrence of fulfillment incongruence as a result of obligation incongruence. This idea draws from Morrison and Robinson's (1997) work where they argue that one of the underlying reasons that employees often believe that their organization has breached one or more terms of the psychological contract is that the two parties have incongruent perceptions about what those obligations are. The idea of fulfillment incongruence goes beyond the notion of perceived breach, however, in highlighting the other party's lack of recognition or agreement that a breach has occurred, a reality that has implications for how contract breach is responded to and managed.

8.4.2 Perceptual biases and distortions

In addition to differing views of the obligations that exist between the two parties, perceptual biases will also contribute to fulfillment incongruence (Taylor and Brown 1988). Several streams of research have shown that individuals have a tendency to overestimate their own contributions to a relationship, and underestimate the contributions of the other party (Taylor and Brown 1988). This has been referred to as the self-centered bias (Fiske and Taylor 1984). In one study, for example, researchers asked married couples to indicate their own and their spouse's contributions to various household chores (Ross and Sicoly 1979) and they found that each member of the relationship thought that he or she had contributed more than the other thought he or she had. Similar patterns have been found across a variety of joint experiences (Ross and Sicoly 1979).

In organizations, differences in supervisor and subordinate perceptions have also been noted. In particular, employees routinely have self-evaluations that are more positive than their supervisors' evaluations of how well they are performing (Harris and Schanbroeck 1988). In addition, research in the conflict area has shown that people often have self-serving views of fairness that can cause them to not see their own role in a conflict situation, hence feeling that they are being unfairly victimized (Thompson and Lowenstein 1992). Research has also shown that victims and perpetrators in a conflict situation have little awareness of their discrepant perspectives and interpretations (Baumeister et al. 1990).

Taken together, these various streams of research suggest that employees will tend to overestimate their own contributions to the employment relationship, whereas employers will tend to overestimate their contributions (Tekleab and Taylor 2003). These dynamics will widen the gap between employee and employer perceptions of fulfillment.

Another issue contributing to fulfillment incongruence is the fact that "fulfillment" is a concept subject to interpretation. The fulfillment of obligations is rarely evaluated in a yes–no fashion. It entails judgments of amount, quality, and timing. For example, if an employee is evaluating whether his or her employer has provided "support," he or she is considering *how much* support or *how good* is the support. If he or she is evaluating "rapid promotion," the issue of *how fast* becomes relevant. A potential problem here is that employees may often have unrealistic expectations regarding the degree and speed of contract fulfillment. Robinson and Rousseau (1994) found that, among a sample of new MBAs, 55 percent perceived that their psychological contract had been violated within the first two years of employment. One reason for this effect may have been that these individuals had inflated beliefs about what they would receive and how quickly. In support of this idea, Heath et al. (1993) argued that overentitlement is a common problem in employment relationships, stemming from both psychological limitations in judgment as well as strategic distortion by the employer. Although they focused on *employee* overentitlement, it is likely that this phenomenon will sometimes be exhibited by employers as well. For example, organizations and their agents may come to believe that their employees owe them not only a regular work week, but also overtime and a willingness to work weekends when needed.

Morrison and Robinson (1997) discussed how, when evaluating the fulfillment of employment obligations, parties engage in a comparison process whereby they consider both parties' maintenance of the terms of the relationship. This comparison process, however, is affected by many pieces of input, many of them vague or subject to interpretation. Because the two parties have different information available to them, they may reach different conclusions about both their own, and the other side's, fulfillment of obligations. For example, the employer may perceive that the employee overstepped the deadline on a major project, not knowing that the delay was due to external factors beyond the employee's control.

Moreover, because the process of evaluating fulfillment involves interpretation, it is subject to a variety of cognitive and perceptual errors, such as primacy effects, halo error, or selective attention (Schneider et al. 1979; Eagly and Chaiken 1993). For example, an employer may have fulfilled all of its obligations to an employee, yet one inadvertent transgression may lead the employee to notice subsequent failures of fulfillment because he or she is primed to see it; in contrast, the employer would not be as cognizant of such failures.

The two parties may also be using different notions of "balance" when comparing their respective contributions. One party, for example, may evaluate balance in terms of immediate and direct reciprocity, whereas the other may take a more long-term and generalized reciprocity perspective on balance. The former corresponds to more of a transactional view of the relationship whereas the latter corresponds to more of a relational view (Rousseau 1989). If this difference exists, the two parties are likely to have significantly different views about the fulfillment of obligations in their relationship because they are using a different metric to determine fulfillment. As well, some individuals are more sensitive to inequity than others (Huseman et al. 1987). These individuals might be more likely than the other party to the relationship to perceive a slight imbalance as evidence of non-fulfillment.

8.4.3 Social comparisons

An additional reason why assessments about obligation fulfillment may diverge for the two parties is that these assessments are often affected by social comparisons (Festinger 1954). The employee, for example, is likely to look at what other employees are contributing to and receiving from the organization, and based on this information, makes judgments about how well his or her own psychological contract is being fulfilled. Research suggests that social comparison is a vital part of the self-evaluation process, and that in making comparisons individuals look to similar others (Festinger 1954) and to those holding similar structural positions (Erickson 1988). A new assistant professor, for example, will look to other assistant professors in evaluating how well his or her psychological contract is being fulfilled, and will be especially likely to look to those assistant professors with similar areas of expertise and similar demographic characteristics.

Yet there are two different ways in which the social comparison process can work. In some instances, employees may see what similar others are getting or not getting, and assume that they will receive (or not receive) the same thing. For example, if other employees are being laid off despite assurances of job security, an employee may perceive that his or her own promise of job security is not being fulfilled (since job security is now in question). In other cases, employees may make contrasting judgments based on social information. For example, an employee who had viewed his or her 5 percent raise as representing fulfillment of a promise of "fair compensation," may form a very different judgment after learning that a similarly performing colleague received a 10 percent raise. In this case, the contrast between the outcomes received by the two employees is affecting how the focal employee views the fulfillment of his or her psychological contract.

The employer, too, may be making social comparisons. How well a given employee is meeting his or her obligation to "do whatever is needed to help the organization" is likely to be evaluated relative to how well other employees are performing on this dimension. Employers' evaluations of how well they are fulfilling obligations may also be shaped by comparison with other employers. Self-enhancement biases, however, might cause organizational agents to make "downward" social comparisons (Wills 1981) that suggest that the organization is doing a better job in fulfilling its obligations to employees. For example, agents may do this by comparing their organization to competitors that treat employees less favorably. Employees, however, will be unlikely to exhibit this bias when evaluating the organization's fulfillment of obligations, a factor that may widen the gap between the two parties' perceptions.

8.5 Implications of incongruence

Thus far, we have explicated the nature of both obligation incongruence and fulfillment incongruence, and have discussed why these two forms of incongruence come to exist. Given the prevalence and inevitability of incongruence, a critical question to ask is what are the implications of this incongruence. Past research has discussed how obligation incongruence is one of the factors that give rise to perceived psychological contract breach and resulting feelings of contract violation (Morrison and Robinson 1997) and a recent empirical study lends support to this idea (Tekleab and Taylor 2003). Perceived breach and violation, in turn, have been shown to affect employee trust, commitment, perceptions of organizational support, in-role and extra-role performance, and turnover (Robinson and Rousseau 1994; Robinson and Morrison 1995; Robinson 1996; Coyle-Shapiro and Kessler 1998; Bunderson 2001; Lester et al. 2002). Here, we argue that obligation incongruence can have an additional effect of causing the parties to the employment relationship to misallocate energy and resources. As well, we propose that fulfillment incongruence often leads to misunderstood conflict and tension in employment relationships.

8.5.1 Squandered resources

One of the more obvious effects of obligation incongruence is an employee or employer eventually perceiving that the other party is undercontributing to the relationship (Morrison and Robinson 1997) and thus the impact of psychological contract breach, as noted above, comes into play. A less obvious effect of obligation incongruence is that it may cause one or both parties to overcontribute to the relationship in a way that is wasteful. That is, obligation incongruence not only makes it more likely that one party will feel that the other has failed to fulfill obligations, but it may also make it likely that one party will provide inputs and take actions that are unnecessary and unappreciated. For example, the employer may be providing career development opportunities that the employee is neither aware of nor expects to receive. Similarly, the employee may be repeatedly engaging in time consuming tasks with the belief that they are required, whereas organizational agents might not see these tasks as an employee obligation, and in fact, might prefer the employee to spend time on alternative activities.

In a sense, unnecessary effort and resources may be expended because the two parties have different understandings of what they are suppose to be providing to one another. As such, these contributions may go unnoticed, unused, and unappreciated by the recipient. The resources and effort are inefficiently or suboptimally allocated. As we see in research on ineffective negotiations, the collective outcomes that the two parties receive are Pareto-inefficient in that some resources are allocated to the wrong individual and thus are not used to their full extent (Raiffa 1982; Neale and Bazerman 1991). A likely result is that neither party will be satisfied with the outcomes being received. In such circumstances, the contributing party is not given credit for providing the unexpected resources, and may be criticized for not providing those things that were expected. The receiving party feels shortchanged whereas the contributing party feels resentment and frustration because their contributions are not being appreciated.

8.5.2 Conflict and tension

Fulfillment incongruence has the potential to produce ongoing tension in the employment relationship, even when feelings of contract violation do not surface. When the two parties have different understandings of how well their obligations to one another are being fulfilled, confusion and frustration are likely to arise. In relationships characterized by fulfillment incongruence, both parties are likely to develop these negative feelings because their needs are not being met.

Specifically, one or both parties may be attempting to follow through on their side of the bargain, but reactions by the receiving party may suggest they are failing or doing something wrong. Whether implicitly or explicitly communicated, the contributing party receives negative feedback when positive feedback was expected. Whereas the contributing party might be anticipating gratitude, acknowledgment, or positive reciprocity, she or he receives none. Confusion and negative affect may then result.

At the same time, the party not receiving what he or she feels entitled to receive may develop an unease that is not actually a sense of violation but rather, a disappointment or confusion as the other party seems to repeatedly come up short on his or her side of the bargain (Kotter 1973). Alternatively, one party may be feeling that the contract between them has been violated, yet the other party may feel that the relationship is fine, which may further frustrate the aggrieved party. It is bad enough to be let down by another party, yet it is even worse when that party fails to acknowledge the transgression or show remorse. In these circumstances, individuals are likely to experience feelings of injustice (Lind and Tyler 1988), involving both a sense of distributive injustice, in not receiving what was expected, and a sense of procedural injustice, in not experiencing fair treatment.

In sum, neither party will be fully satisfied, yet they may not understand why the relationship is not working as it should. What develops is similar to covert conflict (Pondy 1967), because the parties are thwarting each other's goals yet neither party is aware of the misunderstanding that is occurring nor why the tension is present. Moreover, even if parties are able to acknowledge this conflict, attempts to discuss and thus repair the relationship may go awry because neither party will necessarily comprehend that the other party sees the situation differently.

8.6 Managing incongruence

Given the inevitability of incongruent perceptions between employer and employee, and the effects that these incongruent perceptions can have, it is important that organizations work toward bridging the gap between employee and employer views of their mutual obligations and of how well these are being met. In this section, we discuss some ways by which incongruence can be minimized and managed.

8.6.1 Coordination among sources

As noted, incongruence between employee and employer expectations and perceptions emanates in part from the fact that these expectations and perceptions come from multiple sources. As such, it is critical for organizations to identify the various information sources that influence the construction of employees' psychological contracts, and to strive for consistency between the messages conveyed by those sources (e.g. recruiters, supervisors, co-workers, employee manuals, compensation systems), as well as consistency between these messages and what the organization can actually do for employees.

For example, organizations can try to ensure that there is coordination between the organizational agents who are responsible for creating, maintaining, and executing the terms that are at the foundation of employees' psychological contracts. Many times the agents who make promises to employees, such as recruiters or human resources managers, are not the ones who later have to fulfill those promises. Those parties making promises to employees may be unaware of constraints on the ability of others in the organization to fulfill those obligations. Moreover, supervisors may sometimes be unaware of promises made by others, even when they could be easy promises to deliver. Unless these various agents communicate, and ensure agreement and consistency among themselves, incongruent expectations and beliefs are very likely (Rousseau 1995).

8.6.2 Frequent communication

To reduce and effectively manage incongruence, it is important that employees and organizational agents meet on a regular basis to discuss and communicate their mutual obligations. Certain critical junctures are ideal times to discuss mutual obligations, such as during recruitment (Kotter 1973; Robinson and Morrison 2000), after a promotion or change in reporting structure, and during the annual performance appraisal meetings (Rousseau and Greller 1994). However, it is also valuable for communication to take place throughout the year on a regular, frequent, and informal basis (Frese and Schalk 1996).

Support for the importance of communication for reducing incongruence can be found in Kotter's (1973) early work on psychological contracts where he argued that "mismatches" are partly a function of the two parties not discussing their expectations and hence not understanding each other's views. Further support comes from a recent study by Tekleab and Taylor (2003), which found that tenure and the quality of the leader–member exchange relationship both reduce incongruence. Tekleab and Taylor argued that these two variables mitigate incongruence by allowing for more information sharing.

Ongoing communication is important for reducing incongruence because, at a minimum, it can help to dispel the false consensus effect (Ross et al. 1977), reminding both parties that there are likely multiple understandings of the obligations between them. Frequent regular communication also allows for ongoing adjustment of the parties' psychological contracts (Robinson and Brown, forthcoming). Moreover, these communication opportunities can help the parties to identify divergent expectations and perceived obligations and allow them to resolve those disagreements (Morrison and Robinson 1997). Communication can also help to offset the impact of fulfillment incongruence. If, through communication, managers can influence employees' perceptions and attributions about why they did not receive what they expected to receive, the likelihood of perceived breach and feelings of violation may be reduced. As Turnley and Feldman (1999) found, when employers communicated to employees adequate justifications for contract breach, it lessened the impact of the breach.

Although regular communication is important in almost any context for reducing incongruence, it may be more important under some conditions than others. One such condition is during periods of organizational change. This is because organizational change may affect the degree of uncertainty surrounding obligations as well as the ease with which the parties can fulfill various obligations to one another. For example, during a restructuring, questions regarding obligations about promotion may arise because the restructuring may limit new opportunities for promotion.

Furthermore, with a shuffling of managers, it may no longer be clear who is responsible for ensuring those promotions.

Another context where communication is especially important is when there is a strong basis for expecting that employee and employer have very different prior schemas about employment relationships. For instance, when a new employee has worked in a very different cultural context or industry, he or she may not be "on the same page" as the employer with respect to mutual expectations. Explicitly discussing these different starting assumptions, and working to bridge the gap, can be helpful for mitigating subsequent incongruence.

Communication can take numerous forms, and organizations can play various roles in facilitating communication. For example, they can encourage employees to raise questions when they arise and encourage supervisors to initiate informal discussions about obligations and expectations. A more structured approach that organizations can take would involve encouraging supervisors and subordinates to discuss these issues in the context of yearly performance evaluations or when establishing quarterly performance goals. The use of forums to convey a consistent message to groups of employees may sometimes be valuable as well. In addition, periodic memos or e-mails that detail existing policies to employees can be useful for offsetting contract drift.

To conclude, the process of communicating and aligning the perceptions and beliefs of employees and organizational agents is an ongoing part of managing the employment relationship. It is akin to weeding a garden; it needs to be done on a regular basis and is never complete. Constant and frequent attention to employees' psychological contracts, and the extent to which they converge with the perceptions of organizational agents, is critical to managing incongruence and thus enhancing the health of the employment relationship.

8.7 Conclusion

The goal of this chapter has been to highlight the concept of incongruence in employment relationships, discuss the various forms it takes, and identify its implications for both employees and organizations. Although the notion of incongruence has appeared throughout the psychological contract literature, to date scholars have not fully or systematically explored this important aspect of employment relationships.

As we have sought to demonstrate, obligation and fulfillment incongruence are common and inevitable in employment relationships. They stem from both the very nature of the obligations that exist within that relationship and the perceptual and cognitive processes that affect how employees and organizational agents determine what each party owes the other and how well those obligations are being maintained. Moreover, these forms of incongruence have significant implications for employees, organizations, and their managers, as well as the scholars who study employment relationships. Although the causes of incongruence are rooted in the very nature of psychological contracts and employment relationships, we have identified a number of ways by which organizations may be able to reduce the incidence and severity of incongruence, and thus its impact. We hope that this chapter will encourage others to recognize the role of incongruent perceptions about employment obligations and to study this important phenomenon in future empirical studies.

References

Argyris, C. (1960). *Understanding Organizational Behavior*. Homewood, IL: Dorsey Press.

Athanassiades, J. C. (1973). "The distortion of upward communication in hierarchical organizations." *Academy of Management Journal*, 16: 207–26.

Baumeister, R. F., Stillwell, A., and Wotman, S. R. (1990). "Victim and perpetrator accounts of interpersonal conflict: Autobiographical narratives about anger." *Journal of Personality and Social Psychology*, 59: 994–1005.

Bunderson, J. S. (2001). "How work ideologies shape the psychological contracts of professional employees: Examining doctors' responses to perceived breach." *Journal of Organizational Behavior*, 22: 1–25.

Coyle-Shapiro, J., and Kessler, I. (2002). "Exploring reciprocity through the lens of the psychological contract: Employee and employer perspectives." *European Journal of Work and Organizational Psychology*, 11: 69–86.

Eagly, A. H., and Chaiken, S. (1993). *The Psychology of Attitudes*. New York: Harcourt Brace Jovanovich.

Erickson, B. H. (1988). "The relational basis of attitudes," in B. Wellman and S. D. Berkowitz (eds.), *Social Structures: A Network Approach* (Cambridge: Cambridge University Press), 99–121.

Festinger, L. (1954). "A theory of social comparison processes." *Human Relations*, 7: 114–40.

Fiske, S. T., and Taylor, S. E. (1984). *Social Cognition*. New York: Random House.

Freese, C., and Schalk, R. (1996). "Implication of differences in psychological contracts for human resource management." *European Journal of Work and Organizational Psychology*, 5: 501–9.

Goldman, B., Lewis McClear, K., and Taylor, M. S. (1996). "Supervisor and employee perceptions of the psychological contract: The predictors and consequences of multiple perspectives." Presented at Society for Industrial and Organizational Psychology meeting.

Griffin, D. W., and Ross, L. (1991). "Subjective construal, social inference and human understanding," in D. M. Zanna (ed.), *Advances in Experimental Social Psychology*, Vol. 24 (San Diego: Academic Press), 319–59.

Harris, M. M., and Schaubroeck, J. (1988). "A meta-analysis of self-supervisor, self-peer, and peer -supervisor ratings." *Personnel Psychology*, 41: 43–62.

Heath, C., Knez, M., and Camerer, C. (1993). "The strategic management of the entitlement process in employment relationships." *Strategic Management Journal*, 14: 75–93.

Herriot, P., Manning, W. E. G., and Kidd, J. M. (1997). "The content of the psychological contract." *British Journal of Management*, 8: 151–62.

Hofstede, G. (1980). *Culture's Consequences: International Differences in Work-Related Values*. Beverly Hills, CA: Sage.

Huseman, R. C., Hatfield, J. D., and Miles, E. W. (1987). "A new perspective on equity theory: The equity sensitivity construct." *Academy of Management Review*, 12: 222–34.

Kotter, J. (1973). "The psychological contract: Managing the joining-up process." *California Management Review*, 15: 91–9.

Krackhardt, D., and Porter, L. W. (1986). "The snowball effect: Turnover embedded in communication networks." *Journal of Applied Psychology*, 71: 50–5.

Lester, S. W., Turnley, W. H., Bloodgood, J. M., and Bolino, M. C. (2002). "Not seeing eye to eye: Differences in supervisor and subordinate perceptions of and attributions for psychological contract breach." *Journal of Organizational Behavior*, 23: 39–56.

Levinson, H., Price, C., Munden, K., Mandl, H., and Solley, C. (1962). *Men, Management, and Mental Health*. Cambridge, MA: Harvard University Press.

Lind, E. A., and Tyler, T. R. (1988). *The Social Psychology of Procedural Justice*. New York: Plenum Press.

Marks, G., and Miller, N. (1987). "Ten years of research on the false consensus effect: An empirical and theoretical review." *Psychological Bulletin*, 102: 72–90.

Meyer, G. W. (1994). "Social information processing and social networks: A test of social influence mechanisms." *Human Relations*, 47: 1013–36.

Morrison, E. W., and Milliken, F. (2000). "Organizational silence: A barrier to change and development in a pluralistic world." *Academy of Management Review*, 25: 706–25.

—— and Robinson, S. L. (1997). "When employees feel betrayed: A model of how psychological contract violation develops." *Academy of Management Review*, 22: 226–56.

Neale, M., and Bazerman, M. (1991). *Cognition and Rationality in Negotiations*. New York: Free Press.

Pondy, L. (1967). "Organizational conflict: Concepts and models." *Administrative Science Quarterly*, 2: 296–320.

Raiffa, H. (1982). *The Art and Science of Negotiation*. Cambridge, MA: Belknap Press.

Rice, R. E., and Aydin, C. (1991). "Attitudes toward new organizational technology: Network proximity as a mechanism for social information processing." *Administrative Science Quarterly*, 36: 219–44.

Roberts, K. H., and O'Reilly, C. A. (1974). "Failures in upward communication in organizations: Three possible culprits." *Academy of Management Journal*, 17: 205–15.

Robinson, S. L. (1996). "Trust and breach of the psychological contract." *Administrative Science Quarterly*, 41: 574–99.

—— and Brown, G. (forthcoming). "Psychological contract breach and violation: A review," in R. W. Griffin and A. M. O'Leary-Kelly (eds.), *The Dark Side of Organizational Behavior* (San Francisco: Jossey Bass).

—— and Morrison, E. W. (1995). "Psychological contracts and OCB: The effects of unfulfilled obligations." *Journal of Organizational Behavior*, 16: 289–98.

—— and Morrison, E. W. (2000). "The development of psychological contract breach and violation: A longitudinal study." *Journal of Organizational Behavior*, 21: 525–46.

—— and Rousseau, D. M. (1994). "Violating the psychological contract: Not the exception but the norm." *Journal of Organizational Behavior*, 15: 245–59.

—— Kraatz, M. S., and Rousseau, D. M. (1994). "Changing obligations and the psychological contract: A longitudinal study." *Academy of Management Journal*, 37: 137–52.

Ross, L., Greene, D., and House, P. (1977). "The 'false consensus effect': An egocentric bias in social perception and attribution processes." *Journal of Experimental Social Psychology*, 13: 279–301.

Ross, M., and Sicoly, F. (1979). "Egocentric biases in availability and attribution." *Journal of Personality and Social Psychology*, 37: 322–37.

Rousseau, D. M. (1989). "Psychological and implied contracts in organizations." *Employee Responsibilities and Rights Journal*, 2: 121–39.

Rousseau, D. M. (1995). *Psychological Contracts in Organizations: Understanding Written and Unwritten Agreements*. New York: Sage.

—— (2001). "Schema, promise and mutuality: The building blocks of the psychological contract." *Journal of Occupational and Organizational Psychology*, 74: 511–41.

—— and Greller, M. M. (1994). "Human resource practices: Administrative contract makers." *Human Resource Management*, 33: 385–402.

—— and McLean Parks, J. (1993). "The contracts of individuals and organizations," in L. L. Cummings and B. M. Staw (eds.), *Research in Organizational Behavior* (Greenwich, CT: JAI Press), 1–43.

Salancik, G. R., and Pfeffer, J. (1978). "A social information processing approach to job attitudes and task redesign." *Administrative Science Quarterly*, 23: 224–50.

Schein, E. H. (1965). *Organizational Psychology*. Englewood Cliffs, NJ: Prentice Hall.

Schneider, D. J., Hastorf, A. H., and Ellsworth, P. C. (1979). *Person Perception*. Reading, MA: Addison-Wesley.

Shore, L. M., and Barksdale, K. (1998). "Examining degree of balance and level of obligation in the employment relationship: A social exchange approach." *Journal of Organizational Behavior*, 19: 731–44.

—— and Tetrick, L. E. (1994). "The psychological contract as an explanatory framework in the employment relationship," in C. L. Cooper and D. M. Rousseau (eds.), *Trends in Organizational Behavior* (New York: Wiley), 91–109.

Taylor, S. E., and Brown, J. D. (1988). "Illusions and well-being: A social psychological perspective on mental health." *Psychological Bulletin*, 103: 193–210.

—— and Crocker, J. (1981). "Schematic bases of social information processing," in E. T. Higgins, C. P. Herman, and M. P. Zann (eds.), *Social Cognition: The Ontario Symposium* (Hillsdale, NJ: Erlbaum), 89–134.

Tekleab, A. G., and Taylor, M. S. (2003). "Aren't there two parties in an employment relationship? Antecedents and consequences of organization–employee agreement on contract obligations and violations." *Journal of Organizational Behavior*, 24: 585–608.

Thompson, L., and Lowenstein, C. (1992). "Egocentric interpretations of fairness and interpersonal conflict." *Organizational Behavior and Human Decision Processes*, 51: 176–97.

Triandis, H. C., Bontembo, R., Villareal, M. J., Asai, M., and Lucca, N. (1988). "Individualism and collectivism: Cross-cultural perspectives on self-ingroup relationships." *Journal of Personality and Social Psychology*, 54: 323–38.

Turnley, W. H., and Feldman, D. C. (1999). "The impact of psychological contract violations on exit, voice, loyalty, and neglect." *Human Relations*, 52: 895–922.

Tsui, A. S., Pearce, J. L., Porter, L. W., and Tripoli, A. M. (1997). "Alternative approaches to the employee–organizational relationship: Does investment in employees pay off?" *Academy of Management Journal*, 40: 1089–121.

Wills, T. A. (1981). "Downward comparison principles in social psychology." *Psychological Bulletin*, 90: 245–71.

9

Job Creep: A Reactance Theory Perspective on Organizational Citizenship Behavior as Overfulfillment of Obligations

LINN VAN DYNE AND JENNIFER BUTLER ELLIS

9.1 A reactance theory perspective on OCB as overfulfillment

"Doing more with less" characterizes many employee jobs and employment relationships in most organizations these days. This is because competitive pressures have triggered downsizing, reorganization, flattened hierarchies, and layoffs (Cappelli et al. 1997; Rousseau 1997). Large numbers of employees have lost their jobs and many fear the possibility of future cutbacks (Brockner et al. 1986). Accordingly, employees often feel they must protect their employment status by making sure that their contributions to the organization exceed their obligations. Overfulfillment of contributions such as organizational citizenship behavior (OCB) signals commitment and loyalty—causing employees to believe or hope that they are enhancing their job security. When employees feel ongoing pressure to do more than the requirements of their jobs, we refer to this as "job creep." We define job creep as the slow and subtle expansion of employee job duties that is not officially recognized by the organization. Job creep changes the fundamental nature of the employment relationship by causing supervisors and work group peers to assume that a specific employee will take responsibility for certain tasks or activities, even though this is not part of the job and even though they get no formal tangible or intangible recognition.

In this chapter, we develop a theoretical model based on reactance theory (Brehm 1966; Brehm and Brehm 1981) that predicts consequences of job creep for employees and their work group peers (see Figure. 9.1). This conceptual approach complements existing work on employment relationships and psychological contracts because fulfillment of obligations is a critical indicator of the quality of employment relationships. For example, the expanding literature on psychological contracts (Rousseau 1989, 1990, 1995) conceptualizes employment as based on two-way exchanges where employees and organizations have mutual obligations.

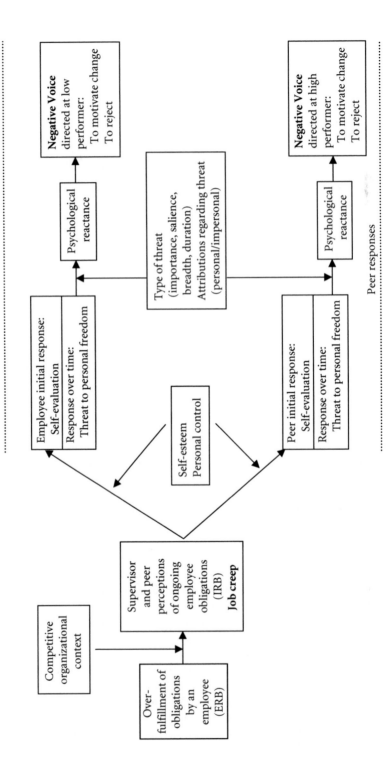

Figure 9.1. *Job Creep—a reactance theory perspective on OCB as over-fulfillment of employee obligations.*

Consistent with this emphasis on mutual obligations, the OCB literature draws on social exchange theory and the norm of reciprocity (Blau 1964) to predict and explain the positive relationship of organizational commitment, job satisfaction, and fair treatment with citizenship (Organ 1988). Thus, a series of reciprocal exchanges characterizes ongoing employment where both employees and organizations expect to have their contributions recognized and reciprocated. In this chapter, we focus on situations where employees feel that the norm of reciprocity is not applied. Sometimes managers may not notice employee OCB. Furthermore, managers may not view OCB as overfulfillment of obligations. Alternatively, managers may be constrained (budget constraints, promotion freezes, downsizing that requires everyone to do more with less) and unable to provide tangible or intangible recognition to employees. Finally, in some cases, managers may intentionally fail to recognize OCB, knowing that there are few job alternatives in the external labor market. In each of these examples, employees perceive that they overfulfill their obligations to the organization. They also perceive that the organization does not respond according to the norm of reciprocity, and thus they experience job creep. In sum, the model in this chapter focuses on situations where employees perceive that the employer is violating the norm of reciprocity.

To date, the majority of research on psychological contracts has focused on employee perceptions that the employer has violated the psychological contract (Robinson et al. 1994; Morrison and Robinson 1997; Robinson and Morrison 2000; Bunderson 2001; Thompson and Bunderson 2003). Violation occurs when employees believe that employers have not fulfilled their obligations. This is an important stream of research because it demonstrates that lower satisfaction, commitment, organizational citizenship, and intention to remain in the organization typically follow perceived violation of obligations (Robinson and Rousseau 1994; Robinson 1996; Turnley and Feldman 1999a). More recently, scholars have expanded their thinking about psychological contracts and employment relationships. For example, Coyle-Shapiro (2002) and Coyle-Shapiro and Kessler (2002) emphasized the two-way nature of employment relationships and the benefits of considering more than just the employee's perspective. This could include the employer's perspective, as well as the perspective of work group peers. Other recent approaches have begun to consider the effects of fulfillment (Turnley et al. 2003), discrepancies and excess in inducements and contributions (Turnley and Feldman 1999b; Lambert et al. 2002), escalating citizenship (Bolino and Turnley 2002), and acts of positive deviance (Spreitzer and Sonenshein 2003). These new approaches are promising and consistent with our model of job creep.

In this chapter, we have three objectives generally aimed at advancing research on employment relationships. First, responding to contemporary pressures on employment relationships, we introduce the concept of job creep which we define as the slow and subtle expansion of employee job duties such that extra-role behavior (ERB) becomes viewed as in-role behavior (IRB) and employees feel ongoing pressure to do more than the official requirements of their jobs. Based on changes in perceived obligations, we propose that job creep changes the fundamental nature of the employment relationship. Second, we draw on reactance theory to develop an initial theoretical framework that predicts the consequences of job creep for employees and their work group peers. Third, we differentiate two types of negative voice and predict that job creep can lead to negative voice when employees try to regain a sense that their overfulfillment does not represent obligations but instead is discretionary behavior.

In this research, we integrate concepts from the literatures on psychological contracts, organizational citizenship, and reactance theory. Thus, this framework is distinctive based on this specific theoretical integration. In addition, two aspects of our approach to the employment relationship differ from that of most prior research. First, most psychological contract research has focused on underfulfillment of obligations (i.e. violation and breach) and emphasizes a negative discrepancy. In contrast, we focus on overfulfillment of obligations (excess contributions) and emphasize a positive discrepancy (Ellis 2001; Lambert et al. 2002). Second, prior research has primarily emphasized the employee perspective and has only recently considered multiple perspectives on employment relationships (Lester et al. 2002). In our research, we include both actor (employee) and observer (peer) perspectives. Thus, we explicitly acknowledge that employment relationships occur within a system of relationships where the behavior of one employee has spillover effects on others in the work group (Howard 1995). In sum, combining past research with our framework should help scholars advance our understanding of employment relationships because fulfillment can be equal to, more than, or less than obligations, and because employment relationships occur in a complex system of relationships involving individual employees and their work group peers.

The remainder of this chapter is organized as follows. We start by describing job creep in more detail and link it to existing literature on psychological contracts and extra-role behavior. We then draw on reactance theory to develop our initial model of employee reactions to job creep. The model includes specific propositions describing how job creep influences employee self-evaluations, leading to employee reactance and negative voice based on employee efforts to regain a sense that excess contributions are indeed discretionary rather than obligations. We then shift our focus from the employee to the work group peers and describe similar reactance processes for the peers that again lead to negative voice. We conclude by discussing theoretical and practical implications, making recommendations for future research.

9.1.1 Job creep

Job creep is the gradual and informal expansion of role responsibilities where discretionary contributions (such as OCB) become viewed as in-role obligations by supervisors and peers. Drawing on the social cognition literature, we suggest that job creep is influenced by the persistence of expectations and people's tendency to expect past behavior to continue in the future (Anderson 1955; Ross et al. 1975). In other words, if an employee repeatedly exceeds role obligations, observers such as supervisors and work group peers develop schemas that this behavior will persist.

Accordingly, observers expect the overfulfillment to continue. These heightened expectations for contributions represent job creep because they are not formally recognized or rewarded. Instead, employees experience ongoing pressure to make contributions that exceed their formal role obligations. In sum, job creep blurs the boundary between ERB and IRB.

The large literature on OCB (Organ 1988) is relevant to job creep because it shows that employees often make contributions to their organizations that are not explicitly specified as job requirements (Podsakoff et al. 2000; LePine et al. 2002). For example, some employees fulfill work obligations at exceptionally high levels (unusually high conscientiousness), assist co-workers with heavy work loads (helping), and speak up to make suggestions for change (voice). Research demonstrates three primary reasons why employees engage in OCB. First, employees may be reciprocating positive inducements they have received from the organization (Organ 1988). Second, they may be fulfilling their own needs (such as concern for others or prosocial values) (McNeely and Meglino 1994; Rioux and Penner 2001). Third, they may be engaging in impression management to conform to group norms or to enhance their own self-interest (Bolino 1999). Regardless of motive or combination of motives, none of these behaviors are included explicitly in job descriptions. They require judgment and initiative because they cannot be specified in advance and they are not explicitly rewarded (Van Dyne et al. 1995). Sometimes referred to as discretionary behaviors, organizational citizenship is increasingly important to organizations because contemporary approaches to management such as work teams and empowerment emphasize the benefits of proactive employee behavior and initiative (Farr and Ford 1990; Spreitzer, 1996; Morrison and Phelps 1999; Seibert et al. 2001; Campbell 2000; Crant 2000).

Several other literatures beyond the domain of OCB also provide insights that are relevant to our focus on job creep. Here, we focus on other types of proactive employee efforts to influence the nature of their jobs and the role boundaries of these jobs. One of the earliest literatures to address this issue is Katz and Kahn's (1966, 1978) work on spontaneous role behavior. Graen (1976) described employee role-making (i.e. efforts to modify job scope to fit personal idiosyncratic preferences) and West (1987) studied role innovation at work. More recently, Frese and colleagues have described the concept of initiative (Frese et al. 1996; Frese and Fay 2001). Finally, a recent theoretical framework described job crafting as the process employees use to change job boundaries to reconceptualize their jobs in ways that are personally meaningful (Wrzesniewski and Dutton 2001).

Also important to the idea of job creep is the literature on role boundaries. An interesting set of papers in the OCB literature addresses the issue of role obligations and OCB. For example, researchers have demonstrated that employees and supervisors often have different views about what is a role obligation and what is discretionary behavior (Morrison 1994; Lam et al. 1999). Van Dyne et al. (1995) developed three conceptual explanations for why role perceptions can vary: (a) across persons (actors and observers); (b) across contexts; and (c) across time. In addition, Parker et al. (1997), Parker (1998), and Welbourne et al. (1998) have argued that organizations often deliberately encourage employees to expand their role conceptualizations proactively. When this occurs, employees take initiative to do more than what has been traditionally specified in their job descriptions. Overall, these arguments are consistent with Tepper et al.'s (2001) results demonstrating higher frequency of behaviors construed by employees as IRB.

Overall, we view our work on job creep as complementary to these other approaches and suggest that the combined consideration of OCB, ERB, spontaneous behavior, role-making, job crafting, and job creep will further enrich our understanding of employee initiative and employment relationships. At the same time, we emphasize that job creep is not the same as these proactive behaviors. Instead, we propose that job creep is a consequence of these behaviors—job creep occurs when employees overfulfill obligations and perceive that the organization does not respond based on the norm of reciprocity. Several examples may help to clarify the difference between job creep and OCB. Although there is evidence that OCB is sometimes viewed as IRB by employees (see e.g. Morrison 1994), Podsakoff et al. (2000) concluded (based on their in-depth review of the literature) that OCB is generally viewed as non-required or volitional behavior that is not specified in advance. Examples of OCB include helping co-workers with heavy workloads, staying late to finish a special report, and making suggestions that might improve work processes. In each case, OCB emphasizes employee judgment and choice. Thus, the behaviors are typically viewed as discretionary.

In contrast, examples of job creep would include the following. Job creep could occur when supervisors encourage employees to help co-workers who are behind in their work on an ongoing basis, but provide no extra tangible or intangible recognition (violating the norm of reciprocity). For example, although helping might not be formally written into a job description, supervisors can use a variety of techniques (such as direct commands, threats, persuasion, requests, and peer pressure) to reinforce expanded role responsibilities. When employees feel ongoing pressure to help those with heavy workloads, what was originally a volitional or discretionary behavior becomes transformed into an obligation. Similarly, if one employee develops a reputation for speaking up and making constructive suggestions for change, work-group peers could develop the habit of waiting for this person to take the initiative and suggest solutions to problems. In each of these cases, pressure from supervisors and peers reduces the employee's sense that the behavior is volitional. Instead, ongoing overfulfillment becomes expected behavior, part of the job, and an employee obligation. In sum, we propose that ERB can become transformed into IRB, resulting in informal expansion of job responsibilities and increased employee obligations.

Proposition 1   *Overfulfillment of obligations by an employee (e.g. OCB) leads to job creep (higher supervisor and peer perceptions of employee obligations).*

9.1.2 Context

We do not, however, propose that ERB will always be transformed into IRB. Instead, consistent with our emphasis on contemporary trends in organizations and in employment relationships (Rousseau 1997), we acknowledge the important role of context (Cappelli and Sherer 1991). Although scholars have recommended increased attention to the role of context for many years (Mowday and Sutton 1993), it is only recently that context has become a key consideration in theory development (Johns 2001; Rousseau and Fried 2001). In our model, we propose that context is a critical consideration because job creep will be more likely to occur when external factors increase competitive pressures (Cappelli 1997).

For example, when pressure to improve performance causes an organization to downsize and reorganize, the remaining employees typically must pick up additional responsibilities. Similarly, in a weak economy where employees have relatively few alternative job opportunities, two simultaneous processes may increase the likelihood that discretionary behavior will be transformed into role obligations. First, when employees have few job options, they have less bargaining power and organizations may expect more from these employees (Hulin et al. 1985). At the same time, a weak economy with few job alternatives may induce employees to overfulfill their obligations as an attempt to increase job security. In other words, these two forces combine to increase the probability of job creep, based on context. Thus, we propose that the competitive nature of the external organizational context will moderate the relationship we have proposed in Proposition 1 such that job creep (transformation of ERB into IRB) will be more likely when organizations are under severe competitive pressure to cut costs, improve products and services, and increase profits.

Proposition 2 *Transformation of ERB into IRB will be more likely when organizations are under heavy competitive pressure.*

9.2 An initial model of employee reactions to job creep

In this section of the chapter, we develop propositions for the consequences of job creep for employees and for their work group peers. Drawing on reactance theory, we propose that social comparison of self with others (in this case with work group peers) will cause those who overfulfill their obligations to experience psychological reactance. When discretionary behavior becomes viewed as a role obligation, reactance theory predicts that employees will take action to regain their sense of personal freedom (Wicklund 1974; Brehm and Brehm 1981). In considering behavioral responses to psychological reactance, we introduce the concept of negative voice. Negative voice (such as complaints and criticism) occurs when reactance causes those who experience job creep to speak up in an effort to regain a sense of personal control. For example, the employee might use voice directly to motivate peers who do not engage in overfulfillment to improve their performance (LePine and Van Dyne 2001a). Alternatively, the employee might use voice indirectly to criticize, reject, or ostracize peers who do not overfulfill their obligations. In each of these cases, the employee is using voice to transform IRB back into ERB.

We propose a similar reactance process for work group peers who observe a colleague overfulfill obligations. To work group peers, the employee who overfulfills obligations represents a threat to personal freedom because the peers may experience pressure to change their own performance and also start to overfulfill their contributions. This is consistent with the logic proposed by Bolino and Turnley (2002) in their discussion of escalating citizenship behavior. Consistent with reactance theory, our model predicts that peers will also engage in negative voice. This could include voice intended to motivate the high performing co-worker to reduce contributions so that the discrepancy no longer exists. It also could include voice directed at rejecting or ostracizing the employee who has overfulfilled the obligations.

9.2.1 Employee reactions to job creep

When job creep occurs, employees may initially feel pleased that others entrust them with additional responsibilities. Expanded job scope can imply competence and capability, leading to positive self-evaluation. When supervisors and/or peers act as though an employee has additional, ongoing responsibilities, social comparison processes should cause a sense of pride and superiority, leading to self-enhancement (Gecas 1982; Brewer and Weber 1994; Mussweiler and Bodenhausen 2002). This would be consistent with the Lake Wobegon effect that suggests most people judge themselves as "better than average" (Zuckerman and Jost 2001). Thus, we propose that when job creep occurs, similarities and differences between co-workers become increasingly salient. For example, if supervisors act as though some employees have greater obligations than others, the employee who has been overfulfilling obligations may feel exceptional and deserving of special treatment.

Furthermore, the desire to appear "better than average" often leads employees to make self-serving comparisons (Taylor and Brown 1988; Dunning et al. 1989; Zuckerman and Jost 2001) that yield personal psychological benefits. In the case of job creep, employees who overfulfill obligations will experience self-enhancement by comparing themselves to work group peers. This increases self-worth and indicates their centrality and importance in organizational networks (Krackhardt, 1987). In sum, those who overfulfill obligations will experience self-enhancement.

Proposition 3a   *Higher supervisor and peer perceptions of an employee's ongoing obligations will lead initially to positive self-evaluation by that employee.*

Although we have predicted that initial reactions to job creep will be positive for employees who overfulfill obligations, we now need to qualify the time frame for this prediction. Here, we propose that if employees feel ongoing pressure to work longer hours or if they feel others always expect them to assume responsibility for unexpected projects, their initial positive feelings of self-enhancement will weaken over time and be replaced by a sense of threat to personal freedom. Freedom is the belief that an individual can choose to participate in a specific behavior (Brehm and Brehm 1981: 35). When job creep occurs, employees lose the feeling that their behavior is optional and in addition, they receive no raise or promotion. Instead, they feel obligated to make specific contributions and no longer have freedom of choice.

When employees feel that they must regularly perform additional responsibilities (but without formal recognition), their behavior is not discretionary. In addition, overfulfillment can be personally costly. For example, regularly working longer hours reduces time available for family and personal interests. Trying to "do more with less" all the time is stressful. In contrast, if an employee chooses occasionally to stay late or take on an extra project, this is discretionary behavior that enhances self-evaluation. When contributions that were initially intended as discretionary become an unofficial but ongoing part of the role, the employee's freedom is restricted. In sum, we predict that job creep (the informal but ongoing expansion of role obligations) represents a personal threat to employee discretion, judgment, and freedom.

Proposition 3b *Over time, higher supervisor and peer perceptions of an employee's ongoing obligations will threaten that employee's sense of personal freedom.*

Reactance theory emphasizes the important moderating role of individual differences in strengthening or weakening the intensity of threat to personal freedom. For example, Brehm and Brehm (1981) theorized that internal locus of control, type A personality, and self-consciousness would accentuate the effect of threat to personal freedom. Although empirical results for type A and self-consciousness are inconsistent, results for internal locus of control are strong. For example, Cherulnik and Citrin (1974) demonstrated stronger reactance for those with internal locus of control.

Extending prior research and theory, we focus on the more contemporary concept of self-esteem as a key individual difference that most likely influences reactance processes. This is because our focus is employee behavior in organizations and because research demonstrates that self-esteem moderates employee reactions and behavior at work (Brockner 1988). Self-esteem is an individual's degree of positive self-worth (Coopersmith 1981). It indicates the degree to which individuals believe they are capable, significant, successful, and worthy. Those with high self-esteem exhibit more initiative and assertiveness than those with low self-esteem (Crandall 1973). They also conform less (Wells and Marwell 1976). Applying this to our model suggests that job creep (the unofficial expansion of perceived role obligations) will represent a greater threat to personal freedom for those with high self-esteem than for those with low self-esteem.

A second individual difference that is relevant to employee attitudes and behaviors at work is personal control (Greenberger and Strasser 1986; Greenberger et al. 1989). Personal control is an individual's cognitive beliefs about ability to influence the environment. Unlike locus of control (Rotter 1966), however, personal control is not a stable individual difference. Instead, personal control beliefs can change over time. Past research in work organizations has demonstrated that personal control triggers cognitive, emotional, and behavioral responses. In general, those with higher personal control are more proactive in their responses to the environment and in their attempts to influence their environment (Greenberger et al. 1988; Greenberger et al. 1989).

Recognizing the emphasis placed by Brehm and Brehm (1981) on the role of individual differences in the reactance process, we combine the above two paragraphs to predict that self-esteem and personal control will moderate the relationship between job creep and threat to personal freedom. We expect that job creep will be more threatening to the personal freedom of those with high self-esteem and to those with high personal control (compared to low self-esteem and low personal control). Thus, the relationship between job creep and threat to personal freedom will be stronger for those with high self-esteem (than those with low self-esteem). It also will be stronger for those with high personal control (than those low in personal control).

Proposition 4 *Self-esteem and personal control will moderate the relationship between job creep and threat to personal freedom, such that the link will be stronger for employees with high self-esteem and high personal control.*

9.2.2 Psychological reactance

According to Brehm and Brehm (1981), threat to personal freedom triggers reactance. Psychological reactance is an internal, psychological state that includes self-perceptions as well as subjective beliefs about personal abrogation of freedom. Reactance is a motivational state that can be intense and can represent strong urges. Furthermore, reactance is not a generic reaction to loss of freedom and is not a diffuse emotional state. Instead, "the direct manifestation of reactance is behavior directed toward restoring the freedom in question" (Brehm and Brehm 1981: 4).

In our case, employees who overfulfill obligations undoubtedly start out feeling that their behavior is volitional. If job creep occurs, however, the scope of the job is informally expanded and what was discretionary becomes an obligation. Over time, these unrecognized obligations may cause the employee to feel overwhelmed, exhausted, frustrated, cynical, and angry (Maslach and Leiter 1999) because their personal freedom is reduced. When people expect to control or influence an outcome and then feel that they have lost this freedom, reactance occurs such that larger perceived losses increase reactance (Brehm and Brehm 1981). In applying this to our model, we suggest that the greater the loss of perceived freedom associated with unofficial job creep, the stronger the reactance feelings of injustice, frustration, anger, and hostility (Miller 2001). If employees perceive little threat to their freedom, there will be little psychological reactance. On the other hand, if employees perceive significant threat to their independence, psychological reactance will be stronger.

Proposition 5 *The larger the perceived threat to personal freedom, the stronger the employee's psychological reactance.*

Other characteristics of the threat (beyond magnitude) also influence the intensity of reactance. For example, reactance theory research has demonstrated that type of threat and attributions about the threat intensify the level of reactance. We discuss each below.

Reactance theory stresses four specific attributes of threat to personal freedom that accentuate the effects of threat on psychological reactance: importance, salience, breadth, and duration. If an individual views a threat as personally relevant, the link between threat and reactance will be stronger. If job creep focuses on an area of work that is related to an employee's identity or core values (importance), this will strengthen the effect of the magnitude of the threat on reactance. For example, the more value an employee places on freedom to choose whether or not to engage in ERB, the stronger the reactance when ERB is transformed into IRB.

Threats also vary in terms of their visibility (salience), scope (breadth), and time horizon (duration). Each of these, according to reactance research, will strengthen the relationship between magnitude of threat and reactance (Brehm and Sensenig 1966). For our job creep application, this suggests a moderating role for more obvious threats such as explicit requests to expand obligations without recognition (salience). It also suggests an interaction between size of threat (magnitude) and scope (breadth) of threat. Finally, for threats with an ongoing pattern of loss such as implied permanently expanded obligations (duration), the effect of magnitude of threat on reactance will be further strengthened. Thus, we propose a moderated relationship.

Proposition 6a   *The link between threat to personal freedom and psychological reactance will be stronger when the threatened freedom is important, salient, broad, and ongoing.*

Individual attributions for whether the loss of freedom is personal or impersonal is another important characteristic that influences psychological reactance (Brehm and Brehm 1981). For example, if an individual imputes an impersonal motive as the reason for the loss of personal freedom, this will weaken the link between threat and reactance. If employees believe that others in the organization have expanded role obligations (job creep), this will weaken the effects of perceived loss. On the other hand, if specific employees feel that they have been singled out for job creep and that others do not have additional informal obligations, their attributions and sense-making will accentuate the link between threat and reactance. According to reactance theory and research, personal attributions imply intentional and ongoing loss of freedom whereas impersonal attributions imply unintentional and temporary loss of freedom. In other words, the negative effect of threat to personal freedom on reactance will be stronger when employees make personal attributions than when they make impersonal attributions.

Proposition 6b   *The link between threat to personal freedom and psychological reactance will be stronger when attributions are personal.*

9.3 Negative voice as a response to psychological reactance

9.3.1 *Voice and types of voice*

Existing management research on voice has adopted two contrasting conceptualizations of voice. The first approach uses the term voice to describe speaking-up behavior such as when employees proactively make suggestions for change (Rusbult et al. 1988; Withey and Cooper 1989; Farrell and Rusbult 1992; Van Dyne et al. 1995; Janssen et al. 1998; LePine and Van Dyne 1998; Frese et al. 1999; Zhou and George 2001). These verbal expressions are intended as positive suggestions. The second conceptualization of voice describes the presence of due process procedures that enhance justice judgments and facilitate employee participation in decision-making (Folger 1977; Bies and Shapiro 1988; Lind et al. 1990). Although both conceptualizations have merit and address important managerial issues, we focus in this paper on the first conceptualization (i.e. voice as an employee behavior rather than an organizational process) due to our interest in employee behavior directed at increasing personal freedom and control (Brehm and Brehm 1981).

In addition, the management literature uses a variety of terms to refer to employee voice behavior. Of these, the most common term is the word voice itself. This includes research on the exit, voice, loyalty, and neglect (EVLN) framework (Hirschman 1970; Farrell 1983; Rusbult et al. 1988; Withey and Cooper 1989). It also includes more recent work that focuses specifically on voice as proactive and con-structively intended speaking-up behavior (Van Dyne et al. 1995; LePine and Van Dyne 1998, 2001*b*; Van Dyne and LePine 1998; Zhou and George 2001; Avery and Quinones 2002).

In addition to the above research that uses the specific term of voice, there are a number of other voice-like constructs that emphasize speaking up and making suggestions. This includes the civic virtue form of organizational citizenship (Organ 1988; Graham 1991, 2000; Robinson and Morrison 1995; Robinson 1996) that includes proactively speaking up and participating in organizational affairs. Advocacy participation, a similar voice-like construct, has been defined as a con-structive and proactive voice such as expressing high standards, challenging others, and making suggestions for change (Van Dyne et al. 1994). Another positive, change-oriented construct is constructive suggestions that include actively proposing ways to improve individual, group, or organizational functioning (George and Brief 1992; Frese et al. 1999; Zhou and George 2001). Other relevant, prosocial behaviors such as championing, taking charge, issue selling, and reformist dissent also involve verbal expressions intended to benefit the larger collective (Howell and Higgins 1990; Dutton and Ashford 1993; Parker 1993; Morrison and Phelps 1999). In sum, although these constructs have not been explicitly labeled "voice," each represents verbal expression of ideas, information, and opinions with the goal of making positive and cooperative contributions to the organization.

9.3.2 Negative voice

In commenting on the voice literature, Withey and Cooper (1989) speculated that prior research may have combined different types of voice into one construct and that this may have confounded research findings. Accordingly, they suggested the benefits of developing a more fine-grained conceptualization of employee voice. Following up on this recommendation, Van Dyne et al. (2003) introduced a multidimensional framework that differentiated prosocial voice (i.e. other-oriented expression of ideas, information, and opinions for constructive ways to improve work and work organizations, based on cooperative motives), defensive voice (i.e. self-protective expression, based on fear), and acquiescent voice (i.e. disengaged expressions based on resignation). Further extending this framework, we now focus on negative forms of voice that may have relevance to job creep and reactance.

When roles and obligations expand (e.g. ERB becomes transformed into IRB), employees may engage in non-problem focused reactance by complaining and communicating their frustration (expressive voice). Alternatively, they may use problem-focused expressions to try to change the situation (instrumental voice). These two responses parallel the differences between expressive aggression and instrumental aggression (Buss 1961) and between expressive complaints and instrumental complaints (Kowalski 1996). For expressive voice, the focus is self-oriented catharsis (e.g. venting frustrations and personal feelings). For instrumental voice, the focus is other-oriented attempts to change the situation and reduce perceived threats to personal freedom (Brehm and Brehm 1981).

For this section of our framework, we draw on LePine and Van Dyne's (2001a) typology of employee responses to low performing peers that emphasized helping directed at peers. In this chapter, we extend their conceptualization to include negative voice that is directed at low performing peers. We focus on two forms of instrumental voice and exclude expressive voice because our predictions are based on reactance theory and instrumental employee efforts to increase feelings of personal control and freedom (rather than simply venting frustrations). The two types of instrumental voice that we address are: (a) voice directed at *motivating* change so that peers also overfulfill obligations; and (b) voice directed at ostracizing or *rejecting* peers who do not overfulfill obligations. In both cases, the objective is to enhance perceived personal freedom by reducing pressure to overfulfill obligations. We refer to these forms of voice as negative voice because they can appear aggressive and may harm others in the workplace. By explicitly differentiating types of voice, we aim to improve our ability to predict and understand voice behavior.

We also contrast motivating voice and rejecting voice in terms of directness. Direct voice occurs when an employee complains or criticizes directly to the target of their loss. For example, an employee may feel that their obligations have been expanded because low-performing co-workers do not fulfill their work responsibilities. In this instance, direct voice would include complaints or criticism made directly to low-performers to motivate them to increase their contributions. As another example, direct voice could be used to motivate others to overfulfill obligations so that extra work is distributed more equally across employees. This could include verbal threats, harsh or punitive feedback (Moss and Martinko 1998), motivational exhortations to increase contributions, warnings such as "I'm not going to help you next time," or directive pep talks (LePine and Van Dyne 2001a). If successful, these motivating forms of voice would increase personal freedom and allow employees a greater sense that overfulfillment is volitional and not an obligation.

Indirect voice occurs when an employee complains or criticizes a peer to others (not directly to the target). This could include gossiping and scapegoating about a co-worker to others in efforts to ostracize or reject the peer from the group (LePine and Van Dyne 2001*a*). As an example, Morrison and Milliken (2000) suggested that employees may respond to a lack of control by engaging in workplace sabotage. This could include complaining about a low performing co-worker or engaging in work-related, professional gossip to harm the peer's reputation (Kurland and Pelled 2000). Alternatively, indirect voice could focus on those who do not overfulfill obligations. In this case, an employee could retaliate by covertly complaining to others and blaming the target peer for inequitable distribution of work (Skarlicki and Folger 1997). Indirect voice should cause the target peer to feel rejected and feel more of an outsider than an insider (Stamper and Masterson 2002). Over time, this should increase the likelihood of the target peer voluntarily or involuntarily leaving the work group. In either case, these indirect forms of voice cause the target peer to be ostracized and rejected, while simultaneously reducing pressure on others to overfull obligations (Kowalski 1997).

In sum, we propose that job creep expands role responsibilities, threatens perceived freedom (the personal choice to engage or not engage in discretionary behavior), and leads to psychological reactance which triggers instrumental voice (motivating voice or rejecting voice) aimed at restoring personal freedom. Consistent with reactance theory research (Brehm and Brehm 1981), we predict that the higher the psychological reactance, the more likely the use of instrumental voice to eliminate the need for ongoing overfulfillment. When people feel pressure to overfulfill their obligations (e.g. their helping is no longer discretionary), they may comply at first but will eventually develop feelings of reactance and resistance. Over time, psychological reactance will be directed at restoring the specific freedom that has been threatened (the choice to engage in ERB). Accordingly, the higher the reactance, the more the individual will want to re-establish feelings of control directed at the threatened freedom.

Proposition 7   *The higher the psychological reactance, the more likely the employee will engage in negative forms of voice (e.g. trying to motivate a peer to overfulfill or trying to reject a low performing peer) so that overfulfillment is no longer needed.*

9.4 Peer reactions to job creep

Thus far, we have focused on the effects of job creep on those who overfulfill obligations. Extending our model, we now propose that work group peers are also subject to reactance processes. Basically we use the same logic and propose parallel relationships, with one primary exception. In contrast to the initial positive reaction of employees who overfulfill obligations (Proposition 3a: Self-enhancement), we argue that spillover effects will be negative for work group peers. This is for three reasons. First, peers who are not subject to job creep may feel ignored or unappreciated by the supervisor because they were not entrusted with additional job responsibilities.

Second, this may cause peers to question their value to the organization and engage in negative self-evaluation. Self-evaluation depends heavily on comparisons with others (Brewer and Weber 1994; Mussweiler and Bodenhausen 2002). In our situation where one employee overfulfills obligations, other members of the work group suffer from contrast effects. This may lead to self-deprecation and feelings of failure and incompetence. Accordingly, we propose that having a co-worker who experiences job creep will trigger contrast effects and negative reactions from peers, leading to self-deprecation. Furthermore, peers may feel that this discrepancy in contributions may threaten their job security or put pressure on them to increase their contributions (such as engaging in overfulfillment themselves). Over time, these contrast effects will reduce the peers' sense of personal freedom.

Proposition 8a *Higher supervisor perceptions of an employee's ongoing obligations will lead to negative self-evaluation by work group peers (self-deprecation).*

Proposition 8b *Over time, higher supervisor perceptions of an employee's ongoing obligations will threaten work group peers' sense of personal freedom.*

For the remainder of the model illustrated in Figure. 9.1, the logic and form of our propositions for peers parallel that of the employee who overfulfills obligations. Thus, individual differences will also intensify peer reactions to observed job creep such that those with high self-esteem and high personal control will experience a more intense threat to personal freedom when a work group peer overfulfills role obligations.

Proposition 9 *Individual differences will moderate the relationship between supervisor perceptions of an employee's ongoing obligations and the reactions of work group peers, such that the link will be stronger for peers with high self-esteem and personal control.*

Similarly, magnitude of threat will influence psychological reactance of peers such that larger perceived threats trigger stronger reactance. For example, if overfulfillment by one employee causes the supervisor to raise expectations for all employees, this creates pressure for peers to stay late, take on additional assignments, and increase their contributions without formal recognition (no promotions and no raises). This increase in obligations represents a personal threat to employee discretion, judgment, and freedom, such that greater threats heighten peer reactions. Likewise, characteristics of the threat and attributions regarding the threat will also moderate the relationship between threat and reactance.

Proposition 10 *The larger the perceived threat to personal freedom, the stronger the peers' psychological reactance.*

Proposition 11a *The link between threat to personal freedom and peer psychological reactance will be stronger when the threatened freedom is important, salient, broad, and ongoing in duration.*

Proposition 11b *The link between threat to personal freedom and peer psychological reactance will be weaker when peer attributions are impersonal (compared to personal).*

9.4.1 Peer use of negative voice as a response to job creep

When peers experience psychological reactance because a co-worker overfulfills obligations and creates pressure on them to increase their contributions, these peers may use negative forms of instrumental voice in efforts to restore the freedom and control they have lost (Barker 1993; Hackman 1992). Thus, work group peers might use direct voice to try and motivate the high performing peer to conform and stop overfulfilling obligations (Kiesler and Kiesler 1969). This would reduce the discrepancy and negative contrast effects, thus reducing pressure to increase contributions. By minimizing the variance in performance, work group peers can regain freedom to perform at status quo levels and increase their feelings of control and personal freedom. In extreme cases, peers may sabotage the work of an employee who overfulfills obligations (Analoui 1995).

Alternatively, work group peers might use indirect voice to try and reject or eject the high performing peer from the group. This could include making disparaging comments or gossiping to other co-workers about the high performer. In addition, peers could use indirect voice to sabotage the reputation of a co-worker who overfulfills obligations. This would isolate and ostracize the high performer, reducing contrast effects and threats to personal freedom of the peers. Ultimately, peer pressure might cause the high performer to change behavior or leave the group. By motivating the high performer to change (i.e. reduce their work contributions) or by rejecting the high performer and encouraging them to leave the work group, peers regain freedom to work at status quo levels. In sum, we propose that peers will use proactive negative voice to enhance their sense of influence and feelings of personal freedom.

Proposition 12   *The higher the psychological reactance, the more likely peers will engage in negative forms of proactive voice (such as trying to **motivate** those who overfulfill obligations to conform to typical performance levels or trying to **reject** the high performer so that the individual leaves the group or is ejected from the group) so that comparisons are no longer negative.*

9.5 Discussion

This chapter integrates past literature on psychological contracts, organizational citizenship, and reactance theory to develop a framework for predicting employee reactions to job creep. Job creep is the gradual and informal expansion of role responsibilities that occurs when employee contributions to the organization exceed their formal obligations (overfulfillment of obligations). One key contribution of this chapter is introducing the construct of job creep. We suggest that job creep has increasingly salient implications for employees, supervisors, and work group peers during economic downturns. In addition, this chapter makes several important contributions to the literature on employment relationships.

First, our research is distinct because it focuses on fulfillment of employee obligations. In contrast, most existing research on psychological contracts and most research on individual–organizational relationships tend to focus upon perceptions that the employer has violated their obligations (Robinson and Rousseau 1994; Robinson 1996; Morrison and Robinson 1997; Robinson and Morrison 2000; Turnley and Feldman 2000; Thompson and Bunderson 2003). Second, our approach is unique in its focus on positive discrepancies or overfulfillment of employee obligations. In contrast, most prior research has emphasized negative discrepancies (i.e. perceived employer violations and insufficient fulfillment of obligations). Third, most research on employment relationships and failure to fulfill obligations has adopted the employee perspective. Because the employment relationships and psychological contracts are necessarily embedded in a broader context and involve multiple two-way obligations, it is also important to examine additional perspectives (such as that of work group peers).

Thus, this chapter has examined previously neglected aspects of work relationships, including positive discrepancies and overfulfillment of obligations, as well as multiple perspectives of employees, peers, and supervisors. Although a few recent papers acknowledge overfulfillment, positive violations, and positive discrepancies (Ellis 2001; Lambert et al. 2002; Turnley et al. 2003), more research and theoretical development is needed to explore the antecedents and consequences of the overfulfillment of obligations. Furthermore, it is important to consider both employee and observer perceptions (e.g. supervisor and peers) on fulfillment because they represent the other half of the relationship. In sum, this theoretical framework is another step toward a more complete view of employment relationships.

Another important contribution of the chapter is the conceptualization of two specific forms of negative voice (motivating voice and rejecting voice). Based on reactance theory, we have predicted that one employee response to job creep and threats to personal freedom is proactive voice directed toward restoring the lost freedom. Thus, we have argued that employees and their work group peers will use complaints and criticism (both directly and indirectly) in attempts to reduce the sense of threat and personal loss (Brehm and Brehm 1981). In the case of job creep, where an employee's exceptional contributions become viewed as in-role obligations by supervisors and peers, we have predicted that the high performing employee will use negative voice directly to try and motivate others to increase their contributions or indirectly to reject others from the group so that contributions are distributed more equitably across employees and so that overfulfillment is discretionary behavior and not an obligation.

Adopting multiple perspectives, we have also proposed that work group peers will experience feelings of reactance when a co-worker overfulfills obligations. To work group peers, the employee who overfulfills obligations represents a threat because contrast effects create peer pressure on others to change performance and increase contributions. Adopting an approach that parallels the employee part of the model, we predicted that peers will use direct and indirect negative voice to regain their own sense of personal freedom and control. Thus, peers will use direct voice to motivate those who overfulfill obligations to lower their contributions. In addition, peers will also use indirect voice to reject those with exceptionally high performance so that contributions are distributed more equitably and so that overfulfillment is discretionary behavior and not an obligation.

Thus, a key point in our model is that employees and their work group peers both use negative voice in efforts to restore personal freedoms. To the high performing employee who overfulfills obligations, low performers are perceived as deviant and thus become the most salient targets for negative voice. In contrast, for work group peers, the high performer is the deviant who becomes the most salient target of direct and indirect negative voice. In both cases, employees and their peers are motivated to regain a sense of personal control over ongoing obligations and restore personal feelings of freedom to choose whether or not to engage in overfulfillment of obligations.

9.5.1 Future research

In our model, we have applied reactance theory to organizational work settings where employees have embedded and ongoing relationships. To date, most of the prior research on reactance has been done in laboratory settings. This has been useful in establishing the fundamental principles that form the core of reactance theory. To test our model, however, we recommend that researchers focus primarily on field research. This is because our predictions are based on embedded and ongoing work relationships among employees, their supervisors, and their work group peers.

Although our model is relatively complex, it is under-identified. Future research should consider additional antecedents, consequences, and perspectives to expand and enrich this initial framework. In addition, future research could consider additional factors that trigger or strengthen reactance. Perhaps reactance to job creep is influenced by employee initial motives for overfulfilling obligations. For example, those who are motivated by impression management goals may be more sensitive to job creep than those who are motivated by personal values such as prosocial orientation. Additionally, it would be beneficial to consider an expanded set of individual difference factors that may influence the reactance process. For example, those who are high in dominance, extroversion, or equity sensitivity may be more assertive in their attempts to restore personal freedom whereas those who are high in benevolence might have weaker reactions. Another idea for future research is considering boundary conditions that may limit peer reactance to overfulfillment. For example, weak group norms for performance (leading to greater variance in employee fulfillment of obligations) may reduce conformity pressures on peers, reduce their feelings of reactance, and reduce their use of negative voice. Alternatively, when work group peers have weak role identity, negative social comparisons will be less salient to them and less likely to generate reactance. Finally, it is possible that job creep is more common in some industries, some types of jobs, or some cultures.

There also would be benefits to considering other consequences of reactance. For those who overfulfill obligations, this could include stress, emotional exhaustion, decreased motivation, lower job satisfaction, and burnout. For example, if employees feel overwhelmed by their expanded obligations and unable to accomplish their work, this can lead to burnout or emotional exhaustion (Maslach and Leiter 1999;

Demerouti et al. 2001; Cropanzano et al. 2003). On the other hand, work group peers may experience feelings of guilt when confronted with a co-worker who regularly overfulfills obligations (Baumeister et al. 1994). Over time, feelings of guilt may develop into feelings of resentment. Other peer reactions could include decreased satisfaction, motivation, and a desire to leave the organization. Future research also could consider other targets of employee and peer reactance such as supervisors, family, and friends. In sum, we view this model as a first step in thinking about responses to job creep.

9.5.2 Summary and conclusion

In this chapter, we have introduced the concept of job creep and, based on reactance theory, have developed a theoretical framework that predicts employee and peer reactions to job creep. Given competitive pressures to "do more with less," we have argued that job creep occurs for many employees in many organizations. Job creep is the gradual and informal expansion of role responsibilities such that discretionary contributions (e.g. OCB) become viewed as in-role obligations by supervisors and peers. Job creep changes the fundamental nature of the employment relationship between employees and other parties to the relationship (peers, supervisors, and the organization) by changing perceptions of what an employee is obligated to contribute to the organization. When job creep occurs, employees experience pressure to overfulfill their obligations on an ongoing basis. In other words, job creep blurs the boundary between ERB, which is composed of discretionary contributions, and IRB, which is composed of required contributions. We conclude by recommending that future research should refine this initial conceptualization of job creep and test the predictions in the model.

References

Analoui, F. (1995). "Workplace sabotage: its styles, motives and management." *Journal of Management Development*, 14(7): 48–65.

Anderson, C. A. (1995). "Implicit personality theories and empirical data: Biased assimilation, belief perseverance and change, and covariation detection sensitivity." *Social Cognition*, 13: 25–48.

Avery, D. R., and Quinones, M. A. (2002). "Disentangling the effects of voice: The incremental roles of opportunity, behavior, and instrumentality in predicting procedural fairness". *Journal of Applied Psychology*, 87: 81–6.

Barker, J. R. (1993). "Tightening the iron cage: Concertive control in self-managing teams." *Administrative Science Quarterly*, 38: 408–37.

Baumeister, R. F., Stillwell, A. M., and Heatherton, T. F. (1994). "Guilt: An interpersonal approach." *Psychological Bulletin*, 115(2): 243–67.

Bies, R. J., and Shapiro, D. L. (1988). "Voice and justification: Their influence on procedural fairness judgments." *Academy of Management Journal*, 31: 676–85.

Blau, P. (1964). *Exchange and Power in Social Life*. New York: Wiley.

Bolino, M. C. (1999). "Citizenship and impression management: Good soldiers or good actors?" *Academy of Management Review*, 24: 82–98.

—— and Turnley, W. H. (2002). "Escalating citizenship: The pressure of the 'good solider' syndrome." Paper presented at the meeting of the Academy of Management, Denver.

Brehm, J. W. (1966). *A Theory of Psychological Reactance.* New York: Academic Press.

—— and Sensenig, J. (1966). "Social influence as a function of attempted and implied usurpation of choice." *Journal of Personality and Social Psychology*, 4: 703–7.

Brehm, S. W., and Brehm, J. W. (1981). *Psychological Reactance: A Theory of Freedom and Control.* New York: Academic Press.

Brewer, M. B., and Weber, J. G. (1994). "Self-evaluation effects of interpersonal versus intergroup social comparison." *Journal of Personality and Social Psychology*, 66: 268–75.

Brockner, J. (1988). *Self-esteem at Work: Research, Theory, and Practice.* Lexington, MA: Lexington Books.

—— Greenberg, J., Brockner, A., Bortz, J., Davy, J., and Carter, C. (1986). "Layoffs, equity theory, and work performance: Further evidence of the impact of survivor guilt." *Academy of Management Journal*, 29: 373–85.

Bunderson, J. S. (2001). "How work ideologies shape the psychological contracts of professional employees: Doctors' responses to perceived breach." *Journal of Organizational Behavior*, 22: 717–41.

Buss, A. H. (1961). *The Psychology of Aggression.* New York: Wiley.

Campbell, D. J. (2000). "The proactive employee: Managing workplace initiative." *Academy of Management Executive*, 14: 52–66.

Cappelli, P. (1997). *The Changing Nature of Work.* Boston: Harvard Business Press.

—— and Sherer, P. D. (1991). "The missing role of context in OB: The need for a meso-level approach," in L. L. Cummings and B. M. Staw (eds.), *Research in Organizational Behavior*, 13: (Greenwich, CT: JAI Press), 55–110.

—— Bassi, L., Katz, H., Knoke, D., Osterman, P., and Unseem, M. (1997). *Change at Work.* New York: Oxford University Press.

Cherulnik, P. D., and Citrin, M. M. (1974) "Individual difference in psychological reactance: The interaction between locus of control and mode of elimination of freedom." *Journal of Personality and Social Psychology*, 29: 398–404.

Coopersmith, S. (1981). *The Antecedents of Self-esteem.* Palo Alto, CA: Consulting Psychologists Press.

Coyle-Shapiro, J. A. M. (2002). "A psychological contract perspective on organizational citizenship behavior." *Journal of Organizational Behavior*, 23: 927–46.

—— and Kessler, I. (2000). "Consequences of the psychological contract for the employment relationship: A large scale survey." *Journal of Management Studies*, 37(7): 903–30.

—— and —— (2002). "Exploring reciprocity through the lens of the psychological contract: Employee and employer perspectives." *European Journal of Work and Organizational Psychology*, 11(1): 69–86.

Crandall, R. (1973). "The measurement of self-esteem and related constructs," in J. P. Robinson and P. R. Shaver (eds.), *Measures of Social Psychological Attitudes* (Ann Arbor, MI: Institute for Social Research), 45–167.

Crant, J. M. (2000). "Proactive behavior in organizations." *Journal of Management*, 26: 435–62.

Cropanzano, R., Rupp, D. E., and Byrne, Z. S. (2003). "The relationship of emotional exhaustion to work attitudes, job performance, and organizational citizenship behaviors." *Journal of Applied Psychology*, 88(1): 160–9.

Demerouti, E., Bakker, A. B., Nachreiner, F., and Schaufeli, W. B. (2001). "The job demands—Resources model of burnout." *Journal of Applied Psychology*, 86(3): 499–512.

Dunning, D., Meyerowitz, J. A., and Holzberg, A. D. (1989). "Ambiguity and self-evaluation: The role of idiosyncratic trait definitions in self-serving assessments of ability." *Journal of Personality and Social Psychology*, 57: 1082–90.

Dutton, J. E., and Ashford, S. J. (1993). "Selling issues to top management." *Academy of Management Review*, 18: 397–428.

Ellis, J. B. (2001). "Psychological Contracts: Assessing Similarities and Differences in Perception of Quality Communication and Work-life Promises for Blue-collar and White-collar Employees." Unpublished doctoral dissertation, Michigan State University.

Farr, J. L., and Ford, C. M. (1990). "Individual innovation," in M. A. West and J. L. Farr (eds.), *Innovation and Creativity at Work* (Chichester: John Wiley).

Farrell, D. (1983). "Exit, voice, loyalty, and neglect as responses to job dissatisfaction: A multidimensional scaling study." *Academy of Management Journal*, 26: 596–607.

—— and Rusbult, C. E. (1992). "Exploring the exit, voice, loyalty, and neglect typology: The influence of job satisfaction, quality of alternatives, and investment size." *Employee Responsibilities and Rights Journal*, 5: 201–18.

Frese, M., and Fay, D. (2001). "Personal initiative: An active performance concept for work in the 21st century," in B. M. Staw and R. I. Sutton (eds.), *Research in Organizational Behavior*, 23: (New York: JAI Press), 133–87.

—— Kring, W., Soose, A., and Zempel, J. (1996). "Personal initiative at work: Differences between East and West Germany." *Academy of Management Journal*, 39: 37–63.

—— Teng, E., and Wijnen, C. J. D. (1999). "Helping to improve suggestion systems: Predictors of making suggestions in companies." *Journal of Organizational Behavior*, 20: 1139–55.

Folger, R. (1977). "Distributive and procedural justice: Combined impact of 'voice' and improvement on experienced inequity." *Journal of Personality and Social Psychology*, 35: 108–19.

Gecas, V. (1982). "The self concept," in M. R. Rosenzweig and L. W. Porter (eds.) *Annual Review of Psychology*, 8 (Palo Alto, CA: Annual Reviews.), 1–33.

Graen, G. (1976). "Role-making processes within complex organizations," in M. D. Dunnette (ed.), *Handbook of Industrial and Organizational Psychology* (Chicago: Rand-McNally.), 1201–45.

Graham, J. W. (1991). "An essay on organizational citizenship behavior." *Employee Responsibilities and Rights Journal*, 4(4): 249–70.

Greenberger, D. B., and Strasser, S. (1986). "Development and application of a model of personal control in organizations." *Academy of Management Review*, 11: 164–77.

—— —— and Lee, S. (1988). "Personal control as a mediator between perceptions of supervisory behaviors and employee reactions." *Academy of Management Journal*, 31: 405–17.

—— —— Cummings, L. L., and Dunham, R. B. (1989). "The impact of personal control on performance and satisfaction." *Organization Behavior and Human Decision Processes*, 43: 29–51.

Hackman, J. R. (1992). "Group influences on individuals in organizations," in M. D. Dunnette and L. M. Hough (eds.), *Handbook of Industrial and Organizational Psychology*: Vol. 3, 2nd ed. (Palo Alto, CA: Consulting Psychologists Press), 199–267.

Hirschman, A. O. (1970). *Exit, Voice, and Loyalty: Responses to Decline in Firms, Organizations, and States.* Cambridge, MA: Harvard University Press.

Howard, A. (1995). *The Changing Nature of Work*. San Francisco: Jossey-Bass.

Howell, J., and Higgins, C. (1990). "Champions of technological innovation." *Administrative Science Quarterly*, 35: 317–41.

Hulin, C. L, Roznowski, M., and Hachiya, D. (1985). "Alternative opportunities and withdrawal decisions: Empirical and theoretical discrepancies and an integration." *Psychological Bulletin*, 97(2): 233–50.

Janssen, O., de Vries, T., and Cozijnsen, A. J. (1998). "Voicing by adapting and innovating employees: An empirical study on how personality and environment interact to affect voice behavior." *Human Relations*, 51: 945–67.

Johns, G. (2001). "Commentary: In praise of context." *Journal of Organizational Behavior*, 22: 31–42.

Katz, D., and Kahn, R. L. (1966, 1978). *The Social Psychology of Organizations*. New York: Wiley.

Kiesler, C. A., and Kiesler, S. B. (1969). *Conformity*. Reading, MA: Addison-Welsey.

Krackhardt, D. (1987)."Cognitive social structures." *Social Networks*, 9: 109–34.

Kowalski, R. M. (1996). "Complaints and complaining: Functions, antecedents, and consequences." *Journal of Applied Psychology*, 119: 179–96.

—— (1997). "Aversive interpersonal behaviors: An overarching framework," in R. M. Kowalski (ed.), *Aversive Interpersonal Behaviors* (New York: Plenum Press), 215–33.

Kurland, N. B., and Pelled, L. H. (2000). "Passing the word: Toward a model of gossip and power in the workplace." *Academy of Management Review*, 25: 428–38.

Lam, S. S., Hui, C., and Law, K. S. (1999). "Organizational citizenship behavior: Comparing perspectives of supervisors and subordinates across four international samples." *Journal of Applied Psychology*, 84: 594–601.

Lambert, L. S., Edwards, J. R., and Cable, D. M. (2002). "Breach of the psychological contract: Consequences of deficient and excess inducements and contributions." Paper presented at the Annual Meeting of the Academy of Management, Denver.

LePine, J. A., and Van Dyne, L. (1998). "Predicting voice behavior in work groups." *Journal of Applied Psychology*, 83: 853–68.

—— and —— (2001a). "Peer responses to low performers: An attributional model of helping in the context of groups." *Academy of Management Review*, 26: 67–87.

—— and —— (2001b). "Voice and cooperative behavior as contrasting forms of contextual performance: Evidence of differential relationships with big five personality characteristics and cognitive ability." *Journal of Applied Psychology*, 86: 325–36.

—— Erez, A., and Johnson, D. E. (2002). "The nature and dimensionality of organizational citizenship behavior: A critical review and meta-analysis." *Journal of Applied Psychology*, 87: 52–65.

Lester, S. W., Turnley, W. H., Bloodgood, J. M., and Bolino, M. C. (2002). "Not seeing eye to eye: Differences in supervisor and subordinate perceptions of an attributions for psychological contract breach." *Journal of Organizational Behavior*, 23: 39–56.

Lind, E. A., Kanfer, R., and Earley, P. C. (1990). "Voice, control, and procedural justice: Instrumental and noninstrumental concerns in fairness judgments." *Journal of Personality and Social Psychology*, 59: 952–59.

Maslach, C., and Leiter, M. P. (1999). "Burnout and engagement in the workplace: A conceptual analysis." in T. C. Urdan, M. L. Maehr, and P. R. Pintrich (eds.), *Advances in Motivation and Achievement: The Role of Context*, Vol. 11 (Stamford, CT: JAI Press), 275–302.

McNeely, B. L., and Meglino, B. M. (1994). "The role of dispositional and situational antecedents in prosocial organizational behavior: An examination of the intended beneficiaries of prosocial behavior." *Journal of Applied Psychology*, 79: 836–44.

Miller, D. T. (2001). "Disrespect and the experience of injustice." *Annual Review of Psychology*, 52: 527–53.

Morrison, E. W. (1994). "Role definitions and organizational citizenship behavior: The importance of the employee's perspective." *Academy of Management Journal*, 37: 1543–67.

—— and Milliken, F. J. (2000). "Organizational silence: A barrier to change and development in a pluralistic world." *Academy of Management Review*, 25(4): 706–25.

—— and Phelps, C. C. (1999). "Taking charge at work: Extrarole efforts to initiate workplace change." *Academy of Management Journal*, 42: 403–19.

—— and Robinson, S. L. (1997). "When employees feel betrayed: A model of how psychological contract violation develops." *Academy of Management Review*, 22: 226–56.

Moss, S. E., and Martinko, M. J. (1998). "The effects of performance attributions and outcome dependence on leader feedback behavior following poor subordinate performance." *Journal of Organizational Behavior*, 19: 259–74.

Mowday, R. T., and Sutton, R. I. (1993). "Organizational behavior: Linking individuals and groups to organizational contexts," in L. W. Porter and M. R. Rosenzweig (eds.), *Annual Review of Psychology*, Vol. 44 (Palo Alto, CA: Annual Reviews), 195–229.

Mussweiler, T., and Bodenhausen, G. V. (2002). "I know you are, but what am I? Self-evaluative consequences of judging in-group and out-group members." *Journal of Personality and Social Psychology*, 82(1): 19–32.

Organ, D. W. (1988). *Organizational Citizenship Behavior*. Lexington, MA: Lexington Books.

Parker, L. E. (1993). "When to fix it and when to leave: Relationships among perceived control, self-efficacy, dissent, and exit." *Journal of Applied Psychology*, 78: 949–59.

Parker, S. K. (1998). "Enhancing role breadth self-efficacy: The roles of job enrichment and other organizational interventions." *Journal of Applied Psychology*, 83: 835–52.

—— Wall, T. D., and Jackson, P. R. (1997). "That's not my job: Developing flexible employee work orientations." *Academy of Management Journal*, 40: 899–929.

Podsakoff, P. M., MacKenzie, S. B., Paine, J. B., and Bachrach, D. G. (2000). "Organizational citizenship behaviors: A critical review of the theoretical and empirical literature and suggestions for future research." *Journal of Management*, 26: 513–63.

Rioux, S. M., and Penner, L. A. (2001). "The causes of organizational citizenship behavior: A motivational analysis." *Journal of Applied Psychology*, 86: 1306–14.

Robinson, S. L. (1996). "Trust and breach of the psychological contract." *Administrative Science Quarterly*, 41: 574–99.

—— and Morrison, E. W. (1995). "Psychological contracts and OCB: The effect of unfulfilled obligations on civic virtue behavior." *Journal of Organizational Behavior*, 16: 289–98.

—— and —— (2000). "The development of psychological contract breach and violation: A longitudinal study." *Journal of Organizational Behavior*, 21: 525–46.

—— and Rousseau, D. M. (1994). "Violating the psychological contract: Not the exception but the norm." *Journal of Organizational Behavior*, 15: 245–59.

—— Kraatz, M. S., and Rousseau, D. M. (1994). "Changing obligations and the psychological contract: A longitudinal study." *Academy of Management Journal*, 37: 137–52.

Ross, L., Lepper, M. R., and Hubbard, M. (1975). "Perseverance in self-perception and social perception." *Journal of Personality and Social Psychology*, 32: 880–92.

Rotter, J. B. (1966). "Generalized expectancies for internal versus external control of reinforcement." *Psychological Monographs*, 80 (1, Whole No. 609).

Rousseau, D. M. (1989). "Psychological and implied contracts in organizations." *Employee Responsibilities and Rights Journal*, 2: 121–39.

Rousseau, D. M. (1989). "New hire perceptions of their own and their employer's obligations: A study of psychological contracts." *Journal of Organizational Behavior*, 11: 389–400.

—— (1995). *Psychological Contracts in Organizations: Understanding Written and Unwritten Agreements.* Thousand Oaks, CA: Sage.

—— (1997). "Organizational behavior in the new organizational era," in J. T. Spence, J. M. Darley, and D. J. Foss (eds.), *Annual Review of Psychology*, Vol. 48 (Palo Alto, CA: Annual Reviews.), 515–46.

—— and Fried, Y. (2001). "Location, location, location: Contextualizing organizational research." *Journal of Organizational Behavior*, 22: 1–13.

Rusbult, C. E., Farrell, D., Rogers, G., and Mainous, A. G., III. (1988). "Impact of exchange variables on exit, voice, loyalty, and neglect: An integrative model of responses to declining job satisfaction." *Academy of Management Journal*, 31: 599–627.

Seibert, S. E., Kraimer, M. L., and Crant, J. M. (2001). "What do proactive people do? A longitudinal model linking proactive personality and career success." *Personnel Psychology*, 54: 845–73.

Skarlicki, D. P., and Folger, R. (1997). "Retaliation in the workplace: The roles of distributive, procedural, and interactional justice." *Journal of Applied Psychology*, 82: 434–43.

Spreitzer, G. M. (1996). "Social structure characteristics of psychological empowerment." *Academy of Management Journal*, 39: 483–504.

—— and Sonenshein, S. (2003). "Becoming extraordinary: Empowering people for positive deviance," To appear in K. Cameron, J. Dutton, and R. Quinn (eds.), *Positive Organizational Scholarship*. San Francisco: Berrett-Koehler, 207–24.

Stamper, C. L., and Masterson, S. S. (2002). "Insider or outsider? How employee perceptions of insider status affect their work behavior." *Journal of Organizational Behavior*, 23: 875–94.

Taylor, S. E., and Brown, J. D. (1988). "Illusion and well-being: A social psychological perspective on mental health." *Psychological Bulletin*, 103: 193–210.

Tepper, B. J., Lockhart, D., and Hoobler, J. (2001). "Justice, citizenship, and role definition effects." *Journal of Applied Psychology*, 86: 789–96.

Thompson, J. A., and Bunderson, J. S. (2003). "Violations of principle: Ideological currency in the psychological contract." *Academy of Management Review*, 28: 571–87.

Turnley, W. H., and Feldman, D. C. (1999*a*). "The impact of psychological contract violations on exit, voice, loyalty, and neglect." *Human Relations*, 52: 895–922.

—— and —— (1999*b*). "A discrepancy model of psychological contract violations." *Human Resource Management Review*, 9: 367–86.

—— and —— (2000). "Re-examining the effects of psychological contract violations: Unmet expectations and job dissatisfaction as mediators." *Journal of Organizational Behavior*, 21: 25–42.

—— Bolino, M. C., Lester, S. W., and Bloodgood, J. M. (2003). "The impact of psychological contract fulfillment on the performance of in-role and organizational citizenship behaviors." *Journal of Management*, 29: 187–206.

Van Dyne, L., and LePine, J. A. (1998). "Helping and voice extra-role behavior: Evidence of construct and predictive validity." *Academy of Management Journal*, 41: 108–19.

Van Dyne, L., Graham, J. W., and Dienesch, R. M. (1994). "Organizational citizenship behavior: Construct redefinition, measurement, and validation." *Academy of Management Journal*, 37: 765–802.

—— Cummings, L. L., and McLean Parks, J. (1995). "Extra-role behaviors: In pursuit of construct and definitional clarity (a bridge over muddied waters)," in B.M. Staw and L. L. Cummings (eds.), *Research in Organizational Behavior*, 17 (Greenwich, CT: JAI Press), 215–85.

Van Dyne, L., Ang, S., and Botero, I. C. (2003). "Conceptualizing employee silence and employee voice as multidimensional constructs." *Journal of Management Studies*, 40: 1359–92.

Welbourne, T., Johnson, D. E., and Erez, A. (1998). "The role-based performance scale: Validity analysis of a theory-based measure." *Academy of Management Journal*, 41: 540–55.

Wells, L. E., and Marwell, G. (1976). *Self-Esteem*. London: Sage.

West, M. A. (1987). "Role innovation in the world of work." *British Journal of Social Psychology*, 26: 305–15.

Wicklund, R. (1974). *Freedom and Reactance*. Hillsdale, NJ: Erlbaum.

Withey, M. J., and Cooper, W. H. (1989). "Predicting exit, voice, loyalty, and neglect." *Administrative Science Quarterly*, 34: 521–39.

Wrzesniewski, A., and Dutton, J. E. (2001). "Crafting a job: Revisioning employees as active crafters of their work." *Academy of Management Review*, 26: 179–201.

Zhou, J., and George, J. M. (2001). "When job dissatisfaction leads to creativity: Encouraging the expression of voice." *Journal of Applied Psychology*, 44: 682–96.

Zuckerman, E. W., and Jost, J. T. (2001). "What makes you think you're so popular? Self evaluation maintenance and the subjective side of the 'friendship paradox.'" *Social Psychology Quarterly*, 64(3): 207–23.

10

Perceived Organizational Support

ROBERT EISENBERGER, JASON R. JONES,
JUSTIN ASELAGE, AND IVAN L. SUCHARSKI

10.1 Introduction

Research on perceived organizational support (POS) began with the observation that if managers are concerned with their employees' commitment to the organization, employees are focused on the organization's commitment to them. For employees, the organization serves as an important source of socio-emotional resources, such as respect and caring, and tangible benefits, such as wages and medical benefits. Being regarded highly by the organization helps to meet employees' needs for approval, esteem, and affiliation. Positive valuation by the organization also provides an indication that increased effort will be noted and rewarded. Employees therefore take an active interest in the regard with which they are held by their employer.

Organizational support theory (OST) (Eisenberger et al. 1986; Shore and Shore 1995; Rhoades and Eisenberger 2002) holds that in order to meet socio-emotional needs and to assess the benefits of increased work effort, employees form a general perception concerning the extent to which the organization values their contributions and cares about their well-being. Such POS would increase employees' felt obligation to help the organization reach its objectives, their affective commitment to the organization, and their expectation that improved performance would be rewarded. Behavioral outcomes of POS would include increases in in-role and extra-role performance and decreases in withdrawal behaviors such as absenteeism and turnover.

Although there were relatively few studies of POS until the mid-1990s (Shore and Shore 1995), research on the topic has burgeoned in the last few years. Rhoades and Eisenberger's (2002) meta-analysis covered some seventy POS studies carried out through 1999, and an additional fifty studies were performed by the end of 2002. The meta-analysis found clear and consistent relationships of POS with its predicted antecedents and consequences. In contrast, the theory underlying POS has received only limited coverage (e.g. Eisenberger et al. 1986; Shore and Shore 1995; Rhoades and Eisenberger 2002; Aselage and Eisenberger 2003). In this chapter, we address this need by describing the key concepts of OST, discussing the theory's relationship with other social exchange approaches and providing suggestions to extend the theory.

10.2 Nature and formation of POS

POS is assumed to be a global belief that employees form concerning their valuation by the organization. Based on the experience of personally relevant organizational policies and procedures, the receipt of resources, and interactions with agents of the organization, an employee would distill the organization's general orientation toward him or her. Although the organization's positive valuations of one's contributions and concern for one's well-being are logically distinct, exploratory and confirmatory factor analyses indicate that employees combine these into a unitary perception (Rhoades and Eisenberger 2002). Employees evidently believe that the organization has a general positive or negative orientation toward them that encompasses both their contributions and their welfare.

POS provides the basis for trust in the organization to observe and reward extra effort carried out on its behalf (Eisenberger et al. 1990; Shore and Shore 1995). Shore and Shore (1995) argued that employees are aware that, because they are disadvantaged in their exchange relationship with the organization, they run a high risk that their efforts on behalf of the organization will fail to be adequately compensated. According to Shore and Shore, this is because: (a) the employee is the less powerful partner in the exchange; (b) there is often a delay inherent in employer fulfillment of obligations; and (c) multiple agents may influence whether obligations are fulfilled. Indeed, an employer may simply incorporate one's added effort into normal job responsibilities without added compensation. By reducing perceived risk, POS serves to enhance employees' willingness to go beyond their normal job responsibilities on behalf of the organization.

OST assumes that the development of POS is fostered by employees' personification of the organization (Eisenberger et al. 1986). Levinson (1965) suggested that employees tend to attribute the actions of organizational representatives to the intent of the organization rather than solely to the personal motives of its representatives. This personification of the organization, suggested Levinson, is abetted by the organization's legal, moral, and financial responsibility for the actions of its agents; by rules, norms, and policies that provide continuity and prescribe role behaviors; and by the power the organization exerts over individual employees. Thus, to some degree, employees think of their relationship with the organization in terms similar to a relationship between themselves and a more powerful individual.

OST maintains that employees use attributional processes similar to those used in interpersonal relationships to infer their valuation by the organization. Gouldner (1960) reasoned that favorable treatment would convey positive regard to the extent that the individual receiving the treatment considered the act to be discretionary. From this perspective, an employee would infer higher regard from favorable treatment if the treatment appeared discretionary rather than the result of such external constraints as government regulations, union contracts, or competitive wages paid by alternative employers (Eisenberger et al. 1986; Shore and Shore 1995). Accordingly, the positive relationship between POS and favorable job conditions was found to be seven times greater when the presence of those conditions were attributed to the organization's discretion rather than to external constraints (Eisenberger et al. 1997).

Thus, the organization's discretion is important for determining the extent to which different treatments most impact POS. For example, union workers might receive excellent wages and benefits. However, if these benefits resulted from difficult contested negotiations, employees would consider the benefits to have been provided involuntarily, and the benefits would have little influence on POS. This suggests that organizations should not automatically conclude that well-treated employees will have high POS. Favorable treatments that organizations provide to employees must be perceived as voluntary if they are to influence feelings of support. To the extent that the organization effectively conveys favorable treatment as discretionary, POS will be enhanced.

Correspondingly, unfavorable treatment that is perceived to be beyond the organization's control will have a less negative effect on POS. For example, management could attribute lower annual pay raises to low profits associated with weak economic conditions. By shifting the responsibility for the cutbacks from the organization itself to external circumstances over which the organization had little control, the deleterious effect of the cutbacks on POS would be reduced.

The importance of the discretion attribution for employees' attitudes toward the organization has practical implications. In extensive consulting with a large retail sales organization, we found that most salespeople reported a high level of stress at work. When we investigated more closely, we found these employees generally attributed their stress to the nature of sales jobs, leading them to believe that there was little that the organization could do to alleviate the stress. Because stress was an aspect of the job that employees believed the organization could not control, the sales employees' POS was not adversely affected by this unfavorable job condition. According to the sales employees, improvements in other features of the job that the organization could control, such as more weekend days off and higher pay, were more important to them. Thus, some unpleasant aspects of one's job are taken for granted by employees and not blamed on the organization. Employees are practical; they are generally concerned with improving working conditions and benefits that management can readily change.

The literature on social accounts (Sitkin and Bies 1993; Cobb and Wooten 1998) suggests additional ways in which organizations may cast negative treatment of employees in a better light and thereby minimize the loss of POS. Organizations may legitimize their actions with exonerating accounts that appeal to higher-order norms and values or they may use reframing accounts which alter employees' perceptions of the unfavorableness of the treatment.

One type of exonerating account attempts to make salient superordinate goals and values. For example, an employee who is asked to work unwanted overtime may be told how important his or her contribution is for meeting a specific objective to which the entire work group is contributing. Of course, the invocation of shared sacrifice by management for the greater good of the organization is likely to be greeted cynically if management does none of the sharing.

Exonerating accounts may also be used to take advantage of the proclivity of individuals to accept unintended consequences of well-meant actions (Sitkin and

Bies 1993). Forgiveness for such errors is fostered when the account giver explains the good intentions behind his or her actions, acknowledges that those actions had deleterious consequences, and expresses sincere regret for the harm done. Exonerating accounts should weaken the negative effects of unfavorable treatment on POS in two ways. First, unfavorable treatment carries less blame when unintentional (Ferguson and Rule 1982). Second, the apology indicates a concern with the employee's welfare.

Additionally, using reframing accounts, organizations may attempt to alter employees' perception of the favorableness of treatment by encouraging them to select a new standard of comparison (Sitkin and Bies 1993). Social reframing can be used to direct employees' attention to other individuals who are less well off. For instance, after an organization decides to reduce health benefits, it can point out other similar organizations that have reduced their health benefits more substantially.

Temporal reframing can be used to place a current negative outcome in a more favorable light by comparing it with an unfavorable past outcome or by drawing attention to a more favorable possible future outcome (Sitkin and Bies 1993). For example, in cases where budgetary shortfalls result in few resources for employees, an organization can construe the budget as less unfavorable by underscoring previous budgets that were even more stringent. Alternatively, the same organization might be in a position to state with some assurance that the following year's budget will be more favorable. Reframing should lead employees to view unfavorable treatment as less unfavorable or less significant, thus reducing the detrimental effects of such treatment on POS.

10.3 Antecedents of POS

We will focus on three general forms of favorable treatment [fairness, supervisor support, human resource (HR) practices] that enhance POS. The empirical evidence linking these three antecedents to POS has been reviewed elsewhere (Rhoades and Eisenberger 2002). Thus, we will concentrate here primarily on conceptual issues.

10.3.1 Fairness of treatment

Fairness is often discussed in terms of two types of justice: distributive and procedural. Distributive justice involves fairness in the distribution of outcomes, whereas procedural justice involves fairness in the procedures used to determine the distribution of outcomes (Greenberg 1990). Shore and Shore (1995) argued that repeated fair treatment would have a strong cumulative effect on POS by indicating a concern for employees' welfare. Further, they maintained that procedural justice might have a stronger influence on POS than distributive justice. This is because the receipt of outcomes such as promotions and pay raises occur infrequently. However, employees are exposed to instances of procedural justice (e.g. being included in decision-making and receiving consistent performance evaluations) on a more regular basis. Procedural justice and favorable outcomes have both been positively linked to POS (Rhoades and Eisenberger 2002). Of the two dimensions of fairness, procedural justice has been found to contribute more strongly to POS than distributive justice (Fasolo 1995; Wayne et al. 2002).

Shore and Shore (1995) suggested that perceptions of fairness surrounding a particular decision contribute to a more global history of support. Although employees would remember a few important organizational decisions that contribute to POS, less important decisions that also contribute to POS would tend to be forgotten. The accumulated history of decisions would operate through POS to influence employee attitudes and performance. In accord with this view, Moorman et al. (1998) found that POS fully mediated the association between procedural justice and extra-role behavior. Longitudinal research to assess the causal direction of the relationship between POS and fairness would be helpful to provide more definitive evidence concerning these relationships.

Research on fairness has also considered the relative contributions made by procedural justice and interactional justice to POS. Interactional justice refers to employees' perceptions of the favorableness of an interpersonal interaction accompanying decisions of resource allocation (Bies and Moag 1986). Masterson et al. (2000) reasoned that because procedural justice results from actions of the organization, and interactional justice results from individuals' actions, the two types of fairness should differentially influence employees' social exchange relationships with the organization and with representatives of the organization. Supporting these hypotheses, Masterson et al.'s study of university employees found that procedural justice was predictive of POS, whereas interactional justice from supervisors was predictive of the quality of employees' exchange relationship with their supervisors.

10.3.2 Support from organizational representatives

According to OST, employees incorporate the favorable treatment received from various organizational agents and units into an overall perception of organizational support. OST assumes treatment received from an organizational agent contributes to POS to the extent that the representative's actions are believed to be sanctioned and promoted by the organization, as opposed to being seen as idiosyncratic motives of the agent. In general, the higher the status or standing the employee believes the organizational agent has within the organization, the more the employee should attribute the actions of that agent to the intent of the organization. The actions and words of high status employees are seen as closely conveying the favorable or unfavorable orientation toward employees of the personified organization.

The perceived status of an agent would be influenced by the agent's formal position in the organizational hierarchy. However, perceptions of status are also influenced by the agent's treatment by others, allowing individuals with similar job titles to differ markedly in the extent to which they are viewed to represent the organization. Organizational agents' status would be influenced by the extent of the positive valuation and regard extended to them by the organization, the degree of job autonomy afforded them, and their influence in important organizational decisions (Eisenberger et al. 2002). Favorable or unfavorable treatment received from high-status representatives, who would be strongly identified with the organization, would have an increased influence on POS. Accordingly, Eisenberger et al. found that the relationship between perceived supervisor support and POS increased with the status employees attributed to them.

According to OST, support from the supervisor results in a favorable relationship between the employee and the *organization*. In contrast, leader–member exchange theory (Liden et al. 1997; see Chapter 8) proposes that positive interactions between supervisor and subordinate contribute to a constructive working relationship between the two interacting parties. Both views would seem to be correct, as supervisors are able to jointly influence the exchange relationships that they have with the employee and that the employee has with the organization. Because the supervisor is an important source of information, she is able to influence whether employees attribute favorable or unfavorable treatment to the actions of the supervisor, the organization, or both.

10.3.3 Human resource practices

Systematic organization-wide policies and procedures directed toward employees, or HR practices, should make an important positive or negative contribution to POS because they are specifically oriented toward employees. Favorable HR practices that signify an investment in human capital and demonstrate recognition of employee contributions have been suggested to promote POS (Allen et al. 2003). Indeed, POS has been found to be related to HR practices such as job security, autonomy, training, participation in decision-making, and opportunities for rewards and promotions (Rhoades and Eisenberger 2002; Allen et al. 2003). The favorableness of a specific HR practice should increase POS to the extent that it is attributed to the voluntary, intentional actions of the organization.

Tsui et al. (1997) proposed that organizations have different strategies concerning the human resources they are willing to invest in employees and the returns they expect on these investments. According to Tsui et al., organizations may have one of four HR investment strategies. The first two strategies are balanced strategies, with the first characterized by the organization's and the employee's exchange of few valued resources, and the second strategy defined by the mutual exchange of highly valued resources. The remaining two strategies are unbalanced, wherein the organization either provides the employee with few resources while expecting much in return, or provides many resources while expecting little from the employee in return.

In a study of employees from multiple organizations, Tsui et al. (1997) found that employees whose organizations invested many valued resources in employees, such as assurances of job security and developmental opportunities, showed greater affective commitment and higher performance. As noted above research on HR practices and POS has shown that strong investments of resources in employees may contribute substantially to POS. Consistent with this view, Shore and Barksdale (1998) found that employees who reported strong mutual obligations between themselves and their organization had higher levels of POS than employees who reported low mutual obligations between themselves and their work organization.

10.4 Psychological outcomes of POS

POS was originally assumed to create a felt obligation to help the organization reach its goals, increase affective commitment to the organization, and strengthen performance–reward expectancies (Eisenberger et al. 1986). More recently, attention has been given to the role of POS in reducing aversive psychological and psychosomatic reactions to stressors by indicating the availability of material aid and emotional support when needed to face high demands at work (George et al. 1993; Robblee 1998). Below we consider the conceptual basis for these outcomes of POS, together with supporting evidence.

10.4.1 Felt obligation

When one person treats another well, the norm of reciprocity obliges the return of favorable treatment (Gouldner 1960). The reciprocity norm may also apply to employee–employer relationships, compelling employees to recompense advantageous treatment they receive from their work organization (see Chapter 1). Because POS provides a broad and valued set of socio-emotional and impersonal resources to employees, the norm of reciprocity should, in turn, produce a general felt obligation to help the organization achieve its goals (Eisenberger et al. 1986; Shore and Shore 1995). In accord with OST, Eisenberger et al. (2001) found a positive relationship between postal employees' POS and a general felt obligation to help the organization. Supporting the notion that reciprocity is involved in this process, the relationship between POS and felt obligation increased with employees' exchange ideology, which is the endorsement of the reciprocity norm as applied to the employee–employer relationship.

10.4.2 Affective organizational commitment

OST holds that POS fosters affective organizational commitment by meeting employees' socio-emotional needs, such as the needs for esteem, approval, and emotional support (Eisenberger et al. 1986; Armeli et al. 1998). The fulfillment of these needs should facilitate the incorporation of employees' organizational membership and role status into their social identity, thereby creating a strong emotional attachment to the organization. A longitudinal panel study found that while POS was related to temporal changes in affective commitment, affective commitment was unrelated to temporal changes in POS (Rhoades et al. 2001). Also, the obligation that arises because employees feel the need to reciprocate the support they receive should also lead to affective commitment to the organization (Rhoades et al. 2001). Thus, Eisenberger et al. (2001) found that felt obligation mediated the relationship between POS and affective commitment.

10.4.3 Performance–reward expectancies

OST proposes a reciprocal relationship between POS and performance–reward expectancies (Eisenberger et al. 1986; Shore and Shore 1995). By providing employees with favorable opportunities for rewards, the organization would convey high regard for its employees and increase POS. In turn, POS would increase employees' expectancies that high performance will be rewarded by the organization. Accordingly, Eisenberger et al. (1990) found a positive relationship between POS and performance–reward expectancies. However, cross-lag panel studies have not yet been conducted to assess the proposed reciprocal relationship between POS and performance–reward expectancies.

10.4.4 Stress

In stressful situations, POS might reduce psychological strain by indicating the availability of emotional and tangible support (George et al. 1993; Robblee 1998). Thus, POS weakened the relationship between nurses' degree of contact with AIDS patients and negative mood at work (George et al. 1993), and tempered the negative relationship between British pub-workers' experiences of threats and violence by patrons and their work-related well-being (Leather et al. 1998). It is also possible that POS could decrease employees' strain at both low and high exposure to stressors (cf. Viswesvaran et al. 1999). Negative relationships have been reported regarding POS and fatigue (Cropanzano et al. 1997), burnout (Cropanzano et al. 1997), anxiety (Venkatachalam 1995; Robblee 1998), and headaches (Robblee 1998). The potential for POS to have direct effects on the reduction of stress in the workplace is an important area of research that needs further investigation. The preventative health benefits that employees would receive could result in substantial savings on the part of the organization regarding absenteeism and slowed production due to overly stressed employees.

10.5 Behavioral outcomes of POS

OST assumes that felt obligation, fulfillment of socio-emotional needs, affective commitment, and performance–reward expectancies all contribute to increased performance and decreased withdrawal behavior. Accordingly, Rhoades and Eisenberger's (2002) meta-analysis reported that POS had highly reliable effects on in-role performance, extra-role performance, and turnover. In view of possible biases in supervisors' performance ratings, of particular interest were positive relationships found between POS and objective performance measures, including the constructive suggestions made by steel company employees (Eisenberger et al. 1990) and speeding tickets issued and driving-under-the-influence arrests made by state police patrol officers (Armeli et al. 1998).

The felt obligation that POS is presumed to produce should enhance performance. Accordingly, Eisenberger et al. (2001) found that felt obligation mediated the positive relationship between POS and extra-role behavior. It also follows that the relationship between POS and behavioral outcomes should be stronger among employees who strongly endorse the reciprocity norm as applied to employee–employer relationships. Consistent with that belief, Armeli and colleagues (1998) reported that the negative association between teachers' POS and absenteeism increased with the strength of their exchange ideology. Because POS should meet employees' socio-emotional needs, employees with strong socio-emotional needs should place more value on POS. Consequently, these employees should more strongly reciprocate the organization's support. In agreement with this view, Armeli et al. (1998) found that among police officers, the incremental relationship between POS and issuance of speeding and driving-under-the-influence citations was greater among officers with strong needs for esteem, affiliation, emotional support, and approval.

10.6 Future research directions

We now turn to five research areas in which the extension of OST would, we believe, be particularly useful for understanding employee–employer relationships. First, we consider possible relationships between OST and another social exchange approach to employment relationships, psychological contract theory. We then examine the development of POS in the early stages of the employee–employer relationship. Next, we cover attributional processes that employees may use in addition to the voluntariness of treatment to determine the organization's support. In view of the strong influence of perceived voluntariness of treatment on POS, these other attributional processes hold considerable promise for future research. We then discuss POS in part-time and temporary employment, job types that have yet to receive much attention in the organizational support literature despite their increasing representation in the workforce. Finally, we provide suggestions for future research on the relationships between HR practices and POS.

10.6.1 Psychological contract theory

Psychological contract theory (Rousseau 1995; Morrison and Robinson 1997) maintains that employees develop a set of perceived mutual obligations between themselves and their work organizations, called a psychological contract. Based on the norm of reciprocity, psychological contract theory holds that the strength of employees' obligations to the organization and their willingness to fulfill them depend on employees' belief that the organization has fulfilled its obligations to them (Coyle-Shapiro and Kessler 2002; Robinson et al. 1994). Consistent with this view, contract breach, or employees' beliefs that the organization has failed to fulfill its contractual obligations to them, is associated with decreased supervisor-rated in-role performance (Lester et al. 2002), decreased self-reported extra-role behaviors (Robinson and Morrison 1995; Robinson 1996; Turnley and Feldman 2000), and increased turnover rates (Robinson and Rousseau 1994).

As social exchange approaches to the employee–employer relationship that emphasize the norm of reciprocity, OST and psychological contract theory are similar in several major respects. For the most part, theory and research associated with POS and the psychological contract have proceeded apart, with a few notable exceptions. In our view, the two theories have focused on different aspects of the employee–employer relationship that are interdependent. We introduce here some ways in which POS and psychological contracts may be related. A more detailed theoretical integration may be found in Aselage and Eisenberger (2003).

Psychological contract theory assumes that promises conveyed by organizational agents form the basis for employees' psychological contracts (Rousseau 1995). The favorableness of the promises included in the psychological contract might play a role in the development of POS (Aselage and Eisenberger 2003). Employees who believe their organization has promised them numerous valued resources, such as training opportunities and job security, would be expected to have higher levels of POS than would employees who believe their organization has promised little to them. However, perceptions that the organization promised highly favorable treatments might only influence POS when employees trust that the organization will deliver on its promises.

Guzzo et al. (1994) and Coyle-Shapiro and Kessler (2000) suggested that employees' beliefs that the organization had kept its contractual promises should result in increased POS. Supporting this contention is Coyle-Shapiro and Kessler's study in which British public sector employees' POS was found to be influenced by the extent to which the organization was perceived to have fulfilled a variety of obligations to them, such as training, equitable pay, and fringe benefits.

We suggest that increased POS tends to produce a positivity bias in employees' evaluation of whether the organization has fulfilled the terms of the psychological contract. In many cases, promises may lack specificity, leading to uncertainty about whether the organization has fulfilled its obligations. For instance, organizations may promise prospective employees *substantial* future pay raises or *frequent* promotions. In subsequently evaluating whether the organization has fulfilled such qualitative promises, employees with high POS may be inclined to give the organization the benefit of the doubt in determining whether the contract has been fulfilled (Coyle-Shapiro 2001). Additionally, employees with high POS may be less likely to monitor the organization for contract breaches and therefore observe them less frequently (cf. Rousseau 1995; Morrison and Robinson 1997; Coyle-Shapiro 2001).

Economic downturns, external pressures from the organization's competitors, or internal changes in the organization's objectives may prompt the organization to try to increase the employee's obligations or decrease its obligations to employees under the psychological contract (Rousseau 1995). Criteria for employee evaluations, promotions, pay raises, and job retention may change greatly, increasing employees' uncertainty about their future. Attempts to greatly alter the terms of the psychological contract at employees' expense may result in strong resistance to change.

POS may influence employees' acceptance of alterations of the psychological contract. Because of a history of positive regard by the organization, employees with high POS may be less likely to believe that changes made by the organization result from malevolent intent. For instance, employees with high POS might be more likely to accept the organization's position that the elimination of promised salary increases resulted because of hard economic times rather than a lessening concern with the employees' welfare. As such, employees with high POS would be more accepting of rationales given by the organization and so would be inclined to adapt to organization-initiated changes to the psychological contract (Aselage and Eisenberger 2003).

POS might also reduce the psychological strain experienced by employees when the organization proposes fundamental changes to the psychological contract. Shore and Tetrick (1994) reasoned that one function of the psychological contract is to reduce stress because it provides employees with a sense of predictability and control. By boosting self-esteem and assuring employees that aid is available when needed, POS might lessen perceived loss of control and consequent strain when employees experience major organizational change (Aselage and Eisenberger 2003).

10.6.2 Early employee socialization

Longitudinal research has indicated that POS is subject to systematic changes throughout employees' tenure in organizations (e.g. Rhoades et al. 2001; Eisenberger et al. 2002). However, we know little about the development of POS very early in employees' tenure. During pre-employment, a period that stretches from an individual first hearing about a prospective employer through the hiring process, and during the subsequent early stages of employment, newcomers typically have little information about their employing organization. Newcomers are motivated to find out more about the organization's general culture, their roles in the organization (Morrison 1993*a,b*), and the organization's general benevolence or malevolence toward its employees.

Potential employees may rely on sources outside the organization, such as friends, family, and career counselors, for credible information regarding the organization's overall reputation in the community (Fisher et al. 1979; Cable et al. 2000). Information gathered from social networks outside the organization should be especially potent in framing employees' initial levels of support, because the information is communicated by familiar individuals who likely have little vested interest in portraying the organization in an inaccurate light (cf. Popovich and Wanous 1982). However, the strength of the contribution of information from outside sources to employees' initial level of POS would be contingent upon the amount and depth of information available from the source. For instance, the views of a friend who is a former employee of the organization should contribute more to initial POS than the views of another who has a vague recollection of something favorable or unfavorable about the organization.

As previously noted, promises made to employees and requests denied during job recruitment and negotiations would be expected to influence POS (Aselage and

Eisenberger 2003). If interviews for the job are carried out at the organization's facilities, discussions with supervisory personnel and future co-workers should influence expectations concerning treatment and therefore initial levels of POS. The influence of pre-employment information on POS is a promising direction for future research.

Although organizational information obtained from pre-employment sources may play a role in shaping new employees' initial levels of POS, employees continue to engage in information seeking upon entry to corroborate and expand upon the information received prior to entry (Ashford and Cummings 1983; Morrison 1993*a,b*). The continued seeking of information would serve to further reduce their uncertainty concerning the organization's norms, values, and favorable or unfavorable orientation toward its employees. Employees would elicit the knowledgeable views of veteran employees concerning organizational support and to begin to judge the organization's benevolence or malevolence through observations of the treatment of others and themselves.

Employees seek out information about the organization via inquiry, wherein employees directly ask other employees for information, or through monitoring, in which employees attend to others and the environment to obtain informational cues (Ashford and Cummings 1983; Morrison 1993*b*). Morrison (1993*b*) found that new employees seek information about organizational norms and values through monitoring more often than inquiry, and tend to rely on co-workers as opposed to managers and supervisors for such information. She proposed that monitoring serves as a less intrusive mode of information seeking than inquiry, which may lead others to perceive the seeker as incompetent, insecure, and bothersome. Moreover, it was suggested that employees rely on co-workers as opposed to managers or supervisors for this information because co-workers are more likely to view the organization from a perspective similar to that of newcomers.

We suggest that newcomers engage in similar processes to infer the degree to which the organization generally values the contributions and cares about the well-being of its employees. Specifically, once new employees have begun work, they would engage in daily routines that provide direct observations of how their co-workers are treated by the organization. In addition to obtaining information by observing the treatment of others, the attitudes conveyed by co-workers would significantly influence new employees' attitudes (Salanick and Pfeffer 1978; Klein et al. 2001). Co-workers readily convey attitudes to new employees through stories of favorable and unfavorable treatment they and others have received. Thus, we would expect new employees' direct observations of the treatment of others, opinions offered by co-workers concerning their histories of treatment, and their own initial treatment to contribute to POS.

The information that new employees obtain from co-workers early in their tenure may have a lasting impact on POS by serving as a lens through which they view subsequent treatment by the organization. However, as new employees gain experience in the organization, they encounter more instances of first-hand treatment. As such, over time, employees may rely less on the views and treatment of co-workers, and infer POS more from the manner in which they are personally treated by the organization.

As employees become more confident in their opinions concerning the regard in which they are held by the organization, favorable or unfavorable treatment of greater magnitude may be required to alter POS measurably. However, even after an employee has become confident of a given level of support by the organization, sudden changes in treatment having high symbolic or tangible importance would greatly influence POS. Examples would include unexpected promotions, demotions, or layoffs.

10.6.3 Attributions of positive valuation

The extent to which favorable or unfavorable treatment is perceived as discretionary has a major influence on the treatment's contribution to POS. Eisenberger et al. (1986) noted several additional attributional heuristics that employees may use to gauge the extent to which the favorableness of treatment signifies that the organization values their contributions and cares about their well-being.

First, favorable treatment that comes at a substantial cost to the organization would indicate greater positive valuation of employees than treatment requiring little sacrifice by the organization (cf. Gouldner 1960; Eisenberger et al. 1986). From this perspective, the establishment of a program to pay for employees' education would contribute less to POS in a highly profitable company than a similar program in a firm with lesser fiscal resources. Second, OST suggests that treatment delivered at a time of great need to an employee should contribute more to POS than the same practice introduced at a time of lesser need (cf. Gouldner 1960). For example, material or socio-emotional aid given to an employee suffering from a life-threatening illness or grieving the loss of a family member would contribute substantially to POS. Similarly, the opportunity for employees to convey their opinions and suggestions to upper management might contribute more to POS while a tumultuous merger produces concerns for their future than during less stressful times. Moreover, when the organization responds benevolently to a variety of employees in times of great need and such aid becomes well known, the POS of employees not directly impacted by the organization's benevolent actions might also be enhanced.

In a related vein, OST proposes that treatment specific to an employee's needs should be especially valued, and should therefore contribute considerably to POS (cf. Schopler 1970). From this perspective, certain types of favorable treatment may be more important in leading to POS for some employees than others. For instance, flexible scheduling may be more beneficial for a single parent of young children than for an employee without children or other substantial non-work responsibilities. As a result, flexible scheduling may contribute more strongly to POS for the former employee than the latter. As another example, favorable opportunities for promotions and career advancement may be more strongly associated with POS among employees with a strong need for achievement. These examples highlight the potential importance of employees' attributional processes in the relationships of favorable treatment with POS. Based on these processes, the favorableness of treatment might be considerably increased or attenuated as a source of POS. Besides the attributional heuristic of the voluntariness of the organization's treatment (Eisenberger et al. 1997), evidence has yet to be gathered on remaining attributional heuristics described above.

10.6.4 Contingent employment relationships

The central tenets of OST have been generally applied to regular employment relationships, wherein employees work for their organizations on a full-time, long-term basis. However, contingent employment relationships, such as part-time and temporary work, are becoming more common in the contemporary workplace (Nollen and Axel 1996; Rousseau 1997; McLean Parks et al. 1998). Many service organizations, such as restaurants, rely heavily on part-time employees (Stamper and Van Dyne 2001). Employers may be less prone to invest resources in short-term and part-time employment relationships (Tsui et al. 1995; McLean Parks et al. 1998), and managers and supervisors may be less likely to convey their appreciation for the accomplishments of such individuals.

Despite the fact that organizations may be less inclined to offer favorable resources to contingent workers, we suggest that the provision of impersonal and socio-emotional resources nonetheless strengthens contingent employees' POS. As is the case with regular employees, contingent employees would be expected to respond favorably to the receipt of socio-emotional and impersonal benefits. Moorman and Harland (2002) found that temporary employees' perceptions of favorable treatment by the organization were predictive of extra-role behaviors, affective organizational commitment, and felt obligation to the organization. Among contingent employees, POS might mediate such relationships.

Because of management's hesitance in many organizations to provide highly favorable treatment for contingent employees, POS should be higher for regular employees than contingent employees in some organizations. However, this result would be expected to be far from universal. In many organizations, the POS of regular employees is not particularly high (Eisenberger et al. 1990), and may not be higher than for contingent employees. Regular employees may expect more from the organization than contingent employees and therefore may be more prone to dis-appointment. According to psychological contract theory (Rousseau 1995), regular employees believe that the organization is obliged to provide favorable levels of resources of various kinds to employees. To the extent that these resources are not afforded, employees would believe that their reciprocal exchange relationship with the organization had been violated. Such contract violation may reduce POS (Aselage and Eisenberger 2003). Thus, greater POS by regular employees than contingent workers would depend on the organization's fulfillment of its added obligations to them.

The voluntariness of the contingent employees' work status (Feldman et al. 1995) may influence POS. Voluntary contingent employees pursue part-time or temporary jobs because they desire these work arrangements. A college student working part-time to earn extra money would be designated a voluntary contingent employee. By contrast, involuntary contingent employees work on a part-time or temporary basis but desire regular employment. A new college graduate who takes a part-time job after failing to find regular work would be denoted an involuntary contingent employee. Because attaining regular employment is a salient need for involuntary contingent workers, they may attribute the organization's failure to offer them regular employment as an indication of low valuation. This would be more likely if the organization were known to make use of contingent employees on a continuing basis. In such cases, it would be expected that involuntary contingent employees will tend to have lower levels of POS than voluntary contingent workers.

Work status may also play a role in determining how contingent workers choose to reciprocate POS. Due to the brevity of their expected tenure with the organization, temporary employees may be less inclined than regular employees to volunteer for ambitious projects. Rather, temporary employees may be likely to repay the organization by working harder or more carefully in their in-role activities or by engaging in short-term ad hoc extra-role behaviors. Many voluntary part-time employees may have been drawn by the opportunity for more free time for their personal life. For these employees, activities outside of work, such as child-rearing or education, may take precedence over work. Therefore, part-time employees may be less inclined to volunteer for tasks that would impinge on their personal lives, such as overtime work assignments.

10.6.5 Human resource practices

POS has implications for the strategic human resources literature, which emphasizes the effects of an organization's HR package on employee performance (Huselid et al. 1997). Strategic HR investigators have concentrated on such practices as hiring from within versus from outside the organization, formal training programs, appraisal systems, profit sharing, employment security, opportunities for employees to voice their views, and scope of job responsibilities (Delery and Doty 1996). Delery and Doty (1996) noted that HR researchers have investigated the link between strategic HR practices and performance but have given little attention to possible mechanisms responsible for this relationship.

While it is generally assumed that effective HR practices contribute to performance by enhancing employees' knowledge, skills, and abilities (Schuler and Jackson 1987; Jackson and Schuler 1995), favorable strategic HR practices may also enhance performance by increasing POS. Investing in employees' development and recognizing their contributions would indicate the organization's positive valuation by the organization of employees' contributions and its commitment to a strong employee–employer relationship, thereby enhancing POS. On the basis of the norm of reciprocity, POS would promote a heightened sense of obligation among employees to help meet the organization's objectives. This increased obligation should result in greater work effort and heightened performance (Eisenberger et al. 1986;

Shore and Shore, 1995). Future research should examine the mediational role of POS in the strategic HR practices–performance relationship (cf. Wayne et al. 2002).

Other research might address the relative influences that individual- and group-based HR practices have on POS. Some HR programs reward individual achievement, such as pay for performance plans and bonuses tied to productivity. When such practices highlight the performance of individuals in a favorable or unfavorable manner, they will tend to have strong effects on POS (Shore and Shore 1995). For instance, a retail organization may choose to recognize the superior performance of its top salesperson by rewarding him or her with praise and approval, along with a monthly bonus. Based on social comparison (Festinger 1954), such individual recognition is especially informative to an employee that his or her efforts are appreciated by the organization.

Other HR practices provided to entire groups of employees should affect POS, albeit to a lesser degree (cf. Shore and Shore 1995). Group rewards, such as team-based bonuses, are not directly informative of individual achievement but nevertheless indicate a positive valuation of the individual as a member of a class and should contribute to POS. Other HR practices, such as healthcare benefits, while not based on performance, are nevertheless indicative of the organization's favorable or unfavorable orientation toward employees and should also affect POS. Social identification theory (Tajfel and Turner 1979, 1986) holds that because employees work interdependently and are subject to similar organizational policies and procedures, they are likely to identify with their co-workers as members of their in-group. As a result, employees would value the organization's favorable treatment of co-workers as an indicator of the organization's concern for themselves. Therefore, the treatment groups to which one belongs in the organization would affect POS. The stronger the identification with a particular group within the organization, the greater would be the influence of favorable treatment of the group on POS.

10.7 Conclusions

OST provides a social exchange account of the development of the employee–employer relationship based on the central assumption that in order to meet socio-emotional needs and gauge the utility of increased efforts on behalf of the organization, employees form global beliefs concerning their valuation by the organization. Such POS would depend on favorable discretionary acts carried out by the organization. Based on the norm of reciprocity, employees would respond to favorable treatment with an increased felt obligation to help the organization achieve its obligations and a greater affective commitment to the organization. These factors and enhanced performance–reward expectancies stemming from POS would lead to greater performance and to reduced withdrawal behaviors such as absenteeism and turnover.

A substantial empirical research literature suggests that, consistent with OST, major categories of favorable treatment received by employees are positively related to POS which, in turn, is associated with outcomes favored by employees and the organization. Further progress in this line of research, we believe, will depend greatly on the theory's elaboration and evolution to explain a greater diversity of employee behavior. In the preceding, we detailed OST and indicated possible bases for its integration with other recent social exchange accounts. As additional directions for theoretical development we suggested a consideration of relationships between POS and employee socialization, employee attributions of positive valuation by the organization, contingent employment relationships, and strategic human resources management. These are but a few of the new directions we hope researchers will explore in extending organizational support theory.

References

Allen, D. G., Shore, L. M., and Griffeth, R. W. (2003). "The role of perceived organizational support and supportive human resources practices in the turnover process." *Journal of Management*, 29: 99–118.

Armeli, S., Eisenberger, R., Fasolo, P., and Lynch, P. (1998). "Perceived organizational support and police performance: The moderating influence of socio-emotional needs." *Journal of Applied Psychology*, 83: 288–97.

Aselage, J., and Eisenberger, R. (2003). "Perceived organizational support and psychological contracts: A theoretical integration." *Journal of Organizational Behavior*, 24: 491–509.

Ashford, S. J., and Cummings, L. L. (1983). "Feedback as an individual resource: Personal strategies of creating information." *Organizational Behavior and Human Performance*, 32: 370–98.

Bies, R. J., and Moag, J. S. (1986). "Interactional justice: Communication criteria of fairness." *Research on Negotiation in Organizations*, 1: 43–55.

Cable, D. M., Aiman-Smith, L., and Edwards, J. R. (2000). "The sources and accuracy of job applicants' beliefs about organizational culture." *Academy of Management Journal*, 43: 1076–85.

Cobb, A. T., and Wooten, K. (1998). "The role social accounts can play in a justice intervention." In W. Pasmore and R. Woodman (eds.), *Research in Organizational Change and Development*, Greenwich, CT: JAI Press, 73–115.

Coyle-Shapiro, J. A. M. (2001). "Managers: Caught in the middle of a psychological contract muddle." Paper presented at the Annual Meeting of the Academy of Management, Denver.

——and Kessler, I. (2000). "Consequences of the psychological contract for the employment relationship: A large scale survey." *Journal of Management Studies*, 37: 903–30.

——and —— (2002). "Exploring reciprocity through the lens of the psychological contract: Employee and employer perspectives." *European Journal of Work and Organizational Psychology*, 11: 69–86.

Cropanzano, R., Howes, J. C., Grandey, A. A., and Toth, P. (1997). "The relationship of organizational politics and support to work behaviors, attitudes, and stress." *Journal of Organizational Behavior*, 22: 159–80.

Delery, J. E., and Doty, D. H. (1996). "Modes of theorizing in strategic human resource management: Tests of universalistic, contingency, and configurational performance predictions." *Academy of Management Journal*, 39: 802–35.

Eisenberger, R., Huntington, R., Hutchison, S., and Sowa, D. (1986). "Perceived organizational support." "*Journal of Applied Psychology*," 71: 500–7.

—— Fasolo, P., and Davis-LaMastro, V. (1990). "Perceived organizational support and employee diligence, commitment, and innovation." *Journal of Applied Psychology*, 75: 51–9.

—— Cummings, J., Armeli, S., and Lynch, P. (1997). "Perceived organizational support, discretionary treatment, and job satisfaction." *Journal of Applied Psychology*, 82: 812–20.

—— Armeli, S., Rexwinkel, B., Lynch, P. D., and Rhoades, L. (2001). "Reciprocation of perceived organizational support." *Journal of Applied Psychology*, 86: 42–51.

—— Stinglhamber, F., Vandenberghe, C., Sucharski, I., and Rhoades, L. (2002). "Perceived supervisor support: Contributions to perceived organizational support and employee retention." *Journal of Applied Psychology*, 87: 565–73.

Fasolo, P. M. (1995). "Procedural justice and perceived organizational support: Hypothesized effects on job performance," in R. Cropanzano and K. M. Kacmar (eds.), *Organizational Politics, Justice, and Support: Managing Social Climate at Work* (Westport, CT: Quorum Press), 185–95.

Feldman, D. C., Doerpinghaus, H. I., and Turnley, W. H. (1995). "Employee reactions to temporary jobs." *Journal of Managerial Issues*, 7: 127–41.

Ferguson, T. J., and Rule, B. G. (1982). "An attributional perspective on anger and aggression," in R. G. Geen and E. I. Donnerstein (eds.), *Aggression: Theoretical and Empirical Reviews. Vol. 1: Theoretical and Methodological Issues* (New York: Academic Press), 41–74.

Festinger, L. (1954). "A theory of social comparison processes." *Human Relations*, 7: 114–40.

Fisher, C. D., Illgen, D. R., and Hoyer, W. D. (1979). "Source credibility, information favorability, and job offer acceptance." *Academy of Management Journal*, 22: 94–103.

George, J. M., Reed, T. F., Ballard, K. A., Colin, J., and Fielding, J. (1993). "Contact with AIDS patients as a source of work-related distress—effects of organizational and social support." *Academy of Management Journal*, 36: 157–71.

Gouldner, A. W. (1960). "The norm of reciprocity: A preliminary statement." *American Sociological Review*, 25: 161–78.

Greenberg, J. (1990). "Organizational justice: Yesterday, today and tomorrow." *Journal of Management*, 16: 399–432.

Guzzo, R. A., Noonan, K. A., and Elron, E. (1994). "Expatriate managers and the psychological contract." *Journal of Applied Psychology*, 79: 617–26.

Huselid, M. A., Jackson, S. E., and Schuler, R. S. (1997). "Technical and strategic human resource management effectiveness as determinants of firm performance." *Academy of Management Journal*, 40: 171–88.

Jackson, S. E., and Schuler, R. S. (1995). "Understanding human resource management in the context of organizations and their environments," in M. R. Rosenweig and L. W. Porter (eds.), *Annual Review of Psychology*, Vol. 46 (Palo Alto, CA: Annual Reviews), 237–64.

Klein, K. J., Buhl, A. B., Smith, D. B., and Sorra, J. S. (2001). "Is everyone in agreement? An exploration of within-group agreement in employee perceptions of the work environment." *Journal of Applied Psychology*, 86: 3–16.

Leather, P., Lawrence, C., Beale, D., and Cox, T. (1998). "Exposure to occupational violence and the buffering effects of intra-organizational support." *Work and Stress*, 12: 161–78.

Lester, S. W., Turnley, W. H., Bloodgood, J. M., and Bolino, M. C. (2002). "Not seeing eye to eye: Differences in supervisor and subordinate perceptions of and attributions for psychological contract breach." *Journal of Organizational Behavior*, 23: 39–56.

Levinson, H. (1965). "Reciprocation: The relationship between man and organization." *Administrative Science Quarterly*, 9: 370–90.

Liden, R. C., Sparrowe, R. T., and Wayne, S. J. (1997). "Leader–member exchange theory: The past and potential for the future," in G. R. Ferris (ed.), *Research in Personnel and Human Resources Management*, Vol. 15 (Stamford, CT: JAI Press), 47–119.

Masterson, S. S., Lewis, K., Goldman, B. M., and Taylor, M. S. (2000). "Integrating justice and social exchange: The differing effects of fair procedures and treatment on work relationships." *Academy of Management Journal*, 43: 738–48.

McLean Parks, J., Kidder, D. L., and Gallagher, D. G. (1998). "Fitting square pegs into round holes: Mapping the domain of contingent work arrangements onto the psychological contract." *Journal of Organizational Behavior*, 19: 697–730.

Moorman, R. H., and Harland, L. K. (2002). "Temporary employees as good citizens: Factors influencing their OCB performance." *Journal of Business and Psychology*, 17: 171–87.

—— Blakely, G. L., and Niehoff, B. P. (1998). "Does perceived organizational support mediate the relationship between procedural justice and organizational citizenship behavior?" *Academy of Management Journal*, 41: 351–7.

Morrison, E. W. (1993a). "Longitudinal study of the effects of information seeking on newcomer socialization." *Journal of Applied Psychology*, 78: 173–83.

—— (1993b). "Newcomer information seeking: Exploring types, modes, sources, and outcomes." *Academy of Management Journal*, 36: 557–89.

—— and Robinson, S. L. (1997). "When employees feel betrayed: A model of how psychological contract violation develops." *Academy of Management Review*, 22: 226–56.

Nollen, S., and Axel, H. (1996). *Managing Contingent Workers*. New York: American Management.

Popovich, P., and Wanous, J. P. (1982). "The realistic job preview as persuasive communication." *Academy of Management Review*, 7: 570–8.

Rhoades, L., and Eisenberger, R. (2002). "Perceived organizational support: A review of the literature." *Journal of Applied Psychology*, 87: 698–714.

—————— and Armeli, S. (2001). "Affective commitment to the organization: The contribution of perceived organizational support." *Journal of Applied Psychology*, 86: 825–36.

Robblee, M. (1998). "Confronting the threat of organizational downsizing: Coping and health." Unpublished Master's thesis, Carleton University.

Robinson, S. L. (1996). "Trust and breach of the psychological contract." *Administrative Science Quarterly*, 41: 574–99.

—— and Morrison, E. W. (1995). "Psychological contracts and OCB: The effect of unfulfilled obligations on civic virtue behavior." *Journal of Applied Psychology*, 16: 289–98.

—— and Rousseau, D. M. (1994). "Violating the psychological contract: Not the exception but the norm." *Journal of Organizational Behavior*, 15: 245–59.

—— Kraatz, M. S., and Rousseau, D. M. (1994). "Changing obligations and the psychological contract: A longitudinal study." *Academy of Management Journal*, 37: 137–52.

Rousseau, D. M. (1995). *Psychological Contracts in Organizations*. Thousand Oaks, CA: Sage.

—— (1997). "Organizational behavior in the new organizational era." *Annual Review of Psychology*, 48: 515–46.

Salanick, G. R., and Pfeffer, J. (1978). "A social information processing approach to job attitudes and task design." *Administrative Science Quarterly*, 23: 224–53.

Schopler, J. (1970). "An attribution analysis of some determinants of reciprocating a benefit," in J. Macaulay and L. Berkowitz (eds.), *Altruism and Helping Behavior* (New York: Academic Press), 231–8.

Schuler, R. S., and Jackson, S. E. (1987). "Linking competitive strategies with human resources management practices." *Academy of Management Executive*, 1: 207–19.

Shore, L. M., and Barksdale, K. (1998). "Examining degree of balance and level of obligation in the employment relationship: A social exchange approach." *Journal of Organizational Behavior*, 19: 731–44.

—— and Shore, T. H. (1995). "Perceived organizational support and organizational justice," in R. S. Cropanzano and K. M. Kacmar (eds.), *Organizational Politics, Justice, and Support: Managing the Social Climate of the Workplace* (Westport, CT: Quorum), 149–64.

—— and Tetrick, L. E. (1994). "The psychological contract as an explanatory framework in the employment relationship," in C. Cooper and D. Rousseau (eds.), *Trends in Organizational Behavior*, Vol. 1 (New York: Wiley), 91–109.

Sitkin, S. B., and Bies, R. J. (1993). "Social accounts in conflict situations: Using explanations to manage conflict." *Human Relations*, 46: 349–70.

Stamper, C. L., and Van Dyne, L. (2001). "Work status and organizational citizenship behavior: A field study of restaurant employees." *Journal of Organizational Behavior*, 22: 517–36.

Tajfel, H., and Turner, J. (1979). "An integrative theory of intergroup conflict," in S. Wohrchel and W. Austin (eds.), *The Social Psychology of Intergroup Relations* (Monterey, CA: Brooks/Cole), 33–47.

—— and Turner, J. C. (1986). "The social identity theory of intergroup behavior," in S. Worchel, and W. G. Austin (eds.), *Psychology of Intergroup Relations* (Chicago: Nelson-Hall), 7–24.

Tsui, A. S., Pearce, J. L., Porter, L. W., and Hite, J. P. (1995). "Choice of employee–organization relationship: Influence of external and internal organizational factors." *Research in Personnel and Human Resources Management*, 13: 117–51.

—— —— —— and Tripoli, A. M. (1997). "Alternative approaches to the employee–organization relationship: Does investment in employees pay off?" *Academy of Management Journal*, 40: 1089–121.

Turnley, W. H., and Feldman, D. C. (2000). "Re-examining the effects of psychological contract violations: Unmet expectations and job dissatisfaction as mediators." *Journal of Organizational Behavior*, 21: 25–42.

Venkatachalam, M. (1995). "Personal hardiness and perceived organizational support as links in the role stress–outcome relationship: A person–environment fit model." Unpublished doctoral dissertation, University of Alabama, Tuscaloosa.

Viswesvaran, C., Sanchez, J. I., and Fisher, J. (1999). "The role of social support in the process of work stress: A meta-analysis." *Journal of Vocational Behavior*, 54: 314–34.

Wayne, S. J., Shore, L. M., Bommer, W. H., and Tetrick, L. E. (2002). "The role of fair treatment and rewards in perceptions of organizational support and leader–member exchange." *Journal of Applied Psychology*, 87: 590–8.

The Role of Leader–Member Exchange in the Dynamic Relationship Between Employer and Employee: Implications for Employee Socialization, Leaders, and Organizations

ROBERT C. LIDEN, TALYA N. BAUER, AND
BERRIN ERDOGAN

11.1 Overview of the employer–employee relationship and leader–member exchange

11.1.1 Employer–employee relationship: "Who" is the organization?

We define the employer–employee relationship as a reciprocal exchange in which employees engage in work-related behaviors that benefit the organization in return for resources and support provided by the organization. The employee "side" of the relationship has been treated both theoretically and empirically as employees' perceptions of what they receive from the organization and corresponding attitudes and behaviors directed toward the organization that are thought to be appropriate, given the perceived level of support obtained from the organization. The employer "side" of the relationship has presented a challenge to researchers of the employer–employee relationship because of difficulties in defining "who" is the organization. Researchers often personify the organization as an entity that varies in terms of the degree to which "it" cares about and supports employees. Organizations are described as recruiting, selecting, socializing, and developing subordinates, without explicitly identifying who personifies the organization in these activities. It has been substantially more difficult to conceptualize and measure the employer side of the employer–employee relationship. In fact, researchers of psychological contracts and perceived organizational support (POS) have not yet made an attempt to develop theory or measurement for the "employer" side of the employer–employee relationship. For example, Rousseau (1989) stressed that psychological contracts represent employee perceptions of their relationship with the organization, and that it is these perceptions, rather than reality, that guides employee attitudes and behaviors.

Similarly, in the POS literature (Rhoades and Eisenberger 2002), the focus has been on *perceptions* of organizational support, and in this research, the organization maintains a rather mysterious identity.

We contend that employees' global view of the organization is based on a complex mixture of organizational culture and the nature of interactions with others in the organization, including immediate leaders, co-workers, subordinates, and contacts outside of focal individuals' functional area. Through their interactions with organizational agents, employees receive support from the organization, and develop obligations to reciprocate. In other words, the employer–employee relationship may be viewed as the perceived amount of support from the organization, and the perceived degree to which the employee feels an obligation to reciprocate. The support received from and obligation felt toward the organization in turn leads to a number of attitudes and behaviors with important consequences for the organization.

Although all are salient in shaping employee perceptions of the organization, in this chapter we focus on the immediate leader. Specifically, we rely on the leader–member exchange (LMX) theory of leadership, and discuss the role of LMX in the development of the employer–employee relationship. Indeed, the immediate leader may represent a key agent of the organization. We contend that the immediate leader has an important role in the socialization of newcomers to the organization, as it is during this period that employees develop perceptions of the employer–employee relationship. The outcomes of the socialization process are perceived obligation to and perceived support from the organization, which lead to organizational attitudes and behaviors.

11.1.2 Defining LMX

As implied above, we feel that it is not possible to adequately describe the employer–employee relationship without discussion of the integral role that the immediate supervisor/leader plays as a representative of the organization and as a purveyor of resources and support. LMX represents one of the main theoretical approaches to the study of dyadic leader–subordinate relationships (e.g. Dansereau et al. 1975; Dienesch and Liden 1986; Graen and Scandura 1987; Bauer and Green 1996; Gerstner and Day 1997; Liden et al. 1997; Erdogan and Liden 2002). The major premise of LMX theory is that rather than treating all subordinates alike, leaders differentiate between subordinates, forming relationships that range from being based strictly on the employment contract to relationships that involve the exchange of resources and support that extend beyond the formal job description (Liden and Graen 1980). Leaders' differentiation between subordinates implies that low LMX employees perceive less support from the organization than high LMX employees. Because of the reciprocal nature of these relationships, it follows that low LMX employees should feel less committed to the organization and less likely to engage in as many organizationally beneficial behaviors than would high LMX employees.

11.1.3 *Immediate superior as an agent of the organization*

Research exploring both POS and LMX has found the two to be reciprocally related (Wayne et al. 1997), suggesting the quality of the relationship with the immediate superior helps employees in their evaluation of support provided by the organization. In fact, Eisenberger et al. (2002) found that perceived supervisor support predicted POS measured six months later, but POS assessed at the earlier time period did not predict perceived supervisor support measured six months later (also see Eisenberger et al., Chapter 7, this volume). Thus, it appears that the immediate supervisor plays a critical role as a key agent of the organization through which members form their perceptions of the organization. Reinforcing this position, Jablin (2001: 778) commented that the immediate leader "is a central source of information related to job and organizational expectations ... and is pivotal in the newcomer's ability to negotiate his or her role." The immediate leader typically plays a role in the socialization of newcomers that begins during recruitment and extends through disengagement/exit (Bauer 1994; Jablin 2001). In this chapter, we view socialization as a key mechanism through which newcomers develop perceptions concerning the employer–employee relationship and accompanying psychological contract (Rousseau 1990). We argue that the immediate superior plays a critical role in the socialization process, and thus is instrumental in the formation of employees' psychological contracts.

Despite the acknowledgment that immediate leaders are of importance in the socialization of newcomers, the literature could be significantly advanced by research on *specific* behaviors that leaders use to socialize newcomers, and how these behaviors affect specific adjustment/socialization outcomes and contribute to employee interpretations of the employer–employee relationship. There is also a lack of understanding about how socialization is influenced by interactions *between* various agents. Sparrowe and Liden (1997) theorized that leaders may sponsor select subordinates by introducing them to key individuals within their social networks. However, they contended that sponsorship of this nature could either help or hinder the progress of subordinates based on the nature of their immediate leader's social networks. Subsequently, Sparrowe and Liden (1999) demonstrated empirically that when members' leaders enjoyed centrality in advice and trust networks, sponsorship benefited subordinates by increasing their control over decisions and resources. On the other hand, when members' leaders suffered from centrality in avoidance networks (i.e. tended to be avoided by others), sponsorship was a "curse" because it tended to reduce control over decisions and resources.

Further supporting the importance of social networks during socialization, Morrison (2002) found that networks cutting across functional areas of the organization provided greater organizational knowledge and also served to increase role clarity. Evidently, when exposed to information from multiple areas of the organization, individuals are better able to understand the specific part that they play in the organization. Morrison (2002) also found, consistent with Sparrowe and Liden's (1999) results, that job and role learning was enhanced when the immediate leader was included in the individual's social network. Thus, learning about the organization, its norms, and accepted views of employer and employee obligations to one another appear to benefit greatly from the development of a diverse set of network contacts. Furthermore, it has been demonstrated that centrality in advice networks is positively related both to in-role and extra-role performance (Sparrowe et al. 2001), suggesting that network structure influences both socialization and subsequent job behaviors. Hence, studies that address the full range of insiders that newcomers encounter, and that consider them in concert via social network methods, will contribute to a fuller understanding of the socialization process, and accompanying employer–employee relationship.

Mentors may also serve as agents of the organization. Although immediate leaders often assume mentoring roles, especially in high LMX relationships (Scandura and Schriesheim 1994), individuals may have one or more mentors other than the immediate leader. Research has shown that having a diverse set of mentors more positively influences career progression than does reliance on only one mentor, or worse still, not having a mentor (Seibert et al. 2001). This finding appears to be related to results showing that protégés' mentoring needs change across socialization periods (Seibert 1999). Mentors may provide information and advice that assists newcomers in forming beliefs about their obligations to the organization as well as what the organization owes them in return. Mentors may also be instrumental in providing protégés with guidance in how to secure the most resources and support from the organization (Green and Bauer 1995). It has been suggested, however, that the benefits of mentoring may be thwarted when the immediate leader has formed a negative relationship with one or more of an individual's mentors (Sparrowe and Liden 1997). Empirical research is needed to test ways in which the influence of the immediate leader and mentors combine/interact to determine the quality of newcomer socialization and formation of beliefs concerning the employer–employee relationship and associated obligations.

11.2 LMX and the employer–employee relationship across socialization stages

Beginning with on-site job interviews, the "future" immediate superior plays a key role in providing recruits with a framework for the employer–employee relationship. In this way, leaders may supply key information to recruits that they use to determine the psychological contract. According to Rousseau (1989), psychological contracts are perceptions formed by employees concerning expectations of the obligations one has to a dyadic partner, such as the organization, and what that dyadic partner is obligated to provide in return. In a later article, Rousseau (1998: 152) challenged LMX researchers to look inside the black box, which she defines as the "exchange itself." Similarly, Liden and colleagues (1997) asked what happened to the *exchange* in leader–member *exchange*, and argued that exchange processes need to be reintroduced to the LMX research. Consistent with this argument, Rousseau (1998) suggested that researchers should explicitly examine the psychological contracts of leaders and members to uncover their perceived obligations to one another.

The specific nature of the employer–employee relationship and accompanying psychological contract will evolve as newcomers become socialized into the organization and role expectations become refined (Katz and Kahn 1978). Reflecting changes in the employer–employee relationship, it has been shown that attitudes of newcomers, such as commitment to the organization, may change as newcomers become integrated into the organization (Vandenberg and Self 1993). Furthermore, the determinants of outcomes also change (Toffler 1981), causing newcomers to make adjustments to accommodate discrepancies between initial job expectations and subsequent perceptions of reality. We argue that the degree to which the immediate leader, vis-à-vis LMX, is involved in assisting newcomers deal with such challenges will help to determine the socialization success of newcomers. In our discussion, we focus on leader effort in building LMXs, and discuss the process by which LMX shapes the employer–employee relationship. Figure 11.1 provides an overview of the mechanisms through which leaders influence the different socialization stages of employees.

11.2.1 Anticipatory stage

In 1976, Feldman proposed a model of socialization, arguing that anticipatory variables should influence the accommodation stage of socialization. Anticipatory variables summarize how well the newcomer "fits" (Edwards 1991) with the organization and also, how realistic the newcomer's view of organizational reality is upon entry. These variables are called anticipatory because they occur prior to actual entry into the organization.

Research results suggest that what happens during this anticipatory pre-entry period does indeed influence post-entry attitudes and behaviors. For example, Lee et al. (1992) found that commitment propensity measured at pre-entry was positively related to commitment at five points in time following entry and negatively related to turnover across a four-year period following entry. Furthermore, in addition to providing support for relations between commitment propensity measured at pre-entry and later commitment and turnover, Pierce and Dunham (1987) found commitment propensity to be positively related to subsequent employee perceptions of leader consideration behavior. These results are suggestive of the role that the relationship between leader and member may have on job attitudes, starting prior to entry into the organization. Similarly, it has been found that job expectations at pre-entry are related to subsequent perceptions of LMX (Bauer 1994; Major et al. 1995), suggesting the importance of future leader and member interactions prior to entry into the organization.

The "future" immediate superior is typically involved in the recruitment process, if not in the initial interview, almost always in on-site job visits (Bureau of National Affairs 1988). Despite this, research has generally not been conducted on the effects of recruitment interactions between the future leader and members on subsequent

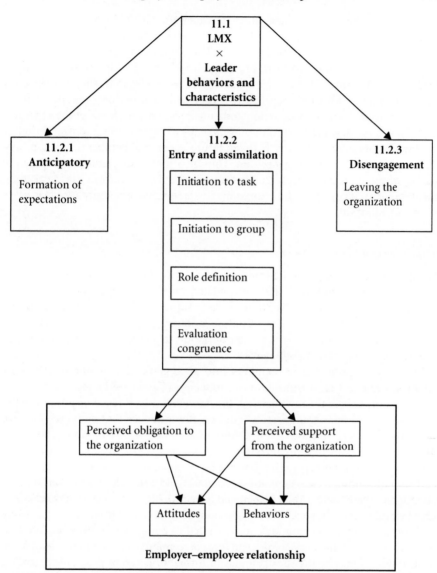

Figure 11.1. *The role of LMX in the development of the employer–employee relationship.*

LMX quality. This is consistent with a lack of attention in the employment interview literature on site-interviews, as the preponderance of interview research has been conducted on campus interviews or in the lab (Parsons et al. 2001). Investigations on post-entry LMX development have discovered that the quality of the relationship between leader and member is established within the first two months of the relationship (Dansereau et al. 1975; Bauer and Green 1996), with one study demonstrating that LMX quality had already been determined during the first five days of dyads' existence (Liden et al. 1993). These results suggest that it is likely that LMX relationships begin to form pre-entry, based on initial interactions between leader and member during recruitment. It is likely that the influence of pre-entry interactions between future leader and member become increasingly important to post-entry socialization and outcomes at higher levels of the organization. This is because the recruiting process tends to extend over a longer period of time with more interaction time between future leader and member than is typically true at lower levels of the organization. Thus, new hires' expectations regarding the nature of the employer–employee relationship may begin to form during recruitment, influenced largely by the future immediate superior, especially at higher levels of the organization.

11.2.2 Entry and assimilation

During the entry stage, sometimes referred to as the accommodation period, newcomers learn about social and work-related issues. It is during the accommodation period that newcomers "learn the ropes" of working and interacting within the organization (Schein 1968). The accommodation stage of socialization consists of four variables: Initiation to the group, initiation to the task, role definition, and congruence of evaluation (Feldman 1976).

The socialization of new members into an organization is one of the most vital processes that an organization can influence (Cascio 1991). Recruitment and selection only supply the raw material, the new employee. What transpires once the employee enters the organization should greatly influence that employee's tenure (Van Maanen 1975; Wanous 1980; Campion and Mitchell 1986; Jablin 2001) and performance within that organization (Van Maanen 1975; Wanous 1980). While organizations routinely spend billions of dollars on employee orientation programs and formal training (Goldstein and Ford 2002) and researchers give considerable attention to these topics (Van Maanen and Schein 1979), they have been rated as not very helpful to the adjustment or socialization process (Louis et al. 1983). It is likely that formal orientation programs are not rated as being helpful because they lack information with which newcomers can form perceptions of the employer–employee relationship. It may be the shortcomings of formal orientation programs regarding the employer–employee relationship that cause new hires to turn to immediate supervisors for clarification of their roles and what can be expected in return from the organization. Indeed, supervisors have been rated as the most helpful agent of socialization (Louis et al. 1983), yet relatively little attention has been paid to the supervisor as a socialization agent (Fisher 1986). Similarly, only recently has the immediate supervisor been studied as an intermediary between the employee and the organization (Rhoades and Eisenberger 2002). Yukl's (2002) taxonomy of leader behaviors offers a vehicle for the potential integration of the leadership and socialization literatures. The purpose of this section of our chapter is to integrate these two disconnected literatures and make specific predictions about how leadership, specifically LMX, can influence the socialization process and the formation of the employer–employee relationship.

Many leader behaviors may contribute to newcomer socialization. Leaders may act as role models (Weiss 1990), leaders may serve as valuable information sources (Morrison 1995), or as mentors (Green and Bauer 1995), and may filter downward organizational communications (Jablin 2001). We argue that a special role that leaders play in the socialization of newcomers is to provide information germane to the formation of perceptions of the employer–employee relationship, often labeled psychological contracts (Rousseau 1989). Specifically, three of Yukl's leader behavior categories (Yukl 2002) should influence the accommodation stage of socialization, a period characterized by the formation of psychological contracts.

Initiation to the group, defined as the extent to which the employee feels accepted and trusted by co-workers (Feldman 1976; Fisher 1986), may be compared to Yukl's (2002) integrating taxonomy of managerial behavior. Behaviors that target "building relationships" are closely related to making an employee feel accepted and, therefore, foster positive working relationships. Within this behavior category is the management of conflict, internal team building, networking with others both internally and externally, and supporting employees. Some empirical support for these relationships exists. For example, social support from the supervisor is usually associated with higher job satisfaction and involvement (La Rocco and Jones 1978; Seers et al. 1983). These outcome variables are often preceded by accommodation variables in socialization research (Fisher 1986). Further, Bauer and Green (1998) found that relationship-oriented manager behavior (supporting), consistent with high LMX relationships, predicted relational accommodation. These results are consistent with Maslyn and Uhl-Bien's (2001) discovery that effort devoted to the relationship on the part of both members of the dyad was related to met expectations. Therefore, it seems reasonable to suggest that social support should also increase a new employee's initiation to the group.

Proposition 1 *To the extent that a leader exerts effort toward building a high LMX relationship with a new employee, that employee should feel a greater level of initiation to the group than for leaders who exert less effort in building the relationship.*

Another accommodation variable is initiation to the task. This has been defined as the extent to which an employee feels competent and accepted as a full work partner (Feldman 1976; Fisher 1986). Again, Yukl's taxonomy addresses this accommodation variable. This effect should be realized via leader behaviors that are classified as "influencing people." This includes motivating employees as well as recognizing and rewarding their performance. A relationship should exist between these leader behaviors and an employee's feelings of initiation to the task. Research on work motivation suggests that employees who receive feedback and rewards for work that is done well will be more motivated in the future (Hackman and Oldham 1975). Also, theory suggests that feedback contributes to the building of self-efficacy (e.g. Gist and Mitchell 1992; Paglis et al. 1998), and empirical research demonstrates that receipt of feedback and rewards is related to self-efficacy regarding the ability to complete tasks successfully (Saks 1992). Self-efficacy has also been proposed to be positively related to LMX (Scandura and Lankau 1996), and support for this proposition has been found (Murphy and Ensher 1999). Further, it has also been demonstrated that LMX is positively related to subordinate creativity (Tierney et al. 1999).

Proposition 2   *LMX is positively related to the newcomer's level of initiation to the task.*

We also contend that the leader's cultural orientation will play an important role in the initiation of employees to their groups and tasks. Previously, Bauer et al. (1998) delineated several cultural propositions using Hofstede's (1980) typology. Building on that work, for the purposes of this chapter, we focus on cultural dimensions from Adler's (1997) typology. Adler (1997) argues that variance in basic perceptions underlies national cultures. Basic perceptions are captured by six dimensions that differentiate cultural orientations. The six dimensions are: People's qualities as individuals, people's relationship to nature, people's relationship to others, people's primary type of activity, orientation towards space, and orientation in time (Lane and diStefano 1992). Each dimension reflects a value with behaviors and attitudes.

For example, the way people see themselves affects their cultural orientation, which in turn affects socialization characteristics. The perception of people as "good" as described by Theory Y, or as a mixture of "good" and "bad," leads to an emphasis on the value of learning and development. We expect that in orientations perceiving human nature as positive, successful socialization processes are those that encourage learning. Organizational commitment and performance are derived through shaping newcomers' attitudes and behaviors. A supervisor with a perception of people as "bad" as described by Theory X, however, will diminish learning opportunities and emphasize lengthy, well-structured selection processes for socialization as a waste of resources.

Proposition 3   *Relative to the negative perception of peoples' nature, a supervisor with a positive perception of peoples' nature will be more helpful to newcomers' initiation to the group and task.*

The third accommodation variable is role definition. This is an implicit or explicit agreement with the work group on what tasks one is to perform and what the priorities and time allocation for those tasks is to be (Feldman 1976; Fisher 1986). Giving and seeking information are ways a leader may influence a new employee's level of role definition. These behaviors include monitoring the performance of the employee, clarifying task objectives, deadlines, and performance expectations for the employee, and informing the employee of relevant information about important decisions, plans, and activities. Again, Yukl's leader behaviors should greatly influence the role definition process. If a leader is effective at communicating these roles and objectives, the new employee can focus on how to perform well rather than focusing on what should be done. Further, findings related to the amount of initiation of structure that a supervisor engages in would suggest this relationship as well

(Yukl 2002). Predictably, Bauer and Green (1998) found that role clarity was predicted by manager clarifying behavior. In addition, it has been found that LMX is positively related to role clarity (Graen and Schiemann 1978). Therefore, we propose that the more a leader attempts to clarify roles, the more role definition an employee should experience.

Proposition 4 *To the extent that a leader effectively engages in giving and seeking information behaviors, LMX should be related to a new employee's perception of role definition.*

Individuals from cultures in which the primary mode of activity is "doing" are likely to work hard, be high achievers, and maximize their time at work. Conversely, in a "being" mode of activity individuals are likely to work only as much as needed to be able to live (Adler 1997). We expect that an organization with supervisors functioning in a "doing" mode will define a successful socialization process as comprehensive, broad with depth, and one with criteria, and performance measures reflecting expectations of hard work. We also believe that an organization functioning in a "being" mode may not even define successful socialization. Where a definition does exist, we expect that the socialization carries different expectations regarding productivity.

Proposition 5 *Relative to a supervisor with a "being" mode, a supervisor with a "doing" mode will engage in socialization processes that will reflect expectations of hard work, leading to a clearer role definition.*

Finally, the fourth accommodation variable is congruence of evaluation. This refers to the extent to which an employee and a supervisor similarly evaluate the employee's progress and performance in the organization. In this case, no single set of behaviors seems to be able to capture the "dynamic" and "relational" character of this variable. Three of Yukl's categories seem to be related. Giving and seeking information, building relationships, and influencing people all seem to have something to add in the prediction of perceived congruent evaluation. The more a leader seeks work-related, specific samples of an employee's work, the more accurate the evaluation should be (Komaki 1986). The more "positive" an employee feels about the leader, as is true with high LMX relationships (Liden et al. 1997), the more likely that individual will want to remain a member of that work group and, therefore, the more likely the employee should be to accept the leader's evaluation of performance (Forsyth 1990). These findings may be stronger in cases in which the leader and member are in agreement about the LMX status of their relationship (Cogliser et al. 1999). In addition, it seems reasonable to posit that the more the leader recognizes and rewards an employee as well as motivates him or her, the more likely that employee will agree when the leader makes positive or negative evaluations in the future.

Proposition 6 *LMX will be positively related to congruence of evaluation.*

When newcomers to the organization feel that they have been provided with guidance and support during pre-entry and entry phases of socialization, they should feel a greater sense of obligation to the organization than is true of new hires who perceive a lower degree of support (Gouldner 1960). This sense of obligation should in turn translate into behavioral and attitudinal outcomes that benefit the organization.

Proposition 7   *Initiation to the group, initiation to the task, employee perception of role definition, and leader–member congruence of job performance evaluation should all be positively related to perceived support from the organization, and perceived obligation to the organization.*

Proposition 8   *Degree of perceived obligation to the organization and perceived support from the organization are positively related to job satisfaction, commitment, intention to stay, job performance, and creative behavior.*

11.2.3 Disengagement/exit

A wide range of antecedents of employee turnover has been discovered (Griffeth and Hom 1995), but findings for leadership as an antecedent are inconsistent. Although some studies have found a negative relation between LMX and turnover (Graen et al. 1982; Ferris 1985), the overall consensus based on Gerstner and Day's (1997) meta-analysis is that there is not a reliable relation between the two variables. One possible reason for the lack of consistency in this relationship may be that low LMX employees are often successful in switching supervisors. In this case, employees may withdraw from the dyad, but not from the organization.

One possible research approach that might be taken to better understand the role that leaders may play in subordinate exit decisions is to integrate psychological contracts theory with LMX as recommended by Rousseau (1998). Perhaps over time, the employer–employee obligations as identified through leader–member interaction may no longer be satisfying to the subordinate. Perhaps resources and support that were instrumental to subordinates early in their tenure in the organization are not seen as being as useful after newcomers transition into becoming incumbents. The focus on career commitment over organizational commitment among many employees today may lead individuals to build as much career-enhancing knowledge, skills, and abilities (KSAs) as possible in an organization, and then move on to another organization where additional KSAs can be obtained. Such behaviors are consistent with the concept of "boundaryless careers" (e.g. Arthur and Rousseau 1996). Individuals who view their careers as boundaryless tend to exit the organization when they feel that progress toward their long-term career needs is not being made. In essence, employees view the employer–employee relationship as temporary, such that there is no felt obligation to remain in the organization when the organization can no longer provide desired career enhancement opportunities or support. To the extent that leaders understand the boundaryless careers perspective adopted by many employees, they will endeavor to provide as many career-enhancing opportunities as possible to high LMX members as a way of retaining them for a longer time.

Most LMX research has employed cross-sectional designs, and the few longitudinal studies have tended to focus on the first year of employment. The emphasis has been on the antecedents and consequences of LMX, with little attention being paid to the maintenance of LMX relationships across long periods of time (cf. Lee and Jablin 1995). Longitudinal research is needed that examines LMX over the full tenure of dyads (e.g. Wakabayashi et al. 1988) to better understand processes related to the maintenance or decline of leader–member relationships and the concomitant perceptions of the employer–employee relationship. For example, it is likely that after newcomers understand their roles as well as group and organizational norms, and have developed their own network contacts, the immediate superior may no longer play the dominant role in their organizational and career development that was evident earlier in their tenure. After becoming acclimated into the organization, employee views of the organization may be based more on self-observation and conversations with mentors and colleagues than with the immediate superior per se. Similarly, employee perceptions of the employer–employee relationship may be less based on the influence of immediate superiors.

11.3 The moderating influence of socialization tactics on the relation between LMX and the employer–employee relationship

So far, we have discussed the role of LMX in shaping and defining the relationship between the employee and the organization. Studies have shown that LMX quality has important relations with affective reactions of employees to their jobs and the organization, as well as work behaviors of employees (Gerstner and Day 1997; Liden et al. 1997; Erdogan and Liden 2002). In addition, when employees have high LMXs, they tend to perceive higher levels of support from the organization (Eisenberger et al. 2002). Thus, LMX is related to the development of a high-quality relationship between the employee and the organization, as evidenced by greater obligations and contributions to the organization, and greater perceived support received from the organization.

Given its relationship with important employee attitudes such as job satisfaction, organizational commitment, and turnover intentions, and employee behaviors such as employee performance, creativity, and innovative behaviors (Gerstner and Day 1997; Liden et al. 1997; Erdogan and Liden, 2002; Tierney and Farmer, in press), LMX is an important factor shaping the nature of the relationship between the employee and the organization. However, it is important to remember that leaders as socialization agents operate within the context of the broader organizational socialization programs. Organizations have different approaches to socializing newcomers. Some organizations adopt a more formal and systematic approach to employee socialization, whereas other organizations deal with each newcomer in a unique way. The ability of leaders to influence employee outcomes may be enhanced or limited, based on the organizational context in which the leader–member relationship develops. Therefore, we now turn our attention to the characteristics of organizational socialization programs, and their potential effects on the way in which LMX influences the development of the employer–employee relationship for newcomers. An overview of the relationships we propose in this section is presented in Figure 11. 2.

11.3.1 Socialization tactics

Van Maanen and Schein (1979) developed one of the most well-known typologies describing the different approaches organizations utilize when socializing their new employees. We will use this typology to examine the differing role of LMX for employer–employee relationships in different organizations. Van Maanen and Schein defined six organizational socialization tactics, each of them consisting of a bipolar continuum. Organizations adopting a *collective* (as opposed to individual) approach to socialization group newcomers together and put them through common experiences, rather than presenting each newcomer with unique experiences. *Formal* (versus informal) socialization tactics involve removing the newcomer from the reality of the actual work environment, rather than training newcomers on the job. In organizations following *sequential* (versus random) tactics, newcomers follow a pre-defined set of steps to reach their target position, instead of following steps that are ambiguous or changing. *Fixed* (versus variable) socialization tactics present newcomers with detailed and specific information regarding the career steps available to them, rather than presenting newcomers with a variable timetable and little information regarding the time to complete each step. In organizations following *serial* (versus disjunctive) tactics, newcomers benefit from having role models who prepare them for their future roles. Finally, *investiture* (versus divestiture) tactics accept employees as they arrive into the organization and

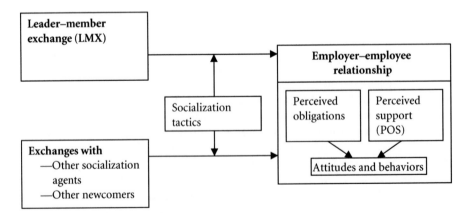

Figure 11.2. *The moderating influence of socialization tactics on the relation between LMX and the employer–employee relationship.*

attempt to utilize their existing skills, as opposed to trying to modify the identity of newcomers to fit the organizational mold.

Jones (1986) suggested that collective, formal, sequential, fixed, serial, and investiture tactics could be classified as "institutionalized" socialization efforts, whereas individual, informal, random, variable, disjunctive, and divestiture tactics could be referred to as "individualized" tactics. In other words, organizational socialization tactics range from those adopting a formal, structured, and planned program of newcomer socialization, to those using a unique, relatively unplanned, and loosely structured approach. Even though Jones (1986) showed that the six tactics were highly correlated, there are arguments against abandoning these six dimensions in favor of a single continuum. Bauer et al. (1998) suggested that the overlap among six dimensions might be due to overlap in items, as opposed to insufficient conceptual distinctiveness. Furthermore, Ashforth et al. (1997) showed that the six-factor model fit better to data compared to the one-factor model. For ease of presentation, we refer to collections of tactics as individualized and institutionalized, without assuming that the six tactics can be collapsed for measurement purposes.

Although Van Maanen and Schein (1979) did not discuss factors that determine why organizations select one tactic over another, we can expect that this selection will be heavily influenced by national culture (Taylor et al. 1996). For example, there are likely to be systematic differences in socialization tactics between organizations in highly individualistic cultures and those in highly collectivist cultures. Within an individualistic culture like that in the United States, people learn at a very early age to value and assert their individuality and independence (Hofstede 1980). Within a collectivist culture, on the other hand, individuals learn to value group membership, loyalty, and conformity, and to subjugate their individual interests to the interests of the group (Hofstede 1980).

As Bauer et al. (1998) noted, the most obvious difference related to collectivism/ individualism pertains to the use of the individual versus collective tactic of socialization. We can expect that relative to organizations within individualist cultures, those within collectivist cultures will be more likely to adopt *collective* forms of socialization, where newcomers are put through a common set of experiences as a group (Van Maanen and Schein 1979).

An extension to the collectivism/individualism diversity is found between universalistic societies and particularistic societies (Hofstede 1980). The devotion to ethics and respect for tradition is the "Confucian Dynamism," shifting on a continuum from pluralistic to universalistic societies. While particularistic societies relate to laws as for everyone at all times, universalistic societies perceive rules as important yet adaptable to circumstances (Hofstede and Bond 1988). Relationships with friends or family members will affect one's obedience to laws. The social contract is not detailed; the strength of the relationship maintains commitment. Because the psychological contract is intentionally unstructured, we predict that particularistic organizations, more than universalistic ones, will adopt unstructured tactics. These unstructured tactics are flexible in that they reduce the use of written and formal components of the social–psychological contract to yet be determined by relationships among the newcomers and between newcomers and all others.

Proposition 9 *Relative to supervisors and newcomers within universalistic cultures, those within pluralistic cultures will be likely to encounter unstructured tactics of socialization.*

11.3.2 Socialization tactics as a moderator of the relationship between LMX, POS, and perceived obligations toward the organization

Socialization tactics provide the context in which individuals react to and benefit from the relationships they form with their leaders. In organizations that adopt a structured, collective, and formal approach to socialization, LMX will have a relatively limited effect on shaping the employer–employee relationship. Instead, employees will interact with, and receive information and support from, multiple agents including the immediate supervisor, other managers in the organization, other newcomers in the organization, and the organization itself, as represented by departments involved in the formal socialization processes. Therefore, we contend that in organizations utilizing institutionalized tactics, employees will be able to differentiate the relationships they form with their leaders and with the overall organization. Immediate supervisors will be perceived as one agent among many that constitute the "employer" side of the employer–employee relationship. Thus, employees will have a lower tendency to equate the support they receive from their immediate supervisor to the support they receive from the organization. In other words, the positive relationship observed between LMX and POS (Eisenberger et al. 2002) will be weaker. Consequently, in organizations utilizing institutionalized tactics, the link between LMX and perceived obligations toward the organization will be weaker.

On the other hand, in organizations utilizing individualized socialization tactics, LMX will exert a more important impact on the development of the employer–employee relationship. Given that employees need to gather the resources, information, and support to perform well and adjust to their new jobs through their individual means, the success of an individualized socialization program will depend strongly on the LMX quality of the newcomer. Thus, under individualized systems, LMX will have a stronger effect on the development of the employer–employee relationship. Consequently, newcomers will have a greater tendency to equate supervisory support with organizational support, leading to higher levels of obligations resulting from LMX.

Proposition 10 *LMX will be more positively related to POS and perceived obligations toward the organization when the organization uses individualized tactics. The positive relationship between LMX, POS, and perceived obligations toward the organization will be weaker when the organization is using institutionalized tactics.*

11.3.3 Socialization tactics as moderators of the relationship between LMX and employee attitudes

Employee attitudes such as job satisfaction, organizational commitment, and turnover intentions are important indicators of the employer–employee relationship for newcomers. Studies have shown that institutionalized and individualized tactics have different effects on employee attitudes. Institutionalized tactics have been positively related to job satisfaction/attachment to job (Baker and Feldman 1990; Ashforth and Saks 1996; Ashforth et al. 1998), organizational attachment (Allen and Meyer 1990; Baker and Feldman 1990; Laker and Steffy 1995; Ashforth and Saks 1996; Ashforth et al. 1998), and information acquisition (Saks and Ashforth 1997), and negatively related to turnover intentions (Ashforth et al. 1998; Riordan et al. 2001). There are at least three alternative explanations for this consistent finding. First, institutionalized tactics may give newcomers the impression that the organization cares about its employees. Individuals perceive greater organizational support when the organization provides them with discrete, developmental experiences (Wayne et al. 1997). Because institutionalized tactics represent a more structured, planned, and systematic approach to newcomer socialization, employees may perceive the organization as providing greater support to them and caring about them when the organization adopts institutionalized tactics. Supporting this explanation, Riordan et al. (2001) showed that organization-based self-esteem mediated the relationship between several institutional tactics and employee attitudes. Second, studies showed that institutionalized tactics were positively correlated with perceived value congruence (Grant and Bush 1996), person–organization fit (Cable and Parsons 2001), and actual changes in the newcomer (Ashforth and Saks 1996; Cable and Parsons 2001), and person–job fit mediated the relationship between institutional tactics and attitudes (Riordan et al. 2001). By providing newcomers with systematic and well-planned, consistent, and formal socialization programs, organizations may facilitate employee adjustment to the organization, and may modify employee values to fit with those of the organization. When employee values are congruent with those of the organization, employees will experience less internal conflict, and will have more positive attitudes. Finally, institutional tactics are related to lower levels of role ambiguity and conflict (Jones 1986), suggesting that institutional tactics may lead to more positive attitudes through reduced stress.

Some of the benefits of institutional tactics may be supplied, and some of the disadvantages of individualized tactics may be alleviated, through the relationships individuals form with their leaders. Thus, we expect socialization tactics to moderate the effects of LMX on employee attitudes. In organizations following individualized tactics, the success of newcomer socialization will be an important function of the relationships newcomers form with their leaders. Therefore, the immediate supervisor will be a central organizational agent affecting the process by which the employer–employee relationship is shaped for newcomers.

Under individualized tactics, the organization does not provide structure or control the socialization experiences of newcomers. Therefore, the degree to which the socialization is successful depends on the extent to which newcomers receive support, information, and developmental experiences that allow them to learn the ropes and be incorporated into organizational networks. As opposed to benefiting from information, training, and role modeling provided to all newcomers in a uniform manner, newcomers in organizations using individualized tactics are left to get these resources and support through other means. Therefore, LMX quality should have a strong and positive relation with the development of positive attitudes for newcomers. Studies show that LMX is positively related to perceptions of support from the organization (Wayne et al. 1997) and mentoring (Scandura and Schriesheim 1994; Thibodeaux and Lowe 1996), and negatively related to job stress (Gerstner and Day 1997; Bernas and Major 2000). Thus, under individualized social-ization, employee affective relations will depend on the relationship quality between leaders and members such that there will be a positive relation between LMX and employee attitudes.

We expect a different pattern of relationship between LMX and employee affective reactions in organizations using institutionalized socialization tactics. Individuals who are unable to form high LMXs with their leaders will experience lower levels of dissatisfaction if the organization is using institutionalized tactics. These low LMX individuals will benefit from the systematic information provided to them and the planned and structured treatment they receive from the organization, especially because they do not have access to the important resources provided to high LMX members. However, high LMX employees may find that the institutional tactics sub-stitute for some of the information and support they receive from their leaders. Forming a high-quality exchange with the leader will still be satisfying, and thus will be positively related with employee attitudes, but employees are no longer depend-ent on receiving information, mentoring, or support from their leaders to reduce their stress levels, to assess perceived organizational support, or to fit with their jobs or the organization. Thus, we expect that LMX will show a positive but weaker rela-tion with employee attitudes, owing to the information and guidance received from the organization as part of the institutional efforts to socialize the new employee.

Proposition 11   *The relation between LMX and employee attitudes (job satisfaction, organizational commitment, and intentions to stay) will be more positive when the organization uses individualized tactics. In organizations using institutionalized tactics, LMX will exhibit a positive, albeit weaker relation with employee attitudes.*

11.3.4 Socialization tactics as moderators of the relationship between LMX and employee behaviors

Employee behaviors are important indicators of employer–employee relationships and demonstrate the degree of effort the employee is willing to spend to further the goals of the organization. Socialization tactics have been related to employee behav-iors, as well as attitudes. An interesting conclusion of these studies is that, even though institutional tactics are positively related to employee attitudes, they are also related to a "custodial role orientation," or accepting the status quo and a narrow role definition, whereas individualized tactics have been related to innovative role orien-tation (Allen and Meyer 1990; Ashforth and Saks 1996), goal-oriented behaviors (Laker and Steffy 1995), and superior performance (Ashforth and Saks 1996). It seems that while institutionalized tactics have the benefit of providing employees with more direction, ensuring employee fit with the organization, indicating support for newcomers and reducing their stress levels, they also have the disadvantage of providing employees with more exact performance standards, and limiting the range of behaviors employees are expected to demonstrate.

Ashforth and Saks (1996) argued that institutionalized methods might also be used to teach newcomers innovative behaviors. According to this argument, there is nothing inherent in institutionalized tactics that would lead to low levels of performance or creativity, and institutionalized socialization is merely a process by which employees learn the expectations of the organization. However, through collective, formal, sequential, fixed, and serial tactics, institutionalized approaches reinforce a limited range of behaviors employees are expected to demonstrate, and these behaviors are usually derived from the dominant behavioral patterns in the organization. Given that innovativeness and flexibility may not always go hand in hand with procedures and structure (Tesluk et al. 1997), it is reasonable to expect that institutionalized tactics will limit the range of behaviors employees may demonstrate. Supporting this argument, Ashforth et al. (1998) found that mechanistic organizations, or organizations that encourage repetitive production of goods and services, were more likely to use institutionalized socialization tactics. They also demonstrated that organic organizations, or organizations designed to be adaptive and fluid, were more likely to use individualized socialization tactics. Thus, we contend that institutionalized tactics would be associated with lower levels of creative behaviors.

We also expect a negative relation between institutionalized socialization tactics and contextual performance. Contextual performance includes behaviors that are not prescribed by role descriptions and support the organizational social system (Borman and Motowidlo 1993). Examples of contextual performance include organizational citizenship behaviors such as helping train new employees and cooperating with team members. Contextual performance requires employees to go beyond their narrow job descriptions and perform behaviors that are not explicitly prescribed. Thus, we expect lower levels of contextual behaviors in organizations utilizing institutionalized socialization tactics.

Proposition 12 *Institutionalized socialization tactics will be negatively related to employee creative behaviors and contextual behaviors.*

LMX has also been positively related to employee behaviors such as job performance (Gerstner and Day 1997), organizational citizenship behaviors (Settoon et al. 1996; Wayne et al. 1997; Tierney et al. 2002), and employee creativity/innovative behaviors (Basu and Green 1997; Tierney et al. 1999). Two theories that have been useful in explaining the relationship between LMX and work behaviors are social exchange and expectancy theories. Consistent with social exchange theory (Gouldner 1960; Blau 1964), when individuals form high-quality exchanges with their leaders, they have a desire to reciprocate with their leaders by behaving in ways that will benefit the leader. Therefore, LMX is likely to be related to positive employee behaviors benefiting the leader, such as job and contextual performance. In addition, based on expectancy theory (Vroom 1964), employees will be more motivated to perform when they perceive high levels of effort–performance and performance–reward linkages. High LMX employees may receive greater levels of information, support, and other resources from their leaders and, therefore, they may perceive greater effort–performance linkage. Supporting this argument, supervisory support has been found to be related to creative self-efficacy of employees (Tierney and Farmer 2002). In addition, studies show that high LMX employees receive higher performance ratings than is warranted by their objective performance (Duarte et al. 1994), and experience faster salary progression (Wayne et al. 1999) and, therefore, they may perceive greater performance–reward linkage. Thus, provided that there are no constraints on individual performance, LMX is likely to be positively related to employee behaviors.

In organizations with individualized socialization tactics, high LMX individuals are likely to perform at high levels given the lack of constraints on their behaviors and their greater motivation to perform. In these organizations, performance of low LMX individuals is likely to suffer. Low LMX individuals will not feel the desire to reciprocate to their leaders in a positive way, given the limited amount of support low LMX employees usually receive from leaders. In addition, the effort–performance linkage is likely to be weak for low LMX individuals in organizations using individualized socialization. Because the organization does not provide individuals with a systematic and planned experience to prepare them for their new jobs or to ensure fit with the job and organization, the newcomers are left to the discretion of their leaders and other organizational agents who may teach them the ropes, show them acceptable behaviors, and provide them with essential resources. For low LMX individuals, these resources and experiences are likely to be missing, leading to low levels of performance and citizenship behaviors. In summary, we expect a strong, positive relation between LMX and employee positive behaviors in organizations utilizing individualized socialization tactics.

In organizations using institutionalized socialization tactics, we expect a different pattern of relationship between LMX and behaviors. Institutionalized tactics teach employees a given set of behaviors and provide greater fit with the job and the organization. In those organizations using institutionalized tactics, employees are taught a set of acceptable behaviors they will have to demonstrate in their new jobs. Because institutionalized tactics will likely lead to greater levels of homogeneity in the performance of newcomers, the relationship between LMX and employee work behaviors will be much weaker in these organizations. Both low LMX and high LMX employees will demonstrate acceptable levels of performance under institutionalized tactics, because they will learn what is expected of them and will demonstrate those behaviors in a satisfactory manner. Low LMX employees will most likely demonstrate higher performance than they would under individualized tactics, given that they will receive support, information, and resources from the organization. High LMX employees will experience some performance loss under institutionalized tactics compared to individualized tactics. The specific information regarding how to do their jobs will limit the range of behaviors they may demonstrate. Furthermore, they will not be able to benefit from their high LMX status under a fixed and serial system in which their advancement opportunities are predetermined as opposed to flexible and negotiable. Thus, we expect work behaviors of high and low LMX employees not to differ substantially from each other in organizations using institutionalized systems.

Proposition 13 *The relation between LMX and employee work behaviors (creative behaviors, task performance, and contextual performance) will be positive when the organization uses individualized tactics. In organizations using institutionalized tactics, LMX will not be significantly related to employee work behaviors.*

In summary, we contend that under institutionalized socialization tactics, LMX will have a smaller role in the development of the employer–employee relationship, as evidenced by a weaker relationship between LMX, employee attitudes, behaviors, and support received from the organization. An important question at this point is to recognize the agents and exchanges that will replace LMX, when institutionalized tactics are being used. When organizations use institutionalized tactics, employees interact with a multitude of organizational agents. Because they go through the socialization process together with other newcomers, their exchanges with these team members will gain importance in determining the development of the employer–employee relationship. Because employees are removed from the actual work environment, they will interact with the training department or trainers frequently. The career stages they will follow may be communicated to them through the HR department, which will constitute an important agent affecting the attachment of new employees to the organization. Thus, exchanges newcomers form with the organizational agents who are part of the newcomer socialization process (*socialization agents*), as well as other newcomers with whom they interact, will have a strong relationship with employee attitudes, behaviors, and support received from the organization.

Proposition 14 *When the organization is using institutionalized tactics, the support received and relationships formed with socialization agents, and with other newcomers will have a stronger relation with employee attitudes, behaviors, and POS. When the organization is using individualized tactics, the relationships formed with socialization agents and other newcomers will reveal a weaker relation with employee attitudes, behaviors, and POS.*

11.4 Conclusion

Leaders play a critical role in the socialization of new employees, and a key function of socialization is to assist the newcomers in developing a realistic sense of the obligations that employers and employees need to fulfill for one another. Although we portrayed the immediate leader as being more salient to newcomer socialization than formal, institutionalized socialization practices, we offered propositions suggesting that these formal practices may moderate the relations between leader socialization behaviors and outcomes. Finally, we proposed that organizational and national culture may influence the role of leaders in the socialization process.

References

Adler, N. J. (1997). *International Dimensions of Organizational Behavior*. Boston: PWS/Kent.

Allen, N. J., and Meyer, J. P. (1990). "Organizational socialization tactics: A longitudinal analysis of links to newcomers' commitment and role orientation." *Academy of Management Journal*, 33: 847–58.

Arthur, M. B., and Rousseau, D. M. (1996). "The boundaryless career as a new employment principle," in M. G. Arthur and D. M. Rousseau (eds.), *The Boundaryless Career: A New Employment Principle for a New Organizational Era* (New York: Oxford University Press), pp. 3–20.

Ashforth, B. E., and Saks, A. M. (1996). "Socialization tactics: Longitudinal effects on newcomer adjustment." *Academy of Management Journal*, 39: 149–78.

—— Saks, A. M., and Lee, R. T. (1997). "On the dimensionality of Jones' (1986) measures of organizational socialization tactics." *International Journal of Selection and Assessment*, 5: 200–14.

—— Saks, A. M., and Lee, R. T. (1998). "Socialization and newcomer adjustment: The role of organizational context." *Human Relations*, 51: 897–926.

Baker, H. E. III, and Feldman, D. C. (1990). "Strategies of organizational socialization and their impact on newcomer adjustment." *Journal of Managerial Issues*, 2: 198–212.

Basu, R., and Green, S. G. (1997). "Leader–member exchange and transformational leadership: An empirical examination of innovative behaviors in leader–member dyads." *Journal of Applied Social Psychology*, 27: 477–99.

Bauer, T. N. (1994). "A longitudinal test of recruiting and leadership influence on newcomer socialization and performance." Dissertation Abstracts International (UMI No. 9512926).

—— and Green, S. G. (1996). "Development of leader–member exchange: A longitudinal test." *Academy of Management Journal*, 39: 1538–67.

—— and Green, S. G. (1998). "Testing the combined effects of newcomer information seeking and manager behavior on socialization." *Journal of Applied Psychology*, 83: 72–83.

—— Morrison, E. W., and Callister, R. R. (1998). "Organizational socialization: A review and directions for future research," in G. R. Ferris (ed.), *Research in Personnel and Human Resource Management*, Vol. 16 (New Greenwich, CT: JAI Press), pp. 149–214.

Bernas, K. H., and Major, D. A. (2000). "Contributors to stress resistance: Testing a model of women's work–family conflict." *Psychology of Women Quarterly*, 24: 170–8.

Blau, P. M. (1964). *Exchange and Power in Social Life*. New York: John Wiley & Sons.

Borman, W. C., and Motowidlo, S. J. (1993). "Expanding the criterion domain to include elements of contextual performance," in N. Schmitt and W. Borman (eds.), *Personnel Selection in Organizations* (New York: Jossey-Bass), pp. 71–98.

Bureau of National Affairs, Inc. (1988). Recruiting and selection procedures (PPFS No. 146). Washington, DC.

Cable, D. M., and Parsons, C. K. (2001). "Socialization tactics and person-organization fit." *Personnel Psychology*, 54: 1–23.

Campion, M. A., and Mitchell, M. M. (1986). "Management turnover: Experiential differences between former and current managers." *Personnel Psychology*, 39: 57–69.

Cascio, W. F. (1991). *Managing Human Resources*. New York: McGraw-Hill.

Cogliser, C. C., Schriesheim, C. A., Scandura, T. A., and Neider, L. L. (1999). "Balanced and unbalanced leadership relationships: A three-sample investigation into the outcomes associated with four different types of leader-member exchanges." Paper presented at the National Meeting of the Academy of Management, Chicago, August.

Dansereau, F., Graen, G., and Haga, W. J. (1975). "A vertical dyad linkage approach to leadership within formal organizations: A longitudinal investigation of the role making process." *Organizational Behavior and Human Performance*, 13: 46–78.

Dienesch, R. M., and Liden, R. C. (1986). "Leader–member exchange model of leadership: A critique and further development." *Academy of Management Review*, 11: 618–34.

Duarte, N. T., Goodson, J. R., and Klich, N. R. (1994). "Effects of dyadic quality and duration on performance appraisal." *Academy of Management Journal*, 37: 499–521.

Edwards, J. R. (1991). "Person-job fit: A conceptual integration, literature review, and methodological critique," in C. L. Cooper and I. T. Robertson (eds.), *International Review of Industrial and Organizational Psychology*, Vol. 6 (New York: Wiley), pp. 283–357.

Eisenberger, R., Stinglhamber, F., Vandenberghe, C., Sucharski, I. L., and Rhoades, L. (2002). "Perceived supervisor support: Contributions to perceived organizational support and employee retention." *Journal of Applied Psychology*, 87: 565–73.

Erdogan, B., and Liden, R. C. (2002). "Social exchanges in the workplace: A review of recent developments and future research directions in leader–member exchange theory," in L. L. Neider and C. A. Schriesheim (eds.), *Leadership* (Greenwich, CT: Information Age Publishing), pp. 65–114.

Feldman, D. C. (1976). "A contingency theory of socialization." *Administrative Science Quarterly*, 21: 433–52.

Ferris, G. R. (1985). "Role of leadership in the employee withdrawal process: A constructive replication." *Journal of Applied Psychology*, 70: 777–81.

Fisher, C. D. (1986). "Organizational socialization: An integrative review," in G. R. Ferris (ed.), *Research in Personnel and Human Resource Management*, Vol. 4 (Greenwich, CT: JAI Press), pp. 101–45.

Forsyth, D. R. (1990). *Group Dynamics*. Pacific Grove, CA: Brooks/Cole.

Gerstner, C. R., and Day, D. V. (1997). "Meta-analytic review of leader–member exchange theory: Correlates and construct issues." *Journal of Applied Psychology*, 82: 827–44.

Gist, M. E., and Mitchell, T. R. (1992). "Self-efficacy: A theoretical analysis of its determinants and malleability." *Academy of Management Review*, 17: 183–211.

Goldstein, I. L., and Ford, J. K. (2002). *Training in Organizations: Needs Assessment, Development, and Evaluation*, 4th edn. Belmont, CA: Wadsworth/Thomson Learning.

Gouldner, A. W. (1960). "The norm of reciprocity: A preliminary statement." *American Sociological Review*, 25: 161–78.

Graen, G., Liden, R. C., and Hoel, W. (1982). "Role of leadership in the employee withdrawal process." *Journal of Applied Psychology*, 67: 868–72.

—— and Scandura, T. A. (1987). "Toward a psychology of dyadic organizing." *Research on Organizational Behavior*, 9: 175–208.

—— and Schiemann, W. (1978). "Leader–member agreement: A vertical dyad linkage approach." *Journal of Applied Psychology*, 63: 175–208.

Grant, E. S., and Bush, A. J. (1996). "Salesforce socialization tactics: Building organizational value congruence." *Journal of Personal Selling & Sales Management*, 16: 17–32.

Green, S. G., and Bauer, T. N. (1995). "Supervisor mentoring by advisers: Relationships with doctoral student potential, productivity, and commitment." *Personnel Psychology*, 48: 537–61.

Griffeth, R. W., and Hom, P. W. (1995). "The employee turnover process." *Research in Personnel and Human Resources Management*, 13: 245–93.

Hackman, R. J., and Oldham, G. R. (1975). "Development of the job diagnostic survey." *Journal of Applied Psychology*, 60: 159–170.

Hofstede, G. (1980). *Culture's Consequences: International Differences in Work Related Values.* Beverly Hills, CA: Sage.

—— and Bond, M. H. (1988). "Confucius and economic growth: New trends in culture's consequences." *Organizational Dynamics*, 16: 4–21.

Jablin, F. M. (2001). "Organizational entry, assimilation, and disengagement/exit," in F. M. Jablin and L. L. Putman (eds.), *The New Handbook of Organizational Communications: Advances in Theory, Research, and Methods* (Thousand Oaks, CA: Sage), pp. 732–818.

Jones, G. R. (1986). "Socialization tactics, self-efficacy, and newcomers' adjustments to organizations." *Academy of Management Journal*, 29: 262–79.

Katz, D., and Kahn, R. L. (1978). *The Social Psychology of Organizations*, 2nd edn. New York: John Wiley & Sons.

Komaki, J. (1986). "Toward effective supervision: An operant analysis and comparison of managers at work." *Journal of Applied Psychology*, 71: 270–9.

Laker, D. R., and Steffy, B. D. (1995). "The impact of alternative socialization tactics on self-managing behavior and organizational commitment." *Journal of Social Behavior and Personality*, 10: 645–60.

Lane, H. W., and Distefano, J. J. (1992). *International Management Behavior, From Policy to Policy to Practice*, 2nd edn. Boston: PWS-Kent.

La Rocco, J. M., and Jones, A. P. (1978). "Co-worker and leader support as moderators of stress-strain relationships in work situations." *Journal of Applied Psychology*, 63: 629–34.

Lee, J., and Jablin, F. M. (1995). "Maintenance communication in superior-subordinate work relationships." *Human Communications Research*, 22: 220–57.

Lee, T. W., Ashford, S. J., Walsh, J. P., and Mowday, R. T. (1992). "Commitment propensity, organizational commitment, and voluntary turnover: A longitudinal study of organizational entry processes." *Journal of Management*, 18: 15–32.

Liden, R. C., and Graen, G. (1980). "Generalizability of the vertical dyad linkage model of leadership." *Academy of Management Journal*, 23: 451–65.

—— Sparrowe, R. T., and Wayne, S. J. (1997). "Leader–member exchange theory: The past and potential for the future." *Research in Personnel and Human Resources Management*, 15: 47–119.

—— Wayne, S. J., and Stilwell, D. (1993). "A longitudinal study on the early development of leader–member exchanges." *Journal of Applied Psychology*, 78: 662–74.

Louis, M. R., Posner, B. Z., and Powell, G. N. (1983). "The availability and helpfulness of socialization practices." *Personnel Psychology*, 36: 857–66.

Major, D. A., Kozlowski, S. W., Chao, G. T., and Gardner, P. D. (1995). "A longitudinal investigation of newcomer expectations, early socialization outcomes, and the moderating effects of role development factors." *Journal of Applied Psychology*, 80: 418–31.

Maslyn, J. M., and Uhl-Bien, M. (2001). "Leader–member exchange and its dimensions: Effects of self-effort and other's effort on relationship quality." *Journal of Applied Psychology*, 86: 697–708.

Morrison, E. W. (1995). "Information usefulness and acquisition during organizational encounter." *Management Communication Quarterly*, 9: 131–55.

Morrison, E. W. (2002). "Newcomers' relationships: The role of social network ties during socialization." *Academy of Management Journal*, 45: 1149–60.

Murphy, S. E., and Ensher, E. A. (1999). "The effects of leader and subordinate characteristics in the development of leader–member exchange quality." *Journal of Applied Social Psychology,* 29: 1371–94.

Paglis, L., Green, S. G., and Bauer, T. N. (1998). "The influence of Ph.D. student socialization on the careers of scientists." Paper presented at the Society for I/O Psychologists Meeting, Dallas.

Parsons, C. K., Liden, R. C., and Bauer, T. N. (2001). "Person perception in employment interviews," in M. London (ed.), *How People Evaluate Others in Organizations* (Mahwah, NJ: Lawrence Erlbaum), pp. 67–90.

Pierce, J. L., and Dunham, R. B. (1987). "Organizational commitment: Pre-employment propensity and initial work experiences." *Journal of Management,* 13: 163–78.

Rhoades, L., and Eisenberger, R. (2002). "Perceived organizational support: A review of the literature." *Journal of Applied Psychology,* 87: 698–714.

Riordan, C. M., Weatherly, E. W., Vandenberg, R. J., and Self, R. M. (2001). "The effects of pre-entry experiences and socialization tactics on newcomer attitudes and turnover." *Journal of Managerial Issues,* 13: 159–76.

Rousseau, D. M. (1989). "Psychological and implied contracts in organizations." *Employee Responsibilities & Rights Journal,* 2: 121–39.

—— (1990). "New hire perceptions of their own and their employer's obligations: A study of psychological contracts." *Journal of Organizational Behavior,* 11: 389–400.

—— (1998). "LMX meets the psychological contract: Looking inside the black box of leader–member exchange," in F. Dansereau and F. J. Yammarino (eds.), *Leadership: The Multiple-Level Approaches* (Stamford, CT: JAI Press), pp. 149–54.

Saks, A. M. (1992). "A self-efficacy theory of organizational socialization and work adjustment." Paper presented at the 52nd Annual Academy of Management Meeting, Las Vegas.

—— and Ashforth, B. E. (1997). "Socialization tactics and newcomer information acquisition." *International Journal of Selection and Assessment,* 5: 48–61.

Scandura, T. A., and Lankau, M. J. (1996). "Developing diverse leaders: A leader–member exchange approach." *Leadership Quarterly,* 7: 243–63.

—— and Schriesheim, C. A. (1994). "Leader–member exchange and supervisor career mentoring as complementary constructs in leadership research." *Academy of Management Journal,* 37: 1588–602.

Schein, E. H. (1968). "Organizational socialization and the profession of management." *Industrial Management Review,* 9: 1–16.

Seers, A., McGee, G. W., Serey, T. T., and Graen, G. B. (1983). "The interaction of job stress and social support: A strong inference investigation." *Academy of Management Journal,* 26: 273–84.

Seibert, S. E. (1999). "The effectiveness of facilitated mentoring: A longitudinal quasi-experiment." *Journal of Vocational Behavior,* 54: 483–502.

—— Kraimer, M. L., and Liden, R. C. (2001). "A social capital theory of career success." *Academy of Management Journal,* 44: 219–37.

Settoon, R. P., Bennett, N., and Liden, R. C. (1996). "Social exchange in organizations: The differential effects of perceived organizational support and leader member exchange." *Journal of Applied Psychology,* 81: 219–27.

Sparrowe, R. T., and Liden, R. C. (1997). "Process and structure in leader–member exchange." *Academy of Management Review,* 22: 522–52.

Sparrowe, R. T., and Liden, R. C. (1999). "Sponsorship: A Blessing and a Curse." Paper presented at the National Meetings of the Academy of Management, Chicago, August.

Sparrowe, R. T., Liden, R. C., Wayne, S. J., and Kraimer, M. L. (2001). "Social networks and the performance of individuals and groups." *Academy of Management Journal*, 44: 316–25.

Taylor, S., Beechler, S., and Napier, N. (1996). "Toward an integrative model of strategic international human resource management." *Academy of Management Review*, 21: 959–85.

Tesluk, P. E., Farr, J. L., and Klein, S. R. (1997). "Influences of organizational culture and climate on individual creativity." *Journal of Creative Behavior*, 31: 27–41.

Thibodeaux, H. F., III, and Lowe, R. H. (1996). "Convergence of leader–member exchange and mentoring: An investigation of social influence patterns." *Journal of Social Behavior and Personality*, 11: 97–114.

Tierney, P., Bauer, T. N., and Potter, R. (2002). "Extra-role behaviors among Mexican employees: The impact of leader–member exchange (LMX), group acceptance, and job attitudes." *International Journal of Selection and Assessment*, 10: 292–303.

—— and Farmer, S. M. (2002). "Creative self-efficacy: Its potential antecedents and relationship to creative performance." *Academy of Management Journal*, 45: 1137–48.

—— and Farmer, S. M. (in press). "The Pygmalion process and employee creativity." *Journal of Management*.

—— Farmer, S. M., and Graen, G. B. (1999). "An examination of leadership and employee creativity: The relevance of traits and relationships." *Personnel Psychology*, 52: 591–620.

Toffler, B. L. (1981). "Occupational role development: The changing determinants of outcomes for the individual." *Administrative Science Quarterly*, 26: 396–418.

Vandenberg, R. J., and Self, R. M. (1993). "Assessing newcomers' changing commitments to the organization during the first 6 months of work." *Journal of Applied Psychology*, 78: 557–68.

Van Maanen, J. (1975). "Police socialization: A longitudinal examination of job attitudes in an urban police department." *Administrative Science Quarterly*, 20: 207–28.

—— and Schein, E. H. (1979). "Toward a theory of organizational socialization." *Research in Organizational Behavior*, 1: 209–64.

Vroom, V. H. (1964). *Work and Motivation*. New York: Wiley.

Wakabayashi, M., Graen, G., Graen, M., and Graen, M. (1988). "Japanese management progress: Mobility into middle management." *Journal of Applied Psychology*, 73: 217–27.

Wanous, J. P. (1980). *Organizational Entry: Recruitment, Selection, and Socialization of Newcomers*. Reading, MA: Addison-Wesley.

Wayne, S. J., Liden, R. C., Kraimer, M. L., and Graf, I. K. (1999). "The role of human capital, motivation, and supervisor sponsorship in predicting career success." *Journal of Organizational Behavior*, 20: 577–95.

Wayne, S. J., Shore, L. M., and Liden, R. C. (1997). "Perceived organizational support and leader–member exchange: A social exchange perspective." *Academy of Management Journal*, 40: 82–111.

Weiss, H. M. (1990). "Learning theory and industrial and organizational psychology," in M. D. Dunnette and L. M. Hough (eds.), *Handbook of Industrial and Organizational Psychology*, 1st edn. (Palo Alto, CA: Consulting Psychologists Press), pp. 171–222.

Yukl, G. (2002). *Leadership in Organizations*, 5th edn. Upper Saddle River, NJ: Prentice Hall.

PART III

DEVELOPING AN INTEGRATIVE PERSPECTIVE OF THE EMPLOYMENT EXCHANGE; CREATING A WHOLE THAT IS MORE THAN THE SUM OF INDIVIDUAL PARTS; LOOKING TOWARD THE FUTURE; DEVELOPING A RESEARCH AGENDA

This volume is organized to provide a logical progression for readers seeking to understand the employment relationship literature. Part I presented a set of chapters on the disciplines that have provided the theoretical underpinnings for the employment relationship literature while Part II presented chapters on various constructs that focus on exchange in the employment relationship. This final part of the volume provides a forward-looking perspective on the employment relationship. With this goal in mind, each of the chapters in Part III seeks to address implications for the future of the employment relationship literature.

Chapter 12 by Taylor and Tekleab provides a comprehensive review of the psychological contracts literature as a basis for considering how this literature may best be developed in the future. They begin with a review of the varied perspectives on the meaning and conceptualization of the psychological contract over time, and discuss the implications of these historical changes. The chapter then describes some troublesome conceptual issues in the psychological contracts literature, and suggests some ways of addressing these issues prior to outlining a future research agenda.

Chapter 13 by Schalk examines changes in the employment relationship over time. He starts his chapter by tracing societal and organizational changes and the implications of these changes for the employment relationship. Schalk proposes that a new psychological contract of exchanging flexibility for employability is replacing the old exchange of security for loyalty. He also highlights changes with respect to the employee, by first examining organizational socialization, and then focusing on the changes that may occur in an employee's life course and the impact these changes may have on the employment relationship.

Chapter 14 by Tetrick focuses on measurement and research design issues pertaining to the employment relationship. She begins her chapter by discussing various conceptualizations of the employment relationship, and how these conceptualizations have been measured in the literature. She points out that while multiple measures exist for assessing the employment relationship, they differ as to whether they focus on content or process. The literature also provides many more measures of the individual-level perspective than the organization-level perspective. Tetrick concludes by providing a number of methodological suggestions for moving the employment relationship literature forward.

Chapter 15 by Hannah and Iverson focuses on implications of the employment relationship for policy and practice. At the beginning of their chapter, they discuss employment relationship as an exchange of employer inducements (HR practices and policies) and employee contributions. They then present the view that the national context influences the availability and type of HRM policies and practices that employers may use as inducements. Aspects of the national context that they highlight are employment laws, policies, regulations, and cultures. Subsequently, Hannah and Iverson discuss how the HRM policies and practices chosen by managers in organizations can influence employees' views of their employment relationships, and their attitudes and behaviours. They finish by discussing the importance of taking into account the national context when designing HRM strategies for managing the employment relationship.

In the final chapter, the editors begin by discussing the preceding chapters, and point out some implications for future research suggested by each chapter. They subsequently provide a synthesis across chapters, and suggest implications for future research in the employment relationship literature more generally.

Taking Stock of Psychological Contract Research: Assessing Progress, Addressing Troublesome Issues, and Setting Research Priorities

M. SUSAN TAYLOR AND AMANUEL G. TEKLEAB

12.1 Psychological contracts

Once the individual and the organization have chosen each other . . . the usually complex and often difficult adaptation period begins. The new employee and the organization must mutually learn to adjust to each other. In some instances, the "marriage" settles down into an easy comfortable relationship. In others, there is an abrupt separation that leaves scars with both parties. In between these two extremes are the remaining majority of cases of individual–organization adaptation; flexible accommodations that result in a never-ending series of compromises—the individual never completely obtaining all that he wants from the organization, and the latter never fully utilizing him for its own purposes. Yet each has the chance to gain something from the continuing interaction. The nature of this relationship has been characterized as a sort of psychological contract (Porter et al. 1975: 160).

Exponential growth in the psychological contract literature within the last fifteen years has made it an increasingly important domain within the organizational sciences, one that generated more than 148 citations from the literature review conducted in preparation for writing this chapter. Our opening quotation by Porter et al. (1975) is taken from the early, that is, pre-1988, references to the psychological contract appearing in the literature. It presents the contract as the nature of the exchange relationship between two parties, an individual employee and his or her organizational employer, spawned by each party's dependence on the other for the fulfillment of desires or needs, some brought into the relationship at entry, others modified or evolving over time. Being responsive to the changing needs of both parties over time through a series of flexible accommodations, the relationship often endures for a lengthy period because "each has the chance to gain something (of value) from the continuing interaction." Thus, one might assume that the relationship will end when one or both parties no longer perceive the chance of gaining something of value from the continuing exchange. While this quotation typifies many of the early references to the psychological contract, as we later explain, it also differs in several important respects from a more recent conceptualization published after 1988.

Without question, the explosion of research on the psychological contract that developed from this conceptualization has deepened our understanding of how the employment relationship functions on a day-to-day basis, is violated at some point in most relationships, and in some cases results in a severing of the relationship itself.

Yet, with these insights has come an exclusive focus on the employee's view of the psychological contract, evidence of potential conceptual redundancy, and confusion about the nature of contract violations. Thus, our objective in writing this chapter is to "take stock" of psychological contract theory and research by reviewing primarily academic writing on the topic from the earliest references appearing in the 1960s to the literature published in early 2003. We seek to: (a) determine how the contract has changed in meaning and conceptualization over time and the implications of these changes; (b) identify troublesome conceptual issues in contract research and propose ways of addressing them; and (c) on the basis of the review, set priorities for future research.

A roadmap of our chapter begins with a focused review of early references to the psychological contract and the identification of a common set of meanings, conceptualizations, and implications. Next, we explore the more recent research on the psychological contract led by the work of Denise Rousseau, identify changes in the conceptualization of the contract from recent and past research, focus on several important elements of Rousseau's conceptualization of the contract, review research testing propositions related to these elements, and recommend ways of addressing troublesome contract issues. We conclude with recommendations for future conceptual and empirical research priorities.

12.2 Early references to the psychological contract

Earliest references to the psychological contract began with the research and writing of Chris Argyris (1960) who examined the relationship that evolved between plant foremen and their employees. Argyris (1960) observed that when a foreman adopts an "understanding" management style that respects the informal culture of the employees' work group, a relationship between employees and management would evolve whereby employees would exchange higher productivity and fewer grievances for the foreman's willingness to deliver acceptable wages and employment security. Argyris (1960: 95–6) termed this relationship the *psychological work contract* and observed that it essentially simplified a foreman's relationship with his employees as well as the nature of the leadership skills required of him. At least two important points may be drawn from Argyris' early writing on the psychological work contract. First, his use of the term "psychological work contract" was intended to refer to an exchange relationship that was quite different from that associated with subsequent references to the psychological contract, one occurring between a *work group of employees* rather than an individual, and a member of management, the foreman. Second, although information about the terms of exchange is fairly limited, the terms of the exchange described by Argyris were fairly economic and specific in nature, including wages, employment security, productivity, grievances, and absenteeism.

A second early reference to the psychological contract appears in the writings of Harry Levinson and his associates (Levinson et al. 1962). These researchers used an interview methodology and examined a sample of more than 800 employees of a privately owned public utility to learn the kinds of experiences that employees undergo at work and their implications for the individuals' mental health. Early findings revealed two important results: (a) the organization tended to reciprocate employee efforts that were devoted to obtaining a satisfactory, interdependent relationship with the company, developing comfortable interpersonal relationships at work, and dealing with change; and (b) each party held strong expectations of one another in the work context and the anticipated satisfaction of these expectations motivated the continuity of the employment relationship. Borrowing from the work of Karl Menniger on the intangible aspects of contracting between therapist and patient (Menniger 1958), Levinson and his colleagues conceptualized a typically informal agreement between an individual employee and his or her employing organization whereby each party held expectations of the other that originated prior to employment, and if fulfilled, satisfied their needs in the relationship. Thus, they viewed reciprocation as the process through which the contract unfolded and was enacted from day to day. Several noteworthy points emerged from Levinson et al.'s (1962) study of the psychological contract including:

1. The two parties involved in the contract are an individual employee and the organization, represented primarily through its managers.

2. The motivation underlying the contract's formation and continuation is driven by each party's desire to fulfill a set of expectations that could not be fulfilled without the cooperation of the other. The expectations of one party were forceful in nature, compelling the other party into action. Thus, reciprocity plays an important role in the day-to-day unfolding of the psychological contract between employee and organization, such that the contribution made by one party in an attempt to fulfill the requirements of the recipient subsequently induces a return contribution by the recipient.

3. Different managers representing the organization will tend to articulate the same set of expectations, a set that is derived from its history and external environment.

4. The expectations covered by the psychological contract are complex and compelling in nature, covering a range of issues, some widely shared, others quite individualized—some highly specific and others quite general in nature.

5. Psychological contracting is a dynamic process whereby parties negotiate changes in their expectations over time due to changes in their circumstances, and an initially limited understanding of the contributions of the other.

Psychologically, the contract provides the structure and support that each party needs to satisfy a natural need for dependence, while also allowing them to negotiate a satisfying and more secure interdependent relationship over time. The development of a quality relationship frees individual energy that can be diverted into organizational behaviors such as enhanced task productivity, the assumption of greater organizational responsibility, and further growth and development.

Schein (1965, 1970, 1980) was also an important early contributor to the literature on the psychological contract. Schein viewed the contract as providing a critical foundation for the *employment relationship*; his conceptualization of it was much the same as Levinson et al. (1962). Yet Schein (1970) made unique contributions to the contract literature in the following ways: (a) by being the first to discuss the importance of a strong match between the expectations of each party and the contributions of the other and the consequences of a poor match; (b) by proposing the importance of allowing each party to retain some power to enforce its view of the contract; and (c) by emphasizing the criticality of the contract as an interaction between two parties, and thus the importance of considering the perspective of each.

In terms of the match between each party's expectations and the other's contributions, Schein proposed that a poor match would affect employees' job satisfaction, commitment, loyalty, and job performance. This match, or its inverse, has become known as contract violation in the literature, and Schein himself seems to have made the earliest known reference to *contract violations*, proposing that violations of implicit expectations closely related to an employee's sense of self-worth were likely to evoke the strongest reactions or responses. Schein (1970) also argued the importance of forming employment relationships that permitted both the employee and the organization some power to enforce their views of the contract; otherwise, he believed that employees were unlikely to accept and honor the organization's authority in the work setting. He also emphasized the nature of the expectations covered in the contract, proposing that it was essential for the contract not only to satisfy an employee's economic and social needs, for example, pay, benefits, job security, workplace harmony, satisfying work relationships, etc., but also to provide opportunities for self-actualization through providing discretion on the job and opportunities for self-development.

Finally, Schein (1980: 99) emphasized the criticality of viewing the contract as an interaction between two parties and its accompanying psychological dynamics. He argued:

ultimately the relationship between the individual and the organization is interactive, unfolding through mutual influence and mutual bargaining to establish and reestablish a workable, psychological contract. We cannot understand the psychological dynamics if we look only to the individual's motivations or only to the organizational conditions and practices. The two interact in a complex fashion that demands a systems approach, capable of handling interdependent phenomena.

Thus, Schein (1980) stressed the interactive nature of the contract and was the first to caution about a tendency to focus on only one party's perspective, if one truly hoped to understand the interdependent nature of the relationship.

Last but not least, Porter et al.'s (1975) writing on the psychological contract is quite consistent with the work of Levinson et al. (1962) and Schein (1965, 1970, 1980). The uniqueness of Porter et al.'s (1975) contribution came in recognizing that the nature of the contract might often be limited by the fundamental design of most organizations. This design makes the joint optimization of both individual and organizational requirements impossible, and in encourages each party to sub-optimize their outcomes. To address this problem, they proposed a major redesign of organizational structure and processes, a redesign further developed by Lawler (1987) in his book *High Involvement Management.* The researchers also identified the process of individual adaptation as a mechanism whereby the individual could leave his or her imprint on the employing organization, thus creating a better overall match between both parties' expectations and contributions.

The early literature on the psychological contract includes virtually no empirical studies beyond the exploratory work of Argyris (1960) and Levinson et al. (1962), described above. One noteworthy exception is research conducted by Kotter (1973), who was heavily influenced by the work of Schein (1970), and examined the degree of match between the expectations and contributions of a ninety-manager sample and their employing organizations. His results supported hypotheses that greater employee job satisfaction, greater productivity, and reduced turnover result from contracts where there was a stronger match between what each party expected and the other intended to contribute, rather than simply from the absolute level of met expectations. Kotter's (1973) study is discussed in greater detail in Chapter 8 of this volume on the topic of incongruence.

In addition, our literature review revealed one conceptual article, Nicholson and Johns (1985), integrating the psychological contract concept into the literature on the determinants of absenteeism. Departing from traditional individual difference-based views of absenteeism, Nicholson and Johns (1985) proposed a typology of absence contexts based on two dimensions: (a) the salience of the organization's or subunit's absence culture, defined as "the set of shared understandings about absence legitimacy . . . and the established custom and practice of employee absence behavior and its control" (p. 136); and (b) the level of trust in the psychological contract (operationalized as high or low discretion tasks with their accompanying expecta-tions). Our review identified no empirical tests of propositions relating the employ-ees' trust in the psychological contract to their absence behavior, but the Nicholson and Johns (1975) paper remains a precursor of subsequent work that has begun to use the psychological contract as part of the conceptual explanation advanced for a growing range of phenomena (West and Cardy 1997; McGaughey and Liesch 2002).

Finally, we note one applied article from this period, Dunahee and Wangler (1974), that provided an interesting discussion of how a spiraling series of negative actions and counteractions between parties may result when an employee, generally possessing less power to enforce his or her view of the contract (Schein 1980), decides that the contract is inequitable, decreases his or her contributions to it, and is unresponsive to organizational attempts to enforce its view of the agreements. Dunahee and Wangler's (1974) presentation of a downwardly spiraling set of increas-ingly severe actions that ultimately result in the termination of the contract is interesting in its implications for assessing validly the state of the employment rela-tionship and preventing its unnecessary termination.

12.2.1 Summary

Overall, the early period of psychological contract development is characterized by limited conceptualization, virtually no empirical research, and one attempt to integrate the contract into conceptual explanations of other phenomena, in this case employee absence from work (Nicholson and Johns 1985). Excepting Argyris (1960), all early references to the psychological contract conceptualized it as an exchange relationship between an individual employee and his or her organizational employer (represented most commonly by individual managers). The contract provides a structure to the employment relationship and is motivated by the parties' desire to satisfy a set of valued expectations, both implicit and explicit, through their relationship with one another. Contract expectations are strong in nature and compel the other party to action, while covering a wide range of content including economic, social, intrinsically motivating, and developmental outcomes. The level of match between each party's expectations and the other's contributions or its inverse, contract violation, was predicted (Schein 1970, 1980) and found (Kotter 1973) to have important implications for the employee's attitudes, performance, and continuance behavior. In general, parties are hypothesized to be most sensitive to the violation of expectations reflective of their self-worth (Schein 1980). The employee who purposefully violates a psychological contract believed to be inequitable but unchangeable may unwillingly trigger a downward spiral of increasingly severe negative actions that ultimately terminate the relationship. Finally, the psychological contract is an ongoing interaction that introduces dynamics of interdependence on the other for the satisfaction of important expectations; thus, it cannot be fully understood or affected by relying solely on the perspective of either party.

12.3 Taking stock of recent psychological contract research (1988 to 2003)

Led by the efforts of Rousseau (1989, 1990, 1995), recent, post-1988 research on the psychological contract has brought significant changes with respect to both the amount of published research and the conceptualization of the contract (Roehling 1996). Without question, Rousseau's research (e.g. 1989, 1990, 1995, 2001) has made the greatest single contribution to the conceptual development of the psychological contract and has stimulated more interest in and research on the contract in the last fourteen years than at any point in its forty-three-year history. As one reviewer of Rousseau's (1995) book noted, "*Psychological Contracts in Organizations* is not a rehash of previous ideas but a timely treatment and relevant extension of previous behavioral understandings of contracting" (Phelps 1996: 488).

Nevertheless, Rousseau's research also introduced significant changes into the very essence of the psychological contract concept as a foundation for the employment relationship. In the remainder of this section, we examine: (a) the contract definition and parties' expectations or obligations; (b) social exchange theory as one conceptual explanation for the contract and two specific social exchange relationships, perceived organizational support (POS) and the leader–member exchange (LMX), that may overlap the contract domain; (c) different assessments of the dimensionality of the contract; (d) psychological contract violations; and (e) the cognitive basis of the contract (Rousseau 2001). We identify these elements, discuss subsequent extensions proposed by other researchers where possible, review recent research testing propositions related to them, and make recommendations for addressing any controversial issues relevant to them. Note, however, that we do not focus on the employer's perspective of either the psychological contract or the employment relationship in general in this section. The literature on the employer's perspective is an important and substantial domain in and of itself, is addressed within Chapter 7 of this volume.

12.3.1 Definition and conceptualization

Consistent with most of the early contract literature reviewed above (e.g. Levinson et al. 1962; Schein 1965, 1970, 1980; Porter et al. 1975), Rousseau's (1989, 1990, 1995, 2001) writing conceptualizes the psychological contract as an unwritten agreement about the reciprocal elements of exchanges existing between an individual employee and the employing organization. Specifically, Rousseau defines the contract as "*individual beliefs*, [emphasis added] shaped by the organization, regarding the terms of an exchange agreement between individuals and their organization" (Rousseau 1995: 9). Thus, some aspects of the psychological contract between a given individual and his or her organization might differ noticeably from that of another employee in the same department, unit, or work group, while other aspects might be virtually identical. This definition has been adopted by most (e.g. Robinson et al. 1994; Robinson 1996; Morrison and Robinson 1997; Turnley and Feldman 1999) but not all researchers publishing on the contract after 1988.

Note that one aspect of Rousseau's contract definition and conceptualization stands in stark contrast to early research, that which views the psychological contract as an entity existing purely in the perceptions or eyes of the individual employee. Clearly, Rousseau's conceptualization conflicts with Schein's (1980) caveat that a focus on any single party's perspective of the contract, whether employee or organization, is unlikely to lead to a full understanding of its underlying psychodynamics. Further, as Pearce (1998) noted in reviewing Rousseau's (1995) book, "By placing the deal so thoroughly in the employee's mind, she has tended to treat any differences in perceptions between the organization's representatives and the employee as faults of the organization" (p. 185). Still other researchers, predominantly British social scientists (e.g. Herriot and Pemberton 1997; Guest 1998; Guest and Conway 2002), have argued that this "single beholder" definition has led researchers "to say [little] about the nature of the contracting process" (Guest and Conway 2002: 22). Thus they continue to define the contract according to the perceptions of both parties. For example, Guest and Conway (2002) adapted Herriot and Pemberton's (1997) definition of the contract, that is, "the perceptions of both parties to the employment relationship—organization and individual—of the reciprocal promises and obligations implied in that relationship" (Herriot and Pemberton 1997: 45). Subsequently, the resulting inconsistency in contract definitions across researchers and studies led one researcher to label the definitional confusion as one of the major stumbling blocks in the (post-1988) psychological contract research (Arnold 1996).

Psychological contract scholars also tend to attribute a second change in the conceptualization of the contract to Rousseau, specifying that the contract is based on "promised-based obligations" instead of "expectations"—another major difference between pre- and post-1988 contract research. Both Rousseau and her current or former students (Robinson 1996; Rousseau and Tijoriwala 1998) have argued that the "obligations" terminology more clearly conveys that the terms of the contract are not solely shaped by the beliefs, values, imagination, and desires of one party, as typically tends to be the case with one's *expectations*, but instead are influenced, at least in part, by the actions—promises—of the other party. Thus, Robinson (1996: 575) states, "only those expectations that emanate from perceived implicit or explicit promises by the employer are part of the psychological contracts." Virtually all contract researchers have adopted this conceptualization.

Nevertheless, there is reason to argue that a focus on promised-based obligations, rather than expectations for the terms of the contract, may constitute little if any change in the prior (pre-1988) conceptualization of the contract. Considering Levinson et al.'s (1962) descriptions of the nature of expectations in general as those compelling the other party to act and of specific expectations as "normative" in nature, we argue that this change is not, in fact, a radical departure from historical meanings of the word "expectations." Thus, we concur with Roehling (1996: 13) that "the theoretical distinction made between obligations and 'mere expectations' by contract researchers may indeed be much ado about nothing."

Nevertheless, Rousseau and Tijoriwala (1998) cite two studies (Robinson et al. 1994; Robinson 1996) as providing empirical evidence that the assessment of contract terms as promised-based obligations yields higher predictability of various attitudinal and behavioral outcomes than does their assessment as expectations. We note also that research by Turnley and Feldman (2000), on a sample of more than 800 managers, found that perceived contract violations assessed through the measurement of promised-based obligations displayed a significant relationship to outcome variables that was not fully mediated by measures of unmet expectations or job satisfaction. Thus, these findings also suggest that obligations, rather than expectations may be the more powerful measure of contract terms.

A comparison of the measures used to assess contract obligations with those used to assess expectations in both the Robinson (1996) and the Turnley and Feldman (2000) studies (we do not find an empirical comparison of expectations and promised-based obligations in the Robinson et al. 1994 study) causes us to take issue with such a conclusion. In each case, the items assessing contract obligations are both far more specific in nature and far greater in number (Robinson: seven versus two; Turnley and Feldman: sixteen versus four), a fact that makes it likely that the obligation measure more completely tapped the domain of contract terms, and thus emerged as a more powerful predictor of outcome variables, than did the expectation measure. Further, the one known study using a long (twenty-nine item) and specific expectation measure of contract terms as expectations (i.e. Kotter 1973) reported that the overall level of fit or match between individual expectations and organizational contributions significantly predicted employee productivity (positive), job satisfaction (positive), and turnover (negative). Unfortunately, this study did not assess measures of promised-based obligations, and thus does not permit comparison of predictability. Finally, contract research conducted on samples of British army soldiers repeatedly found that use of an obligation terminology to assess contract terms was confusing to pilot groups taken from their population and this type of measure was ultimately abandoned for an expectation-based one. Thus, given the current view of the psychological contract as promissory in nature (Rousseau and McLean Parks 1992), promised-based obligations are a more conceptually valid operationalization of contract terms than are traditional expectation measures. However, we also conclude that there is most likely very little difference between the current conceptualization of contract terms as promised-based obligations and their historical treatment as compelling expectations that force the other party to action. Empirically, the jury is still out as to which type of measure is likely to be a more powerful predictor of attitudinal and behavioral outcomes, but it is quite important to conduct such empirical tests on a level playing field where measures of both types are equally specific or general in nature and equal in length. We suspect, that subsequent empirical tests will reveal equivalent predictability, and encourage future research will address this issue. We turn now to social exchange theory as a conceptual basis for the psychological contract and other related concepts.

12.3.2 Social exchange theory as a conceptual foundation

Rousseau and her students frequently have referenced social exchange theory as one conceptual foundation for the psychological contract (Rousseau 1989; Rousseau and McLean Parks 1992; Robinson et al. 1994). Indeed, like the contract, social exchange theory deals with the exchange of resources, "whether tangible or intangible, and more or less rewarding or costly between at least two persons" (Homans 1961: 13). Further, Blau (1964: 91) defines social exchange in a manner quite appropriate for the exchange between employee and employer under the psychological contract, that is, as the "voluntary actions of individuals that are motivated by the returns that they are expected to bring and typically do bring from others." Blau also notes that social exchanges differ from strictly economic exchanges by entailing *unspecified* obligations such that the exact nature of how one is to reciprocate an obligation is typically not specified, and feelings of trust and trustworthiness develop as one party first trusts the other to reciprocate a preceding exchange over time and the other establishes his or her trustworthiness by doing so (Blau 1964).

Our literature review identified several studies offering indirect support for the social exchange prediction of reciprocity in one party's contract obligations and the other's contract fulfillment/violation over time. For example, in a two-measurement longitudinal study, Robinson et al. (1994) predicted and found that recent college graduates' perceptions of the extent to which their employer violated (failed to fulfill) their psychological contracts two years after the initial measurement were related to the decrease in the graduates' own obligations to the employer from Time 1 to Time 2. Thus, one might conclude that over time, a change in felt obligation by one party will lead to behaviors that reduce their contributions to the other, and subsequently, perceptions of violations by the other party, and ultimately, changes in their own contributions to the originating party. Similarly, in a longitudinal study assessing both employee perceptions of contract terms as well as employer perceptions (as reported by the employees' immediate manager), Coyle-Shapiro and Kessler (2002) found that employers' perceptions of their obligations to the employee at Time 1 were related to employees' perceptions of the level of fulfillment in these same obligations at Time 2, and vice versa. Their results again provide indirect support for the psychological contracting process as a social exchange relationship. Finally, consistent with social exchange theory predictions about the role of trust in these relationships, we note Robinson's (1996) findings regarding the significant mediating and moderating roles that new employees' initial trust of their new employer play in the psychological contract process over time.

Much like the case of the psychological contract, POS, defined as employees' "global beliefs concerning the extent to which the organization values their contributions and cares about their well-being," also relies on a social exchange theory foundation (Eisenberger et al. 1986). In the past, at least three studies (Guzzo et al. 1994; Guzzo and Berman 1995; Barksdale and Renn 1997) have operationalized the psychological contract with a well-established measure of POS (Eisenberger et al. 1986). This fact, plus the observation that both variables involve exchange relationships between individual employees and their organizational employer, naturally raises concerns about the discriminant validity of the two concepts. Nevertheless, a comparison of their respective definitions leads one to conclude that psychological contracts are concerned with the terms and conditions of the employment relationship, as perceived through the eyes of the individual employee, while POS addresses the employee's global or general assessment of how much their employer cares about their welfare and values their contributions. Thus, we argue that while the psychological contract and POS are conceptually distinct, they are likely to be moderately related since one would expect the terms and conditions of the psychological contract to convey information to employees regarding how much their employer values their contributions and cares about their well-being. Direct support for these proposals is provided by Coyle-Shapiro and Kessler's (2000) results showing that contract terms, assessed as contract fulfillment along three dimensions, transactional, relational, and training, were moderately related to POS. Indirect support comes from the research of Wayne et al. (1997) who found that employees' perceptions of the investment that the organization made in their development in terms of assignments, special attention from managers, the number of self-reported promotions over a six-year period, and their years of organizational tenure predicted their level of POS. Each of these three "investment" variables might reasonably be viewed as terms of the psychological contract, and indeed they have been treated as such in prior studies (Rousseau 1990; Coyle-Shapiro and Kessler 2002).

Further, we believe that POS essentially provides an assessment of employees' overall evaluation of the quality of the organization as an exchange partner, an evaluation that one might logically expect to influence their own long-term attitudes and behaviors toward the organization. Given the absence of similar variables in current conceptualizations of the contract, we propose that POS could be a valuable addition to the psychological contract literature and discuss this point further in the last section of this chapter. Once again, however, we note our disagreement with the use of POS as a surrogate measure for the psychological contract. For further information, we refer the reader to Chapter 10 on POS within this volume.

LMX is a second social exchange relationship that is relevant to the psychological contract literature. LMX is defined as the quality of the interpersonal relationship that evolves between the employee and his or her immediate manager within a formal organization (Graen and Scandura 1987). Its relevance for the contract lies in the fact that employees' immediate manager is the organizational agent who is frequently charged with forming, maintaining, and monitoring a social exchange relationship with the employee. Since LMX research has provided strong support for the existence of a social exchange relationship between employees and their immediate managers (Graen and Uhl-Bien 1995; Liden et al. 1997), it is relevant to ask whether it is possible for the manager to simultaneously enact two independent social exchange relationships with the same employee. In research presented in other forums (Tekleab and Taylor 2000; Lewis and Taylor 2001), we have hypothesized, and provided evidence to support, the moderating effects of LMX on each party's assessment of and reaction to contract violations by the other. We shall not delve more deeply into proposals about the role of LMX in the psychological contract here but conclude that it is a relationship worthy of more conceptual development and empirical study. We also refer the reader to Chapter 11 within this volume on LMX for greater illumination of the concept.

12.3.3 Measuring the nature of psychological contracts

Rousseau (1989, 1990, 1995) proposed that a two-dimensional framework, relational and transactional, underlies the psychological contract and developed a content-based measure consisting of contract terms to assess it. Relational contracts are focused around open-ended relationships where both parties make considerable investments (e.g. employees, the development of company-specific skills and long-term career development; organization, the provision of extensive employee training), have a high level of mutual interdependence, and experience constraints in terminating their relationship (Rousseau 1995). Rousseau (1990) predicted and found that more relational psychological contracts were positively correlated with employees' level of tenure in the organization.

Conversely, transactional contracts focus on short-term, economically based exchanges, with limited personal or emotional investment and a short-term time frame. Thus, more transactional contracts are hypothesized and have been found to relate positively to careerist attitudes (those viewing a job as only a short-term stepping stone to the next position) on the part of new recruits (Rousseau 1990). Although initially viewed as the end of the same continuum (Rousseau 1989, 1995), the relational and transactional concepts subsequently have been established as two separate dimensions and utilized to characterize the nature of the psychological contract in many different studies (e.g. Guzzo et al. 1994; Robinson and Rousseau 1994; Robinson et al. 1994; Robinson and Morrison 1995; Cavanaugh and Noe 1999).

Nevertheless, researchers have questioned the transactional and relational dimensions on methodological grounds. Roehling (1996) criticized the measures used in early contract studies (Rousseau 1989, 1990) because they included items that inconsistently "crossed-over" to load on different transactional and relational dimensions, depending on the particular set of data. While Rousseau and Tijoriwala (1998) have argued that one might naturally expect "cross-over" items, given the amount of change in employment relationships over the last 12–14 years, our literature review revealed that problems with inconsistent replications of the transactional and relational dimensions have repeatedly plagued psychological contract researchers (Rousseau 1990; Robinson et al. 1994; Taylor 1996; Barksdale and Shore 1997; Coyle-Shapiro and Kessler 2002; Tekleab 2003). Further crossover seems to occur even when item content is similar. One study, Coyle-Shapiro and Kessler (2002), identified a three-dimensional factor structure, relational, transactional, and training dimensions, which the researchers maintained was in fact consistent with earlier findings by Arnold (1996). The researchers concluded, "Our results suggest that training obligations are neither transactional nor relational but rather a distinct component of the psychological contract" (Coyle-Shapiro and Kessler 2002: 114, 116). The three-factor findings remind us of Schein's (1980) hypothesis concerning the importance of having some contract terms relating to employee development and self-actualization, as well as economic and social terms.

Rousseau and Tijoriwala (1998) note that some researchers (Robinson and Wolfe Morrison 1997) have achieved greater stability in factor structures by identifying stable dimensions for employer obligations, for example, enriched job, fair pay, supportive work environment, etc., and then choosing items to cluster conceptually around them. We observe, however, that the development of stable scales for contract terms does not necessarily ensure that the scale-based measures will yield the desired two-dimensional relational and transactional structure. Thus, it is not surprising that other ways of assessing the nature of the psychological contract have begun to emerge.

One of these developing measurement schemes assesses the degree of balance present between the contributions both parties make to the employment relationship and is grounded in the organizational fairness proposals that, in general, balanced relationships lead to more positive outcomes at the individual and organizational levels of analysis. We term this the balanced/unbalanced relationship approach. The first study to use this approach was conducted by Tsui et al. (1997), who assessed the nature of the employee–organization exchange relationship based on the employer's perspective. In the study, managers, as representatives of the employer, described the level of contributions that the employer expected of employees and the level of inducements that employers made to employees. The researchers then established a four-cell typology by establishing the median rating for each dimension and dividing it into high and low levels. The two balanced cells, the high–high and low–low relationships, were hypothesized to yield more positive outcomes in terms of employee attitudes and behaviors; findings were somewhat consistent with predictions.

In a later study, Shore and Barksdale (1998) adopted a derivative of the balanced/unbalanced relationship-based approach in order to "to move away from the focus in the literature on contract terms, with inherent problems of situation-specificity, to a focus on the general form, or pattern, of the exchange relationship" (p. 732). Using data from 327 part-time, working MBA students, these researchers cluster analyzed scores on a fifteen-item measure of transactional and relational contract dimensions by Rousseau (1990) to identify different patterns of relationships between employee and employer obligations. Their findings partially supported those of Tsui et al. (1997) and provide some additional support for the utility of this measurement approach.

Finally, McLean Parks et al. (1998) proposed another set of dimensions for classifying the psychological contract based on features of the psychological contracts themselves; we term these feature-based dimensions. These researchers argued that prior measures based on relational and transactional dimensions have limited applicability to individuals working within emerging employment types (such as contingent work arrangements) as well as those working in different cultures, and proposed six dimensions: Stability, scope, tangibility, focus, time frame, and particularism, along with a set of measures. Limited research has been conducted on the dimensions proposed by McLean Parks et al. (1998), and some research has found them to demonstrate low internal consistency reliability (e.g. Moye and Bartol 2001). At this point in time, it is impossible to assess the usefulness of this feature-based measurement approach until more research has examined it. See Chapter 14 on measurement and methodology in this volume for more information on this issue.

12.3.4 *Psychological contract violations*

The contract violation concept reminds us that perceived obligations are not always fulfilled in the eyes of the employee and has been defined by Rousseau (1989: 128) as the "failure of organizations or other parties to respond to an employee's contribution in ways the individual believes they are obligated to do so." She also notes that failure to meet the terms of a psychological contract may signal damage to the relationships between the employee and the organization, as trust and good faith are likely to be undermined by perceived violations. Rousseau proposed that employees' perceptions of violation may take one of three forms: (a) inadvertent violation, where divergent interpretations of the contract between employee and the organization leads one party to fail to fulfill its obligations, despite its willingness and ability to do so; (b) disruption to the contract, where circumstances make it impossible for one or both parties to fulfill their obligation of the contract, despite a willingness to do so; and finally (c) reneging or breach of contract, where one party deliberately refuses to fulfill its obligations despite being capable of doing so. Drawing on the social accounts literature (Bies and Moag 1986), Rousseau (1995) proposes that whether the source of violation is due to the violating party's unwillingness or inability to comply, it will have a powerful effect on the experienced violation of the other party and that party's response. Thus, one would expect that contract violations, like obligations, are seen through the eyes of the beholder.

It appears that employee eyes tend to see violations fairly frequently. For example, Robinson and Rousseau (1994) found that 55 percent of an MBA graduate sample reported experiencing contract violation within the first two years on the job. Similarly, in a diary-keeping study of forty-five individuals who were either part-time MBA students or bank employees, Conway and Briner (2002) reported that 69 percent of their sample identified at least one broken promise over the ten-day research period. Finally, Lester et al. (2002) investigated a combined sample of part-time working MBA students and telecommunications employees, and found that 65 percent of their sample reported that employer contributions failed to meet the level promised to them.

Fortunately, given the incidence of contract violations by the organization, Rousseau (1995) also developed a model explaining how employee perceptions of contract violations develop. She proposed a basic chain of events whereby an employee's perception of a contract outcome discrepancy results in a perception of the size of the loss resulting from the violation. Then, the size of loss perception and the employee's perception of the voluntary or involuntary nature of the organization's action both yield employee's perception of contract violation. However, Rousseau (1995) also proposed a number of factors affecting each of the major variables in the chain. For example, the level of employee monitoring of employer obligation fulfillment is hypothesized to affect the perception of contract outcome discrepancies, and the level of remediation displayed by the employer is predicted to impact the perceived size of loss. Similarly, both relationship strength at the time of the violation and the procedural justice underlying the organization's decision not to meet its obligations are predicted to affect the perception of violation (see Rousseau 1995: chapter 5).

In terms of the consequences of contract violation, Rousseau (1995) characterized employee reactions to violation using Hirshman's (1970) "Exit, Voice, and Loyalty" typology of employee responses. She proposed that behavioral responses to violation are shaped by personal predispositions and situational factors. Personal dispositions include such things as the tendency to value the employment relationship and to attempt to save it even at high costs versus the tendency to have a low tolerance for even slight inequities occurring in the relationship. Situational factors are composed of variables such as the availability of behavioral models, i.e. other employees who chose to leave the organization once evaluating discrepancies as contract violations. Exiting the relationship, classified as an active but highly destructive response to violation, is hypothesized to be most probable under the following conditions: (a) when the contract is more transactional than relational in nature; (b) when many other potential jobs are available; (c) when the relationship is a relatively new one; (d) when other employees are also exiting; and (e) when attempts to remedy the violation have failed. In addition, Rousseau and McLean Parks (1992: 36) proposed that contract violations erode trust, undermine the employment relationship, lower employee contributions such as performance and attendance, and lower employer investments such as retention and promotion. Once relational contracts are violated, they are expected to become transactional contracts.

Responding to the growth in the psychological contract literature after 1988, Morrison and Robinson (1997) proposed their own model of contract violation development. Like Rousseau's framework, Morrison and Robinson's model (1997) proposes that contract violations ultimately result from a chain of events beginning with the employee's perception of unmet employer promises, but the two researchers also identified a larger set of factors believed to underlie this perception. These include the concepts of unavoidable (lacking the ability to prevent) reneging and incongruence (Rousseau's inadvertent violation), as well as the moderating effects of the salience of broken promises and the vigilance with which employees monitor the organization's fulfillment of the contract. Unlike Rousseau's (1995) model, however, Morrison and Robinson inserted a mediating variable in the chain of variables between perceived unmet promises and contract violation; this mediator, termed "contract breach," was defined as the *cognition* that promised obligations have not been met. They proposed contract breach as the most direct predictor of contract violation, defined as "an emotional and affective state that *may* result from the belief that one's organization has failed to adequately maintain the psychological contract" (Morrison and Robinson 1997: 230).

Primary differences between the contract violation models of Rousseau (1995) and Morrison and Robinson (1997) are the latter's greater development of the process through which employees perceive unmet organizational promises; their addition of contract breach to the chain of variables between the employee's perception of unmet promises and contract violation; and their identification of several moderators of the relationship between unmet promises and contract breach and between contract breach and contract violation. In addition, Morrison and Robinson's (1997) contract violation model does not discuss the consequences of contract violation, other than the emotional response of violation itself, whereas Rousseau's model and writing specifies particular consequences.

Empirical research examining the antecedents and consequences of contract violation has increased dramatically from 1994 to the present. Regarding the consequences, in a longitudinal study of ninety-six MBA graduates at two time points, Robinson et al. (1994) tested Rousseau and McLean Parks' (1992) predictions about the impact of contract violations on subsequent perceptions of perceived obligations. Violations were assessed in a manner more consistent with Rousseau's (1995) definition than that of Morrison and Robinson (1997), that is, more cognitively than emotionally, and measured as employees' evaluation of the extent of the organization's contract fulfillment. Findings confirmed hypotheses that contract violations were more likely to result in a decrease in employees' relational obligations than their transactional ones. These results are consistent with Rousseau and McLean Parks' (1992) predictions that violations cause contracts to become more transactional than relational in nature. A second longitudinal study by Robinson and Rousseau (1994) also examined a group of MBA graduates, both shortly after their acceptance of a post-graduation job and after two years on the job. Their results supported the propositions of Rousseau and McLean Parks (1992), revealing that perceived violations at Time 2 were negatively related to employees' trust in their employer, satisfaction with employment, and intentions to remain with the employer, and positively related to actual turnover. Research by Robinson (1996) further tested the proposed negative effects of contract violations on employee reactions. Using a three-measure longitudinal design on a similar sample of MBAs, she found that employees' initial trust of their organizational employer at the time of hire both mediated and moderated the effects of contract breach. High initial trust was negatively related to perceived contract breach at Time 2 and subsequent trust at Time 2 mediated the effects of contract breach at Time 2 on employees' reactions at Time 3. Initial trust moderated the relationship between contract breach and subsequent trust such that those with low initial trust experienced a greater decrease in trust after experiencing a perceived employer violation at Time 2. Finally, perceived contract breach was negatively related to employee contributions in the form of self-reported organizational citizenship behaviors (OCBs) directed toward the organization (civic virtue scale) and positively to intentions to remain and actual turnover. Note, also, that contract breach was a significant and negative predictor of the attitudinal outcome variables. Finally, a study by Lester et al. (2002) also found that employees' perceptions of contract breach were negatively related to their level of affective commitment and their performance as rated by their supervisor.

In perhaps the best test to date of Rousseau's (1995) hypothesized employee reactions to contract breach, Turnley and Feldman (1999) examined the reactions of a sample of 800 managers to perceived contract breach on behaviors related to the exit, voice, and loyalty typology, as well as the effects of several situational moderators. Violations were assessed in a manner consistent with Rousseau's definition, rather than the affect-emphasizing one posited by Morrison and Robinson (1997). Turnley and Feldman's (1999) results supported the negative relationship of perceived contract violations to employees' self-reports of exit intentions, voicing displeasure and neglect of in-role performance, as well as their positive relationship to self-reported expressions of loyalty in representing the organization to outsiders. Further, they found partial support for the moderating effects of several situational variables proposed by Rousseau on the relationship between perceived contract violations and the exit response. Significant moderator effects were found for the availability of employment alternatives, insufficient justification of the violation by the organization, and the procedural justice of the organization's decision-making practices. However, the moderating effects were limited to the dependent variable of exit, operationalized in their study by self-reported job search behavior. Tekleab and Taylor (2000) reported another moderating effect on the violation–outcome relationship. They found that LMX negatively moderated the relationship between contract violation and job satisfaction. Research by Coyle-Shapiro and Kessler (2000) on a sample of British public-sector employees also supported the contract violation–outcome relationships hypothesized by Rousseau (1995). These researchers found that contract fulfillment, considered by many to be the opposite of contract violation, was positively related to employees' affective organizational commitment and self-reported organizational citizenship behavior directed toward the organization.

Two studies have tested the antecedents of the psychological contract violation as proposed by the Morrison and Robinson (1997) model. The best test to date is that conducted by the researchers themselves (Robinson and Morrison 2000) in a study examining 147 managers in a longitudinal design beginning at the time they started their jobs and ending after eighteen months on the job. The study assessed both contact breach, as the cognition of unmet promises by the organization, and contract violation, as an emotional and affective state that may result from contract breach. Findings supported discriminant validity of breach and violation, and confirmed hypothesized effects for declining organizational performance (inability to meet promised obligations), low employee performance (as a motivator of opportunistic behavior by the organization to renege on obligations to the employee), alternative employment opportunities, and a past history of contract breaches. All of these variables were positively related to employees' reports of contract breach, while formal socialization and greater interactions with organizational representatives (as constraints on incongruence of contract terms between parties) were negatively related to breach. Hypotheses regarding the positive effects of organizational change and the implicitness of organizational promises on contract breach were not supported. Robinson and Morrison's (2000) findings also supported the hypothesized positive relationship between contract breach and violation ($r = 0.68$), as well as a two-way, but not the predicted single moderating effect of interactional fairness and the attribution of breach to reneging on the relationship between breach and violation.

The second study, Guest and Conway (2002), provided a more indirect test of the Morrison and Robinson (1997) model of contract violations by examining the types of communication used by organizations to convey information about the organization's perspective on the mutual obligations of the psychological obligations. Presumably, effective communication of the organization's perspective about mutual obligations would reduce the likelihood of contract breach by decreasing the likelihood of incongruent obligations between employee and organization. A survey of 1306 senior

HR managers revealed that their ratings of communication effectiveness were positively related to their rating of the explicitness of the psychological contract. Further, the effectiveness of two types of communication, that occurring during recruitment as well as that concerning job and personal communication at work, were negatively related to HR managers' perceptions of experienced contract breach.

Two studies have examined the implications of both exceeding promised obligations and breaching them. In the first study, Conway and Briner (2000) used a diary-keeping methodology to investigate the frequency of perceived contract breaches, fulfillment, and incidences of exceeding promises and the emotions attached to them. Findings revealed that contract breaches and exceeded promises both occurred frequently, with some 69 percent of their forty-five person sample reporting at least one breach over the ten-day study period and 62 percent reporting at least one exceeded promise. Breaches were more likely to yield feelings of betrayal than hurt and exceeded promises to yield feelings of self-worth than surprise. Breaches had a stronger effect on participants' mood than did exceeded promises. Somewhat consistent with the Morrison and Robinson (1997) model, the importance of the breached promise to the relationship with the organization was the stronger predictor of emotional reactions, as compared to the explicitness of the promise, whether it was the other party's responsibility, and whether it had occurred previously in the past. Further, the results provide general support for the model's distinction between breach and violation. However, Conway and Briner (2002) also criticized the Morrison and Robinson (1997) model of contract violation development for its less than parsimonious nature. Specifically, they criticized the model for the sheer member of proposed moderating effects and the failure of several studies to support them, including Conway and Briner (2002) and Morrison and Robinson (2000). The second study, Lester et al. (2002), compared supervisor and employee perceptions of and attributions for contract breach. Supervisors were more likely to attribute the causes of breach to situations beyond the organization's direct control (breach due to unavoidable reneging), while employees were more likely to attribute breach to willful reneging. Somewhat surprisingly, given the Conway and Brinier (2002) findings, Lester et al. (2002) found that fulfilled and exceeded promises led to higher levels of employee performance and affective commitment than did contract breach.

In summary, since 1994, a growing body of research has examined the consequences and antecedents of psychological contract violation. Findings from these studies generally support Rousseau's (Rousseau and McLean Parks 1992 and Rousseau 1995) proposals concerning the negative effects of perceived contract violation on employee attitudes, such as organizational commitment, trust in the organization, and job and organizational satisfaction, and on employee behaviors, including in-role performance, OCBs, and turnover, and the movement of the contract from a more relational to a more transactional nature. Further, a limited number of indirect empirical tests are generally supportive of reneging (both willful and forced) and incongruence as antecedents of contract breach and the discriminant validity of the breach and contract violation concepts proposed by Morrison and Robinson (1997). However, the breach and violation concepts are highly intercorrelated and existing model propositions do not clearly establish whether a given outcome would be best predicted by breach or violation. We now discuss Rousseau's conceptualization of the cognitive basis of the psychological contract.

12.3.5 A cognitive explanation of contract development

Observing that the antecedents and building blocks of psychological contracts have received relatively little attention from researchers, Rousseau (1995, 2001) proposed a cognitive basis for the psychological contract that is grounded in the concept of prototypical mental models or schema. Rousseau (2001) believes that contract schema originate in individual's past histories and develop slowly over time with their accumulation of additional information about contract obligations from the work setting. She notes that different contract schema may develop within the same organization, depending on the clarity of information and trustworthiness and consistency of available sources. Moreover, schema observed or heard from other sources may prominently influence the development of psychological contracts in cases where individuals possess incomplete information about the new job setting. Thus, an employee may incorporate aspects of the schema held by others such as co-workers and managers to determine what he or she owes to the organization and the organization's obligations to him or her. The idea that others' schema vicariously affect an employee's own contract schema over time may partially explain the effects of socialization processes documented by prior researchers (Feldman 1976), whereby information gathered from co-workers, supervisors, and personal observations play significant roles in shaping the individual's own belief structures.

Rousseau (2001) posits that once fully formed and tested for accuracy by feedback from the environment, contract schema become quite resistant to change. Prior research on schema outside the psychological contract area suggests that changes are more likely when individuals are highly motivated to alter their schema through the provision of rewards and new opportunities. Left to their own devices, however, individuals tend to look for information supporting their schema, rather than to search openly for disconfirming information. Rousseau (2001) believes this resistance to changes on contract schema may explain why organizations wishing to adopt more innovative work or management practices often choose to build new facilities in rural locations that permit the hiring of new employees whose contract schema are likely to be more open to the new practices.

At this point, no research has directly examined the role of schema in psychological contract formation, although Rousseau (2001) identifies Bunderson's (2001) findings of two distinct ideologies, market oriented and professional, among health care workers as an example of how two distinct contract schema may arise in a single work organization. Similarly, the idea that newcomers may benefit from the existing contract schema of established employees may provide an indirect explanation for the results of Thomas and Anderson (1998) regarding changes in the psychological contracts of British army soldiers during their first two months in training. Further, recent work by Tekleab (2003) found that higher levels of socialization decreased the organizational obligations reported by new telemarketing employees during their first three months of employment.

12.3.6 Summary and conclusions on review of five contract elements

Led by Rousseau's (1989, 1990, 1995, 2001) conceptual and empirical research on the psychological contract, much has been accomplished during the 1988–2003 period of psychological contact research. Researchers have explored differences between the conceptualization of contract terms as expectations versus promised obligations, proposed and tested different dimensions for the contract and the underlying exchange relationship, and linked them to various attitudinal and behavioral outcomes. They also have begun to examine models identifying the antecedents and consequences of psychological contract breaches and violations, and have proposed and indirectly tested hypotheses concerning the underlying cognitive structure for contracts, as a structure based on employees' past work experience guides the subsequent assimilation of new information. We are frankly a bit awed by the amount of progress occurring in this research stream during the last fourteen years. Nevertheless, we believe that this progress makes it more important to refresh our memory of knowledge gleaned from early research on the contract, and set conceptual and empirical research priorities for the immediate future. We turn to this task in the final section of this chapter on research priorities.

12.4 Research priorities for the psychological contract

In order to continue the relatively fast pace of discovery within psychological contract research over the last fifteen years, we suggest the following priorities. With the exception of measurement and methodology issues, we list them in order of importance.

12.4.1 Bringing the employer's perspective into the contract

Both the social exchange theory foundation of the contract as well as its earliest historical references support Schein's (1980) assertion that the employment relationship cannot be well understood by research addressing the perspective of only one party to the contract, that of the employee. While the exclusive focus on the employee's perspective throughout the recent period of research on the contract has advanced our understanding of that perspective in all of the ways reviewed earlier, it has also distracted researchers' attention away from the perspective of the employer and from an integration of the two perspectives that is badly needed for a comprehensive understanding of the employment relationship. We argue that knowledge about the interdependent interactions and reactions of both parties are important determinants of the nature of the employment relationship, its quality, and ultimately its longevity. Thus, we are delighted by the Fall, 2003 issue of the *Journal of Organizational Behavior* dedicated to the topic of the employment relationship, the inclusion of Chapter 7 on the organizational perspective in this volume, and the evidence of considerable ongoing research on this issue that can be found in a growing number of symposia and presentations given at national meetings, such as the Academy of Management and the Society of Industrial and Organizational Psychology (SIOP) over the last three years.

Nevertheless, an integration of the employer's perspective into psychological contract research will require considerable time and effort for researchers to address a myriad of issues, such as which organizational representative is best able to articulate that perspective for particular research questions, what is the appropriate obligation set for the employer, what actions does it undertake during the contracting process, and what are relevant outcome variables or consequences from the organization's perspective. We think it important that this perspective be addressed from both macro- and micro-levels. At the macro-level, researchers must study how the decisions and actions of upper-echelon leaders shape and enact the contract and for what purposes, for example, because of its contributions to the reduction of uncertainty, facilitation of goal achievement through strategy implementation, attainment of speed and flexibility in market responses, and/or optimization of organizational resources. At a micro-level, we suggest that it is the values and behaviors of employees' immediate managers that are deserving of further research attention. Researchers must understand the impact of these managers on how psychological contracts between organization and individual employee are formed, maintained, changed, and ultimately terminated. We posit that the macro-perspective of the contract will be most important for predicting organizational level performance on a variety of indicators, economic, turnover, quality of products and services, etc., while the micro-perspective will be most important for predicting the attitudes and behaviors of individual employees. We hypothesize that both levels ultimately contribute to the organization's reputation, as outsiders' perceptions are shaped by its public persona, as experienced through the media and through one-on-one interactions with its employees, either personally experienced or related by trusted friends and associates.

What does it mean to research the integration of these two perspectives, employee and organization, on the psychological contract? At this point, we can only speculate, but we posit that it has both process and content implications. In part, studying the integration might mean examining the process of day-to-day contract enactment to discern whether each party has some power to enforce its view of the contract as Schein (1980) discussed and whether individual employees, generally recognized as having less power in the relationship, are able: to affect changes in organizational contributions to the contract, as proposed by Porter et al. (1975). A process orientation would also include investigating whether contract changes occur as a result of changes in the situations of the two parties, and whether and through what means the relationship between parties demonstrates the ability to rebound in response to contract violations, rather than spiraling toward unnecessary and unwanted termination. Contentwise, researching the contract from an integrative perspective means assessing how well the expectations of each party are met in the relationship, their level of satisfaction with it, overall evaluation of it, and their reactions to its termination. Perhaps most importantly, we believe it will include making some determination, given the interests/desires and contributions of each party, of how much joint value was left unrealized by the parties from the contract and from the overarching employment relationship.

Given our expectation that the development of research on the psychological contract from an integrated perspective of employee and organization will take some time to design, conduct, interpret, and assimilate into the existing body of knowledge on the contract and employment relationship, the primary question then becomes: "What should be done in the interim with research on the psychological contract, from the employee's perspective?" Our response is that researchers should continue to strengthen and extend this body of work in the immediate time frame by clarifying concepts, addressing potential conceptual overlap, revising existing models to incorporate new findings, and addressing measurement and methodological problems. In this way, research on the employee's psychological contract will continue to contribute to the literature on the employment relationship and may, though offering its own conceptual models, findings, measures, and methodologies as exemplars, facilitate the more rapid development of research integrating both perspectives, the employee's and the organization's.

12.4.2 Developing more comprehensive conceptual models

Seemingly, extant research on the individual's psychological contract has progressed sufficiently to inform the development of more comprehensive conceptual models identifying the nature of the contract, its antecedents, mediators, and consequences. The development of such models should provide greater direction for future research while also suggesting important avenues for the integration of employee and organizational perspectives of the contract. Based on the literature review in this chapter, we take a first, but far from final step in the specification of a comprehensive model (see Figure 12.1). Hopefully other researchers may find our model a stimulus for their own thinking and input toward this end.

As Figure 12.1 shows, antecedent variables and processes such as the employees' past work experience, pre-entry information, socialization processes, co-worker schema, and the performance and history of the organization result in the formation of the employee's psychological contract, depicted at this point as a cognitive representation of the relational and transactional dimensions, the balanced or unbalanced nature of the exchange, and the intrinsic and developmental nature of exchange content. Over time, the nature of the contract then directly affects the

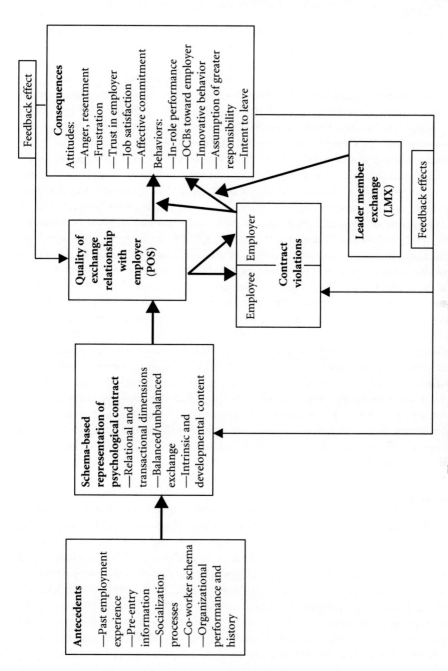

Figure 12.1. *An integrative psychological contract model.*

employee's assessment or evaluation of the quality of the exchange relationship with the employer, which we propose is very similar to the current POS concept (Eisenberger et al. 1990). Thus, the experience of a more relational contract, a balanced or overfulfilled exchange, and/or organizational contributions that provide intrinsic job characteristics and opportunities for employee development will contribute positively toward the employee's perception of a high-quality exchange relationship. The employee's assessment of the quality of the exchange relationship with the employer then directly yields a number of attitudinal and behavioral outcomes that includes trust of the employer, elements of Hirschman's (1970) voice, exit, loyalty framework, negative emotional reactions such as anger, resentment, frustration, trust in employer (diminished) identified by Morrison and Robinson (1997), and Levinson et al.'s (1962) suggestions of innovative work behavior and the assumption of greater organizational responsibility and innovative behavior. However, violations of the contract by the employer, the antecedents of which are discussed in other models (Rousseau 1995; Morrison and Robinson 1997), are hypothesized to negatively moderate the relationship between the perceived quality of the exchange with the organization and resulting attitudinal and behavioral consequences, such that, for example, the positive effects of a high-quality relationship on consequences such as trust of employer, commitment, etc., will be negatively moderated by the perception of a contract violation. Employer contract violations themselves are predicted to have a direct effect on a variety of outcomes, including reducing trust of employer and attitudes such as commitment and job satisfaction, while increasing anger and resentment, and negatively affecting a variety of contribution behaviors. However, we posit that the employee's exchange relationship with his or her immediate manager, LMX, will negatively moderate the employer contract violation–consequence relationship, denoting a tendency by the employee to react more negatively toward violations by those in whom one places a high level of trust. Our inclusion of both POS and LMX in the comprehensive model of psychological contract denotes the importance we believe they play within the psychological contract process.

In addition, consistent with Rousseau's (1995) hypothesis that a favorable or positive relationship between organization and employee will yield a tendency for the employee to scan for violations less frequently and a willingness to give the organizational partner the benefit of the doubt if evidence of a violation is perceived, we also predict a negative effect of relationship quality on the employee's perception of contract violations by the organization. Finally, the model depicts feedback loops running from consequences to: (a) contract violations by the employee, positing that the consequences experienced as a result of an employer violation will serve to stimulate a return violation by the employee; (b) the quality of the exchange relationship with the employer, proposing that the consequences experienced will also directly affect the quality of the exchange relationship over time; and finally (c) the nature or representation of the psychological contract itself, as the negative consequences of a violated contract tend to increase the transactional nature of the exchange, affecting perceptions of exchange balance.

Although a rough representation, Figure 12.1 incorporates contract research from the early and later periods in an attempt to model more comprehensively the antecedents, mediators, moderators, and consequences of the psychological contract process. We hope it not only suggests future areas for research but also encourages continuing efforts to model these relationships by others.

12.4.3 Merging and revising contract violation models

The topic of psychological contract violation has attracted the most research attention during the recent post-1988 period and has proven to be a powerful determinant of employee attitudes and behaviors. Thus, we believe it important to encourage further exploration of the contract violation models. Given continued organizational restructuring in the United States and throughout much of Asia and Europe, and the current economic downturn, we encourage more research on the consequences of willful versus forced reneging. Consider situations such as the ill-fated attempt of then American Airlines CEO Don Cardy to convince employees and their four labor unions to accept pay and benefits cuts in order that the airline might avoid declaring bankruptcy. Not surprisingly, when employees and their unions learned that instead of proportional cuts, airline executives were being awarded large supplemental pension and cash retention bonuses, they rapidly withdrew their agreement to accept such cuts (Click 10.com, 2003). We suggest that this situation might be viewed as one where circumstances that were presented by the organization's social accounts as disruption (Rousseau 1995) or unavoidable reneging (Morrison and Robinson 1997) subsequently proved to be willful reneging and ultimately backfired, resulting seemingly in more negative attitudinal and behavioral responses on the part of its employees.

We also propose the need for a friendly merger between the two existing violation development models of Rousseau (1995) and Morrison and Robinson (1997), whereby a common terminology for the antecedents of contract breach is adopted and serious consideration is given to a parsimonious reduction of proposed moderating variables. Perhaps the variables associated with the comparison process thought to moderate the unmet promises—contract breach relationship, along with the process itself, offer a possible place to start. In addition, we encourage careful scrutiny of the distinction made between contract breach and contract violation by Morrison and Robinson (1997). While not denying the role of emotion in the experience of violation, we question why it is important to separate the two when there is no conceptual reason to suggest that they lead to different consequences. At least one empirical finding has shown they are quite highly correlated ($r = 0.78$; Robinson and Morrison 2000), and a growing number of studies find contract breach to be a significant predictor of many different attitudinal and behavioral consequences (Turnley and Feldman 1999; Tetrick et al. 2002).

Finally, the findings of Tsui et al. (1997) regarding the positive outcomes associated with the overinvestment cell (from the employer's perspective), along with recent results from Lester et al. (2002), suggest that the overfulfillment of contract promises may lead to positive attitudinal and behavioral consequences. Thus, we encourage further research on the meaning and consequences of a level of fulfillment exceeding that promised by the organization.

12.4.4 Attending to contract development

We concur with Rousseau (2001) that it is time to devote greater attention to the process through which the psychological contract develops. Her proposals concerning the role of schema in contract development and resistance to change are important ones to pursue in this effort. Yet we note that only two published studies have examined the nature of changes in contract obligations over time (Robinson et al. 1994; Thomas and Anderson 1998). Thus, we suggest that research by Tekleab (2003), examining RJP and socialization effects on changes in the nature of the new employees' psychological contracts over time, as well as that by De Vos et al. (2003) examining contribution and reciprocity effects during the encounter stage of socialization, may be useful models in this respect.

Further, we encourage readers to attend to Herriot and Pemberton's (1997) proposals about the contracting process in order to increase our understanding of the social interactions between employees and organizational representatives that shape the contract. Hopefully, subsequent reviews of the contract literature will reveal gains in the area of contract development similar to those on the issue of contract violation.

12.4.5 Becoming more thoughtful about contract consequences

The growing body of research examining consequences of the psychological contract process and contract violations seems at times to be stuck on a specific grouping of outcome variables including job satisfaction, organizational commitment, performance, OCBs, and turnover intentions. We do not deny the importance of these variables and include them in our own integrative model and research. However, we suggest it is time to become more thoughtful about the outcomes that may be considered consequences of the contract and more selective about choosing consequences that are most relevant to the research questions of interest. We point to the research of Turnley and Feldman (1999) on the exit, voice, loyalty consequences of contract violation as well as a recent paper by Tetrick et al. (2002), as good examples of thoughtful selectivity and conceptual justification and encourage readers to consider as well Levinson et al.'s (1962) suggested outcomes, the assuming of greater responsibility and innovative work behaviors.

12.4.6 Improving contract measures

Our literature review revealed that weak measures of the nature of the contract's dimensionality continue to threaten the validity of empirical research. In order to

address this issue, researchers will be forced to make decisions about the most important conceptualizations of the nature of the contract. Earlier we suggested that
research evidence to date supports the validity of the relational and transactional
dimensions along with the balanced/unbalanced nature of the exchange. To add to
these, we remind the reader of Schein's (1980) proposals regarding the importance of
intrinsically motivating and developmental obligations. At this point in the development of contract measures, we urge researchers to be creative and fairly comprehensive in their attempts to measure the contract in order to avoid overlooking important
aspects of the contract's fundamental nature. As research samples continue to investigate populations beyond the overly sampled MBA graduates, it is very possible that
untapped characteristics of the contract may take on an even greater importance.
Thus, we conclude that at the present time it is critical to be both creative in using a
variety of conceptualizations to assess the nature of the contract, and diligent in
strengthening the psychometric properties of contract measures. Surprisingly, we are
aware of only one study, Coyle-Shapiro and Kessler (2000), that has examined the
discriminant validity of psychological contracts from other similar constructs, such as
POS, trust, and perceptions of fairness; we suggest that additional examinations of
discriminant validity are warranted. In addition, we refer the reader to Chapter 14 in
this volume on measurement for further discussion of this issue.

12.4.7 Varying research methodologies

Our literature review for this chapter has caused us to note, with more than a little
exasperation, that much psychological contract research seems to have fallen into
a methodological rut. We have seen (and conducted) far too many studies with
correlational, albeit longitudinal, research designs, samples of MBA graduates or
students, established but unreliable measures, single sources of data, and hierarchical
regression analysis. Yet newspaper articles and neighbors' comments suggest many
opportunities to study naturally occurring field experiments on the changing nature of
the psychological contract. By combining correlational field studies with field experiments, experimental scenario studies, and/or creative lab experiments researchers
might both make full use of available field research opportunities and also draw
stronger conclusions about causality. We urge researchers to think more creatively
about research methodologies at this stage in the development of contract research.

12.5 Conclusions

In conclusion, this chapter reviewed the literature on psychological contract, as an
important foundation of the employment relationship, in order to "take stock" of its
progress and suggest future research priorities. The good news is that there has been
rather remarkable progress during the last fifteen years both in conceptualizing the
contract from the employee's perspective and in researching this conceptualization.
To a great extent, this progress must be attributed to the work of Denise Rousseau

and her current and former doctoral students who have consistently proposed and researched new ways to think about the contract and its related elements, as well as its implications throughout the post-1988 period. The somewhat bad news resulting from our literature review is that contract researchers have focused more on the empirical testing of existing propositions than on the refinement of conceptual proposals and the development of more comprehensive conceptual models. They also have become rather lax in their reliance on established but unreliable contract measures, longitudinal, correlational research designs, and samples of MBA graduates. Thus, we have recommended substantive and methodological research priorities infused with suggestions derived from both early and recent psychological contract research in order to address these weaknesses.

Overall, we conclude that research on the employee's psychological contract is relatively well and thriving *but* that it currently exists in a kind of vacuum that fails to consider the organization's perspective of the contract, and thus the way the contract develops, is enacted on a day-to-day basis, is violated, and even results in termination. This, we believe, is the significant downside of the decision to reconceptualize the contract as the employee's perspective almost fifteen years ago. Much like Schein (1970), we argue that to ignore the basis of the psychological contact as an *interaction occurring between two parties* is to overlook something fundamentally important about the richness and complexity of their continuing interdependence. Unfortunately, conceptual explications of the employer's perspective and studies integrating the two are largely absent from the current literature, and substantial time will be needed for it to develop, yield consistent findings, and become assimilated into our current understanding of the psychological contact. Thus, our tack in this chapter has been to identify problematic issues and gaps in the conceptual and empirical literature on the *employee's psychological contract* in the hope that it will prove a useful model for conceptual and empirical research on an integration of the two. We have high hopes for the continued development of the psychological contract literature, although we anticipate that it is about to experience another discontinuity similar to the one occurring around 1988 with the publication of Rousseau's early contract work "Let The Games Begin."

References

Argyris, C. (1960). *Understanding Organizational Behavior*. Homewood, IL: Dorsey Press.

Arnold, J. (1996). "The psychological contract: A concept in need of closer scrutiny?" *European Journal of Work and Organizational Psychology*, 5: 511–20.

Barksdale, K., and Renn, R. W. (1997). "A field study of the effects of a new pay-for-performance compensation plan on perceived organizational support and attendance: A psychological contract and justice perspective." Working Paper, Department of Management, Robinson College of Business, Georgia State University, Atlanta.

—— and Shore, L. M. (1997). "A typological for examining psychological contracts." Working Paper, Department of Management, Robinson College of Business, Georgia State University, Atlanta.

Bies, R. J., and Moag, J. S. (1986). "Interactional justice: Communication criteria of fairness," in M. H. Bazerman, R. Lewicki, and B. Sheppard (eds.), *Research on Negotiations in Organizations* (Greenwich, CT: JAI Press).

Blau, P. (1964). *Exchange and Power in Social Life.* New York: Wiley.

Bunderson, J. S. (2001). "How work ideologies shape the psychological contacts of professional employees: Doctors' responses to perceived breach". *Journal of Organizational Behavior,* 22: 717–41.

Cavanaugh, M. A., and Noe, R. A. (1999). "Antecedents and consequences of relational components of the new psychological contract". *Journal of Organizational Behavior,* 20: 323–40.

—— (2003). "American Airlines' turbulent drama continues". Click 10.com, April 23, 7:52 AM.

Conway, N., and Briner, R. B. (2002). "A daily diary study of affective responses to psychological contract breach and exceeded promises". *Journal of Organizational Behavior,* 23: 287–302.

Coyle-Shapiro, J., and Kessler, I. (2000). "Consequences of the psychological contract for the employment relationship: A large scale survey". *Journal of Management Studies,* 37: 903–30.

—— and —— (2002). "Exploring reciprocity through the lens of the psychological contract: Employee and employer perspectives". *European Journal of Work and Organizational Psychology,* 11: 69–86.

De Vos, A., Buyens, D., and Schalk, R. (2003). "Psychological contract development during organizational socialization: Adaptation to reality and the role of reciprocity". *Journal of Organizational Behavior,* 24: 537–60.

Dunahee, M. H., and Wangler, L. W. (1974). "The psychological contract: A conceptual structure for management/employee relations". *Personnel Journal,* 518–48.

Eisenberger, R., Huntington, R., Hutchison, S., and Sowa, D. (1986). "Perceived organizational support". *Journal of Applied Psychology,* 71: 500–7.

—— Fasolo, P., and Davis-LaMastrro, V. (1990). "Perceived organizational support and employee diligence, commitment, and innovation". *Journal of Applied Psychology,* 75: 51–9.

Feldman, D. C. (1976). "A contingency theory of socialization". *Administrative Science Quarterly,* 21: 433–52.

Graen, G. B., and Scandura, T. A. (1987). "Toward a psychology of dyadic organizing," in L. L. Cummings and B. Staw (eds.), *Research in Organizational Behavior,* vol. 9 (Greenwich, CT: JAI Press), 175–208.

Graen, G. G., and Uhl-Bien, M. (1995). "Relationship based approach to leadership: Development of leader–member exchange (LMS) theory of leadership over 25 years: Applying a multi-level multi-domain perspective". *Leadership Quarterly,* 6: 219–47.

Guest, D. (1998). "Is the psychological contract worth taking seriously?" *Journal of Organizational Behavior,* 19: 649–64.

—— and Conway, R. (2002). "Communicating the psychological contract: An employer perspective". *Human Resource Management Journal,* 12(2): 22–38.

Guzzo, R. A., and Berman, L. M. (1995). "At what level of generality is psychological contract fulfillment best measured?" Academy of Management meeting, Vancouver, August.

—— Noonan, K. A., and Elron, E. (1994). "Expatriate managers and the psychological contract". *Journal of Applied Psychology,* 79: 617–26.

Herriot, P., and Pemberton, C. (1997). "Facilitating new deals". *Human Resource Management Journal,* 7: 45–56.

Hirschman, A. O. (1970). *Exit, Voice, and Loyalty.* Cambridge, MA: Harvard University Press.

Homans, G. (1961). *Social Behavior.* New York: Harcourt, Brace and World.

Kotter, J. P. (1973). "The psychological contract: Managing the join-up process". *California Management Review*, 15: 91–9.

Lawler, E. E. (1987). *High Involvement Management*. San Francisco: Jossey-Bass.

Lester, S. W., Turnley, W. H., Bloodgood, J. M., and Bolino, M. C. (2002). "Not seeing eye to eye: Differences in supervisor and subordinate perceptions of and attributions for psychological contract breach". *Journal of Organizational Behavior*, 23: 39–56.

Levinson, H., Price, C. R., Munden, K. J., Mandl, H. J., and Solley, C. M. (1962). *Men, Management and Mental Health*. Boston: Harvard University Press.

Lewis, K., and Taylor, M. S. (2001). "Reciprocity from the organization's side". Paper presented at Society of Industrial/Organizational Psychology (SIOP) Meetings, May.

Liden, R. C., Sparrowe, R. T., and Wayne, S. J. (1997). "Leader–member exchange theory: The past and potential for the future". *Research in Personnel and Human Resources Management*, 15: 47–119.

McGaughey, S. L., and Liesch, P. W. (2002). "The global sports-media nexus: Reflections on the 'super league saga' in Australia". *Journal of Management Studies*, 39: 383–416.

McLean Parks, J. M., Kidder, D. L., and Gallagher, D. G. (1998). "Fitting square pegs into round holes: Mapping the domain of contingent work arrangements onto the psychological contract". *Journal of Organizational Behavior*, 19: 697–730.

Menniger, K. A. (1958). *Theory of Psychoanalytic Technique*. New York: Basic Books.

Morrison, E. W., and Robinson, S. L. (1997). "When employees feel betrayed: A model of how psychological contract violation develops". *Academy of Management Review*, 22: 226–56.

Moye, N., and Bartol, K. (2001). "The dimensionality of the psychological contract". Paper presented at Society of Industrial/Organizational Psychology Meetings (SIOP), San Diego.

Nicholson, N., and Johns, G. (1985). "The absence culture and the psychological contract— who's in control of absence?" *Academy of Management Review*, 3: 397–407.

Pearce, J. (1998). "Psychological contracts in organizations: Understanding unwritten agreements". *Administrative Science Quarterly*, 43: 184–6.

Phelps, S. (1996). "Psychological contracts in organizations: Understanding unwritten agreements". *Personnel Psychology*, 49: 487–90.

Porter, L. W., Lawler, E. E., and Hackman, J. R. (1975). *Behavior in Organizations*. New York: McGraw-Hill.

Robinson, S. L. (1996). "Trust and breach of the psychological contract". *Administrative Science Quarterly*, 41: 574–99.

—— and Morrison, E. W. (1995). "Psychological contracts and OCB: The effect of unfulfilled obligations on civic virtue behavior". *Journal of Organizational Behavior*, 16: 289–98.

—— and —— (2000). "The development of psychological contract breach and violation: A longitudinal study". *Journal of Organizational Behavior*, 21: 525–46.

—— and Rousseau, D. M. (1994). "Violating the psychological contract: Not the expectation but the norm". *Journal of Organizational Behavior*, 15: 245–59.

—— and Wolfe Morrison, E. (1997). "The development of psychological contract breach and violation: A longitudinal study". Working Paper, New York University, Stern Business School, Department of Management.

—— Kraatz, M., and Rousseau, D. M. (1994). "Changing obligations and the psychological contract: A longitudinal study". *Academy of Management Journal*, 37: 137–52.

Roehling, M. V. (1996). "The origins and early development of the psychological contract construct". Paper presented at the Annual Meeting of the Academy of Management, Cincinnati.

Rousseau, D. M. (1989). "Psychological and implied contracts in organizations". *Employee Responsibilities and Rights Journal*, 2: 121–39.

—— (1990). "New hire perceptions of their own and their employer's obligations: A study of psychological contracts". *Journal of Organizational Behavior*, 11: 389–400.

—— (1995). *Psychological Contracts in Organizations: Understanding Written and Unwritten Agreements*. Thousand Oaks, CA: Sage.

—— (2001). "Schema, promise and mutuality: The building blocks of the psychological contracts". *Journal of Occupational and Organizational Psychology*, 74: 511–41.

—— and McLean Parks, J. (1992). "The contracts of individuals and organizations," in L. L. Cummings and B. M. Staw (eds.), *Research in Organizational Behavior* (Greenwich, CT: JAI Press), 1–43.

—— and Tijoriwala, S. A. (1998). "Assessing psychological contracts: Issues, alternatives and measures". *Journal of Organizational Behavior*, 19: 679–95.

Schein, E. H. (1965). *Organizational Psychology*. Englewood Cliffs, NJ: Prentice Hall.

—— (1970). *Organizational Psychology*, 2nd edn. Englewood Cliffs, NJ: Prentice Hall.

—— (1980). *Organizational Psychology*, 3rd edn. Englewood Cliffs, NJ: Prentice Hall.

Shore, L. M., and Barksdale, K. (1998). "Examining degree of balance and level of obligations in the employment relationship: A social exchange approach". *Journal of Organizational Behavior*, 19: 731–44.

Taylor, M. S. (1996). "Restoring the faith: The impact of procedural justice on psychological contract violations". Paper presented at Society of Industrial and Organizational Psychology (SIOP) Meetings, San Diego.

Tekleab, A. G. (2003). "The role of realistic job previews and organizational socialization on newcomers' psychological contract development". Dissertation, University of Maryland at College Park.

—— and Taylor, M. S. (2000). "Easing the pain: Determinants and effects of psychological contract violation". Paper presented at the Annual Conference of the Academy of Management, Toronto.

Tetrick, L., Shore, L. M., Bommer, W. H., and Wayne, S. J. (2002). "Effects of perceptions of employer's failure to keep their promises: An application of ELVN-P". Paper presented at Society of Industrial/Organizational Psychology (SIOP) Meetings, Toronto.

Thomas, H. D. C., and Anderson, N. (1998). "Changes in newcomers' psychological contracts during organizational socialization: A study of recruits entering the British Army". *Journal of Organizational Behavior*, 19: 745–67.

Tsui, A. S., Pearce, J. L., Porter, L. W., and Tripoli, A. M. (1997). "Alternative approaches to the employee–organization relationships: Does investment in employees pay off?" *Academy of Management Journal*, 40: 1089–121.

Turnley, W. H., and Feldman, D. C. (1999). "The impact of psychological contract violations on exit, voice, loyalty, and neglect". *Human Relations*, 52: 895–922.

—— and Feldman, D. C. (2000). "Re-examining the effects of psychological contract violations: Unmet expectations and job satisfaction as mediators". *Journal of Organizational Behavior*, 21: 25–42.

Wayne, S. J., Shore, L. M., and Liden, R. C. (1997). "Perceived organizational support and leader–member exchange: A social exchange perspective". *Academy of Management Journal*, 40: 82–111.

West, M. S., and Cardy, R. L. (1997)). "Accommodating claims of disability: The potential impact of abuses". *Human Resource Management Review*, 7: 233–46.

13

Changes in the Employment Relationship Across Time

RENÉ SCHALK

13.1 Introduction

This chapter examines changes in the employer–employee relationship from three perspectives: Societal changes; organizational changes; and individual changes in employees' desires. The first perspective is the influence of the societal environment in which the employment relationship is embedded. Arguably, changes in the employment relationship occur as a consequence of developments in our society overall. In addition, characteristics of the context in which employment relationships are embedded exert an influence on the exchanges between employer and employee. For example, the specific situation in a certain country with respect to the legal system and the state of the economy has an impact on the employment relationship. Other examples are the influence of cultural norms and values related to exchanges, and the role of the unions and the state with respect to agreements and rules around employment relationships (see Rousseau and Schalk 2000). The societal environment is the context for the exchange between employer and employee (see Figure 13.1).

The parties directly involved in the employment relationship, the organization and the employee, provide the second and third sources of potential change on the employment relationship. While the employer/organization and the employee are part of society, they are influenced by the same structural factors and dynamic change processes. Nevertheless, they have a unique perspective on the employment relationship, which is also subject to change over time. For example, the needs and desires of the organization and the employee may not necessarily converge nor might there be agreement on the obligations of each party to the relationship. For example, organizations may need organizational flexibility to cope with increasing competition and this may require employees to develop specific skills. Organizations might also try to change rules for the standard age of retirement, working hours, etc.

Similarly, employees' expectations and desires from employment may change. An employee who has a family with young children will consider the employer's flexibility to provide a good balance between work and private life as an important issue. Freese and Schalk (1995) argue that individuals attach differing degrees of saliency to what an employer offers based on their non-work life. Consequently, society, the employer, and the employee are involved in a dynamic and changing interaction process over time.

Figure 13.1. *Framework: Society, organization, and employee.*

The structure of the chapter is as follows. First, changes in society and the employment relationship are described. Specifically, a key issue is whether there has been a fundamental shift in the employment relationship and whether we can speak of a new psychological contract. We start with describing changes over time on the societal level, including changes in employment relations across time in the past. More specifically, our attention will be focused on the present situation related to the question of whether there is a fundamental shift in the content of the terms of employment relations: Is a new psychological contract taking over from the old deal of security in exchange for loyalty? Second, given organizational trends towards greater flexibility and employability, does this give rise to greater differentiation in contract forms and what are the consequences of contingent work on employee attitudes and behavior? Third, what are the implications of changes in an individual's life course for the employment relationship? Finally, different phases in the process of exchange between employer and employee are discussed. How the employment relationship evolves in the first period after organizational entry is described, as well as the development in later stages. The latter part of the chapter is devoted to the consequences of these processes and developments for managing and fostering good employment relationships.

13.2 Society

The industrial and information revolution have fundamentally changed the world of work and this has had a profound impact on the employment relationship. Looking back in history, fundamental changes in employment relations can be observed. At first, the predominant model for the employment relationship was the world of work of small businesses of craftsmen (sometimes organized in strongly tied network-like systems like the Guilds), with a master–student relationship as a basic model. The industrial revolution introduced the manufacturing model. Strong employer power, "carrot and stick" motivational approaches, and paternalistic management of the factory owner characterized employment relationships of that period. Greater attention to the human factor and the growing power of the unions were driving factors that acted as a counterbalance to the power of employers. The employer–employee relationship subsequently became embedded in an elaborated system of labor laws created by governments. In addition, central agreements between employer organizations and the unions determined and limited the zone of negotiability for large groups of workers (Rousseau and Schalk 2000), thus limiting the freedom to create individual labor contracts.

More recently, the technological and information revolution highlighted the importance of knowledge in organizations with knowledge being recognized as a crucial competitive factor. Furthermore, growing worldwide competition made companies more vulnerable and sensitive to their complex and dynamic environment and employees' knowledge was increasingly recognized as an important asset for organizations. Breakthroughs in the field of technology and information, increasing global competition, and escalating interdependence between organizations have created new fundamental "rules" for organizations.

Organizations today are facing rapid successions of unpredictable changes. As a reaction to these pressures, new trends in management are emerging such as greater market orientation, a stronger focus on cost reduction and efficiency, and closer cooperation between organizations. To respond to these types of pressures, management strives for greater organizational flexibility and at the same time greater employee commitment to organizational goals. On the other hand, employees want more individualized opportunities that fit their own goals in relation to career development and work–family relationships (Rousseau and Schalk 2000). We now witness a situation in which both employer and employee are seeking more flexibility in line with their own goals, which may conflict. Thus, finding a "match" between employees' and employers' needs may be difficult, but is necessary to guarantee positive organizational outcomes.

13.2.1 Global trends

There seems to be a global trend that traditional labor laws are less influential in determining the employment relationships in many countries. Declining unionization worldwide (see e.g. Kabanoff et al. 2000; Sels et al. 2000) and increasing numbers of individuals being employed in sectors not covered by traditional labor statutes means that fewer employees' working conditions are regulated by (legal) standards. The implication is that there is more scope for organizations and employees to bargain over individual terms and conditions of employment. The pressures for greater firm-level flexibility have led to significant changes in employment relations within firms. The degree to which these changes have occurred is linked to societal factors.

In general, employment relationships are becoming more diverse within firms, more idiosyncratic between people, and more directly shaped by market-related factors (Rousseau and Schalk 2000). Contemporary employment relationships are changing as a consequence of these developments. Changing the conditions under which firms are likely to be more successful affects the critical features of the employment relationships these firms create (Anderson and Schalk 1998).

Employers' rising need for organizational flexibility is leading firms to establish diverse employment arrangements to cope with fluctuations in organizational production capacity. Some of the trends include the use of temporary workers, on-call contracts, and fixed-term contracts, as well as hiring workers through employment agencies. Flexibility also means a changing allocation of business risks as firms transfer risk to employees through the adoption of performance-related pay, allowing employees equity stakes in the company, and the differentiation between highly valued core workers and peripheral contingent employees.

In sum, employers are making increasingly greater demands upon their employees' flexibility in order to be able to better anticipate the dynamics of the environment. There is an ongoing process of change in the nature of employment relationships between employers and employees, resulting from changes in the economic and social environments in which organizations operate (Roehling et al. 2000; Sparrow 2000).

13.2.2 Changing psychological contract?

The changes outlined above have consequences for the exchange relationship. Some authors suggest that a "new deal" and, consequently, a "new" psychological contract is emerging in employer–employee relationships (see e.g. Hiltrop 1995; Anderson and Schalk 1998). The "old" core issues of the twentieth century psychological contract, the offer of job security and continuity in exchange for loyalty, seem to make room for a more transactional relationship with a greater emphasis on flexibility and employability (Anderson and Schalk 1998; Roehling et al. 2000; Sparrow 2000).

In the "new deal," employers are supposed to put greater emphasis on the development of the broad skills of the employees and employees' willingness to change jobs and be flexible (Sparrow 2000). Employees are expected to seek more opportunities to develop their competencies and skills, in order to increase their "market value." They should focus less on job security provided by the organization, and more on job security based on their value on the labor market (Gaspersz and Ott 1996). This is supposed to be typical for "modern" contractual relationships. For employers to meet their goals, they need to place more emphasis on eliciting autonomy, cooperation, responsibility, and creativity from employees and at the same time, in meeting these organizational goals employees experience more work pressure and less job security, and seek a balance between responsibilities at work and at home.

How do employees react to these fundamental changes in employment relationships? Do their perceptions of what their employer is obligated to provide them and what they feel they owe their employer change accordingly? Is a new "psychological contract" emerging? We will discuss these questions based on the results of a recent large-scale study on the mutual obligations between employer and employee as perceived by the employee (the psychological contract) in the Netherlands (Huiskamp and Schalk 2002).

In twenty-seven Dutch organizations in 1999–2000, a standard questionnaire was distributed among groups of employees. The data of 1331 employees were gathered creating a sample that was reasonably representative for the Dutch working population. The percentage of males was slightly higher than the Dutch working population, and there was an underrepresentation of younger and older employees, as well as an overrepresentation of the group between 25 and 44 years of age. Also, the degree of education was higher than in the Dutch working population as a whole. The questionnaire for individual employees assessed individual characteristics, job and contract characteristics, employee obligations toward the organization, and employer obligations toward the employee (including fulfillment of these obligations).

Tables 13.1 and 13.2 give an overview of the degree to which the employees in the sample perceived that they themselves or their employers were obligated to deliver certain issues (on a five-point scale). Employees felt a very strong obligation to deliver good work in terms of quality and quantity, to protect confidential information, to provide a good service, and to work well with others. They felt that they had few obligations with respect to issues related to switching jobs or making a transfer. The scores for working extra hours when needed to get the job done, volunteering to do non-required tasks if necessary, and not supporting the organization's competitors were rated around the mean score.

With respect to the opinions of employees about the obligations of the employer towards them, Table 13.2 represents the mean scores on these obligations. The scores for obligations with respect to the "soft" issues of candid and fair treatment and open and direct communication were higher than scores on "hard" issues such as the provision of job and income security, a challenging and stimulating job, opportunities for promotion, and bonuses based on performance. In comparison to the employee

Table 13.1. *Means of employee obligations*

Employee obligations	Mean
Deliver good work in terms of quality and quantity	4.57
Protect confidential information	4.55
Provide a good service	4.44
Work well with others	4.24
Work extra hours if that is what is needed to get the job done	3.84
Volunteer to do non-required tasks if necessary	3.61
Not support the organization's competitors	3.25
Provide advance notice if taking a job elsewhere	2.83
Accept an internal transfer if necessary	2.75
Accept a transfer to another geographical location if necessary	2.22
Total mean employee obligations	3.63

Source: Huiskamp and Schalk (2002).

obligations, the range between the highest and lowest score was much smaller (employee obligations ranged from 4.57 to 2.22, whereas employer obligations ranged from 4.35 to 3.60).

In addition, using the employees' opinions about the fulfillment by the employer of the employer's obligations, the degree of fulfillment of the psychological contract was assessed. The mean scores are shown in Table 13.3. Overall, the psychological contract was better fulfilled with respect to the work climate, job and income security, and provision of training and education. The fulfillment scores were lowest on open and direct communication, opportunities for promotion, and, especially, candid and fair treatment. The highest mean score on fulfillment was 3.17, much lower than the highest mean scores for employee (4.57) and employer (4.35) obligations. The employees evaluated the fulfillment on issues of open and direct communication

Table 13.2. *Means of employer obligations*

Employer obligations	Mean
Candid and fair treatment	4.35
Open and direct communication	4.29
A competitive salary	4.29
Respect	4.15
Training and education	4.02
Good work climate	4.02
Job and income security	3.88
A job that is challenging and stimulating	3.66
Opportunities for promotion	3.61
Bonuses based on performance	3.60
Total Mean employer obligations	3.99

Source: Huiskamp and Schalk (2002).

Table 13.3. *Means of fulfillment of employer obligations*

Fulfillment of employer obligations	Mean
Good work climate	3.17
Job and income security	3.16
Training and education	3.14
A competitive salary	3.08
A job that is challenging and stimulating	3.05
Respect	2.98
Bonuses based on performance	2.81
Open and direct communication	2.77
Opportunities for promotion	2.67
Candid and fair treatment	2.64
Total mean fulfillment of employer obligations	2.95

Source: Huiskamp and Schalk (2002).

and candid and fair treatment as low. Considering that these issues were indicated as strong obligations of the employer, this is an important point to note.

What do these results tell us about the emergence of a new psychological contract? These results seem to be partly in line with a "new style" of employment relationship, characterized by an emphasis on responsibility and cooperation, and a more transactional exchange relationship. However, the picture is complex, and certainly not clear-cut. The general ethical issue of "protecting confidential information," for example, seems to have a timeless high rating. In contrast to what would be expected from a "new deal" relationship, the willingness to comply with the employers' wishes with respect to "employability" (transfer of job or location) is low. This implies that, with respect to employee obligations, the "new" deal certainly is not fully recognizable: Issues of the "old" psychological contract are still considered important, and, on the contrary, some issues related to the "new" psychological contract are considered as not very important.

Employees, in general, believe that employers are strongly obliged to provide candid and fair treatment, to communicate in an open and direct manner, to offer a competitive salary, and to treat employees with respect. These issues are considered more important than having job and income security, opportunities for promotion, a challenging and stimulating job, and bonuses related to performance. Open communication is considered typical of the "new," individualized employment relationship (Roehling et al. 2000), while job and income security (characteristic of the "old" contract) are considered less important. However, issues that are not directly linked to the new psychological contract, such as candid and fair treatment, a competitive salary, and respect, also score high. In contrast to what would be expected of a "new deal," having opportunities for promotion and a challenging and stimulating job, which would increase the employee's employability, obtain low scores as employer obligations. The inevitable conclusion is that, with respect to employer obligations, the "new" contract is certainly not fully recognizable and visible.

The employees considered the fulfillment of the psychological contract as sufficient with respect to "traditional" issues such as a good work climate, job and income security, and training and education. However, the psychological contract is least well fulfilled with respect to "modern" issues such as open and direct communication, and opportunities for promotion.

Thus, the overall picture seems to indicate that employers are perceived as fulfilling obligations that are considered important within the "old" psychological contract, but at the same time, seem to do less well on issues of the "new" psychological contract. These data do not provide strong support for the assumption that a "new" psychological contract has replaced the "old" psychological contract in the Netherlands as a whole. In other countries, the situation might be different. We have no reason, however, to assume that this is the case. Countries all over the world are facing the same global developments and global changes (see Rousseau and Schalk 2000).

Within a country, there may be many differences, of course, between different sectors of employment or occupational groups. In some sectors, new contracts may be prominent, whereas in other sectors issues of the old contract may be more prevalent. Still, we believe that many contract terms can be considered as timeless and important in all sectors and across time. Fairness, communication, and respect are apparently related to basic human values that are valued irrespective of time. These issues are clearly related to the nature of the relationship between the individual and the group (organization), and responsible behavior that preserves the social fabric. These two issues are considered as fundamental dimensions of human values related to work (see Schwartz 1999). On other, more concrete terms, such as pay and security, there is perhaps more variation possible over time. The provision of these issues is mainly considered in relation to the context of societal developments that have an impact on the employment relationship. Job security, for example, will only become an issue when economic prospects are uncertain. Pay will be considered in relation to the standards for costs of living in a certain region, country, and time.

In summary, the influence of society on employment relationships is twofold. First, characteristics of the formal and informal institutions in society determine employment relationships and the zone of negotiability when creating employment relationships. Second, with respect to the terms included in employment relations and the changes therein over time, there seems to be a difference between rather stable "timeless" issues and other issues that are more prone to changes in society. The next section of this chapter will focus on changes in the employment relationship from the perspective of the organization, in the context of the trends and changes at the societal level we have described above.

13.3 The organization

As a consequence of changes in the environment, organizations adjust their ways of organizing with implications for employment relationships. We will discuss here two main issues: The diversification of contract forms and the implications of organizational changes for employment relationships.

13.3.1 Diversification in contract forms

Organizations are increasingly using more differentiated contract types. The numbers of employees with a permanent position and a full-time contract are declining, while the numbers of part-time workers and workers on a contingent basis are steadily, although not very rapidly, increasing. Across EU countries, for example, there was a growth from 9.1 to 13.4 percent in the proportion of workers on fixed-term contracts between 1983 and 2000 (EUROSTAT data, cited in EIRONLINE 2002). The 1995 U.S. mini census data (Cohany 1996) indicate that contingent workers, defined as having jobs in which individuals do not have explicit or implicit contracts for long-term employment (Polivka 1996: 4), make up 4.9 percent of the U.S. workforce. According to Cohany (1996), in the United States, workers with alternative employment arrangements made up 10 percent of the workforce, and only 1 percent were employed in temporary help agencies.

One reason organizations strive to diversify employment contracts is to achieve greater flexibility to anticipate peaks in production or service needs of customers, for example, seasonal employment. Contingent employees are also hired by organizations when a temporary growth of production is expected, or to replace workers who are expected to be absent for a period of time, for example, because of maternity leave. In addition, there is a growing tendency by organizations to initially offer contingent contracts as a way of evaluating the performance of potential permanent employees prior to offering them permanent contracts (Donker van Heel 2000).

Flexibility for the organization often implies the absence of job security for employees. The type of contract offered has consequences for job related outcomes. Contingent employees have fewer career opportunities, less opportunities for education and training, and lower wages (Van Breukelen and Allegro 2000; Zant et al. 2000). Coyle-Shapiro and Kessler (2002) found that in a sample of government employees in the United Kingdom, permanent employees reported higher numbers of obligations and inducements than temporary employees. Temporary employees are likely to perceive their contracts as more transactional than relational (Millward and Hopkins 1998). Temporary jobs are often regarded as stepping-stones to permanent jobs, especially by younger workers (Tremlett and Collins 1999; Goudswaard et al. 2000). As workers get older, the chance of getting a permanent contract as a follow-up to a temporary contract declines (Muffels and Steijn 1998; Zant et al. 2000; Remery et al. 2002).

There are two important factors that predict whether people will be employed on a flexible contract or on a permanent contract. The first factor is the previous labor market position. When an individual's previous job is temporary, or when an individual has been unemployed, the chances of that individual getting a temporary contract are much higher than getting a permanent job. The second factor is the length of the training period required for the job. Employees on jobs that require long periods of on-the-job training have a very high chance of being offered a permanent contract. Organizations have to invest in the employees' training, work experience, and specific competencies, and workers with a great deal of company-specific knowledge constitute the core of the organization (Remery et al. 2002). Workers with little education, those who are unskilled, previously unemployed, or employed in temporary positions, have only a slight chance of obtaining a permanent contract.

13.3.2 *Characteristics of contingent work*

Contingent contracts are used to enhance flexibility. Therefore, one would expect to find higher employability, mobility, and intention to leave among contingent employees. The labor market mobility of contingent employees seems to be higher in comparison to permanent workers (Dekker and Dorenbos 1997; Muffels and Steijn 1998; Zant et al. 2000; Schippers et al. 2001; Remery et al. 2002). In the Netherlands, almost 50 percent of the workers in flexible jobs have a permanent job a short period later in time, while the number of permanent employees moving to a flexible contract is very low. However, the number of flexible workers finding a qualitatively better job is, in fact, rather small. This might be due to the fact that temporary employees in general have low education, limited skills, and little work experience. Therefore, they are less likely to acquire a permanent job (Muffels and Steijn 1998).

This brings us to the question of whether the contingent contract is the contract of choice for contingent employees. For approximately one-third of the employees on contingent contracts this seems to be the case. In the United States, around 30 percent of those in temporary employment seem to have a preference for temporary work (Polivka 1996; Barringer and Sturman 1999). In the United Kingdom, a survey indicated that just under a quarter of temporary employees did not want a permanent job (Tremlett and Collins 1999). Several other studies indicate that the majority of workers employed in temporary contracts would rather have a permanent contract (Russo et al. 1997; Muffels et al. 1999; Steijn 1999; Miedema and Hesselink 2000; Gustafsson et al. 2001; Remery et al. 2002; Van Ginkel et al. 2002). The main reasons for this preference have to do with (future) security and fulfilling obligations towards family and society. Employees on a permanent contract acquire more benefits and rights, ranging from pensions to better career opportunities and greater respect.

De Feyter et al. (2001), who interviewed 2501 Dutch employees by telephone, found that contingent employees who have a preference for contingent work have a higher preference for external mobility. In a sample of 540 Dutch temporary agency workers, there is some evidence that these employees are willing to work for several organizations (Slinkman 1999), especially among younger employees. The main reason they gave for this was that they wanted to improve their employability. A study by Van der Toren et al. (2002) sheds some light on individuals' motives for working on a contingent basis. In a sample of 234 employees, 15 percent indicated they opted for this kind of contract because of the freedom involved. Twenty-four percent of respondents indicated that they were unable to find a permanent job and 13 percent reported that contingent work allowed them greater possibilities to combine work and life. Limited availability to the labor market was an important reason for 15 percent, to gain experience was indicated by 4 percent, and earning an additional income by 12 percent. Other reasons totaled to 17 percent (Van der Toren et al. 2002: 35).

Tremlett and Collins (1999) cited as main reasons for contingent employment in the United Kingdom "not wanting the commitment that goes with permanent employment" (21 percent), the loss of freedom to choose the work they wanted to do (18 percent), being too old (18 percent), and not being interested in permanent employment (18 percent). This general trend is supported by data on the satisfaction with labor contracts of a large sample (11,351) of Dutch employees (Goudswaard et al. 2000) (see Table 13.4).

Temporary workers who had no prospect of a permanent position were less satisfied with their contract than permanent employees. Temporary workers with the chance of getting a permanent appointment were less satisfied than permanent employees, but more satisfied than temporary contract workers without the prospect of getting a permanent contract. Temporary agency workers were not very satisfied with their contract (Goudswaard et al. 2000). Other studies confirm the finding that

Table 13.4. *Satisfaction with type of contract of Dutch employees*

Employment contract	Satisfied (%)	Not satisfied (%)
Permanent contract	91.1	8.9
Temporary contract with prospect of permanent	84.0	16.0
Temporary < 1 year without prospect	66.3	33.7
Temporary > 1 year without prospect	63.1	36.9
Permanent on-call	82.6	17.4
Temporary on-call	80.6	19.4
Temporary agency worker	69.1	30.9
Other flexible contracts (seasonal)	86.7	13.3
Freelancers	78.1	21.9

Source: Goudswaard et al. (2000: 74).

temporary workers with the prospect of a permanent contract were more satisfied than employees without prospects (Hesselink et al. 1998; Sanders et al. 2002). An explanation for these results might be that the downside of flexibility is job insecurity. Many authors conclude that perceived job insecurity of contingent workers is high (Fluit and Knegt 1999; Klandermans and Van Vuuren 1999; Hesselink and Van Vuuren 1999; Guest and Conway 2000, 2001; Miedema and Hesselink 2000; Van den Bos 2000; Van der Toren et al. 2002). Often this is not only a perception, but also a reality. In the Netherlands, for example, temporary employees have a much greater chance of becoming unemployed in comparison to permanent workers, 17 versus 9 percent (Steijn 1999). However, not all contingent workers experience high employment insecurity. In a sample of 199 permanent employees and 24 flexible contract employees in the American aerospace industry, voluntarily choosing a flexible contract had no impact on perceived security (Pearce 1993; Pearce and Randel 1998). Guest et al. (2000) found that temporary workers reported lower job security, but agency workers reported higher security than permanent employees.

Organizations, in general, provide less opportunities and benefits for contingent employees than for permanent employees (De Feyter et al. 2001). Contingent workers receive less education, training, and appraisals, and their tasks remain the same. Often, contingent employees have to pay the expenses of their education and training activities themselves (Delsen 1998).

13.3.3 The effects of contingent work on employee well-being and performance

Based on the data of a large-scale longitudinal survey of approximately 4000 Dutch employees over the period 1986–1996, an analysis was made of changes in job satisfaction among contingent and permanent employees (Zant et al. 2000). On average, the satisfaction with a contingent contract was stable over the years, but significantly lower than the average satisfaction with a permanent contract. In support of these findings, a significant increase in job satisfaction was found when employees obtained a permanent contract, and a decline in job satisfaction after shifting from a permanent to a contingent contract. Several other studies confirm these findings (Muffels and Steijn 1998; Miedema and Hesselink 2000; Kaiser 2002; Sanders et al. 2002).

Regarding commitment to the organization, Coyle-Shapiro and Kessler (2000) found that temporary workers displayed lower levels of commitment to the organization. Goudswaard et al. (2000) found higher commitment among temporary workers with a chance of getting a permanent appointment, as compared to permanent workers. In this study, there was a small difference, however, between the commitment of short-term temporary workers without an outlook on a permanent contract and permanently employed workers. Several other studies confirm that the general assumption of lower organizational commitment among temporary employees (Dercksen 1997) but this does not seem to hold in all situations (Pearce 1993; Schalk et al. 1998*b*; Guest et al. 2000; Miedema and Hesselink 2000; Steijn 2000; Torka 2000; Torka and Van Riemsdijk 2001; Koster et al. 2002; Sanders et al. 2002).

With respect to performance, a study by Van Breukelen and Allegro (2000) in the transport sector, in which employees were asked to give a self-report on their performance, found no significant differences in performance based on type of contract. In addition, Van Breukelen and Allegro asked managers to rate the performance of their subordinates. According to managers, temporary agency workers did not perform as well as permanent workers. Managers were of the opinion that temporary agency workers were less competent and less skilled than permanent workers. The managers noticed not only negative, but also positive points: According to the managers, temporary workers as a group (in this case including agency workers) made a clear contribution to the performance of the departments and were fun to work with.

Quinlan et al. (2001) give an extensive review of contingent work and reported that there was a positive relationship between contingent work and both accidents and poor work-related health. With respect to accidents at work, a Dutch union report (Warning and Van der Straten 2001) indicated that according to their sample of 88 union representatives, contingent workers caused 8.5 percent of the accidents in their organizations. In another 11.3 percent of the accidents, contingent employees were perceived to be involved one way or another. It was indicated that this could be attributed to insufficient instructions being given to contingent employees since most of the time they were excluded from regular company training programs. Hesselink et al. (1998) found that agency workers were significantly less informed about safety at work compared to permanent workers and directly employed temporary workers.

A report of the Dutch government investigating accidents in the workplace with a lethal ending in the period from 1997 to 2000 (Martens 2001) showed a declining trend of accidents among temporary agency workers, despite an upward trend in the total number of accidents. However, the percentage of lethal accidents for temporary agency workers (8 percent) was twice as high as the percentage of agency workers in the labor population as a whole (approximately 4 percent).

From an organizational perspective, hiring contingent employees seems to be attractive to increase flexibility. Most employees on those contracts, however, seem to prefer a permanent position. There is also a group of employees that prefer the positive opportunities they perceive in having a contingent contract. In general, permanent employees seem to have better attitudes and organizational behaviors as compared to contingent employees. A positive exception to this rule is the group of temporary employees that are looking for a permanent position: They often perform better and have more positive attitudes towards work than their permanent colleagues.

13.3.4 Organizational changes

In many companies, there is an increasing organizational pressure for greater employee flexibility linked with decreasing job security. Employers are demanding greater worker innovation and contribution and at the same time they are putting more emphasis on assessing the added and demonstrable value each worker provides. Many organizational changes (e.g. flattening of the organizational structure to ensure a flexible and decisive organization) imply a fundamental change in the relationship between employer and employee (McLean Parks and Kidder 1994; Schalk and Freese 1997). Such changes influence individual beliefs about the mutual obligations of employer and employee (Rousseau 1990). When an employee observes a discrepancy between the situation after an organizational change and the expectancies based on the original contract, the psychological contract will be perceived as violated, leading to a decrease in satisfaction and motivation to work (Robinson and Rousseau 1994). In addition, there is a chance that an employee will feel less involved in the organization (Schalk et al. 1995).

Violations of the psychological contract arise in periods of change. A violation of the psychological contract arises when the employee perceives a discrepancy between the actual fulfillment of obligations and the promised obligations. Since a psychological contract is based on promised obligations and it is assumed that both parties will keep their promises, a violation of the psychological contract can have severe consequences (Robinson and Rousseau 1994).

Restructuring and decentralization may have an enormous effect on the psychological contracts of employees (Kissler 1994; Morrison 1994; Anderson and Schalk 1998). This occurs when traditional beliefs, like job security and a fixed salary in exchange for hard work and loyalty of the employee, are being replaced by other, often more unclear, mutual obligations between employer and employee (Sims 1994). As a consequence, according to Hiltrop (1995), the psychological contract is moving towards the transactional end of the continuum, implying a decrease in loyalty and commitment to the organization (Wiesenfeld and Brockner 1993; Hiltrop 1995). Furthermore, the turbulence and insecurity of the environment leads to a situation in which it becomes difficult for the organization to fulfill all obligations expected by employees (McLean Parks and Kidder 1994). These factors can lead to violations of the psychological contract.

During organizational changes, employees can experience a decline in the fulfillment of employer obligations and employees' personal obligations towards the organization, resulting in an increase in the number of violations of the psychological contract (Robinson and Rousseau 1994). A decline in the fulfillment of obligations and an increase in violations of employer obligations in the psychological contract can go hand in hand with decreasing commitment to the organization (Kessler and Undy 1996; Coyle-Shapiro and Kessler 2000) and a growing intention to quit (Schalk et al. 1995; Turnley and Feldman 1999). A loss of trust (Robinson 1996) and lower job satisfaction (Turnley and Feldman 2000) are other consequences. These changes negatively affect employee contributions to the organization, such as organizational citizenship behavior (Coyle-Shapiro 2002).

When organizational changes lead to violations of psychological contracts, negative consequences for organizational performance can be expected. The negative changes in employee attitudes and behavior will have consequences for the organization as a whole. On the other hand, organizational change might lead to a better functioning of the organization and improvement of work processes. If, in the process of implementation, attention is paid to communication, support, and participation of employees (Schalk et al. 1998*a*), this could have positive effects on employees. With respect to the general characterization of the psychological contract as more transactional or relational, it is suggested that, because of organizational change, the psychological contract can become more transactional (Wiesenfeld and Brockner 1993; Hiltrop 1995).

An example of the effects of organizational changes is a study on the impact of a merger on changes in the psychological contract and workplace attitudes (Schalk et al. 2001). Data were gathered in two health care organizations involved in a merger before (time 1) as well as after (time 2) implementation of organizational changes related to the merging process. The results of the study show that before and after the organizational changes, the employees' view of the fulfillment of employer obligations, the number of violations of organizational obligations, and their reported obligations toward the organization was about the same (Schalk et al. 2001). However, in general, employees felt less affectively committed to the organization at time 2. There was no clear increase in the intention to leave the organization and no universal shift towards a more transactional relationship (although there was a shift to a more transactional relationship among the full-time employees). To explain these findings we take a closer look at change processes of the psychological contract.

Psychological contracts are relatively stable and have a rather broad margin regarding acceptability and appropriateness within the current contract (see Schalk and Freese 1997). Fluctuations can occur within the margins without fundamentally changing the psychological contract. Work-related attitudes (like affective commitment) will obviously follow roughly the same fluctuation patterns in a positive and a negative direction. Violations will not occur until the limits of the current psychological contract are passed. Once the current contract can no longer be kept, either the contract will be revised and a new, balanced psychological contract will be created or the current contract will be abandoned (explicitly or implicitly terminated). An employee can resign, or stay on and work without dedication, or even thwart the organization (see Schalk and Freese 1997).

For many employees, organizational changes may temporarily lead to a negative fluctuation in their psychological contract, but not to a fundamental change of the contract. Another possibility is revision of the psychological contract. These processes may explain why in the study of Schalk et al. (2001) the content and violations of the psychological contract seemed not to have been affected, while affective commitment to the organization was lower. No general violation of the psychological contract is experienced, linked to a shift toward a more transactional relationship and higher intention to leave.

The general conclusion of the study of Schalk et al. (2001) is that the overall level of experienced employer obligations did not change. However, Schalk et al. (2001) did find interesting differences when they considered specific items of the psychological contract for specific groups of employees. In certain groups, several specific aspects were affected by the organizational changes. The data showed, for example, that after implementation of the organizational changes, employees with few contract hours experienced more problems (violations) in gearing to their private situation, in opportunities to meet other people, and with respect to job security. This could be attributed to the attempts of the organization to improve customer orientation and the changing organizational strategy with respect to permanent contracts. To improve customer orientation, clients did get more say in how care hours were filled in. This led to clients buying more care during family "peak hours," for example, from 8 to 9 a.m. and from 5 to 6 p.m. This resulted in a deterioration of working times for employees because most of them had few working hours and had to deal with family "peak hours" themselves. In addition, because of the changing organizational strategy towards providing permanent contracts, job security might have been affected.

For the group with full-time jobs, particularly "work pressure," "communication channels are open, direct, and clear," and "you receive the information you need" were felt as more problematic after the changes (more violations experienced). In this respect, the way the changes were implemented was not successful. This could also be the reason why the relationship with the organization among these employees shifted in the direction of a more transactional one.

In summary, it seemed that the merger led to a decrease in affective commitment and a shift towards a more transactional relationship with the organization only in the group with a full-time contract. At the same time, the perception of mutual obligations and perceived violations of employer obligations, and the intention to leave the organization did not change dramatically in the organization as a whole, indicating that, in general, the psychological contract had either been revised or not fundamentally affected. However, specific differences between groups with different working hours did emerge. The groups showed different reactions to the changes implemented, depending on their original psychological contract with the organization and the features of their relationship with the organization.

Several conclusions emerge from the above description of the organizational perspective on the employment relationship. Developments in the environment of organizations are driving factors for a greater diversification of contracts and organizational restructuring and change. The (limited) evidence we have now shows that contingent work, especially when not the contract of choice, which seems to be the case for the majority of employees on contingent contracts, is related to lower employee well-being and performance. Organizational changes and restructuring are likely to breach the ideas of employees about what the organization promised them in the past. This may lead to violations of the psychological contract, with adverse effects on employee attitudes and behaviors, and thus on organizational performance.

13.4 The employee perspective

Every individual employee's ideas about the employment relationship changes over time. Newcomers gradually develop rather stable ideas about their employment relationship. Employees make sense of what is happening during their first period at work, the socialization period. And later, when the employment relationship evolves, these ideas will be put to a test and change over time.

In this part, we will discuss two main issues. We will first examine which mechanisms explain changes in newcomers' perceptions of the promises they have exchanged with their employer, that is, the process of psychological contract formation. After that, we will elaborate changes in ideas about the employment relationship related to life course.

13.4.1 The formation of the psychological contract

The process of psychological contract formation has received limited empirical attention. There are only a few studies in this area (Robinson 1994; Thomas and Anderson 1998; De Vos 2002). Robinson et al. (1994) and Thomas and Anderson (1998) found that during the socialization process, newcomers came to perceive that their employers owed them more. In addition, Robinson et al. (1994) found that newcomers came to perceive that they owed less to their employers. These findings support the idea that newcomers change their psychological contract perceptions based on the reality they encounter after entry.

In a four-wave longitudinal study among 333 new hires during the first year of employment, De Vos et al. (2003) showed that changes in newcomers' perceptions of the promises they have made to their employer are affected by their perceptions of their own contributions as well as by their perceptions of inducements received from their employer. Psychological contract formation can be conceived of as a sense-making process taking place during organizational socialization (Louis 1980). Central to the conceptualization of the psychological contract is that it is a perceptual cognition that exists "in the eye of the beholder" (Rousseau 1989). In the sense-making framework, changes in newcomers' perceived promises are associated with their interpretations of experiences encountered after organizational entry. The socialization period is generally considered as an important stage in the formation of employees' psychological contracts (e.g. Nelson et al. 1991; Shore and Tetrick 1994;

Rousseau 1995; Anderson and Thomas 1996; Thomas and Anderson 1998). Socialization research has shown that during this period, sense-making plays an important role in the adjustment of the newcomer to the organization, especially during the first months after entry (Morrison 1993*a*,*b*; Saks and Ashforth 1997). In general, during the socialization process newcomers actively make sense of promises based on their interpretations of experiences encountered in the work setting.

More specifically, there is evidence for the occurrence of a unilateral and a reciprocal adaptation process (De Vos et al. 2003). First, unilateral adaptation refers to changes in perceived promises conveyed by one party based on the interpretation of that party's actions. Newcomers change their perceptions of what their employer has promised them based on their perceptions of the employer inducements actually received. They also change their perceptions of what they have promised their employer based on their perceptions of what they actually contribute to their employer. This implies that newcomers use their experiences within the work environment as feedback about their initial expectations and that they are flexible in adapting their initial expectations based upon this feedback. The evidence for unilateral adaptation of perceived promises provides a confirmation of the importance of sense-making processes after organizational entry put forward in existing theoretical models on psychological contract formation (Shore and Tetrick 1994; Rousseau 1995, 2001). It is important for organizations to pay attention to newcomers' first experiences within their new employment relationship. Active communication about what employees can expect and what is expected of them can enhance changes in perceived promises that are in line with organizational objectives.

Newcomers also change their perceptions of promises based upon their interpretations of the other party's actions in the work setting, that is, reciprocal adaptation. A greater level of perceived employer inducements received is associated with a greater level of perceived employee promises over time. Thus, newcomers not only adapt their promises based on their perceptions of what they contribute to the organization but also as a function of their perception of the inducements they receive from their employer. This supports the validity of the norm of reciprocity (Gouldner 1960) as a central element in explaining the dynamics of the psychological contract. It supports the notion of the psychological contract as an exchange construct (Shore and Tetrick 1994; Rousseau 1995). It confirms earlier findings on the role of reciprocity in explaining the relationship between psychological contract evaluations and employee attitudes and behaviors (e.g. Robinson and Morrison 1995; Robinson 1996; Conway and Briner 2002; Turnley et al. 2003).

The study of De Vos et al. (2003) extends this research by demonstrating that reciprocity also operates during the stage of psychological contract formation and that it explains changes in newcomers' psychological contract perceptions. Moreover, De Vos et al. (2003) showed that it is important to take into account both employee contributions and employer inducements when studying the dynamics of psychological contract changes.

During the first year after entry, newcomers' interpretations of their experiences within the work setting are associated with changes in their perceptions of the terms of their employment deal. This implies that newcomers' psychological contracts are not formed once and for all at the time they enter the organization. They evolve and are periodically revised as a result of sense made of experiences encountered after entry.

13.4.2 Changes in the life course

Employees' needs and ideas about important obligations of the employer (and themselves) change over time. At different ages, employees have different priorities. The content of these priorities, and the changes over time, are related to career stages and events in private life. The seasons of a man's life (Levinson et al. 1978), as well as of course those of a woman's life (Gallos 1989) bring forward different ideas about what is important in the employment relationship.

We use the model of the stages in male adult development that has been proposed by Levinson et al. (1978) and Levinson (1986) as a starting point. Although, in our opinion, only few individuals have a life course that strictly follows Levinson's scheme, it is a useful scheme to illustrate typical changes that might occur in the course of life. Levinson conceives of the adult life course as a sequence of structure-building periods and structure-changing periods (or transitions). In the structure-building periods the central task for a person is to create a (renewed) life structure, that is, an underlying pattern or design in one's life based on primary relationships. According to Levinson, such a period usually lasts six or seven years, up to ten years maximum. After each structure-building period, there is a period of transition to a next structure-building period. Much of the structure of the previous phase is then abolished. The person's views of self and the world are reexamined, and choices are made, creating a new life structure. These transition phases usually last about five years. Each transition is both the ending of a previous phase and the beginning of the next.

The phases discerned by Levinson are:

Preadulthood age	8–17
Early adult transition	17–22
Entry life structure for early adulthood	22–28
Age 30 transition	28–33
Culminating life structure for early adulthood	33–40
Mid-life transition	40–45
Entry structure for middle adulthood	45–50
Age 50 transition	50–55
Culminating life structure for middle adulthood	55–60
Late adult transition	60–65

A person is constantly giving up elements of the younger age period and acquiring new elements for the next one. In the beginning of the career in early adulthood, the needs and expectations (the basis for the exchange of obligations between employer and employee) are related to the central theme of "testing your own capabilities." An employee has to learn by experience if he or she can and wants to be part of the organization, and has the capabilities required for fulfilling the work obligations (Schein 1988). In later stages of the career, these needs and expectations shift to discovering the work area, in which the employee wants to build a career (specialization) and acquire a professional identity. In addition, the employee expects that the organization will recognize the contribution.

The major issue for men in early adulthood is, according to Levinson (1978), building a career and family, with the career often taking precedence. The age-30 transition is often directed at improving one's lot in the career realm. For men, it is often not until the mid-life transition that they begin to deal in a deep way with family issues and with the conflicts between career and family. In a later stage of the career, in which the employee is most productive, he expects to get recognition and rewards from the organization. In the last phase of the career, when the position and contribution to organizational activities of an employee are less prominent, the need for security is high, and the expectations center on the theme of not being made redundant.

A successful career implies being able to be creative, take on a broad array of tasks, acquiring all-round knowledge. In the second half of the career, employees attach a different value on having a career and to the sacrifices they have to make to reach their goals in their social lives. Work pleasure, self-actualization, social recognition, and being able to use creative sources seem to be more important for employees in later career stages (Freese and Schalk 1995). In short, the meaning attached to work changes.

Women appear to have a different cycle of development as well as different correlates of development (Gallos 1989). The central issues for women with respect to growth and career are that they are based on interdependence and relationships. Bardwick (1980) refers to the male sense of self as egocentric and the female sense as interdependent. By egocentric she means an orientation of autonomy and concern for task achievement, and internal focus on one's work. By interdependent she means being oriented toward relationships, working with and helping others, and defining oneself in terms of the other people in one's life.

According to Bardwick (1980), the most important differences in male and female career development stages occur in the thirties and forties. These two decades reflect the following concerns for women. Women between the age 28 and 39 experience the age-30 transition and the settling-down period of the second adult life structure. Women probably experience a more profound and prolonged transition than men at the same age because of the effects of factors such as the "biological time clock" and the effects of growing families (children). Women at this age experience strong career changes, whether they have just established a career or are in mid-career, as well as strong life and family changes.

According to Bardwick (1980) at age 40–50, the mid-life transition and middle adulthood, women are feeling more secure and settled in their relationship and are moving toward more autonomy. Men are moving in just the opposite direction; as career and task demands diminish, they are able to become more sensitive to interpersonal relationships and to their internal psychological needs. Each gender is moving toward greater balance of autonomy and interdependence, but from different directions (Sekaran and Hall 1989).

Male and female careers and family issues should be conceived of as an integrated whole. An individual career should always be considered in the context of other life roles. That is, each person is part of a social environment and has a life outside work. Especially with respect to career issues, the circumstances of "private" life should be taken into consideration. For example, families' developmental needs may produce career dynamics. Work and family linkages are often so strong and pervasive that they simply cannot be ignored.

This is not only the case for men, but also for women. Women increasingly are entering the labor force with the intentions of staying there. The number of dual-career families is increasing. Dual-career families have to deal with the problem of adjustment of two careers. It is clear that couples' careers might be asynchronous at various stages life. The careers do not have to start at the same point, and when they do they might progress at different rates (Sekaran and Hall 1989). Organizational policies might make it difficult for couples to intertwine their family and work interests and goals in a smooth way. As an illustration of differences in importance over the life course, especially at older ages and later career stages, we present in Table 13.5 data on differences related with age based on Huiskamp and Schalk (2002).

Table 13.5. *Correlations of employee, employer, and fulfillment of employer obligations with age (based on data from Huiskamp and Schalk 2002)*

Employee obligations	
Work well with others	0.15***
Provide a good service	0.11***
Protect confidential information	0.07**
Volunteer to do non-required tasks if necessary	0.17***
Work extra hours if that's what is needed to get the job done	0.13***
Accept an internal transfer if necessary	0.07**
Not support the organization's competitors	0.07*
Deliver good work in terms of quality and quantity	0.10***
Employer obligations	
Good work climate	0.10***
Respect	0.06*
Open and direct communication	0.10***
Candid and fair treatment	0.09**
Bonuses based on performance	0.11***
Fulfillment of employer obligations	
Opportunities for promotion	−0.06*
Good work climate	−0.09**
Respect	−0.08**

*p < 0.05; **p < 0.01; ***p < 0.001.

In general, older employees indicate higher levels of obligations, especially with respect to their own obligations. This could be an indication that older employees in general have a "stronger" psychological contract. Van den Brande (2002) makes a distinction between several types of psychological contracts. These types are "strong" and "weak" psychological contracts, in which mutual obligations are high or low, respectively. Next to these types, Van den Brande (2002) also makes a distinction between instrumental and investing psychological contracts, which differ mainly in degree of employee obligations toward the employer (low versus high). The last two types are "loyal" and "loose" contracts; this distinction refers to the time frame of the contract and the related investment.

It seems that older employees indeed have a better psychological contract then younger employees (Freese and Schalk 1995). Older employees feel especially obligated to work extra hours if that is what is needed to get the job done, work well with others, provide a good service, and deliver good work in terms of quality and quantity. On the other hand, they feel that their employer is more obligated (compared to younger employees) to provide them with a good work climate, bonuses based on performance, and open and direct communication. Older employees feel that the organization fulfills its obligations less than younger employees when it comes to opportunities for promotion, good work climate, and respect.

Thus, from the employee perspective, the ideas about the employment relationship change over time. This is because of changes related to aging and progression through the life course, changes and events in private life (e.g. the career pattern of the partner), and changes related to the development of the employment relationship itself (socialization, renegotiation, changing jobs, or leaving for another organization).

13.6 Conclusion

Our society influences the basics of the exchange processes in the employment relationship. The creation, regulation, and ending of employment relationships is embedded in societal institutions, laws, regulations, norms, and values. Since these characteristics of societies are rather stable, and not prone to change, the central issues of employment relationships are to a large degree fixed. Nevertheless, over time, some changes occur. We have seen that the nature of the employment relationship over time has changed. There is an increasing diversification of the types of employment relationships, with an increasing variety of different—more individualized—terms, and with a greater differentiation in the division of the degree of power between the parties involved. Organizations react to current societal developments and ask more flexibility of employees and, in addition, the willingness to comply with organizational changes and take more responsibility for their own career and development. Needs and wants of individual employees change throughout their life course, as a function of individual development and family issues.

Because of these dynamics, the employment relationship changes over time. The developments on the societal level, organizational changes, and processes of change in individual employees and their home situation create the need to readjust the type of relationship between employer and employee on a regular basis.

Many of the changes with an impact on the employment relationship are predictable. There is, for example, certainly at least a general idea about the impact of the socialization process and of the changes that may occur in an employee's life course on perceptions on the employment relationship. The potential negative effects of offering certain types of contracts and the downside of organizational change processes are also clear. Certain organizational changes (especially restructuring, downsizing) can lead to experienced violations of the psychological contract, with adverse consequences for the employment relationship. But the fact that many changes are predictable does not imply that the dynamics of the adjustment process are well understood. Keeping a fit and agreement between the psychological contracts of employer and employee is difficult. It is certain that simplistic models of employment relations fail to represent the complex reality of the dynamic change process. What makes things even more complicated is that in this process multiple contract makers are involved; there is an array of parties having interest to the employment relationship of any given worker.

Variation at the individual level has been increasing as a function of the growth of different employment arrangements. Accepted variations in employment arrangements also make it more likely that firms can combine full-time, part-time, contingent, and other employees under one roof. We expect that in the future employers and workers will bargain over a broader range of terms (including work/family balance, the worker's stake in the company, the employer's rights to worker knowledge and intellectual products, etc.; see Schalk and Rousseau 2001).

Since on the societal level interorganizational relationships are becoming more prominent, the parties involved in employment relationships are expected to become more diverse. There will be more differentiation between workers, because of the involvement of contacts with clients, joint ventures, occupational groups, professions, start-up ventures, etc. An important question is how societies will respond to the apparently competing goals of promoting flexibility for both employer and employee, while keeping social harmony. The relative power of workers and employers is getting more differentiated, and different patterns will emerge. As the workforce places a greater emphasis on employability and makes employees more responsible for their own career paths, both within and outside of organizations, some employers will become more powerful because they have more means to "set the rules." On the other hand, knowledge workers may be in a more powerful position when negotiating the terms of employment—they often find themselves in a seller's market where they have the upper hand. We expect that the intersection of the market mentality with greater market power for some workers will require firms to pay even closer attention to trends in the larger labor market in order to remain competitive for scarce, valuable workers. This pattern may result in a greater variation in psychological contract terms, particularly as negotiated by workers in more valued sectors of the labor market. In these sectors the zone of negotiability is higher.

The zone of negotiation determines the focus of negotiations about the employment relationship. For example, working conditions and pay levels are less highly regulated for higher-level jobs (managerial, professional) than for lower-level jobs (white- or blue-collar). Therefore, negotiations for higher-level jobs focus less on pay and working circumstances and more on opportunities for development, additional benefits, job content, and so on, while negotiations for lower-level jobs focus more on the former.

This has implications for the boundaries of what is considered acceptable within the agreement made. Breaches of the contract will have different meanings to employees in different positions, as a result of the generally different focus in terms of the exchange relationship. Next to this, there is another process involved: Employers will accept more from, and be willing to offer more for, hard-to-get workers. Employers recruiting in a difficult labor market may gain an advantage by communicating that they are willing to negotiate customized psychological contracts. But an employer who offers idiosyncratic arrangements should take into account that between employees they are procedurally as well as distributively fair.

The results presented in this chapter highlight several potential implications for employers. They imply that employers should pay more attention to their strategy of offering certain types of contracts, and to the way they manage change processes in their organization. Management of employees' psychological contracts, starting with paying attentions to newcomers' beliefs regarding the promises they have exchanged with their new organization and extending to later phases of the exchange between employer and employee, should be considered as a central issue in human resource management. The relationship between organizational actions and changes in newcomers' perceptions of both employer and employee promises indicates that it is important for employers to be aware of the impact of their human resource policies on employees' expectations and on their intended contributions. Employers can manage employees' perceptions of their own promises directly by providing them concrete information and feedback about their own contributions within the work setting.

The chapter points out some potential negative effects of organizational changes on workplace attitudes. In implementing changes, communication about the psychological contract plays a particularly important part. We underscore the importance of taking into account specific effects for categories of employees with different contract patterns. If no attention is paid to differences between groups, violations of the psychological contract and negative effects on workplace attitudes can be the consequence.

In the future, a critical question is how to balance a greater differentiation of contracts that try to match organizational and individual needs, while keeping fairness in terms of the contract between employees, especially in situations where employees are interdependent. Integrating employer and employee flexibility, promoting individual employability, and at the same time promoting organizational cooperation, while keeping clear boundaries for individual psychological contracts, is the main task.

A greater variety of contract types, including more "individualized" results of contract negotiations, will exist. The management of employment relationships means building "people-building" rather than "people-using" organizations, in an organizational climate characterized by trust and a life-long perspective for the employee. Matching individual and organizational needs in a changing society is the core task of a dynamic approach to employment relationships.

References

Anderson, N., and Schalk, R. (1998). "The psychological contract in retrospect and prospect." *Journal of Organizational Behavior*, 19: 637–47.

—— and Thomas, H. D. C. (1996). "Work group socialization," in M. A. West (ed.), *Handbook of Work Groups* (Chichester: John Wiley and Sons), 423–50.

Bardwick, J. (1980). "The seasons of a woman's life," in D. G. McGuigan (ed.), *Women's Lives: New Theory, Research and Policy* (Ann Arbor, MI: University of Michigan, Center for Continuing Education of Women), 35–55.

Barringer, M., and Sturman, M. (1999). "Contingent workers and the multiple foci of organizational commitment: A social exchange perspective." Paper presented at the Academy of Management Conference, Chicago, August.

Cohany, S. (1996). "Workers in alternative employment relationships." *Monthly Labor Review*, October, 31–45.

Conway, N., and Briner, R. (2002). "A daily diary study of affective responses to psychological contract breach and exceeded promises." *Journal of Organizational Behavior*, 23: 287–302.

Coyle-Shapiro, J. (2002). "A psychological contract perspective on organizational citizenship behavior." *Journal of Organizational Behavior*, 23: 927–46.

—— and Kessler, I. (2000). "Consequences of the psychological contract for the employment relationship: A large scale survey." *Journal of Management Studies*, 37: 903–30.

—— and —— (2002). "Contingent and non-contingent working in local government: Contrasting psychological contracts." *Public Administration*, 80: 77–101.

De Feyter, M., Smulders, P., and de Vroome, E. (2001). "De inzetbaarheid van mannelijke en vrouwelijke werknemers." *Tijdschrift voor Arbeidsvraagstukken*, 17: 47–59.

Dekker, R., and Dorenbos, R. (1997). "Flexibel werk aan de onderkant van de arbeidsmarkt." *Tijdschrift voor Arbeidsvraagstukken*, 13: 103–12.

Delsen, L. (1998). "Zijn externe flexibiliteit en employability strijdig?." *Tijdschrift voor HRM*, 1: 27–45.

Dercksen, W. J. (1997). "Flexibel aan het werk," in G. Faber and J. J. Schippers (eds.), *Flexibilisering van arbeid* (Bussum: Coutinho), 16–28.

De Vos, A. (2002). "The Individual Antecedents and the Development of Newcomer's Psychological Contracts During the Socialization Process: A Longitudinal Study." Gent: University of Gent, Ph.D. thesis.

—— Buyens, D., and Schalk, R. (2003). "Psychological contract development during organizational socialization: Adaptation to reality and the role of reciprocity." *Journal of Organizational Behavior*, 24: 537–60.

Donker van Heel, P. A. (2000). "Inleenmotieven van werkgevers." *Bedrijfskunde*, 72: 49–57.

EIRONLINE (European Industrial Relations Observatory On-Line) (2002). "Non-permanent employment, quality of work and industrial relations." www.eiro.eurofound.ie

Fluit, P., and Knegt, R. (1999). "Flexibilisering en arbeidsbescherming." *Sociale Wetenschappen*, 42: 26–42.

Freese, C., and Schalk, R. (1995). "Het Psychologisch contract en leeftijdsbewust petsoneels management." In R. Schalk (ed.), Oudere werknemers in een veranderende wereld. Utrecht: Lemma, 207–23.

Gallos, J. V. (1989). "Exploring women's development: Implications for career theory, practice, and research," in M. B. Arthur, D. T. Hall, and B. S. Lawrence (eds.), *Handbook of Career Theory* (Cambridge: Cambridge University Press), 110–32.

Gaspersz, J., and Ott, M. (1996). *Management van employability.* Assen: Van Gorcum/Stichting Management Studies.

Goudswaard, A., Kraan, K. O., and Dhondt, S. (2000). *Flexibiliteit in balans. Flexibilisering en de gevolgen voor werkgever én werknemer.* Hoofddorp: TNO Arbeid.

Gouldner, A. W. (1960). "The norm of reciprocity: A preliminary statement." *American Sociological Review,* 25: 161–78.

Guest, D., and Conway, N. (2000). *The Psychological Contract in the Public Sector.* London: CIPD.

—— and —— (2001). *Organizational Change and the Psychological Contract.* London: CIPD.

—— Mackenzie Davey, K., and Patch, A. (2000). "The impact of new forms of employment contract on motivation and innovation." Working paper OP 277, Birkbeck, University of London, Department of Organizational Psychology.

—— —— and —— (2003). "The Psychological Contract, Attitudes and Behaviour of Workers on Temporary and Permanent Contracts." London: King's College, Management Centre Working paper.

Gustafsson, S., Kenjoh, E., and Wetzels, C. (2001). *Employment Choices and Pay Differences between Non-Standard and Standard Work in Britain, Germany, Netherlands and Sweden.* Amsterdam: Tinbergen Institute, 086/3.

Hesselink, K. D. J., and Van Vuuren, T. (1999). "Job flexibility and job insecurity: The Dutch case." *European Journal of Work and Organisational Psychology,* 8: 273–93.

—— Koppens, J. L. G., and Van Vuuren, T. (1998). *Flexibiliteit van de arbeid: achtergronden en effecten.* Hoofddorp: TNO Arbeid.

Hiltrop, J.-M. (1995). "The changing psychological contract. The human resource challenge of the 1990s." *European Management Journal,* 13: 286–94.

Huiskamp, R., and Schalk, R. (2002). "Psychologische contracten in arbeidsrelaties: De stand van zaken in Nederland." *Gedrag en Organisatie,* 15: 370–85.

Kabanoff, B., Jimmieson, N. L., and Lewis, M. J. (2000). "Psychological contracts in Australia: A 'fair go' or a 'not-so-happy' transition?" in D. M. Rousseau and R. Schalk (eds.), *Psychological Contracts in Employment: Cross-national Perspectives* (Thousand Oaks, CA: Sage), 29–46.

Kaiser, L. C. (2002). *Job Satisfaction: A Comparison of Standard, Non-standard, and Self-employment Patterns Across Europe with a Special Note to the Gender/Job Satisfaction Paradox.* Colchester: University of Essex.

Kessler, I., and Undy, R. (1996). *The New Employment Relationship: Examining the Psychological Contract.* London: Institute of Personnel Development.

Kissler, G. D. (1994). "The new employment contract." *Human Resource Management,* 33: 335–52.

Klandermans, B., and Van Vuuren, T. (1999). "Job insecurity: Introduction." *European Journal of Work and Organisational Psychology,* 8: 145–53.

Koster, F., Sanders, K., and Van Emmerik, H. (2002). "Solidariteit van tijdelijke werknemers: de affecten van temporale en netwerkinbedding op universitaire junioronderzoekers." *Gedrag en Organisatie,* 15: 240–54.

Levinson, D. J. (1986). "A conception of adult development." *American Psychologist,* 41: 3–13.

—— Darrow, C. N., Klein, E. B., Levinson, M. H., and McKee, B. (1978). *The Seasons of a Man's Life.* New York: Knopf.

Louis, M. R. (1980). "Surprise and sense-making: What newcomers experience and how they cope in unfamiliar organizational settings." *Administrative Science Quarterly*, 25: 226–51.

Martens, P. J. M. (2001). *Arbeidsongevallen met dodelijke afloop*. Den Haag: Arbeidsinspectie.

McLean Parks, J., and Kidder, D. L. (1994). " 'Till Death Us Do Part . . .' Changing Work Relationships in the 1990s," in C. L. Cooper and D. M. Rousseau (eds.), *Trends in Organizational Behaviour*, Vol. 1 (New York: John Wiley and Sons), 111–36.

Miedema, E. P., and Hesselink, K. D. J. (2000). *Uitgezonden of uitgezonden worden*. Hoofddorp: TNO Arbeid.

Millward, L., and Hopkins, L. (1998). "Psychological contracts, organizational and job commitment." *Journal of Applied Social Psychology*, 28: 1530–56.

Morrison, D. E. (1994). "Psychological contracts and change." *Human Resource Management*, 33: 353–372.

Morrison, E. (1993*a*). "A longitudinal study of the effects of information seeking on newcomer socialization." *Journal of Applied Psychology*, 78: 173–83.

——(1993*b*). "Newcomer information seeking: Exploring types, modes, sources, and outcomes." *Academy of Management Journal*, 36: 557–89.

Muffels, R., Dekker, R., and Stancanelli, E. (1999). "Een Flexibele baan: Opstap naar een vaste baan of eindstation?" *Sociale Wetenschappen*, 42: 43–65.

Muffels, R. J. A., and Steijn, A. J. (1998). *Flexible and Permanent Jobs on the Dutch Labour Market*. Utrecht: Netherlands School for Social and Economic Policy Research.

Nelson, D. L., Quick, J. C., and Joplin, J. R. (1991). "Psychological contracting and newcomer socialization." *Journal of Social Behavior and Personality*, 6: 55–72.

Pearce, J. (1993). "Toward an organizational behavior of contract laborers: Their psychological involvement and effects on employee co-workers." *Academy of Management Journal*, 36: 1082–96.

—— and Randel, A. (1998). "The actual job insecurity of contingent workers: Effects of trust and social capital." Paper presented at the Academy of Management Conference, San Diego, August.

Polivka, A. (1996). "Into contingent work and alternative employment: By choice?" *Monthly Labor Review*, 10, 55–74.

Quinlan, M., Mayhen, C., and Bole, P. (2001). "The global expansion of precarious employment, work disorganization, and consequences for occupational health: A review of recent research." *International Journal of Health Services*, 31: 335–414.

Remery, C., Van Doorne-Huiskes, J., and Schippers, J. (2002). "Labour Market flexibility in the Netherlands: Looking for winners and losers." *Work, Employment and Society*, 16: 477–96.

Robinson, S. L. (1996). "Trust and breach of the psychological contract." *Administrative Science Quarterly*, 41: 574–99.

—— and Morrison, E. W. (1995). "Psychological contracts and OCB: The effect of unfulfilled obligations on civic virtue behavior." *Journal of Organizational Behavior*, 16: 289–98.

—— and Rousseau, D. M. (1994). "Violating the psychological contract: Not the exception, but the norm." *Journal of Organizational Behavior*, 15: 245–59.

—— Kraatz, M. S., and Rousseau, D. M. (1994). "Changing obligations and the psychological contract: A longitudinal study." *Academy of Management Journal*, 37: 137–52.

Roehling, M. V., Cavanaugh, M. A., Moynihan, L. M., and Boswell, W. R. (2000). "The nature of the new employment relationship: A content analysis of the practitioner and academic literatures." *Human Resource Management*, 39: 305–20.

Rousseau, D. M. (1989). "Psychological and implied contracts in organizations." *Employee Responsibilities and Rights Journal*, 2: 121–39.

—— (1990). "New hire perspectives of their own and their employer's obligations: A study of psychological contracts." *Journal of Organizational Behavior*, 11: 389–400.

Rousseau, D. M. (1995). *Psychological Contracts in Organizations. Understanding Written and Unwritten Agreements.* Thousand Oaks, CA: Sage.

—— (2001). "Schema, promise and mutuality: The building blocks of the psychological contract." *Journal of Occupational and Organizational Psychology*, 74: 511–41.

—— and Schalk, R. (eds.) (2000). *Psychological Contracts in Employment: Cross-national Perspectives.* Thousand Oaks, CA: Sage.

Russo, G., Gorter, C., and Moolenaar, D. (1997). Temporary Jobs and Temporary Workers. Amsterdam: Tinbergen Institute Discussion Papers, 3/23: 97–133.

Saks, A. M., and Ashforth, B. E. (1997). "Organizational socialization: Making sense of the past and present as a prologue for the future." *Journal of Vocational Behavior*, 51: 234–79.

Sanders, K., Nauta, A., and Koster, F. (2002). "De invloed van tevredenheid met type en omvang van het contract op de betrokkenheid van medewerkers." *Gedrag en Organisatie*, 14: 456–72.

Schalk, R., and Freese C. (1997). "New facets of commitment in response to organizational change: Research trends and the Dutch experience," in C. L. Cooper and D. M. Rousseau (eds.), *Trends in Organizational Behaviour* (New York: John Wiley and Sons), 107–23.

—— and Rousseau, D. M. (2001). "Psychological contracts in employment," in N. Anderson, D. S. Ones, H. Kepir Sinangil, and C. Viswesvaran (eds.), *Handbook of Industrial, Work and Organizational Psychology; Volume 2, Organizational Psychology* (Thousand Oaks, CA: Sage), 133–42.

—— Freese, C., and Van den Bosch, J. (1995). "Het psychologisch contract van part-timers en full-timers." *Gedrag and Organisatie*, 8: 307–17.

—— Campbell, J. W., and Freese, C. (1998a). "Change and employee behaviour." *Leadership and Organization Development Journal*, 19: 157–63.

—— Freese, C., and De Bot, M. (1998b). *Differences in the Perception of the Employment Relationship Between Contingent and Non-contingent Employees.* Academy of Management Conference, San Diego.

—— Heinen, J., and Freese, C. (2001). "Do organizational changes impact the psychological contract and workplace attitudes? A study of a merger of two home care organizations in the Netherlands," in J. De Jonge, P. Vlerick, A. Büssing, and W. B. Schaufeli (eds.), *Organizational Psychology and Health Care at the Start of a New Millennium* (München und Mering: Rainer Hampp Verlag), 23–38.

Schein, E. H. (1988). Organizational Psychology (3rd edition). Englewood Cliffs, NJ: Prentice-Hall.

Schippers, J. J., Remery, C., and Vosse, J. (2001). "Tien jaar flexibilisering in Nederland: tussen onderzoek en beleid," in P. Ester, R. Muffels, and J. Schippers (eds.), *Flexibilisering, organisatie en employability* (Bussum: Coutinho), 19–39.

Schwartz, S. H. (1999). "A theory of cultural values and some implications for work." *Applied Psychology: An International Review*, 48: 23–47.

Sekaran, U., and Hall, D. T. (1989). "Asynchronism in dual-career and family linkage," in M. B. Arthur, D. T. Hall, and B. S. Lawrance (eds.), *Handbook of Career Theory* (Cambridge: Cambridge University Press), 159–80.

Sels, L., Janssens, M., Van den Brande, I., and Overlaet, B. (2000). "Belgium: A culture of compromise," in D. M. Rousseau and R. Schalk (eds.), *Psychological Contracts in Employment: Cross-national Perspectives* (Thousand Oaks, CA: Sage), 47–66.

Shore, L. M., and Tetrick, L. E. (1994). "The psychological contract as an explanatory framework in the employment relationship," in C. L. Cooper and D. M. Rousseau (eds.), *Trends in Organizational Behavior*, Vol. 1 (New York: John Wiley and Sons), 91–109.

Sims, R. R. (1994). "Human resource management's role in clarifying the new psychological contract." *Human Resource Management*, 33: 373–82.

Slinkman, E. (1999). "Hoe employable zijn uitzendkrachten?" *Tijdschrift voor Arbeid en Participatie*, 21: 14–27.

Sparrow, P. R. (2000). "The new employment contract: Psychological implications for future work," in R. J. Burke and C. L. Cooper (eds.), *The Organization in Crisis: Downsizing, Restructuring and Privatization* (Oxford: Blackwell).

Steijn, B. (1999). "De arbeidsmarktpositie van flexibele werknemers: bewijs van een gesegmenteerde arbeidsmarkt?" *Sociale Wetenschappen*, 42: 90–105.

—— (2000). "Betrokkenheid, bij veranderende organisaties." Paper presented at the TvA/Weswa-Congress, Amsterdam.

Thomas, H. D. C., and Anderson, N. (1998). "Changes in newcomers' psychological contracts during organizational socialization: A study of British recruits entering the British Army." *Journal of Organizational Behavior*, 19: 745–67.

Torka, N. (2000). "De metaal: een betrokken sector met flexibiliteit?" *Bedrijfskunde*, 72: 20–6.

—— and Van Riemsdijk, M. (2001). "Atypische contractrelatie en binding: een paradox?" *Tijdschrift voor HRM*, 1: 59–76.

Tremlett, N., and Collins, D. (1999). "Temporary employment in Britain." London: DfEE Reseach Report, 100.

Turnley, W. H., and Feldman, D. C. (1999). "The impact of psychological contract violations on exit, loyalty and neglect." *Human Relations*, 52: 895–922.

—— and —— (2000). "Re-examining the effects of psychological contract violations: unmet expectations and job dissatisfaction as mediators." *Journal of Organizational Behavior*, 21: 25–42.

—— Bolino, M. C., Lester, S. W., and Bloodgood, J. M. (2003). "The impact of psychological contract fulfillment on the performance of in-role and organizational citizenship behaviors." *Journal of Management*, 29: 187–206.

Van Breukelen, W., and Allegro, J. (2000). "Effecten van een nieuwe vorm van flexibilisering van de arbeid." *Gedrag en Organisatie*, 13: 107–24.

Van den Bos, K. (2000). "Omgaan met onzekerheid: het belang van rechtvaardigheid in organisaties." *Gedrag en organisatie*, 13: 249–59.

Van den Brande, I. (2002). Het psychologisch contract tussen werknemer en werkgever: Een survey-onderzoke bij Vlaamse werknemers. Ph.D. Thesis, University of Leuven.

Van der Toren, J. P., Evers, G. H. M., and Commissaris, E. J. (2002). *Flexibiliteit en zekerheid: Effecten en doeltreffendheid van de Wet flexibiliteit en zekerheid*. Den Haag: Ministerie van Sociale Zaken en Werkgelegenheid.

Van Ginkel, M. A., Van Lin, M. H. H., and Zwinkels, W. S. (2002). *Temporary Agency Work: National Reports: The Netherlands*. Dublin: European Foundation for the Improvement of Living and Working Conditions, 1–27.

Warning, J., and Van den Straten, J. (2001). *Veiligheid op papier*. Utrecht: FNV Bondgenoten.

Wiesenfeld, B., and Brockner, J. (1993). "Procedural unfairness and the psychology of the contingent worker." Paper presented at the Academy of Management Meetings, Atlanta, August.

Zant, W. R., Alessie, R., Oostendorp, R., and Prahan, M. (2000). *Flexibiliteit op de Nederlandse Arbeidsmarkt: een empirisch onderzoek op basis van OSA- vraag- en aanbodpanels*. Den Haag: SDU.

14

Understanding the Employment Relationship: Implications for Measurement and Research Design

LOIS E. TETRICK

14.1 Introduction

Scholars have long recognized that clear conceptual definitions of constructs are necessary for developing reliable and valid measures of constructs as well as designing sound, valid research to test theoretical relations among constructs. The preceding chapters have addressed several issues concerning the employment relationship that suggest clear conceptual definitions may only now be emerging; as a result many of the measures do not capture the full domain of the employment relationship. For example, most measures focus on the individual employee and do not incorporate the organizational perspective. Similarly, some measures focus on the elements or specific obligations of the employment relation whereas others focus on the underlying exchange process.

The purpose of this chapter is to review the various definitions and measures of key constructs for understanding the employment relationship. A framework for assessing the employment relationship and designing research to further our understanding of the employment relationship is provided and methodological considerations discussed.

14.2 Conceptual frameworks/definitions and measurement issues

The employment relationship is conceptualized as an exchange between the employer and the employee. In its most basic form, it might be described as the employer pays the employee in exchange for the employee's labor. Approaches to measuring the employment relationship generally have assessed the relationship focusing on either content or process as reflected by the rows in Figure 14.1. Content approaches focus on the elements of the employment relationship. These elements have been characterized as specific obligations or investments and contributions of both parties to the employment relationship. That is, content approaches attempt to enumerate the specific obligations (or contributions) of employees to the employer

Focus of the assessment of the relationship	Individual employee	Organization or group
Content	Psychological contract	Inducements–contributions
Process	Exchange relationship	Perceived organizational support

Figure 14.1. *Conceptual framework for assessing the employment relationship.*

and the specific obligations (or investments) of employers to the employees. The process approach, on the other hand, focuses on mechanisms by which the employment relationship is developed and maintained rather than the specific elements or promises contained in that relationship. These approaches generally draw on social exchange theory and the norm of reciprocity to examine the process of the employment exchange.

In addition to the focus on content or process, measures of the employment relationship differ in the perspective taken as reflected by the columns in Figure 14.1. Some measures have looked at the employment relationship from an individual employee's perspective where other measures have assessed the employment relationship from an organizational, departmental, or group perspective. It is important to note that there has been relatively little research on the employment relationship from an organizational perspective, and there has been even less research that incorporates both the organizational and the individual perspective. Therefore, while the framework presented here recognizes the importance of considering the organizational perspective, discussion of specific measures necessarily will be disproportionately focused on the individual level.

When considering the individual and organizational perspectives, it is clear that understanding the employment relationship requires a multilevel approach. That is, the employment relationship is a function of organizational factors including Human Resource Management strategies, departmental or work group factors including relationships between managers and their employees and the relationships between co-workers, and individual factors including individually negotiated agreements, perceptions of promises made by the organization or its agents, and previous employment experiences. For example, as shown in Figure 14.2, one can conceptualize there being individual specific employment relationships as reflected by psychological contracts. These psychological contracts may be influenced by as well as influence departmental/group/team relationships and job/occupational group relationships. The organizational level employee–employer relationship may influence

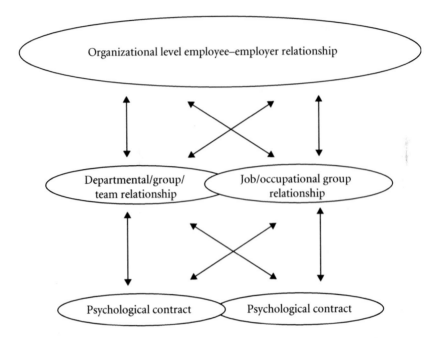

Figure 14.2. *Multilevel conceptualization of the employment relationship.*

and be influenced by the group level. As was the case with the paucity of research on the employment relationship from the organizational perspective, research incorporating multiple levels of analysis is extremely rare and is discussed in the part on methodological considerations.

Using the framework reflected in Figure 14.1, a brief overview of existing measures of the employment relationship is presented. The measures are categorized as content or process approaches. Within each approach, measures are further categorized as taking an individual or group/organizational perspective.

14.2.1 Content approaches

As indicated above, content approaches to assessing the employment relationship attempt to identify the specific elements of the employer–employee relationship either as specific obligations of the organization to employees and of employees to their employers or investments in employees by the organization and contributions from employees to their employers. Psychological contracts, which Rousseau (1989) defined as the individual's perception of the mutual obligations of the employee to the employer and the employer to the employee, reflect a content approach at the individual level of analysis. The original measure included fifteen specific obligations that were based on interviews with recruiters of MBA students graduating from a Midwestern university in the United States (Rousseau 1990). A canonical correlation analysis of these obligations supported the existence of two aspects of psychological contracts: Relational and transactional. Relational contracts are based primarily on a social exchange and are generally considered to be open-ended and long-term in nature. Transactional contracts are primarily based on economic exchange and are generally considered to be more specific without a long-term focus. Subsequent research using specific obligations generally has supported the existence of two types of obligations although which obligations reflect which type of relational or transactional obligations varies somewhat from study to study (Rousseau and Tijoriwala 1998).

More recently, Rousseau (2000) has refined and extended the measure of the psychological contract. The Psychological Contract Inventory (PCI) assesses employer obligations and employee obligations based on four types of contracts: Transactional, relational, balanced, and transitional. These four types have been identified in samples of employees from the United States and Singapore (Rousseau 2000) and China (Hui et al. forthcoming) although further evaluations of the dimensionality of the PCI are needed.

Another content approach to assessing the employee–employer relationship is the investments–contributions model (Tsui et al. 1997). This model assessed specific investments in employees made by the organization and the specific contributions to the organization expected from the employees. This model takes an organizational perspective rather than an individual employee perspective focusing on the job level rather than the individual employee. That is, supervisors were asked what investments were made in individuals holding particular positions in the organization based on the organization's human resource practices. Additionally, supervisors were asked what contributions were expected for employees, as a group, holding a particular position based on human resource practices that focused employees' attention on their work units, labeled employee unit focus. Tsui et al. found that there was more agreement among supervisors rating investments and contributions for the same job than for supervisors rating different jobs, supporting the notion that specific employment relationships exist for employees in particular positions in the organization. Based on a median split on the dimensions rated by the supervisors, four employee–employer relationship approaches were formed to reflect (a) quasi-spot contracts, (b) underinvestment, (c) overinvestment, and (d) mutual investment. The relationship was categorized as a quasi-spot contract when employee unit focus and employer investment in employees were both below the median. An under-investment relationship was defined as occurring when employer investment was below the median and employee unit focus was above the median. Overinvestment, on the other hand, was defined as above the median on employer investment and below the median on employee unit focus. Lastly, a mutual investment relationship was defined as one where both employee unit focus and employer investment were above the median. Therefore, in this approach, the employee–employer relationship is strategically defined by the organization.

Unfortunately, no other studies were located that used this specific assessment approach. Porter et al. (1998), however, took a similar approach. They had top executives provide information on organizational inducements provided by their individual organizations with the specific inducements included being those that were expected to be relevant across organizations, jobs, and industries. Employees were also asked to indicate the extent to which their organization provided these specific inducements. Contributions expected from the employees were not assessed, and thus, Porter et al. did not attempt to categorize the employee–employer relationship as was done by Tsui et al. (1997). Rather, Porter et al. focused on perceptual gaps between organizational representatives (the top executives) and employees. Therefore, evidence for the validity and generalizability of the organizational perspective taken by Tsui et al. is limited to one study. This creates some concern since the four types of relationships were determined based on the sample data by using median splits. If future studies continue to use median splits, then the level of investments and contributions could differ across studies for determining whether the type of employment relationship is a quasi-spot contract, underinvestment, overinvestment, or mutual investment. Essentially, the definition of the four categories of employment relationships would be study specific, making comparisons across studies inappropriate.

14.2.2 Process approaches

The above approaches were categorized as content approaches because they focused on the specific obligations, investments, and contributions. These approaches to assessing the employment relationship do not capture the actual exchange per se that underlies the notion of an employee–employer relationship. Instead, they rely on the correlation between specific obligations to reflect the exchange and frequently the specific obligations or investments and contributions are used individually rather than jointly thus not capturing the effects of the employment relationship on either organizations or individuals. Alternatively, there have been some attempts to measure the actual exchange process underlying the relationship. These approaches have focused on the linking of specific obligations from the employee to the employer and from the employer to the employee or the mechanism by which the employment relationship is developed and maintained.

Shore and Barksdale (1998) sought to capture the exchange more directly by linking employee and employer obligations. They hypothesized that there would be four groups of employees based on perceptions of (a) mutually high employee and employer obligations, (b) mutually low obligations, (c) employee overobligation in which employee obligations are high and employer obligations are moderate to low, and (d) employee underobligation in which employee obligations are moderate to low and employer obligations are high. These four categories are similar to those developed by Tsui et al. (1997) but are based on individual employee perceptions. Cluster analysis supported the presence of these four groups of employees among MBA students. As was the case with the Tsui et al. (1997) study, however, the definition of the groups was statistically obtained for this particular sample, raising questions as to the generalizability of the findings for future studies.

Another approach to assessing the exchange relationship at the individual level is reported by Shore et al. (forthcoming). Rather than taking a statistical approach to assessing process underlying the exchange relationship, Shore et al. took a more direct approach. Scales were developed to assess social and economic exchanges in the employment relationship using items that actually reflect exchanges. For example, one of the economic exchange items is "My relationship with [my organization] is strictly an economic one—I work and they pay me." One of the social exchange items is "The things I do on the job today will benefit my standing in [this organization] in the long run." Validity and reliability evidence were obtained in a study of MBA students and a study of employees working in a small aerospace company. In addition, Gakovic and Tetrick (2003) used these scales in a study of the relation of work status to several exchange constructs among working people who were attending college. Support was found for the two dimensions of social and economic exchange and each scale had acceptable reliability. Social exchange was strongly positively related to perceived organizational support and economic exchange was moderately negatively related to perceived organizational support. Additional support for the validity and reliability of the social exchange scale was provided by Rupp and Cropanzano (2002). In their study, social exchange was found to mediate the relation between justice and job performance and organizational citizenship behaviors.

A third approach to assessing the underlying exchange process in the employer–employee relationship is by assessing reciprocity in the exchange relationship. Tetrick et al. (2003), drawing on Sahlins (1972), Sparrowe and Liden (1997), and McLean Parks and smith (1998), developed a measure of generalized, balanced, and negative reciprocity. Generalized reciprocity is indicated by a high degree of interest in the other party and indefiniteness in the obligation to reciprocate relative to the equivalence of resources exchanged and the immediacy of the return. Balanced reciprocity is reflected by mutual interest among the parties, an equivalence of resources exchanged, and a relatively short time frame for return. Negative reciprocity is essentially the opposite of generalized reciprocity with a high degree of self-interest, equivalence of resources exchanged, and a high immediacy of return. Evidence of the reliability and validity of this measure was obtained in three samples: Undergraduates attending a southwestern university in the United States, MBA students attending a southeastern university in the U.S., and MBA students attending several universities in China. Generalized reciprocity was positively related to perceived organizational support, and negative reciprocity was negatively related to perceived organizational support in all three samples as would be expected (Eisenberger et al. 1986). Balanced reciprocity, however, was negatively related to perceived organizational support in the two U.S. samples and unrelated to perceived organizational support in the China sample. The pattern of relations was consistent with reciprocity existing on a continuum from generalized reciprocity to balanced reciprocity to negative reciprocity.

The last process measure to be discussed is perceived organizational support. As indicated above, many measures of the employee–employer relationship have been related to perceived organizational support, which itself is an exchange construct.

Perceived organizational support reflects the treatment of individual employees by the organization. It reflects the process by which the organization communicates that it respects and values the individual and is committed to the employee (Eisenberger et al. 1986). Rousseau and Tijoriwala (1998) classified perceived organizational support as an evaluation-oriented measure of the psychological contract based on its use as an indicator of psychological contract fulfillment (Guzzo et al. 1994) or at least the expectation that the organization will fulfill the obligations to employees (Shore and Barksdale 1998). I have chosen to include perceived organizational support as an assessment of the exchange process focused at the organizational level since it reflects the quality of the exchange at least on the part of the organization to the individual. Admittedly, it is an individual level variable; however, it has the potential to be treated as an organizational level variable. For example, if there were agreement among employees as to the level of perceived organizational support, then perceived organizational support could be conceptualized as an organizational level phenomenon rather than an individual level construct. This would be a comparable procedure used to develop measures of organizational climate.

14.3 Measures of fulfillment of the terms of the employment relationship

The preceding discussion has focused on assessing the employment relationship. A preponderance of research appears to examine the failure of organizations to fulfill the terms of the employment relationship from the individual employee's perspective ignoring the effect of failure of employees to fulfill the terms of the employment relationship from the organizational perspective.

14.3.1 Measures of fulfillment of the employment relationship— employee perceptions

The employment relationship reflects mutual obligations on the part of employees and their employers. It is recognized that these obligations may change or simply not be met by either or both parties to the employment relationship. Robinson and Rousseau (1994) reported that psychological contract violation was "not the exception but the norm" in their follow-up study of MBA graduates and most of the investigations of psychological contract violation have focused on failures of organizations to fulfill their obligations and, to a lesser extent, employees failure to fulfill their obligations to their employers (Tetrick et al. 2002). This negative perspective may reflect issues with the measurement scale as suggested by Robinson (1996) and methodologies as suggested by Conway and Briner (2002), which are discussed below, or it may reflect the context of the past decade in which organizations have downsized and restructured displacing workers and managers.

Three general approaches have been taken in the assessment of psychological contract fulfillment. The first approach is a global assessment of psychological contract breach, that is, the perception that the organization has not lived up to its obligations in exchange for the employee's contribution (Morrison and Robinson 1997). Using this approach, employees are asked how well they have kept their promises to their organizations and how well their organizations have kept their promises to them overall (Robinson and Rousseau 1994). This approach makes no distinction as to the relational or transactional nature of the psychological contract nor does it examine the specific obligations in the psychological contract. It would be expected that if the nature of the employment relationship matters, then it would be important to determine whether the social aspects of the exchange or the economic aspects of the exchange are not being met or whether the specific obligations that are not being fulfilled reflect relational or transactional obligations (Craig and Tetrick 2001).

Use of global measures of psychological contract violation, either explicitly or implicitly, result in overfulfillment of some obligations offsetting underfulfillment of other obligations. Turnley and Feldman (1999, 2000) took a more specific approach to measuring psychological contract violation. They had participants indicate how important each of the obligations were as well as the amount they had actually received compared to what they had been promised. The obligations were those typically included in content measures of the psychological contract (Rousseau 1990). In the 1999 article, Turnley and Feldman used a multiplicative weighting fulfillment of each obligation by the importance of that obligation to the participant, but in the 2000 article, they did not weight obligation fulfillment by importance. In both studies, it is reported that this multi-item measure correlated 0.70 with the overall global assessment of psychological contract breach discussed above. Therefore, weighting the specific obligation's fulfillment by the importance of that obligation to the individual employee does not appear to be necessary. It may be that the response scale used which asked participants to indicate how much they had received relative to what they were promised captures the relative importance and thus weighting by importance is redundant. Further, the response scale Turnley and Feldman used for respondents to indicate fulfillment of specific obligations allowed for responses of overfulfillment as well as underfulfillment as recommended by Robinson (1996). Therefore, summative scores of fulfillment allow overfulfillment of specific obligations to compensate for underfulfillment of other obligations. However, it may be that overfulfillment operates differently from underfulfillment. If this were the case, then it would be important to distinguish between the two to further our understanding of the effects of fulfillment of obligations in the employment relationship, at least at this stage in our understanding of the employment relationship.

Coyle-Shapiro and Kessler (2000) noted that measures of contract fulfillment typically assumed that the specific obligation existed and felt that this may contaminate the measure. To eliminate this assumption in the measure, they developed two alternate measures of contract fulfillment. The first method had respondents first indicate whether specific obligations existed on the part of their organization. Then respondents were asked to indicate the extent to which the organization had met each obligation. A discrepancy score was then computed for each obligation removing the ambiguity as to whether the obligation actually existed. In addition to this measure, Coyle-Shapiro and Kessler obtained a direct assessment of contract fulfillment using an additional response category of "not obligated to provide." Results of a factor analysis indicated that these two approaches yielded the same factor structure suggesting that they are equivalent in capturing psychological contract fulfillment.

Using a similar approach to Turnley and Feldman (1999, 2000) and to Coyle-Shapiro and Kessler (2000), Kickul et al. (2002) first asked participants which of several obligations their organizations had promised them. Then, for each promised obligation, the participants indicated the extent to which the organization had fulfilled their promises. This two-step approach avoids the confounding between fulfillment and whether the individual indeed perceived that a specific obligation existed. Recognition that different employees may have perceived different obligations, this procedure conceivably could result in the measure of psychological contract fulfillment being based on a different set of items for each respondent, although it was not clear from the text of the article if this was indeed the case. If so, this reflects the idiosyncratic nature of the psychological contract although it creates potential concerns about measurement equivalency for comparison across individuals. It would be interesting to be able to make a direct comparison of the results of Kickul et al. with the earlier study of Coyle-Shapiro and Kessler (2000), to see if the two-step process yielded different results compared to simply adding a response option of "not obligated to provide," since Coyle-Shapiro and Kessler found support that these two approaches are equivalent.

Most of the research on psychological contract violation has been cross-sectional requiring individuals to recall events that signaled whether the organization had fulfilled the terms of the psychological contract. Schemas and other cognitive biases may distort the perception of fulfillment or the recall of fulfillment of obligations (Rousseau, 2001) and cross-sectional studies cannot address the extent of these distortions. Notable exceptions are Robinson and Rousseau (1994), Robinson et al. (1994), Robinson and Morrison (2000), Conway and Briner (2002), and De Vos et al. (2003). Robinson and Rousseau (1994) and Robinson et al. (1994) compared perceptions of obligations upon graduation but prior to starting work with business school alumni two years later. Robinson and Morrison (2000) used an eighteen-month time interval, which reduces the memory load somewhat although it is not clear how substantial a reduction that might be. De Vos et al. collected data at four points in time—two weeks, three months, six months, and twelve months after joining the employing organizations. This was the only longitudinal study to provide a theoretical basis for the intervals between measurements, which was based on the organizational socialization literature. Conway and Briner (2002) conducted a study using a daily diary approach in which respondents reported broken promises and their emotional reactions at the end of each working day for ten consecutive working days. This approach allowed a more direct link between broken promises and the respondents' reactions to these broken promises, offsetting concerns with previous longitudinal studies in which it was not possible to determine how long a psychological contract breach had occurred prior to assessing the reaction to that psychological contract breach. Further, the design enabled Conway and Briner to examine within-person variability as well as between-persons variability in psychological contract breach and exceeded promises, which is more consistent with the present theory.

As is the case when measuring a phenomenon across multiple groups, it is important to consider measurement equivalence over time (Golembiewski et al. 1976; Vandenberg and Lance 2000). For example, as the employment relationship develops, an employee's perceptions of the extent to which the organization made certain promises may shift and employees may redefine their obligations to the organization. Also, it is possible that over time, employees may reinterpret the meaning of specific obligations. For example, in the early stages of the employment relationship, a raise may reflect an economic exchange. However, as the employment relationship matures, a raise may reflect that the organization values the individual and wants to maintain a long-term relationship thus signifying a social exchange. Therefore, while these longitudinal studies are to be applauded, more research directly assessing measurement equivalence across time is needed.

Another concern with the few longitudinal studies that have been reported is that they generally have included only two times of measurement. With only two points of measurement, it is not possible to detect non-linear trends and the interval between measurements may mask effects. Only the Conway and Briner (2002) study had the potential to examine non-linear trends although this was not the purpose of the study and no assessments were reported. Further, although the daily approach was useful in linking specific incidents of broken promises with emotional reactions, it is possible that there may be residual or cumulative effects of broken promises. Theory needs to be expanded to address "when things happen" as well as how they happen (Mitchell and James 2001), and then studies designed based on the theory as was done by De Vos et al. (2003).

One last issue that has emerged is the distinction between psychological contract breach and violation. Prior to 1997, there was no distinction made and most studies of psychological contract violation actually measured psychological contract breach. According to Morrison and Robinson (1997), psychological contract breach is the perception that promises have not been kept. Psychological contract breach may then result in feelings of psychological contract violation. Psychological contract violation entails emotional reactions of betrayal and hurt. Robinson and Morrison (2000) conducted a factor analysis of the eight items measuring perceived breach and feelings of violation. The results supported two factors; however, the scores on the two scales were strongly correlated with each other (Robinson and Morrison 2000) suggesting that there may be conceptual overlap. Conway and Briner (2002) reported partial support for the Morrison and Robinson's model of breach and violation. Broken promises were related to negative emotional reactions such as betrayal and hurt and exceeded promises were related to positive emotional reactions such as self-worth and a sense of being cared for, and the likelihood of experiencing negative emotional reactions as a result of broken promises was, at least in part, a function of the importance of the promise.

14.3.2 Measures of contract fulfillment—employer perceptions

Most studies of contract fulfillment, breach, and violation have been conducted at the individual level of analysis based on employee perceptions. However, there are few studies that have assessed contract fulfillment from the organization's perspective. Only four such studies were identified.

Lewis-McClear and Taylor (1997) found that employees and their managers differed in their perceptions of employee obligations in the employment relationship. Discrepancies in this study were operationalized in two ways—discrepancies in the obligations where the employee perceived an obligation to be important but the supervisor did not and discrepancies in the obligations where the supervisor perceived an obligation to be important but the employee did not. Sums of the number of instances for a given dyad, in which either the supervisor or the employee indicated that the obligation was important and the other indicated that the obligation was not important, were used thus avoiding the use of difference scores. The results suggested that discrepancies where the employee felt the obligation was important but the supervisor did not were related to supervisors' perceptions of contract violations, but discrepancies where the employee felt the obligation was not important but the supervisor thought it was important were not. Coyle-Shapiro and Kessler (2000) used manager or supervisor ratings of psychological contract breach and also found some differences between managers and employees on perceptions of the obligations in the employment relationship. Where differences existed, managers tended to see fulfillment of obligations as higher than the employees. Lester et al. (2002) also compared supervisors' and subordinates' perceptions of psychological contract breach. Not surprisingly, supervisors reported that the organization had fulfilled the terms of the psychological contract to a greater extent than the employees although there was no difference on some of the psychological contract elements. All three of these studies found there were discrepancies between supervisors and subordinates in their perceptions of the employment relationship and the extent to which the obligations of the employment relationship were met. The discrepancies varied across the studies although one consistency was that managers and supervisors were more positive concerning organizational fulfillment of obligations. Each study used different sets of obligations and different methods for computing discrepancy or congruence between supervisors and subordinates making comparison across the studies difficult.

The fourth study by Porter et al. (1998) rather than focusing on the supervisor–subordinate dyad asked executives at the topmost levels in each of the sampled organizations to act as representatives of their organizations. It is noted that divisions rather than the total organization were used. The ratings of the executives were then aggregated to form an indicator of organizational inducements. Unfortunately, no information was provided as to the extent of agreement among these executives. As was the case with the three studies discussed above, a different set of inducements were used making comparison difficult. Considering all four studies together, it is clear that managers and supervisors do not agree with employees on the terms of the employment relationship and these discrepancies are negatively associated with performance and organizational citizenship behaviors. Interestingly, none of these studies examined the correlates of these discrepancies on organizational level variables.

14.4 Methodological considerations

Different approaches to measuring the employment relationship raise additional methodological considerations. In this section, three such considerations are discussed: Measurement equivalence across studies and across time, measurement of discrepancies in parties' perceptions of the employment relationship, and incorporating a multilevel perspective to understanding the employment relationship.

14.4.1 Measurement equivalence

As is apparent from the above discussion, there are several existing measures that have been used to assess the employee–employer relationship. These measures include both content (e.g. specific obligations) as well as process underlying the relationship and they focus on either the individual perspective or the organizational perspective. For measures focusing on content, the specific obligations included have varied across studies. Not surprisingly, the dimensionality has varied and even when the same number of factors is evident, specific obligations may load inconsistently on a particular factor.

In order to assess measurement equivalence, research using content-based measures needs to use consistently the same set of obligations. The original set of obligations was based on interviews with HR professionals and recruiters (Rousseau 1989). Subsequent lists of obligations have extended this set to include additional obligations from the literature and conversations with employees. Potential explosion in the number of specific obligations reminds one of a similar phenomenon that occurred in the early development of need theories where the number of basic needs proliferated. Perhaps more research attempting to identify the content of the psychological contract like that reported by Herriot et al. (1997) using representative samples of employees and managers would help identify if the content domain has been adequately sampled. Alternatively, the lack of stability that has occurred with measuring specific obligations may arise because specific obligations have symbolic meaning and this meaning may change across organization and individuals and across time within organizations and individuals.

It is also the case that published research has assumed a particular measurement model. This is evident by the use of coefficient alpha as an index of internal consistency and the use of factor analysis, either exploratory or confirmatory, to determine the dimensionality of the items included in the measures. These approaches are essentially using a reflective measurement model in which responses as to the extent of specific obligations are "caused" by the underlying factor such as employer relational obligations. Based on this reflective model, the extent to which an organization or an employee has certain obligations should be correlated reflecting a common underlying source (i.e. the employment relationship) of these obligations. For example, if organizations invest in employees in a strategic Human Resources Management sense, then this might be a reasonable assumption. The obligations to or investments in employees are driven by the strategy taken by the organization in building the employment relationship. If an organization wants to develop a social exchange relationship with its employees or perhaps only a subgroup of its employees, then the investments in its employees would be selected to indicate this social exchange relationship. However, since certain obligations may not necessarily reflect a particular, consistent strategy but rather multiple strategies along multiple dimensions this assumption may not hold. This assumption should be critically evaluated both theoretically and empirically, especially for content approaches for measuring the employment relationship.

An alternative to the reflective measurement model is the formative model (Edwards and Bagozzi 2000; Edwards 2001*a*). In a formative model, the indicators actually create the construct. With respect to the employment relationship, for example, specific obligations an organization has promised to provide to employees or employees have promised to the organization creates the construct, in this instance the employment relationship as shown in Figure 14.3. Essentially, the reflective and

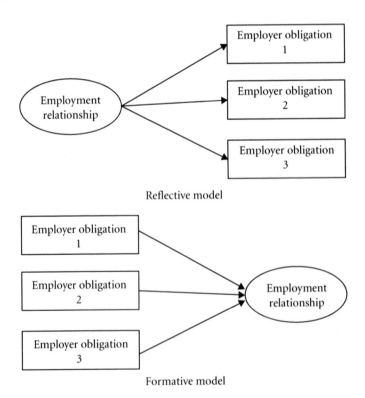

Reflective model

Formative model

Figure 14.3. *Reflective and formative measurement models of the employment relationship.*

formative models differ in causal direction. Are the investments and obligations determined by the underlying employment relationship or do the investments and obligations create the employment relationship (the formative model)? No published studies were found that explicitly addressed this possible alternative measurement model, although certainly theory suggests that the formative model is plausible.

14.4.2 Use of difference scores to measure discrepancies (i.e. perceptual gaps)

Several studies have included measures of "perceptual gaps" to either identify the extent to which something was promised in contrast to the extent to which it was fulfilled, or gaps between supervisors' and subordinates' perceptions of the employment relationship. These gaps were operationalized as difference scores either at the item level or the scale level. Despite the concerns that have been expressed about the use of difference scores (Edwards 2001b), it was surprising that only two studies made an attempt to address these concerns. First, Coyle-Shapiro and Kessler (2000) compared the item-level difference score measure with a direct measure of psychological contract breach and found that the factor structures were similar in that the same number of factors was retained for both measures. Second, Porter et al. (1998) specifically addressed the conditions Edwards (1994) recommended before proceeding to use difference scores. Although the data did not meet all of the conditions, Porter et al. elected not to use the polynomial regression method of addressing fit or congruence (Edwards 2001b). Thus, the potential richness of their data in relating perceptual gaps to outcomes may not have been realized.

Polynomial regression is theoretically consistent with much of the literature on the employee–employer relationship and psychological contracts. It allows one to assess not only the interaction terms but also the quadratic relations of the variables resulting in a response surface that reflects the more configural relation among the variables. It might be useful in assessing the "perceptual gaps" between organizational representatives and employees as well as between promises and fulfillment or the relation between breach and violation.

Only one study was found that had employed this approach to examining the effects of agreement in employees' and managers' perceptions of their mutual obligations. Tekleab and Taylor (2003) incorporated the full polynomial regression model which allows one to examine non-additive effects as well as providing information as to whether it is important as to which party has higher levels of perceived obligations. Tekleab and Taylor found that agreement on employee obligations was curvilinearly related to managers' perceptions of employee violations such that when employees and managers generally do not agree or when they strongly agree with each other, managers are more likely to perceive that employees have not lived up to their end of the bargain. Further, the results suggested that when managers perceived employees' obligations to be less than the employees perceived their obligations to be, the managers were most likely to perceive employees had not met their obligations.

Another potentially informative use of polynomial regression analysis might be in the establishment of a typology of the employment relationship. Several studies have attempted to categorize employee–employer relationships based on the relation of inducements and contributions (Tsui et al. 1997) or employee obligations and employer obligations (Shore and Barksdale 1998). In both of these instances, the categories were derived based on the sample data and then differences in other variables based on these categories were examined. Polynomial regression could have directly tested these relationships without the need to form categories thereby facilitating the comparison of results across studies. For example, inducements and contributions could both be entered into the regression equation. Then in the next step, the interaction between inducements and contributions as well as the squared values for inducements and contributions could be entered. A significant increase in R^2 would suggest that there is a curvilinear relation between inducements and contributions. The shape of the response surface would then describe the nature of the curvilinearity. Maintaining the full continuous nature of inducements and contributions bypasses the need to categorize the data. Similarly, employee relational obligations and employee transactional obligations as well as employer relational obligations and employer transactional obligations could be entered into the polynomial regression analysis. The response surface based on the polynomial regression equation would depict the nature of the exchange among employee and employer obligations. This approach thus would allow us to examine more complex relations between the employment relationship and relevant antecedents and consequences.

14.4.3 Multilevel analysis

The last methodological issue that I would like to discuss is the incorporation of a multilevel perspective. As reflected in Figure 14.2, individuals are nested within departments, groups, supervisors, occupational groups, and jobs. These groups are nested within the larger organization. Research, to date, has not explicitly examined the potential effects of these dependencies.

The literature on psychological contracts and the emerging literature on the employee–employer relationship expressly acknowledge the importance of social interactions in defining the employment relationship. Interestingly, the measures and methodologies used in the research have not been consistent with the contextual or configural approach suggested by the theory. Not only is it important to consider contextual effects in understanding the employee–employer relationship, but it is also important to consider temporal and emergent processes (Kozlowski and Klein 2000).

Most of the multilevel research to date has taken a contextual, top-down approach to recognizing the interdependencies among observations in organizational research (Kozlowski and Klein 2000). That is, organizational factors such as culture or strategy may affect individual behavior. Or, the top management team's decisions or behavior may affect first line managers' behavior, which affects employees' attitudes and behaviors. This same perspective seems to permeate much of the literature on the employee–employer relationship. The employer drives the relationship from recruiting to HR practices, etc., and the employee reciprocates. The question of who speaks for the organization is unclear since "the organization" is composed of multiple individuals. The literature identifies the top management team (again multiple individuals whose responses would need to be aggregated in some way) and supervisors. However, if one views the employee–employer relationship as a social interaction, other individuals such as peers and subordinates might affect the employee–employer relationship.

Kenny and his colleagues (Kenny 1996; Kenny et al. 2001; Bond and Kenny 2002) have developed social interaction models that allow partitioning of variance attributable to individuals and interactions among individuals based on the general framework of generalizability theory. Detailed discussion of these models is beyond the scope of this chapter; interested readers are referred to the work of Kenny and his colleagues. The value of this model is that it explicitly recognizes multiple sources of variance in interpersonal relationships, which can stem from individual characteristics, roles of the individuals, and reciprocity between the interacting individuals. Incorporating these social interaction models into Figure 14.2, one would conceivably want to be able to assess the variance in the employment relationship that could be attributable to individuals, groups, jobs, supervisors, organizations, and all possible interactions of these factors. The complexity of such a model would tax most statisticians' capabilities; however, without examining at least the most likely sources of variance, our understanding of the employee–employer relationship is limited. Based on the literature today, it would appear that supervisors, as the most proximal agents of the organization, and the top management team, as more distal representatives of the organization, minimally should be included in measurement and design.

Multilevel modeling offers methods for accounting for the dependencies among individuals and higher organizational groupings, and there exist several statistical techniques for assessing these contextual effects. They include analysis of variance (ANOVA), within and between analysis (WABA), hierarchical linear modeling (HLM), and random coefficient modeling (RCM). A full discussion of each is beyond the scope of this chapter. Interested readers are referred to Kozlowski and Klein (2000) for a brief description of each along with relevant references. In these procedures, effects of higher-level groupings on individual responses can be examined. As indicated above, supervisors acting as agents of the organization may be a primary source of individual employees' psychological contracts. To the extent that supervisors communicate the terms of the employment relationship to employees as suggested by Tsui et al. (1997), multilevel modeling is useful in partitioning the effects of a supervisor's deal with multiple employees and the idiosyncratic aspect of a specific individual's employment relationship.

Most investigations of context have taken a top-down perspective; that is, organizational factors are proposed to influence group factors and behavior, which in turn influence individual factors and behavior. Although not examined to date in the employment relationship literature, bottom-up processes may also occur. These processes explain how lower-level properties result in collective phenomena such as individual perceptions of psychological climate reflecting organizational climate when aggregated, at least to the extent there is agreement among the individual employees. The interpersonal relationships literature and social information processing would suggest that a bottom-up or emergent processes approach could enhance our understanding of the employee–employer relationship. Social exchange is based on the norm of reciprocity and is assumed to be a two-way exchange. Therefore, theoretically one would expect top-down and bottom-up processes to be operating simultaneously. Organizations offer inducements in expectation of contributions from employees and employees contribute to the organization in expectation of inducements. Interestingly, very few studies have examined employees' fulfillment of their obligations to the employer and the literature remains silent on the possible effects of employees' reciprocation on the employer's perspective of the employment relationship.

Adoption of a multilevel perspective has implications for measurement, design, and analysis. First, theory has to guide the level of measurement. If the construct is at the group level, the measure should be at the group level. Although Kenny suggests that we should not aggregate data, it is common practice for individuals to report on a group level phenomenon. Then if there is sufficient within-group agreement (Bliese 2000), individual responses are aggregated based on some compositional model such as the mean or variance (Chan 1998; Kozlowski and Klein 2000). To date, most of the more sophisticated statistical techniques such as HLM and RCM can identify top-down effects; however, these techniques have not addressed bottom-up processes. Fortunately, statistical techniques to assess these bottom-up, emergent processes are currently being developed (Kozlowski and Klein 2000).

14.5 Conclusion

This chapter has described existing measures and methods for assessing the employee–employer relationship. Multiple measures exist for assessing the employment relationship, and they differ as to their focus on content or process. Most of the measures treat the employment relationship as an individual level phenomenon although the reference in many cases is the organization. Measurement of the employer perspective is considerably less developed. In addition to the underdevelopment of the measurement of the employer perspective, the theory, measures, research design, and statistical techniques have limitations with a reliance on difference scores to measure perceptual gaps, sample dependent methods to measure balance in the relationship, and consideration of only a single level of analysis. It is suggested that consideration of measurement equivalence across studies and time, non-linear techniques such as polynomial regression analysis, and multilevel statistical techniques would move our understanding of the employee–employer relationship forward.

References

Bliese, P. D. (2000). "Within-group agreement, non-independence, and reliability: Implications for data aggregation and analysis", in K. J. Klein and S. W. J. Kozlowski (eds.), *Multilevel Theory, Research, and Methods in Organizations: Foundations, Extensions, and New Directions* (San Francisco: Jossey-Bass), 349–81.

Bond, C. F., and Kenny, D. A. (2002). "The triangle of interpersonal models". *Journal of Personality and Social Psychology*, 83: 355–66.

Chan, D. (1998). "Functional relations among constructs in the same construct domain at different levels of analysis". *Journal of Applied Psychology*, 83: 234–46.

Conway, N., and Briner, R. B. (2002). "A daily diary study of affective responses to psychological contract breach and exceeded promises". *Journal of Organizational Behavior*, 23: 287–302.

Coyle-Shapiro, J., and Kessler, I. (2000). "Consequences of the psychological contract for the employment relationship: A large scale survey". *Journal of Management Studies*, 37: 903–30.

Craig, D. D., and Tetrick, L. E. (2001). "Psychological contract breach and violation: the role of the employment exchange relationship and organizational justice." Paper presented at the Academy of Management Meetings, Washington DC, August.

De Vos, A., Buyens, D., and Schalk, R. (2003). "Psychological contract development during organizational socialization: Adaptation to reality and the role of reciprocity". *Journal of Organizational Behavior*, 24: 537–60.

Edwards, J. R. (1994). "The study of congruence in organizational behavior research: Critique and a proposed alternative". *Organizational Behavior and Human Decision Processes*, 58: 51–100.

—— (2001*a*). "Multidimensional constructs in organizational behavior research: An integrative analytical framework". *Organizational Research Methods*, 4: 144–92.

—— (2001*b*). "Alternatives to difference scores: Polynomial regression analysis and response surface methodology", in F. Drasgow and N. Schmitt (eds.), *Measuring and Analyzing Behavior in Organizations* (San Francisco: Jossey-Bass), 350–400.

—— and Bagozzi, R. P. (2000). "On the nature and direction of relationships between constructs and measures". *Psychological Methods*, 5: 155–74.

Eisenberger, R., Huntington, R., Hutchison, S., and Sowa, D. (1986). "Perceived organizational support". *Journal of Applied Psychology*, 71: 500–7.

Gakovic, A., and Tetrick, L. E. (2003). "Perceived organizational support and work status: A comparison of the employment relationships of part-time and full-time employees attending university classes". *Journal of Organizational Behavior*, 24: 649–66.

Golembiewski, R. T., Billingsley, K., and Yeager, S. (1976). "Measuring change and persistence in human affairs: Types of change generated by OD designs". *Journal of Applied Behavioral Science*, 12: 133–57.

Guzzo, R. A., Noonan, K. A., and Elron, E. (1994). "Expatriate managers and the psychological contract". *Journal of Applied Psychology*, 79: 617–26.

Herriot, P., Manning, W. E. G., and Kidd, J. M. (1997). "The content of the psychological contract". *British Journal of Management*, 8: 151–62.

Hui, C., Lee, C., and Rousseau, D. M. (2003). "An analysis of the forms and outcomes of psychological contract in China". *Journal of Applied Psychology*.

Kenny, D. A. (1996). "The design and analysis of social-interaction research". *Annual Review of Psychology*, 47: 59–86.

—— Mohr, C. D., and Levesque, M. J. (2001). "A social relations variance partitioning of dyadic behavior". *Psychological Bulletin*, 127: 128–41.

Kickul, J., Lester, S. W., and Finkl, J. (2002). "Promise breaking during radical organizational change: Do justice interventions make a difference?" *Journal of Organizational Behavior*, 23: 469–88.

Kozlowski, S. W. J., and Klein, K. J. (2000). "A multilevel approach to theory and research in organizations: Contextual, temporal, and emergent processes", in K. J. Klein and S. W. J. Kozlowski (eds.), *Multilevel Theory, Research, and Methods in Organizations: Foundations, Extensions, and New Directions* (San Francisco: Jossey-Bass), 3–90.

Lester, S. W., Turnley, W. H., Bloodgood, J. M., and Bolino, M. C. (2002). "Not seeing eye to eye: Differences in supervisor and subordinate perceptions of and attributions for psychological contract breach". *Journal of Organizational Behavior*, 23: 39–56.

Lewis-McClear, K., and Taylor, M. S. (1997). "Not seeing eye-to-eye: Implications of discrepant psychological contracts and contract violation for the employment relationship". *Academy of Management Proceedings*, 335–9.

McLean Parks, J., and Smith, F. (1998). "Organizational contracting: A 'rational' exchange". In J. J. Halpern and R. N. Stern (eds.), Debating Rationality: Nonrational Aspects of Organizational Decision Making. Ithaca, NY: Cornell University Press, 125–54.

Mitchell, T. R., and James, L. R. (2001). "Building better theory: Time and the specification of when things happen". *Academy of Management Review*, 26: 530–47.

Morrison, E. W., and Robinson, S. L. (1997). "When employees feel betrayed: A model of how psychological contract violation develops". *Academy of Management Review*, 22: 226–56.

Porter, L. M., Pearce, J. L., Tripoli, A. M., and Lewis, K. M. (1998). "Differential perceptions of employers' inducements: Implications for psychological contracts". *Journal of Organizational Behavior*, 19: 769–82.

Robinson, S. L. (1996). "Trust and breach of the psychological contract". *Administrative Science Quarterly*, 41: 574–99.

—— and Morrison, E. W. (2000). "The development of psychological contract breach and violation: A longitudinal study". *Journal of Organizational Behavior*, 21: 525–46.

—— and Rousseau, D. M. (1994). "Violating the psychological contract: Not the exception but the norm". *Journal of Organizational Behavior*, 15: 245–59.

——, Kraatz, M. S., and Rousseau, D. M. (1994). "Changing obligations and the psychological contact: A longitudinal study". *Academy of Management Journal*, 37: 137–53.

Rousseau, D. M. (1989). "Psychological and implied contracts in organizations". *Employee Rights and Responsibilities Journal*, 2: 121–39.

—— (1990). "New hire perceptions of their own and their employer's obligations: Study of psychological contracts". *Journal of Organizational Behavior*, 11: 389–400.

—— (2000). Psychological Contract Inventory. Technical Report, #3. Carnegie Mellon University, Heinz School of Public Policy.

—— (2001). "Schema, promise and mutuality: The building blocks of the psychological contract". *Journal of Occupational and Organizational Psychology*, 74: 511–41.

—— and Tijoriwala, S. A. (1998). "Assessing psychological contracts: Issues, alternatives and measures". *Journal of Organizational Behavior*, 19: 619–95.

Rupp, D. E., and Cropanzano, R. (2002). "The mediating effects of social exchange relationship in predicting workplace outcomes from multifoci organizational justice". *Organizational Behavior and Human Decision Processes*, 89: 925–47.

Sahlins, M. (1972). *Stone Age Economics*. New York: Aldine De Gruyter.

Shore, L. M., and Barksdale, K. (1998). "Examining degree of balance and level of obligation in the employment relationship: A social exchange approach". *Journal of Organizational Behavior*, 19: 713–44.

——, Tetrick, L. E., Lynch, P., and Barksdale, K. (forthcoming). "Measuring exchange processes underlying the psychological contract". *Journal of Applied Social Psychology.*

Sparrowe, R. T., and Liden, R. C. (1997). "Process and structure in leader–member exchange". *Academy of Management Review*, 22: 522–52.

Tekleab, A. G., and Taylor, M. S. (forthcoming). "Aren't there two parties in an employment relationship? Antecedents and consequences of organization–employee agreement on contract obligations and violations". *Journal of Organizational Behavior*, 24: 585–608.

Tetrick, L. E., Shore, L. M., Bommer, W. H., and Wayne, S. J. (2002). "Effects of perceptions of employer's failure to keep their promises: An application of ELVN-P". Paper presented at the Annual Meeting of the Society for Industrial and Organizational Psychology, Toronto, April.

—— —— Tsui, A. S., Wang, D. X., Glenn, D., Chen, N., Liu, H., Wang, X., and Yan, H. (2003). "Development of a measure of generalized, balanced, and negative reciprocity in employment relationships". Paper presented at the International Association for Chinese Management Research conference, Beijing.

Tsui, A. S., Pearce, J. L., Porter, L. W., and Tripoli, A. M. (1997). "Alternative approaches to the employee–organization relationship: Does investment in employees pay off?" *Academy of Management Journal*, 40: 1089–121.

Turnley, W. H., and Feldman, D. (1999). "The impact of psychological contract violations on exit, voice, loyalty, and neglect". *Human Relations*, 52: 895–922.

—— and —— (2000). "Re-examining the effects of psychological contract violations: Unmet expectations and job dissatisfaction as mediators". *Journal of Organizational Behavior*, 21: 25–42.

Vandenberg, R. J., and Lance, C. E. (2000). "A review and synthesis of the measurement invariance literature: Suggestions, practices, and recommendations for organizational research". *Organizational Research Methods*, 3: 4–70.

15

Employment Relationships in Context: Implications for Policy and Practice

DAVID R. HANNAH AND RODERICK D. IVERSON

> Each participant and group of participants receives from the organization inducements in return for which he makes to the organization contributions .... each participant will continue his participation in an organization only so long as the inducements offered him are as great or greater than the contributions he is asked to make.
>
> Simon et al. (1950: 381–2)

15.1 Introduction

As the date of this quote demonstrates, scholars have long recognized that in order for employers to get desired contributions from their employees, they must provide appropriate inducements (March and Simon 1958; Schein 1965). But it has never been easy for employers to know what kinds of inducements will influence employees to make desired contributions. There are multiple reasons why this has proved to be such a difficult challenge for employers. One reason is that employees have varying conceptions of their employment relationships with their employers, and as a result, inducements can affect different employees in different ways (Robinson 1996). One employee may exert greater effort if promised a promotion; another may do so if he or she is offered a pay increase. A second reason is that organizations have an extremely broad range of inducements that they can provide, and it can be difficult to know which inducements are most appropriate when trying to elicit certain prosocial behaviors. This is complicated by the fact that how organizations offer inducements, and sometimes when they offer them, can substantially alter the impact of those inducements. A third reason is that organizations exist within national contexts that influence the range of inducements that organizations are permitted to offer and shape how individuals react to those inducements.

In this chapter, we explore how external inducements influence employees' attitudes and behaviors. We address the complexities noted in the introduction by developing a "contextualized" model of employment relationships, in which those relationships reside within broader organizational and national contexts. We begin by discussing briefly the nature and substance of employment relationships.

15.2 Employment relationships

As seen in many of the chapters of this book, scholars have frequently conceptualized the employment relationship between employer and employee as an exchange relationship where employees provide their contributions in exchange for inducements from their employers (Rousseau and McLean Parks 1993; Shore and Barksdale 1998). These conceptualizations have historically fallen into two main types: Dyadic and solo. A dyadic conceptualization of the employment relationship was common among scholars who first introduced the term "psychological contract" to the literature on organizations. Argyris (1960), Levinson (1962), and Schein (1965) used the term to describe an implicit agreement, or overlap of expectations, between the parties to an employment relationship. More recent scholarship has focused on solo conceptualizations where each individual in a relationship has his or her own thoughts about what each party to the employment relationship is expected to provide. When Rousseau (1989) reintroduced the term psychological contract to the literature, she used it to describe this kind of solo conceptualization. Most recent theorizing on psychological contracts has followed Rousseau's lead by focusing on the solo conceptualizations of employees (e.g. Guzzo et al. 1994; Herriot et al. 1997; Thomas and Anderson 1998). Others scholars have focused on managers' solo conceptualizations about what inducements they, acting as agents of their employers, will provide for employees and what contributions are expected in return. Managers' conceptualizations have been called employee–organization relationship strategies (see Chapter 7).

Both employees' and managers' conceptualizations of employment relationships can contain many different kinds of inducements and contributions. For example, inducements may include such HRM practices as pay, benefits, and job security; contributions can include hard work and loyalty. Each inducement and contribution, that is, each component of an employment relationship, can be classified as either "hard" or "soft." Hard components, sometimes called transactional (e.g. Robinson and Morrison 1995; Sapienza et al. 1997), pertain to the economic part of the employment relationship (Blau 1964), and are related to measurable, tangible, and monetizable outcomes (Robinson et al. 1994). Hard inducements include base levels of pay and pay based on performance, and hard contributions include greater work effort and working extra hours without compensation (Rousseau 1989; Robinson 1996). Soft components, sometimes called relational (e.g. Rousseau 1995), are those that are non-monetizable, less tangible, and hard to measure. They are those described by Blau (1964) as being a part of a social exchange. Soft inducements include job security and providing employees with sufficient power and responsibility (Robinson 1996), and soft contributions include loyalty and refusing to support competitors (Rousseau 1989; Robinson 1996).

A manager considering how to elicit desired behaviors from employees can, in theory, choose from wide variety of inducements, both hard and soft, in the hopes of inducing a range of hard and soft contributions from their employees. But in reality, the range of inducements that managers can offer and the effects of those inducements on employees are influenced by other factors. One important factor is the national context that an organization exists in.

15.3 National contexts and HRM "toolkits"

Each subsidiary of a multi-national organization exists in a country. Each country has numerous characteristics (e.g. labor regulations, culture) that influence how people living in that country think and act, both within and outside organizational life. These characteristics are what we call the national context.

There is considerable evidence to suggest that in different national contexts, employers make use of different kinds of HRM practices and policies, and also implement them in different ways. For example, scholars have noted that firms in different countries tend to have varying practices in training and development (Drost et al. 2002), compensation (Lowe et al. 2002), and performance appraisal (Milliman et al. 2002).

In order to help explain why and how national contexts influence the HRM policies and practices of organizations, we borrow a metaphor from Swidler (1986)—the "tool kit." Swidler described organizational cultures as providing employees with "tool kits" of practices and habits that assist employees in making decisions about how they should think and act in an organization. National contexts can also be thought of as providing toolkits for employers. Each national context contains a set of "tools" that employers can draw upon in the pursuit of organizational goals: The tools are the inducements that employers can offer. In this discussion, we will focus on an important subset of the tools that employers have: The human resources management policies in their toolkits. For the sake of brevity, we will call them HRM toolkits. We will focus on two characteristics of HRM toolkits: Their size and their content.

15.3.1 Factors influencing HRM toolkits

The size of an HRM toolkit is an indicator of the number and variety of HRM policies that are available to employers in a given national context. Employers in countries with relatively few laws and regulations will have few constraints on how they choose to operate. For example, firms often relocate to developing nations where they can set levels of compensation that are much lower than what they would be required to pay in more developed countries (Lowe et al. 2002). These firms will take advantage of the larger HRM toolkits afforded to them in those situations.

A larger HRM toolkit in a given country is likely to be positive for the employers located there, but for employees this may not be such a good thing. Many employers, if given the freedom to pay lower wages, will choose to do so. Employers may also choose not to provide overtime pay, and to offer fewer benefits. In theory, employers with large HRM toolkits could exploit that flexibility by being unusually generous to employees, but in practice, it is probably unlikely that employers will do so.

Institutional and legal frameworks

At least two factors at the national level influence the size of toolkits. The first is employment laws, policies, and regulations (see Chapters 3–5). National laws and regulations establish rules for what employers must provide for their workers, such as minimum wage levels, safe working conditions, and certain levels of benefits. National laws may require employers to respect the rights of workers to form unions, and may require that employers bargain collectively with unions when they are formed. Kelly (see Chapter 3) notes that the decline of union density in both Britain and the United States has been associated with a decline in employee participation in decision-making. National laws often also tell employers what they must not do: For example, they may forbid employers from discriminating against workers on the basis of gender or race, and require that employers cannot fire workers without just cause.

There is considerable variance in the size of the HRM toolkits that countries offer to employers. The countries that offer the largest toolkits are often developing countries (e.g. Latin America). They tend to have fewer laws and regulations that constrain the hard inducements employers can offer and the contributions they can demand from employees in return. Such countries may have very low requirements for wages and working conditions, and they are often impoverished to such a degree that workers will willingly go to work in unpleasant or even dangerous working conditions. At the other end of the toolkit size "spectrum" are those nations where organizations face substantially smaller toolkits, due to either extensive amounts of regulation, national cultures that expect employers to provide substantial benefits for employees, or both. Scholars have noted that many European nations, in contrast to American jurisdictions, tend to have higher levels of regulation and government intervention in their operations. Sparrow and Hiltrop (1997) argued that European HRM systems, as compared to North American systems, have higher levels of government intervention and more restricted levels of organizational autonomy. They and others have also noted, however, that European organizations have, in recent years, tried to enlarge their HRM toolkits by striving to liberate themselves from national-level constraints (Sparrow and Hiltrop 1997; Bacon and Storey 2000). The increased role of government has also been noted in Asia. Training and development, for example, is legally mandated in China and Korea (Drost et al. 2002).

National culture
A second factor that influences the size of HRM toolkits is national cultures. While laws and regulations shape what kinds of inducements employers are legally permitted to offer, the belief systems that underlie national cultures influence the kinds of inducements that would be culturally acceptable to—and sometimes even expected by—employees in a given country. National cultures (e.g. individualistic versus collectivist) have an influence on, among other factors, what kinds of skills and competencies are valued by employers, the degree of loyalty employees will show to employers, and the importance of careers to individuals (Sparrow 1996; Sparrow and Hiltrop 1997). They also help us understand the effectiveness of HRM practices such as performance appraisal in the employment relationship (Milliman et al. 2002).

Thus, both national laws and regulations and national cultures influence the size of HRM toolkits. Both also influence the substance of those toolkits—that is, what kinds of inducements are in the kits. Using the terminology of "hard" and "soft" components introduced earlier, it seems logical that national-level laws and regulations will tend to require employers to provide inducements that pertain to the hard side of employment relationships. They usually require employers to meet or exceed minimal levels of wages and benefits. While it is possible that laws might be put into place that require employers to provide soft inducements, it would be difficult for national policy-makers to enforce those laws, because soft inducements, by nature, are difficult to quantify and measure. For example, it would be difficult to quantify the extent to which employers provided employees with sufficient power and responsibility, or with support for employees' personal problems.

National cultures, on the other hand, have such a profound impact on how employees and managers see the world around them (Trice and Beyer 1993) that they can have a powerful impact on every characteristic of a given country's toolkit. Cultures can shape what kinds of inducements—hard and soft—are present in a given nation's toolkit. They do so by legitimizing certain types of HRM approaches over others, and by establishing what the purposes of different types of HRM policies and practices are. For example, Sparrow and Hiltrop (1997) suggest that national cultures have a multitude of effects on European HRM, including how organizations select and train managers, organizations' performance management systems and compensation systems, and how they use feedback systems. These types of cultural effects have been observed in other countries such as Australia, Canada, China, Japan, Korea, Indonesia, Mexico, Taiwan, the United States, and Latin America (e.g. Costa Rica, Guatemala, Panama, Nicaragua, Venezuela) (Drost et al. 2002; Lowe et al. 2002; Millman et al. 2002). Figure 15.1 provides a graphical representation of the arguments advanced to this point.

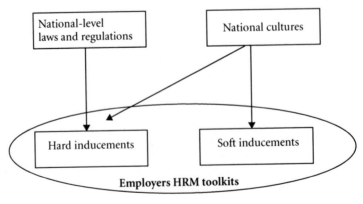

Figure 15.1. *The effect of national-level factors on employers' HRM toolkits.*

15.3 Organizational contexts and employment relationships

To this point, we have discussed how national contexts provide HRM toolkits of inducements that managers in each national setting can choose from. We now discuss how the HRM policies and practices chosen by managers can influence employees' conceptions of their employment relationships, their attitudes, and their behaviors (Rousseau and Greller 1994). We do so in two stages. First, we develop an overall model of how employers' HRM policies and practices, in conjunction with employees' conceptions of their employment relationships, influence employees' attitudes and behaviors. We then examine how several different individual HRM policies and practices can influence employees.

15.3.1 Effects of HRM policies on attitudes and behavior

There are at least three streams of research pertinent to our overall model. First, there is considerable research evidence to suggest that employers' HRM policies and practices influence employees' attitudes and behaviors. The current stream of research on high-performance work systems supports this view. A high-performance work system is defined as a

Set of distinct but interrelated HRM practices that together select, develop, retain, and motivate a workforce: (1) that possesses superior abilities (i.e. superior (a broad repertoire of) skills and behavior scripts); (2) that applies their abilities in their work-related activities; (3) whose work-related activities (i.e. actual employee behaviors/output) result in these firms achieving superior intermediate indicators of firm performance (i.e. those indicators over which the workforce has direct control) and sustainable competitive advantage (Way 2002:765).

At the organizational level, high-performance work systems have been associated with lower turnover rates (Guthrie 2001), higher employee earnings in the steel and apparel industries (Bailey et al. 2001), and increased productivity and financial performance (Huselid 1995). At the employee level, high-performance work systems have been linked to increased job satisfaction (Berg 1999), and decreased employee fatigue (Godard 2001) and occupational injuries (Barling et al. 2003*b*).

Second, numerous scholars have also examined how employers' policies and practices influence employees' conceptions of their employment relationships (Guzzo and Noonan 1994; Sims 1994; Rousseau 1995; Singh 1998). Rousseau (1995) described the process by which organizational policies and practices influence employees' psychological contracts as "contract making." In the contract-making process, when employees believe their employers have promised to provide them with some inducement, that belief becomes part of employees' psychological contracts (Rousseau 2001). Employers' HRM policies can, implicitly and explicitly, convey promises about the inducements that employees will receive. An employee's current job is enlarged with the expectation that this increased responsibility will lead to a promotion at a later date.

Third, employees' conceptions of their employment relationships influence their attitudes and behaviors (Rousseau 1990; Guzzo et al. 1994; Hallier and James 1997).

When employees believe that their employers are failing to uphold their obligations in employment relationships, they respond by adjusting their perceptions of their own obligations by lowering them (Robinson et al. 1994). Such employees are also more likely to leave their employers (Robinson and Rousseau 1994; Robinson 1996) and they self-report lower levels of citizenship behavior (Robinson and Morrison 1995; Robinson 1996).

The findings from these three streams of research are illustrated in Figure 15.2. They are illustrated with the unbroken lines that represent the connections between variables. We have added a fourth path, represented by the dashed line, because we argue that employees' conceptions of employment relationships also moderate the relationship between HRM practices and employees' attitudes and behaviors. We explain our argument below.

15.3.2 Employees' interpretations of HRM practices

Rousseau (2001: 512) theorized that employees' psychological contracts, over time, take "the form of a mental model or schema, which, like most other schemas, is relatively stable and durable." And like other stable, enduring schemas, employees' psychological contracts play an important role in how employees interpret and react to the world around them. Psychological contracts provide employees with an image or conception of their employment relationships: As an exchange of promised inducements and contributions. That conception then serves as a reference point for the interpretation of organizational events, in the sense that employees' attributions about the purposes, meanings, inherent fairness, or other characteristics of events will be shaped by their conceptions of their employment relationships. Put another

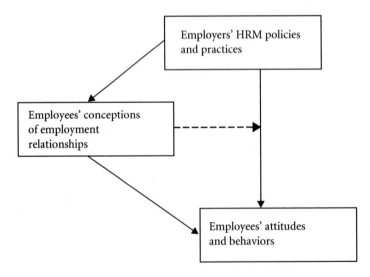

Figure 15.2. *Model of how HRM policies influence employees' attitudes and behaviors.*

way, if something happens to an employee, he or she interprets it by comparing it to relevant characteristics in the schema of their employment relationship. For example, if an employee is passed over for a promotion, her interpretation of that event will be influenced by her belief about whether or not she was promised the promotion as an inducement, and whether she provided sufficient contributions to earn the inducement. If she believes she was promised the inducement, and she worked hard enough to uphold her side of the employment relationship, she is likely to react negatively.

Employees' HRM policies and practices are other "events" that employees in organizations must interpret (Guzzo and Noonan 1994). For example, when employees go through performance appraisals, when they evaluate their benefits packages, or when they receive recognition for their efforts, they will make an interpretation of the experience and that interpretation will influence how they react to it. And, as argued above, that interpretation will be shaped by employees' conceptions of their employment relationships. Therefore, employees' reactions to their employers' HRM initiatives will depend on their conceptions of their employment relationships. Put another way, the relationship between employers' HRM efforts and employees' reactions to those efforts will be moderated by employees' conceptions of their employment relationships.

In the following section, we explore Figure 15.1 in more detail. Other chapters in this book discuss the relationship between employees' conceptions of their employment relationships and their attitudes and behaviors, so we do not revisit that relationship here. Instead, we focus on the three other paths: (a) the relationship between HRM policies and practices and employees' attitudes and behaviors, (b) the relationship between HRM policies and practices on employees' conceptions of their employment relationships, and (c) the moderating effect of those conceptions on the HRM policies–attitudes and behaviors relationship. We do so by exploring these relationships and effects for several kinds of human resources management policies.

In understanding the influence of high-performance systems or individual HRM practices on employees' attitudes and behaviors, it is appropriate to apply a social exchange and norm of reciprocity framework (see Chapter 1 for a comprehensive discussion). Whitener (2001), building on the work of Homans (1961) and Blau (1964), asserts that HRM practices are viewed by employees as a "personalized" commitment to them by the organization, which is then reciprocated back to the organization by employees through positive attitudes and behaviors (Tsui et al. 1997). Other researchers such as Farrell and Rusbult (1981) proposed an investment model, where employees consider HRM practices as rewards. In any event, these exchange relationships shape employees' employment relationships.

Although it is beyond the scope of the chapter to discuss all individual HRM practices we focus on recruitment and selection, performance management, and occupational health and safety, all of which have major impacts prior to and then throughout employees' tenure in the organization (see Rousseau and Greller 1994; Chapter 13, this volume). We do acknowledge the influence of HRM practices such as training and development (Robinson and Rousseau 1994; Thomas and

Anderson 1998), responsibility (Robinson and Rousseau 1994), communication (Guest and Conway 2002), recognition (Porter et al. 1998), and job design (Porter et al. 1998) on the employment relationship. Current research using a high-performance work systems approach has bundled these types of HRM practices (see Becker and Huselid 1998).

15.3.3 HRM practices

Recruitment and selection

The recruitment and selection process involves organizations identifying potential employees, making offers of employment to them, and trying to persuade them to accept those offers. Recruitment has an important influence on employees' later experiences in their new companies. Robinson and Morrison (2000) in a longitudinal study reported that psychological breach was less likely to occur when employees interacted with representatives of the organization during the recruitment process. Employees are likely to begin a recruitment process with a schema of the employee–employer psychological contract already in mind (Rousseau 2001). That general schema will then be shaped and altered by the specific promises that recruiters make to potential employees (Rousseau 1995). When new employees believe that recruiters make promises to them, they expect their new employers will uphold those promises. If the new employers fail to do so, the employees may believe that their psychological contracts have been violated. They are likely to react in ways that go against the interests of their employers (Morrison and Robinson 1997), and in many cases they voluntarily leave the organization (Robinson 1996). On the other hand, if employees exaggerate their own abilities in recruitment, or misrepresent themselves in order to look like they will "fit" with the company, they may find themselves unable or unwilling to adjust to their new circumstances (Beyer and Hannah 2002). This can be costly for both employers and employees.

It is, therefore, important for employment relationships to start off with—and to maintain—congruent expectations between employees and employers. Hom and Griffeth (1995) and Griffeth et al. (2000) in meta-analyses reported the correlation between met expectations and voluntary turnover to be −0.13 and −0.15, respectively. Other research has indicated that unmet expectations are associated with lower performance (Robinson 1996).

These findings illustrate the importance of providing employees with accurate information through realistic job previews and during the orientation processes of new employees. Sims (1994) notes four additional reasons why realistic job previews are important when establishing employment relationships. First, a job candidate may self-select not to take a job if they consider the job will not be personally satisfying. Second, knowing the "good" and "bad" aspects of the job, the candidate on accepting the job becomes committed to their decision. Third, realistic job previews help lower employee expectations, which will in turn reduce the gap between job expectations and reality. In this situation, expectations are more likely to be met, leading to more positive attitudes and behavior. Fourth, and finally, employees can cope better when they are confronted with unpleasant situations that were expected rather than if they were surprises.

The initial schemas of psychological contracts that employees have when they begin the recruitment process will influence how they react to recruitment. If employees have very high opinions about the contributions they will be able to make, and expect that their new employers should offer contributions that are commensurate with that level of contribution, they are likely to expect to be recruited in a certain way. If their expectations are not met, they are likely to react negatively.

Performance management

We focus here on the appraisal and compensation components of performance management. Processes of performance appraisal in organizations involve employers setting performance standards and providing feedback to employees about their levels of performance. Performance appraisals can have powerful impacts on employees' attitudes and behaviors (Boswell and Boudreau 2000; Tziner et al. 2000). Performance appraisals can also influence employment relationships in a number of ways. For employers, they provide an important tool in the management of employment relationships. When an agent of an employer meets with an employee in order to provide feedback about his or her performance, that agent has the opportunity to signal to the employee whether or not they are providing valued contributions in their employment relationships. By doing this, employers can inform employees how they can uphold their side of the employment relationship. Appraisals also give employers the chance to ask whether their employees are satisfied with the inducements provided, and to remedy the situation if necessary. Appraisals can therefore be used to ensure that employees are satisfied that their employers are upholding their side of the psychological contract.

The effect of performance appraisals on employees will depend on employees' conceptions of their employment relationships. Scholars have argued that many employees believe that they are obligated to perform their jobs effectively and in ways that benefit employing organizations (Jackson and Schuler 1985). If this argument is true, it also seems likely that employees will believe that their employers are obligated to tell them how to do this. The performance appraisal provides an opportunity for employers to fulfill this obligation.

Whether or not the appraisal has this effect, though, will probably depend on how the appraisals are conducted. Boswell and Boudreau (2000) observed that whether performance appraisal was used for evaluation or developmental purposes impacted on employees' satisfaction with the process and the appraiser. In addition, the link with compensation is problematic for many employees. Robinson and Rousseau (1994) note that a common problem is the lack of a "line of sight" between positive performance reviews and compensation. This raises the issue of fairness of inducements that applies to many issues throughout the employment relationship (see Chapter 2). Moreover, performance appraisals must be aligned with other HRM practices such as training and career development. Otherwise, employees may perceive injustice in their employment relationships (Rousseau and Greller 1994) and alter their behaviors accordingly (see Chapter 2).

The compensation that employers provide for employees includes payments such as wages, bonuses, and any other direct and indirect compensation (Gerhart and Milkovich 1993). Benefits are part of the indirect financial payments and include such things as health and life insurance, employee assistance plans, and so on. Studies of the composition of employees' psychological contracts have identified "pay" and "pay for performance" as important employers' obligations (Rousseau 1990; Robinson 1996).

The compensation and benefits that employers provide for employees can have a major influence on their conceptions of their employment relationships (Rousseau and Ho 2000). A specific type of compensation system might signal to employees that they are in a specific kind of employment relationship (Rousseau and Ho 2000). Rousseau and Ho matched compensation systems to employees' psychological contracts by identifying two dimensions of the contracts: Their duration (short-term vs. long-term) and the degree to which compensation was tied to specified individual measures of performance (specified vs. unspecified). They identified four types of relationships based on the combinations of these dimensions, and specified the types of compensation systems that were likely to be present in those relationships. First, in short-term relationships with specified measures of performance, compensation is likely to be based on short-term measures of performance such as sales commissions. In these circumstances, employees are also likely to have limited benefits. Second, in short-term relationships with unspecified performance measures, as might be seen in downsizing or restructuring organizations, they theorized that employees' wage levels would decline and benefits would erode as the organization restructured. Third, in long-term employment relationships with specified performance measures, compensation systems would be linked to both short- and long-term performance, for example, by providing workers with sales commissions and skill-based pay, as well as flexible benefits packages that workers could tailor to their own preferences. Fourth, in long-term employment relationships with unspecified performance measures, compensation is likely to be based on factors such as seniority. Benefits would likely be generous, especially for long-term employees.

Rousseau and Ho's ideas also suggest how employees' conceptions of their employment relationships are likely to lead them to expect certain types of compensation. An employee working in a short-term job with specified performance indicators would be more likely to expect compensation based on short-term performance, and could react negatively if that expectation was not met. These ideas also provide insights into how employers could use compensation systems as part of an HRM strategy aimed at establishing certain kinds of employment relationships. For example, an employer that wanted to establish a long-term employment relationship with specified performance measures should structure their compensation system accordingly: With skill-based pay, flexible benefits systems, and a blend of short- and long-term incentives.

Occupational health and safety

An important, but scarcely studied component of the employment relationship is occupational health and safety. The management of occupational health and safety in organizations refers to employers' efforts to promote the physical and emotional health and safety of employees. From the standpoint of many employees, especially those working in countries where organizations are legally required to provide employees with safe working environments, the employer's obligation to provide a safe, healthy working environment is likely to be one of the most important obligations in the employment relationship. In fact, Guest and Conway (2002) found that one of the most important promises made by organizations concerns having a safe working environment. Employers that oversee a dangerous work environment are likely to be viewed by employees as violating their psychological contracts with their employees. They are probably also likely to be seen as failing to provide organizational support for their employees. For both reasons, employees in these work situations would be likely to reduce their own contributions to their employers (see Chapter 10, this volume; Rousseau 1995; Robinson 1996). Barling et al. (2003*a*), in a study using a multioccupational sample, observed that employees, after experiencing a workplace accident, displayed distrust in management.

In addition, the degree to which employees believe employers are obligated to look out for the health and safety of their workers will likely influence how employees react to their employers' health and safety initiatives. For example, some employees may feel that employers are responsible for establishing work situations where employees are not immediately in danger. Other employees may believe that their employers should go even further by considering ergonomically designed work stations that will lessen the likelihood that employees will suffer injuries, such as repetitive strain injuries, caused by repeating the same awkward motions over long periods of time. Still other employees may believe that employers have a responsibility to do everything they can to safeguard the psychological health of their workers. Each group of employees is likely to expect somewhat different levels of attention to health and safety from their employers, and to react in somewhat different ways if their expectations are not met.

15.4 How should organizations manage their human resources?

To this point, we have discussed how national contexts provide "tool kits" of HRM policies and practices for organizations, and how these policies and practices, along with employees' conceptions of their employment relationships, influence employees' attitudes and behaviors. In the remaining section, we will combine the insights derived from these previous sections to offer some normative recommendations for organizations. We base our recommendations on our full, contextualized model of employment relationships in organizations, depicted in Figure 15.3. We focus on two main themes. First, we consider how organizations' HRM strategies should take into account the national context in which they exist. Second, we discuss how those strategies should be congruent with the kind of employment relationship employers want to have with their employees.

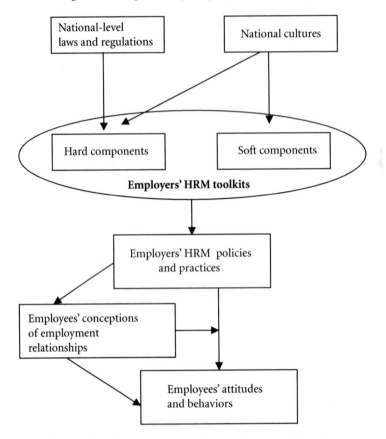

Figure 15.3. *Contextualized model of employment relationships.*

15.4.1 National contexts and HRM strategies

As discussed earlier, national contexts provide HRM toolkits of inducements that organizations can use in order to manage workers. And, as shown in Figure 15.3, the inducements in those HRM toolkits come from two sources in the national context: Laws and Regulations, and National Cultures.

The national context influences the size of HRM toolkits (the number of inducements available to employers) and the content of toolkits (the nature of the inducements themselves). In practice, however, it may be difficult for employers to arrive at an accurate assessment of the size and content of their HRM toolkits. Employers might make at least two kinds of mistakes in assessing their toolkits: (a) they could assume that an inducement is in their toolkit when it is not, and (b) they may not realize that a particular inducement is in their toolkit, and thus avoid using it.

If an employer implements an inducement that is not actually in their toolkit, this can mean one of two things. First, it might mean that the inducement is illegal. If that is the case, then they will have broken laws and may be subject to legal penalties. Second, the inducement could be legal, but culturally unacceptable. Employees might therefore ignore such an inducement, or even react to it in ways that are against the interests of their employers, perhaps by reducing their own contributions to their employers (Robinson et al. 1994), by quitting (Robinson 1996), by stealing from their employer (Greenberg and Scott 1996), or by divulging their employers' secrets (Hannah 2001). Employers should therefore ensure that the HRM policies and practices they implement are contained within their toolkits. In order to do this, organizations must develop what could be called "realistic" toolkits—realistic in the sense that they include all the possible inducements available to them in a certain national context.

In order to ensure realistic toolkits, organizations must ensure that they assemble a complete inventory of both national-level laws and regulations and of relevant features of organizations' cultures. It will probably be easier for organizations to do the former, since laws and regulations are usually made explicit and are published. Organizations should also be aware of the consequences of ignoring a particular law. If a law is on the books but is never enforced, then that may mean that another inducement or inducements are actually in the HRM toolkits even when they would appear to not be. Organizations could also lobby local governments for exceptions to certain laws if those laws restrict organizations from implementing one or more of the key inducements in their HRM toolkits.

Since cultures are often hidden (Trice and Beyer 1993), it is likely to be much more difficult for organizations to learn about how a particular national culture will influence their toolkits. And it may be more important for organizations to learn about cultures than about laws, because organizations may be able to lobby for exemptions to certain laws, but there is no way to escape the effects of cultures.

The question of how organizations should learn how national cultures influence their HRM toolkits brings to light a significant controversy in the literature on how to measure cultures. Many scholars have argued that cultures cannot be measured using quantitative methods such as surveys (Trice and Beyer 1993), yet organizations may not be able to afford the time and effort involved in a qualitative study of a particular national culture. One solution is for employers to use local informants to uncover how the cultures of a particular nation will influence their HRM kits. Many of the influences of that culture on the toolkits might be able to be uncovered by interviewing those informants. But there may also be issues that have achieved a "taken-for-granted" status among the informants, so they may not think to articulate them. It would also be useful for organizations to discuss with other companies in that nation what issues came up in their efforts to manage their human resources. If an organization is the first company in that country or the other companies do not want to discuss their experiences, the organization could initiate their operations on a small scale in order to learn first-hand how culture influenced their HRM toolkits. Presumably any problems experienced while running a small-scale operation could be resolved with fewer negative consequences than if those problems had occurred when an organization was attempting to get its entire operation up and running.

15.4.2 HRM strategies and overall employment relationship goals

Once organizations have developed their HRM toolkits, they then face the task of deciding which of the inducements in those toolkits they will use, and also how they will use them. The inducements they choose will influence the kind of employment relationship they have with their employees. Therefore, organizations should base their choices of HRM policies and practices on their employee–organization relationship (EOR) strategies (see Chapter 7). In this section, we review two different EOR strategies: One based on a primarily transactional, economic approach to the management of employees, and the second based on a more relational, social approach. For each strategy, we discuss what types of HRM policies and practices should be enacted to accompany it. And since the HRM policies and practices chosen by employers will shape employees' conceptions of their own employment relationships, we also discuss the impact of each strategy on these conceptions.

A transactional, economic approach to the EOR, that is, one where employers are primarily concerned with inducing employees to make hard, quantifiable contributions, is likely to involve employers offering hard inducements. Organizations should enact HR systems that emphasize monitoring of employees' performance levels, quantifying the performance of employees in as objective a way as possible, and linking their performance appraisals and their compensation to those quantified levels of performance. In organizations that implement such HR systems, employees are likely to respond by focusing on their own hard contributions in order to reach the hard inducements their employers are providing. But those employees are, therefore, unlikely to feel obligated to make "soft" contributions to their employers. For example, such employees are unlikely to be loyal to their employers, and will probably leave for other opportunities if those opportunities provide better hard inducements such as higher pay.

In contrast, if employers want their employees to provide both hard and soft contributions, for example, they want employees to both work hard and to be loyal, then they should ensure that they provide employees with both hard and soft inducements. One way that organizations can accomplish this is by implementing high-performance work systems, which we discussed in some detail earlier in the chapter. It may be more costly for employers to enact high-performance systems than to enact systems that focus exclusively on hard contributions, but employers who do so will be more likely to get soft contributions in return from their employees.

15.5 Conclusion

In the introduction to this chapter, we discussed one of the most enduring challenges faced by managers: How to use inducements in order to motivate employees to make desired contributions. A number of scholars, including several who are authors and co-authors of chapters in this book, have documented how employees' conceptions of their employment relationships can have a powerful influence on the contributions they make in the course of doing their work. The research and theorizing of the scholars has helped us derive a better understanding of the relationship between inducements and contributions.

In this chapter, we have attempted to place the insights of these scholars into a broader context. Specifically, we explored how factors in the national and organizational contexts influence the inducements–contributions relationship. Our main conclusions can be summarized as follows:

• National-level laws, regulations, and cultures influence the hard and soft inducements that are available to organizations operating in a given country.
• The total set of inducements available to an organization constitutes their Human Resources Management (HRM) "tool kit."
• The HRM policies that employers select from their toolkits and subsequently enact have a direct influence on employees' conceptions of their employment relationships and on their attitudes and behaviors.
• Employees' conceptions of their employment relationships moderate the relationship between HRM policies and employees' attitudes and behaviors, and they also have a direct influence on those attitudes and behaviors.

These conclusions are summarized in graphic form in Figure 15.3.

We hope that our thoughts will provide readers with some ideas for future theorizing and research. We want to emphasize two areas in particular. First, there are numerous issues relevant to the concept of the HRM toolkits that merit additional investigation. Some examples of questions that could be pursued include the following: How do organizations decide what inducements are in their toolkits? How do organizations decide what inducements in their toolkits they should enact? Are organizations with more comprehensive toolkits more able to adapt to new environments? Do organizations have the competencies to implement their toolkits effectively? These are all relevant considerations for organizations.

A second issue concerns the moderating effect of employees' conceptions of their employment relationships on the HRM practices–employees' attitudes and behaviors relationship. This effect has been neglected in the literature on organizations, yet its inclusion in future studies might help us explain more of the variance in employees' attitudes and behaviors. Questions that could be explored include: Why do employees in the same employment relationship display differing attitudes and behavior? How does social information "politicize" the employment relationship by influencing employees' attitudes and beliefs about it? And what influence does the politicization of the employment relationship have on employees' attitudes and behaviors? Future research needs to address these types of issues.

Of course, these are only a few of a multitude of issues pertinent to our chapter that merit additional attention from scholars. We hope that the ideas we have presented herein induce scholars to make their own contributions to the ongoing inquiry into these important issues.

References

Argyris, C. (1960). *Understanding Organizational Behavior*. Homewood, IL: Dorsey Press.

Bacon, N., and Storey, J. (2000). "New employee relations strategies in Britain: Towards individualism or partnership?" *British Journal of Industrial Relations*, 38: 407–27.

Bailey, T., Berg, P., and Sandy, C. (2001). "The effect of high-performance work practices on employee earnings in the steel, apparel, and medical electronics and imaging industries." *Industrial and Labor Relations Review*, 54: 525–43.

Barling, J., Kelloway, E. K., and Iverson, R. D. (2003*a*). "Accidental outcomes: Attitudinal consequences of workplace injuries." *Journal of Occupational Health Psychology*, 8: 74–85.

—— —— and —— (2003*b*). "High quality jobs, job satisfaction and occupational safety." *Journal of Applied Psychology*, 88: 276–83.

Becker, B. E., and Huselid, M. A. (1998). "High performance work systems and firm performance: A synthesis of research and managerial implications," in G. R. Ferris (ed.), *Research in Personnel and Human Resources Management*, 16: 53–101, Greenwich, CT: JAI Press.

Berg, P. (1999). "The effects of high performance work practices on job satisfaction in the United States steel industry." *Relations Industrielles/Industrial Relations*, 54: 111–34.

Beyer, J. M., and Hannah, D. R. (2002). "Building on the past: Enacting established personal identities in a new work setting." *Organization Science*, 13: 636–52.

Blau, P. M. (1960). "A theory of social integration." *American Journal of Sociology*, 6: 545–56.

—— (1964). *Exchange and Power in Social Life*. New York: John Wiley and Sons.

Boswell, W. R., and Boudreau, J. W. (2000). "Employee satisfaction with performance appraisals and appraisers: The role of perceived appraisal use." *Human Resource Development Quarterly*, 11: 283–99.

Drost, E. A., Frayne, C. A., Lowe K. B., and Geringer, J. M. (2002). "Benchmarking training and development practices: A multi-country comparative analysis." *Human Resource Management*, 41: 67–86.

Farrell, D., and Rusbult, C. E. (1981). "Exchange variables as predictors of job satisfaction, job commitment, and turnover: The impact of rewards, costs, alternatives, and investments." *Organizational Behavior and Human Performance*, 28: 78–95.

Gerhart, B., and Milkovich, G. T. (1993). "Employee compensation: Research and Theory," in M. D. Dunette and L. M. Hough (eds.), *Handbook of Industrial and Organizational Psychology* 2nd ed., 3 (Palo Alto, CA: Consulting Psychologists Press), 481–569.

Godard, J. (2001). "High performance and the transformation of work? The implications of alternative work practices for the experience and outcomes of work." *Industrial and Labor Relations Review*, 54: 776–805.

Greenberg, J., and Scott, K. S. (1996). "Why do workers bite the hands that feed them? Employee theft as a social exchange process." *Research in Organizational Behavior*, 18: 111–56.

Griffeth, R. W., Hom, P. W., and Gaertner, S. (2000). "A meta-analysis of antecedents and correlates of employee turnover: Update, moderator tests, and research implications for the next millennium." *Journal of Management*, 26: 463–88.

Guest, D. E., and Conway, N. (2002). "Communicating the psychological contract: An employer perspective." *Human Resource Management Journal*, 12: 22–38.

Guthrie, J. P. (2001). "High involvement work practices, turnover and productivity: Evidence from New Zealand." *Academy of Management Journal*, 44: 180–90.

Guzzo, R. A., and Noonan, K. A. (1994). "Human resources practices as communications and the psychological contract." *Human Resource Management*, 33: 447–62.

—— —— and Elron, E. (1994). "Expatriate managers and the psychological contract." *Journal of Applied Psychology*, 79: 617–26.

Hallier, J., and James, P. (1997). "Middle managers and the employee psychological contract: Agency, protection, and advancement." *Journal of Management Studies*, 34: 703–28.

Hannah, D. R. (2001). "An investigation of the effects of formal control mechanisms and psychological contracts on employees' tendencies to divulge trade secrets." Paper presented at Academy of Management meetings, Washington DC.

Herriot, P., Manning, W. E. G., and Kidd, J. (1997). "The content of the psychological contract." *British Journal of Management*, 8: 151–62.

Hom, P. W., and Griffeth, R. W. (1995). *Employee Turnover*. Ohio: South-Western College.

Homan, S. G. C. (1961). *Social Behavior: Its Elementary Forms*. New York: Harcourt, Brace and World.

Huselid, M. A. (1995). "The impact of human resource practices on turnover, productivity, and corporate financial performance." *Academy of Management Journal*, 38: 645–72.

Jackson, S. E., and Schuler, R. S. (1985). "A meta-analysis and conceptual critique of research on role ambiguity and role conflict in work settings." *Organizational Behavior and Human Decision Processes*, 36: 16–78.

Levinson, H. (1962). *Men, Management, and Mental health*. Cambridge, MA: Harvard University Press.

Lowe, K. B., Milliman, J., De Cieri, H., and Dowling, P. D. (2002). "International compensation practices: A ten-country comparative analysis." *Human Resource Management*, 41: 45–66.

March, J. G., and Simon, H. A. (1958). *Organizations*. New York: John Wiley and Sons.

Milliman, J., Nason, S., Zhu, C., and De Cieri, H. (2002). "An exploratory assessment of the purposes of performance appraisals in North and Central America and the Pacific Rim." *Human Resource Management*, 41: 87–102.

Morrison, E. W., and Robinson, S. L. (1997). "When employees feel betrayed: A model of how psychological contract violation develops." *Academy of Management Review*, 22: 226–56.

Porter, L. M., Pearce, J. L., Tripoli, A. M., and Lewis, K. M. (1998). "Differential perceptions of employers' inducements: Implications for psychological contracts." *Journal of Organizational Behavior*, 19: 769–82.

Robinson, S. L. (1996). "Trust and breach of the psychological contract." *Administrative Science Quarterly*, 41: 574–99.

—— and Morrison, E. W. (1995). "Psychological contracts and OCB: The effect of unfulfilled obligations on civic virtue behavior." *Journal of Organizational Behavior*, 16: 289–98.

—— Kraatz, M. S., and Rousseau, D. M. (1994). "Changing obligations and the psychological contract: A longitudinal study." *Academy of Management Journal*, 37: 137–52.

Robinson, S. L., and Rousseau, D. M. (1994). "Violating the psychologic contract: Not the exception but the norm." *Journal of Organizational Behavior*, 21: 525–47.

—— and Morrison, E. W. (2000). "The development of psychological contract breach and violation: A longitudinal study." *Journal of Organizational Behavior*, 21: 525–47.

Rousseau, D. M. (1989). "Psychological and implied contracts in organizations." *Employee Responsibilities and Rights Journal*, 2: 121–39.

—— (1995). *Psychological Contracts in Organizations*. Thousand Oaks, CA: Sage.

—— (2001). "Schema, promise, and mutuality: The building blocks of the psychological contract." *Journal of Occupational and Organizational Psychology*, 74: 511–41.

—— and Greller, M. M. (1994). "Human resources practices: administrative contract makers." *Human Resource Management*, 33: 385–401.

—— and Ho, V. (2000). "Psychological contract issues in compensation," in S. Rynes and B. Gerhart (eds.), *Compensation Issues in Organizations: Current Research and Practice* (San Francisco, CA: Jossey-Bass).

Rousseau, D. M. (1990). "New Hire perceptions of their own and their employer's obligations: A study of psychological contracts." *Journal of Organizational Behavior*, 11: 389–400.

——— and McLean Parks, J. (1993). "The contracts of individuals and organizations." in L. L. Cummings and B. M. Staw (eds.), *Research in Organizational Behavior*, pp 1–43. Greenwich, CT: JAI Press.

Sapienza, H. M., Korsgaard, M. A., and Schweiger, D. M. (1997). "Procedural justice and changes in psychological contracts: A longitudinal study of reengineering planning." *Academy of Management Best Paper Proceedings*, 1997 Meetings, 354–8.

Schein, E. H. (1965). *Organizational Psychology*. Englewood Cliffs, NJ: Prentice Hall.

Shore, L. M., and Barksdale, K. (1998). "Examining degree of balance and level of obligation in the employment relationship: A social exchange approach." *Journal of Organizational Behavior*, 19: 731–44.

Simon, H. A., Smithburg, D. W., and Thompson, V. A. (1950). *Public Administration*. New York: Alfred A-Knopf.

Sims, R. R. (1994). "Human resource management's role in clarifying the new psychological contract." *Human Resource Management*, 33: 373–82.

Singh, R. (1998). "Redefining psychological contracts with the U.S. work force: A critical task for strategic human resource management planners in the 1990s." *Human Resource Management*, 37: 61–9.

Sparrow, P. R. (1996). "Careers and the psychological contract: understanding the European context." *European Journal of Work and Organizational Psychology*, 5: 479–500.

——— and Hiltrop, J.-M. (1997). "Redefining the field of European human resource management: A battle between national mindsets and forces of business tradition?" *Human Resource Management*, 36: 201–20.

Swidler, A. (1986). "Culture in action: Symbols and strategies." *American Sociological Review*, 51: 273–86.

Thomas, H. D. C., and Anderson, N. (1998). "Changes in newcomers' contracts during organizational socialization: A study of recruits entering the British Army." *Journal of Organizational Behavior*, 19: 745–68.

Trice, H. M., and Beyer, J. M. (1993). *The Cultures of Work Organizations*. Englewood Cliffs, NJ: Prentice Hall.

Tziner, A., Joanis, C., and Murphy, K. R. (2000). "A comparison of three methods of performance appraisal with regard to goal properties, goal perception, and ratee satisfaction." *Group and Organization Management*, 25: 175–90.

Tsui, A. S., Pearce, J. L., Porter, L. W., and Tripoli, A. M. (1997). "Alternative approaches to the employee-organization relationship: Does investment in employees pay off?" *Academy of Management Journal*, 40: 1089–121.

Way, S. A. (2002). "High performance work systems and intermediate indicators of firm performance within the U.S. small business sector." *Journal of Management*, 28: 765–85.

Whitener, E. M. (2001). "Do 'high commitment' human resource practices affect employee commitment? A cross-level analysis using hierarchical linear modeling." *Journal of Management*, 27: 515–35.

16

Directions for Future Research

LYNN M. SHORE, LOIS E. TETRICK, JACQUELINE A-M.
COYLE-SHAPIRO, AND M. SUSAN TAYLOR

The employment relationship can be viewed from many different theoretical perspectives, incorporating several different levels of analysis. The preceding chapters reflected these differing approaches to understanding the employment relationship and many of these chapters have provided suggestions for future research directions. The purpose of the current chapter is to reflect on the richness of these views for understanding the employment relationship by exploring themes, points of integration, and implications for future research. Below, we discuss the first two parts of the book, and conclude with some more general points about the employment relationship.

16.1 Implications of the conceptual frames in Part I

Part I of this book included reviews of literature on social exchange, justice, industrial relations, law, and economics. Each of these approaches has been applied to studies of the employment relationship, but with differing assumptions and applications to the employment relationship literature. Many of the resulting conflicts and commonalities of these approaches were presented in Chapter 6 of this volume. Additionally, Table 16.1 presents a comparative summary of each of these underlying conceptual frameworks, as a point of departure to discuss needed research on the employment relationship.

16.1.1 Individual-level models

Each of the frameworks presented in Table 16.1 is based on different assumptions, with varying implications for the employment relationship. The two frameworks that have focused primarily on the views of the employee (the individual level of analysis) are social exchange and justice. Social exchange emphasizes trust and the norm of reciprocity as the basis for exchange, while justice focuses on fairness of procedures, outcomes, and interpersonal treatment. Both paradigms rely on notions of reciprocity, though within the employment relationship literature, studies based on social exchange have focused primarily on building trust, and those on justice have elaborated on the loss of trust inherent in unfair treatment. While separate streams

Table 16.1. *Comparison of conceptual frameworks*

	Social exchange	Justice	Industrial relations	Legal theory	Economics
Assumptions pertaining to the employment relationship (ER)	Exchange based on norm of reciprocity and trust	Fairness of exchange	Formalized exchange to protect workers	The employment contract with inherent obligations is broad and diffuse	Basis for exchange rational—each party concerned with own benefit
Limitations for understanding ER	Primary focus on employees. Little discussion of context	Primary focus on individual. Little discussion of individual differences	Lack of focus on informal aspects of exchange	Lack of clarity about boundary conditions	Lack of focus on culture and other bases for "non-rational" exchange
Major contribution to ER literature	Basis for explaining trust-building in exchange between individual parties	Basis for understanding the undermining of exchange between individual parties	Provides context for formalized exchange when union is present	Develops implicit aspects of exchange from contract perspective	Provides basis for conceptualizing the strategic role of the organization in ER
Key ER concepts using this conceptual frame	PC, POS, LMX Contract breach and violation	PC, POS, LMX Contract breach and violation	Contract negotiation and administration	PC	ER, EOR
Level of analysis	Individual and group	Individual	Group	Cross-level	Organization

Note: PC, psychological contract; POS, perceived organizational support; LMX, leader–member exchange; ER, employment relationship; EOR, employee–organization relationship.

of literature, both have been associated with psychological contracts, perceived organizational support, and leader–member exchange, though in somewhat different ways. Furthermore, a great deal of evidence supports links between fair treatment and the building of social exchange relationships including perceived organizational support and leader–member exchange (cf. Masterson et al. 2000). Unfair treatment has been associated with psychological contract breach (Tetrick et al. 2002). The consistent associations raise questions about whether models of employee–organization relationships necessitate the inclusion of fair treatment as a critical element.

More careful development of the linkages between justice and the key social exchange concepts of psychological contracts, perceived organizational support, and leader–member exchange is needed. For example, is fair treatment the main basis for building or undermining trust between employees and organizations? There may be norms, other than reciprocity, that affect the employee–organization relationship, such as moral mandates about avoiding harm (see Chapter 2).

Likewise, it is important to evaluate models of social exchange and justice to determine whether the same links apply in groups as they do in perceptions that individual employees have of their relationship with their managers (leader–member exchange, LMX) and employers (perceived organizational support, POS; psychological contract, PC). While Tsui et al. (1997) provided evidence of the value of social exchange for categories of employees as reflected in the employment relationship (i.e. group-level effects), this study did not include fair treatment. Thus, the cross-level issue of whether fair treatment of other employees affects LMX, POS, or PCs is critical to the question of whether models of fairness and social exchange apply beyond the individual level. At a group level, would ill treatment of a category of employees systematically undermine the employment relationship in the manner in which such relationships have been shown at the individual level (see Chapter 10)? While these ideas make sense, current models of justice and social exchange need much more conceptual development prior to empirical testing of such links for categories or groups of employees.

16.1.2 Cross-level models

Roehling's (see Chapter 4) chapter describes several legal models of contracting, with particular emphasis on the value of Macneil's model of relational contracting. As presented, this model seems most relevant to either individual-level models of exchange such as POS and PC, or dyadic models of exchange such as LMX, with the emphasis on obligations and contracting behavior that is embedded in a social context. While Rousseau (2001) proposed that promises are a unique element of psychological contracts, Roehling raises questions as to the value of this approach given Macneil's ideas about the limitations of promise as an explanation for modern forms of contracting. In particular, Roehling points out the assumption in relational contracting theory that these types of contracts are not promise-based. This points to the need for subsequent research that more fully explicates the role of promises and obligations in PCs.

An important question is whether the relational model of contracting can be applied to group-level phenomena, such as the employment relationship. That is, one avenue for future research is to develop the logic for applying the relational contract model to categories of employees, as in the employment relationship. A number of researchers have recently argued for the value of determining organizational obligations from organizational agents to see if such judgments are associated with employee behavior, and employee obligation levels (Tekleab and Taylor 2003). Also the theory as described by Roehling suggests potential applicability to models involving organizational obligations: He says that relational obligations arise based on customs, status, habits, expectations created by the status quo, and social norms, as well as from external sources (e.g. the government regulation of the employment relationship). The explicit role of context in this model suggests potential value for creating cross-level linkages between the organization and either groups of employees (the employment relationship, ER) or the individual employee (the employee–organization relationship, EOR).

16.1.3 Group- and organization-level models

The industrial relations and economics perspectives have generally taken group-level perspectives. The industrial relations literature has looked at the relationship between an employer and group of employers with groups of employees. The economics perspective has tended to examine the relationships between groups of individuals (e.g. the labor force) and organizations at the microeconomic level or groups of organizations at the macroeconomic level. Inherent in the industrial relations approach is the issue of power asymmetry while the economics perspective is comparatively silent about power, assuming information is equally accessible to organizations and labor. Interestingly, the social exchange approaches to understanding the employment relationship have not incorporated power differentials. Future research needs explicitly to consider sources of power among the parties and the potential effects of power asymmetry.

The industrial relations and economics perspectives have also tended to focus on more formal aspects of the exchange underlying the employment relationship. These perspectives thus may be useful in linking explicit contracts with implicit contracts and with psychological contracts and ERs. If we are to form a multilevel model of the employment relationship in which more macro factors are included, we suggest that integration of the industrial relations and economics perspectives with the social exchange, justice, and legal perspectives may be especially fruitful.

16.2 Implications of models in Part II

The chapters in Part II present a number of more recent ways of examining the employment relationship. Each of these chapters presents ideas that have implications for future research. Further, when you consider the chapters as a set, they combine to suggest a number of ideas for additional conceptual development and testing.

Chapter 7 focuses on the value of strategy theories for understanding the relationship between organizations and employees. Shore, Porter, and Zahra use the term EOR to describe the exchange between the employee and the organization. They argue that the agents who represent the interests of the organization within the EOR provide the basis for linking macro-theories of the firm with micro-theories of individual perceptions. They also propose a number of factors that may influence agents in developing the EOR, such as the organization's strategy and the employee's competencies. Building on their ideas, cognitive models of decision-making may be quite valuable in examining factors that influence the agent, and additional research, both conceptual and empirical, would greatly enhance this area of the literature. An aspect of the EOR that was not fully addressed in the chapter is how the employee contributes to the EOR. Future research should examine the processes through which both agents and employees contribute to the development and revision of the EOR. Models of negotiation may be particularly fruitful to address the latter issue.

The focus of Chapter 8 is to understand incongruence of employee and employer perceptions of type and fulfillment of obligations within the psychological contract. The authors argue for the role of cognitive schema about employment relationships in shaping differences between employee and agent perceptions of obligations. Of particular note is the view that these schema develop early in life before people even begin to work. Research examining beliefs about the employment relationship among adolescents would be very useful in determining the role of such schema. Linking young adults and their parents' views of the obligations inherent in the employment relationship to examine similarities also would be quite informative in terms of testing this assumption in Morrison and Robinson's framework. Furthermore, studying the values that underlie such beliefs may be particularly useful in determining the importance of long-held schema about the employment relationship on subsequent perceptions of obligations between agents and employees. The lens of values may help provide greater insights into why agents and employees tend to have limited agreement on types and fulfillment of obligations.

Chapter 9 presents a new model of obligation fulfillment, which is described as "job creep," involving the gradual expansion of role responsibilities such that discretionary contributions become viewed as obligatory. Van Dyne and Ellis focus primarily on citizenship and in-role behavior in their model of job creep, but the model also presents an opportunity to consider a broader array of employee behaviors. As an example, job creep could incorporate negative employee behaviors such that the avoidance of certain initially required aspects of the role causes downward revisions in job requirements. Let us say a professor initially was willing to chair committees if asked, but viewed this as discretionary behavior. Over time with continued avoidance of committee chairing duties, this professor may begin to see chairing of committees as an obligation only for other faculty who volunteered. As posed in Chapter 9, reactance theory predictions would suggest job creep influences both the individual employee (self-evaluation and efforts to change peers) and peers (self-evaluation and efforts to change the employee). Longitudinal research is needed to fully explore the predictions of the job creep model. Of particular interest would be studies of new hires to examine unfolding of job creep, and factors that contributed to increased and decreased levels of employee obligation over time. This model may also be useful for exploring the unfolding of breach and violation of the psychological contract, suggesting the need to expand the job creep model to include agent responses to employee overfulfillment of obligations.

Chapter 10 presents an elaboration of Eisenberger's organizational support theory. In this chapter, Eisenberger and colleagues argue for increased research on a number of issues. One that was particularly interesting was the role of social accounts on perceptions of organizational support. They pointed out that while POS might mitigate certain types of unfavorable treatment, organizations need to consider how best to manage such situations through social accounts. Especially in light of a poor economy and ongoing changes in work arrangements, more research on POS needs to consider ill-treatment as well as favorable treatment. Another area that is ripe for research is that of the role of POS in managing stress. They provide some evidence of the positive impact of POS in stressful situations, including jobs that have inherently stressful components. However, particularly needed is research that explores the role of POS in stressful situations that are discretionary (i.e. under the control of organizational agents), such as pay cuts or job loss. This would allow researchers to test a central component of organizational support theory in a new manner—discretionary treatment that is detrimental to employees and the potential undermining of the social exchange relationship reflected in POS.

Chapter 11 poses an interesting model of the role of socialization and LMX in the development of the employer–employee relationship. An interesting element in this model is the inclusion of multiple agents as contributors to the employer–employee relationship. These include the immediate supervisor, other socialization agents for the organization, and other newcomers. An interesting area of future research would be to explore the differing levels of influence from varying agents during the early employment period. Additional theorizing about the role of newcomer expectations and beliefs prior to entering the organization would be very useful. In addition, some exploration in future research of the unfolding of exchange processes in the early employment period would be quite interesting. At present, Liden, Bauer, and Erdogan's model focuses exclusively on new hires, but could be expanded to include early employment processes whereby the norm of reciprocity underlying exchanges between employees and agents could be used to further develop the model. In such a model, the employee's role in shaping the relationship with agents of the organization could be developed and tested.

There are a number of implications for the chapters in Part II as a set. First, researchers in the employment relationship area increasingly seek ways to understand the context in which this relationship occurs. One area of particular interest is determining "who speaks for the organization." Additional research is clearly needed which discusses agents of the organization in the EOR, including factors that cause continuity in the messages and expectations of agents, and those that contribute to inconsistency across agents. Likewise, but less often discussed, is the importance of examining the EOR within the context of the work group. While Chapters 9 and 11 pose the potential importance of peers in determining the types of employment relationships that are present within and across groups, additional theorizing and research is needed to develop these ideas more fully. Evidence for the importance of peers on the employment relationship is shown in studies of work groups in which both permanent and contract employees are present (Pearce 1993; Ang, Van Dyne, and Begley 2003).

Second, literature on the employment relationship continues to grow, as shown by the incorporation of new paradigms to explain relationships between employees and organizations. Shore et al. use theories of strategy to develop new ways of thinking about the EOR; Van Dyne and Butler Ellis use reactance theory to construct propositions for explaining how obligations shift over time; and Morrison and Robinson discuss the impact of social comparisons on perceived obligations. All of these represent an expansion beyond the more long-standing views of the employment relationship presented in Part I. It is unclear whether these different theoretical perspectives can be integrated into a more encompassing model or whether the theories offer competing propositions that might be empirically tested.

Finally, research on the employment relationship continues to focus primarily on the "usual set of outcomes" (e.g. commitment, performance, and citizenship) when making predictions about the impact of this relationship. Additional models are clearly needed that develop ideas of the many potential influences of the EOR, in terms of consequences for the organization, for the work group, and for the individual employee. It is also possible that the EOR has implications for individuals and groups outside of the focal organization, such as customers or the employee's family. The effects of the employment relationship on the broader community have yet to be explored, but may be important particularly when the employment relationship is viewed at a group or organizational level. As an example, employees who view their employment relationship in a positive manner may "reciprocate" to the broader community in which they live.

16.3 Looking toward the future

Many themes are apparent throughout the book, which we describe below. It is our contention that such themes provide the basis for broader and more integrative approaches to studying the employment relationship.

16.3.1 Basis for the employment relationship

While there are many differences among the chapters in the specific factors incorporated into models of the employment relationship, a key element in all models is the notion of exchange. Some models focus on content—that is, what is exchanged—and others on process—the nature of the exchange. Different theoretical frames may be differentially useful in this regard and integration should increase understanding of the employment relationship. As an example, social exchange and relational contract theories focus primarily on process (i.e. reciprocity and trust building), whereas justice focuses on both process and content (i.e. fair procedures and outcomes). Psychological contract literature, relying on social exchange and relational contract theories as primary theoretical bases, has been limited in its ability to describe content of the exchange (i.e. elements of the PC) in theoretically meaningful ways. Integration with justice theories may allow for a more complete model of PCs with both process and content elements more fully specified.

Likewise, industrial relations and economics models focus on formal and tangible aspects of exchange, without consideration of the meaning of the exchange to the parties involved. For example, increases in pay are likely always viewed as positive by employees, but may have little impact on employee performance or support of organizational initiatives if employees interpret the pay increase as mandated or in some manner forced on organizational agents. The human propensity to view actions of organizational agents in symbolic ways, such as caring about employees (Eisenberger et al. 1986), is well established in some exchange models. Thus, conceptualizations of the employment relationship should consider both formal and tangible aspects of exchange, as well as informal and intangible elements. Most importantly, greater understanding of links between various forms and types of exchange for building or destroying the employment relationship would enhance this literature.

16.3.2 Developing and refining the employment relationship

A number of chapters discuss the development and revision of the employment relationship. Factors forming the basis for change and development can be categorized as falling into the context and the individual. At present, context has been given greater emphasis as a precursor to both development and change of the employment relationship. This is understandable, given the greater power of contextual factors than individual elements in determining the employment relationship. For example, changes in laws or negotiated union contracts present limits within which an organization must operate when establishing relationships with employees. Likewise, the culture in which an organization is embedded creates expectations and imperatives that organizational agents must consider in how they manage the employment relationship with employees. However, as Schalk points out in Chapter 13, individual life changes may also influence the employment relationship. The job creep model (see Chapter 9) presents some ideas about how employees may play a role in the revision of the exchange agreement. However, much more work needs to be done that explicitly develops ways of studying how employees interact with their work environment to develop and revise employment relationships. At the heart of models of the employment relationship are notions of exchange between parties—individual to individual (LMX), individual to group (POS, PC), or group to group (ER, industrial relations)—suggesting that the two parties in an employment relationship each contribute to both development and revision of this relationship.

16.4 A synthesis

A number of serious challenges face researchers seeking to add clarity to the employment relationship literature. First, the study of the employment relationship can take varied forms and approaches, as reflected by the many disciplinary perspectives described in this volume. Each perspective is associated with particular assumptions and both strengths and weaknesses in terms of explanatory power. Second, the employment relationship has been studied at multiple levels of the organization, and has been defined in varied ways. Each of these approaches has enriched our understanding of the employment relationship, while at the same time contributing to a recognition that no one approach is best for explaining this complex and multi-faceted phenomenon. Finally, there are many different factors contributing to the employment relationship, adding to confusion about how best to describe and predict the nature and content of the employment relationship. In this final section, we present two models in which we seek to address some of these challenges, and present some suggestions for future research.

16.4.1 Agents of the organization

Figure 16.1 presents a model of the ER that reflects the many ways in which the ER has been defined, and the many factors that may influence this relationship from the

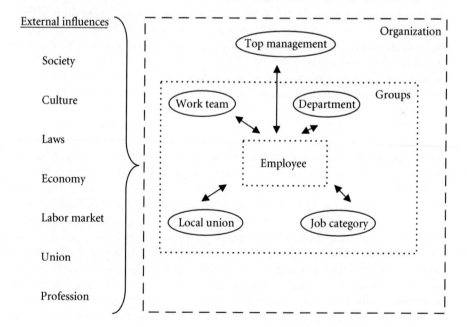

Figure 16.1. *Agents in the employment relationship.*

(*Note*: Dashed lines for boxes suggest permeability; double-headed arrows show mutual influence between agents and employees.)

external environment. First, we discuss groups and individuals that may influence the ER within the organization. We then describe how these varied agents play roles in determining types of ERs that emerge.

As shown in Figure 16.1, the employee is embedded in multiple groups within the organization. The number and types of groups will depend on many different factors, which are beyond the purview of this discussion. Thus, we keep our discussion focused on the types of groups themselves and what they imply for the employment relationship.

Employees typically work within a departmental structure in which there is a direct supervisor and co-workers, both of whom may be important agents in establishing, maintaining, and revising the EOR. As discussed in Liden, Bauer, and Erdogan (Chapter 11), the LMX literature establishes the importance of the manager in determining many of the inducements and contributions reflected in the employee's relationship with the organization. Likewise, the social exchange literature (Coyle-Shapiro and Conway, Chapter 1), and chapters by Morrison and Robinson (Chapter 8) and Van Dyne and Butler Ellis (Chapter 9) point out the importance of peers to the employment relationship. This can occur through social comparison examinations by the employee or through direct pressure exerted by peers to modify employee contributions.

The same sorts of peer and leader influences may occur for employees who additionally work in teams. If the organization has a matrix structure, or if cross-functional teams are used, the nature and form of the exchange relationships within the team may be quite different to those with the department, but with important implications for the employment relationship. Employees likely interact with individuals from other areas and with different functional backgrounds and training. Given the focus on common projects or services, employees may consider the inducements and contributions of peers within such teams when considering their own relationship with the organization. Within a team, the role of the team leader may be quite different than the direct supervisor in relation to the employee–organization exchange, since the team leader is less likely to have a great deal of influence over the "formal or hard" components of the exchange (e.g. pay). Nonetheless, social exchange theory and relational contract theory imply that social exchange relationships between the employee and team leader will likely develop if the relationship continues over a period of time. The team leader may, in fact, seek ways to offer "informal or soft" inducements such as providing interesting work, or treating the employee with respect, in order to gain employee contributions.

Employees are embedded within a job or occupational category, and this categorization is likely to have a strong influence on the EOR. This makes a great deal of sense since most HR systems, such as compensation, rely on job or occupational groupings of employees. HR representatives are important agents of the firm in the exchange based on job categories. Though HR systems may be outsourced by companies, many firms still retain HR generalists to oversee and administer various inducements to employees. Furthermore, HR representatives are often involved in recruitment and socialization activities of new hires, representing a potentially important influence on the employment relationship (Hannah and Iverson, Chapter 15).

If there is a union representing the employee, then the union representatives become important agents in establishing and maintaining many elements in the employment relationship (Kelly, Chapter 3). The union contract does not necessarily cover all aspects of the employment relationship, but many of the "hard or transactional" inducements, such as pay and benefits, are made explicit. Furthermore, union contracts typically contain grievance procedures or other procedural elements that protect the rights of employees. Peer comparisons are most likely when the contract is being negotiated, and employees become aware of how their ER compares with that of employees in other unions.

Another group that has an important role in the employment relationship is top management. As pointed out in Shore, Porter, and Zahra (Chapter 7), top management decisions about organizational strategy exert a strong influence on the employment relationships of individuals and groups within the organization. Agents of the firm typically seek to develop relationships with employees that are supportive of strategic initiatives.

There are many factors that may determine which of these many agents and groups would have the greatest influence on the employment relationship. Clearly, studies of individual-level perceptual variables, such as PCs and POS, need to explicate more fully the role that various agents may play in contributing to these individual perceptions. Likewise, studies comparing group-level employment relationships must also begin to examine the many agents and groups that influence the employment relationships of categories of employee groups. Finally, increasing attention on cross-firm comparisons of the employment relationship would greatly enhance this body of literature.

16.4.2 The employment relationship from an integrative perspective

While exchange seems to be a basis for conceptualizing employment relationships at both micro- and macro-levels of analysis, current research is limited in considering how best to synthesize these varied approaches (see Chapter 14 for a discussion of conceptual and measurement issues). Interestingly, strategic HR researchers have begun to argue the value of the employment relationship within firms as an important means of understanding links between more macro-literatures, such as strategic HR, and more micro-literatures such as HR and OB (Lepak and Snell 1999). As stated by Becker and Gerhart (1996: 793):

Future work on the strategic perspective must elaborate on the black box between a firm's HR system and the firm's bottom line. Unless and until researchers are able to elaborate and test more complete structural models—for example, models including key intervening variables—it will be difficult to rule out alternative causal models that explain observed associations between HR systems and firm performance. We hope to see future research develop these ideas more completely.

Figure 16.2 presents an integrative model of the ER, including multiple organizational levels as well as external influences. As proposed by Hannah and Iverson

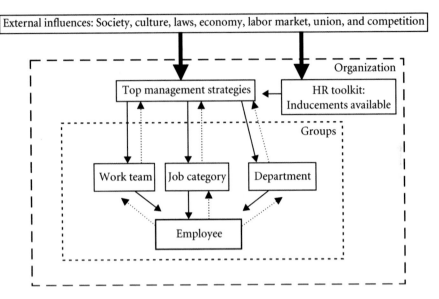

Figure 16.2. *The employment relationship.*

(*Note*: Dashed lines for boxes suggest permeability; inducements between employees and agents are represented by solid arrows, contributions by dashed arrows.)

(Chapter 15), organizations have an HR toolkit with available inducements, depending on a variety of external influences. Top management strategies are likewise influenced by various external factors in the environment. As suggested by Shore, Porter, and Zahra (Chapter 7), top management strategies provide an important basis for the employment relationship. Particular groups will be viewed as more critical to the enactment of corporate and business unit strategies, and those groups will likely receive greater inducements than those who are viewed as less critical. Note, however, that the HR toolkit provides parameters within which management can provide inducements. For example, the presence of a union for some employee groups may enhance or prohibit particular inducements that management would like to provide (e.g. variable pay). Likewise, the labor markets for various groups or in particular regions or nations influences a variety of elements of the HR toolkit, and must also be a consideration in inducements provided.

As suggested in Figure 16.2, the employment relationship for the individual employee is influenced indirectly by top management strategies through membership in various groups. Each group is provided with inducements and in return offers contributions. In turn, the employee is the recipient of inducements as a group member. Note, however, that individual employees within groups are likely to have somewhat different employment relationships depending on their relationships with key individuals within the groups they belong to (e.g. their direct supervisor as suggested by Liden, Bauer, and Erdogan, Chapter 11), the degree to which they are valued by the organization (Eisenberger, Jones, Aselage, and Sucharski, Chapter 10), and the contributions they provide to the organization (Van Dyne and Butler Ellis, Chapter 9).

This model suggests that the employment relationship can be conceptualized as a group- or individual-level phenomenon. Support for this view is shown in the literature on employment relationships. Tsui, Pearce, Porter, and Tripoli's (1997) study shows that organizations offer various categories of employees' different employment relationships, which influence the contributions of those employees. Research on psychological contracts indicates clearly that employees view the relationship with their organizations as reciprocal, and conceptualize that relationship along the lines of mutual obligations reflecting inducements and contributions (Taylor and Tekleab, Chapter 12; Morrison and Robinson, Chapter 8). The evidence that exchange occurs at both individual and group levels suggests the likelihood that these are overlapping processes. Future research is needed that links individual and group ERs.

Figure 16.2 provides a starting point for considering the ER in a more integrated manner. Clearly, more cross-level analyses are needed in future research. Often, models of the ER at the individual level disregard the importance of group membership in determining the types of ERs that are available to particular employees. However, as pointed out by Schalk (Chapter 13) and Eisenberger et al. (Chapter 10), increasing numbers of individuals have alternative ERs, such as part-time, temporary, and contract employment. Note that among permanent employees, there is also a great deal of variety in the ERs offered to various groups, and models of the ER need to reflect these group differences.

16.5 Conclusion

A great deal of research remains to be done on the employment relationship. It is our hope that this volume offers readers both interesting and provocative reading, but also ideas for moving this literature forward. The interdisciplinary nature of the employment relationship literature provides a richness that is rarely available in studies of the workplace. While providing a challenge, it also suggests the importance of the employment relationship to understanding the world of work.

References

Ang, S., Van Dyne, L., and Begley, T. M. (2003). "The employment relationships of foreign workers versus local employees: A field study of organizational justice, job satisfaction, performance, and OCB." *Journal of Organizational Behavior,* 24: 561–83.

Becker, B., and Gerhart, B. (1996). "The impact of human resource management on organizational performance: Progress and prospects." *Academy of Management Journal,* 39: 779–801.

Eisenberger, R., Huntington, R., Hutchison, S., and Sowa, D. (1986). "Perceived Organizational support." *Journal of Applied Psychology,* 71: 500–7.

Lepak, D. P., and Snell, S. A. (1999). "The human Resource architecture: Toward a theory of human capital allocation and development." *Academy of Management Review*, 24: 31–48.

Masterson, S. S., Lewis, K., Goldman, B. M., and Taylor, M. S. (2000). "Integrating justice and social exchange: The differing effects of fair procedures and treatment on work relationships." *Academy of Management Journal*, 43: 738–48.

Pearce, J. L. (1993). "Toward an organizational behavior of contract laborers: Their psychological involvement and effects on employee co-workers." *Academy of Management Journal*, 36: 1082–96.

Rousseau, D. M. (2001). "Schema, Promise and Mutuality: The building blocks of the psychological contract." *Journal of Occupational and Organizational Psychology*, 74: 511–41.

Tekleab, A. G., and Taylor, M. S. (2003). "Aren't there two parties in an employment relationship?" *Journal of Organizational Behavior*, 24: 585–608.

Tetrick, L., Shore, L. M., Bommer, W. H., and Wayne, S. J. (2002). "Effects of perceptions of employer's failure to keep their promises: An applications of ELVN." Paper presented at the Society of Industrial and Organizational Psychology, Toronto.

Tsui, A. S., Pearce, J. L., Porter, L. W., and Tripoli, A. M. (1997). "Alternative approaches to the employee–organization relationship: Does investment in employees pay off?" *Academy of Management Journal*, 40: 1089–121.

Index

absenteeism, and psychological contracts 257
Academy of Management 273
accidents:
    and temporary employees 295
    see also health and safety
accommodation period, and leader-member
        exchange 232–3
Adams, J S, and inequity 36
adaptation, reciprocal and unilateral 300
adult development model 301–4
adverse selection 137
advocacy participation 192
agency theory, *see* strategy theory
Allegro, J 295
American Airlines 277
Amsterdam, Treaty of (1997) 101, 104
anthropomorphization:
    and exchange 23
    see also personification
appraisal, and human resource management
        341–2
Argyris, Chris, and psychological contracts
        254–5
association, freedom of:
    European Union 104
    and labor markets 100–1
authority:
    abuse of 42–3
    and autonomy 30–1, 43
    blank check role of 31, 33, 34, 38, 124
    and employment contracts 30–4, 35
    and fairness 35–6
    legitimacy of 39
    and procedural justice 40
    reactions to 39–40
authority ranking, as relational model 21
autonomy:
    and authority 30–1, 43
    bounded 41–2

balance:
    and exchange 8, 10, 18
    and fulfillment incongruence 172
    and human resource strategies 211
    and psychological contracts 265
    and reciprocity 317

Barksdale, K:
    process approach of 316
    and psychological contracts 265
Becker, B 361
behavior, and habit 23
Belgium:
    and employment regulation 68, 74
    and social pacts 61
    and trade unions 55, 101
    wage levels 54
beliefs, and obligation incongruence
        165–6
benefits:
    and employer's obligations 342
    and exchange relationships 8
    and relational contract theory 82
    value of 9
Berg, J H, and content of exchange relationships
        12–13
Blau, P:
    context of exchanges 11
    distinguishes economic and social
        exchange 7, 8
    groups and exchange 10
    and origins of social exchange theory 7
    and reciprocity 9
Boehm, Christopher:
    and abuse of power 42–3
    on domination 29
bounded autonomy 41–2
bounded rationality 41–2
Brazil, and employment regulation
        74, 75
briefing groups, management-dominated 56
Briner, R B, and contract breach
        270, 320–1
bullying 42–3

Canada:
    and employment regulation 74, 75
    and industrial relations 51
capitalism, varieties of 50–1
Cardy, Don 277
careers, boundaryless 236
civic virtue, and organizational citizenship
        behavior 192

Cohen-Charash, Y, pay and fairness 38
collective bargaining 17, 48, 121, 128, 286
    decentralization of 50
    effects on employees 52–5
    and labor markets 100–1
    and market competition 59
    and pay rates 52–3
    and the United States 52, 106–8
collectivism, and socialization tactics 239
Collins, D 293
commitment:
    and organizational change 297
    and perceived organizational support 212
    at pre-entry 230
    and temporary employees 295
common law, and employment regulation 68, 121
Commons, J R, and employment contracts 84
communal sharing, as relational model 21
communication 340
    and managing incongruence 176–7
    and obligation incongruence 168–9
    and psychological contracts 290, 291
compensation, and human resource
        management 341–2
competitive advantage:
    and dynamic capabilities 141–2
    and resource-based view 138–9
conceptual frameworks, and employment
        relationship 312–14
concreteness, and content of exchange
        relationships 12
conflict:
    and incongruence 174–5
    and industrial relations 48–9
    management of 233
    and self-centered bias 171
consumers, and economic theory 95
consumption, and work decisions 95–6
context:
    and employment relationship 127, 358
    and job creep 186–7
    national 334
        and human resource management
            strategies 344–5
        and human resource management
            tool kits 334–6
    and relational contract theory 88
    see also national cultures
contingent work 294
    and employment contracts 291, 292–4
    impact on employees 294–9
    and perceived organizational support
        219–20

contract breach 15, 16–17, 174, 175, 270, 318–19,
        321, 340
    and contract violation 267
    and obligation incongruence 173
    and organizational citizenship behavior 268
contract drift 167–8
contract law 65, 121–2, 351
    classical 76–7, 86, 122
    comparison of contract theories 84–6
    and employment 66–7
    and employment regulatory schemes 67–75
    and juridification 67
    neoclassical 76–7, 86, 122
    see also relational contract theory
contract violation 183, 256, 265–71, 277–8,
        296–7, 305, 318
contributions:
    types of 333
    see also inducements-contributions model of
        exchange
control systems 137
Conway, N, and contract breach 270, 320–1
Conway, R, and contract violation 269–70
cooperation:
    and industrial relations 48–9
    and relational contract theory 81
coordinated market economies (CMEs):
    and collective bargaining 52
    and industrial relations 51
corporate strategy 135–6
    and upper echelon theory 137–8
corporations:
    as collectivities 102
    legal individuality of 101–2
Council of Ministers, and employment
        regulation 68
Coyle-Shapiro, J:
    and contract fulfillment 319–20, 322
    and psychological contracts 264, 269
    and temporary employees 292
cultural orientation, factors determining 234

De Feyter, M 293
decentralization, and psychological
        contracts 296
Denmark, union density 55
developing countries, and human resource
        management tool kits 335
discrete contracts 79, 82, 90 n3
discrete-relational continuum, *see* transactional-
        relational continuum
discretionary behavior, *see* organizational
        citizenship behavior

discrimination:
  and European Union 104
  and United States 105–6
dismissal, and just cause for 75
disposition:
  and exchange relationships 15–16
  and interdependence theory 22
dispute-resolution, and fairness 36
distributive justice 36, 41, 127
  and pay and conditions 38
  and perceived organizational support 209–10
dominance 29, 42
Dunahee, M H, and psychological contracts 257
dynamic capabilities, *see* strategy theory

economic exchange, definition 7
economics, neoclassical 95, 113, 351
  and employment relationship 94, 123–4
  and exchange 128, 358
  as group-level model 354
  labor demand 96
  labor market 97
  labor market policy 99
  labor supply 95–6
  market failures 98–9
  and reciprocity 128–9
  and regulation 97–8, 129
egalitarianism 43
  and trade unions 53–4
Eisenberger, R:
  and perceived organizational support 119–20, 356
  and reciprocity 16
Emerson, R M:
  and content of exchange relationships 13
  and groups 17
employee-organization relationship 333, 355, 357
  and agency theory 137, 146
  agent and employee influence on 142–6, 150–2, 155, 360
  and dynamic capabilities 141–2, 149–50
  and employment contracts 140–1
  and firm strategy 153, 156
  and inducements 346
  influences on 135–6
  representing the organization 152
  and resource-based view 140–1, 148–9
  and situational dynamics 153–5
  stability of 152–3
  and strategy theory 155
  and upper echelon theory 138, 146–8
employees, and employment relationship 284
employment, relational nature of 83–4

employment agencies 84
employment contracts:
  and agency theory 137
  and authority 30–4, 35
  as blank check 31, 33, 34, 38, 124
  collective 74
  compared with sales contracts 31, 34
  contingent workers 292–4
  continuous renewal of 84
  definition 30, 32
  diversification in forms 291–2
  duration of 74
  and employee-organization relationship 140–1
  and fairness 29, 35–6, 120
  individual 68, 74, 75, 126
  minimum standards 68
  nature of 31–2
  origins of 66–7
  pay and conditions 38–9
  and psychological contracts 162
  rational preference for 32
  regulatory schemes 67–75
  termination of 74–5
  and uncertainty 33, 120
employment protection laws (EPLs), and employment levels 54
employment regulation, *see* regulation
employment relations, *see* industrial relations
employment relationship:
  cross-level models 353–4
  group- and organization-level models 354, 363
  individual-level models 351–3, 362
empowerment, and organizational citizenship behavior 185
equality matching, as relational model 21
equity, and exchange 10
equity theory, and organizational justice 36
equivalence, and reciprocity 8–9
European Court of Justice, and employment regulation 68
European Monetary Union 61
European Union:
  Charter of Fundamental Social Rights 104
  and contingent workers 291
  employment policy 94
  and employment regulation 68, 104, 123
  and human rights 104
  individual rights and employment 101
  individuality of the corporation 102
  paid annual leave 110
  and part-time workers 110–11
  and private property 103
  and trade unions 101, 104

evaluation, congruence of 235
exchange 358
  and employment relationship 357–8
  and psychological contracts 162
  see also social exchange theory
exchange behavior, and relational contract
    theory 83
exchange relationships 333
  basis of 127–8
  and classical contract law 76
  and neoclassical contract law 77
  see also relational contract theory
expectancy theory, and employee behaviors
    243–4
extra-role behavior (ERB), and job creep 183,
    185, 186–7

fairness 120
  and authority 35–6
  and contracts 29
  and dispute-resolution 36
  and employment contracts 29, 35–6, 120
  and forms of justice 36–7
  and justice 351
  and pay and conditions 38–9
  and perceived organizational
      support 209–10
  and psychological contracts 291
  and relational contract theory 82, 86, 88
  and sales contracts 42
  and self-centered bias 171
  and trust 353
false consensus effect 168
  and communication 176
Feldman, D C, and contract breach 268–9, 319
Finland:
  and employment regulation 121
  and social pacts 61
  wage levels 54
firms:
  economic theory of 95
  see also organizations; strategy theory
First National Maintenance Corp v NLRB
      (US Supreme Court) 107–8
Fiske, A P, relational models 21
flexibility:
  and contingent workers 292, 295–6
  and employment contracts 292
  and employment relationship 286, 287
  and job insecurity 294
  pressure for 296
  and psychological contracts 287
  and social harmony 305

Foa, E B and U G 20
  and content of exchange relationships
      12–13
Folger, R, and police-citizen encounters 39–40
France:
  and employment regulation 74
  works councils 103
freedom of contract 75–6, 77, 87
  and neoclassical economics 98
  and property rights 102–3
Frege, C M, and impact of works
      councils 58
fulfillment, measures of:
  employee perceptions 318–21
  employer perceptions 322–3
  see also incongruence

Gakovic, A 317
Gerhart, B 361
Germany:
  and employment regulation 74, 121
  and industrial relations 51
  job insecurity 54–5
  union-profitability connection 58
  wage levels 54
  works councils 56, 103
gift giving, theory of 14
goods, and exchange 12
Gouldner, A W:
  and origins of social exchange theory 7
  and reciprocity 8–9
government:
  and employment regulation 84, 87
      European Union 104
      United States 103–4
Greenberg, M S, and indebtedness 15
groups 360–3
  effect on individuals 11
  and exchange 10, 17–18
  role of 11
Guest, D, and contract violation 269–70
Guilds 286

habit, and social exchange 23
Hall, P A, and varieties of capitalism 50–1
Hall, T H, and transactional-relational
      continuum 78
'Harvard School', and labor-capital
      cooperation 57
health and safety, and human resource
      management 342–3
Herriot, P, and psychological contracts
      259–60

hierarchy:
  and employment contracts 33
  and networks 142
  and organizations 24
high-performance work system 337, 339
Homans, G C:
  equity and exchange 10
  on exchange 5
  exchange and social behavior 7
  and origins of social exchange theory 7
  and process of exchange 8
Huiskamp, R 288–90
human capital:
  and the 'new' psychological contracts 44–5
  and value creation 136, 137
human covenant 41, 42, 128
Human Relations School, groups and
        individuals 11
human resource management (HRM) 48, 313,
        360–1
  definition 50
  effects on attitudes and behavior 337–8
  employees interpretation of 338–40
  and employment relationship goals 346
  and high-performance work system 337, 339
  and inducements 333
  and national context 334, 344–5
  occupational health and safety 342–3
  and perceived organizational support 211–12,
        220–1
  performance management 341–2
  recruitment and selection 340–1
  tool kits 334, 344–5, 362
    institutional and legal frameworks 334–5
    national culture 335–6
  and upper echelon theory 138
human resources:
  and competitive advantage 140
  and dynamic capabilities 141
  and resource-based view 138–9
  and value creation 136
human rights, and European Union 104

in-role behavior (IRB), and job creep 183,
        185, 186–7
incentive programs 137
incongruence 161–2, 257
  communication 176–7
  fulfillment 164, 169–70, 338, 340, 355
    different perceptions of obligation 170
    perceptual biases and distortions 171–2
    and social comparisons 172–3
  implications of 173

conflict and tension 174–5
    squandered resources 174
  managing 175
    coordination of information sources 175–6
  obligation 164
    and different schemata 165–6
    imperfect sense-making processes 166–8
    insufficient communication 168–9
    reasons for 164
  and psychological contracts 163–4
incorporation, and productive exchanges 13
indebtedness, and social exchange 9, 13, 15
indeterminacy 55
  and industrial relations 49–50
individualism:
  and anti-discrimination legislation 105
  and European Union 101
  and socialization tactics 239
  and United States 100
inducements:
  choice of 346
  difficulties with 332
  hard 333
  and human resource management
        337, 344–5
  and national cultures 335–6
  and social exchange theory 7
  soft 333
  types of 333
inducements-contributions model of
        exchange 7, 8, 10, 11–14, 19, 20, 313,
        316, 326, 332
  and habit 23
industrial relations 120–1, 124, 351
  and conflict 49
  context 127
  and cooperation 48–9
  definition 48
  and employee 'voice' 55–7
  and enterprise partnership agreements 59–60
  and exchange 128, 358
  features of 'good' 51
  as group-level model 354
  impact of trade unions 57–8
  and indeterminacy 49–50, 55
  and inequality 49
  and power 49
  and reciprocity 128, 129
  and regulation 50–1, 129
  relevance of 61–2
  and social pacts 60–1
  and works councils 56
  see also collective bargaining

Industrial Revolution 121, 285, 286
  and employment contracts 66–7
inequality:
  and industrial relations 49
  pay rates 53–4
information revolution 285, 286
information-seeking, and perceived organizational
      support 216–17
initiative, and job creep 185
institutions, and industrial relations 50–1
intangible resources, and resource-based
      view 139–40
interactional justice 36–7, 41, 120
  and pay and conditions 38
  and perceived organizational support
      37, 210
  and perceived supervisory support 37
  and police-citizen encounters 39–40
  and psychological contracts 291
interdependence theory:
  and exchange relationships 17–18
  and social exchange 22
interdependency, and exchange relationships 24
International Labor Organization, and
      employment regulation 68
interpersonal conduct, and interactional
      justice 36–7
investment:
  and investments-contributions model 315
  and resource-based view 140
Ireland:
  and social pacts 61
  union density 55
Italy:
  and employment regulation 121
  and social pacts 61
  wage levels 54

Japan:
  and employment regulation 68, 74
  wage levels 54
job crafting, and job creep 185
job creep 184–6, 355–6, 358
  consequences of 194
  context 186–7
  definition 181, 183–4, 196
  employee reactions to 188–90, 199
  and freedom of choice 188–9
  and negative voice 187–8, 193–4
  and organizational citizenship
      behavior 185–6
  peer reactions to 194–6, 197–8, 199
  and personal freedom 189–90, 190–1

  and psychological reactance 190–1, 198–9
  and reciprocity 183, 186
job insecurity 54–5, 181, 294
job security, and employment contracts 292
Johns, G, and psychological contracts 257
juridification 67, 90 n1
  and employment regulatory schemes 67–75
  and freedom of contract 75–6
justice 120, 124, 126, 351
  context 127
  and exchange relationships 127
  and fairness 351
  forms of 36–7
  as individual-level model 351–3
  and pay and conditions 38–9
  and reciprocity 128, 351
  regulation 129
  and relational contract theory 86, 88
  see also distributive justice; interactional justice;
      procedural justice

Kenny, D A 327, 328
Kessler, I:
  and contract fulfillment 319–20, 322
  and psychological contracts 264, 269
  and temporary employees 292
Kickul, J, and contract fulfillment 320
Kimel et al v Board of Regents et al (US Supreme
      Court) 105–6
Kotter, J, and incongruence 163, 257

labor laws, declining influence of 286
labor market 97
  and anti-discrimination legislation 105
  changing trends in 305
  and freedom of association 100–1
  and job creep 187
  labor demand 96
  labor supply 95–6
  and market failure 98–9
  and neoclassical economics 99
  as sellers market 306
  and trade unions 101
Landrum-Griffin Act (USA, 1958) 107
Langley, A, and variance theories 21–2
Lawler, E E, *High Involvement Management* 257
leader-member exchange (LMX) 11, 20, 353
  and content of exchange relationships 13, 14
  definition 227
  and immediate superior 228
  and justice 353
  maintenance of 237
  and organizational citizenship behavior 243

and perceived organizational
    support 228
and psychological contracts 263, 276
and role clarity 234–5
and self-efficacy 234
and social exchange theory 353
and socialization 229–30, 356
    anticipatory stage 230–2
    disengagement 236–7
    and employee attitudes 240–2
    and employee behaviors 242–5
    entry and assimilation 232–6
    and perceived obligations 240
    tactics of 238–40
and turnover 236
leadership:
    and interactional justice 37
    qualities of 43
    see also leader-member exchange
Lester, S W:
    and contract breach 270
    and contract fulfillment 322
Leventhal, G S, and procedural fairness 36
Levinson, Harry:
    adult development model 301
    and psychological contracts 255–6
Lewis-McClear, K 322
liberal market economies (LMEs), and industrial
    relations 51
life course 358
    and obligation 301–4
love, and exchange 12

McLean Parks, J M:
    and contract violation 267
    and psychological contracts 265
Macneil, Ian 353
    on promise framework 89
    and relational contract theory 77–86,
        122–3
Malinowski, B:
    and origins of social exchange theory 7
    and process of exchange 14
management, and upper echelon theory 137–8,
    146–8
March, J G:
    and employee-organization relationship
        9–10
    inducements-contributions model of
        exchange 7
    and origins of social exchange theory 7
    and process of exchange 8
market pricing, as relational model 21

markets:
    and government intervention 103–4, 105
    and market failure 98–9
    and neoclassical economics 95, 123
master-servant relationship 66, 121
Mauss, M:
    and gift-giving 14
    and origins of social exchange theory 7
measurement, *see* methodology
Mediterranean economies (MEs):
    and collective bargaining 52
    and industrial relations 51
memory, organizational 141
Menniger, Karl 255
mentors, impact of 229, 242
mergers, and psychological contracts 297–8
methodology:
    fulfillment measures:
        employee perceptions 318–21
        employer perceptions 322–3
    measurement:
        content approaches 312–13, 314–16
        process approaches 313, 316–18
    measurement equivalence 323–5
    multilevel analysis 326–8
    perceptual gaps 325–6
    and psychological contract research
        279
Mexico, and employment regulation 74, 75
minimum wage 97–8
Mohr, L B, and variance theories 21–2
money, and exchange 12
moral hazard 137
morality:
    moral norms 40–1
    role of 42
Morrison, E W, and contract violation 267, 269
Moss, J E, and transactional-relational
        continuum 78
motivation, and feedback 233
multilevel analysis 326–8
mutual investment 315
    and exchange relationships 18

national cultures:
    factors determining 234
    and human resource management tool kits
        334–6, 345
    influence of 334, 336
    and socialization tactics 239
National Labor Relations Act (USA)
    106–7
negative voice, *see* voice

Netherlands:
  and employment regulation 121
  flexible workers in 292–3
  and industrial relations 51
  and social pacts 61
  temporary workers 294
  works councils 103
networks:
  and employee-organization relationship
    141–2
  and exchange 17–18
  and socialization 228–9
New Zealand, wage levels 54
Nicholson, N, and psychological contracts 257
notice, period of 74

obligation:
  changes over life course 301–4
  Dutch study of 288–90
  fulfillment:
    employee perceptions 318–21
    employer perceptions 322–3
    incongruence 169–73
  and government regulation 84, 87
  and incongruence 163–9
  and leader-member exchange 237
  mutual 181–3
  and organizational change 296–7
  and perceived organizational support
    212, 220
  process approach to 316–18
  and promises 89
  and Psychological Contract Inventory 315
  and psychological contracts 162, 260–1
  and relational exchange 82–3, 299–300
  and social exchange 9, 120
  and socialization 235–6
  types of 315
  see also job creep; transactional-relational
    continuum
organizational behavior (OB) 48
organizational citizenship behavior (OCB) 181
  and civic virtue 192
  and contract breach 268
  and job creep 185–6
  and leader-member exchange 243
  and workplace effectiveness 39
organizational behavior-management, see
    transactional-relational continuum
organizational retaliatory behavior (ORB), and
    workplace effectiveness 39
organizational support theory (OST) 206, 221
  and behavior 213–14

  and contingent employment relationships
    219–20
  and employee socialization 216–18
  and felt obligation 212
  and human resource practices 220–1
  and organizational commitment 212
  and positive valuation 218–19
  and psychological contracts 214–16
  and supervisor support 210–11
organizations:
  agents of 135, 359–61
  competitive environment 286
  and employment relationship 284
  identifying 226–7
  impact of changes in 296–9
  multiple exchanges within 24
  multiple foci of 24
  and perceived organizational support 207–9
  personification of 207, 226
  socialization programs:
    and employee attitudes 240–2
    and employee behaviors 242–5
    and perceived obligations 240
    psychological contract formation 299–301
    tactics 238–40
  strategies of 136
  types of 147
orientation programs, see socialization
overentitlement 171–2
overinvestment 315
  and exchange relationships 18

paid annual leave, and European Union 110
part-time workers:
  and employment contracts 291
  and European Union 110–11
  and perceived organizational support 219–20
  and United States 111
  see also contingent work; temporary workers
particularism:
  and content of exchange relationships 12
  and socialization tactics 239
partnership agreements, and industrial relations
    59–60, 121
paternalism 286
pay rates:
  and collective bargaining 52–3
  and employer's obligations 342
  and fairness 38
  impact of changes in 38–9
  and labor market 97
  and labor market participation 96
  minimum wage 97–8

Pearce, J, and psychological contracts 259
Pemberton, C, and psychological contracts
        259–60
perceived organizational support (POS) 11,
        119–20, 206, 313, 353, 356
    behavioral outcomes of 213–14
    and content of exchange relationships 13–14
    and contingent employment relationships
        219–20
    definition 262
    emphasis on commodities 22
    and employee socialization 216–18
    and employer identity 226
    and fairness 209–10
    and human resource practices 211–12, 220–1
    and indebtedness 16
    and information-seeking 216–17
    and interactional justice 37, 210
    and justice 353
    and leader-member exchange 228
    nature and formation of 207–9
    and positive valuation 218–19
    as process measure 317–18
    and promises 216
    and proximal exchanges 20
    and psychological contracts 215–16,
        262–3, 276
    psychological outcomes of:
        felt obligation 212
        organizational commitment 212
        performance-reward 213
        stress 213
    and social exchange theory 262, 353
    and supervisor support 210–11
    and trust 207
perceived supervisory support (PSS):
    and interactional justice 37
    and perceived organizational support
        210–11, 228
perception:
    and fulfillment incongruence 169–70, 338
    and obligation incongruence 167–8
    and organizational support theory 206
    perceptual gaps 325–6
    and psychological contracts 226–7
performance, and temporary employees 295
performance management, and human resource
        management 341–2
performance related pay 287
personal control, and job creep 189
personification, and organizations 207, 226
police, citizen encounters with 39–40
polynomial regression 325–6

Porter, L M 315–16
    and contract fulfillment 322
Porter, L W, and psychological contracts 256–7
power:
    abuse of 42–3
    and communication 168
    and exchange 10
    and industrial relations 49
procedural justice 36
    and authority 40
    and legitimacy of authority 39
    and pay and conditions 38
    and perceived organizational support 209–10
    and police-citizen encounters 39–40
process theory, and social exchange 22, 25
productive exchanges 13
productivity, and trade unions 58
profit maximization 123, 128–9
    and exchange 8, 10, 21–2
    and neoclassical economics 94, 96
promises 40
    and classical contract law 86
    and contract violation 266
    implicit 167
    and perceived organizational support 216
    and psychological contracts 88–90, 91 n5, 162,
        215, 260–1, 299–300, 353
    and relational contract theory 82
    and unilateral adaptation 300
property rights:
    and anti-discrimination legislation 105
    and European Union 103
    and United States 102–3
proximal exchanges 12, 14, 20
Psychological Contract Inventory (PCI) 315
psychological contracts 11, 13, 25, 33, 143, 253,
        314–15, 333, 353
    changes in meaning of 254–5, 258–61
    and compensation systems 342
    concept of 162–3, 274–7
    contract breach 173, 175, 267, 270, 318–19
    contract development 271–2
    contract making 337
    definition and conceptualization 259–61
    emergence of 'new' 44–5, 287–91
    employee's interpretation of 338–9
    and employer identity 226
    formation of 299–301
    fulfillment 289–90, 318–23
    growth in research on 253–4
    and immediate superior 229–30
    and incongruence 163–4, 257
    and indebtedness 16

psychological contracts (*cont.*)
  interactive nature of 256
  and justice 353
  and leader-member exchange 263
  and life course 304
  literature on:
    early references 254–8
    recent research 258–72
  measuring nature of 263–5
  multiple 18
  and mutual obligations 181–3
  negotiation of 305–6
  and organizational change 296–9
  and organizational support theory 214–16
  and perceived organizational support 215–16,
    262–3
  and promises 88–90, 91 n5, 162, 215, 260–1,
    299–300, 353
  and reciprocity 215, 255, 300
  research priorities 280
    conceptual models 274–7
    contract consequences 278
    contract development 278
    contract measures 278–9
    contract violation 277–8
    employer's perspective 272–4
    methodology 279
  role of 255–6
  and schema 165–6, 271, 278, 338, 341
  and social exchange theory 261–3, 353
  and socialization 230, 233
  violation of 183, 256, 265–71, 277–8, 296–7,
    305, 318, 321
  see also incongruence; transactional-relational
    continuum

quasi-spot contracts 315

rationality:
  and agreement-making 31–2
  bounded 41–2
reactance, psychological 190–1, 198
  and magnitude of threat 195
  and negative voice 191–4, 196
reactance theory 198, 355, 357
  and job creep 181, 184, 187
  and personal freedom 189, 190–1, 195
reciprocity 21, 40, 128
  balanced 317
  Blau on 9
  and exchange 7, 8–9, 10, 13, 14–15, 120, 313
  forms of 128
  generalized 317

Gouldner on 8–9
  and incongruence 163
  and indebtedness 15–16
  and job creep 183, 186
  and justice 128, 351
  and leader-member exchange 227
  measures of 317
  negative 317
  and organizational citizenship behavior 183
  and organizational support theory 215
  and perceived organizational support 212,
    220, 221
  and psychological contracts 215, 255, 300
  and social exchange 262, 351
recognition 340
  and perceived organizational support 207
recruitment:
  and human resource management 340–1
  and leader-member exchange 230–2
reframing, and perceived organizational
    support 209
regulation 120–1
  and employment law 67–75
  and European Union 104
  and freedom of contract 75–6, 87
  and human resource management tool kits
    334–5, 345
  and industrial relations 50–1
  internal and external 129
  and neoclassical economics 97–8
  and United States 103–4
Reichers, A E, and organizations 23–4
relational contract theory 65–6, 77–8, 122–3,
    126, 353–4
  comparison with other theories 86
  and context 88, 127
  discrete contracts 79
  and employment 83–4
  and exchange behavior 83, 127
  and fairness 82, 86, 88
  and justice 86, 88
  overview of 78
  and process 358
  and promises 82, 89
  and reciprocity 128
  and regulation 87, 129
  relational contracts 79–80, 263–4
    benefits and burdens 82
    cooperation 81
    and employment 83–4
    extended duration 80
    involvement of parties 81
    objects of exchange 80–1

obligations 82–3
  scope of 86
  and team leaders 360
  and trust 129
  usefulness of 87
relational contracts, *see* relational
    contract theory
relational models 21
resource-based view (RBV), *see* strategy theory
resource theory:
  and exchange 12–13
  and leader-member exchange
    relationships 14
resources, and resource-based view 138–9
responsibility 340
restructuring:
  impact of 138
  and job creep 187
  and psychological contracts 296, 305
Robinson, S L, and contract violation 267,
    268, 269
role behavior, spontaneous, and job creep 185
role boundaries, and job creep 185–6
role definition, and socialization 234–5
role innovation, and job creep 185
role making, employee, and job creep 185
Rousseau, D M 272, 280
  and contract making 337
  and contract schema 271, 338
  and contract violation 265–9, 276
  and psychological contracts 162, 258–61,
    263–5, 314, 315, 333
  Psychological Contracts in Organizations 258
Rusbult, C E, and interdependence theory 22

Sahlins, M, and reciprocity 14–15
Saint Bonaventura 43
sales contracts 33
  compared with employment contracts 31, 34
  and fairness 42
Schalk, R 288–90, 297–8
Schein, E H, and psychological contracts 256,
    259, 264
schemata:
  contract 165–6, 271, 278, 338, 341
  and obligation incongruence 165–6
self-centered bias 171
self-efficacy 233–4, 244
self-esteem, and job creep 189
self-evaluation:
  and job creep 188, 195
  and self-centered bias 171
  and social comparisons 172–3

sense-making, and obligation incongruence
    166–8
services, and exchange 12
Shore, L M:
  process approach of 316, 317
  and psychological contracts 265
Simon, H A:
  authority and the employment contract 30–3
  and employee-organization relationship
    9–10
  inducements-contributions model of
    exchange 7
  and origins of social exchange theory 7
  and process of exchange 8
social accounts:
  and contract violation 266
  and perceived organizational support 208–9,
    356
social capital, and the 'new' psychological
    contracts 44
social comparison:
  and fulfillment incongruence 172–3
  and job creep 188, 195
social contagion 169
social controls, and networks 142
social exchange, definition 7, 261
social exchange theory 119–20, 124–6, 351
  content of the exchange 7–8, 11–14, 19–21
  context 127
  and employee behaviors 243
  and exchange relationships 127, 313
  as individual-level model 351–3
  limitations of 19–24
  and organizational citizenship behavior 183
  origins of 7
  parties to the exchange 9–11, 17–18, 23–4
  and process 358
  process of the exchange 8–9, 14–17, 21–3
  and psychological contracts 261–3
  and reciprocity 128, 351
  and regulation 129
  and team leaders 360
  theoretical underdevelopment of 5
  and trust 129, 351
  universality of 5
social information processing 169
social pacts, and industrial relations 60–1
socialization:
  anticipatory stage 230–2
  and defining 235
  disengagement 236–7
  and employee attitudes 240–2
  and employee behaviors 242–5

socialization (*cont.*)
entry and assimilation 232–6
and immediate superior 228
and leader-member exchange 227, 356
and networks 228–9
and organizational support theory 216–18
and perceived obligations 240
and psychological contract formation
299–300
tactics of 238–40
society:
and employment relationship 284, 291,
304–5
global trends 286–7
and psychological contracts 287–91
Society of Industrial and Organizational
Psychology 273
Soskice, D, and varieties of capitalism 50–1
Spain:
and collective bargaining 52
and industrial relations 50, 51
and social pacts 61
union density 55
Spector, P E, pay and fairness 38
status:
and communication 168
and master-servant relationship 66
Statute of Laborers 66, 67
Stone, K V W, and new psychological contracts
44–5
Storey, J, and human resource management 50
strategy theory 135, 136–7
agency theory 136, 137, 146
dynamic capabilities 136, 141–2, 149–50
resource-based view 136, 139–41, 148–9
upper echelon theory 136, 137–9, 146–8, 361–2
stress:
increase in levels of 55
and perceived organizational support
208, 213
strikes 51
supervisors, *see* leader-member exchange;
perceived supervisory support
support transactions, visible and invisible 20
Sutton v United Airlines (US Supreme
Court) 106
Sweden:
and trade unions 101
works councils 103
Swidler, A 334

Taylor, M S 322
team-building 233

temporary workers 292, 293–4
and perceived organizational support 219–20
see also contingent work; part-time workers
Tetrick, L E 317
and reciprocity 317
Thibaut, J W, and procedural justice 36
time, and exchange 13
trade unions 126, 286
changes in density 52, 55
and collective bargaining 52–3
decline in 286
and employee 'voice' 55–7
and European Union 101, 104
impact of 57–8
and job insecurity 55
and low paid 54
role of 361
and United States 102, 108–9
and wage inequality 53–4
training 339
as productive exchange 19
*Trans World Airlines (TWA) v International
Federation of Flight Attendants*
(US Supreme Court) 108–9
transaction exchanges 13
transactional-relational continuum 77–8, 90 n2
discrete contracts 79, 90 n3
relational contracts 79–80, 264, 315
benefits and burdens 82
cooperation 81
extended duration 80
involvement of parties 81
objects of exchange 80–1
obligations 82–3
transactional contracts 264, 315
universal applicability of 83
Tremlett, N 293
trust 129
and contract violation 266
and fairness 353
and networks 142
and organizational change 297
and perceived organizational support 207
and social exchange 7, 9, 120, 126, 351
Tsui, A S, and psychological contracts 265
Turnley, W H, and contract breach 268–9, 319
turnover, and leader-member exchange 236
Tyler, T R, and police-citizen encounters 39–40

uncertainty:
and communication 169
and employment contracts 33, 120
and social exchange 261

underinvestment 315
 and exchange relationships 18
unemployment 49
 and employment protection laws 54
United Kingdom:
 and collective bargaining 52, 56
 and contingent workers 293
 decline in employee influence 56
 and employment regulation 68, 74, 121
 and enterprise partnership
  agreements 59–60
 and industrial relations 50, 51
 job insecurity 54–5
 union density 55, 335
 union-profitability connection 57–8
 wage levels 54
United States 123
 anti-discrimination laws 105–6
 and collective bargaining 52, 106–8
 and consumption 95
 and contingent workers 291, 293
 decline in employee influence 56
 employees rights 104–5
 employment policy 94
 and employment regulation 67–8, 74, 75,
  91 n4, 121, 123
 and enterprise partnership agreements 59, 60
 and government regulation 103–4
 impact of unionization 53
 individual rights and employment 100–1
 and individualism 100
 individuality of the corporation 101–2
 and industrial relations 50, 51
 paid annual leave 110
 and part-time workers 111
 and private property 102–3
 and trade unions 102, 108–9, 335
 union-profitability connection 57–8
 wage levels 54
United States Supreme Court:
 and anti-discrimination legislation 105–6
 First National Maintenance Corp v NLRB
  107–8
 Kimel et al v Board of Regents et al 105–6

 Sutton v United Airlines 106
 *Trans World Airlines (TWA) v International
  Federation of Flight Attendants* 108–9
universalism, and socialization tactics 239
upper echelon theory, *see* strategy theory
utility maximization 123, 128
 and employees 95–6
 and neoclassical economics 94

Van Breukelen, W 295
Van der Toren, J P 293
Van Lange, P A M, and interdependence
  theory 22
variance theories 21
voice:
 acquiescent 193
 concepts of 191–2
 defensive 193
 direct 193
 indirect 194
 and industrial relations 55–7
 instrumental 193
 negative 184, 187, 191–4, 196, 197
 and procedural fairness 36
 prosocial 193
 and psychological reactance 191–4, 196

Wade-Benzoni, K A, and transactional-relational
  continuum 78
wages, *see* pay rates
Wagner Act, *see* National Labor Relations Act
Walker, L, and procedural justice 36
Wangler, L W, and psychological contracts 257
Wiebe, F A, and content of exchange
  relationships 12–13
women:
 adult development model 302–3
 and collective bargaining 52–3
work teams, and organizational citizenship
  behavior 185
works councils:
 and European Union 103
 impact of changes in 58
 and industrial relations 56

Lightning Source UK Ltd.
Milton Keynes UK
25 February 2011

168251UK00003B/176/P